WOMEN AND THE **ECONOMY**

SAUL D. **HOFFMAN**

PROFESSOR OF ECONOMICS,
UNIVERSITY OF DELAWARE, USA

SUSAN L. **AVERETT**

CHARLES A. DANA PROFESSOR OF ECONOMICS,
LAFAYETTE COLLEGE, USA

WOMEN AND THE ECONOMY

FAMILY, WORK AND PAY

THIRD EDITION

macmillan education   palgrave

First published 2016 by
PALGRAVE

Palgrave in the UK is an imprint of Macmillan Publishers Limited, registered in England, company number 785998, of 4 Crinan Street, London, N1 9XW.

Palgrave® and Macmillan® are registered trademarks in the United States, the United Kingdom, Europe and other countries.

ISBN 978–1–137–47703–3 paperback

This book is printed on paper suitable for recycling and made from fully managed and sustained forest sources. Logging, pulping and manufacturing processes are expected to conform to the environmental regulations of the country of origin.

A catalogue record for this book is available from the British Library.

A catalog record for this book is available from the Library of Congress.

Printed and bound by CPI Group (UK) Ltd, Croydon, CR0 4YY

To the memory of our friend and colleague, Leslie Whittington,
and to our families—Susan, Jake, and
Nate; Albert, Rebecca, and Natalie.

CONTENTS

PREFACE

We warmly welcome you to the new and improved third edition of *Women and the Economy: Family, Work, and Pay*. In this edition, as in the first two, we take the powerful tools of economics and use them to examine women's lives, from marriage and the family to the labor market. We blend economic theory with discussions of cutting-edge empirical research and contemporary policy issues to offer a fascinating perspective on women's lives in the twenty-first century. Women and economics—what could be more interesting?

New to this Edition

This edition represents a major update and revision of the 2nd edition. This is typically said about a new edition of a textbook whether it is warranted or not, but in this case it is absolutely true. For this edition, we have changed the book's structure so that applications and policy are now integrated directly into the appropriate chapters, rather than separated at the end of the text. As a result, they now fit far more naturally into the core economic analysis. In the process, a few topics were jettisoned, but most are tightened and repositioned. The result is a book that now flows more naturally from theory to application to research to policy.

As part of this restructuring, we added a second, applied chapter to the section on labor force participation and broadened the content of the applied fertility chapter and the earnings policy chapter. We also expanded the content on women in developing countries by dividing one umbrella chapter into separate chapters on marriage and family and on labor market issues.

We have added new more contemporary content throughout. The two marriage chapters now include many new topics, including consumption and investment approaches to marriage, marital search, an economic analysis of cohabitation, and the differential decline in marriage by education. The analysis of fertility issues now includes a discussion of the broad impacts of new contraceptive technologies on women's education, work, and earnings. The new chapter on labor force participation includes new content on taxes and transfers, the "opting out" debate, the impact of race on women's labor force participation, and a fascinating review of the impact of ancient agricultural techniques on contemporary attitudes about women's roles.

Every applied topic that survived to the third edition had to first prove its worth and then was thoroughly reworked to reflect current scholarship. Some old ideas and research—good friends for two editions—were gracefully retired. We reorganized the chapter on the gender gap in earnings to focus on the historical record, examining studies from different decades from the 1950s through the 2010s and noting how the emphasis of the studies and their findings evolved. By the end, students have a clear idea about what was once an important explanation but isn't anymore, and what, as Claudia Goldin writes, the "final chapter in gender convergence" must contain.

Throughout the text, we have simplified the exposition, but still left it lively and informative. We have updated and enhanced our data, figures, and tables. We reread every page, informed by our own teaching experience, with fresh eyes to see what could be strengthened and what could be streamlined. This book contains a great deal more economic theory, including graphs and equations, than other texts in this general area, but everything is accessible to any student who has had a semester of principles of microeconomics. Students without even that background could jump in by reading the overview of economics (Chapter 2) with great care.

We have included more than 30 boxes that discuss specialized material. These boxes include an inventory of famous women economists, past and present (Chapter 1); natural experiments in action (Chapter 2); the division of labor in families and two-sided matching (Chapter 3); the role of gender preference in divorce and fertility (Chapters 4); how a change in citizenship rules affected the quality–quantity trade-off in Germany (Chapter 5); women's work in 1900 and changes in household productivity (Chapter 7); the effect of the Affordable Care Act on work incentives (Chapter 8); biological differences and the gender wage gap (Chapter 10); Sandra Day O'Connor as a real-world example of discrimination in action (Chapter 12); the role of caste and income in India on marriage markets (Chapter 13); and many, many more.

We are confident that the many improvements we have made will help professors and students alike understand and explore the lives of women from an economics perspective.

Distinctive Features

A number of features in this book continue to distinguish it from other textbooks about women and the economy. One is its emphasis on issues outside of the core of work and pay. Five chapters address family issues—Chapters 3 and 4 on marriage, Chapters 5 and 6 on fertility, and Chapter 13 on family issues in developing countries. In other texts, family issues are mostly used to explain labor force trends. Here, they receive the direct attention they deserve. Indeed, we begin the book with the analysis of family issues, because it sets the stage for what follows. Students truly enjoy thinking about these personal issues from an economics perspective, and they find it rewarding and insightful—and a great way to learn economics.

Our treatment of labor supply issues is also distinctive. Other textbooks primarily examine the labor–leisure choice with an emphasis on hours of labor supplied to the market. But that approach makes much more sense for men's labor supply than for women's. We emphasize labor force participation within a labor–leisure–household production model. The virtue of this is that it emphasizes the dimension of labor supply that has changed the most—labor force participation—and integrates changes in the household and in the technology of household activities into the analysis. At the same time, this approach is easier for students, since the theoretical and graphical complexity of indifference curves, budget constraints, and income and substitution effects can be avoided. An instructor who prefers the traditional labor–leisure model will find it in the appendix.

Our discussion of the economics of fertility is sophisticated and fascinating material that is presented in no other textbook of this kind. We introduce the quality–quantity distinction, and analyze the issue thoroughly by using utility, production, and cost functions. The critical effect of the changing value of women's time comes through clearly in influencing the choice of quality and quantity.

Every chapter includes something special. Here are just a few of the highlights:

- Chapter 1 includes an expanded section on women in the economics profession. Women are making great strides in the economics profession, winning three of the last six John Bates Clark awards for the outstanding US economist under age 40. We want students to know their names.
- Chapter 2 includes an introduction to natural experiments in economics as part of a discussion of statistical methods and the difficulties of making causal inferences. Almost every chapter in the text returns to the idea of natural experiments—no-fault divorce (Chapter 4), MTV and teen pregnancy and the uneven access to birth control by young women (both Chapter 6), the lasting effect of World War II on women's work (Chapter 7), and the effect of a change in hiring procedures on the representation of women in symphony orchestras (Chapter 11).
- Becker's supply and demand approach to marriage market equilibrium (Chapter 3). Applications of that approach include a numbers mismatch, the effect of rising wages for women, and a change in attitudes about sexual activity outside marriage.
- Chapter 6 includes a new section on the effect of the oral contraceptive on women's economic lives.

The book also has valuable pedagogical features. The core theory chapters (Chapters 3, 5, and 7) have a common structure. Each begins with an introduction that motivates the material and then turns to the basic empirical magnitudes and trends of, for example, marriage or fertility, in the process emphasizing the broad issues or puzzles that any theory would need to explain. Thus, the marriage chapter emphasizes the decline in the proportion of adults who are married and the fertility chapter stresses the decline in fertility rates. After presenting the facts, each chapter then introduces the relevant economic theory, which is developed with an eye toward explaining the facts—exactly what theory should do! Finally, comparative static analysis is used to explain the key changes and trends that the first section introduced and then empirical work is examined.

The pedagogical goal is to have students appreciate the facts to be explained, see an economic analysis designed to explain the facts, and finally see how well the models perform. By the end of the text, students will not only have seen a great deal of interesting economic analysis, but will have begun to absorb and appreciate the underlying economic approach and distinctive economic way of thinking.

We have pitched the presentation of economic theory to a level consistent with the preparation of students who have completed a standard one-semester course in microeconomics. A basic understanding of supply and demand, opportunity cost, and the idea of maximization is all that is necessary to understand the analyses we present. We have taught this material quite successfully to our students at Lafayette College and the University of Delaware. Students without that background can use the review material in Chapter 2 to get up to speed. There is one requirement, however, whatever the back-ground—the ability to think abstractly and out-of-the-box.

As a practical matter, the main text includes no indifference curves and no isoquants, and no budget lines. The appendix to Chapter 7 does present a traditional analysis of labor supply using indifference curves for instructors who want to use that approach. Very sophisticated economic concepts and economic thinking are used in many places, but not highly technical and graph-intensive expositions. We have worked very hard to make explanations simpler, while still doing justice to the analysis. The analyses of fertility and labor force participation are particularly good examples of this approach.

Using This Book

There are many different paths through this text, as well as different potential audiences. Chapters 2, 3, 5, 7, and 9–11 are the core analysis chapters and we strongly recommend using as many of them as your course schedule allows. They cover core economic thinking and research methods (Chapter 2), marriage (Chapter 3), fertility (Chapter 5), labor force participation (Chapter 7), and earnings (Chapters 9–11). Chapters 4, 6, and 8 are exten-sions of the basic theory, each reviewing applications, policy issues, and new research relevant to the chapter content they follow. The various sections of each of these chapters are largely freestanding and instructors can pick and choose as suits their own interests and emphasis. Chapter 12 is focused on labor market policy issues, while Chapters 13 and 14 rework the core analyses of earlier chapters in the context of developing economies. Those two chapters could be included earlier in the course, following the corresponding earlier chapters.

This text can readily be adapted for courses in economics of the family or in economic demography. Courses like that might use Chapters 2–8, plus Chapter 13. The material here should be accessible to students from disciplines outside economics, for example, advanced undergraduates and graduate students in demography, sociology, public policy, or urban affairs, who want a taste of the economic approach to these issues and the cur-rent research.

We would love to hear from the professors and students who use this book. We can be reached via e-mail at averetts@lafayette.edu or hoffmans@udel.edu. We look forward to hearing from you and we hope you enjoy learning about women and economics.

The authors and publisher wish to thank the following for permission to reproduce copyright material:

- Oxford University Press for Claudia D. Goldin (1990), *Understanding the Gender Gap*. New York: Oxford University Press, Table 2.2.
- The American Economic Association for the excerpt in Box 1.2 from: Barbara Bergmann (1981), "The Economic Risks of Being a Housewife," *American Economic Review*, 71 (2), 81–85.
- The University of Wisconsin Press for Table 11.2 from: Mary Corcoran and Greg J. Duncan (1979), "Work History, Labor Force Attachment and Earnings Differences Between the Races and Sexes," *Journal of Human Resources*, 14(1). Copyright © 1979 by the Board of Regents of the University of Wisconsin System.

ACKNOWLEDGMENTS

When the first edition of this textbook was first conceived and planned in 1999, the authors were Saul Hoffman and Leslie Whittington. Leslie was a very accomplished professor of economics at the Georgetown University Institute of Public Policy. She was an acknowledged expert in tax policy, especially as it affected women and influenced decisions about marriage, cohabitation, and fertility. She wrote a fascinating paper on the tax implications of legalizing same-sex marriages, more than a decade before that was an active political and social issue. Leslie died tragically on September 11, 2001, along with her husband, Charles Falkenberg, and their two young daughters, Zoe and Dana, on American Airlines Flight 77, which was hijacked and crashed into the Pentagon.

Susan Averett joined the textbook project in early 2002. Susan was a good friend and coauthor of Leslie Whittington. Susan and Leslie met in 1986 when they were students in the Ph.D. program in the Department of Economics at the University of Colorado. Leslie was two years ahead of Susan in the program and her successes in the job market and in her research were a source of inspiration for Susan. Professionally and personally, Susan and Leslie were quite close and they published two papers together that are discussed in this textbook. Both papers explore issues that women in the labor market face.

Leslie's many contributions to economics were remembered in a special session of the 2003 annual meeting of the American Economic Association, in a special issue of *The Review of Economics of the Household,* which was published in her honor in 2003, and also in a memorial lecture given annually in her honor at Georgetown University. For a summary discussion of Leslie's work, see *Review of Economics of the Household*, pp. 151–152, 2003, Vol. 1, No. 2. We encourage you to review this journal to see the impact of Leslie's work.

We would also like to thank the team at Palgrave Macmillan, especially our editor, Kirsty Reade, and associate editor, Aléta Bezuidenhout. They both eased our way through this project. We also thank Praveen Gajamoorthy, our project manager at Integra Software Services. He helped us through the production phase with grace and skill. Janel Atlas did a wonderful and thankless job preparing the index. And, lastly, our students at UD and Lafayette made lots of small contributions, most of which they are completely unaware of.

① WOMEN AND THE ECONOMY

Introduction

There is no better way to introduce this book than to turn directly to its main subject—women and their economic lives. It's certainly no secret that women's lives have changed enormously over the past half-century and even more so over the course of the twentieth century and beyond. This change is especially obvious in the broad subject matter of this text—family, work, and pay.

Figure 1.1 shows some of the major changes in marriage, fertility, education, work, and pay for women that occurred between 1960 and the mid-2010s in the United States.

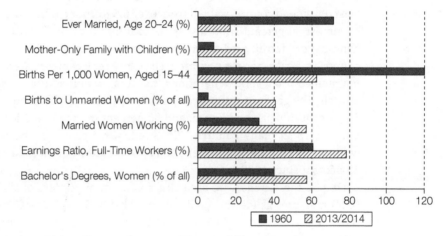

Figure 1.1 *Then and now—changes in US women's lives since 1960.*

Sources: Data from American's Families and Living Arrangements, Table A1 (2014); Current Population Reports, Series PC (2)-4B, Table 2 (1960); National Vital Statistics Reports, Vol. 64, No. 1, Tables 1 and 16; US Bureau of Labor Statistics; US Census Bureau, Historical Income Data, Table P-38; US, National Center for Education Statistics, Digest of Education Statistics, Table 324.40.

In 1960, women's choices and opportunities concerning fertility, marriage, education, and occupation were very different than they are today. Early marriage was the norm: More than 70 percent of women aged 20–24 were or had been married. Fertility was very high; there were about 120 births for every 1,000 women aged 15–44, which works out as more than 3.5 births per woman over her lifetime. The married-couple family was by far the dominant adult family structure and only 5 percent of births were to unmarried women. A married woman's place was in the home, and that's where she spent most of her adult life. Just barely over 30 percent of all married women worked, and only 20 percent of married women with young children did. Many older married women had never worked for pay since their wedding day or shortly thereafter. As a group, women earned considerably less than men, even when they worked full time, and they were heavily underrepresented at colleges and universities.

By the mid-2010s, things have changed substantially. Later marriage is now the norm, with less than 17 percent of women ever-married by ages 20–24. Fertility has fallen sharply to about half its 1960 level. The link between marriage and fertility has been greatly weakened. Births to unmarried women have grown and are now more than 40 percent of all births; consequently, the proportion of families with children that are headed by a single mother has also increased, from about 8 percent to almost 25 percent. Married women have joined the workforce in record numbers, and now nearly 60 percent are working. Many younger women have worked nearly every year since their wedding day, barely leaving the labor force even to give birth. Women are now overrepresented at colleges and universities. The gender gap in earnings remains, although it has been considerably diminished.

The same trends have been seen throughout most of the rest of the world. Over the same time period, the labor-force participation rate for women rose by 20 percent or more in much of Europe. Fertility, measured by the average number of births per woman, fell from a world average of nearly five to a bit over two, and in the poorest, least developed countries it fell from over 6.5 to about 4. In India, births per woman fell by almost 50 percent from nearly six to under three and in China, home of the "one-child policy," fertility fell from about five births per woman to 1.5. In many European countries, births per woman are well below replacement rates, and if those rates are maintained for several generations, the total population in those countries will actually fall. The gender earnings ratio similarly increased, by about 8 percent in Australia, 15 percent in Japan and Korea, and 30 percent in the United Kingdom. Marriage rates plummeted in many countries. In Sweden, for example, the proportion of married women has fallen by 25 percent since 1980, and in France it has fallen by more than 15 percent since 1990.

Despite these trends, we are still far away from gender equality. The United Nations (UN) measures gender inequality on a global basis with the **Gender Inequality Index (GII)**. The GII assesses the extent of gender inequality using three broad factors: women's reproductive health status, measured by maternal mortality and adolescent fertility; women's empowerment, measured by their educational attainment relative to men and their political representation; and their labor-market participation relative to men's. The index is scaled from 0 to 1, where 0 means that men and women fare equally and 1 means that women fare as poorly as possible in all dimensions. The UN interprets the measure as the percentage loss to potential human development due to shortfalls in gender equality.

The measure is certainly imperfect in many ways. It is constrained by the availability of data that are reliable and comparable across countries. For example, the UN notes that the index does not include measures of women's earnings relative to men's, of the extent of their non-market work in the household, and of their ownership of assets. Political representation is based solely on a country's national parliament and thus ignores women's participation at local and regional levels. And there is no perfect way to combine a group of elements into a single composite measure. How much weight should each one have? Equal? Or are some elements more important than others? Still, the GII is useful and informative.

The most recent GII data are for 2013, when Slovenia had the best (lowest) score of 0.021, closely followed by Switzerland, Germany, Sweden, Norway, Denmark, and Austria.

All of the countries in the top 13 were European, including all of Scandinavia. The highest-ranking non-European countries were Singapore, Korea, and Israel, all ranked between 15th and 20th. At the bottom of the ranking were Afghanistan, Chad, Niger, and Yemen, with scores of 0.70 and higher. These countries had maternal mortality and adolescent fertility rates that were 20 to 40 times as high as those in the top group of countries and also very large gender differences in education and labor-force activity. In Afghanistan, for example, only 6 percent of women have at least a secondary level of education, compared to 34 percent of men, and their labor-force activity rate was less than one-fifth that of men. The United States was just 47th, with a GII score of 0.262. The low US ranking reflected its relatively high rates of maternal mortality and adolescent fertility—four to six times those of the top-ranked countries—and its relatively low female participation in government. France ranked 12th, Japan 25th, the United Kingdom 35th, and China 37th.

Figure 1.2 shows the variation in the GII across broad geographic regions. For the world as a whole, the GII is 0.45, while in countries designated as Very High Human Development,[1] it is 0.19, which is still far from equality. The Least Developed Countries and Sub-Saharan Africa have the highest GII values, with Arab states and South Asia also conspicuously high. All four of those groups have a GII value between 0.54 and 0.6. East Asia, the Pacific countries, Europe, and Central Asia have lower values, reflecting greater gender equality.

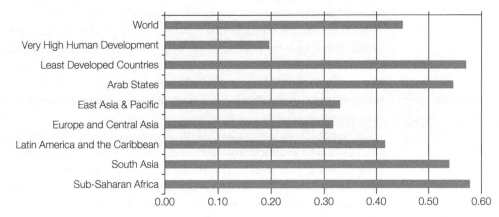

Figure 1.2 *Gender Inequality Index by region, 2013 (higher value = greater gender inequality).*

Source: Data from United Nations Development Reports, *Human Development Report 2014*, Table 4. http://hdr.undp.org/en/content/table-4-gender-inequality-index.

Why study women?

Why is there a separate economics course and textbook on women in the first place? After all, most universities don't offer an economics course on men. There are actually quite a few good reasons. First, many courses in economics are male-oriented, even when they don't explicitly say so. For example, some of the topics discussed in

---

1 This group includes the 49 highest-ranked countries on the UN's Human Development Index. Norway is 1st, the US 5th, and Argentina 49th.

this book are parts of standard non-gendered courses in economics. Labor supply analysis is an important part of courses in labor economics, but those courses almost always emphasize a model of behavior that fits men's choices well and totally misses the mark on women's choices—often without ever saying that this is so. For example, as is explained more thoroughly in Chapter 7, the standard model of labor supply considers an individual who chooses between market work and leisure, thereby excluding from the analysis the activity that has occupied much of women's time for generations—namely, family responsibilities. By incorporating this extra dimension, the analysis in this book provides a much richer framework. In the process, it enables us to make sense of the incredible increase in women's labor-force activity over the course of the last century, something that is impossible to do using the standard (male) labor supply model. In much of the economics curriculum, women are invisible. In this book they are very visible.

Second, women are, frankly, more interesting from an economic standpoint than men. The many changes in women's lives that we saw in Figure 1.1 are great material for economic analysis. In contrast, men's economic lives haven't changed nearly as much. Furthermore, women's economic behavior, especially their participation in the labor force, is still more varied than men's, so, again, additional analysis is important and interesting. Studying women's economic behavior also provides a natural link to interesting public policy issues, especially those relating to family and work. A consistent focus on women helps tie many interesting issues together.

Third, the major topics in this book provide a great opportunity to learn economics, precisely because they seem so far away from traditional economics. At first glance, many of the items shown in Figure 1.1, especially marriage and fertility, are more like the topics traditionally studied in sociology. They may sound less rigorous than the usual fare in economics courses. Make no mistake, though—this is a course in economics.

The approach we use to examine these topics is utterly different from the approach that would be taken in almost any another discipline. You will soon appreciate that economic analysis has a great deal to contribute to the understanding of these topics. Why have marriage rates fallen? Why did fertility fall? Why are more married women working? Why have earnings for women increased relative to men yet they remain stubbornly lower? What economic forces were at work in all these changes? What kind of economic impact did these changes have? The process of thinking about these questions will surely provide a broader understanding of just what economics is.

Fourth, the issues discussed in this book are personal in a way that economics often is not. This book isn't "X-rated," but it does include discussions of marriage, children, and, yes, even sex. The major topics of this book—family and work—are central features of virtually every adult's life. They affect most of us more immediately and more directly than do some of the traditional topics of economics—monopoly vs. competition, the benefits of international trade, and the economics of pollution, to name just a few. Those topics are tremendously important, but they are more abstract and often not part of an individual's daily life in the tangible way that family life is. Thinking analytically—thinking like an economist—about personal issues is fun in a crazy kind of way. We know from personal experience that students learn more about economics when they are personally engaged in the topics.

Economic analysis

The economics used in this book is **microeconomics**, which focuses on the behavior of individuals and firms, as compared to **macroeconomics**, which focuses on the performance of the economy as a whole. Roughly speaking, supply-and-demand analysis and the allocation of resources are central issues in microeconomics, while unemployment and inflation are major topics in macroeconomics. Microeconomic analysis is about how individuals, firms, and other economic agents make the best choices they can, given the constraints they face, and about the market conditions in which they make those choices. Microeconomics is, according to one of the common definitions of economics, "the science of rational choice."

Prices and incomes are usually the most important parts of the constraints that influence choices. Prices play a particularly central role, so much so that microeconomics is sometimes called **price theory**. Prices are the glue that binds all the separate pieces of the economy together. The price system summarizes and conveys vital information about the value of resources to all market participants, allowing each to make decisions on the basis of common information. The prices themselves are determined in markets, which might be competitive, monopolistic, or oligopolistic. In this book, a particularly important price will be the price of time, measured by the wage rate that an individual can earn. Indeed, the change in the price of time is a key element of almost every chapter in this book.

This kind of microeconomic analysis, with its emphasis on choices and constraints, is characteristic of the approach of **mainstream** or **neoclassical** economics. Mainstream economics is the economics practiced by most economists and taught in most economics classes, which is why it is called "mainstream." It is not the only approach to economic analysis, although it is certainly the dominant one by a very substantial margin.[2] It is easy to caricature and exaggerate the rational choice approach. Rationality does not imply that individuals are robots who do nothing but calculate all day. Rather, it means that individuals know their available options and the constraints they face reasonably well, and make the best choices they can. That can apply to shopping at the mall, picking a career, or choosing a spouse. In the next chapter we will discuss the rational choice approach and how economists use it much more thoroughly.

An entire field of economics, called **behavioral economics**, has developed in the past few decades that focuses carefully and rigorously on the ways in which actual economic behavior differs from the simplifying assumptions of basic economic models. Those ideas are best understood as a complement to the basic approach of mainstream economics,

---

2 An alternative approach relevant to this course is **feminist economics**. Like feminist thought in other scholarly disciplines, feminist economics argues that the values and orientation of mainstream economics reflect the values and orientation of its predominant practitioners—men. Julie Nelson, a leading contributor to feminist economics, described the difference between mainstream economics and feminist economics this way: "Traditionally male activities have taken center stage as subject matter, while models and methods have reflected a ... masculine pattern" ("Feminism and Economics," *Journal of Economic Perspectives*, 9 (2), 132, 1995). A well-respected scholarly journal, *Feminist Economics*, publishes research in this area of economics. It is probably fair to say that feminist thought has had less of an impact on economics than it has on some other social sciences.

not as a wholesale rejection of it. This text isn't the proper place to address the issues of behavioral economics, but we encourage you to do so.[3]

An example—economic analysis in action

To understand the kind of analysis that lies ahead, let's think about one of these topics a bit further: Why did fertility fall? Why do women throughout the world have roughly half as many births as 50 years ago—in some cases resulting in fertility rates so low that, if sustained long enough, total population would actually fall? The full analysis is the subject of Chapter 5, but we can catch a glimpse of the answer here. The decline in fertility is a particularly good example of economic analysis because it seems like the kind of behavior that is so personal that economics would have little or nothing to contribute.

An economist would point out that children are expensive, and one of the primary components of their cost is the parental time devoted to their upbringing. Later on in Chapter 5, we will say, more formally, that children are a *time*-**intensive household-produced commodity**. Historically, of course, the time spent in childcare has been primarily women's time. The cost of time is best measured by the earnings that are given up when a woman spends her time in household production—caring for a family full time—rather than working in the labor market. This can be thought of as an opportunity cost; by staying home and raising children, women incur a cost equal to the wages they give up. Over the course of the past 100 years, women's wages have risen by a factor of about 10 to 15, even after accounting for inflation, thereby making children a "good" whose price has risen particularly sharply. Of course, family incomes have risen, too, because both women's and men's earnings have increased. In response to all of these changes, many families have reduced the number of children they choose to have but increased the amount they spend on each child, primarily in the form of spending on goods rather than time. Fertility has fallen, but total spending on children has probably increased: Families have substituted more spending per child for more children. The smaller family is probably here to stay. We present a more detailed model of this in Chapter 5.

Positive and normative economics

Economic analysis attempts to explain the way things are—not the way things should be. In other words, economics focuses on what is termed **positive economics** rather than **normative economics**. In positive economics, we use economic theory to explain what is observed in the real world rather than arguing for or against a particular position or policy. Economists, as individuals, certainly have opinions about what is good and bad, but those opinions are not, and ought not to be, part of economic analysis.

To understand this approach, consider the many trends shown in Figure 1.1. All of them are "facts" (i.e., events/trends that are actually documented with US data). In this book, economic theory is used to explain these trends. Thus, for example, the rise in the labor-force participation of married women, the gender gap in earnings, the falling

---

3   Leading practitioners of behavioral economics include Daniel Kahneman, a Nobel Prize–winning economist and psychologist, and Richard Thaler, who has made numerous contributions to applications of behavioral economics to public policy.

marriage rate, and the rising rate of non-marital childbearing all can, and will, be examined using the tools of economics. The goal is explanation. That is what is meant by "positive economic analysis."

When we discuss these issues, we strive to stay within the realm of positive economics and try not to offer our own opinions about whatever issue we are analyzing. We have opinions, but they belong to us. We hope the analyses in this book help you understand the issues better and have more informed opinions about them.

Overview of the book

Chapter 2 introduces the tools and techniques used in microeconomics and in empirical (or applied) work. It covers many of the analytical and research techniques that we use and discuss throughout the book and thus provides a foundation for what follow.

The rest of the book is organized into three sections. The first consists of Chapters 3 through 6 and focuses on the family—two chapters each on marriage and fertility. The focus then shifts from the family to the labor-market in Chapters 7 through 12. Chapters 7 and 8 focus on women and work. The goal here is to explain the incredible increase in women's labor-force activity over the past century, a change that has reshaped not only the labor-market but family life as well. Chapters 9 to 12 focus squarely on women's earnings. These chapters examine the basis for the gender gap in earnings and consider competing explanations for women's lower earnings. These explanations focus on differences in human capital (e.g., the education and experience that women and men bring to the labor-market) and on labor market discrimination in the form of unequal pay or unequal access to certain jobs based on sex and not on productivity differences. Chapter 11 focuses on how economists measure the extent of wage discrimination, and what the many empirical studies of the gender gap in pay tell us about why the gap exists and how and why it has changed over time. Chapter 12 focuses on employment and wage policies related to women, including anti-discrimination laws, family policies, and Social Security.

Chapters 3 through 12 focus mostly on issues specific to the United States. The analyses we present, however, are broadly applicable to other settings. Each of the major sections of the book includes subsections that examine women's experience in Western Europe. But because women in developing countries often face different constraints, we devote the third section of the book to them. Chapter 13 looks at marriage and fertility and Chapter 14 examines labor-market issues.

Learning more

It is inevitable that statistics change after a book goes to print. All the facts, figures, and numbers included in this volume about marriage, fertility, work, and earnings were the latest available as of the summer of 2015 and usually pertain to 2014 and occasionally 2013. However, by the time you read this, newer figures will have been released and the numbers will have changed.

More often than not, change over a period of a year or two or three is gradual, so that the figures presented will rarely be truly off the mark. At the same time, more current numbers are always better than slightly older ones. Fortunately, official government websites make updating the figures easy. In the process, a few other interesting facts will probably surface. A truly amazing amount of very useful statistical information about women's issues is readily available. Here are the web addresses for the most important data presented in this book:

- Marriage—US Census Bureau at census.gov/hhes/families. Annual data on marriage is presented in a series now called "Families and Living Arrangements." Much of the data are available as Excel spreadsheets.
- Fertility—Vital Statistics Division of the National Center for Health Statistics at cdc.gov/nchs/births.htm. Annual information is available in the National Vital Statistics Reports.
- Labor-Force Participation—US Bureau of Labor Statistics (BLS) at bls.gov. Useful information is available in the Employment and Earnings series at bls.gov/opub/ee/. The BLS also publishes an annual online volume called *Women in the Labor Force: A Databook.*
- Earnings—US Census Bureau at bls.gov/cps/earnings.htm. Annual information on earnings and on poverty status is available in the P-60 Series, "Income and Poverty in the United States."
- Developing Countries—UN, Department of Economic and Social Affairs at esa.un.org/unpd/wpp/index.htm.
- Europe—ec.europa.eu/eurostat/help/new-eurostat-website(Eurostat)andw3.unece.org/pxweb/ (UN Economic Commission for Europe).

If you can't find what you are looking for, try the alphabetical index available on most websites. Sometimes simply locating the entries for "Women," for example, can help you find what you want.

To close this chapter, we offer information on women in the economics profession (Box 1.1) and two views of the essential skills of that totally female occupation—the housewife (Box 1.2).

Box	1.1

Women and the Economics Profession

The Nobel Prize in Economics has been awarded annually since 1969. Through 2014, it has been won by 75 persons, including such pioneers of modern economics as Paul Samuelson, Kenneth Arrow, and Milton Friedman, and well-known contemporary economists such as Paul Krugman (2008) and Robert Schiller (2013). Several men have won the award for work related to women's issues, most prominently Gary Becker, whose work on marriage, fertility, and discrimination will figure prominently in this book, and James Heckman, a labor economist and econometrician who developed groundbreaking statistical methods that are widely used in analyzing women's work choices.

Of the 75 winners, 74 were men; the first and only woman to win the award was Elinor Ostrom, who won the award in 2009. Ostrom was an unexpected winner; she was technically a political scientist rather than an economist, but she had done wonderful research on issues of governance issues concerning natural resources that are on the boundary of these two disciplines. The Nobel committee honored her for her "analysis of economic governance, especially the commons." You can read more about her award at the official Nobel Prize website at www.nobelprize.org/nobel_prizes/economic-sciences/laureates/2009.

In this respect, economics is rather like the hard sciences, where women have traditionally been underrepresented at the highest ranks of the profession. Are there women who could have won the Nobel Prize in Economics? The most obvious overlooked non-winner is Joan Robinson, an English economist who was part of John Maynard Keynes' academic circle. She was famous not only for her contributions to macroeconomics and growth theory but also for developing the theory of imperfect competition (now often called monopolistic competition). For many years she was on the short list of plausible candidates; many economists thought she was a shoo-in in 1975, which had been proclaimed as International Women's Year. Instead, the award that year went to Leonid Kantorovich and Tjalling Koopmans, two men who had made important mathematical contributions to the theory of optimal resource allocation. Still, with no offense to Professor Robinson, her non-award probably wasn't a gross injustice; much of her work was controversial, and many men with arguably stronger credentials haven't won it yet. She died in 1983 and thus is no longer eligible.

What about the future? Who are some prospective candidates to be the second woman (and first full-fledged economist) to receive the Nobel Prize in Economics? Handicapping the future is perilous. There are now many more well-known women economists in both academia and the policy world, although whether any has made the kind of major contribution to the field that merits the Nobel Prize is hard to say. Here's a selective list of well-known women economists, perhaps not laureates-to-be but important and influential nevertheless:

- **Laura Tyson** was the first woman to head the prestigious President's Council of Economic Advisors, serving under President Clinton from 1993 to 1995. She later served as Dean of the Haas School of Business at the University of California, Berkeley and the London Business School.
- In 2014, **Janet Yellen** became the first women to serve as Chair of the US Federal Reserve Board. She previously served as Head of the Council of Economic Advisors under President Clinton and as President of the San Francisco Federal Reserve Bank. She has also made important contributions to the analysis of labor-market contracts and coauthored an interesting and provocative article on the effect of abortion and contraception on non-marital births, which we discuss in Chapter 6. Her coauthor was her husband, the economist George Akerlof, who won the Nobel Prize in 2001.
- **Isabel Sawhill** is an expert in issues involving the family, poverty, the welfare system, and teen childbearing. Currently, she is Senior Fellow and Co-Director of the Center for Children and Families at The Brookings Institution, a Washington, DC, think tank. Previously she served as Associate Director in the Office of Management and Budget during the Clinton administration (1993–1994) and helped found the National Campaign to Prevent Teen Pregnancy. She is the author of *Generation Unbound*, an important 2014 study of family formation among millennials.

- **Alice Rivlin** earned her PhD in economics in 1958, a time when women in economics were incredibly rare. She was the Founding Director of the US Congressional Budget Office in the 1980s and then served as Vice-Chair of the US Federal Reserve Board, and Director of the US Office of Management and Budget in the 1990s. In 1986 she became the first woman (after 88 men) to serve as president of the American Economics Association. She was named one of the greatest public servants of the last 25 years by the Council for Excellence in Government in 2008.
- **Claudia Goldin** has made path-breaking contributions to our understanding of women's economic history, particularly in her book *Understanding the Gender Gap*. She was the first woman to become a tenured full professor in the Economics Department at Harvard and served as President of the American Economic Association in 2013, becoming just the third woman in 116 years. You will read a lot about her work in this book, especially in Chapters 7–11.
- **Susan Athey**, Professor of Economics at Stanford University, became the first woman to win the prestigious John Bates Clark Prize in 2007. That prize is awarded by the American Economics Association to a US economist under the age of 40 who has made "the most significant contribution to economic thought and knowledge." From 1947 to 2009 it was awarded every two years; since then it has been awarded annually. It is widely thought to be a good, if imperfect, predictor of a possible future Nobel Prize; 12 of the first 18 winners did go on to win the Nobel Prize, and many of the others are still young and under consideration. Professor Athey was recognized for her contributions to economic theory, empirical economics, and econometrics, especially in the area of industrial organization.
- Two more women have won the Clark Prize since then—**Esther Duflo**, a tremendously productive scholar who has revolutionized the field of economic development and whose work we discuss in Chapters 13 and 14, and **Amy Finkelstein**, who is a top scholar of health economics and health insurance markets. You can read more about the latter three women and their awards at www.aeaweb.org/honors_awards/clark_medal.php.

Women continue to be underrepresented in the economics profession, although change is afoot. In 1972, the first year that statistics on the status of women in the economics profession were collected, only 6 percent of all faculty in economics departments were women, only 3 percent of full professors were women, and only 12 percent of graduate students were women. By the mid-1990s, this percentage had increased to about one-third, and it has remained at that level ever since. In 2012, women earned 32.5 percent of all new PhDs in economics. Nevertheless, women remain underrepresented in academia. About one-fifth of all tenured or tenure-track economists teaching at universities and colleges are women. Nearly 30 percent of assistant professors are women, but only 12 percent of full professors are. This lower proportion reflects both the age structure of the profession—women in academia are, on average, still younger than men—and also issues relating to retention and promotion, and especially those involving family and work conflict.

Box   1.2

Women's Lives Back in the Day ... but Not So Long Ago

A perfect wife ... according to the textbooks

In the twenty-first century, a clear majority of married women combine family and work responsibilities. But this situation was much less common in the 1950s. And, indeed, being a wife was a sort of occupation. School courses in home economics often served the function of training women in the domestic arts—sewing, cooking, and so on. They also provided some useful tips on how to be a successful wife. The following excerpts come from a home economics textbook published in 1950 and used in a public school in Lincoln, Nebraska.

- "Have dinner ready: Plan ahead, even the night before, to have a delicious meal ... on time. This is a way to let him know that you have been thinking about him and about his needs."
- "Prepare the children: take a few minutes to wash the children's hands and faces ... comb their hair, and, if necessary, change their clothes. They are little treasures and he would like to see them playing the part."
- "Some don'ts: Don't greet him with complaints or problems. Don't complain if he is late for dinner; count this as minor compared with what he might have gone through that day."
- "Make the evening his: Never complain if he does not take you out to dinner or to other places of entertainment. Instead try to understand his world of strain and pressure, his need to be home and relax."
- "The goal: Try to make your home a place of peace and order, where your husband can renew in body and spirit."

Occupation housewife?

Being a housewife isn't traditionally considered an occupation. Household output isn't included in the National Income accounts and women don't receive credit toward Social Security benefits for their household work. But, as Barbara Bergmann, a well-known and early feminist economist, noted in an article in 1981, being a housewife certainly met the dictionary definition of an occupation as "an activity that serves as one's regular source of livelihood." Indeed, as she pointed out, it was undoubtedly the largest single occupation in the United States at that time.

Upon thinking of a housewife as an occupation, it's natural to describe it and compare it to other occupations. Here is what Professor Bergmann had to say about it:

> The housewife's occupational duties ... usually include cooking, dishwashing, housecleaning, laundry work, child care, and a "personal relations" component, which includes sexual relations ... The nonsexual component of housewives' duties are broadly the same as the duties of paid domestic servants, although the housewife usually has more discretion than the servant, and a more responsible role with respect to the children and the finances. A housewife whose "job" ends, either at her own discretion or that of her husband, will probably have to enter some other occupation at least for a time. She will be faced with the fact that the

alternative occupation most like the one she has left, and the one for which she has the most fitting recent experience, is one with both low pay and low status ... They will be at a disadvantage in the job market ... Because of the failure to build up, during their services as housewives, that part of their human capital thought to be most serviceable on non-domestic jobs.

... Like the airline stewardess, part of the housewife's job is being attractive. Unlike the stewardess, however, the housewife's duties clearly include cohabitation ... Of course, sexual cohabitation in this context forms a perhaps vital part of the intimacy of the marriage relationship, with its presumption of caring, consideration, and long-run commitment. It is usually, at the outset at least, considered a highly valued fringe benefit rather than an onerous duty. However, the sex component of the housewife's duties, and the children who may appear as a result of it, make it difficult to go from one "job" to another within the occupation.

The housewife's attractiveness to her husband can be thought of as a component of the human capital needed for her job, and she may be in the position of seeing this part of her portfolio of assets wane in value either gradually or suddenly. Her husband's attractiveness to her may also suddenly or gradually diminish, reducing the value of the intimacy fringe benefit. These possibilities obviously make for high risk both with respect to "working conditions" and tenure.

Another component of a housewife's human capital which contributes to the value of her work is her identity as the mother of the husband's children, and thus as the person usually assumed to be most fitted to give them attentive and loving care. As the number of children born to marriages has ... diminished and as the number of years in which a married couple has preschool children in the home has diminished, this component of a wife's human capital disappears faster, leaving her more open to the threat of displacement from her "job."

... The decline in the value of a wife's services in the home occurs at a time when her husband's earnings and status are usually growing. The discrepancy in economic position and in the social opportunities of a housewife and the man to whom she is married typically grows as they go through their forties.

Final words

Although the focus of this book is women, many, if not most, of the topics considered also involve men. Certainly that is true for most marriages and most births, and also for decisions about working in the labor market. Even if women are from Venus and men are from Mars, their economic lives intersect frequently and in ways that are often of great importance to both of them. So even though the subject of this book is women, it definitely ought to be of interest to both women and men.

Finally, the economics in this book is not the economics that your parents learned when they were in school. Many of the analyses presented here are on the frontier of economics. Topics such as marriage, fertility, and household production are relative newcomers to economics. Why marriage rates have fallen so much for young black men and women, how changes in women's labor-market opportunities affect their well-being in marriage, and how contraception and abortion may have affected the incidence of non-marital births are just a few of the many contemporary issues that are covered in this book. These topics pushed and stretched economic analysis into previously uncharted territory. Not every analysis is fully formed and widely accepted, and you may well find a few quarrels to pick. That's as it should be. You don't have to agree with everything; we don't agree with absolutely everything either, although we think all of it is interesting and provocative, if nothing else. We urge you to think critically and carefully, in this course and elsewhere.

2 ECONOMICS TOOLS AND THINKING

Introduction

The goal in this chapter is to explore the distinctive microeconomic way of thinking. Microeconomics can sometimes be difficult for students to understand. Because it has many graphs, concepts, and definitions, it is certainly possible to lose sight of the forest with all those trees in the way. But the core of microeconomics is relatively simple; even better, it is relatively constant from problem to problem and chapter to chapter. If you can grasp the shape of the forest, you will have much less trouble finding your way through the trees.

We begin by focusing on the core ideas in microeconomics—choice, constraints, maximization, and comparative statics. We then introduce some specific terms and relationships, and review supply-and-demand analysis. The last section of the chapter is a nontechnical introduction to empirical methods widely used in economics, including some new innovative approaches. It is important to understand these methods in order to appreciate and evaluate the empirical research on women's economic issues.

Microeconomics—the basic approach

Choices

Microeconomics is about choosing. The website of the American Economics Association says that "Economics is the study of how people choose to use resources." Alfred Marshall, author of the first famous economics textbook, in 1890, wrote that "Economics is the study of people in the ordinary business of life," a definition that certainly fits the topics of this book. Individuals or firms or workers or whoever else may be the focus of a particular problem make choices about something. For the most part, things don't just happen. Somebody chooses to make them happen.

These choices have some common, though not inevitable and unchangeable, characteristics. First, the choices are usually purposeful and goal-directed. Often, economists assume that the chooser is trying to maximize the value of something. Second, the chooser is assumed to be reasonably well informed so that the actions taken are consistent with the desired goals. Third, the choice is usually made in a context that involves some limits or constraints. Without limits, there isn't much difficulty in choosing—we can have everything.

Now, thinking of objections to this choice-based approach is easy enough. First, sometimes the constraints are so severe that there really isn't much of a choice—certainly no good choices. Sociologists are fond of quoting James Duesenberry, a famous economist, who once wrote that "Economics is all about how people make choices; sociology is all about how they don't really have any choices to make." In a case of extreme poverty, choosing between food and clothing and shelter and healthcare, knowing that choosing one means sacrificing the others, is clearly not an attractive proposition. It may be tempting to think that there is no choice here, but it's much better social science to think of someone choosing even in that setting. Understand that the decision to analyze choices doesn't presume that the choices are themselves particularly attractive. Second, sometimes individuals aren't sufficiently informed; this scenario is certainly the case in some of the issues we'll examine. At what developmental stage do individuals clearly see the implications of their actions so that we might regard them as acting purposefully? When we talk about teen childbearing and try to apply a choice model, the issue of purposefulness is genuine. As we noted briefly in Chapter 1, an entire field of economics, called "behavioral economics," focuses on the limitations of the rational economics approach. Still, for our purposes in this text, sticking to the traditional choice approach but being aware that it may not fit every possible situation is the best approach.

The shorthand economics jargon for the choice situation described above—maximization, reasonably complete information, and a constraint—is **constrained maximization**. The concept of constrained maximization lies at the heart of microeconomic analysis. Let's write this idea out in a very general way. Many, if not most, microeconomics problems have the following general structure:

> Some economic agent (e.g., a person or a firm) chooses the value of some economic variable to maximize something that depends on that variable, subject to a constraint that involves the variable being chosen and usually some other variables as well.

To put this in a yet more compact way, let X stand for the variable to be chosen and V stand for whatever it is that will be maximized. For example, X could be the amount of output a firm produces and V could be its profits. The link between V and X can be written as $V(X)$, which is read "V of X" and means that for every value of X there is a corresponding value of V. Finally, let Z stand for all the other variables in the constraint. Then the constrained maximization problem can be written this way:

> Choose X to maximize $V(X)$ subject to a constraint involving X and Z (2.1)

Two more pieces of jargon will be useful. In a problem like this one, the variable X is called the **endogenous variable**, which means it is chosen inside the model ("endo" = inside). The variables that are "givens" and are not chosen, like Z, are the **exogenous variables**, which means they are determined outside the model ("exo" = outside). The exogenous variables are particularly important, as you will see shortly. Simply keeping track of what's endogenous and what's exogenous is very valuable.

That's it. Most microeconomics problems involve not much more than a clever adaption of equation (2.1) to fit the basic characteristics of a particular problem. We'll look at an example after we examine a few more pieces of the economics approach.

Solutions

Choice problems such as those defined by equation (2.1) usually have a unique solution. That is, there is some value of X that "solves the problem" and yields the maximum value of V given the relationship between V and X and the particulars of the constraint. Call that best choice X^*. We will use the asterisk "*" often, almost always to indicate the solution to a maximization problem.

The solution to a choice problem can be usefully represented in two related ways. First, it is almost always possible to write out a rule or a condition that must hold at the value of X that solves the problem. Typically, this rule involves finding the value of X that causes two different expressions to be equal to one another. These rules are usually called **marginal conditions** because they virtually always involve focusing on the value of the last or "marginal" unit of X. Choosing the amount of X where the marginal benefit of the last unit just equals its marginal cost is a general example of this kind of rule. A firm choosing its output where marginal revenue equals marginal cost is another example that you may have seen in a previous economics class. The marginal conditions are particularly useful for understanding the economic logic behind a solution to a choice problem.

The solution to the problem can also be written in terms of X^* and the exogenous variables in the problem. Generally it looks something like this:

$$X^* = F(Z) \tag{2.2}$$

This equation indicates that the best choice of X depends on (is a function of) all the exogenous variables in the problem (Z). In equation (2.2), F stands for an unspecified function that links the variables in Z to X^*. This solution is derived from the marginal condition; the X^* in equation (2.2) is exactly the value of X that solves the problem, given the particular values of the variables in Z. The relationship between the best choice and the exogenous variables is emphasized in this form.

Expressing the solution in the form of equation (2.2) can often be very useful. Sometimes it is too difficult (at least for many students) to find and understand the marginal conditions of a problem. In that case, however, we can often write the solution as in equation (2.2) if we can express the problem as a constrained maximization problem using equation (2.1) and correctly identify the endogenous and exogenous variables.

Changing choices—comparative static analysis

Finally, economists are often interested in how the best choice of X will change when the exogenous variables change. This is called **comparative static analysis**. The name is not as helpful as might be hoped: "Comparative" refers to a comparison of the before-and-after choices, and "static" means that we are looking at the choices themselves rather than the dynamic process of getting from "before" to "after." A good theory will usually be able to offer a specific prediction about how X^* will change when Z changes.

To analyze this, we use the solution in the form of equation (2.2), in which X^* is a function of the exogenous variables in Z. (The equation is useful already.) The theory might, for example, hypothesize that a positive relationship exists between X^* and one of the variables in Z. Let's call that variable Z_1. Then the predicted relationship can be written as

$$\Delta X^*/\Delta Z_1 > 0 \tag{2.3}$$

In equation (2.3), Δ, the Greek letter delta, stands for "change in." The positive relationship means that X^* increases when Z_1 increases (ΔX^* and ΔZ_1 are both positive) and that X^* decreases when Z_1 decreases (ΔX^* and ΔZ_1 are both negative).

The theory might also suggest a negative relationship between X^* and some other variable, Z_2, which would be written like this:

$$\Delta X^*/\Delta Z_2 < 0 \tag{2.4}$$

The negative relationship means that X^* increases when Z_2 decreases ($\Delta X^* > 0$ and $\Delta Z_2 < 0$) and that X^* decreases when Z_2 increases ($\Delta X^* < 0$ and $Z_2 > 0$).

The comparative static predictions of a theory are absolutely its most important feature. This is true for two reasons. First, it is often exactly what we want to know. For example, we might want to know how an increase in the earnings of women in the twentieth century has affected choices about work, marriage, and family size. Second, it is the way we can tell whether a theory is useful and valid. If a theory predicts a positive relationship between X^* and Z_1, but testing establishes that the relationship is negative or zero, then the theory is rejected. If testing indicates that the relationship is positive, as the theory hypothesized, then the theory is tentatively accepted, pending further testing and possible future rejection. When a theory has been confirmed often enough, it often gains the status of a "law," like the Law of Demand.

The **Law of Demand** is, in fact, a perfect example of precisely how this whole choice apparatus works. In consumer demand analysis, economists attempt to explain the choices that consumers make. Individuals choose the amount of the goods they consume to maximize something called **utility**, which means pleasure or satisfaction. The amount of utility an individual receives depends on the amount of goods he or she consumes; we can write this relationship as $U(X_1, X_2)$, where X_1 and X_2 stand for any two goods. (Economists often use just two goods in a case like this because it substantially simplifies the problem, without distorting it.) The expression $U(X_1, X_2)$ is referred to as a **utility function**. We discuss the idea of a utility function more fully below, but for the moment it should be clear enough that it expresses the idea that the amounts of X_1 and X_2 affect the amount of utility an individual receives.

In choosing the amounts of goods X_1 and X_2, individuals are constrained by their income (I) and the prices of the goods (P_1, P_2). This constraint, which is referred to as the **budget constraint**, limits the amounts of the goods they can afford in a pretty obvious way. They can't, for example, buy goods that cost more than their income. (We're abstracting here from credit cards.)

The constrained maximization consumer demand problem could be written formally this way: *An individual chooses the amounts of goods X_1 and X_2 to maximize $U(X_1, X_2)$ subject to a budget constraint that involves, $P_1, P_2,$ and I.*

A unique best solution to this consumer demand problem can be written in terms of a marginal condition, in this case in terms of something called marginal utility and the prices of the two goods or, in a more sophisticated version, the marginal rate of substitution and prices. The details don't matter; it's enough for now to know that there is *some* best answer. The solution indicates the best amounts of goods X_1 and X_2 to consume to maximize utility.

Let's focus on the demand for good X_1. In this choice problem, X_1 is the endogenous variable and prices, income, and preferences are the exogenous variables. The relationship between the endogenous variable and the exogenous variables, written in the form of equation (2.2), is

$$X_1^* = D\ (P_1,\ P_2,\ I,\ preferences) \tag{2.5}$$

This is the individual's demand function, which is why D is used to represent the function. The demand function indicates that the utility-maximizing choice of the amount of X_1 depends on its own price, the price of the other good, the individual's income, and preferences.

Finally, the most important comparative static relationship is $\Delta X_1^*/\Delta P_1$, which is the response of X_1^* to a change in its own price, holding constant P_2, I, and preferences. Economic theory predicts that $\Delta X_1^*/\Delta P_1 < 0$, which is simply the famous Law of Demand.[1] When the price goes up, the amount demanded falls (and vice versa). Other important comparative static results examine the effect of changes in other prices or income on the demand for X_1.

When economists are doing comparative static analysis, they invariably emphasize changes in prices and/or incomes rather than changes in preferences. Economists do not believe that preferences never change. Clearly, preferences do change—just think about clothing or hairstyles or music, for example. Then why do economists tend to downplay changes in preferences? For one thing, preferences tend to change slowly, so it's often reasonable to think of preferences being constant as prices or incomes change. More importantly, though, resorting to changes in preferences as an explanation for changing behavior is a bit too easy and almost impossible to verify. It's probably prudent to think of preferences as a last explanation, after examining observable changes in prices and/or incomes.

In a nutshell, microeconomics is simply economic agents choosing endogenous variables to maximize something. That choice depends on some exogenous variables that are part of the constraint. The details depend on the particular problem being analyzed. The best solution can be described by both a marginal condition and the corresponding function that relates the best choice to the exogenous variables. The theory predicts how that best choice will change when the exogenous variables change, and those predictions are the comparative static results. If the predictions are wrong, the theory goes into the trash can or at least back to the blackboard or the laboratory for reworking. This are the basic workings of microeconomics.

Theories and models in economics

Like most social and natural sciences, economic analysis relies on theories to explain things observed in the real world. To make a theory easy enough to understand, economists virtually always construct a model of the real-world situation they want to analyze. In doing so, they invariably simplify the problem to be studied by making assumptions that eliminate some real-world factors. A good model in economics or any other subject successfully manages the delicate task of retaining the essence of a problem while simultaneously stripping away all the complicating factors that make the underlying relationships difficult to see. For example, a model of the labor market might assume the absence of government laws (e.g., the minimum wage) and market institutions (e.g., labor unions). It might also assume that all workers are identically productive. The goal is to see how

---

1 More precisely, the Law of Demand holds for **normal goods**, which are goods that an individual buys more of as his or her income increases. For **inferior goods**—goods that an individual buys less of at a higher income—the Law of Demand almost always holds, but that is not a direct prediction of the theory.

the labor market might work in such a setting. What determines labor demand? What influences labor supply? What will the wage rate be? Will there be unemployment? When these questions are answered, an economist might then incorporate minimum wage regulations, labor unions, and productivity differences into the model. This procedure makes seeing the basic economic forces that operate in the labor market possible. It also helps identify exactly how minimum wage laws or labor unions or individual productivity affect the outcome. Another very good example of using models to analyze a very complicated problem is the analysis of the economic impact of labor-market discrimination. See Box 2.1.

The purpose of a model is to explain behavior and outcomes in the real world. Thus after a model is constructed, it is tested against real-world data to see how well it predicts. Those models that don't predict or explain real-world behavior reasonably well are ultimately discarded. A model that repeatedly performs well is accepted. Fortunately, in the area of women's economic behavior, a very substantial amount of data are collected by both the government and private entities. As a result, economists working in this area have ample access to data, which allows them to test their theories. Be aware, however, that the data are seldom perfect, so it is always prudent to be cautious in drawing conclusions. There is a great deal of interesting thinking in economics research right now about how best to carry out economic analysis in the face of imperfect data. Some of the new methods are discussed later in this chapter.

Box	2.1

Using Models in Economic Analysis

The economic analysis of labor-market discrimination, which we will consider in detail in Chapter 10, nicely illustrates the way in which economists use models. Economists typically begin their analysis of discrimination where sociologists, anthropologists, and psychologists stop theirs. Researchers in these fields might investigate such topics as how and why feelings of discrimination develop; how those feelings persist, strengthen, or erode; the forms that discrimination takes, the functions it serves; and its psychological and sociological effects on all parties. They do not, however, usually inquire into how these feelings influence economic behavior and economic outcomes. Those are precisely the topics emphasized by economists in analyzing discrimination, because those are the areas where economic theory can be most usefully applied.

Economists tend to ignore the development of discriminatory attitudes not because that topic is unimportant but because economic theory has relatively little to contribute. Instead the economic approach to discrimination is to pose the problem this way. Suppose that feelings of discrimination take the specific form that employers prefer one type of worker over another, even if the workers were equally skilled and if their wages were the same. How will this affect labor-market equilibrium? Note the important assumption that workers are equally skilled. This is not intended to be realistic. Economists surely know that not all workers are equally skilled. Rather, the purpose of that assumption is to isolate discrimination as the sole source of any wage differences.

The analysis of discrimination also shows the potential value of economic theory. Consider the following two assertions, both of which have their advocates: (1) "Labor market discrimination is a natural outgrowth of the actions of profit-maximizing firms operating in an unregulated, competitive economy;" or (2) "Competitive markets tend to eliminate the effects of discrimination. Discrimination can thrive only when competition is weak." Clearly, only one of the two statements can be correct. The difference is not just academic. The design of effective government policy to eliminate discrimination in the labor market depends critically on which view is correct. Should government restrict competitive behavior, as the first view suggests, or should it encourage competition and seek to strengthen it, following the second? How can we determine which of the two statements is correct?

That is exactly where economic theory comes in. We can save the details for later (Chapter 10), but the basic idea is this. First, economists do not have to start from scratch in analyzing discrimination. There already exists a well-developed model—the competitive model—which has proven useful for analyzing the behavior of profit-maximizing competitive firms in the absence of discrimination. The analytical task, then, is to modify that model by incorporating discrimination and then seeing what difference it makes in the outcomes predicted by the model. How do the results with and without discrimination differ? For example, are discriminating firms more or less profitable than firms that do not practice discrimination? If the model suggested that discriminating firms were more profitable, this would lend support to the first assertion. But suppose that discrimination turned out to require a sacrificing of profits. That would certainly suggest that, in competitive markets, where the profit motive is strong, discrimination might be weak. A good theoretical model of how discrimination affects the behavior of competitive firms should help us to find the answer.

Microeconomics—basic tools and concepts

Not only is there a basic economic approach to many problems, but there are also basic relationships and tools that are common across many analyses. If you learn them, you can get a lot of mileage out of them. In this section we introduce some basic tools and concepts that we will use repeatedly.

Functions

We actually introduced the idea of a function in the previous section where we talked first about the function $V(X)$ and then later the functions $X^* = F(Z)$, $U(X_1, X_2)$, and $X_1^* = D(P_1, P_2, I, \text{Preferences})$. But let's spend a few minutes to understand the ideas and then review two particular functions that appear throughout this book.

Functions are very convenient shorthand ways to show what depends on what. In the function $X^* = F(Z)$, the variable on the left-hand side of the equality (X^*) is postulated to depend on the variable in the parentheses on the right-hand side (Z). If we knew exactly how the variables were related, we might write that explicitly. For example, perhaps $X^* = 3Z_1 + 2.5Z_2$ or $X^* = Z_1 \times Z_2$. But usually we don't know the exact relationship; instead we know only that the variables are related and sometimes also whether the expected effect is positive or negative.

When we don't know the exact relationship, we often use a letter such as F (for "function") to stand for some unspecified relationship between X^* and Z. The letter F doesn't mean anything in particular. In fact, sometimes it's convenient to substitute another letter, such as D for the demand function or S for the supply function.

In the functions $V(X)$ and $U(X_1, X_2)$, there is no equals sign, but the general idea is the same. The value of V depends on X and the value of U depends on X and Y. We could have written $V = V(X)$ or $U = U(X_1, X_2)$, but that is usually not done in some circumstances (e.g., a maximization problem). In the $V = V(X)$ form, the V on the left-hand side is the value of the function and the V on the right-hand side is the function itself.

So the general rule with functional relationships is that whatever is in parentheses affects the other variable, whether that variable is on the other side of the equation or is just a function where the other side of the equation is implicit. The variables inside the parentheses are called the **arguments** of the function. In many economics problems, identifying the arguments of the function is an important first step in the analysis.

Two special functions We will regularly use two special functions—a **utility function** and a **household production function**.

We introduced the idea of a utility function when we discussed the Law of Demand as an example of a choice problem in microeconomics. "Utility" is a concept that comes from nineteenth-century economists and means happiness, satisfaction, or pleasure. Economists assume that individuals make choices in order to maximize their utility – that is, to make themselves as well-off as possible, given their own subjective evaluation of what they like. This doesn't imply that they are totally selfish; an individual might well gain happiness from the happiness of others (e.g., family members).

A utility function is a way of specifying the things that provide utility. These things, which are the arguments of the utility function, will vary, depending on the particular problem being analyzed. The simplest, most general way to write a utility function is

$$U = U(X_1, X_2) \tag{2.6}$$

where, again, we use just two goods rather than many in order to simplify. In equation (2.6), the U on the left-hand side stands for the amount of utility, X_1 and X_2 are consumption goods, and $U(X_1, X_2)$ is the utility function itself. A utility function gives the amount of utility associated with a particular amount of X_1 and X_2. In general, there is a positive relationship between the amount of X_1 or X_2 and the amount of utility.

Utility isn't directly measurable. It doesn't really make any sense to say that a particular meal gave you 11 utility units (sometimes called *utils*) or 27 utility units or any other number. The numbers themselves don't mean anything, but that doesn't matter. The only numerical comparison that matters in utility analysis is that more utility is better than less, so a bigger number is better than a smaller number. This is an ordinal comparison. We will sometimes use numbers to represent utility, but they are just illustrative. The only important feature of one particular number is whether it is bigger or smaller or equal to another number. If individuals want to maximize their utility, they will always prefer more utility to less.

Utility functions are a central element in the economic theory of choice. Suppose an individual is comparing two mutually exclusive situations, which we will call A and B. An individual will do either A or B. A and B could be literally anything—going to college vs. not going, getting married vs. not getting married, and so on. Let's refer to the utility of these situations as $U(A)$ and $U(B)$; $U(A)$ is the utility the individual would receive if she makes choice A, and $U(B)$ is the corresponding utility if she makes choice B. If $U(A) > U(B)$, we expect that she will choose A instead of B; however, if $U(B) > U(A)$, we expect that she will choose B. This simple bit of logic is referred to as a **rational choice model**. It will turn out to be very important reasoning later on. In fact, sometimes we might even work backward. If an individual is observed to choose A when B was available, then it must be true that $U(A) > U(B)$. This idea is referred to as **revealed preference**. The name says it all—the preferences are revealed by the choice.

A **production function** is used to describe the technology of the production process. Originally it was applied to firms to summarize the relationship between the amount of input used and the amount of output produced. In its most general form it can be written as Amount of Output = F (Amount of Input) or $Q = F(L, K)$, where Q is the amount of output, and L and K stand for labor and capital. In the 1960s, Gary Becker proposed a new approach to consumer theory that used production functions to analyze consumer behavior.[2] In his new approach, consumers were producers of what he called **household commodities**. These household commodities, and not market goods and services, were the ultimate source of utility. For example, the food in the refrigerator and pantry doesn't provide utility until it is used, along with time and kitchen capital equipment, to first produce and then consume a meal. The utility comes from the household-produced good—a meal—rather than the raw materials—the food itself.

The point is much broader and not confined to food preparation. In Becker's view, households produced a wide range of very basic goods for themselves—nutrition, health, entertainment, even children—by combining market goods with their own time. The market goods that were previously considered the direct sources of utility are now viewed instead as inputs into the production process. He called the production functions in this process **household production functions**.

A household production function is exactly the same idea as a conventional production function. It shows the maximum amount of output associated with any particular set of inputs. The only difference is that a household production function refers to the household and a conventional production function to a firm. It will often be useful to write out a household production function in the following way:

$$G = G(T, Z) \tag{2.7}$$

In equation (2.7), the G on the left side stands for the amount of household goods produced, T stands for the amount of time, Z stands for the amount of all other inputs, and the G on the right side stands for the production function that links the amounts of T and Z to the amount of G produced. Just as in the traditional production function, there is a positive relationship between the amounts of T and Z used and the amount of G produced.

This idea of household production will be an important concept throughout much of this book. Much of women's lives has taken place in the household rather than in the labor

2 Gary S. Becker (1965), "A Theory of the Allocation of Time," *Economic Journal*, 75, 493–517.

market, and household production is the way to describe what they were, and are, doing there. We use the idea of household-produced goods to describe and explain marriage in Chapter 3, fertility in Chapter 5, and women's labor-force participation in Chapter 7.

Total and marginal curves

When economists work with functions, they are usually interested both in the *total* amount of utility or total amount of output and in the *change* in the total amount when one of the arguments of the function is increased. This latter idea involves looking at what are called **marginal changes**. For example, if we were working with the utility function, $U = U(X_1, X_2)$, we would want to know about the change in utility if X_1 or X_2 increased by a little bit. If we were analyzing household production with the household production function, $G = G(T, Z)$, we might want to know about the change in output if T or Z increased by a little bit. We can write these changes as

$$\Delta U / \Delta X_1 \text{ or } \Delta G / \Delta T \tag{2.8}$$

where, again, Δ stands for "change in."

Totals and marginals are related in a very specific way that will be useful and important to us. Figure 2.1(A) and (B) shows one possible relationship between U and X. Part (A) shows the total function; that is, it gives the total value of U for every value of X. In (A), the total function is a straight line with a constant slope. That slope, like all slopes, is just the change in the vertical-axis variable divided by the change in the horizontal-axis variable (i.e., the rise over the run). So the slope equals $\Delta U/\Delta X$, which is the marginal change. This important idea bears repeating: *For any total function, the associated marginal function equals the slope of the total curve at the particular point at which the change is occurring.* Since the slope in (A) is constant, the marginal change is constant. It is just a horizontal line, whose height is equal to the slope of the total function, as shown in Part (B).

The particular relationship shown in parts (A) and (B) with a linear total curve and a horizontal marginal curve is actually not very common in economic analysis. It implies, not very realistically, that if more of a good is consumed, the same additional amount of additional U is received. It's more likely that the change in U will diminish as the amount of X increases. Think of eating slices of pizza. The first slice, when you are hungriest, tastes best and provides the most utility. Each successive piece is enjoyable, but it is a bit less so than the preceding ones. Eventually, the marginal value is so low that eating another slice of pizza would not be enjoyable. If the pizza were free, we would eat it until its marginal utility was zero. The same idea holds for most goods that are consumed—the marginal value usually declines as you have more and more of them.

This kind of relationship is shown in Figure 2.1(C) and (D). In (C), the total utility function is curved. It gets flatter and flatter as X increases. This is exactly equivalent to saying that the change in U gets smaller and smaller as X increases. But that means that the marginal curve in (D) falls steadily. Each unit of X adds less and less to U. The height of the curve at each value of X in (D) is exactly equal to the slope of the total curve at that same value of X in (C). We've drawn the curve in (D) as a straight line, but it might well be curvilinear; the important point is that it has a negative slope. When the total curve is at its maximum in (C), the marginal curve in (D) equals zero. The vertical dotted line in parts (C) and (D) shows this relationship.

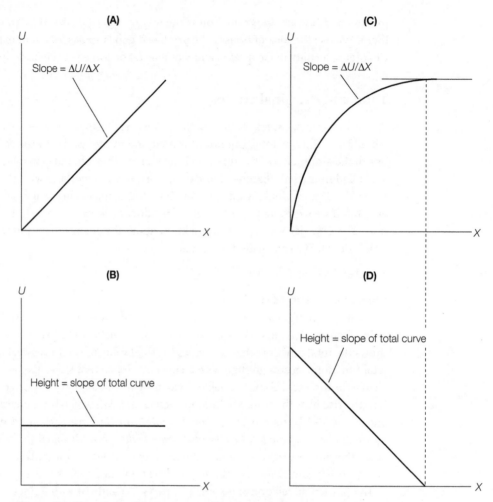

Figure 2.1 *The relationship between total and marginal curves.*

Do not confuse a fall in the marginal curve with a fall in the total curve. When the marginal curve is positive, even if it is falling, the total curve is still rising. If the total curve were falling, the marginal curve would actually be negative.

The increase in utility when the amount of one good increases is called **marginal utility**. We write this as $MU(X) \equiv \Delta U/\Delta X$, where the $\equiv$ means that the expression is an identity, true for all values of X and U by definition. The idea that marginal utility falls as the amount of X increases is called **diminishing marginal utility**. This concept will be important later.

When we work with a production function, the increase in output when one of the inputs increases, with all other inputs held constant, is called the **marginal product**. For the household production function $G = G(T, Z)$, the marginal products are $MP_T \equiv \Delta G/\Delta T$ and $MP_Z \equiv \Delta G/\Delta Z$. Here the idea is that each additional unit of input provides less and less additional output. The marginal product is typically positive—adding more input does increase the amount of output—but declining. This relationship is described in one of the most famous laws in economics, the **Law of Diminishing Marginal Returns**. We will use it later.

The economic details behind diminishing marginal utility and marginal product will be explained later when we use those ideas. For now it is important to realize that a function can be described in two related ways, by looking at either the total function or its associated marginal function. Both provide the same information but they highlight different features. Most functions used in economics will look like Figure 2.1(C) and (D) rather than (A) and (B).

Supply, demand, and market equilibrium

Supply-and-demand analysis is such an important idea in microeconomics that it is worth reviewing here. It is the fundamental, though not exclusive, model for explaining how prices are set in a market economy.

Briefly, a demand function summarizes the relationship between the quantity demanded of a particular good and the various factors that influence that amount. The market demand function is $Q_D^* = D(P, P', I, \text{Preferences})$, where Q_D^* is the utility-maximizing demand of all consumers, P is the price of the good, P' stands for all other prices, and I is income. Holding P', I, and Preferences constant and allowing P to vary traces out the demand curve. The Law of Demand tells us that the price and the quantity demanded vary inversely or negatively. When the price goes up, the quantity demanded goes down. When the price goes down, the quantity demanded goes up.

When the price of a product changes, two things happen at once, and both changes usually operate to cause the negative relationship between price and quantity demanded. First, the **relative price** of the product changes. The relative price is the price of the product compared to the price of other goods that a consumer could buy instead. Second, a change in the price of the product causes a change in consumers' real income – that is, in what they can buy with their income. When the price of a good increases, consumers' real income goes down, because they can no longer buy as much of everything as before. Similarly, when the price of a good decreases, real income goes up—it is as if consumers were a bit richer than before the price decrease.

Suppose, for example, the price of a good goes up. Because the relative price of the good is now higher than before, consumers will typically substitute away from that good and toward goods that are now relatively less expensive than before. This is called the **substitution effect**. In addition, because the price increase reduces real income, consumers typically compensate and buy less of that good and other goods as well. This effect is called the **income effect**. When the price of a good falls, these two effects work in reverse. Consumers substitute toward the now-cheaper good (the substitution effect), and because the lower price makes them richer by increasing their real income, they buy a bit more than before (the income effect).[3]

The supply curve functions in exactly the same way to summarize the amount supplied to the market by profit-maximizing competitive firms. The major influences of supply are the price of the good, the prices of the inputs used in the production process, and the state of the available technology, which affects productivity and hence production costs.

---

3 The income effect described here is for normal goods. It is just the opposite for inferior goods. The Law of Demand may not hold for inferior goods, but it usually does.

The market supply function can be written as $Q_s^* = S\ (P,\ W,\ Z)$, where Q_s^* is the profit-maximizing supply of all producers, W stands for all the input prices, and Z stands for the available technology. Holding W and Z constant and allowing P to vary traces out the firm's supply function. The supply function is just the set of profit-maximizing outputs for each possible price. In general, the relationship between the price and the quantity supplied is positive. When the price increases, so does the quantity supplied. When the price falls, the quantity supplied falls, too.

A competitive market is one in which there are many demanders and many suppliers, none of whom has any meaningful influence over the price of the product. In such a setting, the competitive market equilibrium is the price at which supply and demand just balance. It is a price P^* such that $D\ (P^*,\ P,\ I,\ \text{Preferences}) = S\ (P^*,\ W,\ Z)$; in other words, it is the price at which the amount demanded just equals the amount supplied. This price is the price that is likely to emerge from a competitive market left to its own devices – that is, unregulated by government.

Figure 2.2 illustrates the familiar supply-and-demand diagram. The price is on the vertical axis and the amount demanded or supplied is on the horizontal axis. The demand curve is negatively sloped, while the supply curve is positively sloped. The two curves intersect at P^*, which is the equilibrium price. There—and only there—does the quantity demanded exactly equal the quantity supplied. The associated equilibrium quantity bought and sold is Q^*.

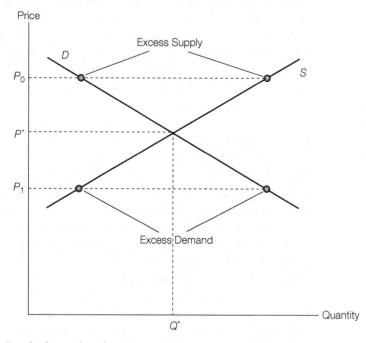

Figure 2.2 *Supply, demand, and market equilibrium.*

At the other two prices shown in Figure 2.2, the market is not in equilibrium because the quantity supplied and the quantity demanded are unequal. At a price above equilibrium such as P_0, the amount supplied is quite large, but the amount demanded is much less. The excess supply is the horizontal distance between the two curves. In this situation the price will usually fall, thereby increasing the amount demanded, decreasing the amount supplied, and moving price and quantity back toward the equilibrium at P^* and Q^*. At a low price such as P_1, the amount supplied is much less, the amount demanded is much more, and a shortage exists, again measured by the horizontal distance between the curves. Now there is likely to be upward pressure on the price, moving it back up to the equilibrium. When the market equilibrium is reached at price P^* and quantity Q^*, there is no reason for any further change unless either the supply curve or the demand curve changes. That is what it means to say that the market is in equilibrium.

Comparative statics of supply and demand

Supply-and-demand analysis is particularly useful for predicting how the equilibrium price and quantity will change if there is a change in one of the two curves. Suppose that demand changes, which would occur if there were a change in a variable in the demand function other than the price of the good—a change in the price of other goods, a change in income, or a change in preferences. These are the exogenous demand variables in a supply/demand model. An increase in demand means that more is demanded at every price or, equivalently, that consumers are willing to pay more for any given quantity. Thought of the first way, the demand curve shifts out to the right; thought of the other way, the demand curve shifts up. The impact is exactly the same in each case. A decrease in demand would be a shift to the left or a shift downward.

Figure 2.3 shows how a demand change affects price and quantity. The two arrows indicate the two ways to represent an increase in demand, as either an outward or upward shift of the demand curve. When demand increases from D_0 to D_1, the equilibrium price and quantity both increase to P_1^* and Q_1^*, respectively. At the original equilibrium price P_0^*, there is excess demand with demand curve D_1, so the price rises. The new equilibrium moves up the supply curve.

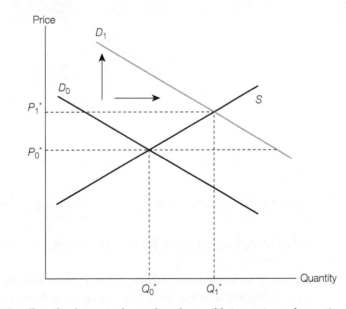

Figure 2.3 *The effect of a change in demand on the equilibrium price and quantity.*

If, instead, demand fell from D_1 to D_0, thereby reversing the process, the price and quantity would fall. Now there is excess supply at price P_1^* with demand curve D_0, which causes the price and quantity to decrease. In summary: when demand increases, the equilibrium price and quantity both rise; when demand decreases, the equilibrium price and quantity both fall.

The effect of a change in supply can be analyzed in the same way. You need to be careful in thinking about what an increase in supply means and how it is represented. Here, an increase means either that the supply curve shifts out (more supplied at the same price, just as for an increase in demand) or that the supply curve shifts down, meaning that any amount will now be supplied at a lower price than before. Figure 2.4 shows the effect of an increase in supply. Again, the two arrows show the two ways to represent an increase in supply. Here, as supply increases, the equilibrium price falls from P_0^* to P_1^*, and the equilibrium quantity increases from Q_0^* to Q_1^*. The price change occurs because, at the original equilibrium price and with the new supply curve, there is excess supply (the horizontal distance between the original market equilibrium and the new supply curve). So the price falls, reducing the amount supplied, increasing the amount demanded, and creating a new market equilibrium at P_1^* and Q_1^*.

If supply decreased, the supply curve would shift to the left (less supplied at any price) or up (any amount now supplied at a higher price). In Figure 2.4, a decrease in supply would be the movement from supply curve S_1 to supply curve S_0. The equilibrium price would increase and the equilibrium quantity would decrease. In summary, when the supply increases, the price falls and the quantity increases; when the supply decreases, the price increases and the quantity falls.

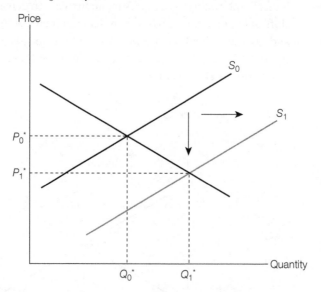

Figure 2.4 *The effect of a change in supply on equilibrium price and quantity.*

Empirical methods in economics: an introduction

Economic theory—indeed, theory of any kind—usually makes a prediction about the relationship between variables. For example, the Law of Demand predicts that the price and quantity demanded are negatively related; the Law of Diminishing Marginal Returns predicts that the amount of an input and its marginal product are negatively related; the Law of Gravity states that the attraction of any two bodies in the universe is positively related to their masses and negatively related to the distance between them. A theory that doesn't make a prediction that can be tested isn't a theory in any scientific sense because it can't be proved or disproved.

A **qualitative prediction** involves the *sign* of the relationship–positive or negative– while a **quantitative prediction** involves the *size* of the relationship. Most theories in economics make a qualitative prediction about the relationship between the two variables; the theories are rarely precise enough to make a quantitative prediction. Thus, for example, the Law of Demand does not say how much quantity demanded will fall when the price rises; it only predicts that the quantity demanded will fall.

For many purposes, however, it is essential to estimate the quantitative relationship between two variables. There are two distinct reasons to do this. First, it tests the qualitative prediction of the model. If we can determine the actual relationship between the variables, we can test whether the prediction of the model is correct. Second, even if the qualitative predictions of the model are supported, it often makes a huge difference whether the relationship is weak or strong. A model may be correct in the sense that its qualitative predictions are borne out, but it may be unimportant if its quantitative effect is small. Economic policy will usually be guided by quantitative estimates.

To estimate quantitative relationships between variables, economists and other social scientists turn to real-world, empirical data and then use statistical methods to estimate the relationship between variables. We begin with an introduction to **regression analysis**, which is a statistical technique for estimating the causal relationship between two or more variables. It is by far the most widely used statistical technique in economics and most other social sciences. We first review the basics, then identify one important way that things can go wrong, and finally discuss a new approach, called **natural experiments**, which can potentially solve some of the problems.

Regression analysis

Suppose a theory hypothesizes that a causal relationship exists between some outcome Y and some variable X. For example, X could be price and Y could be quantity demanded or X could be years of education and Y could be annual earnings. The goal of regression analysis is to estimate the sign and size of $\Delta Y / \Delta X$ from data on Y and X.

To do that we first write the relationship between Y and X as a **regression equation**:

$$Y_i = \alpha + \beta X_i + \mu_i \qquad (2.9)$$

In equation (2.9), Y is the **dependent variable**, X is the **independent variable** (or **causal variable**), and the Greek letter μ (pronounced "mew") is the **error term** of the equation; μ represents all other factors that affect Y but are unobserved by the researcher. μ is assumed to be uncorrelated with X, have a mean of 0, and be normally distributed. A normal distribution is the familiar symmetric bell curve; in this case, it is centered on a value of zero, and is thus equally likely to be positive or negative. Note the "i" subscripts on Y, X, and μ. The subscript means that each person or firm has his/her/its own value of Y, X, and μ.

Finally, α and β are the **regression coefficients**. β shows the sign and size of the relationship between X and Y. If X increases by 1 unit, then Y will change by β units. More generally, $\Delta Y = \beta \Delta X$ or, rearranging, $\beta = \Delta Y/\Delta X$, which is precisely what we want to know. a is called the **constant term** of the equation, just like the Y-intercept in the familiar equation for the slope of a line. It is not multiplied by X; rather, it adds on to create the total value of Y. You can think of it as the value of Y when $X = 0$.

Regression analysis provides an estimate of the best values of α and β, given the actual observed values of Y and X. The estimated values are written $\hat{\alpha}$ and $\hat{\beta}$, pronounced "alpha hat" and "beta hat." The hat or carat indicates that it is an estimated value. Here, the best values of α and β make the predicted value of Y as close as possible to the actual value of Y.[4]

The various terms and relationships are shown in Figure 2.5. This diagram, which visually represents the regression data, is called a **scattergram**. The points represent the hypothetical but entirely plausible relationship between the amount of time spent studying for an exam and the corresponding test score for a group of 30 students; each dot represents a student data point. In this example, five students each studied zero hours, one hour, two hours, three hours, and so on through five hours. The scores at each level of studying have a 20-point distribution between low and high; as is almost always true in real life, there is a range of outcomes associated with any particular level of an independent variable.

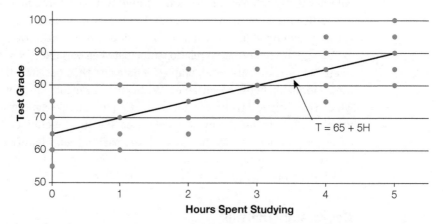

Figure 2.5 *The relationship between test grades and hours spent studying.*

The straight line through the points shows the best relationship between hours spent studying and the test score. Its slope is $\hat{\beta}$, and, as shown, the relationship is strongly positive, which we, as teachers and students, would certainly expect. In this case, the slope is 5, which means that, on average, an individual's test score increases by five points for each additional hour spent studying. $\hat{\alpha}$ is the average test score for a person who didn't study at all; it is equal to 65 in this example. The vertical difference between the predicted value shown by the regression line and the actual value shown by the dots is due to the influence of other unobserved factors that are captured by the error term, μ.

In most real problems, the dependent variable Y is affected by more than one variable. If there are three causal variables, we can write the regression equation as

$$Y_i = \alpha + \beta_1 X_{i1} + \beta_2 X_{i2} + \beta_3 X_{i3} + \mu_i \tag{2.10}$$

---

4   Technically, the estimated values for $\hat{\alpha}$ and $\hat{\beta}$ minimize the sum of the squared errors. The errors are the differences between the actual value of Y and the predicted value of Y, given $\hat{\alpha}$, $\hat{\beta}$, and X.

This kind of analysis is called **multiple regression**, where "multiple" refers to the many explanatory variables. In this case, β_1, β_2, and β_3 represent the effect of a one-unit change in the corresponding X variable, holding constant or "controlling for" the value of all the other X variables. This corresponds exactly to the idea of *ceteris paribus* in economics models—all else held constant. Other than the fact that there are more X variables, the interpretation of multiple regression is exactly the same as the simpler one-variable regression discussed earlier. Note, however, that multiple regression cannot be readily represented by a diagram like Figure 2.5.

Here are some useful details about regression analysis. This material may be valuable as a reference later when examining empirical work or reading supplementary articles.

- Some independent variables, like age or income, are continuous variables, meaning that all numerical values are possible (except possibly negative or extremely high ones). In that case, the regression coefficient gives the effect of a one-unit increase in X on the value of Y. But what about variables such as gender, race, and ethnicity, which are not numeric and only have a few possible "values"? Variables like these can be included in a regression by using a **dummy variable**. A dummy variable for female gender would work this way: Let $X = 0$ if a person is male; let $X = 1$ if a person is female. Now, the regression coefficient for the female gender dummy variable would measure the impact of being female rather than male on the value of Y. For example, if the estimated regression coefficient on a female dummy variable is negative, it means that women have a lower value of Y than men, with all else being equal. Dummy variables are very commonly used in statistical research.

- Dependent variables also come in two types. Some are continuous variables, like a person's wage rate, but others have yes/no values, such as whether an individual is employed, had a teen birth, or is officially poor. Yes/no values are treated much like dummy variables. If we let $Y = 1$ represent an individual who is a yes (i.e., employed, had a teen birth, officially poor) and $Y = 0$ an individual who is a no, then the regression coefficient measures the effect of X on the probability of being a yes.

- Because regression coefficients are estimated from a sample rather than the entire population, they are subject to sampling error. It is possible that the estimate differs from the true regression coefficient. Consequently, researchers compute a standard error of the estimated coefficient. The ratio of the estimated coefficient to its standard error is called a **t-statistic**. The smaller the standard error relative to the coefficient, the greater is the t-statistic and the more reliable is the estimated coefficient. If the t-statistic is greater than 1.65 (in absolute value), then there is only a 10 percent chance that the true coefficient is zero; if the t-statistic is greater than 1.96 (in absolute value), there is only a 5 percent chance that the true value is zero. In these two cases, we say that the estimated coefficient is statistically significant at the 10 percent or 5 percent level. Significance levels bigger than 10 percent are considered too imprecise and researchers will usually report that "the estimated coefficient is not statistically different from zero."

- R^2 is a measure of how well the independent variables explain the variation in the dependent variable. If the points in the scattergram of Figure 2.5 were very close to the regression line, then the independent variable would explain most of the variation in the dependent variable. The more scattered the points in the scattergram are, the less variation in Y is explained by the independent variables. R^2 goes from a minimum of 0 when the independent variables explain none of the variation in Y to a maximum of 1, where all the points lie right on the regression line. A typical R^2 in microeconomic studies might be in the 0.25 to 0.35 range, which means that the independent variables explain 25 percent or 35 percent of the variation in the dependent variable. Don't get too hung up by a low R^2. A low R^2 means that unmeasured factors or unknown factors are important, not that the included independent variables are unimportant or unreliable, or that the coefficient estimates are biased.

Regression pitfalls

Many things can go wrong in regression analysis, leading to wrong answers. The field of **econometrics** is dedicated to these kinds of problem and how to address them. One problem, called **omitted variable bias**, is particularly relevant for the research discussed in this book. Let's consider it in an intuitive, rather than mathematical, way.

In most problems that social scientists examine, a researcher is interested in estimating the causal impact of one particular independent variable on an outcome of interest. In order to do that, however, it is necessary to control for other factors that affect the outcome. This is done by including them in the analysis using multiple regression. Often, however, this is easier said than done; it is hard to measure many of the subtle factors that influence many outcomes of interest.

The important statistical issue is what happens to the estimate of the estimate of the causal effect of X on Y if important variables are omitted. The answer is that it depends. Usually the estimated coefficient of the variable of interest will be biased, which means that it is not equal to the true causal effect of X on Y. In layman's terms, a biased coefficient is a bad estimate. There is a lengthy statistical literature about this kind of bias, but it can be easily summarized: *If variables that affect the dependent variable are omitted from a regression equation, they bias estimates of all variables with which they are correlated.* In this case, the problem is that the included causal variable incorrectly captures some of the causal effect of the omitted variables with which it is correlated. The extent of the bias depends on two things: (1) whether the omitted variable is weakly or strongly related to X and (2) whether the omitted variable is weakly or strongly related to Y. In both cases the stronger the relationship is, the greater the bias.[5] This is a very important idea and it suggests another important insight, one that we will use below: *Omitted variables that are uncorrelated with the causal variable of interest do not bias estimated coefficients of the included variable.*

Omitted variable problems arise quite often in social science research. For example, regression analysis shows that persons with more education earn substantially more than workers with less education. In 2014, median weekly earnings for a college graduate in the United States were more than 60 percent higher than for a high-school graduate. Does that mean that if a typical high-school graduate were to complete college, his or her earnings would increase by 60 percent? Here the concern is that college graduates and high-school graduates might differ in other ways that also affect their earnings. Perhaps the

---

5 The bias is the product of these two terms, so if either one is zero, the bias is zero. Also, because it is multiplicative, it is often possible to predict the sign of the bias.

college graduates have more academic ability than the high-school graduates. If academic ability is omitted and if it is correlated with educational attainment and has its own positive effect on earnings, then the estimated effect of education on earnings will be biased. In this case the estimate will likely be too large, capturing both the effect of education and the correlated effect of ability. This particular omitted variable problem is so well-known in economics that it is called **ability bias**.

A second famous example involves the effect of class size on student achievement. Do students learn more in smaller classes? How much more? This is an important issue in school reform. The problem here is that class size may be correlated with other unmeasured factors that also affect student achievement. For example, schools with smaller class sizes may also have more of other resources too, such as better teachers or greater access to educational technology, and perhaps the students in schools with smaller class sizes are also different from the students in other schools. If these factors are omitted from the analysis of class-size effects on achievement, then the class-size measure will include some of the effect of those variables and would likely overstate the benefit of a smaller class size.

This kind of problem is potentially an issue in many analyses, especially those in which the values of the causal variables that are being analyzed reflect choices made by individuals, firms, or schools. Thus in the two cases discussed above, individuals may choose their education level and schools may choose their class sizes, and these choices may reflect the impact of other variables, known to the individual or school but not the researcher, that also affect the outcome variable.

The best solution to an omitted variables problem is to measure and include the additional variables. But sometimes this is not feasible. In those cases, the problem of omitted variable bias can sometimes be resolved by using experimental methods to provide the data that will be analyzed. In the next section, we review two related experimental methods and explain how and why they can solve the problem.

Experimental methods in economics

Let's start with a non-economics example you may be familiar with. When medical researchers want to determine the effect of a new drug, they often run a clinical trial using an experimental method called **random assignment**. A sample of subjects is enrolled in the trial and then randomly assigned to one of two groups—the experimental or treatment group that receives the drug or the control group that gets either nothing or a placebo. This experimental method is often referred to as a randomized controlled trial (RCT).

In an RCT, to determine the effectiveness of the drug, the researchers need only compare the outcomes for the two groups. The effect of the treatment is $\overline{Y}_T$ (the average outcome for the treatment group) $- \overline{Y}_C$ (the average outcome for the control group). It's that easy.

An RCT isn't a different way to *analyze* data; it's a different way to *generate* data. In fact, the experimental results of a clinical trial can be represented by the regression $Y_i = \alpha + \beta T_i + \mu_i$, where T is a dummy variable equal to 1 if a person was in the treatment group and 0 otherwise. Here the regression estimate for β measures the effect of receiving the treatment; it is exactly equal to $\overline{Y}_T - \overline{Y}_C$.

The virtue of an RCT is to ensure that the only difference between the two groups is the treatment that one group receives. There is no need to measure other factors that might affect the outcome and include them in a multiple regression analysis, because the random assignment guarantees that these variables are uncorrelated with the treatment variable. This is an example of the second rule we presented above: Omitting these variables does not bias coefficient estimates because they are uncorrelated with the causal variable. If random assignment is done properly, the treatment effect is an unbiased estimate of the true impact of the treatment.

In contrast, some medical evidence comes from studies in which individuals report on, for example, their diet or exercise habits and then researchers examine differences in health outcomes associated with those diet or exercise differences. In this case, omitted variable concerns are a major potential issue. Perhaps the individuals with diet habits that appear to provide health benefits differ in other (unobserved) ways than individuals with different diet habits. It is impossible to be sure.

Random assignment, where feasible, is a perfect technique. To see this, consider again the examples about the effects of education and class size discussed earlier. Suppose that some individuals were randomly assigned to acquire more education and others were randomly assigned to have less education. Then other individual differences would be irrelevant because they would be uncorrelated with the "education treatment." The difference in earnings for the two groups would provide an accurate estimate of the causal effect of additional education on earnings. Of course, it would be unethical to restrict education in this way, so the experiment cannot be done. Still, if is often useful to think about how the results of a research study might be different if a random assignment experiment had been done.

In the class-size example, we could run an experiment by randomly assigning some students to smaller class sizes and some to larger ones. If the assignment is truly random, then the two groups of students should be more or less the same except for the difference in class size. An experiment of this kind was actually done in Kentucky in the 1980s. Called Project Star (for Student-Teacher Achievement Ratio), it randomly assigned 6,500 students in kindergarten through third grade into either standard-size classes (22–25) or smaller classes of 13–17. Economist Alan Krueger examined the impact of Project Star and found that students in the smaller classes scored about 5–7 percent higher on standardized tests, which is a considerable boost.[6] Another study found that the students in the small classes were more likely to attend college.[7]

Where ethical problems are not an obstacle, economists now sometimes do experiments with random assignment.[8] A very common use is in development economics, where many policy interventions are tested in a random assignment experiment. Esther Duflo, the second woman to win the John Bates Clark Prize (see Box 1.1), has been instrumental in establishing the importance of this approach. We review some of this research in Chapters 13 and 14.

Another recent well-known example is the Oregon Health Insurance Experiment, which analyzed the effect of the expansion of Medicaid (US government–run health insurance for the poor) on a variety of health and economic outcomes. Previous studies of

---

6 Alan B. Krueger (1999), "Experimental Estimates of Education Production Functions," *The Quarterly Journal of Economics*, 114 (2), 497–532.

7 Raj Chetty, John N. Friedman, Nathaniel Hilger, Emmanuel Saez, Diane Whitmore Schanzenbach, and Danny Yagan (2011), "How Does Your Kindergarten Classroom Affect Your Earnings? Evidence from Project Star," *The Quarterly Journal of Economics*, 126 (4), 1593–1660.

8 The American Economics Association maintains a listing of RCTs at www.socialscienceregistry.org/.

health differences between persons with and without health insurance were undermined by difficulties in controlling for other factors; this is a classic omitted variables problem. In 2008, Oregon expanded its Medicaid program, but it only had enough funding to enroll 10,000 new patients. When 90,000 people signed up on a waiting list to enroll in the program, the state used a lottery to determine who would receive the benefits. The lottery winners who gained access to Medicaid were the treatment group and a portion of the lottery losers were used as a control group. Because the two groups were chosen randomly by the lottery, any resulting differences in health and economic outcomes can confidently be attributed to the expanded access to healthcare. The researchers, who included Amy Finkelstein, the third woman to win the John Bates Clark Prize (see Box 1.1), found that access to Medicaid had positive impacts on a wide range of outcomes, including financial hardship, self-reported health, and access to non-emergency hospital use.[9] See www.nber. org/oregon/index.html for more information on this study and its findings.

In many cases, however, it is either impractical or unethical to do a true random assignment experiment. In those cases, economists look for **natural experiments**, which are like random assignment experiments but with one important difference—they are "natural" in the sense that the researcher doesn't plan and control the experiment. Rather, the experiment occurs naturally, created by a particular policy or by some event. A famous early example of a natural experiment in economics was the Mariel boatlift, in which 125,000 Cubans were allowed to immigrate to Miami between May and September of 1980. This influx of workers, which was large and unexpected, was analyzed to assess the impact of immigration on labor-market outcomes.[10] Earlier research was suspect because immigration was often greatest in those cities with booming labor markets: the booming labor market attracted the immigrants. That problem did not occur in this case, however, because the immigration occurred for reasons quite unrelated to the economic climate in Miami. Another famous example occurred when New Jersey increased its state minimum wage in 1992, while the adjacent state of Pennsylvania did not. This natural experiment allowed researchers to test the effect of a higher minimum wage on the employment of less skilled workers.

In a natural experiment, the treatment and control groups may well have different levels of the outcome of interest before the treatment began. To deal with that, researchers usually compare the *change* in the average outcome for the treatment group with the *change* in the average outcome for the control group. This is called a **difference-in-difference (DID) approach**, which can be written as $(\overline{Y}_{T1} - \overline{Y}_{T0}) - (\overline{Y}_{C1} - \overline{Y}_{C0})$; the first term is the change between time 0 and time 1 for the treatment group and the second term is the change for the control group. If the treatment has a positive effect on the outcome, then the change will be greater for the treatment group; if it has a negative effect, the change will be smaller. The DID approach has the further benefit that it controls for time-related factors that are common to both groups. For example, if group 1 was treated but no control group was included in the analysis, the change in the outcome would reflect both the treatment and anything else that occurred between time 0 and time 1.

---

9   Amy Finkelstein, Sarah Taubman, Bill Wright, Mira Bernstein, Jonathan Gruber, Joseph P. Newhouse, Heidi Allen, Katherine Baicker, and Oregon Health Study Group (2012), "The Oregon Health Insurance Experiment: Evidence from the First Year," *The Quarterly Journal of Economics*, 127 (3), 1057–1106.

10 David Card (1990), "The Impact of the Mariel Boatlift on the Miami Labor Market," *Industrial and Labor Relations Review*, 43 (2), 245–257.

Figure 2.6 shows the structure of a natural experiment with two groups and two time periods. For interesting examples of natural experiments and to see exactly how DID calculations are done, see Box 2.2.

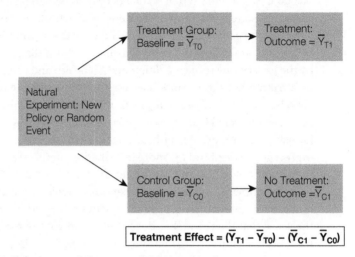

Figure 2.6 *A difference-in-difference model for a natural experiment.*

The general point is this: Sometimes it is possible to identify real-world situations that are very much like random assignment experiments. They aren't literally experiments but they amount to almost the same thing. The key characteristic of a natural experiment is that individuals are either treated or not treated randomly; they cannot choose their treatment status themselves. Natural experiments, when they can be identified, provide data that are well suited to estimating treatment effects. Simply subtract after the numbers are in place.

Box	2.2

Natural Experiments in Action

- In the New Jersey-Pennsylvania minimum wage natural experiment, David Card and Alan Krueger surveyed fast-food restaurants in both states before and after the $0.80 increase in the New Jersey minimum wage. They collected information on the employment of full-time and part-time workers and then used the DID formula above to compute the treatment effect. They found that employment in New Jersey increased by an average of 0.2 workers per store, while in Pennsylvania it fell by 2.7 workers. Thus the DID estimate is $\Delta NJ - \Delta PA = 0.2 - (-2.7) = 2.9$. This positive effect was at odds with the traditional prediction that a higher minimum wage would reduce employment. It initiated a new approach to analyzing the effect of minimum-wage legislation on employment.
- A similar idea was applied by one of the authors of this text in order to analyze the effects on employment of the 2009 increase in the US minimum wage

from $6.55 to $7.25. In the United States, states may set their own minimum wages higher than the federal level, which is exactly what New Jersey did in 1992. When the federal minimum increased in 2009, it had no effect on workers in 17 states that already had a minimum wage above $7.25. In this natural experiment, it was possible to compare what happened to the employment of less-skilled workers—here, teens who were not in college—in states where the minimum wage increased to what happened in states where it did not. 2009 was a recession year, so it is not surprising that employment fell in both sets of states. In states where the minimum wage increased, teen employment fell by 2.4 percent. In states where the minimum did not increase, employment fell by 1.8 percent. Thus the DID estimate of the minimum wage impact on teen employment is $[-2.4 - (-1.8)] = -0.6$ percent.

- The Affordable Care Act ("Obamacare") allowed young adults to stay on their parents' health insurance up to age 25 instead of having their coverage automatically terminated when they completed their education. To measure the impact on coverage, researchers compared the change in the proportion of 19–25-year-olds with health insurance to the corresponding change in the proportion of 26–35-year-olds with health insurance. The "treatment" is the new provision of the Affordable Care Act, which affected only the younger age group. For this younger group, the proportion with insurance increased from 64 percent to 73 percent, while for the older group the proportion with insurance was unchanged. So the DID estimate of the effect of the Affordable Care Act on the coverage of young adults is 9 percent.

- A final example of a natural experiment comes from the Earned Income Tax Credit (EITC), which is the largest anti-poverty program in the United States. (See Chapter 8 for more on the EITC.) In 1993, benefit levels were changed significantly such that families with two or more children experienced a substantial increase compared to families with only one child. Income and health are positively correlated and thus this increase in income from the EITC may have had positive effects on the health of these families. One of the authors of this text found that after the expansion of the EITC, smoking, a leading cause of mortality, declined by 7.6 percent among white, less-educated mothers with two or more children (the treatment group) compared to white, less-educated mothers with only one child (the control group).

Sources:

Susan L. Averett and Yang Wang (2013), "The Effects of Earned Income Tax Credit Payment Expansion on Maternal Smoking," *Health Economics*, 22 (11), 1344–1359.

David Card and Alan B. Krueger (1994), "Minimum Wages and Employment: A Case Study of the Fast-Food Industry in New Jersey and Pennsylvania," *American Economic Review*, 84 (4), 772–793.

Saul D. Hoffman (2014), "Employment Effects of the 2009 Minimum Wage Increase: New Evidence from State Comparisons of Workers by Skill Level," *The B.E. Journal of Economic Analysis and Policy*, 14 (3), 695–721.

Benjamin D. Sommers and Karyn Schwartz (2011), *2.5 Million Young Adults Gain Health Insurance Due to the Affordable Care Act*, US Department of Health and Human Services, Washington, DC.

Summary

In this chapter we have reviewed and surveyed the basic approach of microeconomics and the research methods that economists use to test their theories and to provide quantitative estimates of effects. We have looked at the core concept of constrained maximization with its emphasis on choice, maximization, and constraints. We will use these concepts repeatedly. Economics is not so much difficult as it is relentless. It really is not too much more than the repeated and clever application of constrained maximization to an enormously wide variety of problems. Anyone who can master this approach and apply it creatively is well on the way to becoming an economist.

Most of the economics problems that we will encounter have a four-step structure.

Step 1: Write down the constrained maximization problem in general form, at least indicating what is being chosen, what is being maximized, and what variables are in the constraint. Be certain to distinguish exogenous from endogenous variables. This is where theory is important; it should indicate how variables are related to each other and which ones are likely to affect outcomes.

Step 2: Solve the problem, either for the marginal conditions if possible or for the associated expression in which the endogenous variable is a function of the exogenous variables. Try to understand how the exogenous variables affect the choice.

Step 3: Examine the comparative statics. What happens to the chosen value of the endogenous variable when the exogenous variables change?

Step 4: Test the predictions of the theory, typically using statistical analysis of real-world data. Only when the predictions of a theory have been supported can we have real confidence in the analysis.

We have also developed several useful tools and concepts. Functions express the relationship between variables. A utility function expresses the relationship between the amounts of particular goods or services and the amount of utility that an individual receives. A household production function expresses the relationship between the amounts of particular inputs and the amount of household goods that an individual produces. By using the ideas of household production functions and household goods, economists can apply standard ideas of production economics to the household sector. Economists and other social scientists use regression analysis to test their theories and produce quantitative estimates of causal effects. Natural experiments are an attractive way to generate data, especially when concerns about omitted variables are present.

With such an array of tools at our disposal, we are well prepared to analyze the economic circumstances of women's lives. We begin with marriage and the family.

3 MARRIAGE AND THE FAMILY—AN ECONOMIC APPROACH

Introduction

Marriage is the perfect place to start our analysis of women's economic lives for several reasons. First, it has long been a central feature in women's lives and, indeed, until the past few decades, it was probably *the* central feature. It's true that in a monogamous society, marriage affects an equal number of men. But it has traditionally meant something more for women, usually providing both a change in identity as she adopted her new husband's surname and a new occupation as housewife and mother. In contrast, a man's surname and occupational status usually remained unchanged with marriage.

Second, marriage is a great example of how the core ideas in economics can be used and applied to nontraditional topics. This approach to marriage was introduced into economics by Gary Becker, a Nobel Prize winner whose work will be featured in many places throughout this book. In a well-known and controversial article published in 1973, he applied economic tools to marriage for the first time.[1] At the very beginning of that article he wrote: "In recent years, economists have used economic theory more boldly to explain behavior outside the monetary sector. ... Yet, one type of behavior has been almost completely ignored by economists, although scarce resources are used and it has been followed in some form by practically all adults in every recorded society. I refer to marriage" (p. 813). On the next page he outlined his approach: "Two simple principles form the heart of the analysis. The first is that, since marriage is practically always voluntary ... the theory of preferences can be readily applied, and persons marrying can be assumed to expect to raise their utility level above what it would be were they to remain single. The second is that, since many men and many women compete as they seek mates, a *market* can be presumed to exist. Each person tries to find the best mate, subject to ... market conditions" (p. 814). The language that Becker uses here ought to sound familiar. It is all about choices with constraints, applied to a very personal choice.

Third, a family is in many ways a miniature economy. Like any economy, it makes decisions about consumption and investment, work and leisure, and the allocation of resources among its members. It solves economic problems of allocation and distribution of resources daily. A relatively new area in economics called **economics of the family** focuses on these issues.

---

1 Gary S. Becker (1973), "A Theory of Marriage, Part 1," *Journal of Political Economy,* 81 (4), 813–846.

Finally, marriage and the family are such interesting subjects and far too important to leave to the sociologists and demographers. The ideas we explore in this chapter may well resonate with many readers in very personal ways. Virtually everyone has had some experience with marriage, if not yet their own then that of their parents, brothers, sisters, aunts, uncles, grandparents or friends.

In this chapter we focus on the central elements of the economic analysis of marriage. As we will do in every core chapter, we begin with the facts to provide a focus for the theoretical analysis that follows. We then turn to an analysis of marriage as an economic institution, focusing on the production, investment, and consumption benefits it confers. Next we present a supply-and-demand model of marriage, which offers insights into the underlying factors that determine how the number of marriages and the gains of marriage are shared between husband and wife. Finally, we close the chapter by looking at the distribution of resources within a marriage and an economic analysis of marriage partner search, including a discussion of a theoretical matching mechanism whose author won a Nobel Prize in Economics in 2012. In the next chapter we consider a series of extensions and applications of the basic analyses presented in this chapter.

We offer two important caveats before we begin the analysis. First, the truth is that each marriage is unique in some way and has its individual strengths and weaknesses. Emotional attachments are an important element of marriage and not even the most theoretical economist is blind to that. Still, we will mostly abstract from the details of specific marriages in order to understand better the general structure of marriage as an economic institution. No apologies are necessary: That is exactly what good economic models are supposed to do. To some extent, this caveat applies to all the major analyses we will present, but perhaps nowhere more strongly than for marriage.

Second, marriage, fertility, work, and pay—the central topics of this book—are all deeply interrelated elements of women's adult lives. We can't analyze them all at once, so we have to start somewhere—and marriage is that starting place. Occasionally, however, we will need to refer to ideas that we will develop later about fertility or work in order to explain something about marriage. In the end, we hope you will have a sense of the complex economic interactions among all these topics.

Marriage—facts and trends

Marriage and marriage trends in the United States

Two central facts about marriage as an institution are critical to appreciate and they provide the framework for our analysis. First, marriage is, by far, the dominant form of adult living arrangements in the United States and elsewhere, now and in the past. In the mid-2010s more than 90 percent of US women, aged 55–64, were ever married, and in 2000 more than 95 percent were. Going back further in time, the comparable proportions were 93 percent in 1960 and 92 percent in 1920.

Second, the proportion of adult women (and men) married at a point in time has declined. In 2005, US women crossed a numerical threshold when the Census Bureau reported that for the first time ever more than half of all women age 15 or older were living without a husband. Back in 1950 just 35 percent of women fell into that category. It was big news. The *New York Times* reported it in a front-page story.

Figure 3.1 shows the details of how the marital status of US women has changed between 1950 and 2014.[2] The trends are quite clear. The proportion currently married with their spouse present has fallen steadily and quite sharply, from two-thirds in 1950 to well under 50 percent in the mid-2010s. The official 2014 figure was 47.6 percent; the corresponding figure for men was just over 50 percent, reflecting their higher mortality rate at older ages, which lowers the denominator of the calculation. In the 60+ years since 1950, the proportion married dropped by almost exactly 20 percent, nearly equally divided between an increase in the proportion who had never married (up 9 percent) and an increase in the proportion who were divorced or separated (up 11 percent).

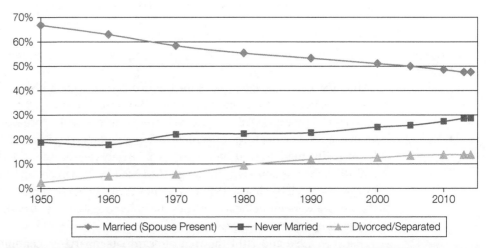

Figure 3.1 *The changing marital status of US women, aged 15 and older, 1950–2014.*

Source: US Census Bureau, Families and Living Arrangements, Table A1, 2000–2014; *Current Population Reports*, Series P-20: #450, Table 1 (1990); #365, Table 1 (1980); #212, Table 1 (1970); Series PC (2)-4B, Table 2 (1960, 1950).

One important factor behind the change in the proportion of women who are currently married is the changing age at which women first marry. These changes are shown in Figure 3.2, which presents the proportion of US women ever married by age bracket in 1960, in 1990, and in the mid-2010s. In 2014, relatively few young women had been married—only about 4 percent by ages 18–19 and about 17 percent by ages 20–24. This latter figure has dropped precipitously in recent years, down 1 percent a year since 2006. The peak age for first marriage is now the late twenties and early thirties, when nearly half of women first marry. The median age at first marriage is 27 for women and more than 28 for men.

---

2 The 1950 and 1960 figures have been adjusted to account for the inclusion of 14-year-olds in the population base. In 1950, women who were separated from their husbands were included in the married category rather than with divorced women. Because divorce and separation were relatively uncommon in 1950, this makes little difference.

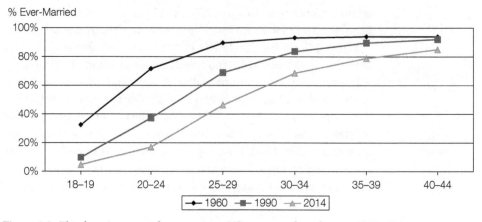

Figure 3.2 *The changing age at first marriage, US women, selected years, 1960–2014.*

Source: Data from US Census Bureau, Families and Living Arrangements, Table A1 (2014), *Current Population Reports*, Series P-20: #450, Table 1 (1990); Series PC (2)-4B, Table 2 (1960).

The first marriage age profiles for the two earlier years are shifted up, indicating far earlier marriage. In 1960, one-third of 18–19-year-old women, 70 percent of 20–24-year-olds, and 90 percent of 25–29-year-olds were ever married. More women married at age 18 than any other single age. The median age at first marriage was 20.3 for women and 24 for men. The trend toward later marriage is already clearly visible by 1990. Between 1960 and 1990, the fraction married by age 18–19 fell by 25 percent and the fraction married by age 20–24 fell by almost 35 percent. But the two lines converge thereafter. By the time the women were in their early thirties the difference was just 10 percent, and by the late thirties it had all but disappeared.

Between 1990 and 2014 the trend toward later marriage continued. At ages 20–24 through 30–34, the difference in marriage rates between the two years is 15–20 percent. The two curves begin to converge at older ages, but the difference is never eliminated. Even at age 40–44 there is still a 7 percent gap between the proportions ever married in 1990 and 2014. The main message here is a shift toward later marriage—down more than 50 percent at age 20–24 and 40 percent at age 25–29 since 1960—but also a much smaller but meaningful decline in marriage at older ages.

These many changes in marriage have deeply affected household and family structure, as well as the lives of children. As shown in Figure 3.3, in 1960, more than nine out of ten US families with children had two parents and just one-twelfth (about 8 percent) were headed by a single woman. Single men heading families with children were barely noticeable at less than 1 percent. In 2014, family structure was quite different. The proportion of families with children with two parents fell to about two-thirds, while the proportions headed by a single woman or a single man increased to about 25 percent and 7 percent, respectively. Thus the proportion of families with children headed by a single parent more than tripled over this time period. Among all families with children, almost one out of three now reside with a single parent.

The changes shown in Figure 3.3 are not just the result of changes in marriage, but also the result of changing fertility outside of marriage. We will have much more to say about that in Chapter 6.

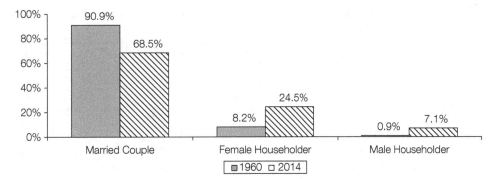

Figure 3.3 *Changes in family structure, US families with children under age 18, 1960–2014.*

Source: Data from US Census Bureau, Family and Living Arrangements, Table F1.

Marriage and marriage trends in Europe

Table 3.1 presents information on marital status of adults in selected countries in Western Europe plus Australia, Canada, and Japan. The statistics shown come from an Organisation for Economic Co-operation and Development (OECD) publication and is based not on official national surveys (like the Current Population Survey in the US) but on a Gallup World Poll.[3] The figures shown are for 2012 and refer to all persons—men and women—aged 15 and older. They are not strictly comparable to the official figures but do provide some useful comparative information. Note, for example, that the US proportion married is 52.5 percent, which is 3 percent more than the official US figure for that year.

With these caveats in mind, the table shows that Italy and Japan rank highest in the proportions married, with Spain and Australia also above average. The United States is in the middle of the pack, while France, the United Kingdom, and especially Sweden are far lower. But Sweden has by far the highest rate of domestic partnership (more commonly known as cohabitation)—almost 20 percent. Cohabitation is a formally recognized status in Sweden and is treated by law as equivalent to marriage. France, the Netherlands, and the United Kingdom also have domestic partner rates above 10 percent. The domestic partnership proportion shown for the United States substantially understates the extent of cohabitation, which tends to be more informal. A rough cohabitation estimate for the United States is closer to 6 percent.[4] Interestingly, the sum of the proportions married or in domestic partnerships is very similar across all the countries. The much narrower range is from 57 percent (Germany) to 65.6 percent (Japan), with five others between 58 percent and 62 percent. Adjusting the US figure to allow for a broader definition of cohabitation puts the United States right in that range.

The higher incidence of divorce in the United States is quite evident in the table. Only Canada and the United Kingdom have proportions close to those of the United States. Japan, the Netherlands, Italy, and Spain are particularly low. Italy and Spain are two of the countries where divorce was limited until recent decades.

Most countries in Europe have followed a demographic trend similar to that of the United States. It is challenging to find consistent statistics for a wide range of countries

---

3 *Society at a Glance 2014: OECD Social Indicators.*

4 About 16 million persons were cohabiting in 2012 out of a population of about 250 million, aged 15 and older.

Table 3.1 *Relationship status of persons aged 15 and over, selected European and OECD countries, 2012.*

	Married	Domestic Partner	Never Married	Divorced/Separated
Australia	54.4	9.9	23.9	6.8
Canada	49.4	9.1	28.4	8.5
France	47.5	12.3	24.5	8.0
Germany	51.5	5.5	26.2	7.6
Italy	63.5	2.0	23.7	4.9
Japan	65.4	0.2	23.4	3.2
Netherlands	52.2	10.8	28.7	4.6
Spain	56.4	4.0	29.9	5.2
Sweden	42.4	19.4	26.7	7.4
United Kingdom	50.6	10.4	22.4	9.4
United States	52.5	1.2	30.8	10.6

Source: Data from *Society at a Glance 2014: OECD Social Indicators.*

and a long time period. Information is available for the **crude marriage rate**, which is the number of marriages per 1,000 persons, and the **crude divorce rate**, defined in the same way. These are, unfortunately, not ideal measures. The marriage rate is sensitive to the proportion of the population in the prime marrying age brackets, which can vary due to changes in fertility or mortality rates. Even worse, the crude divorce rate depends on the marriage rate, since a divorce requires a prior marriage. Bearing those caveats in mind, for the 28 European Union countries as a whole, the crude marriage rate fell by 40 percent between 1970 and 2010, while the crude divorce rate doubled.[5] The marriage rate fell by nearly half in France, Germany, the Netherlands, and the United Kingdom, and by more than that in Italy and Spain. The increase in the divorce rate occurred despite the reduction in the pool of marriages, which would, all else being the same, have produced a lower crude divorce rate. One contributing factor was a change in laws in countries such as Italy, Spain, and Ireland, where divorce had previously been either illegal or very difficult to obtain.

The proportion married at a point in time has been falling in many of these countries, just as in the United States. In Sweden, the proportion of women aged 25–49 who were currently married fell from 69 percent in 1980 to 60 percent in 1990 and 43 percent in 2005. In France it fell from 71 percent in 1990 to 55 percent in 2005. In France in 2012 the number of new domestic partnerships was two-thirds of the number of new marriages.

The economics of marriage

Marriage as an economic institution

The facts and trends presented above make clear what we want to explain: First, why marriage is such a central institution in women's adult lives, and second, why it is considerably less central than in the past.

---

5   These statistics are from ec.europa.eu/eurostat/statistics-explained/index.php/Marriage_and_divorce_statistics.

Before we do that, it is well worth thinking about exactly what marriage is as an economic institution. To an economist, eschewing romance and all of that, marriage is primarily an institutional arrangement that serves as a valuable **intertemporal commitment device**.[6] That phrase—intertemporal commitment device—means that marriage partners commit to one another and, by so doing, adopt a longer-term ("intertemporal") perspective. That perspective enables them to make decisions and take actions that are not always in their short-term interest. In particular, they can more confidently take actions that have long-term payoffs but may involve short-term costs.

How does marriage accomplish this? It typically begins with a public ceremony and declaration, often in front of people the participants care about. The standard language of the ceremony evokes commitment: You agree to take your partner "for better, for worse, in sickness and in health, till death do us part." This is particularly interesting because it implies that the partners ought not to constantly make new calculations if the situation changes, especially for changes that are largely beyond their control. Additionally, marriage is a legal contractual arrangement. It often confers benefits in taxes, eligibility for benefits, and inheritance, just to name a few. Even more importantly, it cannot be undone without considerable cost and effort, far more than are involved in ending any other kind of arrangement between partners. As a result, adults are likely to enter into marriage only when they expect a relationship to last.

None of these things guarantees that a marriage will, in fact, endure, but it is, at least, a public expression of intending that, reinforced by the greater difficulty of undoing it. Therefore it encourages and facilitates adopting a relatively long-term planning and decision-making horizon—in other words, an intertemporal commitment. Keep this idea in mind. It will turn out to be very important. It is what ultimately distinguishes marriage from any other adult living arrangement.

The starting point of an economic analysis of marriage is the benefits or gains of marriage. Because marriage is almost always voluntary, if follows that individuals will marry only when they expect to be better off married than single. This insight follows from the idea of **rational choice**, which suggests that when individuals choose among available alternatives, they choose the one that makes them as well-off as possible. This must be true for both parties to a marriage, not just for the husband or just for the wife. If both parties are better off, then the total well-being provided by marriage must be greater than the sum of what they could have had individually. In other words, marriage must provide genuine tangible benefits to both parties. The demographic fact that marriage is widespread suggests that this condition typically holds, although perhaps less so than in the past. Thus the first task of an economic theory of marriage is to identify the nature of the gains of marriage. What are they and what is their source?

We will examine marriage benefits in three different, complementary ways—in terms of production, investment, and consumption. We begin with the oldest economic approach to the gains of marriage, which emphasizes production and is particularly useful for analyzing marriage in a time when men and women were very different from one another in terms of skills, expectations, and opportunities. It does a great job illuminating the

---

6 The ideas in this paragraph are drawn in part from Shelly Lundberg and Robert A. Pollak (2014), "Cohabitation and the Uneven Retreat from Marriage," in Leah P. Boustan, Carola Frydman, and Robert A. Margo (eds.), *Human Capital in History: The American Record*, Chicago, IL: University of Chicago Press.

benefits of the traditional male breadwinner/female homemaker marriage. It clearly has somewhat less relevance now than in the past, although it still offers some useful insights. Then we turn to the investment and consumption benefits of marriage, both of which are growing in importance.

The gains to marriage: production

We begin by laying out a model of a traditional marriage based on underlying gender differences in productivity. We focus on the choices of a representative man and a representative woman, whom we call Mr M and Ms F—M and F for short. It makes sense for the moment to think of all women being exactly like F and of all men being exactly like M, with no one having a preference for a particular partner. This is a useful simplification that enables us to focus on underlying forces. M and F have a choice of being single or married. We focus on the material standard of living they are able to achieve, leaving old-fashioned sentiments such as love to the side.

Our representative individuals get utility from two broad kinds of things—market goods (C) and household-produced goods (G). Thus they have a utility function $U = U(C, G)$. They have two ways to get these goods—working in the labor market to earn income to purchase market goods (C) and working in the household sector to produce household goods (G).

In the labor market, each individual has some wage rate, $\$w$. We assume, for simplicity, that they can work as many hours as they want. They use their earned income to purchase market goods and services. To keep things simple, we'll let the price of goods be $\$1$, so that they can buy w units of goods with $\$w$; if they earn $\$100$, they can purchase 100 units of goods. Thus the amount of market goods they can consume is $C = w \times T_M$, where T_M is the number of hours worked. In the household sector, the amount of output they can produce depends on the amount of time (T_H) they spend in production. We represent that by a household production function $G = G(T_H)$, a concept we introduced in Chapter 2. Still keeping things simple, we will assume that each hour spent working at home yields h units of household output; thus, $G = h \times T_H$. This assumption is a bit unusual, but it simplifies things without affecting the important predictions of this model.[7]

Let's begin by considering how M and F fare as single individuals. The resulting production and consumption opportunities for M and F as single-person households are shown in Figure 3.4. The two graphs show the amount of market goods they can purchase (Figure 3.4A) and the amount of household goods they can produce (Figure 3.4B) on the vertical axis and the number of hours spent at each activity on the horizontal axis. Since each hour of market work provides $\$w$ of goods, the production possibilities line for market goods is a straight line with slope equal to w. The production possibilities line for household goods is also a straight line (slope $= h$), because each hour spent there is equally productive. If M and F were more (less) productive in the labor market or in the household sector, the corresponding curves would be steeper (flatter). The horizontal dotted line shows the maximum of either good that M or F could have if he or she spent all T hours in that activity—not a very probable or sensible choice, of course, but possible.

---

7   This assumption implies a constant marginal product of time spent in household production, which is not very likely. In a more realistic model, the marginal product would fall—each additional hour spent would yield a smaller amount of output. The results here do not depend on that assumption.

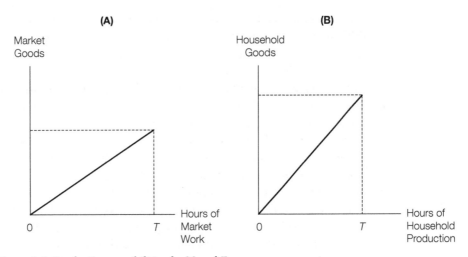

Figure 3.4 *Production possibilities for M and F.*

We can use the information in Figure 3.4 to draw a single graph that summarizes M's or F's production possibilities. Figure 3.5 illustrates a typical **production-possibilities curve (PPC)**. It shows all feasible combinations of market goods (on the vertical axis) and household goods (on the horizontal axis) that M or F could produce, given the total time available and their productivity in the market and household sectors. For example, if all available time (T hours) were spent in the market sector, it would yield a total of $w \times T$ units of market goods; since no time would be available for household production, G would be zero. That point is the endpoint of the PPC on the vertical axis. Similarly, if all time were spent in the household sector, it would yield $h \times T$ units of household goods, but no market goods. That point is the endpoint on the horizontal axis. The straight line connecting the two endpoints shows all combinations of market goods and household-produced goods that are just possible given the wage (w) and household productivity (h).

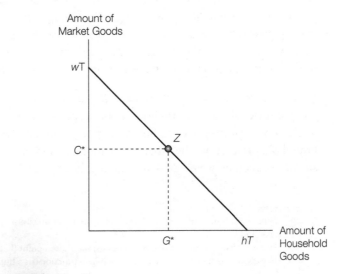

Figure 3.5 *A PPC for M or F.*

All the points on the PPC come directly from Figure 3.4. Points to the northeast of the PPC are unattainable, while points inside the PPC toward the origin are feasible but inefficient in the sense that M or F could have more of one good without sacrificing the other. The slope of the PPC is particularly important. It shows the rate at which M or F could "trade" one kind of good for the other by "trading" time across sectors. For example, he or she could give up wT units of market goods and get hT units of household goods by transferring all T hours from the market to the household sector. The slope of the line is therefore $-(wT/hT)$ or, simplifying, $-w/h$; this tells us that the slope of the PPC depends on the wage rate and household productivity. If w is large relative to h, then the PPC will be steep. In that case, M or F would have to give up a lot of market goods to obtain household goods, and we would say that he or she had a high "price" for household goods. If, instead, h were large relative to w, the PPC would be flat and the "price" of producing household goods would be low. These prices are not the usual kind that you encounter in the market but rather reflect the amount of market goods that must be given up to acquire household goods and vice versa. They are **opportunity costs**, the cost of something measured in terms of what you must give up to get it.

M and F will choose some point along the PPC that maximizes utility. We could write this out as a choice problem, involving decisions about how much time to spend working in the market and how much time to spend working in the household sector.[8] We will do exactly that in Chapter 7 when we analyze women's labor-force participation. For our purposes here, however, the exact choice does not matter. Almost certainly, if M and F were single, each would choose to spend time working in both sectors because almost everyone wants and needs both some household goods and some market goods. Point Z is a possible candidate; the exact details would depend on their preferences for market vs. household goods and on the slope of the PPC.[9] At Z, consumption of the two goods is indicated by the dotted lines to the horizontal and vertical axis. Total consumption is G^* and C^*.

Now consider how marriage between M and F would affect their PPC. We analyze two cases, which capture the key points. In the first we assume that that M and F are economically identical in the sense that they have exactly the same household and market productivity as each other; that is, $w_M = w_F$ and $h_M = h_F$. In the second case, we introduce stereotypical differences in underlying productivity by gender. In both cases we focus on how marriage affects the standard of living they can create for themselves, with the goal of identifying the production gains of marriage and what they depend on.

Case 1: Marriage with equal productivity and wage rates Figure 3.6 shows a PPC for M and F individually and for their joint output if they were married. To keep things simple, let's assume that they have 12 hours a day to potentially allocate to either market work or household production; the other 12 are for sleep and other essentials. To make the analysis more concrete, we have used numbers, but the analysis is perfectly general. Suppose

---

8 Using the language of Chapter 2, the endogenous variables are T_H and T_M and the exogenous variables are w and h.

9 If we were using indifference curve analysis, the chosen point (like point Z) would be where an indifference curve was tangent to the PPC, which here functions as a budget line.

that w and h are both equal to 1, so an hour of work in either sector produces 1 unit of goods. Then, individually, each could produce a maximum of 12 units of market goods or 12 units of household goods if they spent all their work time in one sector. The slope of their PPC is $-w/h$, which in this case equals -1, reflecting the equal productivity in both sectors.

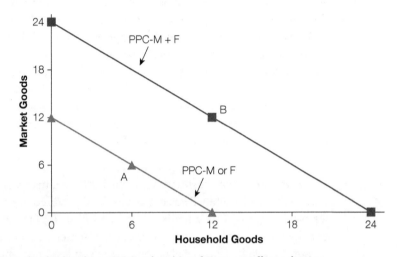

Figure 3.6 *Individual and joint PPCs when M and F are equally productive.*

Because M's and F's PPCs are identical, all the points on the joint PPC are exactly double the corresponding point on the individual PPCs. Thus their joint PPC runs from 24 on the vertical axis (if both M and F spent all available time in market production) to 24 on the horizontal axis (if both spent all available time producing household goods). Similarly, if each produced 6 units of market goods and 6 units of household goods (point *B*), collectively they would have 12 units of market goods and 12 units of household goods (point *A*).

In this situation, M and F have absolutely no reason to specialize in production on the basis of gender. For example, point *A* on the joint PPC could be produced in many very different ways. Our newlyweds could specialize completely on the basis of gender, one working full-time at home and one full-time in the market. If M worked full-time at home, he would produce 12 units of household output, and F could contribute her 12 units of market output. Conversely, F could produce 12 units of household output, and M could contribute 12 units of market output. But combination *A* could also be produced by each one combining market and household work. For example, if each chose a point like *B* on their individual PPC, the sum of their outputs would yield point *A*. Point *A* could be produced with a large range of choices between complete specialization and complete equality. What is true of *A* is true of every other point. Given the underlying productivity of F and M, any desired combination can be constructed in any number of different ways, none of which require or benefit from specialization of task on the basis of gender.

But there is more. Suppose our newlyweds chose a point like *A*, and then shared the resulting goods between themselves equally. That would leave each one consuming a bundle of goods at point B along their own individual PPC. Note that they are no better-off—materially, that is—by linking their production skills via marriage and then sharing what they produce. They end up at a point that they could achieve on their own. And, unless they share equally, one of them will actually be worse off than if he or she were single. The same thing is true of every other point on the joint PPC—dividing the outputs equally leaves each on their original PPC. The reason why marriage does not improve their material lot is that they are economically identical to one another.

Actually, they could possibly be better off, but in subtle and less important ways. If M preferred market work and F preferred household work—or just the opposite—then specialization would leave them happier, because they get to do what they like doing, and if each specialized, they might well get better at what they do. Also, by joining households, they can take advantage of household economies of scale; they likely won't need twice as many resources to provide the same standard of living for themselves if they are living together than if they lived separately. But these are second-order effects.

Case 2: Marriage with unequal productivity and wages The specific case we analyze here is the stereotypical situation in which M has a high wage but is not very productive around the house, while F has high household productivity but a low wage rate. Formally, we have $w_M > w_F$ (his wage is higher) and $h_F > h_M$ (she is more productive at home). For the purposes of this analysis, it doesn't matter whether these gender differences are innate, the product of socialization, or the result of labor-market discrimination; all are possible causes. We focus here on what these differences imply for the gains of marriage.

The particular case described here is called **absolute advantage**, which refers to a situation in which each partner is more productive than the other in one sector. But the same analysis would also hold in the case of **comparative advantage**, in which, for example, M is better than F in both the market and the household sector (or vice versa) but is relatively better in one of them. In that case, M (or F) has an absolute advantage in both sectors but a comparative advantage in the sector in which he or she is relatively better. Unless someone has an equal absolute advantage in both sectors, he or she must always have a comparative advantage in one sector, while the other party will then have a comparative advantage in the other sector. The theory of comparative advantage is the cornerstone of the economic theory of international trade, and it is one of the most famous ideas in economics.

Figure 3.7 shows the PPCs for M and F under these circumstances. Again, we use numbers for concreteness and we continue to assume that M and F have 12 hours to allocate to either market work or household production. The two PPCs are drawn for the case in which M's wage is two times F's, and she is twice as productive as he in the household sector; thus, let $w_M = 2$, $w_F = 1$, $h_M = 1$, and $h_F = 2$. M can produce a maximum of 24 units of market output and 12 units of household output, while F can produce just the opposite. M's resulting PPC is quite steep. This means that, for him, the price of household goods, measured by the amount of market goods he must give up to get them, is very high. In this case, that price equals 2, because he gives up 2 units of market goods for every unit of household output he produces.'

In contrast, F's PPC is flat, because she can produce relatively few market goods but a great deal of household goods. For her, the price of household goods (w_F/h_F) equals ½, because when she gives up 1 unit of market goods, she gets 2 units of household goods in return. Conversely, market goods are expensive for her—they cost $h_F/w_F = 2/1$—while market goods are less expensive for M ($h_M/w_M = 1/2$).

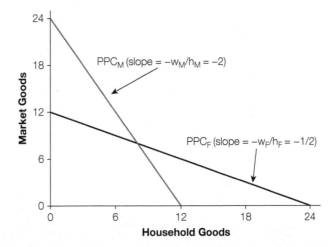

Figure 3.7 *Production possibility curves for M and F when productivity differs.*

This point is so important it is worth repeating. Because M has high market productivity but low household productivity, he faces a high price for household goods but a low price for market goods, where both prices are measured in terms of the amount of the other good that is given up to get it. F is in exactly the opposite situation. Household goods are cheap for her but market goods are expensive.

Figure 3.8 reproduces the two separate PPCs for M and F but adds three additional curves. This is a tricky diagram, so let's go through it carefully, line by line. The two straight lines at the bottom are the PPCs for M and F from Figure 3.7. The two curves at the top—the straight dotted line and the solid kinked one—are possible joint PPCs. (Ignore the lower kinked curve for the moment.) The two endpoints for these curves are easy enough; they are just the sum of the outputs that could be produced if they both devoted full-time to either household or market work. In this case the maximum total market goods output is 36 (24 from M and 12 from F) and the maximum total household goods output is also 36 (12 from M and 24 from F).

The straight dotted line that runs from the two endpoints of the joint PPC represents what M and F could produce together if they each divided up their work time in the same way as the other. For simplicity, we call this the Equal Effort PPC ("Equal" in the figure). Thus, for example, they might both work 8 hours in the labor market and 4 in the household sector or 6 and 6, but always both the same. To derive this curve, start at the endpoint of the PPC on the Y-axis where $G = 0$ and $C = 36$. If M reduced his market work by 1 hour, their total market goods would fall by 2 units, and if F also reduced her market work by 1 hour, their total market goods would fall by an additional 1 for a grand total of 3. Their production of household goods would increase as each switched an hour to household production: M's hour would provide 1 unit and F's hour would provide 2, for a grand total of 3. So the slope of this no-specialization joint PPC in this example is $-3/3$ or -1. The rest of the curve is derived the same way. The curve has a constant slope equal to -1 all the way to the other endpoint.

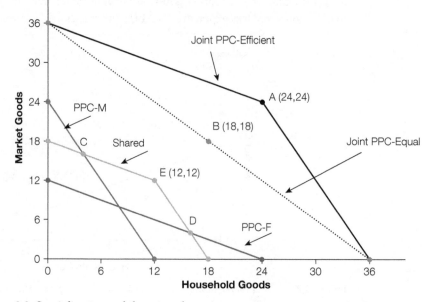

Figure 3.8 *Specialization and the gains of marriage.*

The kinked joint PPC is derived by allocating M and F's time to the sector where it is more productive, rather than allocating it equally. Let's call this the **Efficient PPC**, in the sense that it maximizes the amount of output they can produce together. In this case, starting again at the endpoint on the Y-axis where both are allocating all of their time to market work, it is efficient to reduce F's time in the market first, because she is less productive than M there and also more productive than M in the household sector. If she switches one hour from the labor market to the household sector, market output falls by 1 while household output increases by 2. So the resulting PPC is flatter (slope = $-1/2$). The slope of this part of the line is exactly the same as the slope of her PPC. For every hour that she switches from the labor market to the household sector, M & F's total market output falls by 1 unit and their joint household output increases by 2 units. At the "kink point" (point A), she has transferred all 12 available hours from the labor market to household production, decreasing market goods by 12 (from 36 to 24) and increasing household goods by 24 (from 0 to 24).

The kink point is where each one specializes in the sector in which he or she is more productive—full-time labor market work by M and full-time household sector work by F. It is the bundle (24, 24). This is the classic gender-based division of labor, with one full-time homemaker and one full-time breadwinner.

To the right of the kink point the PPC is very steep, because to produce yet more household goods, M must now transfer his time from the labor market to the household sector. In so doing, the amount of market goods falls sharply (because M is productive there) and the amount of household goods increases slowly (because he is not very productive there). Now, they must give up 2 units of market goods to increase their household goods by 1 unit, so the slope of the PPC is -2. This part of the efficient PPC has the same slope as M's individual PPC.

The kinked efficient-allocation PPC lies above the shared-work PPC everywhere except at the endpoints. The difference between the two joint PPCs shows the gains of specialization. You can see that the gains are greatest when they have fully specialized. There they can produce 24 units of each good (point *A*). If, instead, they each worked 6 hours in each sector, they could only produce 18 units of each good (point *B*).[10]

The kinked curve represents their joint total production opportunities as a married couple, taking efficient account of the differences in their productivity. What point will our newlyweds choose? There are many possibilities.[11] The kink is an obvious candidate, in which case there would be complete specialization along gender lines. M would work only in the market, and F would work only in the household sector; each would specialize in the particular area where they are more productive. But if M and F have a strong preference for market goods, they might choose a point to the left of the kink, along the flat portion of the curve. In that case, M would work only in the market, but F would combine market and household work. On the other hand, if they strongly prefer household goods, they might choose a point like the steep portion of their budget constraint. In that case, M would work in both sectors but F would specialize in household work.

For our purposes it does not matter which choice the happy couple makes. Instead, let's focus on what they can consume. For the moment we assume that they share what they have equally, but this is not essential and later in this chapter and the next we will examine factors that influence how the total is shared.[12] To find the shared PPC, we take half of each point on the joint curve, which produces the lower kinked curve (the one that includes points *C*, *D*, and *E*). Notice that the kink point on this curve is (12, 12), exactly half of the (24, 24) kink point on the total production curve. And the endpoints are exactly half of the corresponding points as well—(0, 18) and (18, 0). Each point is constructed in the same way.

Now here is the key point. We have already seen that specialization yields greater output—a higher standard of living—than an equal allocation of effort by M and F. This is represented by the difference between the two joint PPCs. It also enables both M and F to achieve a higher standard of living than either could achieve by themselves. Note that much of the shared PPC curve—the part between points *C* and *D*—lies above the single-person PPCs available to both M and F. For example, at the kink point on the shared PPC curve, F gets 12 units of market goods and 12 units of household goods, whereas on her own she could get only 6 units of market goods to go with 12 units of household goods. (This is the point on her PPC, directly below the kink point.) Similarly, M gets 12 units of market goods and 12 units of household goods at the kink point, but he can produce only 12 market units and 6 household units on his own. (This is the point on his PPC directly to the left of the kink.)

In other words, M and F can marry, specialize, produce, and share, and in the process increase their material standard of living. Both M and F can end up consuming a bundle of goods that exceeds what they would have if they were single. *They can both be better off by joining forces, specializing, and sharing.*[13] These are the production gains of marriage.

---

10   Every hour in the labor market yields 3 units of market goods—2 from M and 1 from F. Every hour in household production also yields 3 units of goods—now 1 from M and 2 from F. So with 6 hours spent in each sector, the total output is 18.

11   The actual choices here can be shown precisely by using indifference curves that represent their joint preferences.

12   We emphasize that they do not necessarily share the material gains from marriage equally. We return to this point later in this chapter when we discuss bargaining power within the household.

13   This exact point is made in the analysis of international trade. Contrary to much popular opinion, both parties in international trade gain by taking advantage of underlying differences in productivity.

They are in addition to the second-order benefits we noted in the analysis above, which would continue to apply here.

If M and F are in love, that's even better. But as long as they can get along well enough, they have something to gain—they can make themselves a material life that they cannot achieve if they are single. The gains derive from their differences in market and household productivity. Precisely because they are different from one another, they benefit from specializing and "trading." M can "buy" household goods from F, who can produce them at a much lower market goods price than he can. And F can "buy" market goods from M, who can get them at a much lower household goods price than she can. So M and F each benefit by gaining access to a lower-cost producer. Moreover, since they share a household, trading these goods with one another is very simple. Economists would say that the transaction costs of exchange are very low, which is also a good thing.

The gains of marriage with smaller gender differences Figure 3.9 shows the same kind of situation but with much smaller differences in the underlying productivity of M and F. In this example, M is only 20 percent more productive in the market (a maximum output of 24 compared to 20 for F), while F is only 20 percent more productive in the household sector. To make Figure 3.9 simpler, we have omitted the joint PPC with equal allocation of time by both M and F in both sectors and also show only the part of the shared PPC that lies above their individual PPCs. The joint PPC is constructed in exactly the same way as before. The endpoints are now at 44 (= 24 + 20) on both axes. The kink point is still (24, 24) but the curve is much less kinked—the slope doesn't change as much as before, precisely because their productivities are more similar. The shared curve is still kinked at (12, 12) and there is still a region for both to be better off—the lower darkened kinked line. Clearly—and this is the key point—the gains are much smaller now. Compare the parallelogram-shaped areas of "both better off" in Figures 3.8 and 3.9. You can see immediately how they differ.

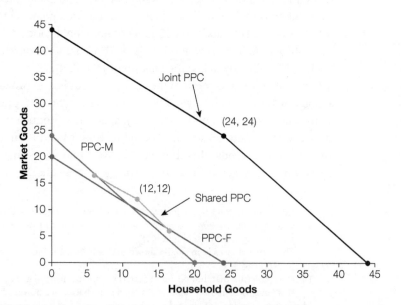

Figure 3.9 *The smaller gains of marriage when gender productivity differences are smaller.*

If we were to redraw Figure 3.9 with even smaller gender differences, the joint PPC would be yet less kinked and the shared PPC would yield yet smaller gains. And certainly that is what has happened to gender differences in recent decades. Women's earnings haven't caught up to men's—see Chapters 9–11 for details—but the gap has narrowed as women's labor-market opportunities and skills have increased. Men, in turn, have managed to acquire some household skills that were previously ceded entirely to women. Technological change and market development have played important contributing roles in narrowing household productivity differences and their importance. The vast arsenal of household technological devices—everything from washers and dryers to vacuum cleaners and microwave ovens—have vastly increased household productivity, so that household production need not be the full-time task it once nearly was. They have also reduced the amount of skill needed to accomplish a task. In addition, markets now do a commendable job of providing many of the goods and services that were formerly produced exclusively in the household—everything from childcare and house cleaning to prepared foods. This, too, has lessened the demands of household productivity.

This brings us back to the key point. As men and women have become more and more like each other in terms of market and household productivity, the traditional gains of marriage, based on specialization of task by gender and within-marriage trade, have shrunk. Perhaps that is one reason why contemporary marriages have become more fragile. They can't rely on sheer increases in the material standard of living to see them through. More on this idea when we discuss divorce in Chapter 4.

It is possible to go too far and dismiss the importance of the gender-based production gains of marriage entirely. Box 3.1 presents evidence that in the United States the gender-based division of labor within families is still alive and well, especially when young children are involved. A partner with a skill set that is different from your own remains valuable, although the skills need not necessarily be those stereotypically linked with gender.

Box	3.1

The Division of Labor by Gender: Declining, but Far from Dead

The 1950s and early 1960s were the heyday of the male-breadwinner, female-homemaker family. This was certainly evident on TV, where traditional nuclear families with a gender-based division of labor ruled the airways in shows such as *Leave It to Beaver*, *Ozzie and Harriet*, and *Father Knows Best*. (If you haven't seen these shows, *Mad Men* provides another look at family life in that time period). It also showed up dramatically in labor-force statistics. In 1960, fewer than three in ten married women with children aged 18 or under were in the labor force and less than 20 percent of those with preschool-age children were. In 65 percent of all married-couple families, including families with children no longer in the household, the husband was the sole earner. The wife was the sole earner in just 1.3 percent of families, usually in situations of a husband's disability or prolonged employment difficulties. Moreover, since married-couple households were the predominant family structure (see Figure 3.3), this traditional structure with its gender-based division of labor really was a valid stereotype.

Of course, times have changed but in some ways less than you might first think. In the mid-2010s the male-breadwinner, female-homemaker family was a much diminished family structure, accounting for just 22.7 percent of all married-couple families, about a third of its 1960 level. With the simultaneous decline in the proportion of all families that are two-parent families, this traditional structure accounts for just over one-sixth of all US families and one-fifth of all families with children.

But the division of labor by gender is not quite dead, especially in families with a child or children less than age 6. As of 2013, both spouses are in the labor force in about 58 percent of those families, but when only one is working, it is almost always the husband. In more than one-third of all US families with children aged 6 or younger, the husband is the sole labor-force participant; the opposite configuration accounted for just 3.7 percent of all married couples with young children.

From the 1950s through about 1995, the division of labor by gender in married couple families with young children declined quite sharply as married women steadily increased their labor-force participation. Since then the trend toward less gender-based division of labor within families has flattened out and stabilized. The proportion of these families in which both parents work dropped by about 4 percent after 1995, while the proportion with only the husband working increased by about 2.5 percent and the proportion with only a wife working increased by 1.8 percent.

We will have much more to say about the labor-force participation of women, especially married women, in Chapters 7 and 8.

Specialization and intertemporal commitment The division of labor and specialization of task is the central idea behind the production gains of marriage. But such a strategy is potentially problematic and even dangerous; specialization entails the risk of "putting all your eggs in one basket" for both parties. The risk to a woman who has specialized in the household sector is obvious. She may have sacrificed her labor-market abilities and thus have far lower earnings potential than she might have had otherwise. Everyone knows stories of women who have put their careers on hold to care for their families. The downside of specialization is also relevant for a man, who may have far fewer household skills than he might otherwise have had. Yes, it is true that the woman's situation appears more perilous.

Specialization only makes economic sense in a living arrangement that has a high probability of enduring for a long time. Of course, no relationship is guaranteed to last forever; there is ample evidence to the contrary all around us. But remember the earlier point about how the institution of marriage serves as an intertemporal commitment device that encourages partners to look to the longer run. To the extent that partners feel more secure about their futures, they can more confidently make decisions, such as specialization, that enhance their joint well-being, even at the expense of some short-term personal risk. Critically, those decisions, in turn, may contribute to the value and stability of the marriage through a feedback effect.

The gains of marriage: investment

While specialization can be valuable and while it is not nearing extinction, there can be little doubt that in modern economies the primary sources of the benefits of marriage for many couples must lie elsewhere. In this section and the next we explore two other approaches to thinking about the benefits of marriage that accrue to couples even if they specialize very modestly or not at all.

The first alternative approach focuses on investments that adults make in themselves, each other, and their relationship. An investment, of course, involves costs that are made in the present in anticipation of benefits that will accrue in the future. Quite naturally, then, investments are far more attractive when the future is more certain – that is, when individuals take a longer-term view in their decision making. Because the investments are then more attractive, they are more likely to be made in the first place. Institutional arrangements that facilitate and nurture long-term perspectives are thus incredibly valuable because they enable individuals to take fuller advantage of productive opportunities. As we have noted regularly, that long-term perspective is exactly what the institution of marriage encourages partners to adopt. This is the view of marriage as an intertemporal commitment device, and it is nowhere more important than in the investment side of marriage.

Married adults make a wide range of decisions that involve investment-like thinking. Buying a home, moving to another city to take advantage of employment opportunities, putting a spouse through school, and having and raising children—these are all examples of activities with large short-term costs and large long-term benefits. They can best be undertaken in an environment that encourages a long-term perspective.

Another example involves **human capital** investments within a marriage. Human capital refers to skills that individuals develop, typically as a result of an investment of time, effort, and resources. Individuals undertake these investments expecting a return in the future. Economists distinguish between two kinds of human capital. **General human capital** refers to skills that are very broadly useful, while **specific human capital** refers to skills that are valuable in a much narrower area. Completely specific human capital is valuable only in a single site, typically the site where it is acquired. Just like all investments, general and specific human capital investments involve current costs and subsequent benefits. Human capital is usually thought of in the context of labor-market skills—we discuss it when we talk about women's earnings in Chapter 10 but it applies to marriage, too.

Investment in specific human capital is particularly interesting in a marriage context. Learning how to dance or cook might well be general marriage human capital—current and potential future spouses might both appreciate those skills. As a result, those investments would be valuable whether or not a marriage endures. Furthermore, an investment in general marriage human capital does little to make the current marriage more attractive than an alternative one since the skill itself is widely transferrable. In contrast, investments in marriage-specific human capital increase the value of the current marriage relative to another one. Developing a relationship with in-laws and a spouse's friends or learning to enjoy a spouse's particular hobbies and activities are examples of investments in marriage-specific human capital. They may be highly valuable in the current marriage but they aren't likely to be as valuable in a subsequent relationship. Because of that, investments in marriage-specific human capital tend to increase the stability of a marriage.

Just as with specialization, investments in spouse-specific human capital make more economic sense when the time horizon is lengthy. Married individuals who have adopted a long-term time horizon can more readily make those investments, secure in the knowledge that they will likely remain valuable for a very long time. Children are often considered the prime example of marriage-specific human capital in the sense that they are almost inevitably more valued by their parents than by anyone else. Children thus raise the value of the current marriage but not typically the value of another marriage. Put differently, they often bind a couple together. Again, if marriage serves as an (imperfect) intertemporal commitment device, it provides improved incentives to make these investments. That, too, is a good thing.

To see the point personally, try to imagine how your own behavior might differ if you were cohabiting with a partner vs. if you were married or even if you were just seriously dating. Cohabitation is like marriage but without the formal legal status and protections, and thus it is a weaker commitment device with a shorter timeframe. Dating is even less of a commitment with an even shorter timeframe. What actions would you be more willing to take in a marriage than in those relationships? Why? More on this in Chapter 4 when we discuss cohabitation.

The gains of marriage: consumption

The final approach to marriage focuses on consumption, specifically the roles of joint consumption and household **public goods**. Married partners typically consume and, indeed, produce many goods together. This applies to everything from dinner and movies to housing and furniture to vacations and children. While successful marriages may be about compromise, the success is easier—that is, the gains of marriage are greater—if marriage partners have more similar preferences for these jointly consumed goods. If you love the beach and hate hiking and camping, while your partner hates the water but loves the backwoods, a jointly consumed mutually enjoyed vacation may be hard to fashion. Ditto if you love museums and your spouse hates them or if you love a small-town atmosphere and your spouse craves the big city. If you are a strict disciplinarian with children and your spouse is the opposite, jointly consumed mutually enjoyed child rearing may be a serious challenge. Religion, movies, and food preferences—vegetarian or carnivore?—are other examples.

In some of these examples, it is feasible for the spouses to actually consume different amounts of the goods. Spouses need not eat the same foods or vacation, watch movies, or worship together. In those cases, having what is called "separate spheres" consumption is feasible but perhaps more costly. Equivalently, the gains of marriage are likely to be smaller in that situation. In some cases, however, it is literally impossible *not* to consume the same amount of the goods as your spouse. In the examples above, choice of residential location is inevitably jointly consumed. Other daily examples include heat and air conditioning—at whatever temperature the thermostat is set, both partners consume that same air temperature—square feet of space, and other features of housing. A more important example—probably the most important—is children. We will discuss parents' decisions about fertility and children in great detail in Chapters 5 and 6, but here let's simply note that it is not possible for parents to have different numbers of biological children or provide them with different amounts of resources, and that both parents can and do gain simultaneous pleasure from their children and whatever they do.

A good like children or residential location that is jointly and identically consumed is called a public good in contrast to a private good. The most important difference between the two kinds of goods for our purposes is that a public good is non-rival in consumption, which means that one person's consumption public good does not diminish (i.e., rival) the amount of it available to others. As a result, both partners consume the same amount of the good.[14] In contrast, if one person consumes a private good, it is no longer available for consumption by the other. Slices of pizza, shirts, and automobiles are examples of private goods. If you consume a piece of pizza or purchase a new blouse, it is no longer available to someone else.

In the case of household public goods, similarity of preferences is essential because both partners are consuming the identical good in identical amounts. Hot or cold? City or country? Small family or large? In the case of private goods, similarity in preferences is a benefit and increases the gains of marriage, but it is not a deal breaker. Thus while the production approach to marriage emphasizes the value of differences between spouses in wages and household productivity, this approach emphasizes the value of similarities between spouses in preferences for consumption goods, especially true public goods.

Another source of the consumption benefits of marriage involves risk-sharing. In most marriages, economic resources are pooled; that is not the case, however, for most room-mates. Pooling of resources reduces the risk of income loss in the event that one partner loses a job. This reduction in the risk of income loss can allow a married couple to see their way through what would be a more serious problem for a single-person household. The value of this was clearly evident during the Great Recession, which hit men more severely than women. If risk-sharing is important, then matching of partners whose income risk is negatively correlated is most valuable. Another form of risk-sharing involves adverse health events, which can befall someone unexpectedly at any point in their life. Married couples are typically in a better position to handle these events because they have a committed partner. Risk-sharing in marriage is particularly important in developing countries, where incomes are often low and highly variable, and health shocks are more common.

Finally, we briefly noted the idea of **economies of scale** in our discussion of the production model of marriage and they fit here as well. Economies of scale exist when the average cost of producing a good falls as more of it is produced. It is quite clear that economies of scale do exist in many areas of household production and consumption. Two-person households don't need twice as many refrigerators, stoves, sinks, toilets, rooms, and so on as a one-person household to reach the same level of household output. It doesn't take twice as long to cook for two as for one. As a result, a two-person household with twice as much income as a single-person household will typically have a higher standard of living.

Household economies of scale are built into the official poverty standards used in the United States to measure the number of persons who are poor. In the United States a household is officially poor if its income falls below a designated income level called the **poverty threshold**. These thresholds are adjusted for family size, such that the threshold for each family size provides an equivalent (low) standard of living. In 2014 the official

---

14 Public goods are also **non-excludable**, which means that an individual cannot be prevented from consuming them even if he/she does not pay for them. In a marriage context, that property is less important. Public goods are typically provided by governments because private markets cannot profitably produce them due to their non-rivalness and non-excludability. National defense is a classic example of a public good.

poverty threshold for a non-elderly single adult was $11,670. For a non-elderly two-adult family the poverty threshold was $15,830, just 29 percent more, rather than twice as much as it would have been in the absence of economies of scale. Similarly the poverty threshold increases by about 50 percent, rather than 100 percent, when family size increases from two to four. These figures are evidence of the existence of considerable economies of scale in household production.

Important as these economies of scale are, formal marriage is not essential to capturing them. Any two persons who are sharing living quarters and facilities benefit from them. They need not be married or have any romantic relationship. So while married couples benefit from this, it is not a benefit of marriage per se.

One thing that should be clear throughout our discussion of the production, investment, and consumption models of marriage is the role of children. They are the common thread that ties together the various strands of the analysis. In modern economies the main reason to specialize in household production is the presence of children. For most couples the biggest marriage-specific investment they will make is having children, and, once a couple has children, since they are a public good, they can jointly "consume" (i.e., enjoy) them.

The marriage market: a supply-and-demand analysis

In this section we present a supply-and-demand model of marriage markets, based on the famous work of Gary Becker. In some countries, well-organized marriage markets exist that look very much like markets for other kinds of goods and services. In China, for example, a marriage market is often a public site where parents post marriage advertisements on behalf of their children to find a suitable spouse. Shanghai and Beijing have marriage markets like that. In India, marriage brokers and marriage bureaus are common as a formal mechanism to pair prospective spouses. In Western economies, however, formal marriage markets are rare, so the idea of a "marriage market" refers to the general process of finding a marriage partner.

Like any economic model of markets, the marriage market model uses supply and demand to identify the equilibrium price and quantity and then to analyze how the equilibrium will change when the underlying determinants of supply-and-demand change. Here the equilibrium involves the number of married persons and the way the gains of marriage are divided between husband and wife. We skirted that issue earlier when we analyzed the gains of marriage. Our goal there was to show that there *were* gains of marriage, and we focused on the case where the marital output was equally divided. Here we examine how the marriage market works and how it determines the way marital output is distributed. We'll examine how well off women (and men) are within marriage and what things cause that to change.

Basic concepts and notation

To start, we need to introduce some basic concepts and notation. Becker assumed that the utility of single men and single women depended on their ability to produce market and non-market goods for themselves, which depended, in turn, on their wage rate and their productivity in the household sector. The PPCs for M and F as single individuals captures this idea. It is, however, also possible to think about the utility as reflecting more broadly life as a single person, and that interpretation will be useful later on. In most of the analysis that follows, however, we will follow Becker and refer to the *output* produced by households rather than their *utility*. An individual's utility depends on the amount of output he or she consumes, so when output is larger, utility is larger as well—and more utility is a good thing.

Becker assumed that there is a single household-produced good called Z; this assumption is obviously false but simplifies the analysis without fundamentally distorting it. The output of single-person households is Z_M for men and Z_F for women. The output of a married-couple household is Z_{MF}.[15] Finally, total marital output Z_{MF} is divided between M and F. S_M is the amount of Z_{MF} that goes to M (the husband) and S_F is the amount that goes to F (the wife). We are not assuming that $S_M = S_F$, as we did when we analyzed the gains of marriage. It will be important later on to recognize that $S_M + S_F \equiv Z_{MF}$, which simply means that all of the marital output goes to either the husband or the wife. Again, the greater Z_M or Z_F is, the better off a single man or single woman is. Similarly, the greater S_M or S_F is, the better off a married man or married woman is.

If marriage is voluntary, then individuals are willing to marry if and only if they expect to be better off. Thus M is willing to marry only if $S_M > Z_M$, and F is willing to marry only if $S_F > Z_F$. These inequalities are just a formal way of representing the idea of rational choice applied to marriage. They also imply that there are gains of marriage: since $Z_{MF} \equiv S_M + S_F$, $S_M > Z_M$, and $S_F > Z_F$, it follows that $Z_{MF} > Z_M + Z_F$.

Supply-and-demand curves for marriage

A supply-and-demand model requires four things—a price and a quantity plus supply-and-demand. In this case the quantity term is easy; it is the number of men and the number of women in the marriage market. They are the prospective "demanders" and "suppliers." The price is far less obvious because there is no literal monetary exchange.[16] As the price term, we will use S_F, the amount of marital output that a woman receives. This term is a measure of how well-off she is in a marriage.

The supply curve of women to marriage shows the number of women willing to marry at each possible value of S_F. To derive that we use the idea that marriage is voluntary and depends on a comparison of utility if married vs. utility if single – that is, whether $S_F >$ or $< Z_F$. Suppose that Z_F varies across women, ranging from quite low to much higher. These differences could reflect differences in wages or differences in preferences or anything that causes a woman's well-being as a single woman to vary.

To construct the supply curve, we let the value of S_F range from low to high and then evaluate how many women would be willing to marry at each particular value of S_F. When S_F is very low, very few women will be willing to marry—only those with the very lowest values of Z_F, for whom even that low S_F exceeds their Z_F. If S_F were a bit higher, a few more women would now join the supply curve; they are the women with values of Z_F just a bit

---

15 The outputs of same-sex households would be Z_{MM} and Z_{FF}. Virtually everything in this analysis could apply to same-sex or cohabiting households.

16 We are ignoring dowries (payments from a bride's family to a groom's family) and brideprices (payments from the groom's family to a bride's family). See the discussion of marriage in developing countries in Chapter 13.

higher than the ones already willing to marry at the low value of S_F. As S_F increases further, more and more women are added to the supply curve. Finally, at some high value of S_F, all women, even those with the best prospects and highest utility as single women, are willing to marry. At that point the supply curve becomes vertical because there are simply no more women. The result is a supply curve of women to marriage that is upward sloping and then vertical. There is a positive relationship between the number of women willing to marry and S_F, what they get in marriage.

We could do exactly the same thing for men, substituting S_M (the amount of marital output that a man receives) for S_F and proceeding in exactly the same way to find a supply curve for men to marriage, but we don't want two supply curves. Instead we need a demand curve of men for wives to go with our supply curve of women willing to marry.[17] This demand curve must depend on S_F so that we can then put the supply-and-demand curves together on the same graph. To do that, note that S_F and S_M are negatively related; this follows because $S_M + S_F \equiv Z_{MP}$, so $S_M \equiv Z_{MF} - S_F$. This expression shows us that when S_F is high, S_M is low, and when S_F is lower, S_M is higher.

When S_F is very high and S_M is consequently very low, relatively few men will be willing to marry. Most will be better off staying single because their share of marital output is so small. However, as S_F falls, more men will find that what they get in marriage exceeds what they would get if they remained single: $S_M > Z_M$. Consequently the demand curve of men for marriage is downward sloping. Finally, when all potential husbands are accounted for, the demand curve becomes vertical.

We illustrate these supply-and-demand curves in Figure 3.10. Part (A) is the supply curve of women to marriage; part (B) shows the demand curve of men to marriage. Like any supply-and-demand diagram, the quantity is on the horizontal axis and the price is on the vertical axis. The horizontal axis shows the number of women or men willing to marry. The price is S_F; the husband then gets the remaining share of marital output, so S_M can be measured in the opposite direction from low at the top of the vertical axis to high at the bottom. Both curves become vertical when a price is reached at which all men or all women are accounted for.

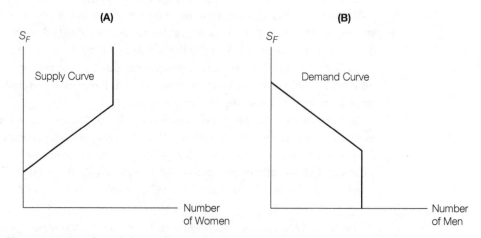

Figure 3.10 *Supply-and-demand curves for the marriage market.*

---

17 It may be natural to think of the demanders as being in charge. Nothing of the sort is implied here.

Marriage market equilibrium

Now let's put the supply-and-demand diagrams together. Our goal is to find the equilibrium price and quantity. Instead of thinking of each couple as negotiating individually over who gets what, imagine instead that the general terms are set by the market. Those terms are the equilibrium values for S_M and S_F, which we'll refer to as S_M^* and S_F^*. Think of them as widely understood social norms for how men and women fare within a marriage. They are something like "this is what married life is like for men and women."

It is important to appreciate that we are not trying to explain who marries whom. In fact, it is useful to think of the men and women in the model as having absolutely no preference for one person over another. Of course, even economists know that's not true, but our goal here is to analyze general forces determining how men and women are treated within marriage, rather than who marries whom.

Figure 3.11 puts the supply-and-demand curves together to find the marriage market equilibrium. When S_F is very high, as at S_{FH}, marriage is a great deal for women but is not so good for men. At this price there is excess supply—more women looking for a husband than men looking for a wife. The excess supply is shown as the horizontal distance between the supply curve and the demand curve at that price. In the same way, when S_F is very low, as at S_{FL}, marriage is a great deal for men but not so good for women. Now the price is too low and there is excess demand—more men looking for a wife than women looking for a husband.

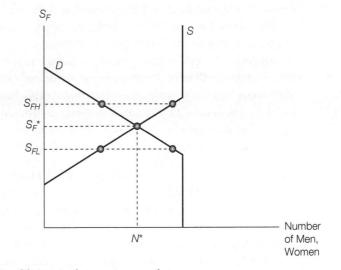

Figure 3.11 *Equilibrium in the marriage market.*

The marriage market equilibrium is at S_F^*, the only price where supply and demand just balance. It's interesting to think about how the equilibrium might get established. At a low price such as S_{FL}, more men are looking for wives than women willing to marry. So a man might figure that if he offered a somewhat better deal by raising S_F, he would improve his chances. The men who don't do that end up without a wife. Eventually, all the men get the message and S_F rises. Now more women are willing to marry but fewer men are, so the surplus of men starts to shrink. Finally, when S_F has increased all the way up to S_F^*, the marriage market is in balance.

Exactly the same kind of logic works starting at a high price such as S_{FH}, where some women are now unable to find husbands. Women would reason that they could find a husband if they got a bit less for themselves. S_F would fall, bringing more men into the market and also reducing the number of women willing to marry. This process would lead back to equilibrium at S_F^*.

In marriage market equilibrium there are N^* married men and an equal number of married women, but not everyone is married. The horizontal distance from N^* to the vertical portion of the demand curve represents the number of unmarried men. They are the men who would marry if they got a better deal, but at the marriage market equilibrium price they are better off single. Similarly, the horizontal distance from N^* to the vertical portion of the supply curve represents the number of unmarried women. They are the women who would marry if they got a better deal, but at the marriage market equilibrium price they prefer to remain single.

Changes in supply and demand: what happens?

The most important and valuable part of a model like this is analyzing what would happen if supply or demand curves changed. The goal is to see how actual real-world changes in the conditions that underlie the supply-and-demand curves of the marriage market affect marriage market equilibrium. Under what circumstances do women fare better or worse in the marriage market? Under what circumstances does the number of married persons increase or decrease? This kind of analysis is called **comparative static analysis**. To brush up on the comparative statics of supply and demand, review the discussion in Chapter 2. The most important point to remember is that the changes we examine affect the outcome indirectly by first affecting either the supply curve or the demand curve. That change, in turn, will affect the equilibrium price and quantity.

We focus here on several interesting real-world changes that would affect the supply and/or demand curve. One is the ratio of men to women. Another is the effect of women's improved labor-market opportunities. Still another is the effect of contraception, abortion, sexually transmitted diseases (STDs), and AIDS.

Sex ratios and the marriage market In Figure 3.11 we considered marriage market equilibrium with equal numbers of men and women, but differences in sex ratios can arise in marriage markets from many different causes. If parents in some countries prefer sons to daughters, then sex ratios in marriage markets can become unbalanced when those babies reach adulthood. (More on this in Chapter 13.) Among the elderly, differential mortality by gender creates far more widows than widowers; in 2013, unmarried US women aged 75–84 outnumbered unmarried men of the same age by 3:1. The US baby boom of the 1950s and early 1960s, which we discuss in Chapter 5, also created a sex ratio imbalance. The sharp increase in fertility rates meant that many years later there were substantially more women aged 25 than men a few years older, who were their traditional marriage partners.

Differences in the sex ratio also exist in several US population subgroups, especially the black population. In 2013, among persons aged 20–44, there were 86 black men for every 100 black women. Among whites, the ratio was 102 men per 100 women. We discuss the gender imbalance in the black population and its effects in detail in Chapter 4. Sex ratios can also vary among recent immigrant groups if men tend to immigrate first.

Figure 3.12 shows how a change in the sex ratio affects the marriage market. To be specific, we focus on an increase in the number of women with no increase in the number of men. Clearly a change like that will affect the supply curve. A parallel analysis could be based on a decrease in the number of men with no change in the number of women. In that case the demand curve would be affected.

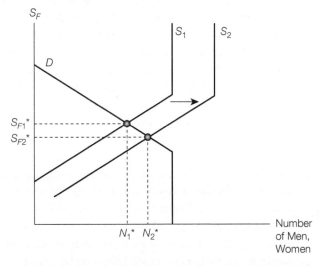

Figure 3.12 *How an increase in the number of women affects the marriage market.*

In Figure 3.12, the original supply curve is S_1, where the sex ratio is in balance and the new supply curve is S_2, representing the increase in the number of women; the curve is just shifted to the right. At the old equilibrium price ($S_{F1}*$) there is now excess supply—more women looking for husbands than men looking for wives. As a result, the equilibrium price will fall to $S_{F2}*$, where the new supply curve and the original demand curve are now in balance. The absolute number of married men and women increases from N_1* to N_2*, representing an increase in the proportion of men who are married but a decrease in the proportion of women. Most importantly, the equilibrium price falls, so that married women are worse off than before, while married men are better off. This confirms what seems like a plausible hypothesis: the group in excess fares worse because the market power tilts in favor of the other group.

If there were a decrease in the number of women relative to men, the situation would be just the opposite. Now the supply curve would shift to the left—fewer women willing to marry at every price. The equilibrium price would rise, men would be worse off, and women would be better off.

The examples of sex ratio imbalances above all fit this analysis very nicely. For example, since older men are almost always scarce relative to older women, they will fare well in the marriage market and widows will fare less well. In China, where gender ratios are seriously askew, there is growing evidence of the difficulties men are having finding spouses.[18]

---

18 There are approximately 120 Chinese men for every 100 women in the prime marrying ages. One study found that Chinese women were very focused on the earnings of potential spouses and that a boom in housing investment by families with sons, taken to be an indicator of earnings, was one result. See Robert Frank, "Supply, Demand, and Marriage," *New York Times*, August 6, 2011. We have more to say about sex-ratio imbalances in Chapter 13.

The rising fertility rates during the US baby boom created a shortage of men a few years older than prospective brides and placed them in an advantageous position.

On US college campuses, women have gone from being underrepresented to overrepresented. When many traditionally all-male colleges first admitted women in the 1960s, men outnumbered women by as much as five or ten to one. Currently, women substantially outnumber men on most college campuses as a result of the gender gap in higher education favoring women. At this particular life stage, marriage isn't the critical issue, but we could reinterpret the model in terms of dating behavior. Would women be treated better when the sex ratio was in their favor than when it favored the men? That's roughly the equivalent of a high value of S_F in our model. What will happen in the 2010s when women substantially outnumber men on most college campuses?

One final note. We analyzed the effect of the sex ratio imbalance situation assuming that all partners were equally desirable. Another way to think about it is that partner desirability varies (as it does in the real world) and that when the ratio is out of balance, the side that is scarce "marries up." They end up with partners that are better than they would have had if the ratio had been more balanced. That is essentially equivalent to what we learned in the model in which all partners were equal. There, the scarce side of the market is better off because it gets a larger equilibrium share of marital output. In this version they are better off because they get a more desirable marriage partner. This is a good example of how to translate the insights of a model from the simplified world of the model to the more complicated world in which we all live.

Women's wages and the marriage market Women's wages and labor-market opportunities have increased steadily and substantially over the past century. We will focus directly on those issues in later chapters, but here we can think about how the changes influenced marriage markets.

Figure 3.13 shows how we might analyze that. An increase in women's wages will increase Z_F, their well-being as single women. Because they earn more, they can support themselves better. This kind of change will shift the supply curve up or in, which is a decrease in supply. It is probably easier to think of shifting the curve up, so that each woman is now just willing to marry at a value of S_F that is higher than before. Or you can think of fewer women being willing to marry at any value of S_F, so the supply curve shifts in. This is exactly the opposite of the change in supply we analyzed in Figure 3.12.

In Figure 3.13, S_1 is the original supply curve, and S_2 is the new supply curve with higher wages for women. Because the number of women doesn't change in this example, the two supply curves eventually join up where all women are accounted for on the new supply curve. The original equilibrium is at S_{F1}^* and N_1^*. When the supply curve shifts, the equilibrium moves up along the demand curve. The new equilibrium price rises to S_{F2}^* and the number of married men and women falls to N_2^*. How do these changes occur? At the old equilibrium price, fewer of the now better-off single women are willing to marry, so there is excess demand by men for wives. So, just as we saw in Figure 3.11, the price must rise. Women gain within marriage precisely because they are better off outside of marriage. Men must treat them better—in our terms, the women get a larger share of marital output—because otherwise the women are better off single and will be unwilling to marry. This is an important conclusion and one that is far from obvious.

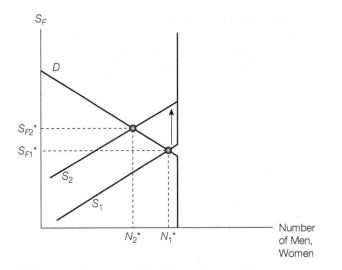

Figure 3.13 *How higher wages for women affect the marriage market.*

Instead of wages increasing, picture the marriage supply curve for women a century or more ago. Their labor-market opportunities were, with rare exceptions, very limited. Their supply curve was therefore positioned very low and the corresponding equilibrium price was very low. The marriage market equilibrium left women with a relatively small share of marital output, again precisely because their non-marriage opportunities were so limited.

Contraception and the sexual revolution Single life has changed in many other ways as well. Not too long ago—in the 1950s and into the 1960s—sexual activity prior to marriage was relatively uncommon, certainly by today's standards. This was not just a matter of different moral standards. Contraception was far less available than it is today and far less reliable. The birth control pill was not yet available. Condoms were behind the counter in the drugstore, not on shelves in broad daylight. In Connecticut, it was illegal even for married couples to buy contraceptives, a provision that was not struck down by the US Supreme Court until 1965. Of course, abortion was illegal and, even where available, often not very safe. As a result, sexual activity outside of marriage carried real risks for both men and, especially, women. More on this in Chapter 6.

Figure 3.14 shows how we can incorporate these changes into our supply-and-demand model. S_1 and D_1 are the original supply-and-demand curves from the 1950s. In this time period, married life and single life are substantially different from one another, precisely because of the unavailability of contraceptives and the associated conservative attitudes about sex. Thus individuals are willing to marry at relatively low values of S_F and S_M. The corresponding equilibrium is at price S_{F1}^* and quantity N_1^*. N_1^* is large—most men and women are married, with early marriage the social norm. That corresponds exactly to what we know about marriage in that time period.

In the changed social environment, married life and single life are no longer as different from one another as before and the value of single life increases, which, in turn, decreases both men's demand for marriage and women's supply to marriage. At any value of S_F and S_M, fewer men and fewer women are now willing to marry than in the

1950s. Both curves (D_2 and S_2) shift inward. In Figure 3.14 we have shifted the women's supply curve by less than the men's demand curve. Because single women inevitably bear greater costs in the event of a pregnancy than single men, the changes might reasonably change their desired choices less than the men's.

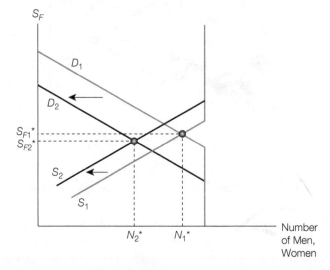

Figure 3.14 *How the sexual revolution affected the marriage market.*

The big change in the equilibrium is in the number of marriages, which falls from N_1^* to N_2^*, a change fully consistent with the actual real-world changes. Quite plausibly, this effect might be greatest for young men and women, who have substantially delayed their entry into marriage. The change in the share of marital output for men and women isn't nearly as great. In the case depicted in Figure 3.14, women end up just a bit worse off because the shift in the demand curve was greater than the shift in the supply curve.

In the mid-1900s and into the 2000s and 2010s, concerns about STDs and AIDS and a somewhat more conservative social order may have shifted the curves again, this time increasing both supply and demand. It will be interesting to see whether age at first marriage falls as a result.

The distribution of resources in marriage

In the supply-and-demand model, we showed that women fared better in marriage under particular circumstances, such as when the sex ratio favored them and when their non-marriage alternatives were better. This latter effect largely reflected their opportunities for self-support through employment; as these opportunities have increased, women are able to be more selective about marriage. We modeled this through a shift in the supply curve and showed that women would be better off in marriage when their non-marriage alternatives improved.

In this section we look at a related idea—the distribution of resources within a marriage and how that is affected by non-marriage alternatives. We examine a situation closer to real married life in which husbands and wives have different preferences and thus do not necessarily always agree about how money should be spent. For example, one spouse might want to save for a bigger or better house, while the other might want to spend on a nicer vacation, something special for the children, or maybe even something for himself or herself that the other spouse doesn't approve of. Issues like these are the stuff of daily life in real marriages. In a situation like that, what happens? What factors influence the result?

To analyze this, economists use **bargaining models** in which a husband and wife with different preferences bargain and negotiate to reach an allocation of resources acceptable to both.[19] How much bargaining power each party has is determined by his or her **threat point**. One particularly important type of threat point is the divorce threat point, which reflects how well off each party would be if the marriage dissolved. The divorce threat point depends upon a number of factors: the labor-market opportunities available to both parties, the availability of welfare benefits to the mother and potential social and family support, and remarriage chances. Laws governing child custody and the terms of divorce, such as how community property is split, also affect the threat point.[20]

In general, the person with the most power in bargaining is the person who has the stronger threat point. Figure 3.15 shows this idea. Once again, M and F are our married couple. The Y-axis shows her utility in the marriage and the X-axis shows his. The curve shown here is a **utility-possibilities curve (UPC)**, which is similar to the PPC that we used in the production model of marriage. The UPC shows all possible combinations of utility for M and F. If F controlled all the resources in the marriage and spent them for things she cared about, her utility would be shown by point A, while if M controlled the resources and spending, his utility would be shown by B. The line AB, which connects the two axes, provides a limit to their utilities such that all the points along the line are attainable, points to the northeast are not attainable, and points inside the line are attainable but inefficient because both individuals would do better if they moved to AB. Each point along AB is what economists call **Pareto efficient** – that is, it gives the maximum utility for one spouse for a given level of the other. Along AB it is impossible to make F better off without making M worse off.

Exactly where along the UPC they will end up depends on their respective threat points—that is, the options they have outside the marriage. In Figure 3.15, these threat points are shown as T_F and T_M. (Ignore T_F' for the moment.) We have drawn these threat points to represent a typical situation from a time period in which men had far better non-marriage opportunities than women because their labor-market options were better. Thus we show $T_F < T_M$. The threat points mean that the relevant utility possibility frontier is now just the portion of the UPC from A' to B'. If F's utility in the marriage fell below T_F, she would be better off exiting the marriage. This eliminates the portion of the UPC between B' and B.

19 The earliest models of family resource allocation adopted a very simple approach called the **unitary model** of the household, which assumed either that a single person (usually the husband) determined the allocation of resources or that all household members had the same preferences. This is not a very satisfying analysis because it completely ignored the internal decision-making process of the family.

20 See Betsey Stevenson (2007), "The Impact of Divorce Laws on Marriage-Specific Capital," *Journal of Labor Economics*, 25 (1), 75–94 and P. S. Carlin (1991), "Intra-Family Bargaining and Time Allocation," in T. P. Schultz (ed.), *Research in Population Economics*, Greenwich, CT: JAI Press.

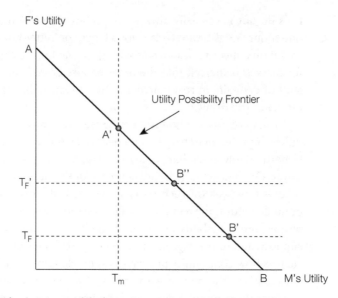

Figure 3.15 *A bargaining model of marriage outcomes with threat points.*

Similarly, if M's utility in the marriage fell below T_M, he would exit the marriage. This eliminates the portion of the UPC between A' and A.

In this example the difference in their threat points moves the likely solution in a direction more favorable to M and less favorable to F. The bargained solution will end up somewhere between A' and B'. Importantly, if F's non-marriage opportunities improved to T_F', perhaps reflecting improved labor-market opportunities, the bargained solution would now have to lie between A' and B'. She would be better off in marriage because she has stronger non-marriage alternatives.

Isabel Sawhill summarized these ideas very nicely in a discussion of women's improving labor-market opportunities and its effect on divorce. She wrote that "A weapon like divorce doesn't have to be used to be effective. The mere threat or availability of the option may be enough to change behavior. Our research, and that of others, provided lots of empirical support for the idea that women's expanding opportunities were simultaneously responsible for rising divorce rates on the one hand and for better—including more egalitarian—marriages on the other."[21]

Evidence Empirical research on this topic has focused on whether the specific source of income—whether it is the husband's or the wife's—affects the way resources are used. Bargaining models suggest that this ought to make a difference. In perhaps the most often cited research, Lundberg, Pollak, and Wales[22] took advantage of a change in the welfare system in the United Kingdom to perform a natural experiment. In the United Kingdom,

---

21 Isabel Sawhill (Summer, 2001), "Reversing Teen Pregnancy and Single Parenthood," *The American Experiment Quarterly*, 77–81.

22 Shelly Lundberg, Robert Pollak, and Terrence Wales (1997), "Do Husbands and Wives Pool Their Resources? Evidence from the United Kingdom Child Benefit," *Journal of Human Resources*, 32 (3), 463–480.

all families receive child benefit. Before 1977, this benefit was essentially paid directly to the father because it was in the form of a deduction from the income tax and thus, if the husband was the breadwinner, it showed up in his paycheck. However, after 1977 the benefit was paid in cash to the mother. Because this change served to increase women's bargaining power within the marriage, Lundberg, Pollak, and Wales examined how it affected household consumption expenditures. They found that after this change, expenditures on children's and women's clothing increased, providing some of the first evidence suggesting that the source of income matters. Numerous other studies, but not all, have verified this finding in other contexts.

Additional evidence for the predictions of the divorce threat models comes from examining how the liberalization of divorce laws affected domestic violence. As we saw above, prior to the advent of unilateral/no fault divorce laws, the spouse who did not want to divorce had the bargaining power, but the shift to the unilateral divorce laws gave the bargaining power to the spouse who wanted to end the marriage. Economists Betsey Stevenson and Justin Wolfers contend that this change in the law shifted the divorce threat points and hence increased women's bargaining power within marriage. They found that the shift to unilateral divorce significantly reduced female suicide rates, domestic violence toward women and the homicide of wives in those states that made the change. They concluded that by giving women more power by being able to exit the marriage without consent from their spouse, the change in the divorce law made women better off within marriage.[23]

Other studies have often found that when income transfers are targeted at mothers, children's health and education outcomes improve.[24] This finding has had tremendously important policy implications particularly in developing countries. To the extent that higher spending on children influences human capital accumulation, these findings suggest that empowering women may also lead to faster economic growth and, thus, there has been a trend toward policies that empower women in the economic sphere. We will have more to say about this in Chapter 13.

Another body of research, primarily within experimental economics, seeks to determine if the husband and wife have differing preferences. This research tends to find that women are more altruistic and more risk-averse than men are.[25] Most of these studies also find that the source of resources does matter.

Marital search

In this section we look at marriage from a different angle by focusing on the process of finding a partner. To do that we use **search theory**, a set of ideas originally applied to the labor market. Up to now we have assumed that all men and all women were alike and that no one had a particular preference for one partner over another. Every possible matching

---

23 Betsey Stevenson and Justin Wolfers (2006), "Bargaining in the Shadow of the Law: Divorce Laws and Family Distress," *The Quarterly Journal of Economics*, 121 (1), 267–288.

24 A review of this evidence can be found in J. Yoong, L. Rabinovich, and S. Diepeveen (2012), *The Impact of Economic Resource Transfers to Women Versus Men: A Systematic Review*, Technical Report. London: EPPI-Centre, Social Science Research Unit, Institute of Education, University of London.

25 C. C. Eckel and P. J. Grossman (2008), "Differences in the Economic Decisions of Men and Women: Experimental Evidence," *Handbook of Experimental Economics Results*, 1, 509–519.

of one partner with another was just as good as any other. That is not realistic, of course, but, like most assumptions in economics models, it was useful in order to isolate and understand more fundamental forces that would continue to hold even in a more complicated and more realistic setting in which individuals differ and have preferences about potential partners.

Search theory was originally developed to analyze employment and unemployment issues in the real world, where both people and jobs differ in many subtle, but important, ways. That analysis, which won the Nobel Prize in Economics in 2010 for economists Dale Mortensen, Christopher Pissarides, and Peter Diamond, developed rules to describe the optimal strategy of job search, especially how long to search and how to decide what wage offer was acceptable. Like most economics problems, optimal searching involves balancing marginal costs and marginal benefits. In the labor market, the marginal benefit of additional searching is the potentially greater income from a better job match in which your skills are better utilized and your income is higher. The marginal cost is the time and resources devoted to searching and the opportunity cost of the lost income of the job that you could have had if you had not continued searching.

These ideas fit the marriage market incredibly well. Certainly people are heterogeneous and some matches are better than others. Most people don't marry the first person they meet. Rather they search among multiple partners; that's called dating. The marginal benefit of searching for one more time period is the potential greater gains of marriage from a better partner match—that is, the difference between the value of marriage to your current partner and the value of the match to a partner you might meet in the next time period, evaluated over the rest of your adult lifetime. The marginal cost is the time and resources devoted to searching (coffee, dinner, a movie, etc.), plus the opportunity cost of the lost value of the current relationship, which it is usually assumed you terminate in order to search. It is, as a practical matter, harder to search for a new partner while involved with a current partner.

Not surprisingly, it makes sense to continue searching as long as the marginal benefit exceeds the marginal cost. Marginal benefits are typically large at the beginning of the search; it is unlikely that the first person you meet is a particularly good match. So continuing to search is usually valuable in finding a better potential match. But those marginal benefits decline as the search continues, for two reasons. First, you have already "sampled" more potential partners, including some who are perfectly decent partners, so the probability of finding a better match is lower. Second, with the passage of time, you will have a shorter and shorter time period over the rest of your life to enjoy the benefits. Marginal costs probably increase over time, mostly because opportunity costs in the form of the lost value of a current relationship increase with searching. The optimal search stopping point is where the marginal benefit of continued searching just equals the marginal cost.

Because marginal cost is always positive, optimal marital searching implies that you stop searching even though the marginal benefit is also positive: $MB = MC$, but because $MC > 0$, $MB > 0$, too. But this means that if you had continued to search, you would likely have found someone better matched to you than your "optimal" partner. By the time you met that person, however, you would likely have too few years together to make that match better in total value than the one you actually make. Your actual marriage partner may be a very good match, maybe even great, but probably not the best. This unromantic conclusion follows from applying search theory to marriage.

It is utterly obvious that search costs have certainly changed enormously over the years. In the distant past, marriage was largely among persons living in the same village or neighborhood because large search costs made it virtually impossible to meet other prospective partners. Urbanization and increasing educational opportunities for women changed that, making it easier (cheaper) to meet prospective spouses. The increase in women's labor-force activity is another factor; it is now possible, indeed common, to meet a future spouse at work. Internet dating sites are the next phase—think about the ease (low cost) with which it is now possible to meet a dizzying array of potential partners.

Some of the more interesting online dating sites are those that arise to serve particular market niches where search costs are likely to be particularly high. These might be "thin" markets—that is, markets with relatively few potential participants on each side of the market. Examples would include marriage markets based on religious beliefs (fundamentalist Christian or Jewish) or a particular lifestyle that might not be for everyone (farmers). You can probably add more examples. In these markets, enabling participants to locate one another greatly reduces search costs.

In addition to the prediction that you probably won't marry your ideal partner, there is one far more optimistic prediction of this approach. Falling search costs means that it is optimal to set a higher bar for an acceptable spouse. You will almost certainly end up with a partner who is a better match for you (and you for him/her) than in a world with higher search costs.

We close this chapter with a description of a mechanism to ensure that the marriage market pairs the right set of partners, where "right" means that no one would rather be paired with someone else. It is a piece of pure theory, but, like the best kind of theory, it turned out to have unexpected practical value in another area altogether. See Box 3.2 about Lloyd Shapley and his Nobel Prize.

Box	3.2

Two-Sided Matching: Marriage, Kidney Exchanges, and School Choice Assignment

In 2012, Lloyd Shapley was awarded the Nobel Prize in Economics for research done 50 years earlier in a famous article, "College Admissions and the Stability of Marriage." Shapley's article is a theoretical analysis of an economic allocation problem called **two-sided matching**. One such two-sided matching involves individuals in the marriage market seeking mates. The same general analysis could be applied to finding a roommate or a date for the senior prom.

The focus of Shapley's paper was whether a mechanism existed that would always produce a *stable* marriage matching. Stability is a technical mathematical property, but it has a natural interpretation in the context of marriage. If means that no two persons who are matched would prefer to be married to another person; if that weren't true, the matching would be unstable, because some marriages would be terminated as individuals found new, more desired partners.

Two-sided matching is potentially quite complicated. You might be someone's first choice, but you might prefer someone else for whom you are a third choice, and maybe that person's first two choices prefer someone else. Shapley showed that a mechanism to identify a stable matching, called a **deferred acceptance algorithm**, did exist and described how it would work. Whether it would or could work in practice is another question, but it is interesting to think about and it has had very important applications in other areas.

Here's how Shapley's deferred acceptance algorithm works in the marriage case. First, each person ranks each potential marriage partner from highest to lowest. Then marriage proposals are made simultaneously. This already stretches reality, but remember that this is a model and he is trying to eliminate superficial complications. Shapley assumed that, as was customary, men would propose to women (more on that below). So each man proposes to his first choice. Some women will likely get more than one proposal, some will get one, and some will get none. Each woman with one proposal *conditionally* accepts it, and each woman with more than one *conditionally* accepts her preferred one and rejects the others. "Conditionally" means that she is deferring her final decision to see if someone better comes along later; Shapley called this "keeping him on a string."

Now, all men who have been rejected in the first round propose to their second choice woman, who, in turn, rejects the offer if she already has one that she prefers or conditionally accepts it. In the latter case, she might reject the person she had on a string, who then goes on to propose to his next most preferred partner in the next round. The process continues round by round with rejections and conditional acceptances. Eventually, when all women have received an offer, each woman accepts the person on her string, who is the most preferred of all who have proposed at any round.

Shapley wrote this in 1962, so he thought of this process occurring iteratively in real time. In one example presented in the article with just four men and four women, it would take ten rounds to reach a stable match. Now we can readily imagine a computer solving this problem if it had all the information about rankings. No one would need to have their feelings hurt by finding themselves kept on a string and then later rejected.

Shapley showed that it often matters whether men or women do the proposing. Typically, for any set of preferences about prospective partners, there is more than one stable matching, and which one emerges depends on the proposing rule. In a simple numerical example with three men and three women, he showed that when men do the proposing, they each end up with their most preferred partner, while the women end up with their least preferred partner. However, with the same preferences, when the women do the proposing, the tables are turned—they get their first choices and the men get their last choices. In practice, the results might be less extreme than this example, which reflects a case in which each man's first choice is each woman's last choice, and vice versa. Why men typically propose to women isn't clear, but the impact is that the men benefit and the women are worse off.

In practice, no one has yet established a clearinghouse of preference rankings to match persons in the marriage market using a deferred acceptance algorithm. But this has been done by Alvin Roth, Shapley's co-winner, and his coauthors in several important real-world instances. Roth modified an existing clearinghouse that matched graduates of medical schools with hospitals providing internships and he developed an improved method for matching New York City students with high schools in a school-choice program. He also designed a mechanism for kidney matching for transplants.

Source: David Gale and Lloyd S. Shapley (1962), "College Admissions and the Stability of Marriage," *American Mathematical Monthly*, 69, 9–15. Shapley's co-author, David Gale, died in 2008 and was not eligible for the Nobel Prize, which is not awarded posthumously.

Summary

The basic message of this chapter is twofold and a bit contradictory. On the one hand, marriage is a social and economic institution of great importance that generates substantial benefits. On the other hand, a declining proportion of women and men are married at any point in time and individual marriages are far less durable than in the past. This is true not only in the United States but in other developed countries as well.

The economic approach to marriage emphasizes the gains of marriage, the existence of which can be inferred by the fact that most men and women still do marry. We examined those gains with a variety of models and approaches—production, investment, and consumption. When men and women have different underlying abilities with respect to market wages and household productivity, marriage enables them to both end up better off than if they were single. They can do this by specializing in either the market or household sector and sharing what they can produce. This explanation fits very nicely with the traditional husband-breadwinner, wife-homemaker marriage structure that was so common a century ago and persisted through the 1950s and beyond. But as underlying differences between the sexes diminish, this source of gains of marriage diminishes as well, although it has not disappeared. The idea that marriage facilitates investment in a relationship by establishing a longer-term time horizon for decision making is critical. That and joint consumption may well be the hallmarks of contemporary marriage.

The supply-and-demand model focuses on decisions about whether to marry or not and on how the gains of marriage are distributed between husband and wife, something we side-stepped in the production model. Supply-and-demand forces definitely matter. The side of the market that is in excess supply or has poorer non-marriage alternatives always fares worse, either in the sense of receiving a smaller share of total marital output or by marrying down.

Finally, we applied search theory to what is, in fact, one of the most important decisions an individual will ever make. Optimal search requires attention to both the marginal costs and the marginal benefits of continued search. Search theory tells us that the lower search costs that are typical today mean that you will likely end up with a better match and a happier marriage. But it also implies that waiting for your ideal spouse is not a good strategy.

4 MARRIAGE—APPLICATIONS AND EXTENSIONS

Introduction

In this chapter we continue our discussion of the economics of marriage and the family. We begin with an overview of research on the gains of marriage, a research area that nicely illustrates many of the statistical issues we raised in Chapter 2. We follow that with discussions of two other important marriage-related demographic decisions—cohabitation and divorce. We then examine two important applied issues concerning sharp declines in marriage for particular demographic groups. We focus on differences in marriage by race and by educational attainment, and the possible causes and consequences of the growing gaps.

The gains of marriage: health, earnings, and happiness

In Chapter 2 we explored the gains of marriage arising from specialization in production, investment, and consumption. In this section we review empirical research on the impact of marriage on health, men's earnings, and happiness.

In all of the research results discussed below, it is important to recognize that there are always two possible explanations of any observed difference between married and unmarried persons. One is that the marriage effect is genuine and is a causal effect of marriage on the outcome. The other is that the effect is just a correlation and that the apparent benefits of marriage simply reflect the kind of men and women who are married, rather than the impact of marriage per se. This is often called a **selection effect**. Obviously, the marital status in which we observe men and women is not the result of a random assignment experiment. Rather, men and women choose whether to marry and whether to remain married on the basis of the benefits they receive. The hard part of the empirical research on the effects of marriage is to distinguish correlation from causation.

Determining which effect dominates has important policy implications. If marriage is the cause of better health, policymakers may want to encourage marriage, as it may have positive externalities in terms of lower healthcare spending and increased labor-market productivity. On the other hand, if marriage is merely correlated with health through selection of the healthier into marriage, then no such positive externality exists.

Marriage and health

In data from the United States as well as many other countries, there is a strong positive correlation between marriage and health. This is such an empirical regularity that it has been described as "one of the most robust in the social sciences."[1] Researchers have theorized that this positive correlation could stem from a **marriage protection effect**: married couples look after each other, making sure that they have regular doctor visits, caring for one another when they fall ill, providing companionship and support in rough times, and keeping each other from engaging in risky behaviors such as smoking and excessive alcohol consumption. The alternative explanation is that married couples are healthier because those who are in better health are more desirable as marriage partners than those who are not, just as we described above.

To determine if marriage is the *cause* of better health, researchers have typically relied on longitudinal data, which includes information about the same individual over a long period of time. This allows a researcher to compare the health of an individual before and after marriage to see if their health changes with a change in marital status. This method controls for factors that are specific to each individual and do not change over time; such factors could include a propensity for risk taking or diligence, or other things that might affect both health and marriage and are difficult to measure.[2] Many social scientists have used this method and have concluded that there is a protective effect of marriage—that is, marriage appears to be the cause of better health.

It is challenging to summarize the findings across these studies because they use many different measures of health or health behaviors and some find a statistically significant effect, while others do not. But some generalizations can certainly be made. Married men and married women have lower levels of negative health behaviors than those who are not married. They report less problem drinking than divorced or widowed men and women. Perhaps not surprisingly, men report far more problems than women regardless of marital status.[3] Married men and women are also more likely to get regular health checkups and engage in preventive healthcare, such as mammograms and dental screenings.[4] They also tend to report better health when they respond to a question asking how they would rate their overall health, and they live longer than their unmarried counterparts.[5]

There are some negative findings, as well. Single individuals may spend more effort maintaining their health and fitness to attract a partner, and so the presence of a committed partner may actually reduce the need to carefully maintain one's health and fitness. This effect has been found to be particularly pronounced for maintaining a healthy weight. Married individuals are more likely to be obese, perhaps because they are no longer searching for a mate and are less inclined to keep themselves physically fit.[6]

---

1 H. Liu (2012), "Marital Dissolution and Self-Rated Health: Age Trajectories and Birth Cohort Variations," *Social Science and Medicine*. 74, 1107–1116.

2 An important shortcoming of this method is that it cannot address the possibility of reverse causality— that is, unhealthy persons may seek out marriage partners to care for them. Economists call this adverse selection.

3 S. L. Averett, L. M. Argys, and J. Sorkin (2013), "In Sickness and in Health: An Examination of Relationship Status and Health Using Data From The Canadian National Public Health Survey," *Review of Economics of the Household*, 11 (4), 599–633.

4 Yuriy Pylypchuk and Edward Miller (2014), "Marital Status, Spousal Characteristics, and the Use of Preventive Care," *Journal of Family and Economic Issues*, 35 (3), 323–338.

5 Chris M. Wilson and Andrew J. Oswald (2005), "How Does Marriage Affect Physical and Psychological Health? A Survey of the Longitudinal Evidence," IZA Discussion Paper No. 1619.

6 Averett, Argys, and Sorkin (2013), op cit. and S. L. Averett, J. Sikora and L. M. Argys (2008),"For Better or Worse: Relationship Status and Body Mass Index," *Economics and Human Biology*, 6 (2), 330–349 both find that marriage increases the probability that an individual is overweight or obese.

The finding that marriage is good for individual health is not universally established in research studies. Two recent studies find that when aggregating several indicators of health together in a single overall index of health and using more sophisticated statistical methods that are beyond the scope of this text, being married was no better for health than being unpartnered.[7] The message from the plethora of research on marriage and health is that although there is a positive correlation between marriage and health, it may not reflect a causal relationship.

Marriage and men's earnings

One possible benefit of marriage for men in a traditional marriage is the ability to specialize in the labor market and potentially earn more. Indeed, for as long as statistics on individual earnings have been analyzed, it has been noted that married men typically earn more than otherwise similar single men, by about 10–20 percent. This finding is referred to as the **male marriage premium**.

This could be a genuine marriage productivity effect, based on specialization, but it could, instead, be a marriage selectivity effect, exactly as in the case of health. In this case, it is possible that married men differ from otherwise similar single men in ways that enable them to have higher earnings and also make them more likely to be married. They could be more industrious, more responsible, more courteous, and so on. These differences and not marriage might be responsible for the male marriage premium.

Sorting out these competing explanations is not simple. Korenman and Neumark[8] examined the male marriage premium in the 1970s and 1980s in a way that allowed the premium to vary with the number of years of marriage. They reasoned that the selectivity effect ought to depend mostly on whether someone was married, rather than how long he was married. In contrast, the productivity effect would likely increase with years of marriage, as the benefits of specialization were realized. They found that the marriage premium did, in fact, increase with years of marriage. The impact of an additional year was about 1–2 percent per year, so that after ten years of marriage, the premium was about 15 percent. They found no evidence of a marital status effect per se. Another study showed that the earnings premium was greater for men whose wives were full-time homemakers compared to men whose wives worked.[9] These findings both suggest that the productivity effect was genuine in this time period.

One interesting possible natural experiment involves marriages that follow a premarital pregnancy—that is, so-called "shotgun" marriages. In that situation the marriage is largely unplanned and selectivity issues might well be less important. Ginther and Zavodny[10] found that the marriage premium for men in shotgun marriages was little different than

7 See Jennifer L. Kohn and Susan L. Averett (2014), "Can't We Just Live Together? New Evidence of the Effect of Relationship Status on Health," *Journal of Family and Economic Issues*, 35, 295–312 and Jennifer L. Kohn and Susan L. Averett (2014), "The Effect of Relationship Status on Health with Dynamic Health and Persistent Relationships," *Journal of Health Economics*, 36, 69–83.

8 Sanders Korenman and David Neumark (1991), "Does Marriage Really Make Men More Productive?" *Journal of Human Resources*, 26 (2), 282–307.

9 Jeffrey S. Grey (1997), "The Fall in Men's Return to Marriage," *Journal of Human Resources*, 32 (3), 481–504.

10 Donna K. Ginther and Madeline Zavodny (2001), "Is the Male Marriage Premium Due to Selection? The Effect of Shotgun Weddings on the Return to Marriage," *Journal of Population Economics*, 14, 313–328.

the premium for other men indicating that the effect is due to marriage and not selectivity. Other evidence on the earnings of identical twins, one of whom was married while the other was not, also shows a beneficial effect.[11]

The male marriage premium in the United States has declined quite steadily since the 1960s. Blackburn and Korenman[12] found that the premium fell by about one-third between the late 1960s and the late 1980s. The decline in the household division of labor by gender (see Box 3.1) is certainly relevant here. If the premium reflected the labor-market gains to men of the division of labor within marriage, then the decline in specialization within marriage would likely reduce those gains. So, as a broad trend, the big increase in married women's labor-force participation fits well with the decline in the male marriage premium.

Finally, we can't leave this topic without mentioning the companion issue—the impact of marriage and children on women's earnings. We talk about that at length in Chapter 11. Suffice it to say here that marriage and especially children have a negative impact on women's earnings. This impact is now often referred to as the **family gap**, reflecting the notion that family issues, rather than skill differences, account for a share of the gender gap in earnings.

Marriage and happiness

While this may seem outside of the realm of economics, there is actually quite a bit of economics research examining happiness. As before, although a positive correlation between marriage and happiness has been documented by many studies, this may be the result of happier people being more likely to marry and stay married. Others have argued that we each have an innate "set point" for happiness and that while we may deviate from that periodically due to particularly good or bad life events, we ultimately return to our own baseline level of happiness, no matter what our marital status is.

A recent study, however, seems to have established that those who are married are happier and that this happiness effect of marriage is long-lasting. This happiness boost occurs for those who cohabit as well.[13] The authors sorted out selection from a causal effect of marriage on happiness by using longitudinal data and by controlling for happiness levels prior to marriage. They report that married individuals are happier and that the happiness benefits of marriage stem from social channels. In particular, spouses who describe themselves as being friends are the happiest. It appears from this research that people can increase their happiness levels by finding support in long-term relationships.

Cohabitation

One particularly interesting demographic development is the emergence of an institutional competitor to marriage—cohabitation. In the United States, cohabiting opposite-sex couples were originally referred to as **POSSLQs** (pronounced "poss-el-queues") for persons of opposite sex sharing living quarters. That classification was based on living

---

11 Kate Antonovics and Robert Town (2004), "Are All the Good Men Married? Uncovering the Sources of the Marital Wage Premium," *American Economic Review*, Papers and Proceedings, 94 (2), 317–321.

12 McKinley Blackburn and Sanders Korenman (1994), "*The Declining Marital-Status Earnings Differential*," *Journal of Population Economics*, 7, 247–270.

13 John F. Helliwell and Shawn Grover (2014), "How's Life at Home? New Evidence on Marriage and the Set Point for Happiness," NBER Working Paper #20794.

arrangements rather than a specific relationship among the individuals, and likely included some persons who were no more than roommates. Beginning in 1995, unmarried partners were identified directly by asking the "householder" about his or her relationship to everyone else in the household; the householder is the person in whose name the housing is owned or rented and who answers the survey. Included among 17 possible relationships are "opposite-sex unmarried partner," and "same sex unmarried partner." "Roomer or boarder" and "housemate or roommate" are both separately identified and thus not included in cohabitation totals. As a result, it is now much clearer who is cohabiting and in a marriage-like relationship and who is not.[14]

In 1977, when the Census Bureau first began counting POSSLQs, there were about 1 million cohabiting opposite-sex couples. In 1996, using the more direct relationship status measure, 2.8 million opposite-sex cohabiting couples were counted. Since then the numbers have increased every year, reaching 5 million in 2006 and over 8 million in 2013. By comparison, there were 61 million married couples, so marriages outnumbered cohabitating couples by seven to one. Cohabitation is most common among younger adults. Among 18–24-year-old women, cohabiters actually outnumber those who are married. About one in nine US women of that age were in a cohabiting relationship in 2013, one in six 25–29-year-olds were, and one in ten 30–34-year-olds. Whites and blacks are approximately equally likely to be cohabiting, Asians less likely, and Hispanics more likely.

Another large nationally representative survey, the National Survey of Family Growth (NSFG), also provides estimates of the time trend in cohabitation for women aged 15–44. It shows an increase in cohabitation from 3.0 percent in 1982 to 7.0 percent in 1995, and 11.2 percent over the 2006–2010 period.[15] The 8 percent increase between 1982 and the late 2000s exactly mirrors the decline in the proportion in first marriages over this time period and suggests that cohabitation is functioning as a near-substitute for marriage. As of the early to mid-2000s, more than half of US women aged 15–44 had ever cohabitated, and about half of all marriages were preceded by a spell of cohabitation.

One very interesting feature of cohabitation in the United States is that it is negatively related to a woman's years of education. For women aged 22–44 in the late 2000s, the NSFG data show that the proportion cohabiting was 20 percent for those with less than a high-school degree, 15.5 percent for women with a high-school degree or equivalent, 11.6 percent for those with some college, and about 6.0 percent for college graduates. The proportions married show the opposite relationship, increasing from an average of about 40 percent for women who are not college graduates to 60 percent for college graduates.[16] The same patterns of cohabitation and marriage by education are also present for men.

Cohabitation and, more recently, marriage have also increased among same-sex couples. A large annual survey of US families called the American Community Survey has provided estimates of the number of same-sex couples annually since 2005. In 2008 it found 565,000 unmarried same-sex couples and in 2012, the most current year available,

---

14 It is still not a perfect measure. If neither cohabitating partner is the householder, they are not counted because the survey only asks about the relationship of the householder to other persons in the household.

15 Casey E. Copen, Kimberly Daniels, Jonathan Vespa, and William D. Mosher (2012), "First Marriages in the United States: Data from the 2006–2010 National Survey of Family Growth," *National Health Statistics Reports*, 49, 1–22.

16 Copen, Daniels, Vespa, and Mosher, op cit, Table 1.

that number had increased to 640,000. The 2010 Census included identifying questions about same-sex marriage and cohabitation, and reported about 510,000 unmarried same-sex couples and another 130,000 married same-sex couples, approximately equally distributed by gender. As of mid-2015 the number of married same-sex couples had tripled to approximately 390,000, according to analyses of survey data by the Williams Institute of the University of California-Berkeley. This increase reflected the changing legal status of same-sex marriage in many US states. In June, 2015, the US Supreme Court ruled in favor of a constitutional right to same-sex marriage, making it legal in all states. It is also legal in 19 countries, ranging from Argentina to Uruguay, and including much of Europe.

Cohabitation raises very interesting economic issues. Like marriage, it enables partners to capture economies of scale in production and consumption, enjoy joint consumption of household public goods, and reduce the transaction costs of maintaining a relationship. The primary difference, of course, is that, at least in the United States, cohabitation does not have a protected legal status and can be terminated unilaterally at will without recourse to the legal system. As a result, it likely does not function as effectively as marriage as an intertemporal commitment device to facilitate coordinated specialization and investment.

This insight helps explain the rise in the incidence of cohabitation, especially when it is linked to the introduction of improved and more reliable forms of contraception. In the 1950s and 1960s, when effective contraception was not widely available, cohabitation was not an attractive living arrangement for couples in a romantic relationship. For most women, the relatively weak commitment that cohabitation created did not offer the protection that many likely deemed necessary in the event of an unplanned pregnancy. It may also not have provided men with sufficient assurance that they could maintain a relationship with their children in the event of a break-up, since cohabitation had no recognized legal status. In that time period, the more realistic relationship choice was between being single and being married and, as we noted in the supply-and-demand model analysis in Chapter 3, these two marital statuses were very different. As contraceptive technology improved—see Chapter 6 for a full discussion—cohabitation became a more attractive option. It was now feasible to enjoy the benefits of co-residence and intimacy without the same risk of pregnancy and possible dependence. For many couples, cohabitation became a kind of trial marriage, focused more on the joint consumption aspects of a shared living arrangement, but still with relatively little specialization or couple-specific investment.

Economists Shelly Lundberg and Robert Pollak have used these ideas to explain the differing patterns of cohabitation and marriage by educational level that we noted above.[17] They argue that ultimately what distinguishes marriage from cohabitation is precisely the longer time horizon of marriage, which facilitates specialization and investment. As long as a relationship is primarily focused on joint consumption, then cohabitation and marriage are very close substitutes. The transition from cohabitation to marriage often occurs with a pregnancy or plans for starting a family, because the presence of children typically leads to both greater specialization and, especially, coordinated investment. Specialization and investment both require a time horizon and commitment that cohabitation does not

---

17 Shelly Lundberg and Robert A. Pollak (2014), "Cohabitation and the Uneven Retreat from Marriage," in Leah P. Boustan, Carola Frydman, and Robert A. Margo (eds.), *Human Capital in History: The American Record*, Chicago, IL: University of Chicago Press.

as effectively provide. As of the mid-2010s, about 60 percent of cohabiting couples in the United States have no children living with them and only about 20 percent have children from their own relationship.

Lundberg and Pollak hypothesize that the commitment feature of marriage is more valuable when parents intend to make greater investments in children. They suggest that better educated parents anticipate making greater investments in their children and these couples thus find the intertemporal commitment feature of marriage particularly valuable. In contrast, if less-educated parents intend to make fewer investments in their children, then cohabitation may be sufficient. As support for this hypothesis, they provide evidence that child-rearing patterns and parental investment in children do differ substantially by the parent's level of education. For example, time diary data show that parents with more education spend more time with their children and that the time spent per child rises sharply with income decile.[18] Furthermore, the proportion of births that are non-marital (which includes births to cohabiting couples) declines very sharply with the education of the mother. As Lundberg and Pollak note, better-educated women are more likely to be able to support a child on their own and yet they do not do so. They interpret this finding as evidence of the relative attractiveness of marriage for better-educated women. There could, of course, be other reasons for the divergent cohabitation and marriage trends by education, so their conclusion should be treated cautiously.

Nevertheless, their analysis is interesting and focuses attention more clearly on the essential ways that marriage now differs from cohabitation. Production-based marriage supported by underlying market and household productivity differences by gender was a central feature for centuries, but it has certainly declined in importance. As it declined, cohabitation has emerged as an institutional arrangement that offers many, although not all, of the benefits of marriage. While they were once very poor substitutes for one another, now they are closer substitutes in many ways, especially involving joint consumption and economies of scale. But they are less similar in matters that inherently involve a longer-term planning horizon, with children being a prime example. From an economics viewpoint, the most salient difference between marriage and cohabitation involves intertemporal commitment.

A final interesting piece of evidence on the difference between cohabitation and marriage involves men. One well-documented health benefit of marriage is that married men are more likely to seek preventive healthcare services, likely because their spouses encourage them to do so. Does cohabitation also have that effect for men? It appears that the answer is "no." Recent research based on a national health survey found that regardless of age or health insurance status, men who were cohabiting were less likely than married men to have had at least one healthcare visit in the previous year.[19] Among men with health insurance, 82 percent of married men and 71 percent of cohabiting men had such a visit. Married men were far more likely to have their blood pressure and cholesterol level checked, and among those with diagnosed hypertension, they were more likely to have had a diabetes screening. These differences were relatively large, amounting to about a 15–20 percent difference. It is impossible to know for certain if these differences are a

---

18 Lundberg and Pollak, op cit.

19 S. J. Blumberg A. Vahratian, and J. H. Blumberg (2014), "Marriage, Cohabitation, and Men's Use of Preventive Health Care Services," NCHS Data Brief, No 154.

causal effect of cohabitation vs. marriage because the men were not randomly assigned to their respective marital statuses and the study doesn't use longitudinal data. Thus we cannot say definitively that this is a causal effect. As is often the case, more research is certainly warranted.

In the above study, men who were cohabiting actually had lower utilization rates than unmarried men, but other studies have found some positive effects of cohabitation on health. Averett, Argys, and Sorkin examined health and marital status in Canada and found that cohabitation had a positive effect on some measures of health for both men and women, but the effect was smaller than for married couples.[20] This is consistent with the idea that cohabitation is not quite the equivalent of marriage in terms of spouses' willingness to invest in each other long term. It will be interesting to follow this as cohabitation spreads in the adult population.

Divorce

Divorce has become a staple of modern family life, common in ways that would have been unthinkable to your grandparents and great-grandparents. Our goal here is to review the facts and then consider possible economic explanations, including the impact of changing divorce laws, as well as many of the ideas developed in Chapter 3.

Facts and trends

We can measure the incidence of divorce by the fraction of women who are divorced at a point in time or by the **divorce rate**, which is calculated as the number of annual divorces divided by the number of existing marriages. Neither measure is ideal. The proportion of women who are divorced at a point in time depends not only on the divorce rate but also on the remarriage rate. The proportion can increase if divorced women are slower to remarry. The divorce rate is a better measure since it adjusts for the population who are married and thus at risk of a divorce and it is not influenced by remarriage. But the US government stopped collecting and analyzing divorce statistics in the mid-1990s. Current data are incomplete and exclude six states, including California.

For most of the first half of the twentieth century, divorce in the United States was extremely uncommon. The 1900 Census counted only 115,000 divorced women out of an adult female population (aged 16 and older) of more than 23 million. Divorcees thus amounted to less than 0.5 percent of adult women. Economists Betsey Stevenson and Justin Wolfers estimate that the divorce rate in the early part of the century was about 0.25 percent.[21] Through the late 1950s, both the divorce rate and the fraction divorced remained low. The divorce rate was well under 1 percent per year, usually 0.5 percent or

20 S. L. Averett, L. M. Argys, and J. Sorkin (2013), "In Sickness and In Health: An Examination of Relationship Status and Health Using Data From the Canadian National Public Health Survey," *Review of Economics of the Household*, 11 (4), 599–633. Other evidence using data from the United Kingdom finds that marriage and cohabitation are not different from each other in terms of overall health, particularly for those under age 45. See Jennifer L. Kohn and Susan L. Averett (2014), "The Effect of Relationship Status on Health with Dynamic Health and Persistent Relationships," *Journal of Health Economics*, 36, 69–83.

21 Betsey Stevenson and Justin Wolfers (2007), "Marriage and Divorce: Changes and Their Driving Forces," *Journal of Economic Perspectives*, 21 (2), 27–52.

lower. The only exception was the 1940s, especially the World War II years and just after, when the rate reached 1.8 percent. In 1950, just 2.4 percent of US women reported themselves as divorced.

But as we saw in Chapter 3, since then the proportion of women married has fallen steadily and the proportions never-married or divorced/separated have increased. Figure 4.1 shows the trend from 1960 to 2013; the figure shows the number of divorces per 1,000 marriages on the left scale and the fraction of women who are divorced on the right scale. Starting in the late 1950s and continuing through the 1960s and 1970s, the divorce rate rose, increasing almost every year from 1960 to 1979. In the process, the rate increased by a factor of 2.5 from 9 divorces per 1,000 marriages in 1958 to 23 in 1979. But since then it has slowly but steadily drifted down, a fact that many in the media seem not to have noticed. As of the mid-2010s, the divorce rate is about 17 per 1,000 marriages, more than 25 percent below its 1979 peak, but still more than 50 percent above the rate in the 1950s and early 1960s.[22] The time trend in the proportion of women who are divorced or separated has also flattened out. After jumping from 2.4 percent in 1950 to 11.8 percent in 1990, it has increased by only 2 percent in the subsequent 25 years and has been unchanged since 2005. As of the mid-2010s, about one woman in seven (13.7 percent) is currently divorced or separated.[23]

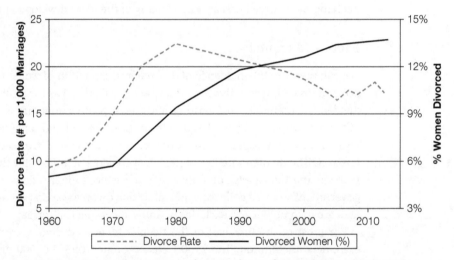

Figure 4.1 *Divorce rate and percent age of women divorced, United States, 1960–2013.*

Sources: Divorce Rate: Monthly Vital Statistics Report, Vol. 43, No. ((S), Table 1 (1960–1990) and author calculations; % divorced: Families and Living Arrangements, Table A1, 2000–2013; Current Population Reports, Series P-20: #450, Table 1 (1990); #365, Table 1 (1980); #212, Table 1 (1970); Series PC (2)-4B, Table 2 (1960).

A divorce rate of 17 divorces per 1,000 marriages is equivalent to a 1.7 percent annual divorce rate. This may sound low but because a marriage is "at risk" of a divorce year after

---

22 This figure is an estimate derived from the reported divorce information and separate information on the number of marriages. The calculation makes assumptions about the divorce and marriage rate in the states that do not report this information.

23 The number of currently divorced women depends not only on the divorce rate but also on the remarriage rate.

year, even a low annual rate cumulates to a relatively large proportion of marriages eventually ending in divorce. Using the higher divorce rates that prevailed in the mid-1980s, demographers predicted that well over half of marriages would end in divorce. That percentage has fallen as divorce rates have fallen since 1979. A 1.7 percent rate implies that about one-third of current marriages will end in divorce within 25 years. New figures show that marriages that began in the 1990s were less likely to end in divorce than those that began in the 1980s, while marriages that began in the 2000s were even less likely to end. Thus the cumulative fraction of current marriages ending in divorce may be lower than one-third and is certainly well below the often-cited 50 percent figure.

The economic analysis of divorce

In at least one respect, divorce is just marriage ... backward. Marriage occurs so commonly because there are widespread gains of marriage. Similarly, divorce will occur when there are no longer gains of marriage or, equivalently, when both parties expect to be better off single than if they remain married.

This is actually a more subtle point than it may seem. The appropriate comparison is between the total benefits of the current marriage and the total benefits of the two potentially single households. If total marital output is greater, then some reallocation of marital output from one party to the other always exists that would leave both parties better off married than single. In this case, reallocation means that one party changes his or her ways in some way, perhaps by eliminating or moderating some particularly annoying behavior, thereby improving the attractiveness of the marriage to the other party. But when the combined single outputs are greater than the marital output, no such reallocation is possible and the marriage will end. To illustrate this point, see Table 4.1.

Table 4.1. *The gains to divorce: three cases.*

	Case 1	Case 2	Case 3
Current Marital Output	M=6/F=6	M=6/F=6	M=6/F=6
Expected Single Output	M=3/F=7	M=7/F=7	M=5/F=8
Analysis	F better off single, but M is worse off. Total Marital Output (12) > Total Single Output (10)	Both are better off single: Total Marital Output (12) < Total Single Output (14)	F better off single, but M is worse off. Total Marital Output (12) < Total Single Output (13)
Expected Result	M could give 2 units of marital output to F. Both are then better off married than single. This marriage can be saved.	No reallocation of marital output can make both partners better off than if single. This marriage should and probably will end.	Any reallocation that makes F better off married than single will make M worse off married than single. This marriage should and probably will end.

The illustrative gains in the married state vs. the single state for men and women in the table are interesting because they suggest that marriage markets match individuals in such a way as to maximize the overall gains that can be achieved, rather than the gains to any particular individual. As the table shows, divorce occurs only when the total gains to the individuals are greater if they are single than if they are married.

For every divorcing couple, we know two things by applying rational choice analysis. First, at some earlier point in time, the gains of this marriage were positive—both parties expected to be better off married to each other than remaining single. We can infer this from the fact that the divorcing couple was married in the first place. Second, at some later point in time, the gains of marriage became negative, so that they are now both better off single than married to each other. The economic analysis of divorce is thus not concerned simply with the fact that the gains of marriage are negative but rather that they were once positive and then became negative. This means that *new* information or *new* developments must be a critical part of the economic analysis of divorce.

Imperfect information One major approach emphasizes the role of imperfect information and costly search. Gary Becker made that point strongly in his analysis of divorce: "Imperfect information ... is often the essence of divorce ... Participants in marriage markets hardly know their own interests and capabilities, let alone the dependability, sexual compatibility, and other traits of potential spouses. Although they date and search in other ways to improve their information, they frequently marry with highly erroneous assessments, then revise these assessments as information improves after marriage." (p. 219).[24] These words were written in 1981. Perhaps things are a bit better in the Internet age, but the general point is certainly valid. It is probably a rule of human relationships that you never fully know what life with your spouse will be like, certainly not beforehand, no matter how much in love you are.

Why, then, don't prospective marriage partners keep searching until they find the perfect partner or at least learn more about their prospective partner? The reason is the one we discussed in Chapter 3. Search is costly, both in money and, especially, in time, and if you wait for the perfect spouse, you may be too old to spend many years together. The utility-maximizing rule for optimal search involves balancing the marginal costs and marginal benefits of continued search and stops well short of complete information. And even with extensive search, the future is still ultimately unknowable.

The information that becomes known after marriage can, of course, be either positive or negative. A simple way to capture this idea is to think of the gains to a particular marriage as following a normal distribution with its peak at the most likely level of gains and its tails representing outcomes that are much better than or much worse than the expected gains. A result on the positive tail of the distribution is a source of great unexpected pleasure—the marriage turned out better than expected. But what would happen if the gains were less than originally expected?

The final ingredient in this analysis comes directly from our earlier analysis of the gains of marriage. We have firmly established that the gains of marriage that derive from specialization have become smaller as men and women have become more alike in terms of market wages and household productivity. Figure 4.2 puts these two ideas together. In both panels, the bell-shaped normal curve represents the distribution of gains of marriage. The two curves are identically shaped, except that the one in Figure 4.2(A) is positioned

---

24   Gary S. Becker (1981), *A Treatise on the Family*, Cambridge, MA: Harvard University Press.

further to the right. This means that the peak in Figure 4.2(A) represents greater gains of marriage and, crucially, also that more of the possible outcomes are positive.

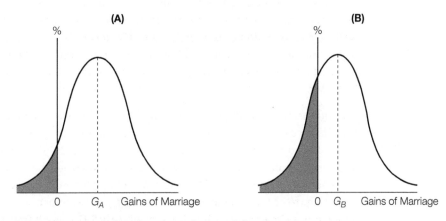

Figure 4.2 *Uncertainty, the gains of marriage, and divorce.*

The expected gains for Figures 4.2(A) and 4.2(B) are G_A and G_B, respectively, where $G_A > G_B$.[25] Roughly speaking, Figure 4.2(A) represents a common situation in the past when the material gains of marriage were substantial, while Figure 4.2(B) represents a common contemporary situation where the material gains are smaller. In Figure 4.2(A) there is substantial room for worse-than-expected outcomes without divorce, which would occur only when the gains were negative (the shaded region to the left of 0). All the area under the curve between 0 and G_A are worse-than-expected outcomes in which the marriage is still better than the alternatives. In Figure 4.2(B), the wiggle room is less: A larger proportion of potential outcomes may lead to divorce. Thus the smaller gains of marriage make the marriage more vulnerable to outcomes less favorable than expected.

Undoubtedly, marriages have always been subject to negative shocks and changing emotional commitments as time passes and new information is acquired. But in the past the gains of marriage were often so large that the marriage could withstand these changes and remain intact. Because the gains are now often smaller in the first place, marriages are more susceptible to these shocks. There is less of a reservoir of material gains to sustain a marriage through changing emotional commitments. As a result, marriages have probably become more fragile, less able to withstand bad times.

One interesting piece of information about the correlates of divorce is quite consistent with these interpretations. Many studies have shown that the probability of divorce is higher when the bride and groom marry at a younger age. Why? People who marry early are typically more uncertain about themselves and their prospective spouses; consequently, they have greater uncertainty about the probable gains of marriage. In terms of our analysis, imagine that the curves in Figure 4.2 had a lower peak and fatter tails, so that there were fewer potential outcomes near the peak and more outcomes further away

---

25 The expected gains are the average of all the possible outcomes. Because the normal distribution is symmetric, the expected gain is the middle of the distribution.

from it. Then it follows that a larger proportion of realized outcomes would be negative and thus lead to divorce.

The rising age at first marriage and the rise in cohabitation are both interesting developments in this respect. The additional search time these changes have allowed may well have resulted in better matches and a lower divorce rate. As pressures to marry fall (e.g., shotgun weddings are a thing of the past as non-marital births are more socially acceptable), people can be more selective about their partners and hence matches may be better.

No-fault divorce During the time that divorce rates were rising, many states liberalized their divorce laws to make divorce easier and less stigmatizing. Starting in the 1970s, many states moved to a no-fault divorce system in which a divorce could be obtained without ascribing a fault, such as adultery to a partner. Instead, the couple could claim to have "irreconcilable differences." Many states also adopted unilateral divorce laws that allowed a marriage to be terminated without the explicit consent of both partners. Although states adopted these laws at differing times, as of early 2015, all 50 states now permit some version of unilateral, no-fault divorce.

These sweeping changes in divorce law, often termed the "divorce revolution," made it easier for partners to dissolve their marriages. Importantly, they also changed the bargaining rights of each spouse. Prior to the change, the partner who wanted to keep the marriage intact (the one who had the most to gain) had the power, since his/her partner would have to convince him/her to agree to a divorce. With the advent of these laws, the balance of power shifted to the spouse who wanted to exit the marriage.

How might this change in divorce laws, which made divorce easier to obtain, be related to the rising divorce rates? Casual observation suggests that these laws actually *caused* the increase in divorce rates during this time period by making divorce easier. Not surprisingly, some religious groups and policymakers criticized the laws for making divorce too easy and undermining the family.

The question that economists have asked is why and how these changes in the law might cause an increase in the divorce rate. If a couple wishes to divorce, does it matter whether fault is ascribed or whether consent is required? The answer is "no" according to Gary Becker and colleagues, who noted that as long as the transaction costs are relatively low, divorce rates should be the same regardless of the change in bargaining power from the individual who wanted to keep the marriage intact to the individual who wanted to dissolve it. This is an application of the **Coase Theorem**,[26] a very famous idea in economics which states that if transaction costs are relatively small, then a change in property rights does not change resource allocation, although it does influence wealth.

If we apply the Coase Theorem to divorce, the transaction costs are the costs (e.g., legal fees) that are incurred when obtaining the divorce, while property rights refer to which person in the couple gets to decide whether he or she wants to divorce. Prior to the passage of unilateral divorce laws, the spouse with the property rights was the one who didn't

---

26 The Coase Theorem is named for Nobel-Prize–winning economist Ronald Coase, who applied this reasoning to the analysis of externalities in his famous paper "The Problem of Social Cost," *The Journal of Law and Economics*, 1960, Vol. III, pp. 1–44.

want a divorce. This spouse could often negotiate a large settlement at divorce—usually a payment from the spouse who did want the divorce. In the 1970s it was usually assumed that the husband wanted a divorce and the wife would consent only if she received a large settlement (i.e., alimony). Thus the divorce settlement is the "wealth" referred to in the Coase Theorem.

The advent of unilateral divorce changed the property rights in favor of the spouse who wanted a divorce. The spouse who did not want one would have to try to convince the other spouse to stay or more often consent to the divorce. According to the Coase Theorem, unilateral divorce would lead to lower alimony payments and lower child support, but not to a change in the actual number of divorces as long as the transaction costs were low.

We can use the information in Table 4.1 to illustrate this point. In case 2 of the table, the couple are better off if they divorce since their combined output as single individuals exceeds their combined marital output. Would this be any different if we evaluated this marriage before the advent of more liberal divorce laws or after? In this case the answer is "no," since both are better off single than married. In case 3 of the same table, F is better off single but M is better off married. In a world with no-fault/unilateral divorce, F will simply divorce M. However, even before the advent of no-fault, unilateral divorce, this marriage would end as well. Why? In this case, M will want to stay married, but F wants a divorce. To get M to agree to a divorce, F can transfer some of her post-marriage wealth to M. How much will it take to get M to agree to a divorce? Economics tells us that M will agree to the divorce if he is at least as well-off divorced as he is married, so F simply has to transfer 1 unit to M after divorce to get him to agree. Thus the law is again irrelevant in determining if the marriage ends, as long as the costs of negotiating the divorce are low.

Note, though, that although the marriage ends in both cases, F is better off in the unilateral divorce regime because she can simply divorce M, whereas if mutual consent prevails, she must transfer some of her post-divorce wealth to M to get him to agree to the divorce. Hence, although the marriage ends in both cases, the distribution of benefits post-divorce does depend on the legal regime that prevails.

Economist H. Elizabeth Peters provided the first empirical test of the applicability of the Coase Theorem to divorce.[27] Peters' analysis was based on a natural experiment, although it actually preceded the introduction of this idea in economics research. Some states adopted no-fault divorce before others. California was the first—its law was effective January 1, 1970. Other states followed at different times during the 1970s and early 1980s. As long as each state adopted the reform for reasons other than the divorce rate in its state, this is a natural experiment in which for no particular reason some states had no-fault laws in some years and other states did not. Her analysis focused on 28 states that adopted unilateral divorce during this time period. Did the change in the law change divorce rates or settlements? Peters found support for the predictions of the Coase Theorem. The divorce law reform did not increase the divorce rate in those states. However, divorce settlements were lower for women in unilateral no-fault states. Peters' work generated a great deal of interest because its findings were clearly not in line with

---

27   H. Elizabeth Peters (1986), "Marriage and Divorce: Informational Constraints and Private Contracting," *American Economic Review*, 82 (3), 686–693.

the beliefs of the general public, many of whom blamed the new laws for the run-up in divorce rates.

Peters' work has been reexamined by other economists, including Leora Friedberg and, most recently, Justin Wolfers.[28] Replication is an important part of social science research. Friedberg found a similar no-effect result in a model like Peters', but, when she modified the model to allow for social and demographic trends within each state, she found a strong effect on the order of a 10 percent increase. This is best understood as an average effect across all the subsequent years. Wolfers focused his attention on the dynamics of the response of divorce rates to the legal reforms. He concluded that the divorce rate rose sharply in the first two years following reform, presumably a consequence of pent-up demand— divorces that would otherwise have occurred earlier but could not. But after that, the divorce rate declined back to its original level. He concluded, like Peters, that the change in the law had no long-run effect and argued that Friedberg's findings reflect only the initial spike in rates and not the subsequent decline.

Economists have also pointed out that the ability of one partner to get a divorce over the objections of the other may create an atmosphere in which people think twice before making marriage-specific investments or other sacrifices that will be costly if the marriage ends. One economist found that in states that allow unilateral divorce, individuals tend to be less likely to invest in marriage-related capital, such as putting the partner through school or having children, and more likely to focus on building individual, portable capital, such as pursuing their own education or job experience.[29]

Finally, it has been argued that now that it is easier for either party to dissolve the marriage, couples who choose to marry are now better matched and hence have greater gains of marriage. If this is the case, we should see a decline in the propensity to divorce following the liberalization of divorce laws.[30]

Employment of married women Another possible explanation for divorce is the improved labor-market opportunities available to women. Rising wages and improved labor-market opportunities for women have made being single a more attractive alternative than it once was. In times past, when these opportunities were far less attractive, women undoubtedly resigned themselves to unhappy marriages because their alternatives were even bleaker.

Economist Terra McKinnish has suggested another way in which the rising employment of married women might affect divorce.[31] As already discussed, imperfect information is an inevitable part of the marriage contract. As time passes, each spouse likely learns more about their partner—sometimes good things, sometimes not. But "new spouse search" while married is a very delicate proposition, if not impossible.

That's where women's work fits in. The labor-force participation rate of married women has increased steadily, something we will talk about in detail in Chapter 7 and, at the same

28 Leora Friedberg (1998), "Did Unilateral Divorce Raise Divorce Rates? Evidence from Panel Data," *American Economic Review*, 88 (3), 608–627. Justin Wolfers (December, 2006), "Did Unilateral Divorce Raise Divorce Rates? A Reconciliation and New Results," *American Economic Review*, 96 (5), 1802–1820.

29 Betsey Stevenson (2007), "The Impact of Divorce Laws on Marriage-Specific Capital," *Journal of Labor Economics*, 25 (1), 75–94.

30 I. Rasul (2006), "Marriage Markets and Divorce Law," *Journal of Law, Economics, and Organization*, 22 (1), 30–69.

31 Terra McKinnish (2007), "Sexually Integrated Workplaces and Divorce: Another Form of On-the-Job Search," *Journal of Human Resources*, 42 (2), 331–349.

time, occupational segregation by sex has declined. As a result, more workers, both men and women, are exposed to contact with the opposite sex on the job. In economic terms, this reduces the cost of partner search. McKinnish noted that workplace contact could increase divorce in several ways. First, an individual could find a more desired mate and dissolve a current marriage in order to remarry that person. Second, office extra-marital affairs might lead to a divorce without an immediate remarriage. And third, even non-amorous exposure to the opposite sex might change an individual's perceptions of his or her own marriage.

McKinnish examined this by linking information from the 1990 Census on an individual's marital status and the proportion of women in his or her occupation and industry. Other independent variables used as controls include characteristics of the individual's occupation and industry (wages, etc.) and personal characteristics such as age, race, education, and urban residence. Because occupations and industries differ in terms of the sex composition of employment, some persons would be more exposed to interactions with the opposite sex than others.

McKinnish found that the sex composition of the workplace was linked to the probability of divorce. In one of her analyses that provides additional control for unmeasured factors (remember this is not a random assignment—people typically choose where they work and sex composition could be one reason), she found that increasing the proportion of men from the level of the 25th percentile to the 75th percentile would increase the probability of divorce by 1.4 percentage points. This is a 7.2 percent increase. For men, the effect is similar, increasing divorce by 7.9 percent. Interestingly, similar results have also been found for workplace sex composition and divorce in Sweden.[32]

Gender preference Does the gender of children affect the likelihood of divorce? See Box 4.1 for some surprising evidence that perhaps it does.

Box	4.1

Gender Preference and the Likelihood of Divorce

Several years ago, two economists, Gordon Dahl and Enrico Moretti, discovered a puzzling finding in US Census data. First-born daughters were consistently less likely to be living with their fathers than first-born sons. Using data from the 1960 through 2000 Censuses, they found that marriages were more likely to end in divorce if the first-born child was a daughter rather than a son. The effects were not very large, but they were statistically significant. In 1960 and 1970, the effect was about 2 percent; in 1980 and 1990, it was about 1.25 percent; and in 2000, it had fallen to 0.5 percent. In addition, single mothers were less likely to marry if the first born was a daughter and more likely to retain custody. The marriage effect was about 1.0–2.5 percent, and the custody effect ranged from 2.5 to 3.9 percent, depending on the Census year. The net effect was that first-born daughters were about 3.5–4.0 percent more likely to have a nonresident father.

---

32 Michael Svarer (2007), "Working Late: Do Workplace Sex Ratios Affect Partnership Formation and Dissolution?" *Journal of Human Resources*, 42 (3), 583–595.

Dahl and Moretti offered three possible explanations for this gender effect. First, it is possible that fathers prefer sons. Second, both parents might recognize the beneficial effect of a father in the household when a boy is present. In that case, both parents might be more willing to marry or especially more willing to remain in a marriage when boys are involved. Custody assignment might also differ, with mothers more likely to have custody of daughters than sons. Finally, they also offer what they call a "differential cost" hypothesis: Perhaps daughters are more costly than sons, so again men are less likely to marry, more likely to divorce, and less likely to seek custody. All explanations are consistent with the basic facts. But using data on the subsequent fertility decisions of parents of daughters and sons, they favored the preferences explanation.

Except for custody, these effects have gotten smaller over time. S. Phillip Morgan, a well-known social demographer, speculated that this might reflect the blurring of sex stereotypes. Girls now play organized sports nearly as much as boys, for example. So perhaps the gender preference has become weaker.

Dahl and Moretti also have some fascinating and provocative things to say about gender preference in the context of fertility. More on that in Chapter 6.

P.S. Dahl has three daughters. No information is available on Moretti's family.

Source: Gordon Dahl and Enrico Moretti (2008), "The Demand for Sons," *Review of Economic Studies*, 75 (4), 1085–1120 and David Leonhardt, "It's a Girl (Will the Economy Suffer?)," *The New York Times*, October 26, 2003.

Race and family structure: an economic analysis

Since the 1970s, large differences in family structure have developed between the white and black populations in the United States. The analysis of race and family structure is very complex and highly controversial. We first present the facts and then examine possible economic causes, using the framework of the marriage models we developed in Chapter 3.

Facts and trends

Table 4.2 summarizes key differences in marriage and family structure for white and black US women and children. Beginning with the 2000 Census, individuals were asked to report the race or races they considered themselves to be; previously, individuals could be of only one race.[33] Information on race is now usually presented in two different ways— persons of a single race alone or persons who are of a race "alone or in combination" (AOIC). The figures shown in the table are for whites and blacks AOIC.

---

33 The US Census Bureau classifies individuals into five racial groups—white; black or African American; American Indian and Alaska Native; Asian; and Native Hawaiian and Other Pacific Islander. "Hispanic" is an ethnicity, not a race, and refers to persons of Spanish, Hispanic, or Latino ancestry; Hispanics can be of any race.

Among white women aged 15 and older in 2014, about half (50.5 percent) were married, spouse present, and just over one-quarter (26.0 percent) were never married. The corresponding figures for black women are almost exactly the opposite—26.5 percent are married and 46.8 percent are never married. This does not appear to be just a matter of differences in the timing of marriage. As seen in the second section of the table, a very substantial proportion of black women—more than 35 percent—were still never married in their early forties, compared to about 12 percent for white women. Two-thirds of white women were married with spouse present at age 40–44 compared to about 39 percent of black women.

These differences in marriage by race mean that family structure and especially the family living arrangements of children will differ as well. The third and fourth sections of the table show this. Among white families with children under age 18, 72.5 percent are two-parent families and 20.5 percent are headed by single women. So, among whites, two-parent families with children outnumber mother-only families with children by about 3.5 to one. Among black families, however, two-parent families are a minority: 40 percent of black families with children are two-parent families, while more than half (51.3 percent) are headed by single women. This means that white and black children are raised in family environments that are quite different, as the fourth section shows. Nearly three-quarters of white children under age 18 are living in two-parent families, while just 41 percent of black children are. Nearly half of black children are in mother-only families.

Table 4.2 *Race differences in marital, family, and economic status, United States women and families, 2014.*

	White	Black
Women, Aged 15+		
Married, Spouse Present	50.5%	26.5%
Never Married	26.0%	46.8%
Women, Aged 40–44		
Married, Spouse Present	66.6%	39.3%
Never Married	11.8%	35.3%
Families with Children ≤ Aged 18		
% Two-Parent	72.5%	40.0%
% Female Householder	20.5%	51.3%
Children		
% Residing with Two Parents	73.5%	41.3%
% Residing with Mother Only	19.2%	48.6%
Median Income, Families with Children ≤ Aged 18**		
Two-Parent Family	$85,783	$73,034
Female-Headed Family	$27,300	$22,575
Poverty Rate, Children, ≤ Aged 18**		
In Two-Parent Family	8.8%	16.3%
In Female-Headed Family	42.1%	53.3%

Note: white and black are AOIC and include persons of more than one race ** = 2013 figures.

Sources: US Census Bureau, *Annual Social and Economic Supplement*, 2013 and 2014 Tables A1, F1, C9, FINC-03 and POV-03.

The main reason to care about these differences in family structure is their impact on the economic resources available to children. The last two rows of Table 4.2 show how family income and poverty rates differ by family structure and race. Family income is more than three times as high in married-couple families as in mother-only families for both white and black families, while the poverty rate is three and a half to four times as high in mother-only families. More than 40 percent of white children and more than half of all black children living in mother-only families are officially poor.

These race differences in family structure developed primarily between 1970 and 1990. In 1950 the difference in marriage proportions by race was relatively small—about 4 percent—and the rates trended downward more or less together through about 1970. During the 1970s, however, the trends diverged sharply. The proportion married dropped a full 10 percent for black women, falling below 50 percent by mid-decade, while for white women the proportion married dipped by just two percent. The trends continued to diverge in the 1980s, although at a slower pace. By 1990 a 20 percent difference developed; since then, the trends have been more similar, leading to the current 24 percent difference. The bottom line, then, is that the proportion married fell for all women, but it fell especially sharply for black women, particularly between 1970 and 1990. Cumulatively, since 1950, the proportion married fell by 16 percent for white women and 36 percent for black women.

The fraction married can fall because of lower rates of marriage (or remarriage) and/or higher rates of divorce. In this case the difference is almost entirely due to lower marriage rates. Over this time period the fraction of women who are currently divorced increased by 10 percent for black women and by about 9 percent for white women. So while the increase in divorce is an important part of the decline in the proportion married for both groups of women, it is not an important source of the increasing *difference* between white and black women in the proportion married. The far more important source is the increase in the proportion of women who are never married. For black women this proportion has increased by more than 25 percent since 1950, while for white women the increase is just over 5 percent.

Economic explanations

Let's begin by thinking like economists about the underlying message of the sharp decline in marriage among black women. Just as in the supply-and-demand model, we assume that men and women choose to marry only when they both expect to be better off married than single—that is, when $U_{MF} > U_{SF}$ and $U_{MM} > U_{SM}$, where U is utility, the first subscript indicates marital status (M or S) and the second indicates gender (F or M).[34] Thus it follows as a matter of economic logic from the lower marriage rates that fewer black men and women today find that those necessary arithmetic conditions hold. That, in turn, tells us that the gains of marriage must have fallen enough for some women and men that marriage is no longer the preferred alternative. There is no other way to reconcile the falling marriage rates with rational choice behavior. As simple as this logic is, it is useful in

---

34 We are using U for utility here rather than Z for output, as in the supply-and-demand model. Using utility is a bit broader, but in general utility will depend on the amount of output Z that is available.

focusing our attention on forces that could have either reduced the gains of marriage or improved the quality of single life.

Within this framework there are three broad economic explanations for the differences by race in family structure. One emphasizes changes in marriage markets, which may have lowered U_{MF} for some women. A second explanation emphasizes the role of the US welfare system, which may have increased U_{SF}. The third emphasizes women's rising wage rates, which have affected both U_{MF} and U_{SF}. The explanations are not mutually exclusive. They may all have occurred; one may have affected some women while another affected a different group of women.

Marriage markets A long line of research has emphasized the deteriorating marriage market prospects of many black women and its impact on marriage decisions. The early research emphasized particularly the declining employment rates of black men, while more recent contributions have focused on high mortality and incarceration rates.

In the late 1980s, the sociologist William Julius Wilson noted that the decline of blue-collar industries such as automobiles, steel, and tires affected black men particularly sharply because they had been heavily employed in those industries at decent wages.[35] Wilson hypothesized that the deteriorating labor-market situation of black men made many of them essentially unacceptable as marriage partners. When men are unable to support a family, he argued, women are unwilling to take them on as husbands. To measure this concept, he computed what he called the **Male Marriageable Pool Index (MMPI)**. The MMPI is the number of employed men per 100 women, computed separately by race and age bracket. In constructing the measure in this way, Wilson assumed, in effect, that women married within their own age bracket and race. Even though there are certainly exceptions, it is probably a reasonable assumption.[36]

The emphasis on the financial gains of marriage may seem old-fashioned and even sexist: It suggests that women (but not men) are seeking financial support in marriage. That criticism absolutely has some merit. Still, a long tradition in sociology, dating back to the Great Depression, documents the impact that unemployment of the "breadwinner" has on marriage and family life.

Wilson showed that MMPIs were, in fact, quite low for black women and that they had fallen in the critical decade of the 1970s when the race gap in marriage developed. In 1970 the MMPI for women aged 25–34 was 88 for whites and 73 for blacks. By 1980 the MMPI had fallen 10 points for blacks but was unchanged for whites. For more recent years the MMPI is easily computed from data on population size and male employment. In 2000, after a long period of substantial economic growth, the MMPI for 25–34-year-olds was 90 for whites but still only 66 for blacks. In 2013, five years after the Great Recession, the MMPIs had fallen to 85 and 59, respectively. Thus, in the years since 1970, the MMPI has been consistently lower for blacks than whites—about 25 points—and low enough that it might plausibly affect marriage rates.

Even without adjustment for employment, there is a basic sex ratio imbalance in the black population. In 2013 there were 83 black men, ages 25–34, in the civilian non-institutional population for every 100 black women of that age. In the white population the

---

35 William Julius Wilson (1987), *The Truly Disadvantaged*, Chicago, IL: University of Chicago Press.

36 In 2013, interracial marriage between whites and blacks accounted for about 1 percent of all marriages.

ratio was 101. The sex ratio difference by race reflects the differential impact of mortality and incarceration. See more on this below.

In terms of our marriage models, these men without employment can offer only household production to a prospective spouse or, perhaps, very modest and uncertain earnings. As a result, the joint PPC of a potential marriage shifts in sharply and the gains of marriage decrease, especially for the women, whose labor-market opportunities did not decline in the same way. In terms of our supply-and-demand model, this is roughly equivalent to a decline in demand, similar in many ways to a sex ratio imbalance problem. As we saw in that analysis, such an imbalance reduces the number of women married and also reduces their share of marital output. In the new marriage market equilibrium, both N^* (the number of men and women marrying) and S_F^* (the share of marital output going to women) will decrease. This means that marriage is now a better deal for men but a worse one for women: because they are in excess supply, they end up having to accept worse terms.

Wilson compared the trends in the MMPI and in marriage rates by race and age separately by region of the country between 1960 and 1980. This is a relatively crude analysis; the geographic scale is too large to approximate a marriage market and there is no control for other factors that could affect marriage rates. Still, the results are interesting and suggestive. The decline in the MMPI was much greater for blacks than whites in every region, and it was particularly large in the Northeast and North Central regions, where job losses in blue-collar employment were especially large. He found that the bigger the decline in the MMPI, the greater was the decline in marriage. Marriage rates fell by more than 20 percent in the Northeast and North Central regions, where the MMPI fell by more, and by less than 7 percent in the South and West, where it fell by less. But there is also clear evidence that something else beside the MMPI is affecting marriage because the decline in the proportion married is more than twice the decline in the MMPI.

In a well-known review article, Ellwood and Crane[37] pointed out that marriage rates fell not only for black men who are not employed (as Wilson's hypothesis suggested) but also for black men who were employed—a finding consistent with the observation that marriage proportions fell by much more than the MMPI. Indeed, between 1960 and 1990, the marriage rate for employed black men fell from over 70 percent to less than 50 percent. Ellwood and Crane argued that employed men should be in greater demand than before, and thus their marriage rate should have increased. Finally, detailed empirical work that examines differences in MMPIs and marriage rates across geographical areas (i.e., local marriage markets) rather than over time has not always supported the relationship between the MMPI and marriage. For example, urban areas with higher MMPIs did not consistently have a higher proportion of married women than areas with lower MMPIs.

In more recent research, Charles and Luoh examined a related idea—the impact of male incarceration on marriage markets.[38] This is an extreme version of the Wilson hypothesis of unmarriageable men. While the analysis is, in principle, race neutral, the male incarceration rate is nine times as high for black men as for white men, and approximately

---

37 David Ellwood and Jonathan Crane (1990), "Family Change Among Blacks: What Do We Know?" *Journal of Economic Perspectives,* 4 (4), 65–84.

38 Kerwin Kofi Charles and Ming Ching Luoh (2010), "Male Incarceration, The Marriage Market, and Female Outcomes," *The Review of Economics and Statistics,* 92 (3), 614–627.

10–12 percent of young black males are incarcerated. Not surprisingly, incarceration rates are not gender-neutral: approximately 10 times as many men are incarcerated as women. Thus the impact on the marriage market could be substantial.

Charles and Luoh focused on the time period between 1970 and 2000, which is when the race difference in marriage rates developed. The big increase in incarceration rates at the national level, however, was between 1990 and 2000, which was after the sharp decline in marriage rates. They compared the marriage rate in a particular marriage market defined by age, race, and state of residence to the corresponding male incarceration rate. They focused on two groups of young adults—women aged 18–25 and 26–33 and men two years older. Their goal was to estimate the quantitative impact of changes in incarceration rates on marriage within these marriage markets. This is a complicated task and requires the use of some sophisticated statistical techniques that go beyond those appropriate for discussion in this textbook.

Using these techniques, they found consistent evidence that incarceration rates for men in a marriage market did affect marriage outcomes for women. A one standard deviation increase in the male incarceration rate in a marriage market was associated with a 5 percent reduction in the marriage rate. This effect was larger for women without a college degree than women with a college degree, which likely reflects the higher incarceration rate for less-educated men, who are their likely marriage partners. They also found evidence that a higher male incarceration rate increased the probability that a woman has more education than her husband. This is another example of "marrying down" when sex ratios are out of balance.

They used these results to estimate the impact of changes in incarceration rates between 1980 and 2000 on marriage rates separately by race. The incarceration rate for black men aged 20–35 increased by 7.4 percent over this time period, while the marriage rate for black women aged 18–33 fell by 17 percent. Certainly, other factor besides the change in the incarceration rate played a role. Depending on the particulars of their analysis, they found that between 13 percent and 27 percent of the decrease in marriage over this time period was attributable to the increase in incarceration.

The welfare system A second argument focuses on the incentives provided by the US welfare system. The main cash assistance program for poor families in the United States is **TANF**, which stands for Temporary Assistance for Needy Families and is pronounced "TAN-EFF." TANF was created in 1996, replacing a program called **AFDC** (for Aid to Families with Dependent Children), which had been in place since the 1930s. The two programs are similar in structure, except TANF imposes strict time limits on lifetime receipt of benefits as well as other requirements that states may choose to impose. We focus our discussion here on AFDC because it was the largest and most important welfare program for poor families during most of the time period when the large changes in marriage occurred. The analysis applies equally to TANF.

The most important feature of AFDC for this analysis is that benefits were largely restricted to poor, mother-only families with children. Married couples, with or without children, and single persons without children, were either ineligible for benefits or eligible for sharply reduced benefits, no matter how poor they were. Father-only families with children were technically eligible for benefits, but they have never accounted for more than a tiny fraction of the welfare caseload. This peculiar feature of the US welfare system primarily reflected the demographic and social context of the time (the 1930s) when the welfare system was established: Men and women were expected to marry and remain married, married men were breadwinners, and married women were homemakers. At that time, mother-only families with children were almost exclusively widows or women who had been abandoned by their husbands during the Depression. They were deemed deserving of support while they raised their children and prior to their expected remarriage. Once they remarried, however, the financial support of the government was to be replaced by the support provided by their husbands.[39]

Because benefits under AFDC were typically quite modest, marriage and/or work were almost always better options than welfare for women with reasonable labor-market skills and/or decent marriage prospects. But for women with poor labor-market and marriage-market prospects, being a single mother and receiving welfare benefits might be a better option. For these women, the welfare system increases U_{SF}, their well-being if single, and thus shifts their marriage supply curve up, reducing their incentive to marry. In addition, the welfare system could increase incentives for married couples to split up, and reduce incentives for women to remarry, again by increasing U_{SF}.[40] Particularly in light of Wilson's hypothesis about the declining marriage opportunities of less-educated black women, this effect might plausibly be greater for black women than white women.

It is easy to construct specific examples of situations in which a woman is financially better off receiving welfare than supporting herself or marrying, but the empirical evidence that this effect was quantitatively important has proved to be quite elusive. Economists have examined this in two ways. First, they looked at the time-series relationship between welfare benefits and marriage rates. Did marriage rates decline as welfare benefits increased over time? Second, they took advantage of a peculiar feature of the US welfare system to examine the cross-sectional relationship between welfare benefits in a state and its corresponding marriage rate. Under AFDC and TANF, each state was allowed to set the cash benefits it provided and benefits have always varied widely. A number of mostly Southern states provided very low benefits—less than $200 per month for a woman with one child—while some Northern and Midwestern states provided more than $500 a month. Some of that reflects cost-of-living differences between the North and the South, but most of it is a genuine difference in support. The differences in benefits provided a kind of natural experiment to test whether marriage rates were lower in states with higher benefits. If welfare benefits were an important influence, marriage rates ought to be lower in states with higher benefits.

It turns out that neither kind of analysis provided much support for the AFDC-marriage hypothesis. Since the proportion of women married fell, especially in the 1970s, we would expect to find that AFDC benefits increased over that same time period, thereby becoming attractive to increasingly more women. In fact, just the opposite happened. AFDC benefits did increase in the 1960s, but after adjusting for inflation they fell throughout

---

39 The notion of families "on the dole" has always been an uncomfortable one in the United States. President Franklin Roosevelt, who helped establish Social Security and the welfare system and who was a champion of the underprivileged, famously called welfare "a narcotic, a subtle destroyer of the human spirit."

40 A well-known version of this argument is Charles Murray (1984), *Losing Ground*, New York: Basic Books.

most of rest of this period. Even adding in the value of food stamps and Medicaid, total benefits fell by about 20 percent. So the two time series go in opposite directions rather than together.

Similarly, differences in marriage rates across states were not strongly related to the difference in the level of welfare benefits. Most studies found effects that were positive, but never quantitatively meaningful. The bottom line here is that the impact of the welfare system on the race difference in marriage was substantially less than one might guess, although it was probably not zero. Robert Moffitt, an expert on this research, put it this way in his summary of the literature on the impact of the welfare system on family structure that time period: "The effects are still generally small in magnitude. In particular ... none of the studies finds effects sufficiently large to explain, for example, the increase in female headship in the late 1960s and early 1970s (p.31)."[41]

Women's wage rates An increase in women's wage rates could affect marriage in two distinct ways. First, the more alike are spouses in terms of their wages and household productivity, the smaller are the traditional productivity and specialization gains of marriage. Remember that the gains occur precisely because each person gains access to a partner whose skills are different from his or her own. Second, as we saw in the supply-and-demand analysis, higher wages for women make being single a more attractive alternative. Higher wages shift the supply curve up, reducing the proportion of women who are married.

Both factors are almost certainly part of the explanation for the declining marriage rate of black women. We discuss wages and work in more detail in later chapters, but we can briefly summarize the relevant facts here. First, the gender earnings gap has historically been smaller for black women. For example, during the 1960s and 1970s, the gender gap was about 40 percent for white women and 25–30 percent for black women.[42] When the gender gap fell in the 1980s, the earnings ratio for black women stayed about 10 to 15 percent above the earnings ratio for white women. As of the mid-2010s, black women who worked year-round full-time (YRFT) earned 88 percent of their male counterparts, compared to 77 percent for white women. Thus the gains of marriage that arise out of the differences between the partners and the specialization of labor are likely to be smaller in general for black men and women than for white men and women.

Second, wages have risen for both white and black women. Between 1967 and the mid-2010s, the median earnings of black women who were YRFT workers increased by more than 75 percent, even after adjusting for the impact of inflation. For white women, the corresponding increase was smaller, about 50 percent. Again, the larger earnings increase for black women suggests that this may have affected the marriage decision of black women more than white women. Higher wages and stronger labor-force attachment also operate by increasing age at first marriage. This effect probably operates most strongly for better-educated women, some of whom delay marriage while they are establishing a career. This decision could help explain why marriage rates have fallen among better-educated black men, a fact that cannot be well explained by Wilson's model.

---

41   Robert A. Moffitt (1992), "Incentive Effects of the US Welfare System: A Review," *Journal of Economic Literature*, 30 (1), 1–61.

42   These figures are for YRFT workers who are employed 35 or more hours per week for at least 50 weeks per year. They are the group usually used in gender earnings comparisons.

Better-educated black men are the likely marriage partners of better-educated black women, and thus the men may find themselves having a more difficult time finding willing and acceptable marriage partners.

Summary If we put all these explanations together, what do we have? Marriage is a very complex phenomenon, and more than one hypothesis could be correct, perhaps for a specific portion of the population. It would be surprising if a single, simple hypothesis were the sole cause of an enormous change such as the decline in marriage. Women and men are too different from one another in their opportunities and preferences for a single explanation to hold for all of them.

More than likely all the factors discussed above have some power in explaining the downward trend in marriage and the growing difference by race. Wilson's emphasis on the marriage market makes an important connection between the labor-market status of men and the formation of two-parent families. The decline in the labor-market outcomes of black men over this time period is genuine and undeniable, and the link to marriage and family formation seems quite plausible. The timing of the downward trend in the MMPI and the downward trend in marriage do correspond roughly. If welfare benefits affected marriage, it could only be among the least well educated—for example, high-school drop-outs. While the evidence is very mixed, the presence of welfare has had an effect, but not a quantitatively large one. The smaller gender wage gap for black women relative to black men may be an added subtle factor contributing to the larger decline among black women. It is easy to see how these factors could have a particularly large effect on less-educated women, whose marriage-market opportunities have declined the most and for whom welfare could be attractive relative to their own labor-market opportunities.

Education and marriage: inequality in the twenty-first century

Throughout most of US history, differentials in socioeconomic status were often drawn most starkly along racial lines. However, in the past several decades, marriage has become a major contributor to inequality in two distinct ways. First, socioeconomic differences are now most pronounced between the married and the unmarried. Second, within marriage, changes in who marries whom have exacerbated the growing income divide between better-educated and less-educated individuals.

Poverty and family income now correlate more strongly with marital status than with race. That can be seen clearly in Table 4.2, which presents information on race differences in marriage and economic status. The poverty rate for a child in a black two-parent family is almost twice as high as for a child in a white two-parent family (16.3 percent vs. 8.8 percent), but it is almost five times as high for a child in a white single-parent family compared with a white two-parent family (41.1 percent vs. 8.8 percent). The same pattern holds for family income: marital status has a far bigger effect than race.

While we have seen that, in general, marriage rates have declined over time, the decline has been very different for women with different levels of education. In 1970, among women aged 25–64, those with less than a high-school degree and those with a college degree were about equally likely to be married. But by the mid-2010s, this pattern had changed. Between 1970 and 2014, the proportion married fell about twice as fast for less-educated women than better-educated women. At the same time the fraction never married increased three times as much for the less-educated women than for their college-educated counterparts (18.7 percent vs. 6.3 percent). In 2014 the difference in the proportion married between these two groups of women was 13 percent (64 percent vs. 51 percent).

Table 4.3 provides additional detail on how marital status varies by education for younger women. This information comes from the NSFG, the same survey that provided information about cohabitation. The sample for the table is women aged 22–44 over the time period from 2006 to 2010. The table shows the sharp divide in marital status between women who are college graduates and all other women. For women who are not college graduates, less than half are married, and for those with less than a high-school degree, the fraction is under 45 percent. In contrast, for college graduates and those with more education, more than 60 percent are married; this is true even though additional education tends to postpone the age at first marriage. Women with less education are more likely than other women to be cohabiting, a relationship we discussed earlier. The difference by education is substantial: among women aged 22–44, those with no college education are three to four times as likely to be cohabiting as college graduates. Divorce also varies with education; women with no college education are about twice as likely to be divorced as women who are college graduates.

Table 4.3 *How marital status varies by education, US women, aged 22–44, 2006–2010.*

Education	Married	Cohabitating	Divorced
Not a HS Graduate	44.3	20.2	16.5
HS Graduate or equivalent	48.7	15.5	15.6
Some College Education	49.5	11.6	12.6
College Graduate	61.6	6.8	6.1
Master's Degree or Higher	67.4	5.5	7.0

Source: Casey E. Copen, Kimberly Daniels, Jonathan Vespa, and William D. Mosher (2012), "First Marriages in the United States: Data from the 2006–2010 National Survey of Family Growth," National Health Statistics Reports No 49, Table 1. Hyattsville, MD: National Center for Health Statistics.

The reasons for the sharp gap in marriage rates by educational attainment are not yet fully understood. Sociologist Andrew Cherlin, an expert on family history, notes that such gaps have been more common in time periods when income inequality was high.[43] Cherlin's analysis actually focuses on marriage rates by occupational category, but occupation and education are sufficiently highly correlated that the pattern he describes certainly applies across education levels, too. A similar pattern of large marriage rate differences apparently existed in the United States at the end of the nineteenth and beginning of the twentieth century, a time period often referred to as the "gilded age" and characterized by very high inequality of incomes. In the middle decades of the century, inequality was lower and marriage rate differences by education were smaller. In the 2000s and 2010s, inequality was at record levels.

---

43 Andrew Cherlin, "The Real Reason Richer People Marry," *New York Times*, December 6, 2014.

Cherlin's explanation harkens back to Wilson's MMPI, which, as we discussed earlier in this chapter, linked marriage rates among black men and women to the ability of men to support a family. The current inequality is largely fueled by a growing earnings gap between college-educated workers and those with a high-school degree or less. The labor-market prospects of less-educated men, who are the likely marriage partners of less-educated women, have been affected most negatively. In Cherlin's words, "college-educated men and women are the privileged players in our transformed economy." Some sociologists argue that men and women have an idealized idea of what marriage ought to be and don't want to enter into it when it can't meet that ideal. In effect, marriage is being treated as a "luxury good," something that is consumed primarily mostly by wealthier families. In its place, Cherlin suggests that less-educated men and women are opting for cohabitation, an idea we have seen several times.

To be sure, economists are more skeptical of that kind of explanation. The old expression that "the perfect is the enemy of the good" may apply here. The benefits of marriage across a range of spheres and for a range of reasons are clear. The old-fashioned production-based gains are certainly smaller on average than in the past, but it remains to be seen if cohabitation can provide the range of benefits that marriage has.

The education gap in marriage may also be a cause of rising inequality via **assortative mating**. This concept refers to the non-random pattern by which marriage partners match up in the marriage market. Positive assortative mating means that likes marry likes, while negative assortative mating means that likes marry non-likes. Production considerations call for negative assortative mating on wage rates and non-market productivity to achieve gains from specialization. But shared consumption and public goods considerations call for positive assortative mating. It is quite likely that as production considerations have diminished in importance as a basis for marriage gains, positive assortative mating has replaced negative assortative mating in importance.

We do see positive assortative mating on many traits, including height, religion, and age. One that is particularly important and that links to concerns about growing inequality in the United States is positive assortative mating on the basis of education. Partly, this reflects the growing educational attainment of women. In the past it was common for college-educated husbands to have more education than their wives, because men had more education than women in the general population. But this has changed—more on this in Chapter 9. In 1970 about 40 percent of college-educated husbands had college-educated wives. By 1990 this had increased to about 55 percent, and by 2000 two-thirds of college-educated husbands had college-educated wives.[44]

Not only has assortative mating on this dimension increased but, as already noted, the economic value of higher education has increased as well. As a result, this form of assortative mating has contributed to increasing family income inequality. Economist David Autor illustrated the potential powerful impact of this second factor in his review of inequality among "the other 99 percent."[45] Since the late 1970s, the earnings difference between college-educated workers and high-school graduates has risen steadily and

---

44 Marriage proportions by education are from Christine R. Schwartz and Robert D. Mare (2005), "Trends in Educational Assortative Marriage from 1940 to 2003," *Demography,* 42 (4), 621–646.

45 David H. Autor (2014), "Skills, Education, and the Rise of Earnings Inequality Among the 'Other 99 Percent,'" *Science,* 344, 843–851.

sharply. Economists attribute most of this trend to technological change that has favored better-educated workers relative to less-educated, although institutional factors, such as the decline in the real value of the minimum wage and the decline in unionization, probably also played a role. In 2012 dollars, the annual educational earnings gap for full-time, full-year working men increased from about $17,000 in 1979 to more than $34,000 in 2012, while the corresponding gap for women increased from about $13,000 to $23,000. At the household level, if all workers had the median earnings for their education, the earnings gap between a college-educated two-earner married couple and a high-school-educated two-earner married couple would have almost doubled, increasing from about $30,000 in 1979 to more than $58,000 in 2012. This, in turn, has enormous implications for the family environments of children born to parents with different education levels.

Summary

This completes a two-chapter unit on the economics of marriage. In the first chapter we identified the gains of marriage and their multiple sources, analyzed the marriage market using a supply-and-demand approach, and looked at optimal marital search. In this chapter we have analyzed two other important marriage-related demographic decisions—cohabitation and divorce. We then examined race differences in marriage and family structure, and also differences by education and the role that assortative mating plays in generating income inequality. We also reviewed the research evidence on the gains of marriage, which suggests that, by and large, married men and women are healthier and happier, and that married men earn more than otherwise similar men.

Still absent from our analysis are those household-produced "bundles of joy" that are a central feature of most marriages—children. In the next two chapters we turn to the economic analysis of fertility. Like marriage, fertility is a newcomer to economic analysis. It may appear that economics could have little to say about how couples make decisions about such an intimate and personal matter. We hope and expect that you will think otherwise after Chapters 5 and 6.

5 THE ECONOMICS OF FERTILITY

Introduction

In 1957, 4.3 million babies were born in the United States, setting a record that held for a remarkable 50 years. One out of every eight women between the ages of 15 and 44 and nearly one out of every four between the ages of 20 and 24 had a birth in that year. In the mid-1950s the average adult woman had 3.65 births over her lifetime.

Some 50 years later, total births reached 4.32 million, exceeding the 1957 figure for the first time. But because the population was so much larger, the proportion of women having a birth was just about half of the 1950s rate. Since then the proportion of women having a birth continued to decline annually through the mid-2010s. Now, on average, a US woman has fewer than two births over her lifetime.

These dramatic changes are not limited to the United States. Fertility has fallen throughout most of Western Europe and also in much of the less developed world. In most of Europe, current fertility rates are well below those in the United States. In Spain, Portugal, and Italy, births per woman are now under 1.5, a rate so low that it will lead to population decline if it continues for a substantial time.

Understanding why and how these changes have occurred is the major goal of this chapter. To do that, we once again step outside the usual domain of economics, applying the tools and methods of microeconomics in very creative ways to another non-traditional subject. In this case we focus on the decisions of adults about the number of children they will have and the resources they will devote to them, surely among the most personal and important decisions that adults make.

In this chapter we focus on the general economic analysis of fertility with a special emphasis on explaining the decline in fertility. In the next chapter we focus on contemporary fertility issues, including teen and non-marital childbearing, the impact of contraceptives on women's lives, and a set of current topics. As always, we begin with the facts.

Fertility facts and trends

Measuring fertility

The study of population issues is called **demography;** economic demography is the subfield of economics that focuses on population issues. Demographers measure fertility in two ways, both as an annual rate and as the corresponding number of births the average woman has over her lifetime. The **fertility rate** is the number of births in a year to women of any age divided by the number of women aged 15 to 44. For ease of expression, this rate is usually expressed as the number of births per 1,000 women. Note that the numerator of the fertility rate includes births to women less than age 15 and older than 44, but the women in those age ranges are not included in the denominator. Even though this isn't quite consistent, it doesn't affect the rate much because there aren't very many births to these women. In 2014 there were 3.98 million births in the United States and the fertility rate was 62.9, meaning that there were 62.9 births for every 1,000 woman aged 15–44. Ignoring multiple births, this means that about 6.3 percent of US women (about one in 16) between those ages had a birth in 2014.

The fertility rate can be computed for different groups of women—for example, by race and ethnicity, as well as by age and marital status. Keep in mind that the denominator is always the population "at risk" for whatever kind of birth is measured in the numerator. When fertility rates are computed by age group (usually five years wide), they are called **age-specific fertility rates**. The teen birth rate, which we will examine in the next chapter, is the age-specific fertility rate for young women aged 15–19. The **non-marital fertility rate (NMFR)** is the number of births to single women divided by the number of single women aged 15–44. This rate has increased substantially over time in the United States and elsewhere; we discuss it further in the next chapter.

The second demographic measure of fertility is the total number of births the average woman has over her lifetime, which is an easier number to interpret directly. This could be determined by collecting retrospective fertility information from a representative sample of women who are about 45 years old. But that means demographers would have to wait a long time to find out what the current trend was.

Thus, instead of that, demographers compute the **total fertility rate (TFR)**, which is the number of births 1,000 women today would have over their lifetimes (from age 10 to 49) if they had the age-specific fertility rates that prevail currently. The TFR is computed this way: $\text{TFR} = 5 \times (\text{FR}_{10-14} + \text{FR}_{15-19} + \text{FR}_{20-24} + \cdots + \text{FR}_{45-49})$, where FR stands for the age-specific fertility rate per thousand women (e.g., a number like 62.9), and the subscripts identify the age group. The age-specific fertility rates are multiplied by five in the formula because a woman spends five years in each age bracket. In 2014 the total fertility rate for US women was 1861.5.[1] While technically the TFR is measured as births per 1,000 women, it is commonly expressed as births per woman by dividing by 1,000. Thus, the TFR in the United States today is approximately 1.9 births per woman.

The TFR isn't a perfect measure because, for example, today's young women might well have a different fertility rate when they are in their thirties than today's 30-year-olds do. When age-specific fertility rates are changing, the TFR will usually be off the mark for the actual experience of a group of young women. This is especially true when fertility is being delayed until later ages, as it has been in recent decades. In that case the TFR understates likely completed fertility. Still, it is very convenient and very widely used.

Zero population growth (ZPG) is the total fertility rate, which, if sustained indefinitely, would cause population growth to come to a halt. Because approximately one of every two babies born is male and contributes no births, each woman has to contribute

---

1   The underlying age-specific fertility rates were 0.3 (age 10–14), 24.2 (age 15–19), 79.0 (age 20–24), 105.7 (age 25–29), 100.8, (age 30–34), 50.9 (age 35–39), 10.6 (age 40–44), and 0.8 (age 45–49). Adding these up and multiplying by five yields a TFR of 1861.5. A quick way to approximate the TFR is to multiply the overall fertility rate by 30, the number of years between 15 and 44. In 2014 the fertility rate was 62.9. $30 \times 62.9 = 1887$; this is within 1% of the official TFR.

an average of two births to keep the population stable. But because some women die before they reach their reproductive years, the ZPG rate is about 2.13 births per woman, or a TFR of 2,130 births per 1,000 women. The TFR in the United States is now below the ZPG mark, although it will take many years at that rate for the natural rate of population increase to reach zero.[2]

In the United States, fertility information is collected by the Vital Statistics System from state birth certificates. The Vital Statistics System is now part of the National Center for Health Statistics, which is itself part of the Centers for Disease Control and Prevention. For more detailed information about US fertility or more current information, check the US Vital Statistics website at www.cdc.gov/nchs/nvss.htm. The UN provides fertility information about the rest of the world at www.un.org/popin. The UN website includes links to the official population information of most member countries, so there is no end to the demographic information you can find.

Changing fertility in the United States

By themselves, these contemporary fertility numbers don't tell us very much. Are they high or low? Figure 5.1 goes back in time and plots the annual number of births in the United States (left axis) and the fertility rate (right axis) since 1940. Some graphs of social phenomena are straight lines—either up, down, or constant—but this one varies widely. Two abrupt changes are obvious: first the **baby boom**, that much-discussed spurt of fertility that defined a generation as well as created problems for everything from school construction to Social Security, and then the somewhat less famous **baby bust** that followed it.

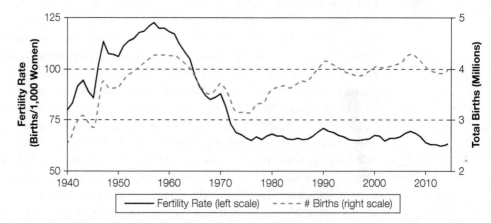

Figure 5.1 *Changing fertility in the United States, 1940–2014.*

Source: Data from J. A. Martin, B. E. Hamilton, M. J. K. Osterman, et al. (2015), "Births: Final data for 2013," *National Vital Statistics Reports* (2015), 64 (6) and 64 (1). Hyattsville, MD: National Center for Health Statistics.

---

2 The reason it takes a long time is because population momentum is built into the age structure of the population. For example, if fertility rates were higher in the recent past, there will be a particularly large group of young women who are in their reproductive years, and this causes population to continue to increase. If the ZPG fertility rate is maintained long enough, however, population momentum is eliminated and population growth ceases.

The exact dates of the baby boom are much debated and depend in part on whether one looks at total births or the fertility rate. The number of births jumped from about 2.8 million in 1945 to 3.4 million a year later—clearly a catch-up of births deferred by World War II. But the number of births kept increasing, finally surpassing 4 million every year from 1954 to 1964. The fertility rate jumped from a prewar level of about 80 births per 1,000 to over 100 births per 1,000 in 1946 and stayed above that figure through 1964. At the height of the baby boom, the fertility rate was about 120 for eight years in a row (1954–1961). The fertility rate peaked at 122.7 in 1957, a rate higher than any year since 1916. The total number of births peaked that year, too, at 4.3 million, setting a record that stood for 50 years.

Just as demographers were absorbing the implications of the baby boom, things changed—and changed dramatically. The baby boom was followed by the baby bust, roughly the years from the early-1960s when the fertility rate, although still high, started to slide, to the mid-1970s, when it stabilized at about 65 births per 1,000. From peak to trough, the fertility rate was nearly cut in half—in just about 15 years.

Since the mid-1970s, the US fertility rate hasn't changed very much. From 1975 to 1990, the rate steadily inched up from 65 births per 1,000 to 71 births per 1,000, but then it fell slowly and steadily seven years in a row. A mini-boomlet in the early 2000s pushed the fertility rate back up to nearly its 1990 level in 2007, but then the rate fell six years in a row. The 2013 fertility rate (62.5) was the lowest ever recorded in the United States. In 2014 the rate increased slightly to 62.9, ending the downward trend.

The total number of births has crept up steadily despite the low fertility rate because the number of women aged 15–44 is now so much larger. By the mid-1970s the leading edge of the 4-million-plus baby-boom birth cohorts had reached their twenties, the prime fertility years. In 1989 the number of births passed 4 million once again, for the first time in a quarter of a century. The year 2007 was the peak year for total births, finally topping the 1957 figure. In the 2010s, total births declined again to just below 4 million.

If we look back even further, to the early part of the twentieth century, the fertility rate trend becomes clearer. The fertility rate was 278 per 1,000 (approximately eight births per woman) at the beginning of the nineteenth century and 184 per 1,000 at the time of the Civil War.[3] In the early twentieth century, the fertility rate was at baby-boom levels—between 115 and 130 births per 1,000 women. But there was a steady slow decline thereafter; from 1910 to 1925, the rate fell almost every year. The decline was accelerated by the Great Depression of the 1930s. There is a bit of a rebound from the Depression and then the giant surge of the baby boom. When examined from this perspective, the baby-boom doesn't fit. Overall, and with allowance for the complicating factors of the Depression and World War II, a pattern emerges of a steady overall decline in fertility.

The TFR followed the changes in the fertility rate. At the peak years of the baby boom, the TFR exceeded 3,500 births per 1,000 women, or 3.5 births per woman. It then fell sharply, bottoming out at 1,738 births per 1,000 women in 1976, about half its baby-boom level. Between 1989 and 2009 the TFR was always above 2,000, except for a few years when it fell just below that level. Since its recent peak in 2007, it has declined slowly, but steadily to its 2014 level of 1,861. Because women are delaying their fertility as

---

3 Infant mortality was much higher then, so actual family size was much smaller than the fertility rates themselves imply.

they acquire education and establish careers, the TFR may well understate the likely experience of young women today: their own fertility rates in their twenties are low, while the fertility rates of those currently in their thirties likely understate the fertility rate of today's 20-year-olds when they reach that age bracket.

US fertility rates do not differ very much by race and ethnicity, with perhaps one exception. Figure 5.2 summarizes this information for the major race and ethnic groups for whom the Vital Statistics System presents separate information. Hispanic is an ethnicity, not a race; race and ethnicity are reported separately on birth certificates.[4]

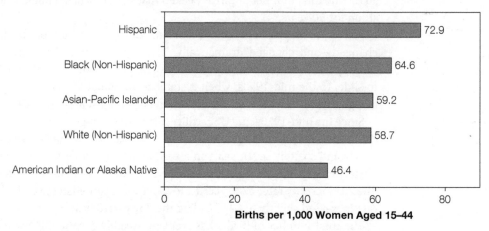

Figure 5.2 *How fertility rates in the United States differ by race and ethnicity, 2013.*

Source: J. A. Martin, B. E. Hamilton, M. J. K. Osterman, et al. (2015), "Births: Final data for 2013," *National Vital Statistics Reports*, 64 (1), Table 1. Hyattsville, MD: National Center for Health Statistics.

As you can see, the fertility rate is quite similar for whites, blacks, and Asian-Pacific Islanders. Native Americans have a lower fertility rate and Hispanics have a substantially higher rate. The fertility of Hispanic women has declined by about one-third since the mid-2000s; much of the drop is due to a decline in the fertility rate of Mexican women.

Changing fertility in the rest of the world

The United States is certainly not the only developed country that has experienced a dramatic fall in fertility. Indeed, fertility in the United States is actually higher than in much of Western Europe. Table 5.1 shows this information for selected countries in terms of the average number of births per woman, computed from the TFR. Fertility fell literally everywhere. In most of the countries shown, births per woman were in the 2.0–2.8 range in 1970, but fell to well under 2.0 by 2013. In Portugal and Spain, average births per woman fell by 1.6, while in Australia, Austria, Greece, Italy and, Japan, births fell by 0.7–1.0. As of 2013, Spain has the lowest fertility of these countries (1.3), with Austria, Germany, Italy, Japan, and Portugal just above it at 1.4. Sweden, France, and the United Kingdom have rates more similar to those of the United States.

---

4 The figures are for 2013, the most recent year for which fertility by race and ethnicity is available as of mid-2015.

Table 5.1 *Declining fertility in Europe and other developed countries, 1970–2013.*

	1970	2013
Australia	2.9	1.9
Austria	2.3	1.4
Canada	2.2	1.6
Denmark	2.0	1.7
France	2.5	2.0
Germany	2.1	1.4
Greece	2.4	1.3
Italy	2.4	1.4
Japan	2.1	1.4
Netherlands	2.6	1.7
Portugal	3.0	1.4
Russian Federation	2.0	1.7
Spain	2.9	1.3
Sweden	1.9	1.9
United Kingdom	2.4	2.0
United States	2.5	1.9

Note: Figures shown are TFR, divided by 1,000.

Source: World Fertility Patterns 1997, UN Publication (ST/ESA/SER.A/165) and Population Reference Bureau, available at www.prb.org/Datafinder.

Fertility remains very high in much of the less developed world, although it is falling in most countries. Figure 5.3 summarizes the time trend in the TFR from 1950 through 2010 for countries by their level of economic development as classified by the UN.[5] In the least developed countries, births per woman averaged more than 6.5 from the 1950s through the early 1970s and then began to fall, slowly through the mid-1980s and then more quickly. Overall, fertility fell for these countries by more than two births per woman to an average of 4.5 as of 2010. For the broader group of less developed countries, fertility started a bit lower, at about 6.0 births per woman from the 1950s through the late 1960s. Fertility fell sooner and more rapidly, narrowing the gap between their own fertility and that in more developed countries from more than three births per woman to just a bit more than one. In the more developed countries, births per woman fell from 2.8 in the 1950s to about 1.7 in 2010.

China is a famous example of falling fertility among developing countries. Births per woman there fell from 5.8 in 1970 to 1.4 by the early 2000s as a result of the "one child" policy. In India, births per woman fell from 5.7 around 1970 to 2.7 in 2010. Other countries

---

5 The Less Developed group includes Africa, Asia (excluding Japan), Latin America, and the Caribbean, plus Melanesia, Micronesia, and Polynesia. The Least Developed countries group includes 34 countries in Africa, 10 in Asia, 1 in Latin America and the Caribbean, and 5 in Oceania. The More Developed region includes Europe, Northern America, Australia/New Zealand, and Japan.

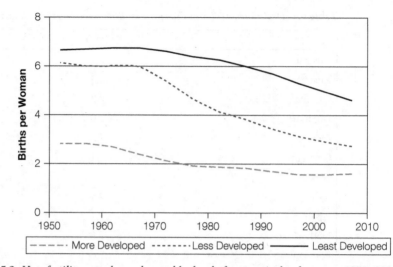

Figure 5.3 *How fertility rates have changed by level of economic development, 1950–2010.*

Source: World Population Prospects: The 2012 Revision, Table F4, Population Division, Department of Economic and Social Affairs, UN Secretariat.

with particularly large drops in fertility include Tunisia, Algeria, Vietnam, and Mexico. The highest fertility rates as of 2010 were in Africa and the Middle East: Niger and Chad both had average births per woman of 7 or above, with Somalia, Uganda, and Afghanistan just below. The lowest fertility rates in the world were in Macao, Hong Kong, Korea, and some of the former Soviet Republics. All have TFR below 1.2 births per woman. We discuss fertility issues in developing countries in Chapter 13.

Fertility—the modern economic approach

The earliest economic approach to fertility is due to Thomas Malthus, an early nineteenth-century economist whose pessimistic theory about population growth outpacing food supplies gave economics its description as the "dismal science." Malthus's theory of population focused exclusively on the effects of income. Higher incomes encouraged earlier marriages, which in turn caused fertility to commence sooner, and also lowered infant mortality. As a result, population grew more rapidly. Eventually, however, the larger population size fed back negatively to reduce wage rates and society fell back toward a subsistence standard of living. That's the dismal part.

The modern economic approach to fertility was developed in the early 1960s, primarily by Gary Becker, whose supply-and-demand model of the marriage market we discussed in Chapter 4.[6] It has since been expanded by many others. In large measure the analysis began with a puzzle: Why did fertility typically fall as family incomes grew? The demand for most goods increases when income rises, but children appear to be a conspicuous exception.

---

6   Gary S. Becker (1960), "An Economic Analysis of Fertility," in *Demographic and Economic Change in Developed Countries.* Princeton, NJ: Princeton University Press.

Becker's key insight was simply thinking of fertility as an application of consumer demand and then applying the core ideas of demand theory—preferences, prices, and utility maximization.

Preferences

The first basic insight is simple: *Most adults want to have their own children.* Sometimes children are useful productive assets. For example, in less developed countries with large agricultural sectors, children can provide both labor and old-age support. In a family business, they can be the next generation of owners. The royal families of Europe required children, preferably male children to ensure the line of succession.[7] But even if parents never expect to get much help from their children or collect a dollar, rupee, or euro from them, they still seem to want them. They are, an economist would find it almost irresistible to say, a source of *utility* or satisfaction to their parents, not to mention their grandparents.

But what kind of source of utility are they? They aren't like a pizza or a good movie, which are sources of utility that are consumed and thereby used up in the process. They are a bit more like an automobile or a house, a durable asset that provides many years' worth of utility. With assets like these, individuals consume and receive utility from the *services* that the asset yields, not the physical asset itself. For example, an individual doesn't literally consume his or her automobile or house; instead, he or she consumes the automobile services and housing services that these goods provide. So let's say that adults get utility from the **child services** provided by their children. We will use that phrase to cover all the many things that children do and that parents gain enjoyment from.

Let's continue with the analogy. The amount of automobile services or housing services depends not only on the *quantity* of automobiles and houses but also on something we might call their *quality*. A couple of Yugos[8] is one thing, a couple of Hondas something else, and several BMWs or Ferraris is something else altogether. The same is true for a house, which could range from modest to opulent, small to enormous, and so on.

How do we apply that concept to children? What might we mean by **child quality** or higher-quality children? We're treading on delicate linguistic ground here because we don't want to disparage any child or any parent. Still, following the same analogy, we might say that higher-quality children are those children who have more child resources devoted to them, just like a BMW has more automobile resources in it than a Yugo (which hardly had any at all). We could, perhaps, call them "high-resource" children, but the standard, if unfortunate, terminology is "high quality." They are not necessarily better children or happier children, although, all else equal, children with more resources available to them probably do better on average. At low resource levels, a positive relationship between the amount of resources and child well-being is reasonably clear and persuasive.[9] More

---

7   Think about Henry VIII and his efforts to produce a male heir, which involved six wives—with no success. He was ultimately followed to the throne by his daughter, Elizabeth I. England no longer gives priority to males in the royal succession.

8   The Yugo was introduced for sale in the United States in 1986 at a price of $4,000, by far the lowest price of any new car at that time. It quickly developed a reputation for very poor quality and was withdrawn from the US market in the early 1990s.

9   It is possible, of course, to spoil a child by giving him or her too many resources.

resources would probably include a broad range of investments in human capital, such as education, healthcare, and nutrition, but also music lessons, summer camp, endless sports practices, and so on.

The result of the analysis thus far is that there are inevitably two dimensions to a family's demand for child services—quantity and quality. Both dimensions provide utility to a parent. Ultimately, adults must make a choice about both quantity and quality.[10] When we think about fertility per se, we are, of course, thinking about just the quantity dimension—the *number* of births a woman has. But because adults care about child services, which depend on both quantity and quality, the analysis of quantity effects is filtered through an additional layer of complexity. This will turn out to be very important.

Adults also get utility from things that have nothing to do with children—food, clothing, entertainment, and so on. Let's lump all these things together and call them A for adult consumption goods. We'll let CS stand for child services, which includes both a quantity and a quality dimension. We therefore write an adult's utility function as

$$U = U(CS, A) \tag{5.1}$$

Equation (5.1) simply states that child services and adult goods are the two broad sources of utility for an adult. Adults can and do have very different preferences about these kinds of things. Some adults may love a household full of children; others prefer few or none at all. All those preferences and then some are perfectly fine.

Production and cost

The second major economic insight about children is also quite obvious: *Children are costly.* This is true for both child quality and child quantity. In saying this, we are referring not to the amount that parents actually spend on their children but rather to something like the cost of one unit of child services. The *total* amount that parents spend on child services is the product of this per unit cost and the total amount of child services that they choose. This total amount of spending is *endogenous*—it is chosen by the family—and depends on the amount of child services that it chooses.

Before we think about the cost of child services, what determines them, and how and why they change, we need to agree on some technical details. First, whenever we talk about the cost of child services, we are talking about the cost of one unit of child services. Exactly how big is one unit of child services? The truth is that nobody knows, but it doesn't matter. We are primarily interested in how a family will change the amount of child services it wants when income or price changes. The actual amount of child services in one unit doesn't make any difference in answering that question. Second, it will simplify things a bit if we assume that the cost of producing one unit of child services is constant, no matter how many units are produced. Essentially, this means that the cost of producing, say, 10 units of child services is ten times the cost of producing one unit, the cost of producing 100 units is 100 times the cost of producing one unit, and so on.

---

10 Sometimes economists assume that parents provide the same quality for each child, which means that each child is essentially treated equally. That's probably roughly correct, except for extreme cases of children with special abilities or special needs. This assumption leads to an interesting interaction between quality and quantity that we discuss in the appendix to this chapter.

Production The costs of child services are, of course, quite different from the costs of most goods and services. Child services cannot be purchased directly at the mall or over the Internet. Rather, they are a household-produced good, an idea we introduced in Chapter 2 and then used in our analysis of marriage in Chapter 3. In many families, child services are *the* single most important household-produced good. So when we talk about the cost of child services, we are actually talking about the cost of *producing* child services, not the cost of *purchasing* them.

The production process for child services, however complicated and varied it may be in practice, can be represented by a household production function with two broad classes of inputs—parental time and market goods. Thus we can write the **child services production function** as

$$CS = F(T_M, T_F, Z) \tag{5.2}$$

where T stands for time, Z for market goods used in child services production, and M and F stand for mother and father, respectively. *Careful: in this chapter the subscripts M and F stand for mother and father, not male and female.* This production function summarizes the general idea that the total amount of child services produced depends on the amount of inputs (time and goods) that are used. More time and/or more goods are necessary to produce more child services.

Without turning this into a class in child development, consider the nature of this production process for children of different ages. The production of child services in infants is almost certainly time-intensive rather than goods-intensive. There are some material costs, such as a crib, toys, and healthcare, but day-to-day goods use is often quite moderate. For one thing, infants eat a lot less than, say, teenagers. Parental time inputs are substantial, to say the least, as any exhausted parent of a newborn or toddler can attest. As children get a bit older, parental time inputs are still required, but the ratio of goods to time almost certainly rises. Teenagers and college students involve almost exclusively goods—things like an iPod, a car, and a college education—rather than parental time, which they often seem to want relatively little of. The idea that the relative amount of time and goods used in the production of child services varies as children grow up is not a deep insight but it will turn out to be important in thinking about the cost of fertility and its quality and quantity components.

Cost What general ideas can we deduce about the cost of producing one unit of child services? The single most important point is this: *The cost of producing one unit of child services depends on the underlying prices of parental time and on the prices of market goods, because these are the inputs used to produce child services.* This is a standard conclusion of production economics: The cost of production depends on the prices of the inputs used to produce a good.

What are the costs of the inputs used to produce child quality? We can write the cost of market goods as P_Z; think of it as capturing the prices of all the market goods that are used in raising children, everything from diapers to books and toys to healthcare and education. What about the cost of the adult time inputs? This is tricky because parents don't literally pay themselves to care for a child. Nevertheless, that time has a cost that is best measured by the wage rate—that is, by what a parent could earn if he or she were not using that time to produce child services instead. This cost is an **opportunity cost**, the cost of something measured in terms of what is given up.

Thus the cost function for the production of child services can be written in very general terms as $C(CS) = C(W_M, W_F, P_Z)$. In words, this equation says that the cost of producing child services is a function of the parents' wage rates and the price of market goods.

Parents must decide how to combine their own time and market goods to produce child services, especially child quality. Public school, private school, or home schooling? Daycare or stay-at-home parent? In making these decisions and thousands of others, they likely will pay attention to the prices of time and goods, trying to economize as much as possible on expensive inputs. Technically, this is a problem involving cost minimization, similar to what a firm does in choosing how much of different inputs to use in production.

The exact details of the cost minimization don't matter much for our purposes, although the general idea is clear: Families will typically use more of inputs that are less expensive and economize on the use of inputs that are more expensive. Whatever choices a family makes, the cost of producing a unit of child services is just the sum of the cost of the time and the market goods used to produce it. Using this idea, we can expand the child services cost function this way:

$$C(CS) = C(W_M, W_F, P_Z) = W_M T_M^* + W_F T_F^* + P_Z Z^* \tag{5.3}$$

In (5.3), the "*" following T and Z means that that these are the actual chosen amounts of the inputs used to produce a unit of child services. The first term on the right side of equation (5.3) is the cost of the mother's time devoted to child services, the second is the cost of the father's time, and the last is the cost of goods and services. Remember that the relevant wage in equation (5.3) is what a parent *could* earn; it is not affected by whether that parent is actually working. Every adult has a price of time, measured by the market wage rate. The higher the wage, the greater the time cost.

For most of human society it has typically been true that $T_M^* > T_F^*$, which is just a formal way of saying that more mother's time than father's time is devoted to the production of child services. This can reflect any number of causes, including differences in wage rates (i.e., time costs), innate preferences, and/or socialization.

Changes in costs When a firm faces an increase in the cost of a factor of production, it typically takes steps to reduce its use of that input and substitute other inputs. But it is a central principle of cost and production analysis that it is never possible to totally eliminate the impact of the increase in the cost of the input. As a result, a firm's average cost of production always rises when the price of an input increases. Importantly, the magnitude of the cost increase depends on two things: (1) how much of that input is used before the increase in cost; and (2) how technologically easy it is to substitute another input for the one whose cost has increased. Thus an increase in the price of a little-used input has a much smaller effect on production costs than an increase in the price of an input that is much more heavily used. Also, where input substitution is relatively easy, it is possible to avoid most (although not all) of the price increase. In contrast, if input substitution is very difficult, nearly the full impact of the price increase is felt.[11] We can summarize these ideas by saying that the impact on cost depends on (1) input intensity and (2) ease of input substitution.

---

11 As a good example of this idea, consider the impact of an increase in the price of gasoline on commuting costs. The impact is larger if an individual has a low-mileage car and/or a long commute so that initial usage is high and if no good transportation alternatives (mass transit, car-pooling) are available, so substitution is difficult.

An increase in the price of parental time or of market goods works in the same way to increase the cost of producing child services, even when families adjust as best they can to find less costly ways of producing those child services. For example, if the cost of parental time increases, families might try to reduce the amount of time used and substitute market goods instead. One good example is using paid daycare or sitters instead of parental care. If the cost of a parent's time is high enough, this makes economic sense. But even when this substitution is done, the cost of child services will increase if the cost of the inputs increases. An increase in input prices always increases the cost of producing child services.

Just as for a regular firm, the quantitative impact of an increase in the price of parental time or market goods on the cost of producing child services depends on input intensity and ease of substitution. In this case, we might well expect a large effect of an increase in the cost of parental time on the cost of child services, since parental time is a very heavily used input in the production process, and good substitutes are not easily available for some time uses. This effect might be especially true for women's wage rates since traditionally, women's time has been the major input into the production of child services. This is a key insight because it suggests that rising wage rates could cause a large increase in the cost of producing child services.

Let's go a step further and think about how an increase in women's wages might separately affect the cost of child quality and child quantity. A family can increase its total amount of child services either by holding quality constant and increasing the number of children or by increasing quality while keeping the number of children the same. Increasing quantity—having a baby—inevitably involves the very time-intensive early years of infancy and early childhood. In contrast, increasing quality often can be accomplished by increasing goods (e.g., educational spending and other less lofty consumption goods) at older ages. That suggests that when women's wages increase, the cost of quantity will increase by more than the cost of quality, because quantity is likely to be more time-intensive than quality. This is an important result that we will use later.

Choosing—the economics of fertility

We can now use our analysis to explain how families make fertility decisions and then to examine the decline in fertility in the United States and around the world. Let's review the key elements thus far:

- Children are like a consumer durable good that provides utility over a long time period in the form of child services. Fertility is one element of child services. The other is child quality or spending per child. Parents care about both quality and quantity.
- Child services are a household-produced good. The price of child services is based on the cost of the time and goods used to produce them. The key price is the price of time, especially women's time, which has traditionally been the primary input in the child services production function.
- If women's wages increase, this will have a very substantial effect on the price of child services, since child services are time-intensive and it is relatively difficult to substitute goods for time in the production of child services. Costs might well increase more for quantity than quality, since additional quantity always involves the very time-intensive infant and early childhood years.

Utility maximization and demand

The adult's utility-maximization problem is a constrained maximization problem, exactly of the form that was introduced in Chapter 2. The adults' utility function, which represents their preferences, is $U = U(CS, A)$, where CS includes both a quality and a quantity element and A is adult goods. As in any consumer choice problem, the prices of the goods and family income are critical elements of the constraint. The most important price is the price of child services. This price, which we will call P_{CS}, is exactly the cost of the parental time and goods used to produce a unit of child services that we analyzed just above. That is, $P_{CS} = C(W_M, W_F, P_Z) = W_M T_M^* + W_F T_F^* + P_Z Z^*$. As the equation indicates, this price depends ultimately on the prices of parental time (W_M and W_F) and the price of market goods used to produce child services (P_Z). Family income will turn out to be a bit more complicated than in the usual case, but let's start by treating it as some fixed amount Y.

As in any utility-maximization problem, the adults will choose an amount of child services and an amount of adult consumption goods in order to maximize their utility, given their preferences, the prices of the goods, and their income. Also, as in any utility-maximization problem, the best choices for the two goods can be expressed in terms of marginal conditions that involve balancing the marginal utility of the last unit of each good with its price. The marginal conditions are interesting, but they are not essential to the main point we want to establish; Box 5.1 has the details of this approach.

Box   5.1

Utility-Maximization and the Demand for Children: Details

The key element in the analysis of utility maximization is the marginal utility derived from child services and adult goods. Marginal utility is the *additional* utility received from the last little bit of something, in this case the last dollars spent on child services and adult goods. In general, the marginal utility of anything falls the more you have of it and this almost certainly applies to child services and adult goods. This property is called **diminishing marginal utility**. For more about marginal utility, see the discussion in Chapter 2.

No matter what the specific consumer choice problem is, the way to maximize utility is to choose exactly the amount of all goods that makes the ratio of the marginal utility of the last unit of a good to its price the same for each good. In terms of child services and adult goods, this rule is written this way: $MU_{CS}(CS^*)/P_{CS} = MU_A(A^*)/P_A$, where CS^* and A^* are the utility maximizing amounts of child services and adult goods. The expression $MU_{CS}(CS^*)$ is the marginal utility of child services when the amount of child services equals CS^*; $MU_A(A^*)$ is the same idea for adult goods. Thus the marginal condition for utility maximization for child services and adult goods is that the marginal utility of child services, evaluated at amount CS^*, divided by its price is just equal to the marginal utility of adult goods, evaluated at amount A^*, divided by its price.

To see why this rule maximizes utility, imagine that instead of CS^* and A^*, a family chooses some other amounts (CS' and A'), where $MU_{CS}(CS')/P_{CS} < MU_A(A')/P_A$. With these choices, the last dollars spent on child services are providing less utility than the same dollars would provide if they were spent on adult goods instead. Total utility could therefore be increased by reducing the amount of child services consumed and increasing adult goods. Doing this would, because of diminishing marginal utility, increase MU_{CS} and decrease MU_A, thus making the two ratios more equal. This is a tricky idea to grasp. The key is that the marginal utility and the amount of a good move opposite to one another. In this case, reducing CS will increase its marginal utility and make the left-hand side of the equation larger, while increasing A will decrease its marginal utility. Unless the two ratios are equal, it is always possible to do better by rearranging consumption from the good with the lower ratio of marginal utility to price to the one with a higher ratio.

A numerical example may help with this idea. Suppose the last dollar spent on child services provides 10 units of utility, while the last dollar spent on adult goods provides 20 units. (These numbers are completely arbitrary; only the comparison of the numbers matters, not their actual value.) If spending on child services is reduced by one dollar, utility falls by 10 units. When that dollar is used to purchase adult goods, utility increases by a little less than 20 units. (It increases by less than 20 because of diminishing marginal utility; for concreteness, let's say it increases by 19 units.) The family is therefore better off by the difference in utility lost and gained—in this case, by 9 units. This process of reallocation of spending can be continued with a resulting improvement in utility as long as the marginal utility of the last dollar spent on the two goods is different. Only when the last dollar spent provides equal marginal utility is it impossible to do better by reallocating spending.

Most parents care a great deal about their children, but even so they typically don't choose to spend all or even nearly all their income on them. If they did that, the marginal utility from spending on children would be very low relative to its price and the marginal utility of spending on adult goods relative to its price would be very high. They could do better by rearranging their spending. Similarly, they don't spend all or most of their income on themselves. Balance in spending is required for utility maximization and that is what the marginal conditions for utility maximization show.

Now consider what would happen if the price of child services increased to P_{CS}'. At the original utility-maximizing choices, $MU_{CS}(CS)/P_{CS}' < MU_A(A)/P_A$ because the denominator on the left-hand side of the equation is now higher than before. What should the family do in order to maximize utility? This is exactly the same as the non-optimal situation involving CS' and A' analyzed above. In order to maximize utility, the family should reduce the amount of child services and increase the amount of adult goods until the necessary equality condition holds once again. Note what we just showed through this exercise: When the price of child services increased, the utility-maximizing amount of child services decreased.

To do a complete analysis of the effect of price changes on the demand for child services, there is one more wrinkle to consider involving a change in the family's income. We discuss that fully in the text.

Instead, let's focus on the corresponding demand function for child services, which represents the utility-maximizing amount of child services demanded, given prices, income, and preferences. We write this demand function as

$$CS^* = D\ (P_{CS}(W_M, W_F, P_Z), P_A, Y) \tag{5.4}$$

This is a complicated-looking expression, so let's take it piece by piece. Ignoring the three terms in the inner parentheses, this equation says that the utility-maximizing demand for child services depends on the price of child services, the price of adult goods, and family income; we know that preferences also matter, but we suppress them because they are usually treated as fixed and not the subject of inquiry. The inner parentheses immediately following P_{CS} indicate that the price of child services depends on W_M, W_F, and P_Z. This term represents the cost and production part of the problem that we analyzed above.

This demand curve is just like a regular demand curve for a standard product that you would buy in the market, but with one final wrinkle that involves the income term (Y). In a typical consumer demand problem, the income term is the earnings that a family has and it is treated as exogenous (fixed) and not analyzed further. That's appropriate because the focus is on spending for consumer goods rather than on how time is used or money is earned. In this case, though, the income term that is appropriate is not what a family actually earns but what it *could* earn. This kind of income is called **full income**. It is *earnable* income rather than *earned* income, a measure of income that is exogenous and does not depend on the work decisions of family members.

The full income for a married-couple family is written this way:

$$Y_{FL} \equiv W_F T + W_M T + V \tag{5.5}$$

In (5.5), Y_{FL} stands for full income, T is total time available (24 hours a day or perhaps the amount left after allowing for some biologically necessary minimum hours of sleep) and V is income from other sources. This is an identity, true by definition for all values of W_F, W_M, and V; note that the two sides of the equation are linked by a $\equiv$, not an equals sign.[12] In words, equation (5.5) simply says that full income is the sum of the maximum income a family would have if everyone worked T hours plus any other income that it has.

As equation (5.5) shows, parental wage rates affect a family's full income. Unsurprisingly, when a wage rate is higher, full income is higher, and when a wage rate is lower, full income falls. The concept of full income is consistent with the idea that time spent in household production is costly and that the cost is measured by the value of time (the wage rate). A family spends its full income partly on time spent in household production and partly on market goods, which it purchases with the income it earns from time spent working in the labor market.

Using the concept of full income, we can rewrite our child services demand function as:

$$CS^* = D\ (P_{CS}(W_M, W_F, P_Z), P_A, Y_{FL}(W_M, W_F, V)) \tag{5.6}$$

Equation (5.6) is almost the same as the demand function in equation (5.4) except that we now are using full income (Y_{FL}) instead of Y and we also show the dependence of full

---

12 In a single-parent family, the expression for full income would have only one wage term on the right side.

income on the two wage rates and other income. Note that the two wage rates appear in two places, affecting both full income and the price of child services. This will be critical later on.

Explaining the decline in fertility

The primary task of any theory of fertility is to explain the decline in fertility. This is an example of comparative statics analysis in which we seek to explain how the outcome of interest (here, fertility and child quality) will change when one of the exogenous variables (here, prices or full income) changes. For example, we might ask: How would a family's demand for child services change if the price of child services changed? How would the number of children—its fertility—change? In this section we analyze the comparative statics of fertility demand, with the goal of explaining the worldwide decline in fertility.

As we analyze this, a few complications about children are worth bearing in mind. First, a household cannot legally reduce the number of children it has once it has acquired them, no matter how its circumstances change. You can't sell your children, no matter what happens to their price, and you can't legally dispose of them in any other way, either.[13] Thus when we analyze the comparative statics of fertility demand, it is best to think of it as what a household would choose to do if it were starting from scratch in a different environment with different constraints.

Second, with the exception of adoption, children typically enter a household at age 0 and grow up, one year at a time. Thus because you can't reduce the number of children once you have them, a decision to have a child is a decision to have a child of each age. Third, the number of children must be an integer number. You really can't have 2.3 children, although we will mostly ignore this inconvenient fact in our discussion. In contrast, the amount of spending on children—their quality—can be chosen at any value at all. Thus the analyses should be cast in terms of finding the desired number of children; fractional amounts must be rounded up or down in practice. Finally, what we are analyzing is desired fertility. Actual fertility could be more or less than desired fertility depending on the efficacy of contraception, the availability of abortion, and/or the existence of biological fertility problems.

An increase in the price of parental time

The most interesting question is how fertility would likely change when the price of parental time, especially mother's time, changed. We focus on women's wages because maternal time has historically been the primary input into the production of child services. Women's wages have, in fact, increased quite steadily and substantially over the course of the twentieth and early twenty-first centuries in the United States and elsewhere throughout the world. (See Box 5.2 for details of the increase in the United States.) An increase in men's wages would likely have a much smaller effect on the price of child services. Why? By now you should have a good answer to that.

---

13 Actually, it is not unheard of for children to be raised by relatives, at least temporarily, if their own parents' circumstances change for the worse. Foster care is another possibility.

Box	5.2

Women's Wages in the United States in the Twentieth Century

In the very early decades of the twentieth century, working women were employed in a relatively small set of occupations. The single largest female occupation was as a servant and waitress, accounting for nearly one in four working women. The largest occupation for better-educated women was teaching, which ranked fifth overall and accounted for about 7 percent of all working women. In 1900, domestic service workers earned an average of $240 per year—about 10 cents an hour. School teachers earned an average of $470 per year; female school teachers probably earned much less. If they earned $300 a year and worked 1,500 hours, that comes out to about 15 cents an hour. Multiplying by 25 puts these figures in approximate current dollar terms, so domestic workers earned the equivalent of $2.50 an hour and school teachers about $3.75 an hour. Yet another way to compute turn-of-the-century wages is to look at the average earnings for all workers, which was $418 in 1900. Women's earnings were probably no more than 50 percent of this—a bit more than $200 a year or about $2.60 per hour in current dollars.

By 1920, domestic service workers were earning an average of about $2.75 per hour, and female school teachers were earning about $3.60, both in current dollars. Women in manufacturing were earning about $4.20 an hour (current dollars), but there weren't very many of them. The average earnings of all workers was about $900 per year; translating this into likely average women's wages, and converting to a current year hourly wage, yields an average hourly wage of $3.60 to $4.00. Even by 1940, domestic service workers were still earning an average of just $3.60 an hour; teachers as little as $7.00 to $8.00 on an hourly basis; and the average woman probably about $6.00 per hour in current dollars.

Wage rates—and the price of time—began to rise in earnest in the post–World War II period. By 1960 a woman who worked full time year-round (roughly 2,000 hours) earned the equivalent of about $11 per hour. By 1970 she was earning about $14 per hour. (Of course, the increase in the amount of education was an important reason for the increase.) Wage growth slowed in the 1970s; in 1980 the median YRFT working woman earned the equivalent of an hourly wage of $15. In 1990 she earned the equivalent of $17.00 and in 2013 she earned about $18.00.[14]

The basic point is clear—in the first half of the twentieth century, wages for US women were very low by twenty-first-century standards. The flip side is that the price of time was low. Over the course of the century, and especially in the years since 1950, women's wages, and thus the price of women's time, have increased tremendously. As the economic theory of fertility suggests, this increase in women's wages would have a substantial effect on the price of child services.

---

14 The dollar figures in this paragraph are median earnings in year 2013 dollars divided by 2,000 hours and are taken from US Census Bureau, Historical Income Tables, Table P-38.

The basic analysis of how a change in women's wage rates affects the demand for child services is shown in Figure 5.4. The price of child services is on the vertical axis and the corresponding amount of child services demanded is on the horizontal axis. Let's start with some price of child services P_{CS}^0 and some full income Y_{FL}^0, both of which reflect specific current values for the underlying wage rates, W_M and W_F, and the price of goods, P_Z. The corresponding utility-maximizing demand for child services is shown as CS_0^* on demand curve D_0.

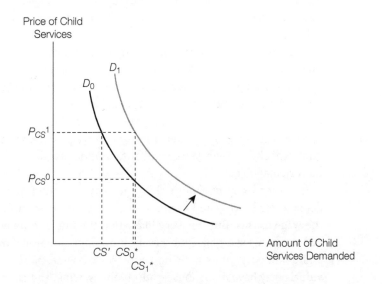

Figure 5.4 *How an increase in women's wages affects the amount of child services demanded.*

When women's wage rates increase, this increases both the price of child services and full income. Consider the two changes one at a time. If the price increased to P_{CS}^1 *and* if full income were unchanged, the amount of child services demanded would fall to CS′, just as the Law of Demand predicts. This is shown in Figure 5.4 as a movement up the original demand curve D_0. The underlying logic is explained in Box 5.1 and involves reducing the amount of child services so that marginal utility is proportional to the new higher price. See Box 5.1 for details.

However, the increase in full income will also affect the demand for child services. When income increases, demand increases for goods that we call **normal goods** and decreases for **inferior goods**. Economic theory doesn't specify whether any particular good is normal or inferior, but it seems quite reasonable that child services are a normal good—that is, a good you want more of when your income is higher, holding the price of the good constant. Inferior goods tend to be things like long-distance bus travel, cheap wine and beer, cheaper cuts of meats, and so on. Children are almost certainly not in that category. Thus the increase in full income will cause an increase in the amount of child services demanded. Since we have already accounted for the change in the price of child services, the effect of the increase in full income is represented in Figure 5.4 as a horizontal shift of the demand curve to D_1. This increases the amount of child services demanded at price P_{CS}^1, shown in the figure as CS_1^*.

We can express the same idea very compactly with variables and arrows this way: (1) $W_M\uparrow \rightarrow P_{CS}\uparrow \rightarrow CS^*\downarrow$ (full income constant), but also (2) $W_M\uparrow \rightarrow Y_{FL}\uparrow \rightarrow CS^*\uparrow$ (price of child services constant). The first part is the effect of a wage increase through the price of child services, and the second part is its effect through full income. The effect through P_{CS} is likely to be large due to input intensity and difficulty of substitution.

We can't be certain whether $CS_1^* >$ or $< CS_0^*$. It is certainly possible that the family will demand more child services at the higher price P_{CS}^1 than at the lower price P_{CS}^0, due to the increase in full income.[15] It is also possible that the negative effect of the price increase will outweigh the positive effect of the full income increase and the amount of child services will fall.

So far we've established that the impact of a wage increase on the total amount of child services demanded could go either way. It's very important to understand that an increase in women's wages need not necessarily lead to a reduction in child services, even though it does increase the price of child services, because the wage increase has conflicting effects operating through the price of child services and full income.

Now, let's turn to the likely impact of a wage increase separately on the quantity and quality of child services. Remember that understanding the fall in fertility (quantity) was our original objective.

It is very likely that both child quantity and child quality are normal goods, so the demand for both would increase due to the increase in full income that an increase in the wage causes. But it is very likely that the full income effect is larger for quality than quantity. This is a typical observation in other situations involving choices about quality and quantity, such as housing, automobiles, wine, clothing, and so on. Wealthier individuals may have *more* houses, automobiles, wine, and clothing, but even more they have *higher-quality* houses, automobiles, wine, and clothing. If that same pattern held for child quantity and quality, which seems plausible, then an increase in full income would have a bigger positive effect on child quality than on child quantity.

It is also likely that the impact of a wage change will be different on the price of child quality than the price of child quantity. When we analyzed the costs of child services, we suggested that an increase in women's wage rates might have a bigger effect on the cost of child quantity than on child quality because additional quantity, which typically involves a newborn, is more time-intensive than additional quality, which can be produced at older child ages with the substitution of goods for time. Thus it is quite plausible that the increase in wage rates would have a *bigger* effect on the price of child quantity than the price of child quality.

If we put together these ideas about the likely different income effects on quality and quantity and the likely differing effects of wage increases on the price of quality and quantity, we reach a very interesting conclusion. As wage rates for women have steadily increased, the large resulting increase in the price of child quantity would reduce desired fertility substantially, while the accompanying increase in full income would have a relatively small positive effect. The likely result is that fertility would fall because the negative impact through price outweighs the positive impact through full income.

---

15 This is not a violation of the Law of Demand because an extra wealth effect is operating here. The Law of Demand applies to a *ceteris paribus* change in price.

In contrast, the same increase in the wage rate would cause a smaller increase in the price of child quality and thus would likely have a smaller negative impact on the demand for child quality. Meanwhile, the increase in full income would have a bigger positive effect. The net result is that child quality might well rise: The positive income effect outweighs the negative price effect.

Figure 5.5 illustrates this analysis; Figure 5.5(A) focuses on child quantity (N) and Figure 5.5(B) examines child quality (L). Let's start with prices P_N^0 for quantity, P_L^0 for quality and full income Y_{FL}^0; just as in Figure 5.4, these values reflect specific current values for the underlying wage rates, W_M and W_F, and the price of goods P_Z. The corresponding utility-maximizing choices are N_0^* and L_0^*. In Figure 5.5(A) an increase in a woman's wage rate increases the price to P_N^1, shown as a relatively large increase because of the historical importance of women's time in the production of child quantity. This price increase would reduce the quantity demanded from N_0^* to N'. The positive income effect on quantity is small, so the demand curve shifts out relatively little. The net effect is a decline in quantity from N_0^* to N_1^*. In Figure 5.5(B) the increase in the price of child quality is smaller (from P_L^0 to P_L^1) because quality is less time-intensive. But because the income effect on quality is larger, the demand curve shifts out further when full income increases. Thus we show a net increase in the demand for child quality from L_0^* to L_1^*.

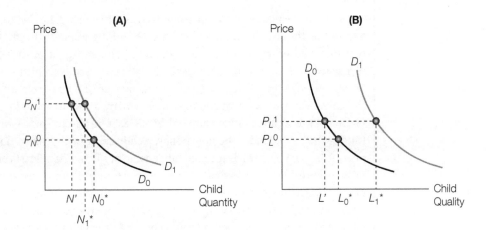

Figure 5.5 *The effect of an increase in women's wages of the quality and quantity of children.*

Using the same variables and arrows as above, we can express these ideas this way:

Child Quantity: $W_M\uparrow\rightarrow P_N\uparrow$ (big effect)$\rightarrow N^*\downarrow$ but also $W_M\uparrow\rightarrow Y_{FL}\uparrow\rightarrow N^*\uparrow$ (small effect)

Child Quality: $W_M\uparrow\rightarrow P_L\uparrow$ (smaller effect)$\rightarrow L^*\downarrow$ but also $W_M\uparrow\rightarrow Y_{FL}\uparrow\rightarrow L^*\uparrow$ (bigger effect)

We have now developed the following important results:

- When wages increase—especially the wages of women, whose time input into the production of child services has been substantial—the total amount of child services demanded could go up or down. The higher price causes families to want fewer child services, but the higher full income allows them to afford more.

- It is quite likely that child quality will increase. This occurs because the negative effect of the price increase is small, while the positive effect of the higher full income is large.
- It is quite likely that child quantity—fertility—will decrease. This occurs because the negative effect of the price increase is large, while the positive effect of the higher full income is small.

That, in a nutshell, is the modern economic argument for falling fertility. When the price of time increases, families opt for fewer children, but spend more on each of them. Fertility falls but child quality increases. Child services may go up or down.

We have focused thus far on how the increase in women's wage rates induced a shift from child quantity to child quality. But government policy can also have the effect of changing the relative prices of quantity and quality and thus affect choices. For an interesting recent example, see Box 5.3.

Box	5.3

The Child Quantity–Quality Trade-Off: Evidence from German Citizenship Policy

In 1999 the German Parliament amended the Citizenship and Nationality Law of 1913 to grant birthright citizenship to children of immigrants. Birthright citizenship means that the children were automatically granted citizenship at birth if they were born in Germany, even if their parents were not citizens. Although birthright citizenship has been granted in the United States since the passage of the Fourteenth Amendment after the Civil War, this was not the case in Germany. Prior to the reform, a child born in Germany was granted citizenship only if at least one parent was a German citizen at the time of the birth. Under the new policy, a child born in Germany to foreign parents on or after January 1, 2000, is granted citizenship at birth if (i) at least one parent has been ordinarily resident in Germany for eight years and (ii) if at least one parent has been granted permanent right of residence. Citizenship provides unrestricted access to the host country labor market, and evidence from many countries shows that immigrants who become citizens in their adopted countries earn more than those who do not.

Economist Ciro Avitabile and colleagues examined the effect of this change on the fertility and investments in children in immigrant families. They interpreted the reform as a decrease in the price of child quality. Because these children now have better economic opportunities, the parents can achieve any desired level of child quality with fewer resources; they no longer have to compensate for the disadvantage of noncitizenship. At this lower price, parents might be more willing to invest in child quality. This decrease in the price of child quality will likely also have a negative indirect effect on the number of children, since the price of quality has fallen relative to quantity, fertility will fall.

To test this they used a DID research design of the sort we discussed in Chapter 2. The treatment group consisted of children in immigrant families where at least one parent had lived in Germany for eight or more years; this is the group whose children benefitted from the reform. As a control group they used immigrant families where one parent was a German citizen at the time of the birth, since these children were granted citizenship prior to the reform and thus were unaffected by the reform. By comparing the outcomes of the treatment group and the control group before and after the reform, they could measure the effect of the change in the law on the child quantity and quality choices made by immigrant parents.

They found that after the reform, fertility in the group which gained citizenship rights for their children fell by 1 percent (or about 12 percent of the mean fertility level), while fertility in the control group was essentially unchanged. To determine the impact on child quality, the authors examined several potential measures of child well-being. They used obesity (as a crude proxy for a child's health) and measures of socio-emotional development, as well as a measure of general child well-being; none of these alone is a perfect indicator of child quality, but each probably captures some dimension of child quality. Indeed, they found that children born to the immigrant group that gained from the reform were less likely to be obese and their socio-emotional outcomes improved, as did their overall well-being. Thus it appears that the German citizenship reform affected both fertility and child quality in ways consistent with the economic approach to fertility: it reduced quantity and increased quality.

Source: Ciro Avitabile, Irma Clots-Figueras, and Paolo Masella (2014), "Citizenship, Fertility, and Parental Investments," *American Economic Journal: Applied Economics*, 6 (4), 35–65.

Other explanations for the decline in fertility

Men's wages What about changes in men's wages during the twentieth century? Men's wages probably affected fertility quite differently than women's wages did. Since men's time was historically not a large input into the production of child services, increases in men's earnings would primarily affect full income and would have only a small effect on the price of child services. The average earnings for men rose by about one-third between 1900 and 1920 and then nearly doubled by 1950. They grew by about 50 percent during the boom years of the 1960s. Since then, men's wages have stagnated. After adjusting for inflation, median men's earnings of YRFT workers are actually about $1,000 lower than in the mid-1970s. Still, over the course of the twentieth century they have increased enormously.

Taken by itself, the change in men's earnings would increase a family's full income and actually increase, not decrease, both the quality and quantity of children. Thus it does not provide a very good explanation for the general trend of declining fertility.

Improved contraception The development of modern means of contraception, especially the birth-control pill, is clearly an important factor. One way to think of its impact is that it lowered the cost of controlling fertility. It made it much easier for families to adjust actual fertility to desired fertility and for women to control the timing of their fertility. Improved contraception has had so many effects on women's lives across multiple dimensions that we discuss it in depth in Chapter 6.

Rising women's labor-force participation It is tempting to explain the decline in fertility as the flip side of the rise in married women's labor-force participation. It's certainly true enough that the trends are related in time. But is the relationship causal? Did rising participation *cause* the fall in fertility? That seems quite unlikely. Both fertility and labor-force participation are choice variables. Because of that, participation could cause fertility only if women first made decisions about labor-force participation and then made fertility decisions, taking as given (i.e., exogenous) the participation decision. That's not impossible, but it doesn't seem particularly sensible. It is far more likely that women jointly and simultaneously make interdependent decisions about work and children, and perhaps marriage, as well, on the basis of truly exogenous variables, such as wage rates and preferences.

Changing preferences for children It is always possible that adult preferences have changed to favor adult goods relative to child services, and that that accounts for the decline in fertility. Economists typically don't give preference-based explanations very much credit because they are very hard to establish or to refute. As a matter of good research protocol it is almost always better to focus on measurable factors, where scientific standards of proof and falsification can be more rigorously applied.

Summary

Very few economists would argue that decisions about children are solely a function of incomes and prices. But we have seen that economic analysis provides an interesting window through which to view fertility decisions. The ideas that families derive utility from children, that children have both a quantity and a quality dimension, and that children are household-produced goods with real costs of production are all genuine and important insights and great examples of how economic thinking can be highly creative.

The economic theory of fertility began with the puzzle of declining fertility in conjunction with rising incomes. Why, unlike most goods, did fertility fall as income rose? Could children really be "inferior goods" that adults wanted less of as their incomes rose? The answer, of course, is "no." The key parts of the answer are the distinction between the quality and quantity of children, and the inextricable link between rising incomes and the rising price of human time. Families have gotten richer but, at the same time, children have gotten more expensive. In response, families have reduced fertility but increased spending per child. The total demand for child services has likely increased, but fertility has fallen.

In this chapter we have focused on developing a broad view of fertility, and especially the economic explanation for declining fertility. In the next chapter we extend the discussion of fertility to focus on related issues, including non-marital and teen fertility, the broad effects of contraception on women's lives, pro-fertility policies, and a potpourri of recent research findings.

Appendix: fertility and the interaction of quality and quantity

The prices of child quality and child quantity are related in an unusual way. In most situations the price of one good doesn't depend on the amount you consumer of some second but, in this case, quantity affects the price of quality and quality affects the price of quantity. This provides another reason why fertility has fallen.

Here is an example that illustrates the nature of a quality–quantity interaction in the context of building a brick patio, where you must choose both the size of the patio and the quality of the bricks you will use. Let A stand for the size of the patio (its quantity) and let Q stand for the quality of the bricks. To be specific, suppose there are medium-quality bricks that cost $1 per brick and higher-quality bricks that cost $2 per brick. The bricks are identical in size but differ in some other way. To make the arithmetic easier, suppose further that a patio of A square feet requires A bricks, so a 100 square foot patio requires 100 bricks. It follows that the cost of building a patio of A square feet is A with the medium-quality bricks and $2A$ with the better bricks. The cost of improving the brick quality—upgrading from medium to high quality—is $2A - $A = A. This is a quality-quantity interaction—the cost of improving patio brick quality depends on the patio quantity (A). If A were small, the cost of increasing quality is small. The larger A is, the greater the cost of increasing the quality is.

The same thing is true for increasing the size of the patio. Suppose you were considering doubling the size of the patio, from A to $2A$. If you were using the medium-quality bricks, this would cost $2A - $A = A. But if you were using the higher-quality bricks, it would cost $4A - $2A = $2A$. Now the cost of increasing patio quantity depends on patio quality.

The same interaction occurs between the quality and quantity of child services, as long as parents provide the same quality of child services to all their children. Here, the cost of increasing child quality is larger if family size is greater, because the family must provide this improved quality to all their children. As a specific example, think about how the cost of a longer beach vacation or private school education or new bike varies with the number of children. The cost is greater when there are more children to feed at the beach, more tuitions to pay, or more bikes to buy. So the price of quality depends on quantity.

The same thing is true for an increase in quantity. Suppose parents have chosen a level of child quality—that is, the time and material resources they will provide to their children. If that level of quality is low, then the cost of having another child—who will get that same level of quality—is relatively low. But if that level of quality is higher, then the cost of having another child is higher because it entails a larger resource expenditure.

We can summarize these two interactions this way:

$$\Delta P_L / \Delta N > 0 \tag{5.7}$$

and

$$\Delta P_N / \Delta L > 0 \tag{5.8}$$

Equation (5.7) says that the price of child quality (P_L) and the amount of child quantity (N) move together. The price of quality goes up when quantity goes up and goes down when quantity goes down. Equation (5.8) expresses exactly the same positive relationship between the price of quantity (P_N) and the amount of quality (L).

This quality–quantity interaction adds another possible way in which a change in the wage rate could cause quality to increase and quantity to fall. We have already argued that an increase in the wage might decrease quantity and increase quality. The decrease in quantity would, in turn, decrease the price of child quality, as shown in equation (5.7), which would cause a further increase in the amount of child quality. Simultaneously, the increase in child quality would increase the price of child quantity, as in equation (5.7). This would cause a further decline in the amount of child quantity.

An increase in family income may also start a chain of events leading to lower fertility. Suppose, as we have already argued, a change in income increases child quality more than quantity. Normally this would be the end of the story, but in this case the new choices cause price changes. The higher quality increases the price of quantity relative to the price of quality. This, in turn, would cause families to choose slightly smaller families with higher quality, which would cause families to choose yet slightly smaller families with higher quality, and so on.

6 THE ECONOMICS OF FERTILITY: APPLICATIONS AND EXTENSIONS

Introduction

In this chapter we examine a set of topics in the economics of fertility. First we examine the other major contemporary development in fertility—the rise in non-marital fertility—and a closely related issue, teen fertility. Then we examine the broad impact of contraception on women's adult economic lives, focusing on the introduction of the oral contraceptive, known popularly as "the pill." Lastly we look briefly at several new research topics in fertility, including gender preference, fertility timing, and ultra-low fertility.

Non-marital and teen fertility: facts and trends

Non-marital fertility

Non-marital fertility is measured by two related terms. The **NMFR** is just like the fertility rate we discussed in Chapter 5, except, obviously, it applies only to single women. It is the number of births to single women divided by the number of single women, aged 15–44, usually expressed as the number of births per 1,000. Some 50 years ago it was common to refer to these births as "illegitimate births." Now these births are usually called by the more neutral descriptive terms, "non-marital births" and "out-of-wedlock births."

The **non-marital birth ratio (NMBR)** is the proportion of all births that are non-marital—that is, the number of births to single women divided by the total number of births. Note that this measure is a ratio rather than a rate. Its denominator is not the number of women at risk of a non-marital birth but rather the total number of births. The NMBR is a tricky measure to interpret because it depends on three separate demographic rates: the **marital fertility rate (MFR)**, the NMFR, and the proportion of women who are married. Changes in any one of these factors will affect the NMBR. The NMBR could go up, even if the non-marital birth rate fell, as long as the marital birth rate fell even more or if the proportion of women who are married fell. See Box 6.1 for more about how the three underlying demographic factors are related and how they contributed to the change in the NMBR in the United States

Box   6.1

"What If?" Analysis and the Non-Marital Birth Ratio

As we noted above, the NMBR depends on three separate factors: the NMFR, the MFR, and the proportion of women who are married. With the benefit of a little bit of algebra, we can use that to compute a quantitative estimate of the importance of each underlying factor in determining the change in the NMBR. This kind of "What If?" analysis is widely used.

To see how the three terms are related, we can expand the NMBR formula as follows. In each term, the population is women aged 15–44.

$$\text{NMBR} = \frac{\#\text{ Births, Single Women}}{\#\text{ Births}} = \frac{\#\text{ Births, Single Women}}{\#\text{ Single Women}}$$
$$\times \frac{\#\text{ Single Women}}{\#\text{ Women}} \times \frac{\#\text{ Women}}{\#\text{ Births}} \tag{6.1}$$

The first term after the second equals sign is the NMFR the second term is the proportion of women who are single, and the third term in the inverse of the fertility rate for all women. (You should be able to see that the additional terms cancel out, so this is a legitimate expansion of the formula for the NMBR.) The last term in the equation is itself a weighted average of the MFR and NMFR, where the weights are the proportions single and married. Using that and simplifying, the formula for the NMBR becomes much simpler:

$$\text{NMBR} = \frac{s \times \text{NMFR}}{s \times \text{NMFR} + (1-s) \times \text{MFR}} \tag{6.2}$$

where s is the proportion of women age 15–44 who are single. Note that the denominator is just a weighted average of the NMFR and MFR, where the weights are the fractions single (s) and married ($1 - s$).

Let's confirm that this formula holds using 2013 data for the United States. 40.6 percent of all births were to single women. The fertility rate for unmarried women was 44.3 births per 1,000 women, the MFR was 86.9 births per 1,000 women and 57.3 percent of women aged 15 to 44 were single. Plugging these figures into the formula, we have NMBR = (0.573 × 44.3)/[(0.573 × 44.3) + (1−0.573) × 86.9] = 0.406 = 40.6 percent. So the formula works.

This formula is very useful for answering what if? questions, such as: What would the NMBR be today if the proportion of women who are single or the NMFR hadn't changed? For example, between 1970 and 2013, the NMBR increased from 10.7 to 40.6 percent. Over the same time period, the proportion of single women aged 15–44 increased from 35.6 to 57.3 percent, the MFR fell from 121.9 to 86.9, and the NMFR increased from 26.4 to 44.3. So what was the separate impact of each change on the change in the NMBR? To answer questions like that, we can use the formula in equation (6.2) to compute a new predicted NMBR for 2013 by substituting in a value for one term from an earlier time period. That isolates the impact of that factor. This kind of exercise is called a simulation or a counterfactual analysis.

First, suppose the NMFR had remained at its 1970 level but everything else changed exactly as it did between 1970 and 2013. To compute what the NMBR would have been, use the formula for the NMBR from above but substitute the 1970 NMFR (in bold) for the 2013 rate: NMBR^1_{2013} = $(0.573 \times \textbf{26.4})/[(0.573 \times \textbf{26.4}) + (1-0.573) \times 86.9)]$ = 0.289 = 28.9 percent. This tells us that instead of increasing by 29.9 percent to 40.6 percent, the NMBR would have increased by 18.2 percent (28.9−10.7 percent) if the NMFR hadn't changed. Thus the rest of the increase in the NMBR—11.7 percent from 28.9 to 40.6 percent—must have been due to the increase in the NMFR.

Suppose instead that the proportion of women who were single in 2013 had remained at the 1970 value, but the MFR and NMFR had their actual 2013 values. Substitute the new value for "s" (in bold) into the formula: NMBR^2_{2013} = $[(\textbf{0.356} \times 44.3)/[(\textbf{0.356} \times 44.3) + (1-\textbf{0.356}) \times 86.9)]$ = 0.220 = 22.0 percent. This means that if the proportion single hadn't changed, the NMBR would have increased by only 11.3 percent (22.0 − 10.7). The actual change in the proportion single from 35.6 to 57.0 percent is responsible for the remainder of the increase in the NMBR. In this case that is 18.6 percent, which is the difference between the actual 40.6 percent NMBR in 2013 and the 22.0 percent rate if the proportion single hadn't changed.

Finally, suppose the MFR had remained at its 1970 level but everything else changed as it actually did. Again use the formula, this time substituting the 1970 MFR (in bold) for the 2013 rate: NMBR^3_{2013} = $(0.573 \times 44.3)/[(0.573 \times 44.3) + (1-0.573) \times \textbf{121.9})]$ = 0.327 = 32.7 percent. In this case the NMBR would have increased by 22 percent. Thus the decrease in marital fertility from 121.9 to 86.9 is responsible for 40.6 − 32.7 = 7.9 points of the increase in the NMBR.

Comparing the results of the three simulations suggests that the biggest factor in increasing the NMBR between 1970 and 2013 was the increase in the proportion of women who were single. This makes sense because the change is very large and it appears in the formula in two places. The next biggest factor was the increase in the NMFR.[1]

The analysis above is a simple example of how this technique works. It can be used in many contexts—and you will see a few others in this textbook.

It is easy to confuse these two measures. The numerator in both cases is the number of non-marital births, but the denominators differ—the number of single women for the NMFR and the total number of births for the NMBR. Remembering that rates have the at-risk group in the denominator should help.

---

[1] This version of "what if" analysis does not provide an exact accounting for the total change in the NMBR. If you note carefully, the estimates of the quantitative impact of each factor add up to more than the total change in the NMBR. The relative sizes of the quantitative impacts are valid, so it is possible to assess the relative importance of each factor.

The link between marriage and fertility in the United States has weakened, to say the least. In 2014, the last year with full information, more than 40 percent of all births were to single women. The NMFR was 44.0 births per 1,000 single women aged 15–44. By comparison, the marital birth rate was 86.9 births per 1,000 married women.

Figure 6.1 shows the historical trend of both measures since 1940. The solid line shows the NMFR and is measured on the left vertical axis; the dotted line is the NMBR and is measured on the right vertical axis. The most obvious point in the figure is that both measures of non-marital fertility have increased enormously, and, for the most part, they have moved together. In 1940 there were just 7 births per 1,000 single women between the ages of 15 and 44 and less than 4 percent of births were non-marital. But the NMFR increased every year from 1940 through 1970, more than tripling in the process. At first the high MFR of the baby boom and the high early marriage rate kept the NMBR from increasing as fast as the NMFR. But both rates rose steadily and sharply from the mid-1970s through the mid-1990s; the NMFR doubled over these years and the NMBR almost tripled, now aided by the declining MFR. From then through the early 2000s, the NMFR leveled out at about 43 to 45 births per 1,000 single women, and the NMBR was nearly constant at about one-third. But from 2002 through 2008, both rates rose again. The NMFR peaked at 51.8 births per 1,000 single women, and the NMBR passed 40 percent. Since then the NMFR has fallen six years in a row to 44.0 births per 1,000 and the NMBR has stabilized at just over 40 percent.

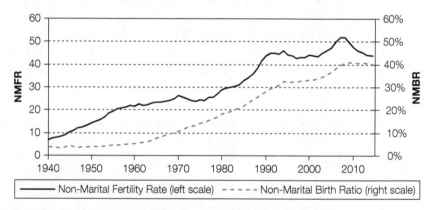

Figure 6.1 *The rise of non-marital fertility in the United States, 1940–2014.*

Source: National Vital Statistics Reports (2015), 64 (1) and 64 (6).

We saw in the last chapter that differences in overall fertility were relatively small across race and ethnic groups in the United States, except for Hispanics, who had a higher fertility rate. But differences in non-marital fertility by race and ethnicity are quite large. This is shown in Table 6.1 for 2013.[2]

---

2 Fertility rates and the NMBR by race and ethnicity for 2014 were not yet available as of mid-2015, although overall rates were.

Table 6.1 *Non-marital fertility by race and ethnicity, United States, 2013.*

Race or Ethnic Group	NMFR (Births/1,000 Single Women)	NMBR (%)
All	44.3	40.6
White	40.8	35.9
Black	61.7	71.6
American Indian or Alaska Native	–	66.4
Asian or Pacific Islander	21.8	17.0
Hispanic	69.9	53.3

Source: National Vital Statistics Reports, Vol. 64 (1), Tables 6 and 15.

The NMFR for black women is about 50 percent higher than the rate for whites, and the rate for Hispanic women, who may be of any race, is higher yet. This difference between white and black women has been narrowing in recent years. The NMFR for black women has fallen by 25 percent from over 90 births per 1,000 single women in 1990, while the rate for whites has increased slowly but steadily. As the last column shows, the NMBRs differ as well. About 36 percent of births to white women in 2013 were non-marital, compared to over 70 percent for black women. The NMBR has been increasing for white women and has held quite steady for black women. For Hispanics the pattern is different yet. The NMFR was stable in the 1990s but has increased sharply since 2002. The NMBR followed a similar pattern, stable and then rising. As seen in the table, Hispanics have a very high NMFR, but a relatively low proportion of births that are non-marital, partly because of their higher MFR. Asian or Pacific Island women have a conspicuously low NMFR and NMBR.

Finally, the rise in non-marital fertility is an international phenomenon. The United States has far from the highest proportion of non-marital births. In 2011, 40 percent of births in the EU countries were non-marital, a figure almost exactly the same as the US proportion. Iceland has the highest proportion at 65 percent, and seven other countries, including Belgium, Denmark, France, Norway, and Sweden, are all above 50 percent. The United Kingdom and the Netherlands are just below 50 percent, with Portugal not far behind. In some of these countries, long-term cohabitation is a substitute for marriage and is responsible for a substantial part of the high ratio. This is true for France and the Scandinavian countries. Greece, at 8 percent, has the lowest NMFR in Europe; it is the only country with a NMFR less than 10 percent. Even in Spain and Italy, which had relatively low rates in the early 2000s and before, 30–35 percent of births are to unmarried women. The time trend in most of these countries with a high NMBR is similar to that in the United States. In France, for example, the ratio has quadrupled since 1970, while in the Scandinavian countries it has doubled or tripled from a higher initial level.

Japan and South Korea are two other developed countries with very low NMBRs. In both countries the proportion of births that are non-marital birth is well under 5 percent.

Teen fertility

In 1960, teen fertility in the United States was quite high. The teen fertility rate in that year was 89/1,000, which means that almost 9 percent of all young women aged 15–19 had a birth. But the NMBR was quite low; 85 percent of the births were to married women. This makes sense given what we already know. Early marriage was the norm—one third of women were already married by age 20—and women's post-secondary educational attainment was low.

Since then, teen fertility has, except for a few short time periods, declined more or less steadily, but its connection to marriage has all but disappeared. In 2014 the teen fertility rate was 24.2 births per 1,000 women, aged 15–19, less than a third of the 1960 rate and the lowest rate ever recorded in the United States. But only about one teen birth in 10 is to a married woman. Unlike non-marital fertility in general, where both the NMFR and the NMBR have moved upward together, here the two trends go in opposite directions.

The recent decline in the teen fertility rate has been extraordinary. Since 1990 the teen fertility rate has fallen in all but two years and for all racial and ethnic subgroups; since its recent peak in 2007, it has fallen by more than one-third. We discuss the possible explanations for this recent trend later in this chapter. The NMBR has continued to increase at about the same rate.

Despite the decline, teen fertility in the United States remains a matter of substantial concern. First, even with the decline, the US teen fertility rate is still far higher than in comparable countries. Figure 6.2 shows the comparison as of the early 2010s for selected countries in Western Europe and Asia. In Western Europe the teen fertility rate was typically less than 10 births per 1,000 teen girls and in Switzerland, Denmark, and the Netherlands it was less than five per 1,000, just one-fifth of the US rate. In China and Japan the rate was also less than 5 per 1,000. Canada, Australia, and the United Kingdom are closest to the United States in teen fertility, with rates about one-third to one-quarter lower than in the United States. No other developed country has a teen fertility rate as high as that of the United States.

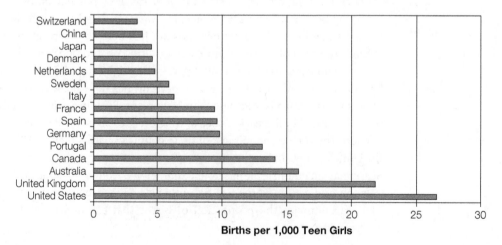

Figure 6.2 *How teen fertility varies: United States and selected other developed countries, 2012.*

Source: Data from *United Nations Demographic Yearbook*, 2012, Table 9.

Second, on average, teen mothers do poorly on a wide range of outcomes, educational attainment, family income, poverty, and welfare usage. Whether teen births are the cause of the problems of teen mothers or just a marker of disadvantage is a more complicated research question; see below for a discussion. But it has, nevertheless, made teen childbearing a focus of public policy. President Clinton called it "our most serious social problem" in his 1995 State of the Union address. At that time the teen fertility rate was about twice as high as now.

Third, the proportion of young women who ever have a teen pregnancy remains very high. About half of teen pregnancies result in births, one-third end in abortion, and one-sixth in a miscarriage. So, for example, even a teen fertility rate of 35 per 1,000 means that about 7 percent of teen girls become pregnant in a year and about one-third ever have a pregnancy over their teen years. The one-third figure reflects the obvious arithmetic that a girl spends five years at ages 15–19, so the cumulative teen pregnancy rate is five times the annual rate, adjusted slightly downward to account for the fact that some girls may have repeat pregnancies. At the 2013 rate of 26.5 births per 1,000 teen girls, about 20–25 percent of teen girls will ever have a teen pregnancy.

Teen fertility in the United States does vary considerably along racial and ethnic lines, although the differences are smaller than the differences for all women. Table 6.2 summarizes the key teen fertility statistics in 2013. The fertility rate for black teens and Hispanic teens is about 50 percent higher than the rate for white teens—39.1/1,000 and 41.7/1,000 vs 24.9/1,000. The rate for Asian or Pacific Islanders is about one-third the rate of whites. The NMBR is uniformly high for teen births across all race and ethnic groups, ranging from a low of about 80 percent for Asian or Pacific Islanders to more than 97 percent for black teen mothers.

Table 6.2 *Teen fertility in the United States by race and ethnicity, 2013.*

Race or Ethnic Group	Fertility Rate	NMBR
All	26.5	88.7
White	24.9	85.8
Black	39.1	97.2
American Indian or Alaska Native	31.1	92.4
Asian or Pacific Islander	8.7	79.7
Hispanic	41.7	87.5

Source: National Vital Statistics Reports, Vol. 64, No. 1, Tables 3, 7, and 15.

The socioeconomic consequences of teen childbearing

On average, teen mothers have far poorer socioeconomic outcomes than women who have a later first birth. They are less likely to be high-school graduates and also have lower family incomes and higher poverty rates. But the poor outcomes alone do not scientifically establish that the teen birth is the cause. The underlying research problem is one that we discussed back in Chapter 2 and keep coming back to—the effect of omitted variables when a random assignment experiment is infeasible, as it certainly is in this case. It is always possible that some critical variable—perhaps family, school, or neighborhood characteristics—is unmeasured and is the cause both of a teen birth *and* of the poorer outcomes for teen mothers. Young women differ from one another in so many ways that it is impractical, if not impossible, to measure them all in representative national surveys.

As always, whether an effect is causal or just a correlation is important for the design of appropriate public policy. If it is causal then a policy that helps delay a first birth can lead to better outcomes for women and children. If it is a correlation, then a delay won't improve outcomes and therefore other interventions, perhaps in schooling or other areas, might be more effective.

To measure the causal impact of a teen birth, researchers have attempted to identify better "natural" comparison groups where omitted variable issues are likely to be less important. One approach compared outcomes for sisters, one of whom had a teen birth while the other did not.[3] Because sisters share many family and neighborhood characteristics that are hard to measure, the difference in outcomes between the sisters ought to be due largely to the difference in their age at first birth. This isn't a perfect comparison, of course, because even sisters differ from one another in ways that might be important.

Another approach compared teen mothers to teens who had a pregnancy but had a miscarriage instead and, thus, had a delay in their age at their first birth.[4] Because most miscarriages are random, those who had a birth and those who had a miscarriage ought to be quite similar in other ways, so the difference in outcomes may, again, be due largely to the difference in their age at first birth. This is quite close to a natural experiment, courtesy of Mother Nature.

These studies do suggest that otherwise unmeasured factors are important and that the generally poor outcomes for teen mothers are due, at least in part, to factors other than their age at first birth. In the studies of sisters, the estimated effects of a teen birth were still negative, but they were not as negative as in earlier studies that used standard regression methods to control for measured family background. For example, the average difference in economic well-being between a teen mother and her (non-teen mother) sister was about one-third, compared to about 40–50 percent in earlier, more traditional studies. There were also reasonably big differences between the sisters in the probability of being poor, receiving welfare, and educational attainment, all to the detriment of the sister who had the teen birth.

The teen birth/miscarriage study provided even stronger and more controversial evidence. This study looked at births and miscarriages to teens aged 17 or younger rather than aged 19 or younger, as in the usual definition of a teen birth, and followed the two groups of women through their early thirties. This allowed the researchers to distinguish between short-term and longer-term impacts, which is an important difference not fully considered in previous research. The researchers found that by their mid-to-late twenties, the teen mothers actually did better over a wide range of outcomes than those who had

---

3 Arline Geronimus and Sanders Korenman (1992), "The Socioeconomic Consequences of Teen Childbearing Reconsidered," *Quarterly Journal of Economics*, 107 (4), 1187–1214; Saul D. Hoffman, E. Michael Foster, and Frank F. Furstenberg, Jr., (1993), "Re-evaluating the Costs of Teenage Childbearing," *Demography*, 30 (1), 1–13.

4 V. J. Hotz, S. W. McElroy, and S. G. Sanders (1997), "The Impacts of Teenage Childbearing on the Mothers and the Consequences of Those Impacts for Government," in R. Maynard (ed.), *Kids Having Kids*, Washington, DC: The Urban Institute Press.

a miscarriage. For example, the teen mothers worked more regularly and earned more than their counterparts and their spouses had higher incomes. Differences in educational attainment (including receiving a GED) and income from welfare between the two groups were very small. So this study suggests that other factors are the primary cause of the poorer outcomes for teen mothers.

Even though this study is careful and thoughtful, it has some weaknesses. First, it is very difficult to obtain reliable information on teen miscarriages from survey data. Some young women might have an understandable incentive to conceal an early pregnancy that did not result in a birth. In fact, miscarriages were substantially underreported in the data they used. Because of this underreporting, the comparison group of teens with miscarriages is very small and potentially unrepresentative. Suppose, for example, that misreporting is highest among young women who viewed their early pregnancy as an unfortunate error and who went on to do relatively well. The sample of women who *reported* a teen miscarriage would be more disadvantaged than the population of women who *had* a teen miscarriage. This would bias the analysis toward finding no effect of a teen birth.

It is also important to understand that this study reflects the experience of teens who had births in the 1970s and that the economic environment then was very different. The labor market was far better for less-educated workers and the welfare system was more generous. Impacts of a teen birth today could well be much more negative. A newer study found that the outcomes were more negative for teens who had their births in the 1980s than in the 1970s, although the impacts are still far less negative than in the older studies.[5]

In an attempt to reconcile some of this evidence, a group of demographers and sociologists[6] used a variety of sophisticated statistical techniques to estimate the causal effect of a teen birth on educational attainment. Their goal was to assess whether differences in method or differences in data or time period were the cause of the wide range of estimates of the effect of a teen birth on educational attainment. The techniques are related to the ones discussed above, but the details are beyond the scope of this book. They find a fairly wide range of estimates, which they interpret as evidence that the different results in the literature largely reflect differences in method and that omitted variables are important. Using their preferred method, they estimate that a teen birth reduces completed education by 0.7 years. This is a relatively large impact.

In a famous and oft-quoted 1968 article, Arthur Campbell wrote that "The girl who has an illegitimate child at the age of 16 suddenly has 90 percent of her life's script written for her."[7] Although the nature of the script wasn't indicated in the quote, it was meant to suggest the inevitability of a tough life of poverty and material deprivation. We know now that this is far too strong a statement. The new research quite appropriately recognizes and focuses attention on the important contribution of other factors, especially

---

5 Saul D. Hoffman (2008), "Updated Estimates of the Consequences of Teenage Childbearing for Mothers," in Saul D. Hoffman and Rebecca A. Maynard (eds.), *Kids Having Kids: Economic Costs and Social Consequences of Teen Pregnancy*, Second Edition, Washington, DC: The Urban Institute Press.

6 J. B. Kane, Philip S. Morgan, K. M. Harris, and D. K. Guilkey (2013), "The Educational Consequences of Teen Childbearing," *Demography*, 50 (6), 2129–2150.

7 Arthur A. Campbell (1968), "The Role of Family Planning in the Reduction of Poverty," *Journal of Marriage and the Family*, 30 (2), 236–245.

difficult-to-measure family and individual characteristics, to the poor average outcomes of teen mothers. But, at the same time, there is no compelling evidence that the causal effects of a teen birth are zero or even just marginally negative.

Non-marital and teen fertility: economic explanations

Now we turn to the difficult task of trying to explain the economic causes of non-marital and teen fertility. Clearly this is a complex and multi-faceted issue and economic factors are likely to be only part of the story. It is also important to understand that teen and non-marital fertility are not quite the same thing, although they share some common features. For both teens and non-teens, the fraction of births that are non-marital has increased sharply. But while non-marital fertility has been generally increasing, teen fertility has been generally decreasing, especially since 2007.

We present below a general economic analysis of non-marital fertility that incorporates a variety of possible causes. One approach emphasizes the costs and benefits of non-marital fertility and how that might vary across women. Another focuses on the introduction of contraception and the legalization of abortion, and how that might have affected the social norm about the responsibility of single men to an unplanned pregnancy of their partner. Finally, we focus on the recent decline in teen pregnancy and teen births, examining the possible role of contraceptive use, sexual activity, and the media.

Rational choice and the opportunity cost hypothesis

Economists analyzing non-marital fertility usually begin with a rational choice approach. We have seen this idea previously applied to marriage. In this case it means that a woman compares the future she might have if she has a non-marital birth with the future she might have if she does not. She then chooses the one that provides greater utility. The utility of each alternative includes all that goes along with it over her lifetime, including the impacts of a non-marital birth on education, work, income, and marriage, as well as, of course, from the child. Obviously the future is uncertain, so this involves making best "guesstimates" of what lies ahead.

When applied to non-marital births, this approach is often called the **opportunity cost hypothesis** because it emphasizes what is given up when one fertility choice rather than the other is made. Within this framework, anything that affects the opportunity cost of having a non-marital birth is logically a potential explanation. If a woman has good alternatives to a non-marital birth, including some combination of education, work, marriage, and a later marital birth, then her opportunity cost of a non-marital birth is likely to be high. With much to lose by having a birth, she might well act in ways that reduce the risk of a birth. Suppose, instead, that she has poor alternatives to having a non-marital birth. Perhaps marriage is not a realistic option or one that makes little economic sense, and even avoiding a non-marital birth will not improve her life options considerably. Then her opportunity cost of a non-marital birth is lower and a birth is more likely. A birth can, of course, also be a direct source of utility, exactly the same as in the model of fertility we presented in Chapter 5. It may also provide a young woman with a sense of accomplishment and an adult identity as a parent.

The same rational choice logic can be applied to the time trend in non-marital births. Since women now are more likely than in the past to have a non-marital birth, it follows that the opportunity costs of having such a birth have likely fallen.

Empirical research about the causes of non-marital births has attempted to identify and quantify the importance of factors that affect these opportunity costs. Economists have typically emphasized the incomes that a woman might typically have with and without a non-marital birth, because income is an important determinant of overall well-being. In practice, this research has focused on two specific kinds of incomes. The first is income from the welfare system, which provides income support to low-income single parents. Many women with non-marital births, especially teen mothers, do end up on welfare. Importantly, these women are likely to be ineligible for welfare if they marry the father of their child. The more generous the welfare system is, the more attractive will be having a non-marital birth because the opportunity costs will be lower. This argument, which is usually associated with more conservative politicians and economists, was prominently made by Charles Murray in his book *Losing Ground.*

The other is income from marriage, including the earnings of a spouse. It is typically true that having a non-marital birth reduces the future probability of marriage, so marital income will likely be higher without a non-marital birth than with one. The worse are a woman's future marriage prospects without a birth, the smaller are her opportunity costs and the more likely she is to have a birth. We saw this idea earlier in Chapter 4 in the work of William Wilson, who emphasized the shortage of marriageable men as an explanation for the lower marriage rates of black women.

Testing the opportunity cost model Let's look first at two simple ways to test for the effect of welfare benefits on teen and non-marital births in the United States. The first is a cross-sectional (i.e., single-year) comparison of NMFRs by state. Because some states have higher benefits than others, then, all else being equal, single mothers will typically have a higher income and be better off in those states than in the lower-benefit states. Thus if the welfare system is an important influence, non-marital fertility ought to be higher in high-benefit states than in low-benefit states. The same should be true for teen births, since most of these are non-marital births.

The simple evidence on this is shown in Figures 6.3 and 6.4. The scattergram in Figure 6.3 shows each state's TANF benefits for a family of three on the horizontal axis and the percentage of births that are non-marital on the vertical axis. Both benefits and the NMBR vary widely across the states. The straight line through the points is the regression line, which shows the best relationship between the causal variable (TANF benefits) and the dependent variable (NMBR). As you can see, the relationship in 2012 was actually slightly negative, not positive as we would expect if the opportunity cost argument holds.[8] Mississippi, Arkansas, and Texas are examples of states with low welfare benefits and high non-marital fertility, while Minnesota, New Hampshire, Vermont, and Wisconsin are states with high benefits and low non-marital fertility. On average a $100 increase in a state's monthly TANF benefits is associated with a 1.5 percent decline in its NMBR.

---

8 This is true for previous years as well.

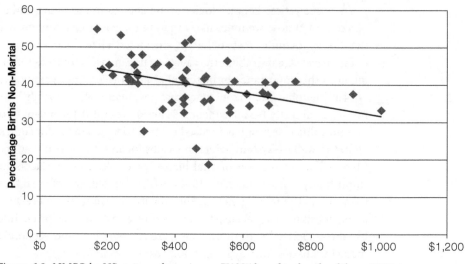

Figure 6.3 *NMBR by US state and maximum TANF benefits, family of three, 2012.*

The relationship is even more negative for a state's teen fertility rate (see Figure 6.4). The states with the highest teen fertility rates are among those with the lowest welfare benefits and vice versa. For teens, a $100 increase in monthly benefits is associated, on average, with a teen fertility rate that is 3.6 points lower. In both figures you can see that there is a great deal of unexplained variation in non-marital fertility as measured by the distance of the points from the regression line. This suggests that other factors may also be important.

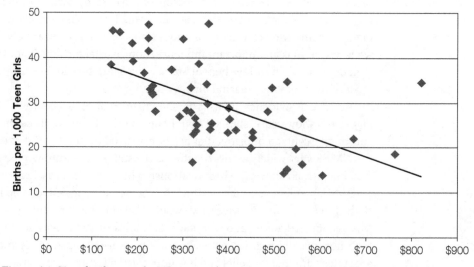

Figure 6.4 *Teen fertility rate by US state and maximum TANF benefits, family of two, 2012.*

The second approach is a time-series comparison. After adjusting for inflation, a family on welfare in the 2000s and 2010s was eligible to receive *lower* benefits than the same family would have received in 1970. The real value of median welfare benefits—their purchasing power—fell by about 45 percent over this time period because most states did not raise their welfare benefits to keep up with inflation. Even adding in the value of food stamps and Medicaid, which have increased in value since 1970, total benefits have fallen about 20 percent. If high welfare benefits are an important cause of teen births, teen NMFRs should have fallen over time. But, in fact, non-marital fertility rose, rather than fell, through most of this time period.

Welfare benefits are just one part of the calculation of opportunity costs, so these simple comparisons, while useful, are incomplete. A fuller analysis would include for each woman not only the welfare benefits she would receive if she had a non-marital birth but also her likely income if she didn't. Measuring what would happen to a woman if she had not had a birth is a challenge, but the general idea is to estimate a likely outcome based on actual outcomes for women who are similar in background and did not have a birth. One of the first and still most thorough studies to do this was by Duncan and Hoffman, who examined births among black teens in the mid-1970s and early 1980s.[9] They tested the opportunity cost hypothesis by comparing the welfare income and the predicted income each woman might likely have if she didn't have a birth.[10]

They found some limited support for the opportunity cost hypothesis. Teens with better non-birth opportunities were more likely to delay their first birth beyond their teen years. Higher welfare benefits were associated with higher rates of teen fertility, but the effect was not statistically significant from zero, which means that the estimate was not very reliable. Neither impact was terribly large, however. For example, they found that a 25 percent increase in AFDC benefit levels would increase the proportion with a teen birth by about 5 percent, while a 25 percent increase in income without a birth would decrease that proportion by about 9 percent. As in much of the research literature in this area, the economic incentives are genuine and statistically significant, but relatively modest in size. Other influences clearly matter a great deal.

Income inequality Research by economists Melissa Kearney and Philip Levine suggests that income inequality may also play an important role.[11] Rising income inequality is one of the most significant labor-market developments of the past few decades. The teen fertility rate varies substantially across US states, with the rate in some states (New Hampshire, Massachusetts, and Connecticut) just about one-quarter that in others (Mississippi, Oklahoma, and New Mexico). Kearney and Levine show that teen fertility rates are higher in states with more inequality; there is a strong positive relationship between a state's rate and its Gini Coefficient, which is an overall measure of income inequality. As we have said many times, correlation does not imply causality.

Kearney and Levine offer an explanation that is a variant of the opportunity cost model. They hypothesize that more extreme inequality creates greater feelings of economic hopelessness, leading young women to view opportunity costs as very low.

9   Greg J. Duncan and Saul D. Hoffman (1990), "Economic Opportunities, Welfare Benefits, and Out-of-Wedlock Births Among Black Teenage Girls," *Demography*, 27, 519–535.

10 In predicting those incomes, they adjusted statistically for selectivity bias, which means that the two groups of women might differ in terms of traits and characteristics that could not be measured.

11 Melissa S. Kearney and Phillip Levine (2014), "Income Inequality and Early Non-Marital Childbearing," *Journal of Human Resources*, 49 (1), 1–31.

When the distance to the middle class is greater and more difficult to traverse, they argue, perhaps some young women conclude that they won't make it there, no matter what they do, so they have little to lose with a teen birth. This could make teen births more likely. Sociologists have emphasized the importance of relative deprivation, which is related to inequality, rather than absolute deprivation.[12] We saw an argument something like this in considering why marriage rates had declined so much for less-educated Americans.

Kearney and Levine test this hypothesis by looking at the relationship between teen births and "lower-tail inequality." This is the ratio of household income, measured at the state level, between a household at the 50th percentile of the income distribution and one at the 10th percentile. Their analysis focuses particularly on the fertility of young women from poorer households, because they are the most likely to be affected by greater lower-tail inequality. They use the education of a young woman's mother, which is correlated with household income, to identify households likely to be poorer or of lower socioeconomic status. This is a common research practice, especially when information about household income is not available. This analysis is not derived from a natural experiment, so instead they control statistically for other potential causes, including state social and policy differences.

They find strong and consistent evidence of an inequality effect on early fertility. The critical comparison in their analysis is between the fertility of young women from poorer households in high inequality states with the behavior of similar women living in lower inequality states. When they divide states into three broad categories by the extent of inequality, they find a clear pattern. In the low inequality states, about 15 percent of teens from households where the mother was not a high-school graduate had a birth. In states with medium lower-tail income inequality, the percentage with a birth was about three percent higher, and in states with high income inequality, it was another five percent higher. The overall difference between the low and high inequality states is about seven percent, which is almost a 50 percent difference. Interestingly, the differences in teen births are much smaller across the three groups of states for young women whose mothers were high-school graduate- and the differences disappear entirely for women whose mothers attended college. This suggests that the differences are not due to something about the states themselves.

Kearney and Levine confirm this relationship in regression analysis of teen fertility that controls for other individual and state characteristics. They find that a one percent increase in lower-tail inequality, which is approximately the difference between low and high inequality states, increases the proportion with a teen birth by 5.3 percent for teens whose mothers were not high-school graduates and by 2.1 percent for teens whose mothers were high-school graduates. They show that other measures of income and income inequality, including upper-tail inequality and average income at the 10th and 50th percentiles, all have a much weaker effect on teen births. The impact of lower-tail inequality is not much affected by controlling for other state characteristics, such as religiosity, the political leaning of the state, or its minority population.

---

12   Tara Watson and Sara McLanahan (2011). "Marriage Meets the Joneses: Relative Income, Identity, and Marital Status," *Journal of Human Resources*, 46 (3), 482–517.

Abortion, contraception, and changing norms

A very different and interesting explanation for the increase in non-marital fertility was presented by Akerlof, Yellen, and Katz (hereafter AYK).[13] They focused on a change in the social norm concerning the responsibility of a single man to the unplanned pregnancy of his unmarried girlfriend. In the 1950s and 1960s, these pregnancies were typically resolved by what were colorfully termed "shotgun" marriages in which a wedding occurred after a pregnancy but before a birth, and ideally soon enough that the bride did not look pregnant. Now such shotgun marriages are very rare.

In order to explain why this social norm changed, AYK analyzed the "bargaining" between single men and women over premarital sex and the man's responsibility in the event of a pregnancy, both before and after the introduction of effective contraception and legal abortion. The birth-control pill was introduced in the mid-1960s, and at about the same time it also became easier for unmarried couples to obtain contraceptives. Abortion was legalized in the *Roe v Wade* decision in 1973. At first thought you might expect these developments to reduce non-marital childbearing, but AYK show why that might not, in fact, happen.

To analyze the bargaining, AYK used **game theory**, an economic approach suitable for situations in which each party has its own interests and strategies—something like a game of chess or even football of baseball. They focused, in particular, on the way in which contraception and abortion altered the bargaining. Because this is a theoretical model and because the topic is, after all, sex, it is necessarily a bit abstract and stylized in order to illustrate a point.

In the AYK model, single women involved in a romantic relationship choose one of three strategies: (1) declining to have sex before marriage; (2) having sex, but only after extracting a (shotgun) marriage promise; and (3) having sex, but without a marriage promise. Men can accept those terms or they can reject them and break off the relationship. In that case, each party searches for another partner in the next time period, hoping to find someone who will offer or accept terms more to their liking. In deciding whether to request a promise of marriage, a woman must take into account the likely response of her partner and whether she can find a better partner. And he, in turn, must assess whether breaking off the relationship and searching for a new partner will yield a better outcome.

AYK analyzed what the likely outcome would be if the men and women each made decisions in their own self-interest, but taking into account the self-interested behavior of the other group. This is a complicated but widely used idea in economics called a **Nash equilibrium** after John Nash, a mathematician and economist who won the Nobel Prize in Economics in 1994 and whose lifelong battle with schizophrenia was the subject of the Oscar award–winning movie *A Beautiful Mind*.

To analyze this, AYK assumed, for simplicity, that there are just two kinds of single women. One group, which they called Type I women, have high opportunity costs of a non-marital birth; presumably, they have bright prospective careers that would be derailed

13 George A. Akerlof, Janet L. Yellen, and Michael I. Katz (1996), "An Analysis of Out-of-Wedlock Childbearing in the United States," *Quarterly Journal of Economics*, 111 (2), 277–317. Akerlof won the Nobel Prize in Economics in 2001 for his work on asymmetric information. Janet Yellen, his wife, was appointed as chair of the US Federal Reserve Board in 2014, becoming the first woman to hold that position.

or reputations that would be tarnished, or they are otherwise not ready for motherhood. The second group, called Type II women, have negative opportunity costs, by which AYK meant that they want to have a baby. They would prefer a husband, too, but would rather have a birth than neither.

Consider the bargaining situation without effective contraception and legal abortion, something like the 1950s and early 1960s. Type I women would refuse to have premarital sex without a marriage promise because the costs for them are too high. Type II women are willing to have sex without a promise because they want to have a child, so a man could refuse to give a marriage promise to a Type I woman, break off the relationship, and attempt to find a Type II woman. But a man's probability of finding such a woman depends on the ratio of Type I women to Type II women. If the ratio is sufficiently high, then this probability will be low; for example, if 80 percent of women are Type I and 20 percent Type II, then the probability of finding a Type II women is just 25 percent (= 20%/80%). AYK show that if the ratio of Type I to Type II women is high enough, then all women will demand marriage promises—including the Type IIs—and all men will make such a promise. The men do so because they are unlikely to do any better—there aren't enough Type II women—and in the meantime they lose the benefits of the current relationship. The Type IIs demand a marriage promise because they know that the men will accept it.

In this time period, premarital sex with a marriage promise is the social norm (or at least the norm among couples who are sexually active before marriage), so shotgun marriages are common and non-marital births are uncommon. This was, in fact, a typical pattern in the 1960s, when 60 percent of all single pregnant women married before the birth of their child.

Once contraception and abortion were available, however, the situation changed. Type I women would adopt the new options because they have high pregnancy costs. As a result they would no longer demand a marriage promise before engaging in premarital sex because they didn't need one. Type II women, however, would not take advantage of contraception or abortion because they were not seeking to avoid a pregnancy. They would still prefer to ask their partners for a marriage promise but now the men would no longer accept it because they could now readily find a Type I woman who would not demand such a promise. Some Type II women would therefore become single mothers and the non-marital birth ratio would increase as births shift from marital to single. The equilibrium or social norm would shift from one with widespread marriage demands, frequent shotgun marriages, and relatively few non-marital births to one with no marriage demands, no shotgun marriages, and far more non-marital births.

In the model that AYK presented, Type II women want to have a birth. But they could just as well be women who lacked access to affordable contraception and abortion or were less effective users of contraception. Either way, they might well end up as single mothers rather than with a shotgun marriage in the new environment.

AYK summarized their finding this way: "The sexual revolution, by making the birth of a child the *physical* choice of the mother, makes marriage ... a *social* choice of the father" (p. 281). Their approach does seem to capture something very interesting and something very different from the narrower economic approaches. It is undeniable that the relationship between young single men and women in this area is very different than it used to be and that these changes have affected marriage and fertility.

Other influences

Another potential economic cause of non-marital childbearing is women's improving labor-market opportunities. As women's wages have increased, it is now possible to have children and a reasonable standard of living without a marriage partner. We should not, however, overstate this impact. Families with a single female householder have substantially lower average income than married-couple families.

Births to women who are cohabiting are technically non-marital, but functionally they are somewhat more like marital births since the child has two biological parents in the family unit. As discussed in Chapter 4, cohabitation among opposite-sex partners is increasing. Some cohabiting relationships are relatively long term and marriage-like, although, as we noted, cohabitation inherently has less of a long-term focus. Information on births to cohabiting couples is not available through Vital Statistics but can be determined for more recent time periods from other data sources. In 2002, 41 percent of non-marital births to US women were to women who were cohabiting. In the 2006–2010 period, this figure increased to 58 percent.[14] It is too early to know whether outcomes for children born to parents who were cohabiting are more like children born to married parents or to single parents.

It is also clear that the social stigma of unwed motherhood has declined substantially, if not disappeared. In Nathaniel Hawthorne's *The Scarlet Letter*, a tale of early American New England life, Hester Prynne was made to wear the letter "A" (for adultery) permanently as punishment for her non-marital birth. In the 1960s it was still common for pregnant teens to be expelled from high school; they were deemed a bad influence who ought not to mix with the rest of the high-school population. Clearly things have changed. As non-marital births became more common, they appeared to become more accepted. Non-marital births among celebrities and other prominent persons in the news are now common and are rarely associated with severe criticism or negative career effects.

Explaining the decline in teen fertility: contraception, abstinence, and MTV

For most of the past two decades, teen fertility has fallen and it has fallen particularly rapidly since 2008. While the United States still has the highest teen fertility rate among developed countries, it has narrowed the gap. In this section we review some potential explanations for why the teen fertility rate has fallen, especially in recent years.

Change in contraception and sexual activity John Santelli and coauthors[15] examined the impact of changes in sexual activity and contraceptive use on the decline in the teen pregnancy rate between 1995 and 2002. This is an important issue because public policy has sometimes emphasized sex education, which includes information about contraceptives, and sometimes emphasized abstinence education, which might influence the extent of early sexual activity.

---

14 Sally C. Curtin, Stephanie J. Ventura, and Gladys M. Martinez (August 2014), "Recent Declines in Nonmarital Childbearing in the United States," NCHS Data Brief, Number 162.

15 John S. Santelli, Laura Duberstein Lindberg, Lawrence B. Finer, and Susheela Singh (2007), "Explaining Recent Declines in Adolescent Pregnancy in the United States: The Contribution of Abstinence and Improved Contraceptive Use," *American Journal of Public Health*, 97 (1), 150–156.

Conveniently, the teen pregnancy rate is the arithmetic product of the proportion of teens who are sexually active and the pregnancy rate for sexually active teens; this latter term is certainly related to the extent of use of contraception.[16] Santelli et al. analyzed information on changes in both factors and supplemented that with information on the **failure rate** for each contraceptive method actually used by teens.[17] The failure rate is the number of pregnancies that would be expected among 100 women using a particular method for one year, based on actual use by women and men rather than ideal conditions. For example, failure rates are 85 percent using no contraception, 13.7 percent for condoms, 7–8 percent for the birth-control pill, and less than 1.0 percent for intrauterine devices (IUDs) and hormonal implants. By knowing the method of contraception actually used by sexually active teens, they could compute what they called a **contraceptive risk index**; the index is a weighted average of the failure rates for each method, where the weights are the proportion of sexually active women using that method. The higher the index, the greater the risk. If teens shifted over time to either greater use of contraceptives or to methods with lower failure rates, the contraceptive risk index would decline.

Over the period studied, the teen pregnancy rate fell by 25 percent. The proportion of young women aged 15–19 who were sexually active declined slightly from 40.5 percent in 1995 to 38.4 percent in 2002; this is a 6.4 percent decline. Among those who were sexually active, the proportion using no contraception at all fell by half (from 34 to 18 percent) and the proportions using a condom, birth-control pill, or hormonal implants all increased. As a result the overall contraceptive risk index dropped from 33.8 in 1995 to 22.3 in 2002, a decline of 34 percent. Given the much larger decline in the contraceptive risk index than in the size of the sexually active population, it makes sense that it is the major cause of the decline in the teen pregnancy rate. Santelli and his coauthors calculate that improved contraception accounted for 86 percent of the decline, with the remaining 14 percent attributed to the reduction in the size of the sexually active population.

This kind of analysis doesn't explain the ultimate causes of the changing behaviors. Why did teen sexual activity decline slightly? Why did contraception improve? It is possible that improved sex education and outreach improved contraceptive use, along with concerns about STDs. It is also possible that a more conservative social climate and less supportive welfare system or the spread of abstinence-based programming discouraged sexual activity and/or increased contraception.

Public policy, the economy, and the media In an important study, Melissa Kearney and Philip Levine—whose work on teen fertility and inequality we discussed above—tried to identify the causes behind the general decline in teen fertility since 1990 and its especially sharp decline since 2008.[18] For the early period they examined a broad set of policies and

---

16   Expressed as an equation, $P \equiv s \times P_s$, where P is the teen pregnancy rate, s is the proportion of the teen population that is sexually active, and P_s is the pregnancy rate for women who are sexually active. The right-hand side of this equation is just (# sexually active/population) × (pregnancies/# sexually active). The two "# sexually active" terms cancel out, leaving pregnancies/population.

17   This kind of sensitive information is collected in the National Survey of Family Growth. It is done in ways that assure confidentiality so that, for example, parents do not know the responses of their teen children.

18   Melissa S Kearney and Phillip B. Levine (2015), "Investigating Recent Trends in the US Teen Birth Rate," *Journal of Health Economics*, 41 (2), 15–29.

laws, including the presence of sex education programs, abortion restrictions, and benefits available through the welfare system. Because these programs varied over time and especially across states—a natural experiment, once again—they could see which had an important impact. They found that only two of these programs had a meaningful effect on teen fertility at the state level. The two were declining welfare benefits and expanded access to family planning services through Medicaid, and even these accounted for just one-eighth (12 percent) of the decline in teen fertility over this time period. This suggests that broader forces common to young women in all states were likely responsible for the decline in teen fertility over this timeframe.

They attributed the more recent sharp decline to two factors. One obvious factor is the Great Recession. Many studies have shown that teen births rise and fall with economic conditions. Their research found that, on average, a 1 percent increase in the unemployment rate led to a 2 percent reduction in the teen fertility rate. Since the unemployment rate increased by 5 percent during the recession, this would cause the fertility rate to decline by about 10 percent, which is about half of the actual decline.

The second factor they examined was the influence of the media. It is easy enough to think of the way in which TV and movies might influence broad cultural attitudes about teen motherhood, but it is very hard to actually measure the impact on teen fertility, whether positive or negative. Kearney and Levine managed to do that, focusing on the impact of MTV's *16 and Pregnant* series, which aired beginning in 2009.[19] The show was an hour-long documentary series that followed teens through much of their pregnancy and portrayed much of it in a very unglamorous light. One sign of its popularity is that it led to three spin-off shows—*Teen Mom, Teen Mom 2,* and *Teen Mom 3.*

To measure the causal impact of *16 and Pregnant,* Kearney and Levine took advantage of yet another natural experiment, this time involving geographic variation in MTV viewership across TV markets *prior* to the airing of *16 and Pregnant.* They used viewership in an earlier time period rather than actual viewership of the program because actual viewership might well be higher in areas where teen births were more common, thereby creating a spurious positive relationship between viewership and teen fertility. Their results are fascinating. Google searches and Twitter messages about *16 and Pregnant* jumped sharply immediately following each episode, by approximately 30–40 percent. Google searches and tweets containing the terms "birth control" and "abortion" also both increased following the airing of each episode and they increased more in geographic areas where searches and tweets about *16 and Pregnant* increased more. Most significantly, they found that the program appeared to affect teen fertility rates. Teen birth rates fell more in areas that had higher MTV viewership. They estimated that *16 and Pregnant* and the *Teen Mom* shows led to a 5.7 percent reduction in teen births that were conceived after the show began and through the end of 2010. This is about one-third of the total decline in teen fertility during this time period.

---

19 Melissa S. Kearney and Phillip B. Levine (2014), "Media Influences on Social Outcomes: The Impact of MTV's 16 and Pregnant on Teen Childbearing," National Bureau of Economic Research Working Paper 19795.

Birth control and women's education, marriage, and work

In 2000 the US Centers for Disease Control ranked family planning as one of the top 10 public health achievements of the twentieth century, right alongside vaccinations, fluoridation of drinking water, and the recognition of the health hazards of cigarettes. The first and still most significant family planning innovation was the oral contraceptive—famously known as "the pill"—which was approved for use by the US Food and Drug Administration in 1960. The introduction of the birth-control pill changed not only fertility but also many other aspects of women's and men's lives. In this section we review some of those changes, focusing on how the pill altered women's economic decision making across many dimensions.

It is important to recognize just how much the introduction of the pill altered daily life for women and men. In the absence of contraception, 85 women out of 100 will become pregnant within a year in a typical sexual relationship with a partner. Fertility-awareness methods (the "rhythm" method) can be effective if perfectly adhered to, but in practice 25 women out of 100 will become pregnant within a year if they rely exclusively on that. Even condoms have high failure rates in practice; about 15 women in 100 will become pregnant in a year. Since most married women use contraception for many years, these pregnancy rates cumulate. After five years of use, 94 out of 100 women will become pregnant with fertility awareness methods and 63 out of 100 using a condom. In contrast, the birth-control pill has a failure rate of less than 1 percent in perfect use and about 8 percent in actual use. Not only was the pill a far more reliable form of birth control, but it was controlled by women and could be used at a time and place separate from sexual intercourse itself. The newest contraceptive developments are LARCs (long-acting reversible contraceptives), which have failure rates of less than 0.25 percent in actual use.[20]

In the absence of reliable effective contraception, the economic theory of fertility that we outlined in Chapter 5 was sometimes just wishful thinking. Families had great difficulty in planning their fertility, including both the total number of births and the spacing between them. The development of more effective family planning methods enabled them to narrow the difference between desired and actual fertility and thus more closely meet their desired level of child quality, as well. It undoubtedly had an impact on children's lives, too.

It is easy to understand how the introduction of much more reliable contraception could have played an important role. In the pre-pill days, single women and men in romantic relationships either abstained from sexual intercourse or married at younger ages and at earlier stages in their relationship—sometimes too early. Indeed, they sometimes married in the shadow of a pregnancy caused by a contraceptive failure—the infamous shotgun marriages. Even within marriage, it was very difficult to control and plan fertility. Since women were the primary providers of infant and childcare, they could not meaningfully plan for an adult life that included both a normal married sexual relationship and a career. With the pill, however, women and men could have a sexual relationship without

---

20   LARCs include the IUD and various hormonal implants. The contraceptive failure rates are from James Trussell (2011), "Contraceptive Failure in the United States," *Contraception,* 83 (5), 397–404 and Gregor Aisch and Bill Marsh, "How Likely Is It That Birth Control Could Let You Down?" *The New York Times,* September 13, 2014.

marriage if they chose to do so, so marriage could be deferred and be based on greater knowledge of and experience with a partner. Within marriage, fertility could be controlled and planned, so women could plan for careers with more certainty that they could achieve the plan. With this increased ability to plan fertility, a woman could make human capital investments in her own education and training. These investments would pay off only in the long run and only if she could expect to be able to work regularly in the labor market, which she could now do. For example, it now made far more economic sense to prepare for a professional career by investing in higher education.

Claudia Goldin and Lawrence Katz, two experts on the economic history of women, studied the impact of the pill on women's economic activity.[21] They argued that the pill also had important indirect effects on women's behavior. It reduced the "musical chairs" aspect of marriage markets in which young men and women married early in order to avoid being the ones left without a partner or with a less attractive one. With the pill, there was no longer the same rush to marriage because the women with a higher level of attractiveness were also waiting as they pursued education and a career. It also likely improved marriage matching, as both men and women now were able to search longer and have more knowledge about their eventual partner. Goldin and Katz described this effect as making the marriage market "thicker—" that is, there were more potential partners left at older ages. In this way the pill had an effect on those not even directly using it. It allowed everyone to wait to get married, wait to have a first child, and pursue a career.

There is no question that shortly after the introduction of the pill, many things changed. Enrollment by women in professional graduate education programs soared from as little as 1–5 percent in the 1960s to 20 percent in the mid-1970s and far higher than that now. (More on this in Chapter 9.) Age at first marriage also started to increase, a change we noted in Chapter 3. The fraction of women who were sexually active by a given age increased as well. But, of course, other factors could have caused those changes. This was a time of major social, legal, and economic change, including the legalization of abortion, the passage of civil rights legislation and equal pay legislation, and changing attitudes about gender roles.

To analyze the effect of the pill on women's marriage and education, Goldin and Katz took advantage of a natural experiment that involved differences in the timing of access to the pill by young women across states. When the birth-control pill was first introduced, prevailing laws in most states prevented it from being prescribed to minors (women under age 21) without parental consent. In 1969 only nine states allowed a woman aged 18 to obtain the pill without consent. But this began to change.[22] By 1971, 30 states allowed younger women access to the pill, and by 1974 only two states did not. As a result of these laws, over this time period in the mid-1960s to mid-1970s, young women in some states had access to the pill before otherwise similar women in other states. These laws had a large effect on utilization of the pill. In 1971, young women living in states with nonrestrictive laws on dispensing the birth-control pill to women under age 21 were 30–50 percent more likely to be using the pill, depending on the particular age group.

---

21 Claudia Goldin and Lawrence Katz (2002), "The Power of the Pill: Oral Contraceptives and Women's Career and Marriage Decisions," *Journal of Political Economy*, 110 (4), 730–770.

22 Goldin and Katz attribute the change partly to the passage of the Twenty-Sixth Amendment, which made age 18 the age of majority for voting.

Goldin and Katz used this variation across states in exposure to the pill to estimate its impact on a number of outcomes. First, they examined its impact on whether a college-educated woman aged 23–45 in 1980 was married by age 23. Some of these women turned 18 before the pill was introduced, while among those who turned 18 after its introduction, some had access at age 18 and some did not. They found that women who lived in a state with a nonrestrictive law were, indeed, less likely to marry by age 23. The difference in the proportion married was about 2–3 percent, depending on the sample and the particular details of the statistical models they used. The overall decline in the percentage married by age 23 between the older women in the sample who came of age before the pill and the younger women who came after its introduction was 8.7 percent. This means that the birth-control pill accounted for about one-quarter or perhaps somewhat more of the decline in early marriage among college-educated women.

Goldin and Katz did a similar analysis on career outcomes of women aged 30–49 in 1970, 1980, and 1990. Again, some women had access to birth control at an earlier age than others and the question is whether this had an impact on their career choices. In this analysis they found strong impacts of this exposure on whether a woman was in a non-traditional professional occupation (i.e., not teaching or nursing) and especially whether she was in an occupation requiring substantial long-term career investment (e.g., lawyer, doctor, dentist, or veterinarian). The effects of early pill usage and exposure were positive and quantitatively important. Their estimates of the pill's impact suggest that it accounted for approximately one-third of the overall increase in the proportion of women in nontra-ditional professional occupations over this time period and well over half of the increase in the proportion in the very heavy investment occupations. Needless to say, these are very considerable impacts.

The exact same approach—variation in access to the pill for women of the same time period due to differences in state law—was also used by Bailey, Hershbein, and Miller to examine the impact of the pill on women's work and wages.[23] We examine women's wages in detail in Chapters 9–11, so here we just focus on the broad story. Bailey, Hershbein, and Miller examined wages from the late 1960s through the 1980s for women who were born between 1943 and 1954. They noted that the pill could affect women's earnings both by increasing formal education and by increasing work continuity and total work experience. Both education and years of work experience are important determinants of earnings for both men and women. As explained above, it is quite plausible that the pill improved women's incentives to invest in further education and skills by making it more likely that they could use their skills throughout their adult lifetimes.

They found lasting life-cycle effects of early access to birth control. Annual earnings for women with early access were 10–13 percent higher, depending on a woman's age range, and hourly earnings were 4–6 percent higher. The bigger impact on annual earnings is consistent with an effect of early access on hours worked. They also found that these women were more likely to enroll in college and be in a nontraditional or professional job. They also ended up with more education—about 0.25 years—and worked more hours per year.

23   Martha J. Bailey, Brad Hershbein, and Amalia R. Miller (2012), "The Opt-In Revolution? Contraception and the Gender Gap in Wages," *American Economic Journal: Applied Economics*, 4 (3), 225–254.

Bailey, Hershbein, and Miller also looked at whether different groups of women, defined by their academic ability, benefitted more from the pill. It might be natural to think that the pill primarily benefitted the most able women, who could most take advantage of the new opportunity to establish careers. But when they divided women into three groups— the bottom, middle, and top third by IQ—they found the biggest positive impact of early access was on wages and work experience for women who were in the middle third of the distribution. They hypothesized that women in the top third of the distribution might have been able to take advantage of career opportunities even without early access, but that women in the middle third were able to establish careers that they would otherwise not have had.

Putting all the effects together, Bailey, Hershbein, and Miller found that the pill may have accounted for one-third of the earnings gains for women in their forties who were born in the 1940s and 1950s. The biggest effect of early pill access on earnings was through its effect on greater and most continuous work experience. This factor accounted for two-thirds of the almost 9 percent advantage in earnings at age 40–45 between women who did and did not have early access to the birth-control pill. Increases in education and in occupation each accounted for about one-sixth of the wage difference.

The various effects of birth control that we have described are just the tip of the iceberg. Health professionals note that family planning improves both maternal and child health outcomes. Women who plan their pregnancies are more likely to have prenatal care and avoid unhealthy behaviors, such as smoking and drinking. Unplanned pregnancies are significantly more likely to result in a preterm birth and have low birthweight, both of which can be indicators of infant health problems. Bailey has found in other work that children also gained from the spread of birth control.[24] She found that children conceived in areas with better access to family planning were more likely to graduate from college and to have higher earnings than children conceived in otherwise similar areas with less access to family planning.

New developments in the economics of fertility

To conclude this section on fertility, we review a set of new development in the economics of fertility, including evidence of gender preference, the effect of government policy on fertility, and the very low fertility in some countries in the 2010s.

Gender preference

Gender preferences in India and China and their effect on fertility have received substantial publicity. Amartya Sen, a famous Nobel-Prize–winning economist, called attention to the "missing women" in Asia and estimated their numbers to be 80–100 million. We discuss that further in Chapter 13. Here we focus on gender issues in fertility in the United States. We previously saw in Chapter 4 that there is some evidence that a first-born male child increased marital stability, which suggested the possibility that "fathers prefer sons."

24 Martha J. Bailey (2013), "Fifty Years of Family Planning: New Evidence on the Long-Run Effects of Increasing Access to Contraception," *Brookings Papers on Economic Activity* 46 (1), 341–409.

Dahl and Moretti, the two economists who did that research, also examined the effects of gender preference on fertility by comparing the subsequent fertility behavior of families that have a son first vs. those who have a daughter first.[25] They focused on third births, because second births are sufficiently common that they are likely no matter what the gender of the first child is. If fathers (or mothers) prefer sons, it is possible that fertility will be higher in daughter-first families than son-first families, as some fraction of the former have a third (or higher) birth in hopes of having a son.

To examine this, they used data from the 1960 to 2000 US Censuses that enabled them to link marital status and fertility. They found a small but statistically significant positive effect of having a first-born daughter on the probability of having three or more children. This is consistent with a small male gender preference effect on fertility. When they used just the 1960 to 1980 Censuses in which they could identify women who were in their first marriage and thereby reduce a downward bias in the data, the effects were about twice as large.[26] Dahl and Moretti estimated that first-born daughters caused approximately an extra 5,500 births per year in the United States between 1960 and 2000.

Other research has looked at the fertility of recent immigrant groups in the United States, especially those from Asian cultures that are known to favor boys traditionally. Jason Abrevaya investigated this, focusing on fertility among Chinese, Korean, and Indian immigrants.[27] Again, the focus is on higher-order births. He examined all births in California from 1970 to 2005 and looked at the proportion of boys in first and second births compared to third and fourth births. If gender preference for boys was present, it would likely appear in higher-order births as families continued their fertility in order to have a boy. For US whites and blacks (i.e., non-immigrants), the proportion of boys was identical in both birth groups. For Chinese, Korean, and Indians, the proportion of boys in third and fourth births was higher than for first and second births. The effect was especially large for Indians, where the percentage of boys in third and fourth births increased 6 percent relative to first and second births. For Chinese and Koreans, the third and fourth male birth effect was about 2 percent. The same analysis done on national data confirmed the gender effect for third and fourth births, although the impact for Indians was not as dramatic. Abrevaya interprets these higher birth male effects as evidence of gender selection, possibly via abortion.

Even more interesting is the effect of the gender of children already born on the gender of subsequent births. This analysis is based exclusively on births in California, where birth records provide information on previous births and the gender of the child. A first-born girl increased the probability that the second birth was male for Chinese and Indians and, again, the Indian effect was particularly strong. Even stronger was the effect of having no sons on the third-birth male probability for Indians. Abrevaya finds that the third-birth boy probability for an Indian family with two daughters was above 60 percent throughout the 1990s and peaked at more than two-thirds in the late 1990s.

25 Gordon B. Dahl and Enrico Moretti (2008), "The Demand for Sons," *The Review of Economic Studies*, 75 (4), 1085–1120.

26 The bias comes from the effect of the sex of the first-born child on divorce.

27 Jason Abrevaya (2009), "Are There Missing Girls in the United States? Evidence from Birth Data," *American Economic Journal: Applied Economics*, 1 (2), 1–34.

Finally, Abrevaya considered how the probability of a third birth varied with the gender of the first child; this is the same kind of analysis that Dahl and Moretti did, but Abrevaya examined it separately by immigrant group. Again, the intuition is that if families have a male gender preference, the likelihood of having a second or third child would depend on the gender composition of prior births. He tested this using Census data from 1980 to 2000. For whites, the fertility behavior suggests no gender preference but rather a preference for variety. The probability of a second birth is very similar whether the first birth is male or female, while the probability of a third birth is higher if the first two births are of the same sex than if they are mixed. But, interestingly, the third-birth probability is the same whether the first two births are male or female. For Chinese, Indian, and Korean families, however, the third-birth probabilities are consistently higher if the first two births are female than if they are male. The average effect is about 10 percent. Overall, Abrevaya concluded that approximately 2,000 Indian and Chinese girls were "missing" in the United States between 1992 and 2004 due to gender-selection in fertility.

Understanding the "lowest low" fertility

Fertility rates differ sharply for countries that are relatively similar to one another in many ways. Case in point: fertility in the United States and the Scandinavian countries is far higher than in Southern Europe and Eastern Europe—about 1.9 births per woman in the United States, about 1.8 to 1.9 in Sweden, Denmark, and Norway, and 1.3 and below in Southern Europe (Italy, Spain, and Greece) and Eastern Europe (Bulgaria, Latvia, Lithuania, and the Ukraine, among others). Fertility in these countries is so low that their population will shrink in half in two generations if the low rate is maintained that long. That level of fertility is now referred to as the "lowest low," levels literally unseen in most of recorded human history.

A full explanation of the differences is well beyond the scope of this chapter and perhaps beyond social scientists as well, but some broad themes are evident. Scandinavia is well known for its history of strong gender equality and substantial government support for families, including paid maternity and paternity leave, and financial support tied to a birth. Italy, Spain, and Greece are known for their more traditional approach to gender roles, plus a weak political system that provides little or no family support policies and funding. In addition, labor markets in these countries are weak and relatively inflexible, with the result that job growth is low. Demographers speculate that these differences, some cultural, some economic, are an important part of the explanation.[28]

The fertility decline in Eastern Europe appears to be something quite different. Most observers attribute it largely to the economic chaos and uncertainty following the break-up of the old Soviet Union and the Communist governments in closely aligned countries. Possibly, this lowest-low fertility is temporary.

What about the United States? What accounts for its high fertility rate relative to almost all countries at or about its level of economic development? It is not a result of

---

28 Interested readers should consult Hans-Peter Kohler, Francesco C. Billari, and José A. Ortega (2006), "Low Fertility in Europe: Causes, Implications and Policy Options," in F. R. Harris (ed.), *The Baby Bust: Who will do the Work? Who Will Pay the Taxes?* Lanham, MD: Rowman & Littlefield Publishers, 48–109.

strong family policy. Indeed, the United States is near the bottom of rankings of family-friendly government policy such as paid family leave, subsidized daycare, and the like, as we discuss in Chapter 12. And its view of gender equality probably places it comfortably between Scandinavia and Southern Europe. But labor markets in the United States work very well compared to most other countries. Finding a job is not an insurmountable problem for most workers, especially younger workers with skills. Perhaps this knowledge enables families in the United States to plan births with the expectation that their economic future will not be derailed even if a wife (or much less often a husband) leaves the labor market temporarily.

Fertility policy

Most governments provide some form of preferential treatment for families with children through either provision of public services or through the tax system. These policies, whatever their form, have the effect of lowering the price of child services. Here we review a few such policies and their effects.

Tax credits in the United States Believe it or not, the week with the most births in the United States is often the week between Christmas and New Year's Day. This seems at first glance like a particularly unlikely time. Parents and relatives are around, and in the future the children will suffer the dreaded fate of having a birthday just days after Christmas. Even the weather isn't ideal for a sudden trip to the hospital. But it is, nevertheless, true. Between 1997 and 2003, this last week of the year was the busiest four times, beating a week in September, the traditional leader.

One possible explanation is the desire to benefit from the income tax advantages of a birth late in the year. Each family member provides an additional personal exemption, valued in 2014 at $3,900. For someone in the 25 percent tax bracket, this is a savings of $925 and it is worth even more for families in higher brackets. A birth also provides eligibility (or increased benefits) for benefits from the Earned Income Tax Credit and the Child Tax Credit. These programs are primarily beneficial to low- and moderate-income families, and they can add up. (We discuss both of these programs in Chapter 8, focusing on their labor-supply effects). The key is that family size for tax purposes is determined as of December 31, so the same benefit is received whether the birth occurs on January 1 or December 31. An early January birth misses out forever on the previous year's tax benefits. A late December birth receives the tax benefits without incurring many of the associated costs that the personal exemption is intended to compensate for.

Economists Stacey Dickert-Conlin and Amitabh Chandra examined this possible effect by looking at births that occurred in the week before and the week after January 1.[29] Their data covered the period roughly from 1979 through 1994, a time when the Earned Income Tax Credit and Child Tax Credit were much less valuable than they are now. For each family having a birth, they computed the likely tax advantages. They found that the tax benefits for the December births were almost 20 percent higher than the January births, which is simple evidence of a possible effect. In regression analyses in which they controlled for

---

29 Stacey Dickert-Conlin and Amitabh Chandra (1999), "Taxes and the Timing of Births," *Journal of Political Economy*, 107 (1) 161–177.

other possible causes, they consistently found that the greater the financial benefit, the more likely the birth occurred in the last week of December rather than the first week of January. All effects were statistically significant. Because their sample was very small—only 170 births—it is sensible to treat these findings cautiously.

Exactly how do expecting couples arrange for late December births? One is the old-fashioned way, counting backwards from December, rather than January, and hoping. The other is via Cesarean births and drug-induced deliveries, both of which can be scheduled within some time range to suit the interests of both obstetricians and couples seeking a tax break. Simply advancing some births from early January to late December might be enough to make the week between Christmas and New Year the annual winner.

Child benefits in Germany More evidence on timing of births comes from the implementation of new, explicitly pro-natalist policy introduced in 2007 in Germany.[30] As we saw in Chapter 5, Germany has one of the lowest TFRs among industrialized countries. The rate was even lower for more highly educated mothers, prompting particular concerns among policymakers. The previous policy was means tested and provided benefits for up to two years after childbirth. The new policy has benefits that are now dependent on a mother's earnings but payable for only 14 months. While the exact change for each mother varied based on her earnings and previous labor-force participation, higher-income households with mothers who were working and who planned to return to the labor force within a year or so after the birth generally experienced higher payments under this revised benefit, while households with mothers who did not work before the birth or had lower earnings generally would have lower benefits under this new program.

The new policy took effect on January 1, 2007. What effect did this benefit change, which was more generous in terms of payment but less generous in terms of the length of the benefit, have on the timing of births? Economist Marcus Tamm analyzed whether the use of a specific cut-off date for the new benefits had the effect of changing the timing of births.[31] His empirical results show that the incentives for the new program led to more than 1,000 births (about 8 percent of all births) being delayed from December 2007 to January 2007 so that the families were eligible for this new benefit. He also reports a sharp decline in stillbirths over this period but an increase in high birthweight babies.

Subsidizing the stork in Canada Kevin Milligan analyzed the fertility effect of a pro-natalist policy adopted in the Canadian province of Quebec between 1988 and 1997.[32] The policy, called the Allowance for Newborn Children, was particularly focused on encouraging third and higher-order births. Families received modest stipends with the birth of a first or second child, but the stipend was four to eight times as great for a third or fourth birth.[33] Milligan estimated that the benefit was equivalent to a 30 percent subsidy rate of average costs of a third child.

---

30 We have more to say about family-friendly policies such as family leave in Chapter 12.
31 Marcus Tamm (2013), "The Impact of a Large Parental Leave Benefit Reform on the Timing of Birth Around the Day of Implementation," *Oxford Bulletin of Economics and Statistics,* 75 (4), 585–601.
32 Kevin Milligan (2005), "Subsidizing the Stork: New Evidence on Tax Incentives and Fertility," *Review of Economics and Statistics,* 87 (3), 539–555.
33 Families received $500 (Canadian) for a first birth, $1,000 for a second birth, and up to $8000 for a third birth, paid over 5 years.

This policy, adopted only in Quebec, was a kind of natural experiment. Milligan compared the fertility response in Quebec before and after the policy with the corresponding fertility response over the same time period in other Canadian provinces that had no policy change. Since the policy change was greatest for higher-order births, he focused especially on families that already had two children. In Quebec, fertility for these families increased by 7.5 percent, while in the rest of Canada fertility increased by 2.3 percent. This yields a DID estimate of the policy equal to 5.2 percent ($5.2 = 7.5 - 2.3$), which is an 18 percent increase in the probability of having a third birth.

In a regression analysis that controlled for other possible factors, Milligan found that fertility increased by 12 percent on average and by 25 percent for families eligible for the maximum benefits. On average, a C$1,000 increase in the stipend was associated with a roughly 17 percent increase in fertility.

Summary

This chapter completes a unit on fertility and the economic approach to fertility issues. In the previous chapter we developed the basic ideas of how demographers measure fertility and how economists analyze it, with an emphasis on the increase in the price of women's time and its effects. Here we focused on further issues in the economics of fertility. We discussed non-marital and teen fertility, two closely related issues. Non-marital fertility has increased steadily in the United States and in Europe. Teen fertility rates in the United States have fallen but are still conspicuously high by international standards. We also considered explanations for the rise in non-marital fertility, with special emphasis on opportunity costs, especially those created by the welfare system and marriage opportunities. We also reviewed the approach of AYK, who showed how the introduction of more effective contraception and the legalization of abortion could, somewhat counterintuitively, have actually increased non-marital fertility by reducing a man's responsibility to his partner in the event of a premarital pregnancy. Finally, we looked at evidence concerning gender preference in the United States, the very low fertility in parts of Europe, and the effects of government policy on fertility.

⑦ WOMEN AT WORK

Introduction

The change in the labor-force activity of women, especially married women, ranks among the most significant labor-market phenomena of the twentieth century. Some might go further and claim that it ranks among the century's most important social phenomena, transforming not only the labor market but family life as well, not only women's lives but also those of the men and children with whom they live. The magnitude of the change is truly staggering. In the early part of the twentieth century, only about one in five women in the United States worked outside the home and fewer than one married woman in ten did. Most of these working women fell into one of two categories—younger women who worked prior to marriage or women who never married. Very few women combined marriage and paid employment, but a century later, all this had changed. Six in ten married women in the United States worked outside the home, and married women were just about as likely to be working as single women.

In this chapter we examine women's labor-force activity in detail in order to understand the underlying causes of the changes as well as the differences that exist today among different groups of women—for example, between better-educated and less-educated women. To do that we first review the facts and trends, and then develop an economic model that can help explain those facts. Our goal is to see how decisions about whether to work outside the home were affected by changes in the economic environment that women faced throughout the course of the twentieth century.

Facts and trends

In the United States, statistics on employment, unemployment, and labor-force participation come from a large monthly survey called the Current Population Survey (CPS), conducted jointly by the Bureau of the Census and the Bureau of Labor Statistics. That survey classifies workers into three mutually exclusive categories—employed, unemployed, and not in the labor market—based on their activities in the previous week. An individual is employed if he or she worked at least one hour for pay, even if he or she would like to work more. An individual is unemployed if he or she is without a job and has made an effort to find work within the past four weeks. Persons who are not employed and have not looked for work are classified as nonparticipants.[1]

The **labor-force participation rate (LFPR)** is the most widely used measure of work activity for different population groups. It is the proportion of individuals, aged 16 or older, in the civilian non-institutional population who are either employed or unemployed:

---

1 Workers who have given up looking for work are officially classified as "discouraged workers" rather than unemployed. Information on labor-force statistics can be found at the BLS website: stats.bls.gov.

LFPR = (E+U)/POP. The unemployed are included because they are deemed to be actively looking for work and thus participating in the labor market.

Table 7.1 presents labor-force participation rates in 2014 for US women and men for all workers and by age, race, and Hispanic origin. The figures shown are the average rates for the whole year. For all persons aged 16 and over, about 69 percent of men and 57 percent of women were in the labor-force. For men and women in the prime working ages (25–54), when work is not much affected either by schooling or by retirement, about 88 percent of men and 74 percent of women were in the labor-force. The difference in participation rates by gender is thus about 12–14 percent. The 2014 figures are down several percent from their pre-recession levels. The recession slightly narrowed gender differences in LFPRs.

When we compare labor-force participation by race, the comparisons depend very much on gender. Black men are less likely to be in the labor-force than white men, while white women are less likely to be in the labor-force than black women. The race difference in participation rates is 7–9 percent for men (higher for whites) and 1–3 percent for women (higher for blacks). For prime-age workers, Hispanic men have the highest labor-force participation rate of all three groups (90.6 percent), while the rate for Hispanic women is a bit lower for all women, but 7–8 percent lower for prime-age workers. Another way to view the race and ethnicity rates is to compute the gender difference within each group. Focusing on the prime-age workers, the gender difference ranges from 23 percent for Hispanics to just 5 percent for blacks. The gender difference for white workers is in the middle at 15 percent.

Table 7.1 *Labor-force participation rates by gender and race, United States, 2014.*

	Men	Women
All		
Age 16+	69.2	57.0
Age 25–54	88.2	73.9
White		
Age 16+	69.8	56.7
Age 25–54	89.4	74.3
Black		
Age 16+	63.6	59.2
Age 25–54	80.7	75.8
Hispanic		
Age 16+	76.1	56.0
Age 25–54	90.6	67.0

Source: US Department of Labor, Bureau of Labor Statistics.

By far the most important thing about women's labor-force participation are the many ways it has changed over time. Figure 7.1 shows the LFPR for US women and men

Figure 7.1 *The changing labor-force participation rates of US men and women, 1900–2014.*

Source: Graph constructed by author from BLS data, available at stats.bls.gov/.

since 1900. At the turn of the twentieth century, more than 90 percent of men aged 16 and older worked, compared to 20 percent of women. Men's labor-force participation rate drifted down very slowly through 1940, jumped up through 1950, and then fell a bit more rapidly after that. The post-1950 decline primarily reflects the falling labor-force participation of older workers as private pensions and Social Security made earlier retirement feasible. Since 1980 the LFPR for men has declined by a total of about 10 percent.

In contrast, women's labor-force participation moved upward slowly but steadily through 1940, and then more rapidly thereafter. The proportion of US women in the labor-force increased by about 10 percent in the first half of the twentieth century, reaching about 30 percent in 1950. It then increased another 30 percent in the next 50 years, topping 60 percent for the first time in 2000. From 1940 through 1990, the trend line is straight, but it noticeably flattens in the 1990s. After increasing an average of 7 percent every ten years between 1940 and 1990, the total increase in the 1990s was less than 3 percent. And since 2000 the LFPR for women actually dropped by almost 3 percent, ending more than 100 years of steady increases. More on this below. Still, there is no minimizing the extent of the change. Over the course of the twentieth century the gap between men's and women's labor-force participation rates narrowed by more than 50 percent, from 65 percent to 12.

Beneath the surface of these overall figures, the nature of women's labor-force participation rates was changing in ways that would change family life permanently. At the turn of the century, participation in the paid labor market was largely an activity of single women. In 1900, when the overall participation rate for women was 20 percent, the participation rate for married women was just 5 percent—just one married woman in 20 worked for pay. (See Box 7.1 for fascinating details about women and work from the 1900 Census.) Single women were 60 percent of all working women between 1900 and 1920. But this was to change, as Figure 7.2 shows. From 1900 to 1940 the participation rate for married women increased slowly but steadily, about 5 percent every two decades. Then, beginning in 1940, their LFPR

Box	7.1

Women at Work in 1900: Tables from the 12th Decennial Census of the United States

The 1900 Census included a special section called Statistics of Women at Work. The 120-page report is available at www2.census.gov/prod2/decennial/documents/00779830ch1.pdf. It makes fascinating reading. Below we show one table and excerpts from several others.

The 1900 Census reported that 4.8 million women were "breadwinners," to use the Census terminology, compared to 22.5 million men (see Table 7.2). More than nine of out ten men worked, but only one woman in five (20.6 percent). Market work for pay was largely confined to women before marriage or women who did not marry; married women were 56 percent of all women but only 16 percent of working women. The specialization of task by gender in married-couple families is evident: 94% of married men worked, compared to just 5.6 percent of married women. Roughly half of never-married and divorced women worked. Almost two-thirds of working women (3.1 million/4.8 million) were never married.

Table 7.2 *Labor-force participation by gender and marital status, United States, 1900.*

Marital Condition	Population 16 Years of Age and Over					
		Male			Female	
	Total	Breadwinners		Total	Breadwinners	
		Number	Percent		Number	Percent
Total	24,851,013	22,489,425	90.5	23,485,550	4,833,630	20.6
Single (incl. unknown)	9,633,157	8,355,666	86.7	6,843,140	3,143,712	45.0
Married	13,955,650	13,150,671	94.2	13,810,057	769,477	5.6
Widowed	1,177,976	907,855	77.1	2,717,715	857,005	31.5
Divorced	84,230	75,233	89.3	114,647	03,436	55.3

Source: US Census Bureau, *Statistics of Women at Work, 1900*, Table VI.

Table 7.3 is an excerpt from the same Census report. It shows how labor-force participation varied dramatically by race, marital status, and age. The categories are verbatim from the report and reflect an era and sensibility quite different than ours. Less than 15 percent of native-born white women whose parents were also native born worked, and only 3 percent of married women of the same background did. White women who were either immigrants or the children of immigrants were more likely to work. Overall about one-fifth to one-quarter of them worked, but if they were married just 3–4 percent worked. black women ("Negro" in the Census Bureau table) were the most likely to be working; 43 percent of all black women worked, including 26 percent of married black women, about eight times the participation rate for the three groups of white women. black women accounted for almost 50 percent of working married women, even though they were just 11 percent of the adult female population. We will offer an explanation for that after we develop a model of labor-force participation decisions.

Irrespective of age, US married women in 1900 were extremely unlikely to be working. Work in the labor market largely ended with marriage. At ages 15–24, 6.4 percent of married women were working. At ages 45–54, less than 4 percent were. Never-married women had relatively high work rates, ranging from 27 percent at ages 15–24 to 55 percent at ages 25–34.

Table 7.3 *Employment of US women by race, marital status, and age, 1900.*

	All	Married	Never-Married
By Race and Parents' Origin of Birth			
Native White, Both Parents Native	14.6	3.0	33.8
Native White, Parent(s) Foreign Born	25.4	3.1	51.6
Foreign Born White	19.1	3.6	70.4
Negro	43.2	26.0	63.1
Indian and Mongolian	15.5	10.7	18.2
By Age			
15–24	29.0	6.4	37.3
25–34	17.2	4.8	55.0
35–44	13.2	4.5	48.1
45–54	12.9	3.9	41.0

Figures shown in table are percentage employed.

Source: US Census Bureau, *Statistics of Women at Work, 1900,* Tables VII and VIII.

Finally, the Census reveals some interesting facts about the jobs US women held in 1900. The single largest female occupation was as servants and waitresses, employing 1.2 million women or nearly one in four working women. Rounding out the top five in order were agricultural workers (456,000), dressmakers (338,000), laundresses (329,000), and teachers (327,000), the sole professional occupation among the top five. Pink-collar employment for women in offices was still relatively limited. About 165,000 women (3 percent of all working women) worked as clerks, copyists, stenographers, or "typewriters." About 90 percent of these jobs were held by men. The Census Bureau report notes that "many of these [clerical and copyist] occupations are not well adapted to the employment of women" (p. 97).

increased more rapidly. From 1950 to 1990 the LFPR for married women increased by almost exactly 10 percent per decade—from 20 percent in 1950 to 30 percent in 1960, 40 percent in 1970, 50 percent in 1980, and nearly 60 percent in 1990. Again, the curve flattens beginning in the 1990s, and especially at the end of the decade. The LFPR for married women peaked in 1997 at 61.6 percent and has been stable or slightly lower ever since; the LFPR for US married women in 2014 was 58.4 percent, just where it was in the early 1990s. The LFPR of never-married women was essentially unchanged from 1900 to 1960, but then it rose steadily and sharply through about 1990, when it leveled off. Just like married women, their LFPR has declined in the 2000s and 2010s, down by a total of 5 percent since 2000. Some of the post-2008 decline is due to the lingering effects of the recession, and some of the effects for single women may reflect their rising educational attainment. But there is certainly evidence that the steady, seemingly inevitable increase in women's LFPRs is over.

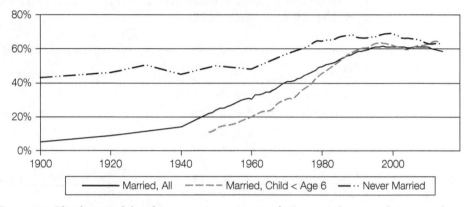

Figure 7.2 *The changing labor-force participation rates of US women by marital status and age of youngest child, 1900–2014.*

Source: Graph constructed by authors from BLS data, at stats.bls.gov/.

Also shown in Figure 7.2 is the LFPR for married women with pre-school-age children. This information is only available from 1948 when the Census Bureau and the Bureau of Labor Statistics began the regular collection of labor-force data. The increasing labor-force participation of these women is particularly interesting and far-reaching in its impacts. Back in 1948, only 12 percent of married women with children aged six and under were members of the workforce. Labor-force participation by married women was still largely either before a first birth or when the youngest child was grown up and gone from the home. Even among women with school-age children, the LFPR was just 26 percent. Labor-force activity increased steadily through the 1950s and 1960s for the married mothers with young children, reaching 30 percent by 1970. During this period the LFPR rose an average of 8 percent each decade. Between the early 1970s and the mid-1990s, their LFPR increased even more rapidly, reaching 63.5 percent in 1995—an increase of more than 1 percent per year. In all the LFPR for married mothers of young children increased by a factor of five in under 50 years, but like the other LFPR trends, this one also plateaued out in the late 1990s. Between 1998 and 2004, the LFPR for married mothers of young children declined in almost every year. But, unlike the other LFPR trends, their LFPR has picked up again since then, rising a total of 4.5 percent between 2004 and 2014.

The most telling statistics about how labor-force participation has become a norm for women is the way that characteristics, especially demographic characteristics, that once predicted work status no longer do so nearly as well. In 1970 the LFPR of women between the ages of 25 and 34, the peak family and childbearing years, was noticeably lower; now a difference is barely evident. In 1970, women with young children had LFPRs barely half that of women with older children; now the difference is less than 10 percent. In 1970, marital status still made a sizable difference; now the effect is very modest. In 1970, race made a difference; again, the effect is now relatively small.

The increase in women's labor-force activity is by no means an exclusively American phenomenon. Indeed, as Figure 7.3 shows, participation rates have increased in most countries throughout Western Europe and North America. Participation rates are highest in the United States, Canada, and Sweden, with Italy the lowest in Western Europe. The LFPR rose in every one of these countries between 1975 and 2012 an average of 12 percent. In Australia, Canada, the Netherlands, and the United States, the LFPR rose more rapidly than that, with the Netherlands at the top with an increase of more than 20 percent. At the lower end, the increase was lowest in Japan, with Sweden, known for its high women's LFPR and greater gender equity, also below average.

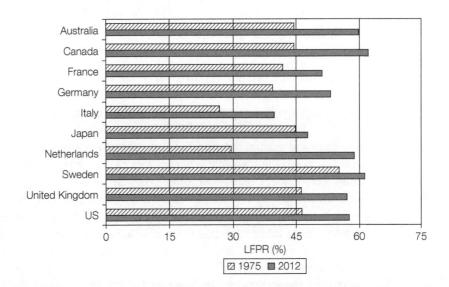

Figure 7.3 *Women's labor-force participation rates, selected countries, 1975 and 2012.*

Source: US Bureau of Labor Statistics, International Labor Comparisons, Table 7.4.

Labor-force participation over the life cycle

Another interesting way to look at labor-force participation is over a woman's life cycle as she ages. Women's life-cycle patterns of labor-force participation have changed substantially over the course of the twentieth century.

Much of what we know about this topic is the result of the path-breaking research of Claudia Goldin, an economic historian whose work we discussed in Chapter 1. Goldin linked data on LFPRs of US women by age from one Census to the next in order to construct a life-cycle picture of labor-force activity over much of the twentieth century. For example, women born in the 10-year period between 1886 and 1895 were aged 15–24 in the 1910 Census, 25–34 in the 1920 Census and so on. By piecing the LFPRs together, she could see exactly what happened to them over the life cycle.

Table 7.4 presents this life-cycle information for white women.[2] The numbers in the table are the LFPRs by age bracket for women born in each successive ten-year period,

---

2 Census data early in the century does not separately identify black women; instead it combines all non-white women in a single category. The data for non-white women follow a somewhat different pattern than the one discussed here for white women.

Table 7.4 *Life cycle labor-force participation rates for white women by age and birth cohort.*

Year of Birth	Never Married	Married			
	Age 15–24	Age 15–24	Age 25–34	Age 35–44	Age 45–54
1886–1895	N.A.	N.A.	7.7	9.8	10.1
1896–1905	46.6	8.2	11.5	13.8	22.2
1906–1915	42.6	13.3	16.7	25.3	38.6
1916–1925	40.8	14.7	21.0	35.4	46.7
1926–1935	42.9	24.9	26.7	44.4	53.4
1936–1945	40.0	30.0	36.2	59.1	—

Source: Claudia D. Goldin, *Understanding the Gender Gap*. New York: Oxford University Press, 1990, Table 2.2.

beginning in the late nineteenth century; we will refer to a group as a **birth cohort.** The first column of figures is the LFPR of never-married women between the ages of 15 and 24; the other columns are for married women by ten-year age brackets. Reading down a column traces out the experience of successive cohorts of women when they were the same age and marital status in different calendar years, ten years apart. Reading across a row traces out the life-cycle experience of each cohort. All the information comes from the US Decennial Censuses as compiled by Goldin.

Consider the experience of white women born between 1896 and 1905. When they were between the ages of 15 and 24, if they were single, nearly half (46.6 percent) worked in the labor market. At the same ages, only about 8 percent of married women worked. What does this tell us about how many women left work more or less just at the time they married? Goldin computes a rough estimate this way. Suppose the married women between the ages of 15 and 24 had the LFPR of the never-married women in the years before the married women were married. Then their own LFPR fell with marriage from 46.6 percent to 8.2 percent, meaning that more than 80 percent ((46.6–8.2 percent)/46.6 percent) of the working single women exited work more or less at the time of marriage.

As late as the 1916–1925 birth cohort, the sharp divergence in labor-force activity with marriage is still apparent among the young women. Almost two-thirds of the single working women in this group ((40.8–14.7)/40.8) likely exited the labor market at about the time of their marriages. The LFPR for young married women doesn't really start to rise until the 1926–1935 birth cohort, and they are between the ages of 15 and 24 in 1950. So it is clear that through most of the first half of the twentieth century, marriage marked the withdrawal of many young working women from the labor-force.

In the early birth cohorts in the table, marriage meant a more or less permanent withdrawal from the labor market. For example, for the women born around the turn of the century, their LFPR increases just 5 percent as they age from 15–24 to 35–44. A decade later, when their children must be largely grown, still barely more than one in five is working. For this early cohort of white women—and for the cohorts who preceded them—participation in the paid labor-force not only largely ceased at marriage but never really again became a particularly important factor in their lives.

That life-cycle pattern of work changed dramatically over the course of the century. For the women in the 1906–1915 cohort, the LFPR is quite low through the 25–34 age bracket (1940) but then jumps up sharply in the 35–44 age bracket and then up sharply again at ages 45–54. LFPRs are high before marriage, drop sharply, and then return almost to their previous level. This marks a new pattern: Paid work still diminishes sharply with marriage, but eventual return to the labor market becomes far more common. Still, note that the percentages imply that perhaps well under half of married women never worked in the paid labor market.

That life-cycle pattern of return to work is clearly evident in the 1916–1925 birth cohort, whose LFPR jumps by more than 20 percent between ages 15–24 and 35–44 and reaches nearly 50 percent at 45–54. Finally, there's a peculiar pattern for the next cohort, those born between 1926 and 1935. Their LFPR as young married women is sharply higher than for the cohort that preceded them, indicating a real break with the historic pattern of work ending with marriage. Now, more often, work ended not with marriage but with motherhood. But the fraction working barely increases as these women aged from 15–24 to 25–34. What was going on? These women, who turned 25 between 1951 and 1960, are precisely the women of the baby boom, who had a fertility rate at that age of nearly 250 births per 1,000. But when their childbearing and child-rearing was over, they returned to the labor-force in unprecedented numbers. Finally, the last cohort shown in Table 7.3 had a relatively modest LFPR until they were in their mid-thirties through mid-forties. With this group, return to the labor market became a clear norm.

Goldin emphasizes the importance of this life-cycle pattern of labor-force participation for understanding the gender gap in wages. As she notes, this pattern means that relatively few married women established careers in the same way that men did. Rather, she writes: "married working women who entered the labor-force in their middle years had, by and large, entered a rather new world …. They were not bringing to the labor market recently acquired skills. Many were, instead, reentering occupations they had left many years, or possibly decades, before, and most were inadequately prepared for their new labor market roles" (p. 23). We return to this issue when we analyze the gender gap in earnings.

Goldin has also presented a fascinating history of the family and work experiences of college-educated women during the first half of the twentieth century. See Box 7.2 for a summary.

Box	7.2

Having It All? Family and Work among US College-Educated Women in the Twentieth Century

In the early decades of the twentieth century, a college education was an uncommon achievement for men or women. Of persons born between 1886 and 1905, only about 5–10 percent of men and 3–5 percent of women were college graduates. We have already seen how rare labor-force participation was for married women at this time. Because combining family and work was enormously difficult, these women faced some very extreme choices. They could work, or they could marry and have a family, but only rarely could they do both. What did they do? Nearly one-third of them never married, compared to just 7 percent of women who did not attend college. (The marriage rates of men were not affected at all by a college education.) Nearly half of them never had children, including more than a quarter of those who were married. Those who never married worked virtually their entire lives. For example, when they were between the ages of 45 and 54, their LFPR was nearly 90 percent, barely below the LFPR for men. They worked primarily as elementary and secondary school teachers; a full 60 percent worked in just those two occupations. These never-married women were the primary source of school teachers through the 1950s. Interestingly, marriage, not children, continued to be a major factor in determining work. Among those college-educated women who were married but had no children, less than one-third worked between the ages of 45 and 54. Goldin has characterized this cohort of college-educated women as facing a "family or work" choice.

According to Goldin's research, this pattern persisted through the birth cohort of 1906–1915, who graduated college in the mid-1920s through the mid-1930s. The choices were not quite so extreme, but still 20 percent never married, and about 40 percent had no children. Thereafter, marriage rates for college-educated women rose, and the gap between them and women with less education narrowed, although it did not disappear. Like other women during the early post–World War II years, college-educated women married when they were quite young—nearly half within a year of their college graduation—and had high fertility rates. Like the others, they returned to the labor market in great numbers after an absence for family responsibilities. Goldin characterizes this cohort of college-educated women as following a "family, then work" pattern.

More recent cohorts of college-educated women have often deferred marriage and children while trying to establish a career. Nearly 20 percent are unmarried between the ages of 35 and 44, and about 25 percent still have no children. Differences in marriage and fertility between these women and women with less than a college education have grown again. Goldin describes them as pursuing a "career, then family" strategy.

Source: Claudia Goldin (1997), "Career and Family: College Women Look to the Past," in Francine D. Blau and Ronald G. Ehrenberg (eds.), *Gender and Family Issues in the Workplace*, New York: Russell Sage Foundation.

An economic model of women's labor-force participation

Overview

Economists are interested in understanding how individuals make decisions about whether to work in the labor market and also about how many hours they want to work. Decisions about hours worked are more often the subject of labor-supply analysis in a typical intermediate-level course in microeconomics or labor economics. Two factors are probably responsible for this emphasis. First, often the real goal of labor-supply analysis is to construct a total market labor-supply curve, and, for that, hours of work are the appropriate dimension. Second, the subject of the analysis is often taken to be men (without necessarily saying so), for whom the LFPR is, as we've already seen, very high. For them, choices about hours of work and how those choices are affected by economic factors such as taxes are the more interesting topic.

But for women the decision about whether to work in the labor market is the more interesting decision because that's where the action has been. This is true in two ways. First, as we have just seen, the proportion of women, especially married women, who are working has changed enormously over the course of the twentieth century and into the twenty-first. Second, because the fraction of women working is still lower than for men, there is more variation among women. Why do some women work in the labor market while others don't? To understand these changes we need to construct a model that illuminates how individuals make decisions about work and what factors influence that decision. In doing so we'll want to apply the standard economics approach—constrained maximization and then comparative statics.

The traditional (male) approach to labor-supply analysis involves the choice between two kinds of time—time spent at work in the labor market and time spent in leisure. A model like that isn't really a particularly good representation of the choices of men in this day and age, but for women it is hopelessly inadequate. What's left out of the model is exactly what has occupied women, especially married women, for many generations—namely, family and household obligations, or what we have called **household production**. Truthfully, for both men and women, the choice of time use is threefold—among leisure, market labor (paid), and household labor (unpaid). But for men, the two-way analysis is (or at least was) often good enough. For women, though, it is impossible to make sense of the experience of the twentieth century without thinking about household production and building it directly into the model.

The model of labor-force participation presented here is a compromise that makes the key points without undue complexity. It incorporates three uses of time, rather than the two that are often used in standard labor-supply analysis. The appendix to this chapter presents an alternative labor-supply analysis that uses indifference curves and the associated budget constraint in the context of a simpler two-time use model.

Assumptions

We begin with the following assumptions, which simplify and clarify the analysis. Remember: models are not intended to be fully realistic but rather to capture just enough of reality to illuminate important relationships.

- A woman's time is spent doing one of three things—working for pay in the labor market (called M, for *market* hours of work), working in the household (H, for *household* hours), or enjoying leisure (called L, for *leisure*). We also assume that market work is neither liked nor disliked in and of itself. For many workers, that may not be strictly true.

    The distinction between H and L can be subtle. L stands for time spent doing something that is clearly and immediately enjoyable in and of itself. In contrast, time spent in household production is valuable because you value what it produces—a good dinner, clean clothes, a clean house, or healthy, well-adjusted children. It is not valued in and of itself. Another distinction between leisure and household production is that you could potentially hire someone to perform household production tasks in your place, while, quite obviously, you can't hire someone to take leisure for you.[3]

- A woman has some potential wage rate (*w*) and she may also have some nonlabor income (V). Nonlabor income is income that a woman would have even when her own market hours of work are zero. It could come from government programs, like welfare or Social Security. In a traditional old-fashioned male-breadwinner marriage, the husband's income could be regarded as nonlabor income for the wife, as long as she makes her decision about working after his.

- A woman can choose to work as many hours in the market as she likes, from just one hour to a very large number. Assuming an unrestricted choice of hours of work may sound terribly unrealistic. But if we fix the hours she can work, we won't have anything left to analyze. And what should we fix it at? Remember, we are trying to determine desired hours of work. Do keep this simplification in mind; more complex economic models do consider limits on the choice of work hours.

- A woman receives utility (satisfaction or pleasure) from three general kinds of commodities—consumption goods and services that are purchased in the market (*C*); household-produced goods (*G*); and leisure time (*L*). We write this utility function as $U = U(C, G, L)$ to represent the link between the amounts of the three goods and the amount of utility. The three uses of time and the three sources of utility are directly related. Hours of market work yield the income needed to purchase consumption goods and services, hours of household production yield household goods and services via a household production function, and hours of leisure are directly enjoyable.

Model details

Each hour of time spent in market work, household production, or leisure produces something of value. Let's call the value of an hour of time the **marginal value of time** (MVT). We have three such expressions, one for each of the three possible uses of time, which can be written as follows:

Leisure: $\text{MVT}_L \equiv \Delta U / \Delta L$ (7.1)

Household work: $\text{MVT}_H \equiv \Delta U / \Delta H$ (7.2)

Market work: $\text{MVT}_M \equiv \Delta U / \Delta M$ (7.3)

In these equations, *U* stands for utility. Utility is measured in units that are called **utils**, but the numbers used are arbitrary—that is, they don't have any real numerical meaning. The only important numerical property of utils is that a bigger number is better than a smaller one. The Δ in the equations is the Greek letter delta; it stands for "change in." We will often think of ΔL, ΔH, and ΔM as being an hour of time, but smaller changes are certainly possible. Note that the two sides of all three equations are linked by a "$\equiv$" symbol,

---

3 An early definition comes from Margaret Reid, one of the first famous women economists and probably the first economist to do research on household production. She defined household production as "those unpaid activities which are carried on, by and for the members, which activities might be replaced by market goods, or paid services, if circumstances such as income, market conditions, and personal inclinations permit the service being delegated to someone outside the household group." See Margaret Reid (1934), *Economics of Household Production*, New York: John Wiley and Sons, 11.

rather than an equals sign. This means that the equations are identities, true for all values. They are just definitions.

Each of these three terms is related to the concept of **marginal utility**, a concept that was introduced in Chapter 2 and that we used in Chapter 5 to analyze fertility choices. As is standard in economic analysis, we will assume that the three goods in our model—leisure, household goods, and market goods—all have the property of **diminishing marginal utility**. This simply means that the first units of each good are more valued than subsequent units. This will turn out to play an important role in the analysis of labor-force participation.

Let's look at the three terms individually to isolate their important properties. For leisure time, what we are calling the MVT_L is, in fact, simply the marginal utility of leisure ($\Delta U/\Delta L$), as shown in equation (7.1). Thus we can conclude that the MVT_L falls as the amount of leisure (L) increases. To express this relationship between MVT_L and L, we write $MVT_L(L)$, which indicates that the marginal value of leisure time is a function of L. Falling marginal utility of leisure makes perfect sense. Wouldn't the first hour of leisure be more valuable than the 24th? Try to imagine how much more you would appreciate the first few leisure hours of a day relative to the last few.

For household and market work, the MVT terms are related to marginal utility, but they are not quite the same thing. To see this, it is useful to expand the expressions in (7.2) and (7.3) to show their components. For household work, we use the now familiar idea of a **household production function**. We write the household production function as $G = g(H; Z)$, which expresses the idea that the amount of G depends on the amounts of H and Z. G stands for the amount of output produced in the household—everything from dinner to clean clothing to healthy children. H is time spent in household production, and Z stands for the available capital goods—things like washing and sewing machines and microwave ovens. The production function has been written with a semicolon between H and Z to emphasize that H is being chosen, but Z is not, although we will think about how it has changed.[4]

We can expand the expression for MVT_H in equation (7.2) by identifying the specific impacts, as shown in (7.2') just below:

$$MVT_H \equiv \Delta U/\Delta H = (\Delta U/\Delta G) \times (\Delta G/\Delta H) = MU_G(G) \times MP_H(H) \qquad (7.2')$$

Look at the two terms in parentheses in the middle part of the equation. The second term, $\Delta G/\Delta H$, is the additional household output (G) produced by an additional hour of household work (H). The first term, $\Delta U/\Delta G$, is the increase in utility from that additional household output. The effect operates from H to G and from G to U. (It is as if the two ΔGs cancel out.) Together, the product of the terms shows how and by how much an increase in household time increases utility. There is both a production effect reflecting how much more is produced and a consumption effect reflecting how much it is valued.

The two terms on the far right of equation (7.2') are just notation for these terms. MU_G is the **marginal utility of household goods**, while MP_H is the **marginal product of household time**. The G in parentheses following MU_G indicates that the marginal utility of household goods depends on the amount of those goods. The H in parentheses following MP_H indicates that the marginal product of household time depends on

---

4 This is a necessary simplification. To treat household technology as something that was chosen would make the model much too complicated without really adding anything essential.

the amount of time spent on household tasks. Just as for leisure, we assume that the marginal utility of household goods declines the more household goods an individual already has. This means that MU_G falls as G increases. This relationship will be important later on.

The marginal product is an important idea in microeconomics, which was introduced in Chapter 2, and used in Chapter 3. It is the additional (or marginal) output produced in an additional hour of work. In virtually every production setting studied by economists, the marginal product falls as more of an input is used. This property of production is called the **Law of Diminishing Marginal Returns**.[5] The same thing is likely to be true here—each additional hour spent working in the household is less productive than the one preceding it; fatigue might be one explanation. Taking the two effects together, it is extremely likely that MVT_H will decline as H increases. Each additional unit of H produces less G because of diminishing marginal returns, and each additional unit of G is valued less because of diminishing marginal utility.

We can expand the expression for time spent in market work in equation (7.3) this way:

$$MVT_M \equiv \Delta U/\Delta M = (\Delta U/\Delta C) \times (\Delta C/\Delta M) = MU_C(C) \times w/p \qquad (7.3')$$

Again, look first at the two terms in parentheses in the middle of the equation. The second term, $\Delta C/\Delta M$, is the amount of additional market goods (C) that can be purchased with an additional hour of market work. The first term, $\Delta U/\Delta C$, is the increase in utility from those additional goods. Here, the effect operates from M to C and from C to U: additional market work (M) yields additional consumption goods (C), which yields additional utility (U). Together, the product of these terms shows how and by how much an increase in market hours of work increases utility.

On the far right of (7.3'), we use MU_C for $\Delta U/\Delta C$; this term stands for the **marginal utility of consumption goods**. The C in parentheses following MU_C indicates that the marginal utility of consumption goods depends on the amount of those goods. Again, we assume that there is diminishing marginal utility, so that as C increases, MU_C falls. The other term, w/p, is not just notation but measures the amount of additional goods that can be purchased with an hour of work. In one hour of work, $\$w$ is earned. If we let p stand for the price of goods and services, then w/p is the amount of additional market goods and services that can be purchased by working one more hour. For this reason, w/p is sometimes referred to as the **real wage**. It is the wage measured in terms of what you can buy. For example, if $w = \$10$ and $p = \$2$, then an hour's work yields 5 units of market goods. Note that if w were higher, more goods could be purchased per hour of work.

Taking these two effects together, it is extremely likely that MVT_M will decline as M increases, just as we saw that MVT_H declined as H increased. In this case, each additional unit of M yields the same amount of additional C, but each additional unit of C is less valued because of diminishing marginal utility.

Figure 7.4 summarizes these ideas graphically. The horizontal axis of each graph measures the amount of time spent in that use, while the vertical axis measures the marginal value of an hour of time. The height of the curve shows the marginal value of each hour.

---

5   When we examined specialization within marriage, we assumed that the marginal product of household time was constant. That was a useful simplifying assumption.

The three MVT curves each are downward sloping, which means that the marginal value of an hour of time in that use declines as the number of hours spent increases. The curves are drawn here as straight lines and are quite similar to one another, but that need not be the case. In addition to the negative slope, the height of the curves will be important when we try to analyze how changes over the course of the twentieth century have affected women's work choices.

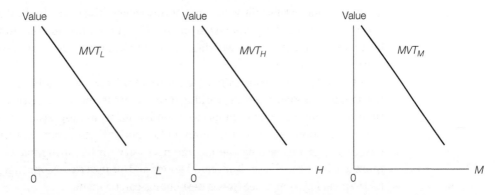

Figure 7.4 *Marginal value of time curves for leisure, household time, and market work.*

Utility maximization and market work

We assume that a woman's objective is to spend her time working in the market, working at home, and/or taking leisure in such a way as to maximize her utility—that is, to make herself and her family as well off as possible in terms of her own preferences and opportunities. Much will depend on her particular situation—her wage rate; whether she is married and, if so, how much her husband earns; whether she has children and, if so, how many and how old they are; and many other details. Later we will see exactly how each of those factors affects her choice. But let's start by examining the general logic behind her choice, a logic that ought to hold no matter what her particular circumstances are.

We can write out her choice problem as follows. She chooses values of three potential uses of time—market work, household work, and leisure—to maximize utility. Utility depends on the amount of consumption goods (C), household-produced goods (G), and leisure time (L). The amount of consumption goods depends on the amount of time spent in market work (M) and also on the amount of nonlabor income (V). The amount of household goods depends on the amount of time spent in household production (H). Finally, L is the time left over not spent in M or H. Putting all this together, the utility function is $U = U(C(M), G(H), L)$, where the terms in parentheses inside the equation reflect the links between the time inputs and the outputs they produce.

Three separate constraints limit what she can choose:

Market goods: $pC = wM + V$ (a)

Household goods: $G = g(H; Z)$ (b)

Time: $M + H + L = T$ (c)

The first of these is *spending*: the amount of spending on goods and services (pC) must equal the amount of income earned (wM) plus nonlabor income (V). In other words, she can't spend more than the amount of income she has. The second constraint is *production*: the amount of household goods that can be produced depends on the amount of time spent and on the technology and capital goods available (Z). Finally, the third constraint is time: there are only so many hours in a day (T), and the total amount of time spent on each activity can't exceed that amount.

The solution to this utility-maximization problem will be the best values for M, H, and L. We will be particularly interested in M^* (remember, the asterisk indicates that it is a best choice) and analyzing whether $M^* = 0$ (no market work) or $M^* > 0$ (some market work).

You can see in the constraints the nature of the choices that have to be made. To have more market goods requires working more hours in the labor market, which means less time is available to produce household goods and/or to enjoy leisure. To have more household production requires more household hours, which means less time is available for leisure and/or for earning the income necessary for acquiring market goods. Similarly, more leisure means fewer household goods and/or fewer consumption goods. Something has to give. Let's try to see how a best choice can be made.

Non-market choices—leisure and household production It is easier to solve this problem in stages. First, consider a woman's choice between leisure and household production, ignoring work in the labor market. We'll establish a rule or condition that ought to guide her choice between those two time uses. Then we'll see if substituting work in the labor market would raise her utility.

What rule should she follow for allocating her time in the household in order to maximize utility? There are three steps.

Step 1: *Think marginally, one hour at a time.*[6] She should compare the value of an hour spent in leisure with the value of that same hour spent in household production. For example, if she were currently taking 24 hours of leisure and zero hours of household work (an odd combination, to be sure), she ought to compare the value of the 24th hour of leisure with the value of the first hour of household work time. Next she would compare the value of the 23rd hour of leisure with the value of the second hour of household work time, and so on and so on. Choices are made on the margin.

Step 2: *Always choose the time use with the higher marginal value of time.* If an hour spent in household production is more valuable than that same hour spent in leisure, then she ought to spend that hour in household production. Why? If she switched the hour from leisure to household production, she would lose utility equal to the lower MVT_H and gain utility equal to the higher MVT_L. In the preceding example, if $MVT_L(1) > MVT_H(24)$—which seems quite likely—then she can make herself better off by switching an hour of time from household production to leisure.

---

6   Again, it may make sense to think of smaller time units.

Step 3: *Equalize marginal values.* Using the logic of step 2 and carrying it to its extreme, the best allocation of non-market time occurs when the marginal value of the last hour spent in leisure just equals the marginal value of the last hour spent in household production. Unless the two marginal values are equal, it is always possible to shift an hour from the use with the lower marginal value to the use with the higher marginal value and increase total utility, while spending the same number of total hours.

These ideas are shown in Figure 7.5, which includes the marginal value of time curves for leisure and household work. Hours of leisure (L) are measured in the usual way from left to right on the horizontal axis from 0 to 24. Hours of household production (H) are shown on the same axis but are measured backward from right to left. We can do that because the sum of leisure and household hours must equal 24, the total amount of time available. Two MVT curves are shown and both exhibit diminishing marginal utility. The height of the curve shows the MVT for that particular hour; both curves are downward-sloping. (Be careful to read the MVT curve for household hours from right to left.) The two curves are drawn as straight lines, but they could just as well be concave or convex, as long as they were downward-sloping. We use numbers for the MVT curves to make the comparisons simpler, but the numbers themselves are just illustrative.

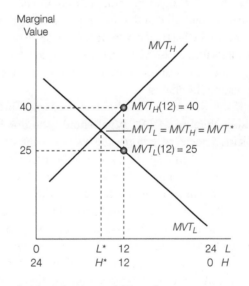

Figure 7.5 *Choosing household production and leisure hours.*

Pick any point on the horizontal axis. That point corresponds to a particular combination of hours of leisure (measured from left to right) and hours of household work (measured from right to left). If you move vertically up to the MVT curves and then over to the vertical axis where utility is measured, you can find the MVTs corresponding to any particular combination of L and H. Look at the (12, 12) combination. Suppose that at that particular combination, $MVT_L = 25$ and $MVT_H = 40$. Since the two marginal values of time are not equal, it is possible to do better. In this case, she should increase H (which will decrease its MVT) and decrease L (which will increase its MVT). She thus moves down the MVT_H curve and up the MVT_L curve, narrowing the difference between MVT_H and MVT_L. The very best combination is always where the two marginal curves intersect. At the intersection point, the MVTs are equal; in addition, all 24 hours are accounted for.

The rule for the utility-maximizing choice of non-market time between leisure and household production is therefore that L and H should be chosen such that $MVT_L(L^*) = MVT_H(H^*)$ and also that $L^* + H^* = T$.[7] This is an example of an **equi-marginal rule** for maximization. If the marginal values are unequal, she can always rearrange her time use, switching time from its less valuable use to its more valuable use, and be better off as a result. Only when the MVTs are equal is it impossible to make a change that makes her better off.

To simplify the analysis of labor-force participation which follows next, let's refer to the particular value of MVT_L and MVT_H that solves this part of the problem as MVT*. That is, MVT* is the value of the last hour of time, when all time is spent on either leisure or household production and when that time is allocated so as to maximize utility.

Labor-force participation Now let's see whether she might be able to do better yet by working in the labor market. The analysis involves the same logic we used for the first part of this problem. If she works one hour—remember, we are assuming for simplicity that she can choose any number of hours of work she likes—she will gain utility equal to the marginal value of that first hour of market time. Because the value for the first hour of work will be particularly important, let's write it as $MVT_M(1)$, where the 1 in parentheses reminds us that the MVT in question is for that particular hour. We could easily substitute some other minimum required amount of work time for one hour without fundamentally changing the analysis.

If she works that first hour, she will gain utility equal to $MVT_M(1)$, and she will lose utility equal to MVT*. What should she do? Using exactly the same kind of marginal decision logic as before, she would want to compare these two marginal values. If $MVT_M(1) < MVT^*$, then she cannot increase her utility by working in the market. Her utility would fall by MVT* and rise by the smaller amount $MVT_M(1)$. In that case she is a utility-maximizing nonparticipant in the labor market. If, however, $MVT_M(1) > MVT^*$, she will be better off by transferring an hour of time from leisure or household production to the labor market. In so doing, her utility will rise by $MVT_M(1)$ and fall by the smaller amount, MVT*. She will end up better off, with a higher utility level.

These simple comparisons yield the utility-maximizing rules for market work. Let M^* stand for the utility-maximizing hours of work. Then, the rules for labor-force participation are:

If $MVT^* > MVT_M(1)$, then $M^* = 0$.   (7.4) This woman does not work in the labor market.

If $MVT^* < MVT_M(1)$, $M^* > 0$.   (7.5) This woman works in the labor market.

---

7 The second condition just means that all time is used. Many combinations of L and H satisfy the equi-marginal rule but don't use up all available hours.

If condition (7.4) holds, the woman would choose 0 hours of market work. If, however, condition (7.5) holds, how many hours should she work? She ought to proceed hour by hour in exactly the same way, always comparing MVT_M, now evaluated at $M = 2, 3, 4$, and so on, with the corresponding MVT in the non-market sector. Two things will happen as hours of market work increase. First, MVT_M will fall because of diminishing marginal utility of goods that her work hours provide: $\mathrm{MVT}_M(3) < \mathrm{MVT}_M(2) < \mathrm{MVT}_M(1)$, and so on. Second, MVT_L and MVT_H will both rise because less time is now being spent in those uses, and the marginal value at fewer hours is always higher. L and H still ought to be chosen so that these two MVTs remain equal, which means that when M increases, both L and H ought to be reduced (although not necessarily equally). The best value for M occurs when its marginal value has fallen enough and the marginal value of leisure and household time have risen enough that all three are exactly equal. In symbols, this best choice, represented by an asterisk (*), is given by the following two conditions:

$$\mathrm{MVT}_L(L^*) \; = \; \mathrm{MVT}_H(H^*) \; = \; \mathrm{MVT}_M(M^*) \tag{7.6}$$

and

$$L^* + H^* + M^* = T. \tag{7.7}$$

Equation (7.6) is the equi-marginal rule for time allocation, when $M^* > 0$. Equation (7.7) means that all time is accounted for. When $M^* = 0$, the corresponding rule is that $\mathrm{MVT}_L(L^*) = \mathrm{MVT}_H(H^*) > \mathrm{MVT}_M(1)$.

Figure 7.6 shows this idea graphically. The figure on the left is the same as Figure 7.5, but now we have added on the right the MVT curve for hours of market work. Two MVT_M curves are shown, one much higher than the other. (We'll see why the position of the MVT_M curve is likely to vary across women shortly.) Both exhibit diminishing marginal value because they slope downward. When all time is spent on leisure or household production, MVT* is shown by the height of the curves where they intersect.

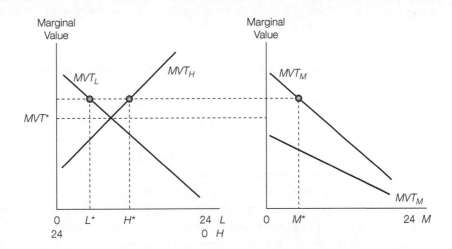

Figure 7.6 *Choosing household production, leisure, and market work hours.*

Now compare that value to the value of market time at $M = 1$. For a woman represented by the lower curve, $\mathrm{MVT}^* < \mathrm{MVT}_M(1)$, so her best choice is to continue to spend all of her time in leisure and household production. For a woman with the higher MVT_M curve, however, it is clear that $MVT^* > MVT_M(1)$. So her best choice is to transfer some time to the labor market. How much? Move up the two MVT curves on the left, keeping them equal at all times, and down the MVT_M curve on the right by an equivalent amount, until all three marginal values are equal. A situation like that is shown by the three points along the higher dotted line in Figure 7.6. Here, leisure (measured from left to right) equals L^*, household work (measured from right to left) equals H^* and hours of market work are M^*. M^* is also equal to the horizontal distance between L^* and H^*.

To recapitulate, we have analyzed the choice of a woman among three uses of time—leisure, household production, and market work. Each is characterized by some marginal value that depends on her preferences, her household productivity, and her wage rate, among other things. She makes a choice that maximizes the utility she obtains from leisure, household-produced goods, and market goods. That choice is determined by comparing the marginal value of time across its uses. Whether she is a labor-force participant depends on that comparison.

We can also write out the solution to this labor-force participation problem in terms of all the exogenous variables in the problem. This will be useful for analyzing the comparative statics of labor-force participation decisions. The exogenous variables are found in the three constraints—the real wage (w/p), the amount of nonlabor income (V) from the spending constraint, and productivity in the household sector, which we can represent through the production function, $g(H; Z)$. Thus we have

$$P^* = P(w/p, V, g(H; Z)) \tag{7.8}$$

where P^* is the utility-maximizing choice of labor-force participation. Equation (7.8) is a woman's labor-force participation equation. In words, it says that a woman's best choice about participating in the labor market depends on her real wage rate, her nonlabor income (which may include her husband's income), and her productivity in the household sector. The next task is to see how changes in these variables affect the participation choice.

Explaining the increase in women's labor-force participation

The most important purpose of a time-use model like this one is to apply it to the real-world situation of women. We can do this in two different ways. First, we can look over historical time—for instance, the course of the twentieth century—to examine the likely changes in the three MVT schedules and the effect of these changes on labor-force participation decisions. For example, we might want to know how an increase in the wage rate for women would affect market work, household work, and leisure. Similarly, there have been enormous changes in the technology of household production and changes in the earnings of husbands, and we certainly would want to examine their likely impact. This approach is called a **time-series analysis**. Second, we can look at a particular point in time and examine how differences among women in their MVT schedules affect their labor-force participation. For example, we can try to explain the differences in LFPR between better-educated and less-educated women or between black and white women. This kind of approach is called a **cross-sectional analysis**.

In analyzing these problems, we continue to focus on labor-force participation decisions rather than on hours of work decisions. It is much easier to analyze participation decisions with the tools we have developed, and, as we've seen, it has changed tremendously in ways that have transformed not only women's lives but also the lives of men and children.

Husband's income

Let's consider the effect of a husband's income on the labor-force participation of a married woman in a setting in which her market work decision is clearly secondary to his. This was certainly true for most married couples through at least the first three-quarters of the twentieth century and it is still true to a lesser extent today. See Box 3.1 for details.

We don't need to change our framework or our decision rule to analyze this. Her husband's income functions like nonlabor income (V) to her. It enables the family to purchase a certain amount of goods and services even when her labor supply hours are zero. Let's call that amount C_H, where the subscript H indicates that it is the consumption made possible by the husband's income. If a woman's husband earns a great deal, then C_H is high; if he earns less, then C_H is lower.

Now think about how this will affect her MVT_M curve. We saw in equation (7.3') that MVT_M is composed of two separate terms, one reflecting her real wage rate and the other the marginal utility of consumption goods that the family consumes based on her earnings. That equation is repeated here:

$$\text{MVT}_M \equiv MU_C(C) \times w/p \tag{7.3'}$$

As long as her work decision is secondary to his, then the appropriate marginal utility of consumption for the goods and services made available by her first hour of work begins at C_H, the goods and services the family *already* has from his income. If C_H is high, then the marginal utility of the additional goods she could provide will be relatively low. This follows directly from the idea of diminishing marginal utility of consumption. If, however, C_H is much lower—her husband is poorer—then the marginal utility of the additional goods she could provide will be much higher. In this case, her income will provide more essential goods that have a higher marginal utility. The critical element is therefore $MU_C(C_H)$, the marginal utility of consumption goods evaluated at the level of goods provided by her spouse.

We want to consider only the effect of having a richer or poorer husband, so imagine that everything else is unchanged. We've just shown that the higher the husband's income is, the lower the entire MU_C curve will be; it begins at $MU_C(C_H)$. This, in turn, means that the value of $\text{MVT}_M(1)$ will be lower. As a result, she is less likely to work in the labor market: $\text{MVT}^* > \text{MVT}_M(1)$, because the latter term will be lower. Thus the model predicts that a wife will be less likely to work outside the home if her husband's income is high and more likely to work if her husband's income is lower.

Turn back to Figure 7.6. The two MVT_M curves there could represent two different women, with the same wage and other characteristics except for the income of their respective husbands. The lower curve would be for a woman with a high-income husband. Her MVT_M curve is lower because the value of the additional goods her earnings would provide is lower. Because the family already has a lot of consumption, she chooses no market work. The higher curve would be for a woman with a lower-income husband. Her MVT_M curve is higher because the value of the additional goods she could provide is higher. So for her, market work is the best choice.

In fact, this pattern is a common one. Consider, for example, the historical difference in the labor-force participation of black married women and white married women. Married black women had substantially higher rates of work; we saw that in Box 7.1 about women's work in 1900, and it was true throughout most of the twentieth century. Why? It certainly was not because black women had more attractive labor-market opportunities. Indeed, they did not. But their husbands fared far worse, on average, than the husbands of white women. Black men earned much less than white men—less than 50 percent in the years before 1940. Thus more black women found themselves in the situation of the woman in Figure 7.6 with the higher MVT curve. Even today, when married women's LFPRs are many times higher than at the beginning of the twentieth century, differences based on the income of a woman's husband still exist.

The effect of husband's income on his wife's labor-force participation is also an important idea in macroeconomics and labor economics, where it is called the **added worker hypothesis**. Here the idea is that in a recession, if a husband loses his job, his wife may enter the labor-force in response. This is just an extreme version of differences in husband's income. In this case the extreme decrease in income caused by unemployment increases a wife's MVT_M curve by increasing the marginal utility of the consumption her earnings would provide.

Over the course of the twentieth century, changes in the average husband's income would have mostly affected women's labor-force participation negatively. From 1900 to about 1975, men's earnings rose steadily, doubling after adjusting for inflation just in the years between 1945 and 1971. Since then, men's average earnings have been relatively stagnant. This tells us that, in general, men's incomes were providing more consumption goods over time, which, taken by itself, would have decreased the MVT_M curve and thus reduced the likelihood that a married woman would work.

This is actually a very important conclusion. People often think of a married woman as being "pushed" into the labor market by the inadequacy of her husband's income. While that may be true in some cases, it really can't explain why more women are working today than in the past because, on average, men's real earnings are so much higher than in the earlier parts of the twentieth century. For an explanation of why women's work increased, we must look elsewhere.

Woman's wage rates

What about women's wages? They, too, have increased consistently and substantially over the course of the century. Because the wage rate is part of the marginal value of market time, that curve is the natural candidate. If a woman has a higher wage rate, then, all else being constant, her MVT_M curve will be higher because she can get more goods and services per hour of work. Equation (7.3'), repeated here once again, shows this:

$$MVT_M = MU_C(C) \times w/p \tag{7.3'}$$

In this case a higher wage rate would increase $MVT_M(1)$, thus potentially putting a woman in the condition of utility-maximizing labor-force participation ($MVT^* > MVT_M(1)$). So we would expect higher wages to increase a woman's labor-force participation.[8]

Again, we can use Figure 7.6, this time interpreting the higher curve as belonging to a higher-wage woman and the lower curve as belonging to a lower-wage woman. The evidence for this general effect is strong. LFPRs are positively related to a woman's level of education. About one-third of women who were high-school dropouts worked in 2013, compared to 45 percent for high-school graduates, more than two-thirds for women with some postsecondary schooling, and more than 70 percent for those with a college degree. Some of this relationship could represent other factors, especially age and cohort—the high-school dropouts are likely to be older and from earlier cohorts. Nevertheless, the relationship is obviously a strong one.

Over the course of the twentieth century, women's wage rates have risen enormously. In Chapter 5 we discussed changes in women's wage rates in the context of fertility; see Box 5.2. The basic point is quite clear—in the first half of the twentieth century, wages for US women were very low by twenty-first century standards. Over the course of the century, and especially in the years since 1950, women's wages have increased tremendously.

Getting more productive—at home

Think about the vast arsenal of household technology that is now a regular part of American family life—everything from washers and dryers to dishwashers and microwave ovens. Perhaps you think they've always been there, but, of course, they haven't. See Box 7.3 for details.

Box   7.3

Household Production: Now and Then

In the early decades of the twentieth century, household technology was incredibly primitive by our current standards. Not more than a fifth of US households had central heating, flush toilets, and electricity, and fewer than half had running water. At midcentury, virtually no households had dishwashers or clothes dryers, and between half and two-thirds had vacuum cleaners, washers, and refrigerators. Microwave ovens had not yet made an appearance.

Greenwood, Seshardi, and Yorukoglu provide a detailed description of what this meant for daily life, especially for a housewife. In 1890 the absence of running water and central heating meant that the average household had to handle and transport seven tons of coal and 9000 gallons of water. Clothes washing was an elaborate and time-consuming ordeal. They write: "Water had to be ported to the stove, where it was heated by burning wood or coal. The clothes were then cleaned via a washboard or

---

8 If we were analyzing the effect of a wage increase on work hours for a woman already working in the labor market, the analysis would be more complicated and would involve conflicting income and substitution effects. Those complications are not relevant here.

mechanical washing machine. They had to be rinsed out after this. The water needed to be wrung out, either by hand or by using a mechanical wringer. After this, the clothes were hung out to dry on a clothes line. Then, the oppressive task of ironing began, using heavy flatirons that had to be heated continuously on the stove" (p.112). They cite the example of one housewife who compared her time input in clothes washing before and after the adoption of an electric washer, dryer, and iron. Using the old technology, it took her 4 hours to do the wash and another 4.5 hours to iron it. With the new technology, it took her 41 minutes to do the wash and 1.75 hours to do the ironing.

Ramey and Francis developed estimates of time spent in household production over the twentieth century. In 1900 the average woman aged 25–54 spent over 50 hours per week in household production; the average man of that age spent 3.7. In 1950, women's average work time had come down to 42.7 and men's had increased to 9.2. Note just how modest those changes were and how great the division of labor by gender was. As of 2005, the last year with data in the study, the average 25–54-year-old woman spent 31 hours in household production compared to 17 for the average man.

Sources:

Jeremy Greenwood, Ananth Seshardi, and Mehmet Yorukoglu (2005), "Engines of Liberation," *Review of Economic Studies*, 72, 109–133.

Valerie A. Ramey and Neville Francis (2009), "A Century of Work and Leisure," *American Economic Journal: Macroeconomics*, 1 (2), 189–224.

How did these changes in household technology affect work choices? In the first instance, they made individuals (usually, of course, women) much more productive. They raised the marginal product of household time in the sense that it became possible to produce many more household goods and services per hour than in the old days. For example, producing clean clothing became a matter of an hour or two rather than a day; a dinner could similarly be produced in a fraction of the time it formerly took.

This change in marginal product affects MVT_H. Recall that the value of household time depends on two things, the marginal product and the marginal utility of household goods. The exact relationship is shown in equation (2'), which is repeated here:

$$MVT_H = MU_G(G) \times MP_H(H) \tag{7.2'}$$

The net change in MVT_H in this case is a bit complicated. Suppose the marginal product of household time exactly doubled so that twice as much could be produced per hour as before. (This is, as we saw in Box 7.3, a substantial underestimate of the actual change in productivity.) Because marginal utility declines the more goods a person has, the total value of an hour of household time won't double—the additional output is not as highly valued. It's not impossible to imagine that the net value of household time is much higher for the first several hours of household work, in which the most highly valued tasks—clean clothing and food on the table—are produced at a high rate. But it's also quite possible that the value of time for yet more hours could actually be lower than in the days of low productivity because the output produced in those last hours is not highly valued. In a sense, so much household output is being produced in the first few hours that the marginal value of subsequent hours is very low. In contrast, when productivity is low, the marginal value of the last hours of household production time is still highly valued. Important and needed goods and services are still being produced in those last hours.

If we drew a picture of this change, the new MVT_H curve would be twisted—well above the original curve at first, but eventually below it. This is shown in Figure 7.7. The straight line is the old MVT_H curve, showing a curve that is relatively low, declining, but not very rapidly. The other curve is much higher at first, but much steeper. It starts well above the old curve, cuts it at H_0, and then is lower for all hours beyond that.

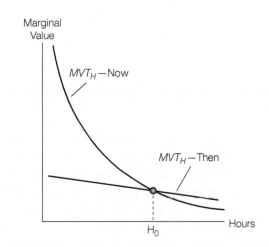

Figure 7.7 *The effect of an increase in household productivity on the MVT_H curve.*

How would this affect labor-force participation? Figure 7.8 captures one possibility. Just as in Figure 7.7, the MVT_H curve twists, and the intersection with the MVT_L curve now shifts to the right, from point A to point B. That change involves a shift from household work to leisure and, more importantly, a fall in MVT^*, the value of the last hour of time in the household. At the situation depicted by point A, it doesn't make sense to work in the labor market because the value of time there is below MVT^*. But at the situation depicted by point B, it now makes sense to work. Thus, in this case, the sharp increase in household productivity has the effect of increasing the LFPR.

Putting it all together

Over the course of the twentieth century there were many changes in economic constraints and opportunities so that virtually all the curves changed. Following is a summary of the most likely set of changes:

- Women's wages increased sharply and consistently. This increased the value of work time for nonworking women, and thus increased their labor-force participation.
- Husbands' wages increased sharply and consistently as well, at least through the early 1970s. This decreased the value of work time for nonworking wives by reducing the

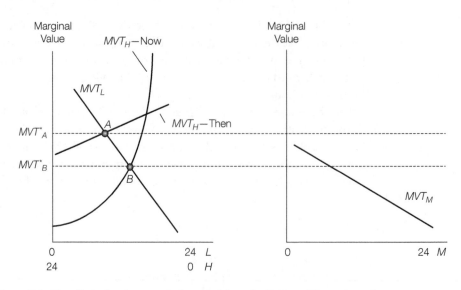

Figure 7.8 *The effect of an increase in household productivity on Women's work.*

marginal utility of the goods and services their earnings would contribute. Taken by itself, this would have reduced women's labor-force participation.

- Household productivity increased many times over. This probably increased women's labor-force participation by reducing the value of the marginal hour of household time. So much more could be accomplished in so much less time that it freed up time for market work.

Figure 7.9 shows a composite now-and-then picture of the forces behind labor-force participation. Figure 7.9(A) describes a time in the first half of the twentieth century, while Figure 7.9(B) describes a time early in the twenty-first century. The two MVT curves for leisure are identical. But the other two curves have changed in the ways described in the summary listing just above. The MVT_H curve in Figure 7.9(B) is higher, but also much steeper than in Figure 7.9(A), reflecting the much higher household productivity, but also its low marginal value. As a result, the value of MVT* is higher in Figure 7.9(A) than in Figure 7.9(B). In the labor-market graphs, the MVT_M curve has also shifted up in Figure 7.9(B). This shift reflects conflicting influences. The enormous increase in women's wages pushes it up; the increase in husband's earnings pushes it down. The net effect is almost certainly a big increase. The result of all these changes is a shift from nonparticipation in Figure 7.9(A) to participation in Figure 7.9(B).

Fertility and labor-force participation—a review and reconciliation

Decisions about fertility and labor-force participation are very closely related for most women, and our analyses of these two decisions are complementary and reinforcing. The approach we have taken in this chapter is a bit different than the way we analyzed fertility, but the results fit together very comfortably, as, of course, they should.

The key difference in the two analyses is that in Chapter 5, when we analyzed fertility decisions, we focused on specific *outputs* of a household production function.

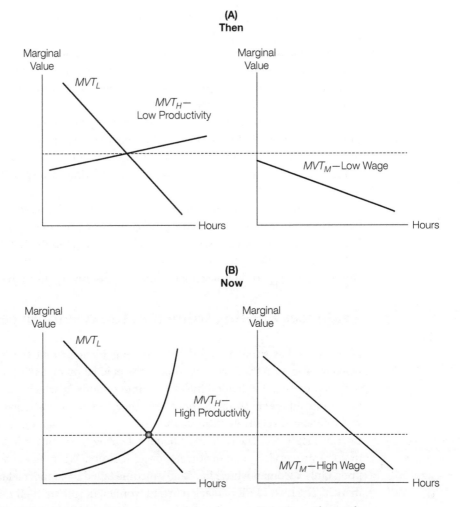

Figure 7.9 *The factors behind women's labor-force participation—then and now.*

Those outputs were child quantity and child quality, while the key input was a woman's time. In this chapter, as we analyzed labor-force participation, we shifted our focus to the *input* side of the household production process, in particular the allocation of a woman's time across alternative uses.

Let's dig a little deeper. In our analysis of fertility decisions in Chapter 5, a woman's wage rate was the price of her time and was the key determinant of the cost of producing child services. Because child services are a very time-intensive household-produced good, their cost increased substantially as women's wages and labor-market opportunities increased. Indeed, we suggested that child quantity (fertility) fell and child quality increased as a result of that increase, reflecting, in part, the different time vs. goods intensity of the two components of child services. In shifting from quantity to quality, women were reducing the amount of time spent in household production of child services. That time had to go somewhere and, although we didn't say so explicitly, it was going from the household sector to the labor market where it provided the monetary resources necessary to provide higher child quality; remember that quality is goods-intensive.

In this chapter we see the same result directly. As women's wages increased over the course of the twentieth- and twenty-first centuries, this sharply increased the value of time spent in the labor market, measured by the MVT_M curve. We showed that often this resulted in a shift of time away from leisure and household production and into market work. Much of a woman's time previously spent in the household was, of course, involved in the production of child services, especially child quantity in an era when fertility was high. The reduction in time spent in household production is the input side counterpart of the reduction in fertility. They go together, reflecting corresponding changes in outputs and input use.

Putting the two analyses together, we see that the increase in the value of time—a woman's wage rate—contributed to the rising price of child quantity and, equivalently, increased the value of time spent in the labor market. On the fertility side, child quantity fell and child quality increased. On the time input side, the corresponding changes were a shift from time spent in household production to time spent in the labor market.

Evidence: working women in the twentieth century

Dora Costa[9] has summarized the empirical evidence about the importance of married women's wages on their participation in the paid labor-force. She suggests that the twentieth century can be divided into three time periods in which the underlying influences were quite different. Through about 1930 the labor-force participation of married women was influenced relatively little by their own potential wage rates. Rather, the income of their husbands was the primary influence. During this time period, most women worked in domestic service, manufacturing, or agriculture. Working conditions were often very poor. Only a woman whose husband's income failed to support a family entered the labor market. The high LFPR of black married women, in spite of their own low wage rates, is a good example of this.

In the middle part of the century, a woman's labor-force participation was more strongly influenced by her own wage rate and the impact of her husband's income diminished. Women with better labor-market prospects began to enter the labor market, while those with poorer prospects tended not to work. By the end of the century and into the twenty-first century, the influence of both her own wage and her husband's income were smaller. Participation became much more of a norm. But do recall the large, positive relationship between a woman's own education and the proportion working. This suggests that wage effects can hardly be unimportant at some wage levels.

The impact of World War II on US women's labor-force activity deserves special attention. Between 1940 and 1945, the male labor-force declined by almost 9 million and the female labor-force increased by 7 million, amounting to nearly a one-third increase. Some have argued that the war was a "watershed" event, permanently changing women's attachment to the labor market and societal values about the appropriateness of married women

---

9 Dora L. Costa (2000), "From Mill Town to Board Room: The Rise of Women's Paid Labor," *Journal of Economic Perspectives*, 14 (4), 101–122.

working. This would be equivalent to an outward shift of the labor-supply curve, meaning that more women were willing to work at a given wage rate than in the past. Others have argued that it was a temporary change, reflecting the unique circumstances of that time period, and that changing wage rates were still the primary mechanism behind women's increased labor-force activity.

Claudia Goldin has analyzed the role of World War II in a set of studies. One took advantage of an unusual data source (the Palmer survey) that provided work histories for women as of 1950 and thus enabled them to link their work status in that year with their work experience during the war.[10] The question she focused on was whether working during the war was strongly related to working after the war. Among white women aged 35–64 in 1950, more than 50 percent who were working in 1950 had been working in 1940, prior to the war. About 20 percent of those working in 1950 had first entered the labor-force during the war, but about half of those who entered during the war were no longer working in 1950. From this evidence, Goldin concluded that the war was not, in fact, a watershed event in women's labor-force participation.

In a newer study, Goldin and Claudia Olivetti[11] looked at the short-run (1950) and long-run (1960) effects of the war on women's labor-force participation and came to a slightly different conclusion. This research took advantage of yet another natural experiment, this one based on differential war mobilization rates for men across US states. Those rates differed because the rate of military deferments varied across states, reflecting differences in employment in agriculture and manufacturing. The average mobilization rate for 18–44-year-old men was 44 percent, but it ranged from a low of 40 percent to a high of 56 percent. The general idea of this analysis is that the different mobilization rates created different labor-market opportunities for women in different states that were unrelated to other factors that might affect labor-force participation. The research question they focus on is whether women in states with higher mobilization rates, who had greater labor-market opportunities during the war, responded differently after the war in the short run (1950) and long run (1960). Instead of linking a woman's labor-force status in 1950 or 1960 to her actual work experience during the war, Goldin and Olivetti link it to her opportunity to work.[12]

This study focused on the labor-force participation of young white women, aged 25–34 in 1950 and 35–44 in 1960. Goldin and Olivetti focus on white women because black women had, as we have seen, much higher LFPRs before the war. They examined impacts separately by education (whether or not a woman was a high-school graduate), marital status, and whether a woman had a child; these factors are all measured as of wartime. For less-educated women there is no effect on subsequent labor-force participation or weeks worked in either 1950 or 1960. Women who were not high-school graduates were no more likely to be working or to work more if they lived in a high mobilization state or a low mobilization state. But for the women who were high-school graduates, they did find

---

10 Claudia Goldin (1991), "The Role of World War II in the Rise of Women's Employment," *American Economic Review,* 81 (4), 741–756.

11 Claudia Goldin and Claudia Olivetti (2013), "Shocking Labor Supply: A Reassessment of the Role of World War II on Women's Labor Supply," *American Economic Review,* 103 (3), 257–262.

12 This eliminates the need to have information on women's work histories, which are not available for that time period.

an impact of the war on subsequent labor-force activity. Married women without children in a high mobilization state worked an average of 2.9 weeks more in 1950 than women in a low mobilization state. This may not sound like much, but it is nearly a 30 percent difference, because the average weeks worked for all women was so low. The impact on married women with children is half as large and is not statistically significant. Single women from high mobilization states worked about 2.6 weeks more. The impacts are similar for labor-force participation—bigger effects for women without children during the war than for married women with children. All of these impacts are relative to the differences between the same groups in 1940, prior to the mobilization.[13]

This difference between women with and without children makes sense. Goldin and Olivetti note that the husbands of married women with children were eligible for a deferment for most of the war, while the husbands of married women without children were not. As a result, married women with children were likely to have had less actual work experience during the war. Thus the postwar impact on them would likely be less. That is exactly what they found.

They repeated their analysis for 1960, when the women were aged 35–44. Here they found bigger effects for women who were married during the war, with or without children, than for single women. The effects are similar in magnitude to those for 1950.

The evidence in this study provides more support for the "war as watershed" interpretation than Goldin's earlier study. To reconcile the two sets of findings, Goldin and Olivetti returned to the Palmer survey data that Goldin had used. The jobs that women in that survey held during the war were closely related to their own education. Women who were high-school graduates typically entered white-collar occupations, such as clerical or secretarial work, while women with less education entered blue-collar assembly line and other manufacturing work. Goldin and Olivetti speculate that when men returned after the war, these opportunities for women in blue-collar jobs vanished. That may be why they found no effect of mobilization rates on subsequent employment for less-educated women. But better-educated women were able to continue in the white-collar (or pink-collar) employment that began during the war. Thus Goldin and Olivetti conclude that the war was a watershed event for the labor-force activity of better-educated women, but not for less-educated women.

Summary

It is no overstatement to call the increase in the labor-force participation of married women one of the most profound labor-market phenomena of the twentieth century. In the United States and throughout most of the developed world, their LFPRs rose from not much more than 10 percent in the early part of the century to 60 percent, 70 percent, or more at the end of the century and in the 2010s. Marriage and children no longer signaled the end of regular labor-force participation for women. In the United States, participation rate differences between men and women dropped from 65 percent in 1900 to about 12 percent in the mid-2010s. The demographic characteristics

---

13   This is a DID analysis similar to what we discussed in Chapter 2. The differencing eliminates the effect of pre-existing differences between women in different states.

that previously dictated low labor-force participation—such things as marriage and the presence of young children—barely make a dent in the participation rate now. We have seen a broad slowdown in the rate of increase in women's labor-force participation since the mid-1990s, and even a decline in participation rates for some groups, especially married women with young children. These trends bear watching. Just possibly, the movement of women into the labor market has reached a threshold. We say more about this in Chapter 8.

The economic approach we took considered market work in the broader context of time-use choices among three potential uses—market work, household production, and leisure. The key concept was the marginal value of time in each of these uses. The decision rule involved choosing amounts of the three time uses so that the marginal values were everywhere equal. If they all weren't equal, a rearrangement of time from a lower-valued marginal use to a higher-valued marginal use would always make an individual better off. This is, in fact, an application of a common economic maximizing rule: to maximize the total value of something, make all marginal values equal. This kind of rule is often called an **equi-marginal rule**.

Just as with the decline in fertility, the primary candidate for explaining the rise in women's labor-force participation is the wage rate. The wage rate determines the value of market work. Women's wage rates have increased many times over since the early decades of the twentieth century. Changes in household productivity are also undoubtedly important. The enormous change in household capital goods paradoxically lowered the marginal value of household production time by making it possible to accomplish so much so quickly. The impact of changes in the earnings of men is most likely to reduce participation because men's earnings have risen over most of the twentieth century. Changes in attitudes and the development of role models are also certainly important parts of the explanation.

The changes in fertility and labor-force participation are best understood as two sides of a coin. The rising price of time raised the marginal value of market time and simultaneously increased the cost of child services. We argued in Chapter 5 that the fertility response was to reduce the amount of time spent producing child services and increase the goods component of fertility—that is, the transition from child quantity to child quality. Women did that primarily by shifting their time from the household sector and the production of child services to the labor market.

In the next chapter we continue our discussion of labor-market issues by focusing on a set of contemporary applied topics.

Appendix: Labor supply analysis—an alternative approach

Introduction

An alternative way to analyze labor supply behavior uses indifference curves and budget constraints. It is a more elegant approach because it emphasizes the role and importance of prices in a way that the model in the chapter does not. It is, however, both more difficult and, at the same time, more limited. The standard model focuses almost exclusively on two time-use choices because that is the natural limit of a graphical approach. Those two choices are typically taken to be market work and leisure; thus household production is ignored. It is possible to integrate household production into the model, but it is difficult to do so and requires some strong simplifications.

In this appendix we present the standard indifference curve/budget constraint approach to labor-supply analysis. We assume familiarity with the basic idea of indifference curves and budget constraints, and focus on applying them to the labor-supply context. We continue to focus on issues of labor-force participation rather than hours of work because that is where the action has been in the twentieth century for women.

The basics of labor-supply analysis

Preferences

We assume that a woman derives utility from two broad categories of goods—leisure time (L) and expenditures on market goods (C). Note that C is measured in money (e.g., dollars or euros) rather than the amount of goods themselves. It is, for example, the amount spent on bananas, not the bananas themselves. This makes the notation a bit easier without changing anything important.[14] Thus we write her utility function as $U = U(C, L)$.

Her preferences for market goods and leisure are represented graphically via a set of **indifference curves**, as shown in Figure A.1. Hours of leisure are measured along the horizontal axis and the amount of consumption goods is measured along the vertical axis. Any particular point represents a specific combination of leisure time and consumption goods. By the definition of an indifference curve, all the combinations of leisure time and consumption goods along a given indifference curve are equally desirable.

These leisure-market goods indifference curves have all the standard properties of indifference curves: they are negatively sloped and convex (bowed inward toward the origin), and more preferred indifference curves are positioned toward the northeast. The slope of the indifference curve ($\Delta C/\Delta L$, holding U constant) represents the **marginal rate of substitution** (MRS).

More carefully, the MRS is the negative (or absolute value) of the slope of an indifference curve: $MRS \equiv -(\Delta C/\Delta L) \mid U$, where "$\mid U$" indicates that utility is held constant. Because this is a definition, we use the identity symbol rather than an equals sign.

The MRS is the rate at which a woman is willing to give up consumption goods to acquire an hour of leisure. The higher the MRS is, the more an hour of leisure is valued. Certainly, different individuals may value leisure differently, but more importantly the MRS will likely also depend on the amount of goods and the amount of leisure that an individual already has. That is, the MRS isn't a constant number, but rather it varies with the amount of leisure and consumption goods one already has.

---

14 An alternative way to think of this is that the price of all goods equals $1, so that the expenditures and amount of goods are equal. This is acceptable because we aren't interested in the details of consumption goods demand.

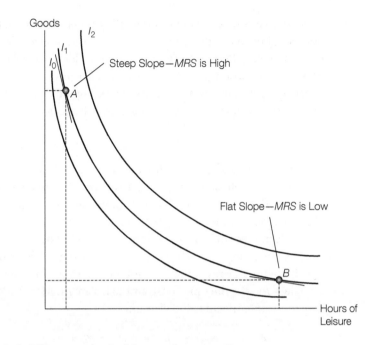

Figure A.1 *Indifference curves for leisure and consumption.*

If a woman currently has very little leisure but a lot of consumption goods, as at point A on indifference curve I_1, then she would probably be willing to give up a great deal of consumption to acquire an hour of leisure because that hour is very valuable. Thus her MRS at A would be quite high and is reflected in the steep slope of the indifference curve there (see the steep tangent line at A). Conversely, if she had relatively little consumption and a great deal of leisure (point B), she would be willing to give up very little consumption to get yet more leisure. Her MRS would therefore be much lower. At B, the indifference curve has a flatter slope; see the flat tangent line at B.

In general the more leisure one has, the less valuable yet another bit of it would be; thus the MRS is lower. This property of preferences is called a **diminishing marginal rate of substitution**. It applies not just to leisure and goods but to almost any pair of goods. The standard shape of an indifference curve—bowed in toward the origin, steeper at the top, and flatter at the bottom—represents a diminishing MRS. In general we will assume that the MRS falls along an indifference curve as L increases and C decreases.

Constraints

She also faces constraints that limit her choice. There are two constraints here, a **time constraint** and a **budget constraint**. A woman's total available time (T) is assumed to be spent either working in the market (M) or enjoying leisure (L). Thus the time constraint is $T \equiv L + M$. This is quite convenient because it means that hours of leisure and hours of work are perfectly negatively related. When L increases, M decreases by exactly the same amount, and conversely. Thus we can analyze hours of work directly, or, if it is more convenient—which it is—we can analyze hours of work indirectly via hours of leisure.

Note what is omitted in both the utility function and the time constraint. There are no household goods in the utility function and no household production time in the time constraint. In addition, time spent at work does not have any direct impact on utility. These are important (and limiting) simplifications.

The budget constraint limits the market goods she can purchase: she cannot spend more than her income. This constraint is written as

$$C = wM + V \tag{7.9}$$

where w is the wage rate, M is hours worked, and V is any additional nonlabor income she may have. The left side of the budget constraint is total spending on consumption goods, while the right side is total income, composed of earnings (wM) plus nonlabor income (V). Nonlabor income is income that a woman receives from a source other than her own work effort. It could be income from stocks or bonds, income from a government income transfer program, or, in some cases, income from her husband.

It is useful and revealing to combine the time constraint and the budget constraint. First, let's rewrite the time constraint to isolate M: $M = T - L$, then substitute this expression for M into the budget constraint:

$$C = wM + V = w(T - L) + V = wT - wL + V \tag{7.10}$$

Finally, move $-wL$ from the right-hand side of the equation to the left-hand side to get

$$C + wL = wT + V \tag{7.11}$$

This interesting and important equation is called the **full-income budget constraint**. Look first at the right-hand side of the equation. The first term, wT, is the income a woman could earn if she worked all T hours of the day. Adding V (nonlabor income) yields **full income**, which is her total maximum income (not to be confused with her total realized income, $wM + V$). Full income is *exogenous*, which means that it does not depend on how many hours she chooses to work, while actual income is *endogenous*.

The left side of the equation contains two terms. The first, C, is, again, the amount of money spent on consumption. The second term, wL, may seem a bit odd but it can be interpreted similarly. It is the amount of full income spent on leisure, where w is the price of leisure. Again, note that *the price of an hour of leisure is the wage rate*. Of course, no one literally pays $\$w$ to purchase an hour of leisure. In effect, an individual buys it from himself. It is an opportunity cost—that is, it is the income that is given up by taking an hour of leisure. It is, nevertheless, a genuine cost.

Figure A.2 is a representation of the budget constraint. We again use L on the horizontal axis and C on the vertical axis and to simplify the diagram we set nonlabor income (V) to 0. Later on we'll add it back in.

If a woman were to take no leisure at all (i.e., $L = 0$) then the maximum C she could consume would be wT, her full income; remember that the full-income budget constraint is $C + wL = wT + V$ and that we are setting $V = 0$. Thus if $w = \$10$ and $T = 24$ hours per day, then full income = $\$240$, and the endpoint of the budget constraint on the vertical axis is the bundle ($L = 0$, $C = wT$); in the numerical example it is the bundle (0, $240). If instead she took all T hours as leisure, her consumption goods would equal 0 because her nonlabor income equals 0. With all T hours taken as leisure, she has no earned income with which to buy consumption goods. Thus the endpoint on the horizontal axis is the bundle ($L = T$, $C = 0$) or (24, 0), continuing with our example.

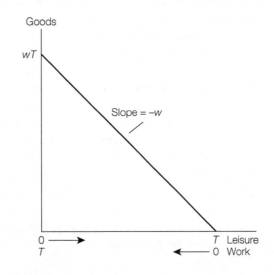

Goods

wT

Slope = $-w$

| 0 | T Leisure |
| T | 0 Work |

Figure A.2 *The full-income budget constraint.*

Finally, the slope of the budget constraint is $-w$. To see why, start at the all-work endpoint on the vertical axis. For every hour of leisure that is taken, $\$w$ of earnings are given up and one hour of leisure is obtained. Equivalently, starting from the endpoint on the horizontal axis and moving up the constraint, every hour of leisure given up yields $\$w$ of earnings. Thus the slope of the budget constraint is $-w/1$ or just $-w$. In the example we are using, the slope is $-\$10$. Another way to find the slope is to use the old geometry formula, Slope = Rise/Run. In this case we have the two points $(0, wT)$ and $(T, 0)$. Thus the rise over run is $(wT - 0)/(0 - T)$. Simplifying, Slope $= (wT)/(-T) = -w$.

All the points on the constraint exactly satisfy the full-income budget constraint. Points toward the origin cost less than the budget constraint, while points above the constraint aren't feasible because they cost too much. Note that there are two scales along the horizontal axis, one for hours of leisure and one for hours of work. Leisure time is measured in the usual way, from left to right. But because leisure and work are the only two uses of time, we can measure hours of work backwards from right to left.

Adding nonlabor income to the budget constraint is easy. The slope of the budget constraint doesn't change because the wage rate isn't affected by the amount of nonlabor income. Thus the budget line with $V > 0$ will be parallel to the budget line with $V = 0$. What about the endpoints of the budget line? Having nonlabor income doesn't change the maximum amount of leisure—that is still T. But it would allow an individual to have some consumption even if $L = T$. Similarly, it increases the amount of consumption possible at the other (all work) endpoint. To be specific, nonlabor income increases possible consumption at every level of L by $\$V$. This means that the whole budget constraint shifts up vertically by an amount equal to V.

If the wage rate changed, the slope of the budget constraint would change. If the wage were higher, the budget line would pivot upward around the point on the horizontal axis. The new budget line would be steeper and the endpoint on the vertical axis would increase. This makes perfect sense: If a woman worked all hours at a higher wage rate, she would earn more and thus be able to consume more. If the wage rate were lower, the budget line would rotate inward, becoming flatter.

The impact of changes in V and w is summarized in Figure A.3. Figure A.3(A) illustrates the impact of a change in nonlabor income, while Figure A.3(B) does the same for a change in the wage rate. In Figure A.3(A) the lowest curve is for $V = 0$, and the other two are for increasing amounts of nonlabor income. Note that the three curves are parallel and also that the curves are chopped off at the lower end at the point where $L = T$. The dotted line shows that. As long as $V > 0$, it is possible to have some consumption even when all time is spent in leisure. For example, the amount a lottery winner might consume could actually be quite substantial. The chopped-off endpoints are precisely those combinations of all leisure and the consumption made possible by nonlabor income.

In Figure A.3(B) the middle budget line is for some initial wage rate. The steeper one represents a higher wage rate, while the flatter one is for a lower wage rate. Note that all three budget lines start at the same point on the horizontal axis (here we have set $V = 0$). The higher the wage rate is, the higher the endpoint on the vertical axis is, or, equivalently, the greater full the income is.

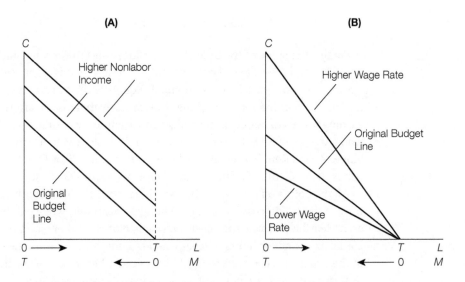

Figure A.3 *The effect of nonlabor income and the wage rate on the full-income budget constraint.*

Choosing hours of work

Now that we have drawn indifference curves and a budget constraint to analyze labor supply, we can solve for the best solution. The full maximization problem is written formally this way:

An individual chooses values for C and L to maximize $U(C, L)$ subject to $C + wL = wT + V$

Figure A.4 illustrates the nature of the solution. Here we have drawn the same indifference curves as in Figure A.1 and the same budget constraint as in Figure A.2. We again set $V = 0$ to keep the graph a bit simpler. The individual's objective is to choose the best combination of leisure and goods along the budget constraint. That is equivalent to finding the highest attainable indifference curve because higher indifference curves are always preferred to lower ones.

In Figure A.4, points A and C along indifference curve I_0 are both feasible choices. But point B along indifference curve I_1 is even better, and it, too, is feasible. We know it is better because it is on a higher indifference curve, and we know it is feasible because it is on the budget constraint. Figure A.4 illustrates two things: (1) No point on any indifference curve higher than I_1 (such as I_2) is feasible, and (2) at point B, indifference curve I_1 is at a tangent to the budget constraint, which tells us that the slopes are equal. Point B is the best available choice. As shown in Figure A.4, this woman would divide her T available hours into L^*_B hours of leisure (measured in the usual way from left to right) and M^*_B hours of work, measured from right to left. As usual, we use an asterisk to indicate that this represents the best choice.

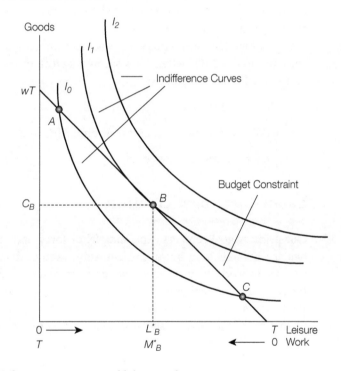

Figure A.4 *Utility maximization and labor supply.*

Let's focus on points A, B, and C more carefully. At B, the slope of the indifference curve just equals the slope of the budget constraint. Recall that the slope of the indifference curve is the negative of the MRS and that the slope of the budget constraint is $-w$. Using this information and the fact that the slopes are equal at B, we can derive the following: (1) Slope of indifference curve at B = slope of budget constraint at B, and (2) by substitution, $-MRS$ at $B = -w$. Multiplying both sides by -1 to eliminate the two negative signs, we have the condition for utility maximization in labor supply: $MRS(L^*, C^*) = w$, where L^* and C^* are the utility maximizing choices of leisure and consumption.

This actually makes a great deal of common sense. The MRS measures how much this woman values an hour of leisure. The wage rate (w) is the price of an hour of leisure.

The equality of MRS and w means that at the margin—for the last hour of leisure taken—its value is just equal to its price.

Points A and C show combinations where the MRS is not equal to the wage rate. These situations will be very useful when we analyze labor-force participation. At A the indifference curve is steeper than the budget line. This means that the slope of the indifference curve is greater (in absolute value) than the slope of the budget line. So, following the same logic as before, this means that the MRS at point $A > w$.

Intuitively, point A can't be a utility-maximizing choice because the value of an hour of leisure (MRS) is greater than its price (w). In that situation a woman could increase her utility by increasing the amount of leisure she takes and, in the process, working less. In doing so she would be moving down the budget constraint from point A toward point B.

At point C the opposite situation exists. The indifference curve is flatter than the budget constraint, so MRS at $C < w$. That is also a bad choice: the last hour of leisure is valued at less than its price. Now, the way to do better is to consume less leisure and to move up the budget constraint toward point B.

Only when MRS just equals the wage is it impossible to rearrange leisure, work, and consumption and do better. Let's summarize the three arithmetic possibilities and the utility-maximizing responses:

$MRS > w$: increase L, reduce M until $MRS = w$

$MRS < w$: decrease L, increase M until $MRS = w$

$MRS = w$: can't do any better

Labor-force participation

Our primary goal remains explaining labor-force participation—that is, whether a particular woman is in or out of the labor-force, rather than the exact number of hours she chooses to work. In this section we draw on and extend the analysis of labor supply to focus on the decision about whether or not to participate in the labor market. We use this analysis to examine the factors that most influence labor-force participation and then tie that to the increase in labor-force participation of married women over the twentieth century.

Basics

The woman represented by Figure A.4 is clearly in the labor-force; for her, $M^* > 0$. The easiest way to see this is to compare the utility at her best choice point when $M > 0$ with the utility she would have with $M = 0$. This is done in Figure A.5, which repeats the budget constraint and indifference curve I_1 from Figure A.4 and adds in indifference curve I_0, which includes point C where all time is spent in leisure. Since I_1 is higher than I_0, there is no question that it is preferred; higher indifference curves are always better. But let's look more carefully at point C. At this point, just as for point C in Figure A.4, $MRS < w$. And, as we saw in Figure A.4, this person will be better off reducing her leisure hours and increasing her hours of work—moving along the budget constraint toward point B.

This figure tells us something about the condition that must hold for a woman to choose to participate in the labor market. If MRS (at $L = T$) $< w$, then it is utility-maximizing to participate in the labor market. Or, put more compactly, if MRS (at $L = T$) $< w$, then $M^* > 0$. In words, if the value of an hour of leisure, evaluated when all time is spent in leisure, is less than the wage rate, an individual can always be better off by choosing to participate in the labor market.

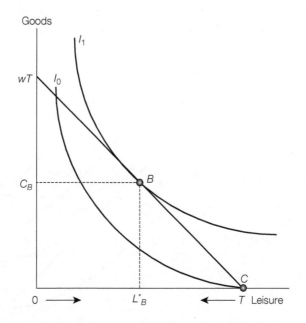

Figure A.5 *Comparing the utility of participation and nonparticipation.*

Conversely, nonparticipation is the better choice if MRS (at $L = T$) $\geq w$. In that case, a woman would want to take yet more leisure and reduce her hours of work. But she is already taking the maximum hours of leisure, so her best choice is all leisure (although, as we see later, it probably wasn't and isn't leisure) and no market work.

Let's summarize these two rules for labor-force participation. If MRS (at $L = T$) $< w$, then $M^* > 0$, and the woman participates in the labor market. If MRS (at $L = T$) $\geq w$, then $M^* = 0$, and the woman does not participate in the labor market

In Figure A.5 it was clear that this woman would be better off participating in the labor market. That will always be true, as long as nonlabor income (V) equals 0, because she is then in the unhappy situation of having no consumption goods at all if she doesn't work. And that is rarely the best (i.e., utility-maximizing) choice.

The labor-force participation of married women

Let's look at the more interesting situation of a married woman, and let's focus on a time period in which her market work decision is clearly secondary to that of her husband. This is a time in which specialization of task on the basis of gender, as discussed in Chapter 3, was widespread. Her husband's income functions like nonlabor income (V), at least as far as her labor supply decision is concerned. That income enables the family to purchase a positive amount of consumption goods and services, even when her own labor-supply hours are zero. As we've already seen, that shifts up her budget constraint without changing its slope.

Figure A.6 shows how this might affect her decision about participating in the labor market. It repeats the original budget line (B_1) with $V = 0$ from Figure A.5 plus two higher budget constraints labeled B_2 and B_3, parallel to the original budget constraint B_1. On budget constraint B_2, the best choice is point D. Hours of work are reduced, but this woman is still better off participating in the labor market. On the highest budget constraint B_3, the best choice is E, where $M^* = 0$.

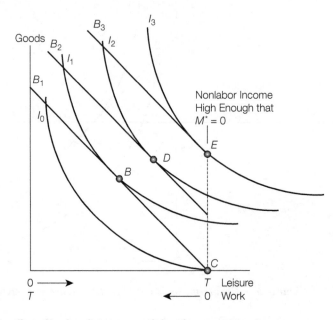

Figure A.6 *The effect of husband's income on labor-force participation.*

Thus Figure A.6 shows that holding the wage rate constant and increasing nonlabor income causes hours of work to fall steadily, and eventually to fall to zero. This is called the **income effect**. In symbols we can express the relationship as $\Delta M^*/\Delta V < 0$. As V increases, holding w constant, hours of work fall. And if V is large enough, hours of work will likely fall to zero. This is true regardless of the source of nonlabor income; it could be husband's income, but it could also be government transfer income or lottery winnings.

Finally, let's look at the effect of a woman's wage rate on labor-force participation, now holding V constant. This is shown in Figure A.7. The original situation is point A on indifference curve I_0 and on the budget constraint with the lower wage rate. With this w and V, this woman would choose not to participate in the labor market. The steeper budget constraint in Figure A.7 is for the same amount of nonlabor (or husband's) income and a higher wage rate. Now, this woman would choose to participate in the labor market. Her best choice is point B on indifference curve I_1.

For a woman who is not currently a labor-force participant, an increase in the wage rate can only have a positive impact on the probability that she will choose to participate in the labor market. Depending on her own particular circumstances, any particular increase in the wage rate might not be large enough to pull her into the labor market. But the impact can only be in the positive direction.

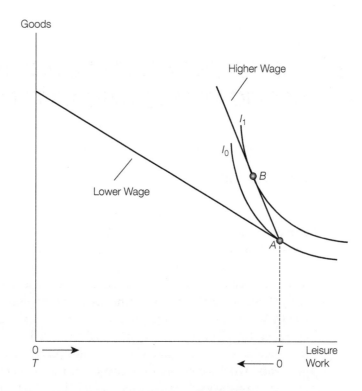

Figure A.7 *The effect of the wage rate on labor-force participation.*

Summary

Using indifference curves and budget constraints, it is possible to analyze labor-force participation decisions with precision and rigor. The great advantage of this approach is making the nature of the constraints and the prices particularly clear. This insight is particularly valuable in going further, especially in thinking about the effect of taxes and government transfers on labor supply decisions. The key lessons of the model are that the wage rate is the price of leisure and that changes in the wage rate over time have clearly had a huge impact on the labor-market participation decisions of women, especially married women.

In a model with just two uses of time (work and leisure), (1) a woman maximizes her utility by choosing hours of work where $MRS = w$; (2) a woman will choose to participate in the labor market if MRS at $L = T < w$; if MRS at $L = T > w$, then she will choose not to work in the labor market; (3) increases in V, holding w constant, increase the probability of nonparticipation; and (4) increases in w, holding V constant, increase the probability of participation.

8 WOMEN'S LABOR–FORCE PARTICIPATION: APPLICATIONS AND EXTENSIONS

Introduction

In this chapter we continue our analysis of women in the labor market, drawing on the economic model we developed in Chapter 7. We begin by thinking about how income taxes and government transfers affect decisions about work. All governments impose taxes on earned income and virtually all provide monetary assistance to families with low and moderate incomes. These policies can have an impact on women's work decisions, especially those of married women, who are often the lower-paid or secondary earner in a family. We then examine the impact of children and childcare costs on women's work decisions. Interestingly, this ties in with the tax analysis, because taxes can have very different impacts depending on whether or not tax revenues are used for programs to support work. We also consider the evidence on a current development regarding the impact of children on the work status of more affluent and highly educated married mothers. This issue, usually referred to as "opting out," touched a nerve and has resonated in the popular media. Finally, we close the chapter with shorter discussions of three issues: why the labor-force participation of US women has fallen behind most other countries in Western Europe, the effect of race on women's labor-force participation, including its historical background, and a big-think discussion of how different technologies adopted in early agricultural societies may still have an influence on norms about gender work roles.

Taxes and transfers

Overview

In a **progressive** tax system, the tax rate increases as family income increases. In a **regressive** tax system, tax rates fall as income increases and in a **proportional** tax system, the tax rate is the same at all incomes. Most tax systems are progressive, at least in principle, although some tax units, such as US states and cities, have proportional taxes.[1] Economists focus special attention on the **marginal tax rate**, which is the tax rate applicable to the last or next bit of earnings that an individual receives. Most economic decision-making depends on marginal values, and that is why the marginal tax rate is so important.

Transfers are like taxes in reverse; they are payments from the government to an individual or family. Usually, transfers decline as earnings increase in order to focus benefits on the neediest families; this kind of transfer program is called a **means-tested transfer**,

---

1 Tax systems are typically less progressive in practice than on paper because of loopholes and preferential treatment of particular kinds of income that are usually more valuable to higher-income households.

where "means" refers to a family's income. Almost every country has some kind of means-tested transfer program. See Box 8.1 for details about the US income tax system and its major transfer programs.

Taxes and transfers potentially affect both men's and women's decisions about work and most of the analysis we present is both perfectly general and gender neutral. There are two differences, though, that make the analysis a bit different and more important for women. First, women are still more often than men the second earner in a married-couple family,

---

Box | **8.1**

An Overview of Taxes and Transfer Programs in the United States

As of 2014, the U.S. federal income tax system has seven tax brackets with marginal tax rates that range from 10 to 39.6 percent. These tax rates are applied to **taxable income**, which is a family's income after subtracting personal exemptions and either the standard deduction or itemized deductions. For a married couple with two children taking the standard deduction, these subtractions amount to $28,000. Each personal exemption is $3,900 and the standard deduction is $12,400 ($6,200 for a single individual). $28,000 = $12,400 + (4 × $3,900). This means that a married couple with two children and with total income of $50,000 would owe tax only on $22,000, the amount above its exemptions and deductions. In 2014 the 10 percent tax rate applied to taxable income up to $18,150 for a married couple and $9,075 for a single individual. Taxable income between $18,150 and $73,800 for a married couple was taxed at a 15 percent rate. The 39.6 percent rate applied to income above $457,600 for a married couple and $406,750 for a single individual. These tax rates apply to earned income; income from capital gains on stocks and bonds is taxed at lower rates. Tax brackets are adjusted annually for inflation to prevent "bracket creep." See Table 8.1 for the full 2014 tax schedule.

Table 8.1 *Taxable income brackets and rates, United States 2014.*

Rate (%)	Single	Married
10	$0–$9,075	$0–$18,150
15	$9,076–$36,900	$18,151–$73,800
25	$36,901–$89,350	$73,801–$148,850
28	$89,351–$186,350	$148,851–$226,850
33	$186,351–$405,100	$226,851–$405,100
35	$405,101–406,750	$405,101–457,600
39.6	$406,751+	$457,601+

Source: Data from 2014 Tax Brackets, The Tax Foundation (available at taxfoundation.org/article/2014-tax-brackets)

The transfer system in the United States, often referred to as "welfare" or the "safety net," is composed of multiple programs. **TANF** (Temporary Assistance to Needy Families) is the primary cash assistance transfer program for low-income able-bodied adults. It is intended primarily for single-parent families with children. TANF was the result of a substantial reform of the welfare system in 1996, under which an older and somewhat controversial program called **AFDC** (Aid to Families with Dependent Children) was abolished and replaced with TANF. Under TANF, families receiving assistance are required to find employment within 24 months and cash assistance is limited to 48 months over a lifetime. In the mid-1990s, nearly 5 million families received benefits from AFDC, but the number of families receiving assistance fell sharply as a result of the changes in TANF and strong economy through the mid-2000s. In 2014 an average of 1.5 million families per month received a total of $9 billion per year, or about $5,800 per family. Benefits vary quite widely across states. In 2012, maximum benefits for a family of three ranged from less than $250 per month in five states to more than $600 per month in ten states.

SNAP stands for Subsidized Nutritional Assistance Program and it provides food assistance to low- and moderate-income families. It is often referred to as "food stamps." Many policy analysts regard it as the bedrock safety net program because it is available without regard to whether an individual has dependent children. In 2014, 23 million families (46 million persons) received SNAP benefits in a typical month. Average benefits per family were $275/month. The **WIC** (Women, Infants, and Children) program provides supplemental food assistance for low-income women who are pregnant, breastfeeding, or have recently given birth. Young children at risk of inadequate nutrition are also eligible for assistance. In 2014, WIC provided benefits to 8.6 million women and children.

The **EITC** (Earned Income Tax Credit) is now the largest cash assistance program in the US for low- and moderate-income families with earnings. In 2012, 27 million families received a total of $63 billion from the EITC. The EITC is actually not a welfare program in the traditional sense but rather a refundable tax credit administered through the Internal Revenue Service. A family with earnings below a specified level is eligible for an income tax credit, which it deducts from its taxes. Unlike most tax credits, the EITC is refundable, so if the credit exceeds the taxes a family owes, it gets a check in the mail for the difference. The EITC is particularly interesting because it has an unusual benefit structure for a transfer program and, as a result, has more varied potential effects on women's labor supply decisions. We discuss it in detail below.

Medicaid, the government-run healthcare system for the poor, covered approximately 42 million non-elderly low-income individuals in 2014, including more than 30 million children. Its enrollment has increased recently because a provision of the **Affordable Care Act** (the healthcare law passed in 2010 and often referred to as "Obamacare") provided financial incentives for states to expand their Medicaid coverage to some non-poor families. The Affordable Care Act is not always included among the safety net programs but it provides financial assistance to help moderate-income families purchase health insurance. Other safety net programs include **Housing Assistance; Nutritional Assistance Programs,** which provide subsidized school breakfast and lunch; and **LIHEAP**, which provides home energy assistance for heating or cooling a home.

SSI (Supplemental Security Income) is an assistance program for disabled adults and children with low and moderate incomes. Because of the special nature of the intended population, it likely does not have labor-supply effects.

and this affects how a progressive tax system affects them. This is not always the case, of course, but it still characterizes a sizable fraction of couples today, especially those with young children; see Box 3.1 on the division of labor in US households. This pattern is certainly many, many times more common than the reverse situation. Second, some transfer programs, especially in the United States, offer benefits primarily to single parents with children. Because those parents are far more likely to be women than men, the impact of transfers on women is likely to be far greater.

Taxes and women's work decisions

In order to be concrete, we focus on the US tax system in 2014 and its effects on a married couple with two children, but the analysis is perfectly general. Let's suppose that the husband earns $50,000 and the wife, who is not working, is considering whether to accept a job offer where she can earn $30,000. Note that in this example her decision about whether or not to work follows his. In this example he is the primary earner and she is the secondary earner.

In 2014 this family would owe no taxes on the first $28,000 of its earnings because of its four personal exemptions ($3,900 each) and the standard deduction of $12,400. The family's taxable income, based on the husband's earnings, is therefore $50,000−$28,000 = $22,000. Using the tax brackets and tax rates applicable in 2014, the first $18,150 of its income would be taxed at a 10 percent rate and the remaining $3,850 would be taxed at a 15 percent rate. Thus this family's total taxes are (0.10 × $18,150) + (0.15 × $3,850) for a grand total of $2392.50. They pay 4.8 percent ($2,392.50/$50,000) of their total family income in federal income taxes.

If the wife decided to accept the job offer, all of her income would be taxed at the 15 percent rate because the personal exemptions and standard deduction have already been applied to her husband's earnings and because her husband's income bumped the family into the 15 percent tax bracket. So she would pay $4,500 (0.15 × $30,000) in taxes. Her effective tax rate is more than three times the rate he pays.[2]

We could, instead, analyze this by assuming that the husband and wife shared the deductions and exemptions and that each paid the same share of their taxable income in taxes. Their total taxes if she works are $2,392.50 + $4,500 = $6892.50, so together they pay 8.62 percent of their income in taxes ($6,892.50/$80,000). Proceeding as if they both paid the same tax rate, her taxes would be 0.0862 × $30,000 = $2,586. But, unfortunately, if she is truly the secondary earner in the family and if the family wants to know how much better off they are financially if she is working (i.e., they are making this decision at the margin), this equal-allocation method doesn't yield the right answer. This method suggests that when the family's income increases by her $30,000, its taxes would increase by only the $2,586 allocated to her. But, in fact, we know that the taxes on her earnings are $4,500—the figure we computed based on her status as the second earner.

There is no getting around the fact that her marginal tax rate is higher than his, as long as she is making her work decision after his. She faces the higher tax rate of the

---

2 Her marginal tax rate would be 25 percent if her husband earned approximately $100,000 and 35 percent if he earned $250,000. Those incomes would put the family in the top 20% and top 5%, respectively, of family incomes in the United States in 2014.

progressive tax system without the protection of the personal exemptions and deductions. Of course, if he were the secondary earner, then he, rather than she, would face the higher marginal tax rate on all of his income. Her average tax rate is also higher than his. He paid 4.8 percent in taxes, while she paid 15 percent.

The higher tax rate is equivalent to a lower net (i.e., after-tax, take-home) wage rate for the secondary earner. Instead of earning \$$w$ per hour, she now earns \$$w \times (1 - t_m)$, where t_m is the marginal tax rate that applies to her earnings; in our example, $t_m = 0.15$, so the tax is equivalent to a wage decrease of 15 percent. In addition to the federal income tax, she would have to pay the 6.2 percent Federal payroll tax used to finance Social Security, the 1.45 percent tax to finance Medicare, and possibly also state or local income taxes. Her marginal tax rate is the sum of all the taxes she faces.

Effects on labor-force participation To analyze how the tax affects her work decision, we can use the framework we developed in Chapter 7. Let's review that quickly. The utility-maximizing choice for market work involves comparing MVT*, the value of time in the household sector when time is optimally allocated between household production and leisure, with the marginal value of time in the labor market (MVT_M), evaluated at the first hour of work. If MVT* > $\text{MVT}_M(1)$, then it does not make sense to work: the marginal value of time in the labor market is less than its marginal value in the household. But if MVT* < $\text{MVT}_M(1)$, then working in the labor market is utility-maximizing.

An income tax lowers MVT_M because that term is the product of two terms: $\text{MVT}_M = MU_C \times w/p$, where w/p is the real wage and MU_C is the marginal utility of the additional consumption goods that can be bought with the earnings from an hour of work. With a tax, MVT_M now equals $MU_C \times (w/p) \times (1 - t_m)$, where t_m is the sum of the income and payroll taxes she faces. This new MVT_M is therefore lower than the original MVT_M curve. Figure 8.1 shows the situation. As always the best decision about labor-force participation involves comparing MVT* with the height of the MVT_M curve shown on the graph on the right. The higher MVT_M curve reflects a no-taxes world, and the lower one reflects the lower wage created by the taxes. With the higher curve, the condition for labor-force participation—MVT* < $\text{MVT}_M(1)$—holds and this woman would work. But with the higher taxes, MVT* > $\text{MVT}_M(1)$ and it is not utility-maximizing to work.

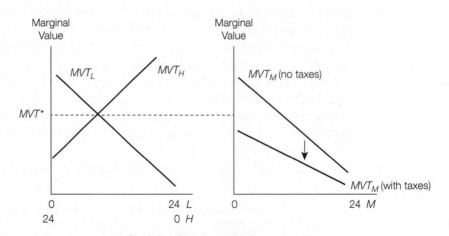

Figure 8.1 *How taxes may affect labor force participation.*

In practice, the taxes might or might not be large enough to reduce MVT_M by enough to affect the decision about whether to work. But we have shown that taxes may reduce labor-force participation by married women, especially if they are the secondary earner in a family and if the difference between MVT^* and $\text{MVT}_M(1)$ is not very large in the absence of taxes.

It's important to add a caveat to this analysis of tax effects on labor-force participation. We've shown that taxes can have important effects on women's decisions about work, especially for those not currently in the labor force, where the impacts are clearly negative. It doesn't follow, however, that income taxes are inherently bad and ought to be eliminated or even sharply cut. First, taxes are necessary to finance the operations of governments at all levels. Countries around the world, including the United States, are having a vigorous policy debate about the appropriate level of goods and services the public sector should provide, the corresponding level of taxes needed to support them, and how those taxes can best be imposed so as to minimize economic distortions. It is clear that the appropriate tax rate is not zero, since that implies zero public sector services. Second, the United States has lower tax rates and lower public spending than most European countries and, moreover, marginal income tax rates in the United States are far lower than they were from the 1950s through the 1980s. The point of the analysis here is to recognize that labor supply effects are a likely consequence of taxation and should be considered when changes in tax policy are contemplated. Third, tax revenues could be used in ways that encourage and support women's work, by, for example, subsidizing the costs of childcare. We discuss this idea further below.

Effects on hours of work[3] We can also use this framework to analyze how a tax change would affect the labor supply of a married woman who was already working, rather than one who was considering whether or not to begin work. Let's focus on the specific case of a tax decrease equal to Δt—for example, a decrease in the marginal tax rate from 0.20 to 0.15; in this example, $\Delta t = -0.05$. Using the same logic as above, the tax decrease is equivalent to a wage increase of w $\times$ $(-\Delta t)$. Note that we write this as $-\Delta t$, so that the effect on wages is positive: tax rates down means after-tax wage rates up and tax rates up means after-tax wage rates down. You might think drawing on the logic of the previous example of the woman who was considering working, that this wage increase caused by the tax decrease would definitely increase her hours of work because an hour of work is now more valuable. But this is actually a more complicated economics problem that involves the famous analysis of income and substitution effects. There are two effects at work, not one.

The first effect of a tax decrease is due to the wage effect of the lower tax rate, which shifts the MVT_M curve up. This is called the **substitution effect** and it captures the change in hours worked when the wage changes, *if total income were unchanged*. Here, the substitution effect operates to increase the number of hours of work she would choose. But there is a second effect because the tax decrease means that she now pays less in taxes at her current earnings. For example, if she earned $30,000 and $\Delta t = -0.05$, her family's taxes would fall by $1,500. This tax decrease is therefore exactly equivalent to an increase in the family's income of the same amount.

---

3 This section covers more advanced material.

This second effect is called the **income effect**; it captures the change in hours worked when income changes, *if the wage were unchanged*. Typically, with a higher income and a constant wage rate, individuals choose to take more leisure and work a bit less. In terms of our model of labor-force participation, the increase in family income from the tax decrease shifts the MVT_M curve down, because the additional income that the tax cut provides means that the marginal utility of the additional consumption her earnings provide is now lower. She and her family are richer than before, so her income is less valuable in terms of the consumption value it provides.

Thus, in the case of a woman who is already working, we cannot predict *a priori* what will happen to the MVT_M curve when the tax rate falls or to her desired hours of work, because the income effect conflicts with the substitution effect. The substitution effect of a tax decrease is an incentive to work additional hours (because of the higher after-tax wage), but the income effect is an incentive to work fewer hours (because of the increased income). The substitution effect increases the MVT_M curve, but the income effect lowers it. If the substitution effect is larger, she will work more at a lower tax rate, but if the income effect is larger, she will work less.

If, instead, taxes were increased, the same two effects occur, but in the opposite direction. The higher tax is equivalent to a lower wage rate, but it also reduces the family's income because the taxes it owes increase. The lower wage rate reduces desired work hours through the substitution effect because work is less valuable. But the higher taxes means that family income is lower and this increases work hours through the income effect. Again, the result depends on which effect is larger.

The earlier analysis of the effect of a tax on the labor-force participation decision of a woman not already working is just a special case of income and substitution effects analysis. In that case there is no income effect, because she had no income to begin with and, thus, is no richer at her current hours of work. The substitution effect is the only effect that operates, so a tax decrease is an incentive to enter the labor market.

Evidence Labor economists have conducted numerous studies to try to identify whether our progressive income tax system reduces hours of work and/or the probability of labor-force participation. What they would like to know is the **elasticity of labor supply**, which measures the responsiveness of labor supply to a change in the wage rate. Two dimensions of labor supply are important to women—first, whether a woman participates in the labor force, and second, how many hours she works if she participates in the labor force. The labor-supply elasticity captures both of these. This elasticity can either be positive or negative depending on whether the substitution effect is larger than the income effect. Estimating this elasticity is difficult because researchers need a change in the tax rate that does not arise from choices about labor supply. One good source of variation like this comes from a change in the tax law such that individuals face different marginal tax rates than they previously did.

A study by Nada Eissa[4] used the tax rate changes created by the 1986 Tax Reform Act (TRA 1986) to examine the impact of taxes on women's labor supply. TRA 1986, which lowered many marginal tax rates, essentially created a natural experiment: Marginal tax

---

4 Nada Eissa (2001), "Taxation and Labor Supply of Married Women: The Tax Reform Act of 1986 as a Natural Experiment," NBER Working Paper No. 5023.

rates changed for some taxpayers but not for all. By observing the labor-supply response of different groups of taxpayers who received different "treatments," she could determine how their labor supply responded to a change in tax rates. She focused on the behavior of women in the top 1 percent of family income because this group experienced the largest tax rate change. Prior to TRA 1986, women in households with a total income over $100,000 (in 1985 dollars) faced a marginal tax rate of 45 percent, but TRA 1986 reduced that to 33 percent. However, women in households with approximately $40,000 in total income saw no change in their marginal tax rate of 28 percent and women earning in between these incomes had smaller decreases. Thus the treatment group was the group of women who faced large tax cuts and the control group was the group that had a small tax rate reduction.

Eissa found that the proportion of high-income women who participated in the labor force increased from 46 to 55 percent and hours worked among those women in the treatment group who were already working increased by 13 percent. Her estimate of the labor-supply elasticity with respect to the after-tax wage is 0.8, which means that for every 10 percent increase in the after-tax wage, a woman worked 8 percent hours more, on average. Eissa noted that about one-half of the responsiveness was due to an increase in participation, and the other half was due to an increase in hours of work.

Research by Francine Blau and Lawrence Kahn[5] demonstrated that the labor-supply elasticity of women declined from a range of about 0.8–0.9 in 1980 to about 0.6 in 1990 and 0.4 by the year 2000. In other words, by 2000, a wage increase had only about half as much effect on women's decisions about how many hours to work during the year as in 1980. Further, married women's work hours became less responsive to their husbands' wages as well—the effect of, say, an increase in their spouses' wages on married women's work hours fell by between 38 and 47 percent. Blau and Kahn attribute this to greater gender equity in the family, so that women were not as regularly treated as the secondary earner.

These findings have implications for the national debate over supply-side tax policy— tax cuts aimed at encouraging more work. If married women's labor supply elasticity has declined, then "the potential for marginal tax rate cuts to increase the labor supply is much smaller now than 20 years ago, since tax rates were much higher then as was married women's labor supply responsiveness," the authors write.

Transfer programs and women's work decisions

Means-tested transfers In a means-tested transfer program, benefits (B) are negatively related to family income (Y). A simple algebraic representation that is typical of many such programs is $B = G - tY$, where G, usually called the **guarantee**, is the amount of benefits a family would get if it had no income and t is the benefit reduction rate.[6] We use "t" to stand for the benefit reduction rate because, as you will see below, it operates exactly like a tax. With this formula, if family income increased by $100, benefits would fall by $t \times \$100$; for example, if $t = 0.50$, then a family would lose $1 of benefits for every $2 of

5   Francine Blau and Lawrence Kahn (2007), "Changes in the Labor Supply Behavior of Married Women: 1980–2000," *Journal of Labor Economics*, 25 (3), 393–438.

6   Sometimes, families are allowed to keep a small amount of earnings before benefits are reduced to cover the costs of working such as transportation and clothing; this amount is called the income disregard. In that case the benefit formula is $B = G - t \times (Y - D)$, where D is the income disregard.

additional earnings. Benefits would fall to $0 when $Y = G/t$; you can compute that by setting $G - tY = 0$ and solving for Y.

Figure 8.2 illustrates a typical benefit schedule for a means-tested transfer program. A family's earnings are plotted on the horizontal axis and its total income after transfers is plotted on the vertical axis. The figures shown are typical of those available to families under the US TANF program with $G = \$6{,}000$ per year and $t = 0.67$. Thus a family with no earnings at all would receive $6,000 and its benefits would fall by $667 for each $1,000 increase in earnings until its benefits were $0 when its earnings reached $9,000. The earnings at which benefits equal $0—here, $9,000—is called the **breakeven income**. Note that the breakeven income equals G/t (=$6,000/0.67$).

Figure 8.2 also shows the family's total income with and without the transfer program. The 45 degree line shows the family's income without transfers; with no transfers its earnings and its total income are the same. The flatter line above it is its income with transfers; it is the sum of the other two lines. The important point to see here is that its total income with transfers increases more slowly than income without transfers. For example, if family income increased from $0 to $6,000, its total income would only increase by $2,000 from $6,000 to $8,000. The reason is that benefits fall so sharply as income increases. In this case the $6,000 increase in income would cause benefits to fall by $0.67 \times \$6{,}000$, or $4,000.

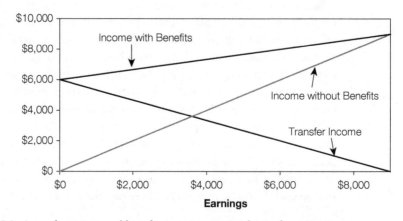

Figure 8.2 *Annual earnings and benefits in a means-tested transfer program.*

Other US transfer programs have a similar structure. SNAP benefits are reduced by $30 for every $100 increase in monthly earnings. The Affordable Care Act (ACA) provides a subsidy to help low- and moderate-income families purchase health insurance, which the ACA requires them to have. But the subsidy is reduced as a family's income increases. The exact formula is complicated and depends on family size as well as income, but marginal tax rates of 10 percent are common for families with incomes between two and four times the Federal Poverty Line.[7]

Effects on labor-force participation A means-tested transfer program creates strong negative work disincentives for recipients. First, the benefit reduction rate lowers the wage rate from w to $w \times (1 - t)$, just as in the earlier tax example. The impact on the wage

---

7 The Federal Poverty Line (FPL) is the official dividing line between poor and non-poor families. In 2014 the FPL for a family of three was $19,790 in the 48 contiguous states and the District of Columbia. It was about 25 percent higher in Alaska and Hawaii to adjust for cost-of-living differences.

rate is huge because the benefit reduction rate is typically 67 percent, which means that a woman's true wage rate, inclusive of the loss of transfer income, is now only one-third of her market wage. This would substantially reduce her MVT_M curve, thus making it much more likely that $MVT^* > MVT_M$ (1). This is exactly like the substitution effect we discussed above in the case of a tax. This is not surprising because the benefit reduction rate—which is an essential feature of a means-tested transfer program—is functionally equivalent to a tax on earnings. It is exactly like having a tax rate of 67 percent, a rate that is far higher than the highest marginal tax rate in the US income tax system, 39.6 percent, that applies to family income in excess of $450,000 for married couples and more than four times as high as the 15 percent rate we used in our tax rate example.

In addition the income guarantee (G) creates an income effect, because a woman has more income at her current hours of work, whether she is not working and receives G or is working and receives $G - tY$. The additional income further lowers the MVT_M curve; not only is she earning less per hour but her earnings are less valuable than before because the transfer income means that the marginal utility of consumption goods is now lower; while she is certainly not rich, she is richer than before. We used this same idea in the tax cut example for a woman already working, where the tax cut made her richer than before. In that case the income and substitution effects conflicted: She had a higher wage rate but also had more income than before. In the case of a means-tested transfer program, both the income effect and the substitution effect provide strong disincentives to work for those eligible for the program: She has a lower wage rate and has more income than before.

Figure 8.3 shows the effect of a means-tested transfer program on work. The left graph shows the marginal value of time curves for leisure and household work and the right graph shows the MVT_M curve. MVT^* is the value of time in the household sector when time is allocated there to maximize utility. Women receiving means-tested transfers often have young children, so that their marginal value of time in the home might well be high. Without a means-tested transfer program, this woman is maximizing her utility by working some hours in the labor market. We see this because MVT^* intersects the MVT_M curve at M^* and $MVT^* < MVT_M(1)$. The introduction of a means-tested program does not change the MVT_L and MVT_H curves, but it does shift down the MVT_M curve because she has a lower wage and more income. Now $MVT^* > MVT_M(1)$, so her best choice is to spend all of her time in leisure in household production.

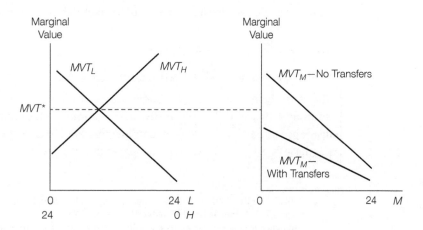

Figure 8.3 *How a means-tested transfer program may affect labor-force participation.*

You may wonder whether anything can be done to reduce the negative work incentives of a means-tested transfer program. For example, perhaps the benefit-reduction rate (t) could be reduced, so that a woman's after-tax wage rate was not as low. Unfortunately, it is not so easy to do this because this would actually have conflicting effects on work incentives for different groups of women. If a woman was receiving benefits and not working, the lower benefit reduction rate would create a positive work substitution effect by increasing her wage rate. For women currently receiving transfer income from the program and working, the same substitution effect would apply but there would also be a negative work income effect because she could keep now more of her benefits than before. To see that, just use the benefit formula $B = G - tY$: if t was lower, than B would be higher for any value of Y. So for these women the income and substitution effects of a lower benefit reduction rate conflict and the effect on work incentives is uncertain. Finally, if t were lower, the breakeven income for the program would increase; the breakeven income equals G/t and is higher if t is lower. But this means that the number of families eligible for the program increases and thus an expanded group of women will find themselves facing negative work incentives. As a practical matter, program costs are usually much higher when the benefit reduction rate is lower because the third effect dominates. In the United States the policy response has been to impose work requirements and limit the amount of time a woman could receive benefits from TANF in her lifetime.

Evidence Empirical studies that have examined the effect of TANF or its earlier incarnation, AFDC, on labor supply strongly support the prediction that the work disincentive is substantial. This primarily reflects the low after-tax wage rate created by the very high benefit reduction rate in these programs.[8] Voluntary work rates (i.e., work in the absence of work requirements) have always been low because it was rarely economically rational to work while receiving welfare. One study found that in 1996, when AFDC was still in place, only 30 percent of single mothers on AFDC worked and only 10 percent worked full-time.[9] The work rate was twice as high for poor single mothers who were not eligible for AFDC and three times as high for non-poor single mothers. There is some evidence that the strengthened work requirements of TANF increased the proportion who worked in the mid-2000s, although the stronger economy (prior to the great recession that started in 2008) may also have played a role.

We noted in Box 8.1 that the Affordable Care Act was a kind of means-tested transfer program. See Box 8.2 for a discussion of its likely labor-supply effects.

Box	8.2

Work Incentives and the Affordable Care Act

The Affordable Care Act ("Obamacare") requires all Americans to have health insurance; this is called the **individual mandate**. Many individuals receive health insurance as part of a package of employment benefits, but those who do not can now purchase it through insurance exchanges that the law created. In order to make the

---

8 Robert Moffitt (2002), "Welfare Programs and Labor Supply," in *Handbook of Public Economics*, Auerbach, A.J. and Feldstein M, (eds). Elsevier, New York.

9 Jeounghee Kim and Myungkook Joo (2009), "Work-related activities of single mothers before and after welfare reform," *Monthly Labor Review*, December 2009.

mandate equitable, families and individuals with income up to four times the official poverty level for their family size receive a subsidy that reduces the net cost. The subsidy is reduced as a family's income rises in order to reduce overall subsidy costs and to limit assistance to those most in need.

In this respect the subsidy of the ACA is exactly like a means-tested transfer program. The benefit reduction rate acts exactly like a tax, reducing the after-tax wage rate. The exact formula is complicated but marginal tax rates—that is, the tax rate that applies to small changes in earnings—in the 8–12 percent range are common in some income ranges.

The ACA could have labor supply effects for several reasons. First, like any means-tested transfer, it reduces the wage rate and simultaneously makes the individual or family better off. Thus it could reduce desired work hours through substitution and income effects. For example, a parent might work part-time instead of full-time in order to accommodate school schedules or help an elderly parent or relative in need. Some others might cut back on a second job. Second, before the passage of the law, some people with serious health issues continued working because they were eligible for group health insurance through their job. If they left their job before they were eligible for Medicare,[10] they would never be able to obtain health insurance in the private market because of their pre-existing health condition. But because the ACA prohibits insurance companies from denying coverage due to preexisting conditions, an individual in this situation could stop working or work less and purchase insurance on the exchanges.

The Congressional Budget Office studied the expected impact of the Affordable Care Act on total hours of work supplied in the labor market. Taking account of all possible effects, the CBO estimated that the law would reduce labor supply by about 1.5–2.0 percent. The effects would be concentrated among workers in families whose income was low enough that they were potentially eligible for a subsidy. The overall impact is large enough that it is worth recognizing, but it is not quantitatively important for the economy as a whole.

Some critics charged that this finding was proof that the law hurt employment, but that is a misinterpretation of the CBO results. The CBO concluded that the "reduction stems almost entirely from a net decline in the amount of labor that workers choose to supply, rather than from a net drop in businesses' demand for labor."

Other studies of the provision of health insurance have found similar effects. In Chapter 2 we discussed the Oregon Medicaid expansion as an example of a true random assignment experiment in economics. As part of that study the researchers examined its impact on labor supply.[11] The Medicaid expansion was equivalent to a huge increase in family income for those lucky enough to win the lottery. Nevertheless, employment fell only 3 percent in response to a nearly 50 percent average increase in income.

---

10 Medicare is the government-run healthcare program for the elderly. It automatically becomes effective for those aged 65 or over.
11 K. Baicker, A. Finkelstein, J. Song, and S. Taubman (2013), "The Impact of Medicaid on Labor Force Activity and Program Participation: Evidence from the Oregon Health Insurance Experiment." NBER Working Paper 19547, Cambridge, MA: NBER.

The earned income tax credit The EITC is interesting because it is the largest transfer program in the United States and also because it has an unusual benefit structure for a transfer program and, as a result, has more varied effects on women's work decisions. In 2012, 27 million families received a total of $63 billion from the EITC, compared to the $9.5 billion received by about 1.5 m families; see Box 8.1 for more information. Unlike a traditional means-tested program that provides maximum benefits to families with no earnings and then reduces benefits as families earn income, EITC benefits increase with family earnings through a portion of the income distribution, before eventually phasing out at higher incomes. Furthermore, families without earnings are not eligible for any EITC benefits, whereas, in a typical means-tested program, they would get the maximum benefits.

The unique EITC benefit schedule is illustrated in Figure 8.4 for a married couple with two children; the schedule is similar in structure but differs in details for families with a different number of children and for single-parent families. The horizontal axis shows family earnings before the credit and the vertical axis shows the credit that a family would receive. Note the three distinct "ranges" of EITC benefits: a **phase-in range** where the credit increases as earnings increase, a **plateau range** where benefits are constant, and finally a **phase-out range** where benefits are reduced as earnings increase. The first two ranges are unique to the EITC, while the third is typical of means-tested transfer programs.

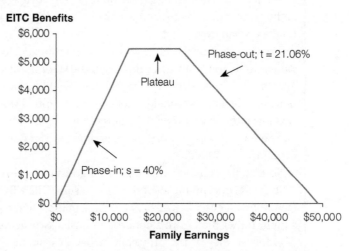

Figure 8.4 *EITC benefits by total family earnings, married couple with two children, 2014.*

In the phase-in range, EITC benefits are exactly like a wage subsidy, so that an EITC-eligible worker's total wage is $w \times (1 + s)$, where w is her hourly wage rate and s is the EITC subsidy rate. If a woman works an additional hour, she earns her hourly wage and also receives a larger EITC benefit. The subsidy rates range from 7.65 percent for families with no children to 34 percent, 40 percent, and 45 percent for families with one, two, and three or more children, respectively, so the after-transfer wage increases created by the EITC can be very substantial. In the plateau region the benefit is constant, so a woman's wage rate is unaffected as earnings increase. In the phase-out range the total wage is

$w \times (1 - t)$, where t is the phase-out rate; now, when she works an additional hour, she earns her hourly wage but loses some of her EITC benefits. The phase-out rates range from 7.65 percent for families with no children to 15.98 percent for families with one child and 21.06 percent for families with two or more children. In 2014 the EITC was worth up to $496 for persons without children, $3,305 for a family with one child, $5,460 for a family with two children, and $6,143 for a family with three or more children.[12]

The EITC has different impacts on a woman's work decisions depending on where on the EITC benefit schedule her family income falls. Consider, first, a single woman with two children who has no earnings at all. Perhaps she is receiving benefits from TANF and is contemplating taking a low-wage job to support herself and her family. Without the EITC, her wage is w. With the EITC, she is eligible for a 40 percent credit subsidy on any earnings. This is exactly like a 40 percent wage increase, which would shift up her MVT_M curve. So if she was earning the 2014 minimum wage of $7.25, her net-of-EITC wage rate would be $7.25 × 1.40, or $10.15 per hour. As a result, it is much more likely that she will now find that the condition for labor-force participation is satisfied: $MVT_M(1) > MVT^*$. Thus we expect that the EITC will increase the LFPR of women, especially low-wage women who will benefit from the EITC subsidy. This is a pure substitution effect. There is no income effect because the EITC provides no income to persons without earnings.

For women who were already in the labor force but earning little enough that they would be on the phase-in range of the EITC schedule, the EITC program has conflicting work incentive effects. On the one hand it operates like a wage increase to increase the MVT_M curve and this is an incentive for additional work. This is the substitution effect that we have seen in the analyses above. But the EITC also increases her total income at her current work hours and this pushes down her MVT_M curve. This happens because the income provided by the credit means that the marginal utility of the additional goods and services she can buy is lower than before. This is the income effect.

In this case the two effects of the EITC conflict. We cannot be certain on theoretical grounds which effect is larger, so the net impact on a woman's hours of work is uncertain. But empirical studies have confirmed that the positive wage subsidy effect outweighs the negative credit income effect. The finding that substitution effects outweigh income effects at low incomes is a typical result.

For women with income on the plateau range, the EITC operates like an increase in income with no change in the after-transfer wage rate. This causes an income effect—she is richer, but has the same wage rate—but no substitution effect. The result is a modest incentive to work less. But because the plateau region is relatively short, this effect is probably not very important.

Finally, the EITC may also have an impact on work decisions among married women with family income that puts them on the phase-out range. Let's again consider the situation of a married woman with two children, whose husband is the primary worker and who earns just enough to leave them near the beginning of the EITC phase-out range.[13] If she works and earns income, the family's EITC benefits will be reduced by $21.06

---

12 The EITC is indexed for inflation, so the dollar amounts increase annually.
13 In 2014 this would have been an income of about $24,000.

for every \$100 she earns. This is equivalent to a decrease in her wage rate from \$$w$ to \$$w \times (1 - 0.2106)$, so her MVT_M curve will fall. In addition, based on her husband's earnings alone, the family might be eligible for a relatively large EITC benefit, perhaps the maximum amount provided. This is exactly the same situation as occurs in a typical means-tested program; the only difference is that with the EITC, this effect occurs at a higher level of family income rather than at \$0. So, in this case, the EITC reduces her MVT_M curve. Both the substitution and income effects will create an incentive to work less: she has a lower wage rate and more income.

Evidence Quite a few studies have examined the effect of increases in EITC benefits on the labor-force participation of single mothers, a group who often face positive work incentives on the phase-in range, and married mothers who often face negative work incentives on the phase-out range. Most of these studies have used a natural experiment framework by looking at responses to changes in the EITC program that affected some women but not others. For example, one comparison is between women with children, who were eligible for larger EITC benefits than women without children. A comparison of work rates before and after the change in the EITC reveals the impact of the EITC.

A number of such studies have all come to the same conclusion: the EITC has had a positive impact on the work decision of single mothers. Eissa and Liebman found that the 1986 EITC expansion from a subsidy rate of just 10 percent to a subsidy rate of 14 percent increased the labor-force participation rate of single mothers by 2–4 percent.[14] Meyer and Rosenbaum found a 6–7 percent increase in employment rate of single mothers between 1990 and 1996 compared to single women without children. And they also found that the change in income taxes that single women paid (primarily the EITC) increased the LFPR of all single mothers by 1.5–2 percent between 1992 and 1996, which was approximately 35 percent of the total change.[15] The EITC is unique among income-transfer programs in having any evidence of a positive impact on work.

For women on the EITC phase-out range, there is evidence that these negative incentives have had an effect. Again, researchers have examined natural experiments, comparing the labor-force participation of married women likely to face these negative incentives with the labor-force participation of otherwise similar women less likely to face those incentives. For example, women with lower-income husbands, lower wage rates, or less education could be compared to women with higher-income husbands, higher wage rates, or more education. Ellwood[16] found that the 1993 EITC expansion and AFDC reform decreased the labor-force participation of low-wage married mothers by 3–7 percent compared to higher-wage married mothers. Eissa and Hoynes found that the EITC decreased the labor-force participation of less-educated married mothers by 2–4 percent.[17]

---

14 Nada Eissa and Jeffrey Liebman (1996), "Labor Supply response to the Earned income Tax Credit," *Quarterly Journal of Economics*, III (2), 605–637.

15 Bruce D. Meyer and Dan T. Rosenbaum (2000), "Making Single Mothers Work: Recent Changes in Policy for Single Mothers and Their Effects," *National Tax Journal*, LII (4, Part 2) 1027–1062.

16 David T. Ellwood (2000), "The Impact of the Earned Income Tax Credit and Social Policy Reforms on Work, Marriage, and Living Arrangements," *National Tax Journal*, LIII (4, Part 2), 1063–1106.

17 Nada Eissa and Hilary Hoynes (2006), "Behavioral Responses to Taxes: Lessons from the EITC and Labor Supply," in James Poterba (ed.), *Tax Policy and the Economy*, Vol., MIT Press, 74–110.

Children, childcare costs, and women's labor-force participation

In this section we examine the effect of children and childcare costs on women's work. We focus on the situation of a married woman with young children or with a large family, both of which require a very substantial amount of parental household production time. Historically, of course, this has been primarily the mother's time. Figure 8.5 shows how we can analyze the effect of this on her labor-force participation decision. The presence of children shifts the MVT_H curve upward because each hour of time spent in household production is now more valuable. This would do three things. First, if all time were spent in the non-market sector, a woman would shift time from leisure to household production. (Ask your mothers, aunts, grandmothers, and older sisters about how little leisure time they had when they were caring for newborns and infants.) Second, the upward shift of the MVT_H curve would increase the value of MVT*—that is, the value of time in the non-market sector when time is optimally divided between leisure and household work. And, third, by increasing MVT*, the presence of children decreases the likelihood that $\text{MVT}_M(1)$ will be greater than MVT*. Thus it reduces the probability of labor-force participation.

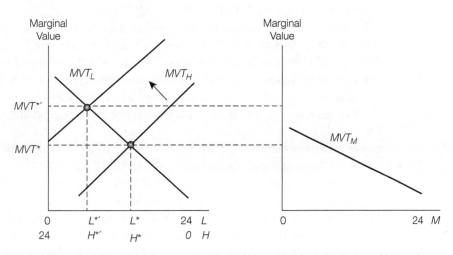

Figure 8.5 *The effect of children on market work, household production, and leisure hours.*

Figure 8.5 shows this analysis. It includes two MVT_H curves; the higher one is for a woman with young children or a large family or other substantial family responsibilities (perhaps an elderly parent or relative). The higher curve intersects the MVT_L curve to the left of the original intersection, so we know that leisure time falls and household work increases; this is the shift from H^* to $H^{*'}$ and from L^* to $L^{*'}$. Note also that MVT* increases to MVT*', reflecting the higher value of time in the non-market sector. With this higher MVT_H curve and with the MVT_M curve shown on the right, MVT*' > MVT_M for the first hour of market work. Thus this woman would not work in the labor market. But a woman with the lower MVT_H curve would work in the labor market.

As children grow older, it is quite likely that the MVT_H curve would fall, thus making it more likely that $\text{MVT}_M(1) > \text{MVT*}$. Just as in the analysis of taxes, we can't be certain whether the change in the MVT_H curve would be large enough to affect the labor-force participation decision, but it certainly might be.

Indeed, women's LFPRs do vary substantially by the age of the youngest child in the family. In 2013, among US women with children, 57 percent whose youngest child was less than a year old were in the labor force. The participation rate increased to 61 percent for women with children age 1–3, 67 percent for women with children age 3–5, and 75 percent for women with children age 6–17.[18] Men's LFPRs were unaffected by the presence of young children.

Childcare costs We can easily add childcare costs into the model. These costs reduce the net wages of a woman working in the formal labor market, as long as she would not have incurred these costs if she were not working. Her wage net of childcare costs is thus $w - c$, where c is the per hour cost of childcare. This reduces her MVT_M curve and makes it more likely that $MVT^* > MVT_M(1)$, which is the condition for not working in the labor market. The relevant graphical analysis is identical to others we have presented where a lower wage rate causes a woman to choose not to work in the labor market; see Figure 8.1 for an example. We could combine this childcare effect with the effect of income taxes that we discussed above. In this case her net wage would be $w \times (1 - t_m) - c$, where t_m is her marginal tax rate. It is not hard to see that under some circumstances, the net wage could be very low indeed, so that $MVT^* > MVT_M(1)$.

Because of that, governments often provide some form of subsidy for childcare costs. While we cover this more fully in Chapter 12, here our purpose is to see how such subsidies would affect the decision to work. This can take the form of direct low-cost direct provision as in France or much of Scandinavia or a tax credit, as in the United States. The US Child and Dependent Care Credit allows a working woman to deduct 35 percent of childcare expenses for children who are under age 13 up to a maximum credit of $6,000. Because this is a tax credit, it directly reduces her taxes dollar for dollar. The subsidy causes an upward shift in the MVT_M curve and, if large enough, she might satisfy the utility-maximizing condition for market work: $MVT_M(1) > MVT^*$.

The basic analysis is shown in Figure 8.6. Let's start by assuming that a woman with children is not participating in the labor market because the costs of childcare lower her wages sufficiently that she is better off not working. In Figure 8.6 this is represented by the MVT_M curve labeled "Before Subsidy." Note that MVT^* is greater than $MVT_M(1)$ for this MVT_M curve. Of course, women who need childcare have small children and thus have a higher marginal value of time in the home, which already means that they are less likely to work, even if they incurred very low childcare costs or commanded high market wages.

However, if a childcare subsidy is available that lowers the cost of care, we would see an upward shift in the MVT_M curve (to "After Subsidy"); if it rose enough, she might reallocate some of her time to market work, as we show her doing in Figure 8.6. A subsidy for childcare lowers the cost of working and this translates into an increased probability of working.

---

18 Statistics are from *Employment Characteristics of Families-2013*, US Department of Labor, Bureau of Labor Statistics.

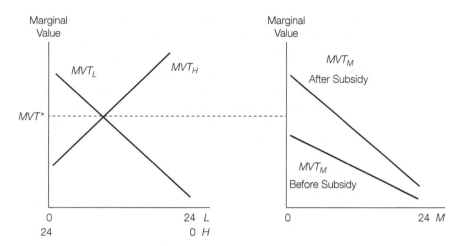

Figure 8.6 *How a childcare subsidy affects a woman's decision to work in the labor market.*

This analysis is an excellent example of the idea that it is not taxes per se that affect labor supply decisions but rather the combination of taxes and spending programs. If taxes are used to support programs that encourage work, they may have a net positive effect. Economist Henrik Kleven makes this point with special reference to Scandinavian countries, where women's LFPRs are high in spite of high marginal tax rates.[19] Kleven notes that these countries "spend relatively large amounts on the public provision and subsidization of goods that are complementary to working, including childcare, elderly care, and transportation" (p. 86) and also on education, which encourages long-run labor supply. He computes what he calls "participation subsidies" across countries due to this kind of public spending and shows that it is strongly positively related to women's labor-force participation. The Scandinavian countries provide the highest subsidies, and the United States, along with Germany, among the lowest.

The changing LFP of women with children

In this section we review the evidence about how children affect a women's labor-market activity, with a special focus on how these effects changed over time and how they differ according to a woman's marital status, and especially her education. We begin by reviewing the facts and trends. We then review the empirical and popular-press research about "opting out," which refers to the decline in work among highly educated married women with young children. *The New York Times* published two widely read and debated articles with this theme and the idea has percolated into contemporary culture.[20]

Figure 8.7 shows how LFPRs changed for selected years between 1975 and 2013 for US women by the age of their youngest child. Much else has also changed between those years. For example, women are more likely to be college graduates,

19 Henrik Jacobsen Kleven (2014), "How Can Scandinavians Tax So Much?" *Journal of Economic Perspectives*, 28 (4), 77–98.

20 Lisa Belkin, "The Opt-Out Revolution," *New York Times Magazine* (October 26, 2003); Louis Story, "Many Women at Elite Colleges Set Career Path to Motherhood," *New York Times* (September 20, 2005). The young women profiled in these articles were students at Princeton and Yale, respectively.

fertility has declined and shifted to older ages, and the proportion married has fallen. In 1975, LFPRs were just over one-third for women whose youngest child was less than age 3, about 10 percent higher for women whose youngest child was age 3–5, and another 10 percent higher for women whose youngest child was age 6–17. The rates moved up in tandem through 2000, each rising about 25 percent in those 25 years. In that year the LFPRs for the three groups were approximately 60 percent, 70 percent, and 80 percent, respectively. But 2000 was near the peak and the LFPRs for all three groups have declined since then. The impact of age of the youngest child is still evident, although it is now weaker than in 1975. About 61 percent of women with a child younger than three were in the labor force, two-thirds of those whose youngest child was age 3–5, and three-quarters of those whose youngest child was age six or older.

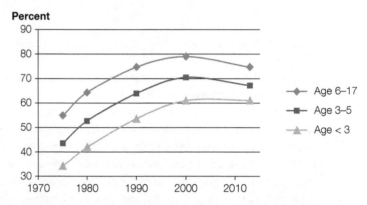

Figure 8.7 *How LFPRs have changed for US women by age of youngest child.*

Sources: Data from US Bureau of Labor Statistics, *Women in the Labor Force: A Databook*, Table 7 and *Employment Characteristics of Families 2013*, Table 4

The decline in women's labor-force participation since 2000 is interesting because it truly marked the end of a very long upward trend. The popular press has suggested that this is a retreat from work and that women, perhaps especially well-educated married women with children, are opting out of the labor market in order to invest more time in their children. This fits nicely with the idea of investment in child quality that we discussed in Chapter 5.

Because so many other factors have changed over time, Figure 8.7 doesn't tell the whole story about how children affect women's labor-force participation and how that relationship has changed. It turns out that the story is a bit more complicated. Heather Boushey[21] examined what she called the "child penalty" on women's LFPRs over this time period, against the backdrop of the opting-out hypothesis. The child penalty is simply the difference in the LFPRs of women with and without children, using regression analysis to control for other factors such as education, age, and race. The general analysis can be written like this:

$$LFP_i = \alpha + \beta X + \delta Children_i + \mu_i \tag{8.1}$$

21 Heather Boushey (2008), "Opting out? The Effect of Children on Women's Employment in the United States," *Feminist Economics*, 14 (1), 1–36.

where LFP is a measure of whether a woman is working in the labor market and X stands for other factors like education, age, marital status, and race that also affect the probability of working. The variable named "Children" in equation (8.1) could be the number of children a woman has or an indicator for the presence of children less than a particular age, and so forth. In general we expect $\delta < 0$, which means that women with children are less likely to be working than otherwise similar women without children. The value of δ is a measure of the child penalty on labor-force participation. The opting-out hypothesis suggests that δ has become more negative over time, especially for particular groups of women.

Boushey estimated an equation like (8.1) for various years from 1979 to 2005 for women aged 25–45, which is the prime age group for women with young children. She found that the child penalty associated with having children under age 18 was more than 20 percent in 1984, declined to 14 points in 1993, and further narrowed to 8 percent in 2004. The corresponding penalties associated with having a child less than age 6 were 25 percent (1984), 23 percent (1993), and about 20 percent in 2004, respectively. Both analyses thus show that the child penalty is genuine, but also that it has declined. The decline is smaller for mothers of younger children. Having children has, according to these analyses, become less of a factor in women's labor-force participation, not more of a factor.

Further analysis by Hoffman[22] confirmed that the child penalty declined over these years but found that the decline was mostly due to the changing work behavior of single women with children. From the mid-1980s through the mid-1990s, children affected the labor-force participation of single mothers much more negatively than married mothers. Over this time period the child penalty was approximately 4–5 percent for married mothers and 10–12 percent for their single counterparts; these effects control, by regression, for age, education, race, and ethnicity. But in the mid-1990s through the early 2000s, the child penalty flip-flopped, falling to essentially zero for single women, but increasing to 12 percent for married women. The rising value of the EITC and the changes in the welfare system over this time period may have been a carrot and stick for single women's labor-force participation. The bottom line: The decline in the child penalty over these years was largely because single mothers were more likely to be working.

Opting out The opting-out hypothesis focuses primarily on labor-force withdrawals by highly educated married women with young children or larger families and usually with high-income husbands. The popular take-away message in the media is that even highly educated women are not as attached to their careers as men are. This hypothesis does, in fact, make some economic sense when analyzed in terms of the model of labor-force participation we have developed. If these women are, indeed, married to high-income men, then the marginal utility of the additional income they earn is relatively low and they also likely face high marginal tax rates. In addition, their own household productivity in producing child quality may be high and the cost of comparably high-quality daycare may be very high, especially in large metropolitan areas. They may also place a high value (i.e., receive high utility from) on high-quality children. It is not far-fetched to conclude that some highly educated women in these

---

22 Saul D. Hoffman (February, 2009), "Married with Children: The Labor Force Participation of Women in the Late 20th and Early Twenty-first Century," *Monthly Labor Review*, 3–14.

circumstances could find that $MVT^* > MTV_M(1)$ and thus decide not to remain in the labor force when their children are young or otherwise may benefit from substantial parental time investment.

It is always possible to find anecdotal evidence that supports an idea—like the *New York Times* article—but social science research findings are always based on broader evidence from nationally representative data. In this case that evidence does not support a widespread pattern of opting-out, although it certainly exists. Table 8.2 shows the change in labor-force participation rates from 1999 to 2014 for married women by their own education and the age of their youngest child. The data are from the Current Population Survey, the nationally representative survey used by the Census Bureau and Bureau of Labor Statistics to measure the unemployment rate and other national economic data. The sample includes all married women age 16 and older whose youngest child is of the designated age bracket.

Table 8.2 *How LFPRs for US married women have changed, 1999–2014, by age of youngest child and mother's education.*

Age of Youngest Child	Not a College Graduate	College Graduate
<3	−7.9	4.9
3–5	−6.9	1.8
6–17	−8.1	−1.5
All	−5.5	−3.8

Figures in the table are the percent change in the LFPR. The "All" category includes women without children. Author calculations from November, 1999 and September, 2014 Current Population Survey.

The table shows quite clearly that the trends in married mothers' labor-force participation since 1999 are quite different by education, but in a direction opposite to the opting-out hypothesis. Over this time period, LFPRs for married mothers with less than a college degree fell by 7–8 percent, more or less independent of the age of their youngest child. For married mothers with a college degree, LFPRs increased by 5 percent if they had children age three or younger and by almost 2 percent if their youngest child was age 3–5. The only group of college-educated married mothers with a decline in their LFPR over this period was women whose youngest child was age six or older and the decline was much smaller than for the corresponding group of mothers without a college degree. So if mothers are opting out of the labor force, it is primarily less-educated women, not highly-educated ones, who are doing so.

The Pew Research Center has examined the opting-out issue in even greater detail, using Census Bureau data.[23] Their research has focused on affluent, very highly educated mothers who are not in the labor market; they define these as mothers with at least a Master's degree, an annual family income of $75,000 or more, and who

---

23 See D'Vera Cohn, Gretchen Livingston, and Wendy Wang, (April, 2014), *After Decades of Decline, A Rise in Stay-at-Home Mothers*, Washington, DC: Pew Research Center's Social & Demographic Trends project, and Gretchen Livingston, "Opting Out? About 10% of Highly Educated Moms Are Staying at Home," Pew Research Center FactTank, May 7, 2014.

indicate that they are not working in order to care for their family, rather than because of labor-market issues.

Their findings echo those in Figure 8.7 and Table 8.2. They find that the number of stay-at-home mothers is increasing after decades of decline. Between 1999 and the mid-2010s, the proportion of married women who were stay-at-home mothers increased from 23 percent to 29 percent. By the Pew definition, "opt-out moms" account for about 4 percent of all stay-at-home mothers; they concluded that most of the increase in the proportion of stay-at-home moms has been due to the decline in labor-force participation by less-educated mothers.

As for the "opt-out moms," the Pew report estimates that in 2012 the number of women in the opt-out mom category totaled 370,000. This is not a tiny number but not a social movement either. Pew estimated that about 10 percent of mothers with a Master's degree or more fit their definition of an opt-out mom. The percentages varied slightly across educational attainment: 11 percent for women with professional degrees such as medicine, law, or nursing; 9 percent for women with degrees; and 6 percent for women with a PhD. Their median family income was about $130,000, half were between ages 35 and 44, and half have at least one child aged 5 or younger. They are overwhelmingly white or Asian. Interestingly, more than one-third of these non-working mothers have more education than their working husbands and 45 percent have the same education.

Economist Joni Hersch has examined opting-out among women who are graduates of elite colleges and finds stronger evidence of opting-out. See Box 8.3 for a summary of her research findings.

While the opt-out phenomenon is, apparently, not widespread, it is, nevertheless, interesting and perhaps instructive. The exact causes are still not fully known. It may reflect a desire to invest heavily in children, but it may also or instead reflect difficulties in resolving family–work conflict satisfactorily, especially in the kinds of work environments that are more common among highly educated men and women. The problem can be compounded by assortative mating if these women's husbands also face difficult family–work conflicts. We will return to this issue in Chapter 11 when we discuss Claudia Goldin's analysis of the gender earnings gap among college-educated men and women and the potential role of occupational characteristics, including job inflexibility, in supporting and maintaining that gap. We also discuss the role of policies, such as maternal leave, that may help with establishing family–work balance in Chapter 12.

| Box | 8.3 |

Opting Out Among Female Graduates of Elite Colleges

While the Pew study identified women by their educational attainment, including postgraduate education, it doesn't focus directly on women from elite schools such as were profiled in the original opting-out stories in the popular press. Joni Hersch used nationally representative data on college graduates to examine whether there women who graduated from more elite colleges and universities were more likely to be opt-out moms than women who graduated from less elite colleges. To do that she used data from a survey of more than 100,000 college graduates, the 2003 National Survey of College Graduates. This is an earlier time period than in the Pew study, but it is still interesting and relevant.

Hersch used external data on college rankings to measure college selectivity. She classified colleges and universities into four distinct tiers of selectivity and then linked that to information on marriage, fertility, and work by female graduates. Tier 1 included the most highly competitive private research universities (e.g., Ivy League universities), Tier 2 included private liberal arts colleges, Tier 3 was most public research universities ("flagship" state universities), and Tier 4 included all other schools. Her study involves a regression analysis of a woman's labor-force status as a function of the quality of her educational institution as measured by its tier, along with typical control measures for her own potential wage rate, her marital status, number of children, spouse earnings, and so on. The analysis is complicated because college quality can operate through its effects on wage rates and spouse earnings, for example. Women who attended higher-quality colleges typically have higher wage rates and possibly also have spouses with higher earnings, courtesy of assortative mating. Hersch suggests that preferences for work may also vary. She argues that women from less privileged backgrounds may attend college only if they are career-focused, while women from more privileged backgrounds who tend to attend the more elite colleges are likely to attend because social norms for college attendance are strong, regardless of their plans for future work.

In general, Hersch finds that female graduates of more elite colleges and universities have lower labor-force attachment across a variety of employment measures than female graduates of less elite schools. For example, graduates of the least elite schools were 8.6 percent more likely to be working than graduates of the most elite schools and, even after controlling for the other factors, the difference was 5.3 percent. Differences by selectivity are larger for women with children than women without children. Hersch also examined the impacts separately by a woman's highest educational degree and its selectivity. Among women with children, she found the largest effects were for those with MBA degrees for more elite schools relative to graduates of less elite schools. Effects were smaller and typically not statistically significant for women with BA or degrees from more elite institutions. No differences by college selectivity were found in this analysis among women with PhDs or MD degrees.

Hersch doesn't offer a full explanation of her findings. The large MBA effects are particularly interesting. She does note the possibility that these women are "pushed out" of the labor market by inflexible working conditions that might be more present at the higher-end jobs they might likely end up in. But she argues that these women would have a wider range of work options, precisely because of their more selective school backgrounds. More on this later in Chapter 11.

Source: Joni Hersch (2013), "Opting Out among Women with Elite Education," *Review of Economics of the Household* 11, 469–506.

Women and work: new research

We close this section on women and work by looking briefly at three interesting issues: How and perhaps why the United States is now falling behind other countries in terms of women's labor-force participation; the effect of race on women's work and its historical causes; and how and why contemporary attitudes about women's work roles may be related to agricultural practices centuries ago. Each of these is the subject of recent economic research.

Women's labor-force participation: is the United States falling behind?

Between 1990 and 2010 the LFPR for US women fell from one of the highest among Western advanced economies to the middle of the pack. As we saw in Chapter 7, women's LFPR increased steadily from about 1940 to 1995, peaked in 1999 and has drifted down slowly since then. The 2014 figure—57.0 percent for all women age 16 and older—is the lowest rate observed since 1998. The same time trend holds for married women, whose 2014 LFPR is the same as their rate in 1990.

Economists Francine Blau and Lawrence Kahn have documented this and offered a possible explanation.[24] Blau and Kahn focused on women aged 25–54 in 1990 and 2010 and compared the LFPR in the United States with that in 22 OECD countries, mostly Western Europe plus Australia, Canada, Japan, and New Zealand. The 1990 US rate (74.0 percent) was the sixth highest, nearly 7 percent above the average of the other countries. By 2010 the US rate had inched up to 75.2 percent (it has since fallen to 73.9 percent), while the average for the other countries jumped to 79.5 percent. The United States now ranks 17th out of 22 countries in its LFPR for 25–54-year-old women. Interestingly, the same general pattern holds for US men, but the change is less extreme. The LFPR for US men aged 25–54 fell from 14th to 22th–dead last. Putting these two trends together, Blau and Kahn emphasize that the gender gap in participation rates fell by about 5 percent in the United States and almost 17 percent in the other countries. The results are not the result of different impacts of the financial crisis; using 2007 as the comparison year yields very similar results.

We discuss employment-friendly family policies in detail in Chapter 12, but suffice it say for the moment that the United States is at the very low end in terms of parental leave—both length and generosity—and public spending on childcare. Many of the countries also have other legislation that grants workers the right to have a part-time work schedule, which could facilitate women staying in the labor force. (It could also increase the cost of hiring a worker, which would likely reduce the amount of employment offered by firms.) Many of the countries also provide part-time workers from protection from discrimination in the workplace. Many of these policies were implemented in the other countries between 1990 and 2010, so they do line up with the time trend in participation rates.

To quantify the impact of these policies on women's labor-force participation over the full 1990–2010 time period, Blau and Kahn used a standard regression analysis, with men's and women's LFPRs as the dependent variable and the various policies as the explanatory

---

24 Francine D. Blau and Lawrence M. Kahn (2013), "Female Labor Supply: Why Is the United States Falling Behind?" *American Economic Review,* 103 (3), 251–256.

variables. Their analysis thus shows whether the apparent differences between the United States and the other countries in these policies are part of the explanation for the changing LFPRs. This is certainly not a random assignment experiment. It is a little like a natural experiment, except that the countries themselves are quite different in ways that are hard to measure and that could be part of the reason that some countries have the policies and others do not. So the results can be viewed as suggestive but not definitive.

They find that all the key policy variables do have a positive effect on women's labor-force participation, although not all the effects are statistically significant, which means they are not reliably different from zero. Measures of the length and generosity of parental leave are positive and reasonably large, but not statistically significant. The two policies related to protections for part-time work both had large positive effects on women's labor-force participation and on the difference between men's and women's rates.

Based on these quantitative estimates of the impact of the policies, Blau and Kahn simulated what the US LFPRs might be if the policies were adopted. They found that the US rate in 2010 would have been almost seven percent higher than its actual value. This would have been enough to make the US rank 11th rather than 17th in women's labor-force participation. On the negative side, Blau and Kahn note that the greater availability of part-time work can lead women into the "mommy track," where they are no longer considered as candidates for higher-level jobs within organizations. Indeed, US women are less likely than women in other countries to work part-time.

We will return to issues of family–work balance in Chapter 11, when we discuss the gender gap in earnings, and in Chapter 12, when we discuss family policy in the United States

Race and women's work: a brief historical analysis

In Chapter 7 we noted the large historical difference in LFPRs between white and black women in the United States. In the 1900 Census, for example—see Table 7.3—the LFPRs for white and black married women were 3 percent and 26 percent, respectively, and the racial LFPR gap was 30 percent for never-married women. The gap narrowed over the twentieth century, actually disappearing in the early 1990s, but it reappeared in the 2000s and 2010s. In 2014 the LFPR for black women was about 2–3 percent higher than for white women, depending on the particular age group being compared. This is true despite the fact that black women still earn less than white women, which often is a disincentive to work.

One obvious explanation for the higher LFPR for black married women in the early part of the twentieth century is the far lower earnings of black men. This was still the aftermath of Reconstruction and Jim Crow laws; racial discrimination in education, housing, and labor markets was widespread, strong, and often legally enforced. As a result the marginal value of black married women's market work (MVT_M) was higher because the goods and services their earnings provided were more critical to a family's standard of living. More formally, it was far more likely that $MVT_M > MVT^*$ for black women than white women. This inequality is the necessary condition for market work to be a utility-maximizing choice.

Claudia Goldin, whose extensive research on women's labor-force participation we discussed in Chapter 7, proposed an explanation for the high rates of labor-force work by black women in terms of what she called the "double legacy" of slavery.[25] The first legacy is the lower earnings of men discussed above. The second is that slavery may have created a norm of work for black women that differed from the norm for white women. Simply put, black women had always worked outside of the home, usually in manual labor and, of course, not always voluntarily. As a result, Goldin proposed that women's manual labor was deemed more acceptable within the black community. White women had no similar experience in working outside the home in this time period and certainly not in manual labor, which was the dominant employment mode in those years.

One way to test this idea empirically is to see whether race is a predictor of a woman's labor-force participation even after controlling for differences in other individual characteristics that typically affect labor-force participation. This is equivalent to estimating a regression like this:

$$\text{LFP}_i = \alpha + \beta X_i + \delta \text{Race}_i + \mu_i \tag{8.2}$$

In (8.2), LFP is a measure of whether a woman worked, X stands for other variables that affect labor-force participation, like a woman's age and education and her husband's income, and Race is a dummy variable equal to 1 if a woman is black and 0 otherwise.[26] The estimated value of δ in equation (8.2) is a test of the double legacy operating through different norms. If the differences between black and white women were fully due to differences in the variables included in X, then δ would be equal to 0. But if $\delta > 0$, then income and family structure are not the whole story and there is an additional effect of race on labor-force participation, possibly reflecting social values.

Regression equations like (8.2) can be run to estimate δ using historical Census data. An analysis by economists Leah Boustan and William Collins[27] used Census data for 1870. Their analysis included as measures of X personal characteristics such as literacy, marital status, the number of children under age five, household wealth, and husband's occupation. They found that the race effect on labor-force participation remained large even after controlling for those variables. For example, differences by race in these measures accounted for only about one-quarter of the 23 percent difference by race in LFPRs for married women. This means that the LFPR of black women in these early years was substantially greater than would be predicted based on their economic and demographic characteristics compared to whites.

Boustan and Collins show that the race effect on labor-force participation continued to exist through much of the twentieth century, although it was diminished. By 1960 the effect of race, controlling for other measures, was about 8 percent and by 2000 it was essentially zero. The rise and expansion of what they refer to as "clean" white-collar occupations in the middle decades of the twentieth century is part of the explanation. These new jobs in clerical and sales positions were less at variance with prevailing norms for appropriate work for white women. In addition, white women were well-suited to enter

---

25 Claudia Goldin (1977), "Female Labor Force Participation: The Origin of Black and White Differences, 1870 to 1880," *Journal of Economic History* 37 (1), 87–108.

26 See the discussion of dummy variables in Chapter 2. This regression equation is similar in structure to the "child penalty" regression shown earlier in Equation (8.1).

27 The discussion in this section draws heavily on "The Origin and Persistence of Black-White Differences in Women's Labor Force Participation," in *Human Capital in History: The American Record*, Leah Boustan, Carola Frydman, and Robert A. Margo, (eds.), University of Chicago Press, chicago.

these fields because they had fuller access to education than black women, who mostly resided in the South and faced segregated and poorly financed school systems. Black women remained heavily concentrated in agricultural and domestic service throughout the first two-thirds of the twentieth century.

In another interesting test of whether work norms were an important factor in the early twentieth century, Boustan and Collins looked at whether black women who were most likely the daughters of slaves were themselves more likely to be working than otherwise similar black women who were not the daughters of slaves. The underlying idea is that daughters of slaves might have a different norm about work, having grown up in an environment in which their mothers did manual labor outside the home. They do, in fact, find support for this hypothesis: The daughters of slaves were 5–9 percent more likely to be working, depending on the particular group analyzed.

In an indirect way, the early race difference in married women's employment had a lingering effect as late as the 1970s. In an analysis of women's labor-force participation in that time period, Boustan and Collins found that women in their late twenties were more likely to be working if their own mothers had worked when the daughters were age 14. This "intergenerational" work effect held even controlling for a broad set of family factors, such as the mother's and father's education. The effect of the mother's work on a daughter's labor-force participation was approximately the same for young white and black women, but because the black women were more likely to have working mothers when they were younger, the difference contributed to the race difference in LFPRs.

The idea that norms are an important part of economic decision making is a relatively new one in economics. Economists tend to downplay differences in preferences in order to focus on differences in more readily observed factors such as incomes and prices, and often this is an appropriate and constructive approach. But norms about gender roles surely matter, too. It is not hard to imagine situations in which a wife's employment was potentially utility-maximizing in terms of the consumption of goods and services it would make possible but did not occur because her husband disapproved. Perhaps he was concerned that he would be thought an "inadequate provider." Adding this negative husband's utility effect into our labor-force participation analysis might well change the wife's behavior.

Agriculture and attitudes: the historical origins of gender roles

In most economies and for most of recorded history, adult men and women have had different economic roles, with men specializing in the labor market and women in the household sector. There are, of course, some exceptions and these differences are narrowing for reasons we understand reasonably well from the discussions in Chapters 3 through 7. But where did the differences come from in the first place? Why did they persist so long? And why do contemporary social norms about women's roles differ so substantially across societies?

These are the kinds of fascinating "big-think" questions that can never be answered definitively. Hundreds of years from now, economists and other scholars will undoubtedly still be debating them. But in an ambitious and provocative article, "On the Origin of Gender Roles: Women and the Plough," economists Alberto Alessini, Paulo Giuliano, and

Nathan Nunn tackled those questions.[28] This is an exercise in economic history on a grand scale and it is not for the faint at heart. It seems a fitting way to conclude this section.

Alessini, Giuliano, and Nunn (AGN for short) note that ideas about appropriate gender roles vary widely across contemporary societies.[29] Their research is a very intensive examination of an idea first proposed by Ester Boserup, an influential Danish economist whose work on women in developing countries we will discuss in Chapters 13 and 14. Boserup hypothesized that historical differences in agriculture between what is called **shifting cultivation** and **plough cultivation** played an important role in defining social perceptions of appropriate gender roles. Shifting cultivation, also known as "slash-and-burn," is labor-intensive but does not require strength that might make men more productive than women. Plough cultivation, however, is more capital-intensive and does require strength to "pull the plough or control the animal that pulls it" (AGN, p. 470). Plough cultivation therefore favored men and it led to greater specialization of production by gender, with women working in the household and men outside it. Boserup suggested that this specialization, in turn, led to the development of norms and beliefs about appropriate gender roles, beliefs that persisted even after that particular form of agriculture declined.[30]

The core of AGN's research is linking ethnographic information about pre-industrial societies to contemporary measures of a society's norms and behavior concerning women working in the market sector of the economy. The underlying information on agriculture comes from a famous anthropology study that has information on early agriculture for 1,265 ethnic groups, including whether or not agriculture used the plough. On the basis of this information, AGN show that women were, indeed, substantially less likely to work in agriculture in pre-industrial times in economies that utilized plough cultivation, but no less likely to be working in activities in the household. They interpret this as empirical support for Boserup's underlying hypothesis about how plough agriculture affected women's work outside the home.

Linking these historical patterns of agriculture to the modern world and its views about gender roles is an enormously difficult task that involves determining the current geographical distribution of the original 1,265 ethnic groups. They do this by linking information on each of 7,612 different current languages and where those languages are now spoken to the 1,265 ethnic groups to get a sense of where the descendants of those ethnic groups now live. Their analysis is far too complex in both data and methods to do justice to here. Needless to say, the data are imperfect. Using a variety of techniques to address the data problems, they develop a country-level measure of ancestral plough use and then link that measure to three gendered outcomes: (1) women's LFPR; (2) the share of firms that are women-owned, which is a measure of women's entrepreneurship; and (3) the share of seats in a national parliament held by women, which is a measure of their political power.

---

28 Alberto Alesina, Paola Giuliano and Nathan Nunn (2013), "On the Origins of Gender Roles: Women and the Plough," *Quarterly Journal of Economics*, 128 (2), 469–530.

29 For example, recent survey responses about whether men have more right to a job than women when jobs are scarce varied from 3.6 percent (Iceland) to 99.6 percent (Egypt).

30 This idea is sometimes referred to as **path dependence** or **lock-in**. An idea that may be functionally valuable at one point in time may persist beyond that time if other ideas and institutions develop that support it. The QWERTY keyboard is often cited as an example of this idea.

To measure the quantitative impact of plough use on these outcomes, AGN used a regression model similar in form to equations (8.1) and (8.2):

$$Y_i = \alpha + \beta X_i + \delta \text{Plough}_i + \mu_i \tag{8.3}$$

In equation (8.3), Y stand for the three outcomes, X are other variables that could affect those outcomes, and Plough is a measure of Plough use in traditional agriculture. If plough use affected attitudes that have persisted and resulted in greater differentiation in gender roles, then δ will be negative. Indeed, that is what they find: in countries with a tradition of plough use, all three measures are lower than in otherwise similar countries (as measured by the X variables). The quantitative impacts are relatively large. They find that a one-standard deviation change in traditional plough use decreases women's labor-force participation by almost 6 percent, women's share of firm ownership by 7 percent, and political representation by 2.25 points. Because the average values of the variables differ—political representation is far lower than the LFPR—the proportional impact ranges from about 10 to 20 percent, depending on the outcome considered.

AGN also consider the effect of traditional plough use on two measures of contemporary gender attitudes from surveys. The first is whether men have more right to a job when jobs are scarce, and the second is whether "men make better political leaders than women." Using a regression structure exactly like equation (8.3), they find that traditional plough use is associated with more conservative attitudes about gender roles. The effects, though, are weaker than in the analyses about economic and political behavior.

You can be certain that this is not the last word on the ever-fascinating conversation about the differences between men and women. It is particularly interesting because it uses contemporary quantitative economic research methods to address that kind of complex issue where these methods are not often employed.

Summary

This concludes our discussion of women's work and work decisions. We have developed a general model of time use in Chapter 7 and used it to identify the likely causes of the enormous increase in women's labor-force participation. In this chapter, we extended the analysis, incorporating the effects of taxes, transfers, children, childcare costs, public policy, and even societal norms.

Having analyzed the movement of women from household production to market work, it is now time to move on to analyze how they have fared in the labor market. We turn to that in Chapters 9, 10, and 11.

9 WOMEN'S EARNINGS, OCCUPATION, AND EDUCATION: AN OVERVIEW

Introduction

Women's wage rates have been a central component of all of our analyses thus far. They helped explain the division of labor within households and the gains of marriage. They were an important factor in thinking about how the marriage market has changed. They played a critical role in explaining declining fertility and rising labor-force participation. Now it is time to examine women's wages directly, rather than as an explanation of these other phenomenon.

The basic economics question about the gender earnings gap is simple: Why do women, on average, earn less than men? There are two very broad possible explanations. Women could have, on average, fewer valuable labor-market skills than men. For example, if women have less education than men on average (in fact, they don't at this point in time) or have less labor-market experience than men (they still do), and if education and labor-market experience are valuable in the labor-market, then these differences could be a source of differences in average earnings. Earnings differences resulting from differences in labor-market skills would exist even if there were no labor-market discrimination at all. Alternatively, the earnings differences could reflect a lower value attached to the skills that women do bring to the labor-market. For example, women might be unable to obtain jobs that match their skills. Outcomes like that would reflect labor-market discrimination.

This chapter begins a four-chapter part on women's earnings. In this chapter we set out the basic facts about the gender gap in earnings and also the gender difference in occupations and education. Then we take a quick survey of how labor-markets work to set wage rates via supply-and-demand analysis. In the next chapter we examine these two alternative explanations of the gender gap in earnings, focusing primarily on investment in human capital and labor-market discrimination. In Chapter 11 we introduce statistical techniques that will help us sort out the quantitative importance of skills vs. discrimination explanations of the gender gap in earnings and then examine empirical research on the causes of the gender gap. Our goal is to be able to answer the questions posed in the preceding paragraph. Finally, in Chapter 12, we review government policies concerning women's work and pay.

The gender gap in earnings

Women earn, on average, considerably less than men, a fact that probably comes as no surprise. The earliest data for the United States for agricultural and manufacturing workers during the first half of the nineteenth century show women earning roughly 30–45 percent of what men earned.[1] More than 150 years later, the gender earnings ratio has risen substantially from that nineteenth-century level, but it is still far short of equality.

Table 9.1 presents the median annual earnings in 2013 for year-round full-time (YRFT) workers by gender and by race and ethnicity in the United States. YRFT workers work at least 35 hours a week and at least 50 weeks in a year; paid vacations count as work weeks. These workers are the standard comparison group for gender earnings because they allow us to compare the earnings of men and women who work fairly similar numbers of hours in a year. The median is a better measure than the mean for this purpose because it is less affected by very high incomes and thus better represents the status of a typical person.

Table 9.1 *The gender gap for US women in 2013: median annual earnings for year-round full-time workers by gender, race, and ethnicity.*

	Women	Men	Women's Earnings as a Percentage of Men's Earnings (%)
All	$39,157	$50,033	78.3
White	$39,013	$50,416	77.4
Black	$33,903	$38,670	87.7
Hispanic	$28,424	$32,243	88.2
Asian	$45,439	$57,148	79.5

Source: US Census Bureau, Current Population Survey, Historical Income Data, Table P-38, census.gov/hhes/www/income/histinc/incpertoc.html

Median YRFT earnings for US women in 2013 were $39,157, 78.3 percent of the $50,033 that the median YRFT man earned. There are interesting and sizeable differences in the earnings ratio by race/ethnicity. Both black women and Hispanic women earned about 88 percent of what men of the same race or ethnicity earned, compared to 77–80 percent for the other two groups. You can also see in Table 9.1 the substantial differences in earnings by race and ethnicity within gender. Whites and Asians earn far more than blacks and Hispanics, and this is true for both men and women.

The overall distribution of earnings for YRFT workers differs substantially by gender. At the low end of the distribution, women were about 50 percent more likely than men to earn less than $25,000 in 2013, while men were more than twice as likely to be earning over $100,000. The gender disparity was even greater at incomes over 250,000, where men outnumbered women by almost a 5 to 1 ratio. Because of the fatter upper tail of the distribution for men, the gender ratio for average earnings was considerably lower than for median earnings; in 2013 this ratio was 72.9 percent, about 5 percent lower than the ratio of median earnings.

The gender gap in annual earnings is larger for all working men and women than for YRFT workers because more women work part-time or part-year than men. In 2013 about three-fifths of all working women worked YRFT, compared to about three-quarters of all working men. Median annual earnings of all working men in 2013 were $39,903,

---

1   Claudia Goldin (1990), *Understanding the Gender Gap,* New York: Oxford University Press, Table 3.1.

compared to $27,736 for all working women, so the gender earnings ratio for all US workers was 69.5 percent. But the usual expectation that men are more likely to be YRFT workers doesn't apply to black men and women. See Box 9.1 for details on this unexpected pattern of labor-force participation.

| Box | 9.1 |

Race, Gender, and Year-Round Full-Time Workers

Gender comparisons of annual earnings focus on YRFT so as to avoid including the lower earnings of the still larger share of women who work part time or part year. But this doesn't work as you might expect for black men and women. More black women are YRFT workers than black men, a relationship not widely recognized or appreciated.

In 2013, 35 million white women and almost 50 million white men were YRFT workers. That means that 40 percent more white men worked YRFT than women. But among black workers, 6.1 million men and 6.7 women worked YRFT, so that women actually outnumbered men by almost 10 percent.

This phenomenon has been developing for many years. In 1970, black men outnumbered black women as YRFT workers by 60 percent. By 1980, this figure had slipped to 30 percent, by 1990 to 11 percent, and finally in 1995 the women caught up to the men. The ratio has bounced around a bit, but black women have outnumbered the men every year since then, usually by 5–10 percent. The peak difference was 11 percent in 2002.

The same general upward trend appears for white women relative to white men, but from a much lower level and with much less increase. In 1970, almost two and half times as many white men worked YRFT as white women. By 1980 this had dropped to approximately twice as many, then to 60 percent more by 1990, and finally to its current figure of about 50 percent more.

What's behind the twisting time trend for black men and women? The deep causes are still matters for research. But we can identify some sources. First, black women have outnumbered black men in the civilian non-institutional population (age 20 and older) by about 25 percent since at least the early 1970s. Even ignoring those over age 65 where women greatly outnumber men but neither are likely to be YRFT workers, the difference is still about 15 percent. But this doesn't explain the trend, because this component has been trendless, although it does differ by race. Second, the LFPR for black women has risen, while the rate for black men has fallen. For example, in 1975 the LFPR for black men was 25 percent higher than for black women; by 2013, the difference had shrunk to just 4 percent. Third, black women have moved from part-time to full-time, full-year work more rapidly than black men. Between 1975 and 2005, the proportion of black working men who worked YRFT increased substantially from 55 percent to almost 69 percent. But over the same time period the YRFT percentage among working black women increased by more, from 43 percent to 65 percent. The net result of these trends is the larger number of black women than black men working YRFT.

In an interesting way, this brings us back to the marriage analysis of Wilson and his MMPI (see Chapter 4), which computed the number of marriageable ("working") black men relative to the number of black women in a specified age range. Wilson was the first to emphasize how out of balance the marriage market was for the black population, with the number of women far exceeding the number of working men. Here we see that the difference is even more profound than indicated by Wilson.

It is important to understand what these earnings ratios do and do not mean. They are not a comparison of men and women doing the same work or with the same qualifications and skills. Rather, the ratios reflect the earnings of the median male and female worker. Median earnings can differ by gender either because average skill levels differ or because men and women earn differ amounts even when they have the same skill levels.

Figure 9.1 shows how the gender earnings ratio has changed since 1960 for both groups of workers. For a period of at least two decades through 1980, the ratio for YRFT workers moved in an incredibly narrow band. In 1960 the ratio was 60.7 percent; in 1980 it was 60.2 percent. In the intervening years it stayed almost entirely between 58 and 59 percent. It is rare to see an economics time series that is so unchanged over such an extended time period. Indeed, the ratio was so constant that the National Organization for Women circulated popular buttons that read "59¢ on the dollar."

Figure 9.1 *How the gender earnings ratio has changed, US workers, 1960–2013.*

Source: US Census Bureau, Current Population Survey, Historical Income Data, Table P-38 & P-41

The YRFT earnings ratio began to increase in the early 1980s. It rose almost every year during that decade, jumping from 60 percent in 1980 to more than 71 percent in 1990. Since then it has risen much more slowly and much less steadily. The ratio has actually fallen in a few years, including, for example, between 1997 and 1999 and again between 2003 and 2004. In the 2000s the ratio barely changed: it was 76.3 percent in 2001 and 76.9 percent in 2010. Between 2012 and 2013, however, the ratio increased by almost 2 percent to the highest figure ever recorded. It is too early to know if this is part of a new trend in the 2010s.

The earnings ratio for all workers has increased more steadily than for YRFT workers, reflecting both the narrowing in gender pay differences and the rapid increase in women's labor-force activity. In 1967, the first year with available data, the ratio of median annual earnings by gender was only 39.1 percent for all workers. The median working woman earned just $2,351, the equivalent of about $18,500 in today's dollars. In 1974 the ratio was still 39.1 percent, but thereafter the earnings ratio moved up quite steadily, 1 percent or more almost every year through the early 1990s. It finally broke the 60 percent threshold in 1992 and the 70 percent threshold 15 years later. In the 1990s the ratio bounced around, actually ending the 1990s lower than the 1992 figure. The ratio rose relatively steadily through the 2000s, peaking in 2010 at just over 72 percent. It has since fallen three years in a row to its 2013 value of 69.5 percent. Again, it is too early to know if this is a trend or just reflects the unsettled economy of the early 2010s.

One well-established fact about the gender earnings gap is that it tends to increase as men and women age. In a study of men and women from 1978 through 1998, Blau and Kahn[2] found that the gender gap increased from ages 25–34 to 35–44, and then often stabilized or even reversed course. For example, in 1988 the gender ratio for hourly earnings for 25–34-year-old YRFT workers was 83 percent. Ten years later, when the workers were 35–44 years old, the women had lost ground and the ratio was 76.1 percent. For an earlier group of 25–34-year-olds in 1978, the earnings ratio started at a much lower 70.3 percent, fell to 68.7 percent at ages 35–44 in 1988, and then increased to 71.6 percent in 1988.

Claudia Goldin[3] has shown the same pattern for college graduates over an even longer time and also more recently. College-graduate women born in the late 1940s and early 1950s earned nearly three-quarters as much as their male peers when they were in their twenties, but the ratio fell steadily to not much more than 60 percent by the time they were in their mid-to-late thirties. Then, as they moved into their forties, the earnings ratio increased, eventually exceeding 70 percent when they were in their late fifties and early sixties. For college-educated women born two decades later—in the late 1960s and early 1970s—the earnings ratio exceeded 80 percent when they were in their twenties, but fell nearly 15 percent by the time they were in their mid-forties. The same pattern holds for women born as recently as the late 1970s and early 1980s. Their earnings ratio declined from about 85 percent in their mid-twenties (the early 2000s) to about 78 percent in their mid-thirties (2010).

This finding suggests that something is happening between roughly ages 25 and 40 that adversely affects women's earnings relative to men, and that this occurred even in time periods in which the overall gender earnings ratio was increasing. There are two obvious candidates—responsibilities associated with marriage and family and labor-market impediments that affect promotion and career paths. We will return to these issues later.

Even within education levels or within occupations, women still earn less than men. Table 9.2 provides some evidence of this. The top part of the table shows the annual median earnings ratio by education for YRFT workers aged 25–64 and the lower part shows the ratio of usual median weekly earnings, also for YRFT workers, in selected occupations.

---

2 Francine D. Blau and Lawrence M. Kahn (2001), "Gender Differences in Pay," *Journal of Economic Perspectives,* 14 (4), 75–99.

3 Claudia Goldin (2015), "A Grand Gender Convergence: Its Last Chapter," *American Economic Review,* 104 (4), 1091–1119.

If education differences were the primary cause of the earnings differences, we would expect to see relatively high gender earnings ratios within each education category. But, in fact, the ratios are all in a relatively narrow range, from just under 70 percent for those with a professional degree to 76.4 percent for high-school graduates. Women with a college degree earned about three-quarters of what college-educated men earned.

The occupational ratios tell a fairly similar story. Men and women do differ in their occupations (more on this in the next section and chapters) and occupational differences are part of the explanation for wage differences, although the role they play is complex. Are the occupational differences the result of different choices or are they the result of constraints and pressures? Leaving that to the side for the moment, the table shows that substantial differences in earnings exist within occupations. Among the group of occupations shown, the gender earnings ratios are mostly in a 10-point range from 72 percent to 82 percent. The highest shown is for post-secondary school teachers (90.2 percent) and lowest for physicians and surgeons (72.7 percent). Occupations are not homogeneous, of course; maybe female physicians and surgeons are doing different things than male physicians and surgeons and similarly for accountants, architects, and the others. Still, the table suggests that the gender earnings differences are widespread and are not just a function of occupational and educational differences.

Table 9.2 *How gender median earnings ratios differ by education and occupation, United States 2013, YRFT workers.*

Education (Age 25–64)	Earnings Ratio (%)
< HS	73.3
HS Graduate	76.4
Associate Degree	73.7
Bachelor's Degree	75.3
Master's Degree	70.1
Professional Degree	69.9
Doctorate	71.6
Occupation	
Accountants and Auditors	81.2
Architecture and Engineering	81.5
Business and Financial Operations	77.5
Computer and Mathematical Occupations	80.9
Lawyers	78.9
Management	75.8
Physicians and Surgeons	71.7
Teachers, Post-Secondary	90.2
Teachers, Secondary School	82.2

Source: Occupation: Labor Force Statistics from the Current Population Survey, Table 39, bls.gov/cps/cpsaat39.htm; Education: US Census Bureau, ASEC, Table PINC-03, census.gov/hhes/www/cpstables/032014/perinc/toc.htm.

Finally, it's interesting to see how the gender earnings ratio in the United States com-pares to the earnings ratio in other countries. Table 9.3 provides information about the earnings gender gap for selected countries in Europe, as well as Australia, Canada, Japan, and New Zealand. The figures shown are an average across 2010–2012, depending on data availability. Chapter 14 includes a full discussion of the gender gap in developing countries.

Table 9.3 *Female/male median earnings ratios, full-time workers, selected developed countries, 2010–2012.*

Country	Ratio	Country	Ratio
Australia	85.4	Japan	72.5
Belgium	93.6	Netherlands	79.5
Canada	81.1	New Zealand	94.3
Czech Republic	84.4	Norway	92.6
Denmark	90.8	Poland	93.3
France	85.9	Portugal	85.7
Germany	83.4	Spain	91.7
Greece	88.7	Sweden	84.9
Ireland	92.9	Switzerland	81.5
Italy	89.4	United Kingdom	81.6
		United States	81.4

Source: Data from OECD Gender Wage Gap, www.oecd.org/gender/data/genderwagegap.htm.

Across these countries, the median gender earnings ratio is 85.1 percent, and the range is from 72.5 percent (Japan) to 94.3 percent (New Zealand). Norway, Denmark, and Ireland are all above 90 percent, while the Netherlands is the only other country with a ratio below 80 percent. The earnings ratio in the United States is below the median for the group as a whole but is comparable to that of the United Kingdom, Switzerland, and Canada. In 1980 the earnings ratio in the United States was conspicuously low; only Japan had a lower ratio. By the mid-to-late-1990s, the earnings ratio in the United States had nearly caught up to that of the other countries. In general, the gender earnings ratio has risen in these countries, as it has in the United States. Among the countries in the table, the largest increases since 1980 were in the United States, the United Kingdom, Canada, and New Zealand, where the ratio increased by 18–21 percent. At the lower end were Australia, France, and especially Sweden. Sweden had the highest gender earnings ratio of all these countries in 1980, but the ratio has increased only 1 percent since then.

Occupational segregation

During the last few decades the face of the American workforce has changed dramatically as more and more women have entered the workforce and sought work in occupations in which women were previously only a small fraction of workers. Yet despite the inroads women have made into traditionally male occupations, it remains a common observation that many of the jobs in the US economy seem to be implicitly tagged for either men or women, but not usually both. Economists term this **occupational segregation** or sex segregation.

Most of us have a sense of occupations that are disproportionately male or female. For example, in the United States in 2013, 80 percent of social workers, 86 percent of paralegals, and 98 percent of kindergarten teachers were women. At the other end of the spectrum, 91 percent of aerospace engineers and electrical engineers were men in 2013.[4] In 2012, of the top 20 occupations for women, over half were 80 percent or more female.[5] Yet women have made considerable inroads into some previously male-dominated fields. For example, in 1972 only about 12 percent of pharmacists were women, but by 2009 that figure had risen to 50 percent. Similarly, in 1972 only 5 percent of lawyers were female and today over 30 percent of lawyers are female.[6]

Measuring occupational segregation: the index of dissimilarity

To measure how much occupational segregation there is and to measure change in the occupational distribution, we can use the **Index of Dissimilarity**.[7] This index is calculated using the following formula:

$$S = \Sigma |M_j - F_j|/2 \tag{9.1}$$

In equation (9.1), M_j and F_j are the percentage of men and women in the labor force who work in occupation j, "| |" is the absolute value indicator, and Σ is the summation indicator. Thus the Index of Dissimilarity is computed by computing the proportion of all men and all women working in each occupation,[8] taking the absolute value of the difference in each occupation, summing across all occupations, and then dividing by two. If there were no occupational segregation, M_j would equal F_j in each occupation, so the Index of Dissimilarity would equal 0. If, at the other extreme, there were complete occupational segregation, then the summed term would equal 200, and after division by 2, the Index of Dissimilarity would equal 100.[9] So the Index of Dissimilarity ranges from 0 when there is no occupational segregation to 100 when occupational segregation is absolute. The Index of Dissimilarity can also be interpreted as the proportion of men or women who would have to change occupations in order to eliminate occupational segregation.

---

4 Bureau of Labor Statistics, *Women in the Labor Force Databook*, www.bls.gov/cps/wlf-databook-2013.pdf

5 Data on the top 20 occupations are from www.dol.gov/wb/stats/20LeadOcc_2012_txt.htm.

6 Institute for Women's Policy Research Briefing Paper, September 2010. Available at: www.iwpr.org/publications/pubs/separate-and-not-equal-gender-segregation-in-the-labor-market-and-the-gender-wage-gap. Last accessed November 18, 2014.

7 The Index of Dissimilarity was created by the sociologist Otis Dudley Duncan. It can be used to measure dissimilarity between any pair of distributions, not just occupation.

8 Be careful—M_j and F_j are the proportion of all men or all women who work in occupation j, not the proportion of workers in occupation j who are male or female.

9 If there were just two occupations, one 100% male and the other 100% female, then $S = (|100 - 0| + |0 - 100|)/2 = 100$.

A simple numerical example will make clear how this formula works. Begin by assuming that there are 100 women and 100 men in the labor-market and that there are four job categories: construction worker, lawyer, teacher, and nurse. Suppose the distribution of men and women among these occupations is as shown in Case 1 in Table 9.4, with men overrepresented in construction and as lawyers, and women overrepresented as teachers and nurses.

Conveniently, in this example, the number of individuals in an occupation is also the percentage in the occupation since there are 100 men and 100 women in the example. The Index of Dissimilarity for this distribution is

$$\text{Case 1: } S = \Sigma |M_j - F_j|/2 = [|60 - 0| + |25 - 10| + |10 - 40| + |5 - 50|]/2 = 75$$

This is a very high degree of segregation; 75 is obviously much closer to 100 than it is to 0. It means that 75 percent of the men or women need to change jobs to eliminate the sex segregation. In this case, 30 of the women teachers and 45 of the women nurses would have to change occupations, becoming, instead, lawyers or construction workers. Alternatively, all 60 construction workers and 15 of the male lawyers would have to change occupations, becoming teachers and nurses. A suitable combination of men and women totaling 75 would also work.

Table 9.4 *Computing the index of occupational dissimilarity.*

Occupation	Case 1		Case 2	
	Male	Female	Male	Female
Construction	60	0	30	10
Lawyer	25	10	25	20
Teacher	10	40	35	35
Nurse	5	50	10	35
Total	100	100	100	100
Index of Dissimilarity		75		25

Now suppose that the occupational distribution changes as shown in Case 2 of the table. On the male side, half of the construction workers have been redistributed to teaching and nursing. On the female side, some of the teachers and nurses have become lawyers and construction workers. In all, 30 percent of the men and 20 percent of the women changed jobs. Now the Index of Dissimilarity is

$$\text{Case 2: } S = \Sigma |M_j - F_j|/2 = [|30 - 10| + |25 - 20| + |35 - 35| + |10 - 35|]/2 = 25$$

This is a much lower estimate of occupational segregation. There is still some disparity among the occupations; men are still overrepresented in construction and women are overrepresented in nursing. But the probability of being male or female in teaching and law is close to being equal.

The Index of Dissimilarity may mask some occupational segregation if the categories are too broad. For example, suppose we take Case 2, but break out several of the categories in more detail, as shown in Table 9.5

Table 9.5 *The index of occupational dissimilarity with more detailed occupational categories.*

Occupation	Male	Female
Construction		
Laborer	25	1
Administrative Staff	5	9
Lawyer	25	20
Teacher		
Elementary	0	20
Secondary	15	15
University	20	0
Nurse	10	35

As is usually the case, the more detailed categories show far more occupational segregation. Now the Index of Dissimilarity becomes

$$S = 1/2 \times (|25 - 1| + |5 - 9| + |25 - 20| + |0 - 20| + |15 - 15| + |20 - 1| + |10 - 35|) = 49$$

This estimate is considerably higher than the earlier estimate of 25 for Case 2. We used the same occupational distribution; we just looked at it in more detail. The point is that by using categories that are too broad, it is possible to overlook the sex segregation that exists within broad occupational categories. Related to this, care must be taken to keep the number of occupational categories consistent when making comparisons over time or across countries. Otherwise, any change in the index could just reflect a change in the number of categories.

Trends and the current magnitude of occupational segregation

As we might expect, more women in the labor force has certainly led to less occupational segregation. Blau, Brummund, and Liu[10] computed the Index of Dissimilarity for US women using a very detailed occupational coding that includes over 500 distinct occupations. As the examples in the tables above show, the measure of dissimilarity is typically far greater when the occupational coding is more detailed. Using a consistent coding of occupations over time, they found that the Index of Dissimilarity for all women declined from about 65 in 1970 to 51 in 2009. The decline was a bit greater for younger women than older women, but the difference was relatively small. Bigger differences were found for women by education. The more education a woman had, the greater was the decline in the index. For college-educated women the index fell from about 62 to 40, while for women with less than a high-school degree, the index fell just 1 percent. The index fell 7–9 percent for women who were high-school graduates or had attended college but did not have a four-year college degree. Despite this fall in

---

10 F. D. Blau, P. Brummund, and A. Y. H. Liu (2013), "Trends in Occupational Segregation by Gender 1970–2009: Adjusting for the Impact of Changes in the Occupational Coding System," *Demography*, 50 (2), 471–492.

occupational segregation, it is still the case that many occupations remain highly segregated by gender today. Interestingly, occupational segregation is even more pronounced in European labor-markets.[11]

Why did the Index of Dissimilarity fall over this time period? As we might expect, researchers found that the major mechanism by which segregation was reduced was through the entry of new cohorts of women during the 1970s and 1980s that were both better prepared for more male-dominated occupations and probably faced less labor-market discrimination. Notably, the reduction in the Index of Dissimilarity slowed down noticeably after the 1980s. It fell 6 percent in the 1970s, 4 percent in the 1980s, and just 3 percent in total since then through 2009.

A number of studies have found that once an all-male occupation receives a large influx of women, the occupation often becomes virtually all female, and this process rarely reverses.[12] For example, bank tellers, secretaries, and teachers were all predominantly male at some point in history and are all today overwhelmingly female. How might this switch come about? An interesting explanation for this "tipping" of occupations from male-dominated to female-dominated comes from an economic model of occupational choice in which men care about the share of women in their occupation. As long as the share of women remains below a certain threshold, men will tolerate an influx of women into the occupation, but once this threshold is reached, the men leave the occupation with the result that the occupation becomes feminized. The threshold at which this occurs is termed the "tipping point." Differing occupations may have differing tipping points, reflecting the level of distaste men in that occupation have for working with women in the same occupation.

Economist Jessica Pan tested the prediction of this model using data from the United States Census for the years 1940–1980, a time period when women's labor-force participation was increasing rapidly.[13] She found tipping points for white-collar occupations that ranged from 30 to 60 percent female, and tipping points for blue-collar occupations which were much lower at just 12–25 percent female. Interestingly, she reported that after an occupation tipped and became more female, this is the only change in the occupation—there is no change in wages or other characteristics of the occupation, but only in the gender composition of the occupation. She also investigated why the tipping points varied across occupations and found some evidence that the tipping points were lower in occupations where men hold more sexist attitudes toward women.

Obviously choosing one's occupation is a personal choice that is complex. Yet occupational segregation by sex is a well-documented source of gender differences in wages since the jobs that have an over-representation of women almost always pay less. When we compare women's earnings to men's earnings in those feminized occupations, we find that women earn less on average even after controlling for education and skills.[14] This suggests

11 J. J. Dolado, F. Felgueroso, and J. F. Jimeno (2002), "Recent Trends in Occupational Segregation by Gender: A Look Across the Atlantic", Institute for the Study of Labor (IZA) Discussion Paper 524, July.

12 Joyce P. Jacobsen (2005), "Occupational Segregation and the Tipping Phenomenon: The Contrary Case of Court Reporting in the United States," Wesleyan University, Department of Economics Working Paper 2005-005.

13 Jessica Y. Pan (2010), "Gender Segregation in Occupations: The Role of Tipping and Social Interactions," Unpublished paper, National University of Singapore.

14 A. Levanon, P. England, and P. Allison (2009), "Occupational Feminization and Pay: Assessing Causal Dynamics Using 1950–2000 US Census," *Social Forces*, 88 (2), 865–891 and *Women in the Labor Force Databook*, Bureau of Labor Statistics, 2013.

that women might be able to increase their absolute earnings by choosing to train for and work in occupations with higher shares of male workers. We address this issue in detail in Chapter 11.

Gender differences in education

Dating back to at least 1940, US women and men have graduated from high school in nearly even proportions, with women 1 or 2 percent ahead through 1970. The overall high-school graduation rate rose over this time period from about one in four to more than four out of five. In 2013, 88 percent of men and 89 percent of women aged 25 or older were high-school graduates.

In terms of college, however, the story is quite different. Figure 9.2 shows the proportion of US men and women aged 25–34 who were college graduates from 1940 to 2014. In 1940, just 7 percent of men and 5 percent of women between the ages of 25 and 34 were college graduates. These men and women were born between 1906 and 1915, and college graduation was a relatively rare event, no matter what the person's gender was. Not much changed during the World War II period, but after the war, the GI Bill led to a sharp increase in college graduation rates for men that was evident by the early to mid-1950s. By 1960, men were nearly twice as likely to be college graduates as women—14.5 percent vs. 7.5 percent. Over the next two decades through 1980, men's and women's college graduation rates moved up together, maintaining about a 7 percent difference. In 1980, about 20 percent of women and 27 percent of men, aged 25–34, were college graduates.

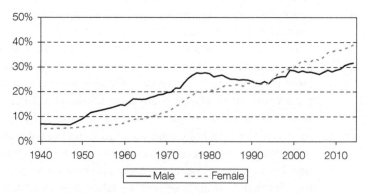

Figure 9.2 *Percentage of college graduates among US men and women, aged 25–34, 1940–2014.*
Source: CPS Historical Time Series, Table A-2.

From that point on, however, men's and women's graduation rates followed very different trends. The men's rate drifted downward steadily throughout the 1980s, falling more than 4 percent, while the women's rate continued upward at a steady, if slower, rate. In 1991, women between the ages of 25 and 34 were for the first time more likely to be college graduates than their male counterparts. The college graduation rate for men started increasing again beginning in the mid-1990s, but the upward trend for women was even greater. In the 2000s, the proportion of those college educated continued to increase for women, jumping by more than 4 percent, while the proportion for men decreased by almost 1 percent. In 2014 the gender gap was more than 7 percent—39.0 percent vs. 31.6 percent.

Women are now more likely to be college graduates at all ages from 25 to 54; men retain an advantage only at ages 55 and older. As a result, we see a different kind of gender gap in college graduation rates among young men and women. In 2013, 38 percent of 25–34-year-old women were college graduates compared to 31 percent of young men. In 2013, men accounted for only 43 percent of new college graduates.

The specifics of women's higher education attainment has changed as well. At the undergraduate level, women have made some inroads into the traditionally male fields. In 1970, women accounted for less than 1 percent of engineering degrees, 10 percent of business degrees, and less than 15 percent of degrees in the physical sciences and in computer and information sciences. By the 2010s, the proportion of women in engineering jumped to 19 percent, the proportion in business to 50 percent, and the proportions in physical sciences and computer and information sciences, to about 40 percent and 30 percent, respectively. But some differences certainly remain.

Women are also far more likely than before to receive advanced degrees—Master's degrees, doctorates, and other professional degrees. In 1962, among all persons with more than four years of college, just over a quarter were women. Some 40 years later, women represent almost half (47 percent) of all persons with an advanced degree. They are now the majority of those with Master's degrees, a third of those with professional degrees, and 35 percent of all people with a doctorate.

The increase in the proportion of women in professional schools has been nothing short of amazing. Figure 9.3 summarizes this information—it shows the proportion of US graduates in dentistry, medicine, law, and business that were female from 1950 through 2012. Through 1970, women were 1 percent of graduates from dental schools, 4–5 percent of graduates from law schools, and about 8 percent of graduates from medical schools and graduate business programs. The 1970s through the 2000s were years of explosive growth in the proportion of women in all of the programs. Over these years the proportion of women graduating in dentistry increased almost forty-fold to 46 percent, in law by a factor of ten to 48 percent, in medicine by a factor of six to 48 percent, and in business by a factor of ten to 46 percent. Veterinarians are another particularly interesting case—in 2013 more than three-quarters of graduates were women. The only professional fields in which men dominate among current graduates are chiropractic and theology.

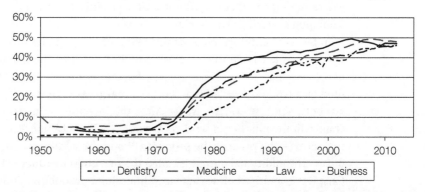

Figure 9.3 *Proportion of women among US graduates of selected professional programs, 1950–2012.*
Source: National Center for Education Statistics, *Digest of Education Statistics*, Table 324.40.

Overall, women no longer lag in Master's and PhD programs either, although some obvious exceptions still exist. In 2012, women were 60 percent of the recipients of Master's degrees and 51 percent of the recipients of PhDs, up from 40 percent and 13 percent, respectively, in 1970. Outliers still include engineering, computer and information sciences, and the physical sciences, where they make up between 20 and 30 percent of Masters, and PhD degree earners.

How labor markets work—an overview

Because the subject of this chapter and the next three is women's wages, it is important to have a basic understanding of how wage rates are set in labor markets. Many factors determine a particular individual's wage rate—education, work experience, race and gender, whether the job is unionized, whether it is in the public or private sector, and so on. It is useful, however, to abstract from many of these factors so that we can focus on the underlying supply-and-demand factors and the way they interact to set the equilibrium wage rate. That approach will help us understand some issues surrounding the gender wage gap and also some of the policy solutions that have been proposed.

The basics—supply and demand in competitive labor markets

A **competitive labor-market** is one in which there are many demanders and many suppliers, none of whom has a significant impact on the market as a whole. This definition follows the way a competitive output market is described. Whenever we use supply-and-demand analysis, there is always a price and a quantity. In the case of labor markets, the price is the wage rate, while the quantity is employment, usually measured by the number of workers. The goal of labor-market analysis is to explain how the equilibrium wage rate and the corresponding equilibrium amount of employment are determined by the interaction of supply-and-demand forces.

The demand for labor comes from firms. Probably the most important thing to understand about labor demand is that it is an aspect of a firm's attempt to maximize its profits. You may be familiar with profit maximization viewed in terms of a firm choosing the best amount of output. For example, firms in competitive markets choose their output where the marginal cost of the last unit produced just equals the price of the product. Monopolies produce where marginal revenue equals marginal cost.

In terms of employment, a similar kind of logic applies. The additional cost of hiring another worker is, in the simplest case, just equal to the market wage rate (plus fringe benefits, which it is useful to ignore for the moment). The additional revenue contributed by a worker is called that worker's **marginal revenue product of labor** (MRP_L). In symbols, $MRP_L \equiv \Delta R / \Delta L$, where ΔR is the increase in the firm's revenues and ΔL is the change in the number of workers (usually 1). The additional revenues are the product of two terms—the price of the product (P) and the additional output that the worker produces. The additional output is called the **marginal product** (MP_L), a concept we used in Chapters 3 and 7 when we analyzed household production. Thus $MRP_L = P \times MP_L$. For example, if adding a worker increases output by 10 units and each unit sells for $1, then her $MRP_L = \$10$.

In a competitive labor-market, the wage rate is determined by the market as a whole rather than by an individual firm. Whatever the wage ends up being, the firm must pay that wage to attract workers and because each firm is a relatively small demander of labor, their own decisions about how much to hire don't affect overall demand enough to change the wage. This is the same idea as the price in a competitive market, which competitive firms take as given. So the firm's only decision is how many workers it wants to employ at that wage rate.

The best way to see the logic of the answer is to think about what would happen if a firm added another worker. It would incur costs equal to the wage rate and it would receive revenues equal to the MRP of that worker. A profit-maximizing firm would be willing to hire that additional worker only if that worker's marginal revenue product was greater than the wage rate—that is, only if $MRP_L > w$. Why? Let's consider the opposite case. If $MRP_L < w$, the worker adds less to the firm's revenues than to its costs, and the firm's profit will therefore fall. If, however, $MRP_L > w$, then profits will rise when the worker is hired, paid w, and the resulting increase in output is sold at price P. Only when $MRP_L = w$ is it impossible for the firm either to add or to subtract workers in an effort to increase its profits. Thus the profit-maximizing rule for employment is to hire workers up to the point where the marginal revenue product of the last worker just equals the wage rate.

In almost all production settings, the marginal revenue product of a worker declines as more workers are employed, even if the potential employees are themselves equally productive. This reflects the idea of declining marginal productivity, an idea we have seen several times already. Additional workers add less and less to a firm's output because the amount of capital is being held constant even as the number of workers is increasing. This is one of the oldest economic laws of production, dating back to the economists of the early nineteenth century. We assumed exactly the same thing when we analyzed the value of time spent in household production: the marginal product of household production time falls as more time is spent in household production. Because $MRP_L = P \times MP_L$, if MP_L declines as L increases, MRP_L will also decline.

If the marginal revenue product falls as more workers are added and if firms are choosing employment at the level where the marginal revenue product just equals the wage rate, then price (here, the wage rate) and the quantity demanded (here, the number of workers employed) will be negatively related. At high wage rates, a firm will hire relatively few employees. Because the cost is high, they will hire workers only up to the point where the marginal revenue product is equally high. At lower wage rates, the firm will be willing to hire more workers—that is, they will be willing to expand employment until the marginal revenue product of the last worker hired is much lower. Falling marginal product, which results in falling marginal revenue product, is the root cause of the negative relationship between wages and employment.

To derive the total demand for labor from all firms, we simply add up each firm's labor demand. Because each firm will hire more workers when the wage is lower, it follows that the market labor demand curve will also have a negative relationship between wages and employment.

The labor supply curve represents the behavior of workers. It is linked to the underlying utility-maximizing decision about whether to work and how many hours to work, similar to the analysis we presented in Chapter 7. Typically, as the wage increases, more and more workers are willing to enter the labor-market. Hours of work decisions may also change as the wage increases. This is a bit more complicated and involves potentially conflicting income and substitution effects, an idea we discussed in Chapter 8 in the context of taxes and transfers. Usually, although not always, higher wages are associated with increases in desired hours of work, but the effect is modest. The net impact of both kinds of change—changes in the number of persons willing to work and changes in hours among those already working—results in an upward-sloping labor-supply curve.

Figure 9.4 shows a typical labor demand and labor-supply curve. The wage rate is measured on the vertical axis and the number of workers is measured along the horizontal axis. The graph in Figure 9.4 could represent the supply and demand for a particular occupation or for a particular labor-market (e.g., all workers with the same underlying skills). It could, for example, be the supply-and-demand curves for college economics professors or nurses or secretaries. Figure 9.4 looks like a conventional supply-and-demand diagram, although the basis for the shapes of the curves is very different than in the usual case of goods and services.

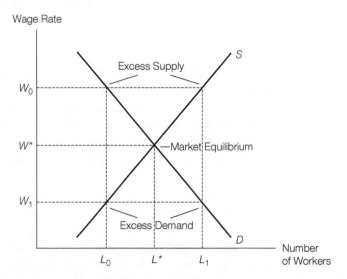

Figure 9.4 *Labor demand, labor supply, and market equilibrium.*

Finding the equilibrium wage

Putting the supply-and-demand curves together shows how the wage rate is determined in a competitive labor-market. As in every supply-and-demand diagram, the equilibrium wage rate and the associated amount of employment is given where the curves intersect. The equilibrium wage rate is the wage at which the amount of labor demanded just equals the amount supplied—that is, where $S^L(W^*) = D^L(W^*)$. Here the curves intersect at a wage of W^* and total employment of L^* workers.

At every other possible wage, the amount of labor supplied and the amount of labor demanded are unequal. If the wage was higher than W^*, as at W_0, then $S^L(W_0) > D^L(W_0)$, and there is an excess supply of labor—more workers looking for work than positions available. This is shown in Figure 9.4 as the horizontal distance between the supply-and-demand curves at W_0. This excess supply can sometimes, although not always, be interpreted as unemployment.[15] Usually the excess supply of labor will put downward pressure on wages, leading back to the equilibrium at W^*. As the wage falls toward W^*, the amount of labor demanded increases and the amount supplied falls, until they are equal at W^*. If, instead, the wage were lower than W^* (like W_1), then $S^L(W_1) < D^L(W_1)$, and there is excess demand or, equivalently, a labor shortage. This is shown in Figure 9.4 as the horizontal distance between the supply-and-demand curves at W_1. In this case we would expect wages to rise back to market equilibrium at W^*, in the process reducing the amount of labor demanded and increasing the amount supplied. Only at a wage of W^* is there no pressure for the wage rate to change. Everything is in balance. Thus W^* is the equilibrium wage rate and L^* is the corresponding equilibrium amount of employment, given these particular supply-and-demand curves.

Comparative statics—how changes in supply and demand affect wages and employment

Changes in labor supply and/or labor demand affect the equilibrium wage and employment in exactly the same way that changes in supply and demand affect prices for goods. An increase in demand may occur either because the workers are more productive (their marginal product is higher) or because there is an increase in the demand for the product that the firm sells. In either case the demand curve would shift up or rightward, with more workers demanded at every wage rate. This situation is shown in Figure 9.5. At the original equilibrium there is now a shortage, and the wage rate will rise, thereby increasing the amount of labor supplied and decreasing the amount of labor demanded. In the new market equilibrium, both wages and employment are higher than before. A decrease in labor demand, represented by a downward or inward shift of the labor-demand curve, would cause wages and employment to fall.

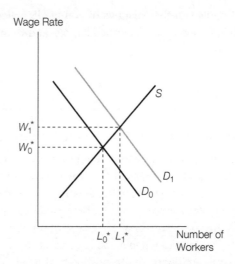

Figure 9.5 *The effect of an increase in demand on wages and employment.*

---

15 To be officially counted as unemployed in the United States, a person needs not only to be jobless but also to have made a specific effort to find work. Jobless persons who are not looking for work are counted as not in the labor force. Some are counted as discouraged workers.

Changes in labor supply involve a shift in the labor-supply curve. An example of an increase in labor supply is shown in Figure 9.6. The supply curve shifts out or down so that there is now excess supply at the original equilibrium. This puts downward pressure on wages, yielding a new equilibrium with lower wages and larger employment, unless there are impediments to reaching equilibrium. In a sense, the wage must fall in order to accommodate the now larger number of people seeking employment in this occupation. If it doesn't, the result will likely be an increase in unemployment, as the labor-market is in a situation of persistent excess supply. A decrease in labor supply would work just the opposite way. The labor-supply curve would shift in or up, and the new equilibrium would feature a higher wage and smaller employment.

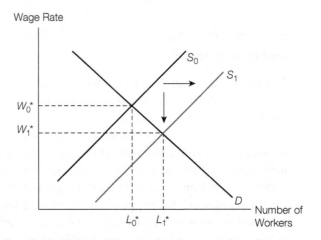

Figure 9.6 *The effect of an increase in labor supply on wages and employment.*

Changes in the earnings of young US college graduates in the period since the 1970s is a great example of applied supply-and-demand labor-market analysis. See Box 9.2 for details.

Box | 9.2

The Relative Wages of Young College Graduates

To fix these ideas about changes in labor supply and labor demand and their impact on wage rates, consider the situation of young college graduates over the time period from 1970 to the 2010s. During the 1970s the wage premium for young college graduates relative to young high-school graduates suddenly fell from 42 to 33 percent in the course of about six years. Many scholars thought this trend spelled the end of the golden era when a college education was a highly valuable economic asset. Then, just as suddenly, the trend reversed itself. The wage gap between young high-school graduates and young college graduates started to rise, eventually exceeding 60 percent in the late 1990s, about where it currently stands. What happened? How can we explain these sharp changes in relative wage?

It turns out that supply-and-demand changes are an important part of this story. During the 1970s there was a substantial and sudden increase in the number of young college graduates. This was due to two factors—rising college attendance rates coupled with an unusually large birth cohort, itself the "echo" of the baby boom of the 1950s. This was followed by a much smaller number of college graduates in the mid-1980s, now courtesy of the smaller birth cohorts that began in the early 1960s. Between 1965 and 1985, the number of college graduates increased annually by 2.4 percent. But in the mid-1970s the average annual growth rate was well above this rate, and in the late-1970s through the mid-1980s the growth rate was considerably below this.

These changes are easily represented in terms of shifts in the supply curve. Typically, the labor demand curve increases over time, reflecting broad increases in productivity. Taken by itself, this change would cause wages to rise. But a sharp increase in supply could outweigh this response, causing wages to fall. In this case, relative wages, not absolute wages, fell. Still, the general idea is the same: The sharp increase in supply caused the relative wages of college graduates to fall in the early 1970s.

Thereafter, two factors caused the relative wages of college graduates to skyrocket. One was the much smaller increase in the supply of college graduates. The other was almost certainly a huge increase in demand, part of what most economists think has been a widespread increase in the demand for more skilled workers. Those ingredients were necessary for the sharp increase in wages, accompanied by an increase in the number of college graduates employed, that has been since the 1980s.

Source: Claudia Goldin and Lawrence F. Katz (2010), *The Race Between Education and Technology*, Cambridge, MA: Harvard University Press.

Thinking about wage rates

Finally, two more points about wage rates are important to appreciate. First, prices are signals that tell the participants in the economy the relative value of various goods. They are highly efficient ways to communicate the value of resources. For example, when the price of a product suddenly rises, perhaps because of an increase in demand, that increase is a signal for consumers to cut back on their use of this product and for producers to increase their production. When utility-maximizing individuals and profit-maximizing firms act upon those signals, the result, under ideal conditions, is economic efficiency. In other words, resources in the economy are allocated where they are most valuable.

The wage rate is also a price, and in exactly the same way the wage acts as a signal to workers and firms. Suppose that the demand for a firm's output fell. Ultimately, the price of the output would fall and that, in turn, would cause the firm's MRP curve to fall because the MRP depends on the price of the output. Following the rule for profit-maximization, this firm would now hire fewer workers. While this wouldn't be a great outcome for the workers, it is absolutely essential from the standpoint of the economy as a whole. Those additional workers in that industry are no longer as valuable to society as before because consumers don't value the output as much as before. It is necessary and proper for those workers to move to a use where they are more highly valued. Wages serve as a signal for that movement. Unless wages can adjust to reflect values, labor resources will be inefficiently allocated.

Second, there is no presumption that the equilibrium wage is a fair wage, a just wage, a living wage, or anything else of the sort. The equilibrium wage is no more and no less than the wage at which labor supply and labor demand just balance. Under the right (or perhaps wrong) circumstances, the equilibrium wage rate can be extremely low or, for that matter, extremely high. If demand is enormous and supply is small—think professional athletes, movie stars, and brain surgeons—the equilibrium wage is certain to be extremely high. If, however, demand is low and supply is large, just the opposite is likely to occur. The equilibrium wage will almost certainly be very low.

Not all labor-markets are in a competitive equilibrium. In some cases the supply of labor to an occupation may be restricted, thus keeping the wage rate above its market equilibrium level. In others, wages may be persistently above equilibrium because of legal requirements such as the minimum wage, union bargaining, or social convention.[16] It is important to understand that even in these circumstances, supply-and-demand analysis continues to operate. If wages are held above the market equilibrium, then there will be persistent excess supply, probably resulting in unemployment. If wages are held below equilibrium, there will almost certainly be persistent labor shortages.

Summary

For as long as labor-market statistics have been collected, women have earned less than men. There is even a biblical reference (Leviticus 27: 1–4) that refers to valuing women at 30 shekels of silver and men at 50 shekels, a ratio eerily similar to the 59 percent figure that held in the United States between 1960 and 1980. In the United States, the earnings ratio of median annual earnings for YRFT workers was well below 50 percent in the nineteenth century, in the 50–60 percent range for the first 80 years of the twentieth century, and above 70 percent since 1990. In the 2010s the ratio is at its historic high, just above 78 percent. The gender gap exists in Europe as well and it is roughly comparable to that in the United States.

Women are still heavily concentrated in just a few large, predominantly female occupations. Almost one in eight working women is a secretary or administrative assistant, registered nurse, or elementary or middle-school teacher. Men's and women's occupational distributions are converging, but they are still quite distinct. Based on a very detailed occupational coding, the Index of Dissimilarity fell from 64 in 1970 to 51 in 2009. This means that 51 percent of men or women would still have to change occupations to make the distributions identical. It is encouraging that the decline in the Index of Dissimilarity was much greater for college-educated women. The current value of the Index of Dissimilarity for them is 40, down from over 60 in 1970.

---

16 For example, it is probably true that the equilibrium wage in some academic disciplines is well below the salary that universities typically pay to new professors. One sign of this is the large number of skilled new PhDs who are unable to find a job. Universities are reluctant to take advantage of this situation by offering a very low starting salary. Starting salaries do differ by academic department, but not by the full amount consistent with market equilibrium.

The educational attainment of men and women has also changed in dramatic ways over the past three to four decades. In 1970, women were much less likely than men to be college graduates, and they were nearly invisible in professional programs in law, medicine, dentistry, and business. Since then, women have overtaken men as college graduates, with a wide margin now existing among 25–34-year-olds. Women are now 40 percent or more of most professional programs, a figure that reflects as much as a forty-fold increase in some fields. Veterinary programs are now predominantly female—over 75 percent in the 2010s.

In the last part of the chapter, we surveyed the basic theory of labor markets and how they operate to set equilibrium wages and employment. The market equilibrium occurs at a wage that just balances supply and demand. Where demand is small and supply is large, the equilibrium might well be at a very low wage. In the opposite circumstances (large demand, small supply), the equilibrium will almost certainly occur at a high wage rate. Changes in labor supply or labor demand inevitably change equilibrium wages and employment. It is worth remembering that the wage rate is a price and, as such, conveys information to market participants about the value of labor in a particular kind of work.

We began this chapter by noting two very broad explanations for women's lower average earnings. Either women could have, on average, fewer valuable labor-market skills or they could receive less pay for the skills they do have. In the next chapter we explore these two possible explanations—and a few others—further.

10

THE GENDER GAP IN EARNINGS: COMPETING EXPLANATIONS

Introduction

In this chapter we turn to explanations of the gender gap in earnings and occupation. First, we examine skill differences, using human capital theory, one of the most widely used and influential parts of economic theory. We examine whether there are any reasons why women might, on average, have less human capital than men. The ideas developed earlier about the division of labor in families will be relevant here. Second, we examine economic models of labor-market discrimination. We consider a set of theoretical models, developed by Gary Becker, that analyze how discriminatory feelings or preferences about an individual's race or sex or other personal characteristic on the part of employers, employees, or customers affect equilibrium wages. Finally, we consider other approaches, including statistical discrimination, gender differences in competitiveness and risk-taking, and theories of occupational segregation.

Human capital—the supply of skills to the labor market

Human capital basics

The phrase **human capital** stands for the skills that workers possess and bring to the labor market and that are the basis for the earnings they receive. The most important characteristic of these skills is that they don't just arise by themselves but rather are the result of costly investments that increase an individual's productivity. Prior to the development of the human capital model,[1] economists mostly viewed workers as "raw labor," a factor of production whose productivity and skills were "givens" of the problem and were not considered further. Why some workers earned more than others was totally outside the realm of economic analysis. Without a way of explaining why some workers were more productive than others, there was no way to explain and account for the personal distribution of income.

The other important factor of production in traditional economic analysis is capital, which represents machinery and the like, and which differs from labor in that it must be produced before it can be used. Firms make investments in capital based on a comparison of its purchase cost to the future benefits (higher profits) that it would provide.

---

1 Some of the central ideas in human capital theory were presented by Adam Smith in the eighteenth century in his famous book *The Wealth of Nations*. The modern treatment was developed in the early 1960s by T. W. Schultz and especially by Gary Becker in his book *Human Capital*. Both Schultz and Becker were awarded the Nobel Prize in Economics for their contributions to the theory of human capital.

From a human capital perspective, individuals are viewed more like capital, with valuable skills that are produced via an investment process. As newborns and young children, most of us know relatively little and have, with rare exceptions, few labor-market skills. But we acquire skills over time, increasing our productivity and our labor-market value. Because acquiring these skills is costly in terms of time and resources, individuals can be viewed as if they were capital in human form or simply, "human capital." The activities that create human capital are called **investments in human capital**.

There are, of course, many important differences between human capital and physical capital.[2] For one thing, human capital is highly mobile, unlike most capital. It naturally and inevitably goes where you go, so immigrants can and do bring their human capital along with them, even if they must leave their physical capital behind. Human capital cannot, however, be inherited or used as collateral for a loan, as other capital goods can.

The two most important forms of human capital investment are education and on-the-job training (OJT). Thinking of education and OJT as investments in human capital focuses attention on their costs and benefits. The costs of an educational investment come in two forms—direct costs and the opportunity cost of foregone earnings. For example, earning a college degree involves substantial direct costs of tuition and books plus the opportunity costs of the earnings that could have otherwise been obtained with full-time work. In contrast, the direct and opportunity costs of finishing fifth grade are often very close to zero, at least for students attending public school in the United States in the twenty-first century.[3] Both kinds of cost are relevant to thinking about the value of the investment. The fact that one kind of cost is out of pocket and the other is an opportunity cost makes no difference.

The labor-market benefits of a college education are the higher earnings that an individual with more human capital receives. Currently, the earnings differential between college graduates and high-school graduates is at an all-time high. Typically, individuals receive these benefits over a long time period—for example, their entire working life. Education may provide other nonmarket benefits as well—for example, appreciating art or music, or even improving parenting skills.[4]

OJT refers to the many skills that workers learn after formal schooling that make them more productive in the labor market. They usually learn these skills at work, which accounts for the name OJT. OJT can be in the form of **general training**, which means that the skills learned will be equally valuable in the firm in which they are received *and* in other firms, or **specific training**, which means that the skills are more valuable in the firm in which they are received than in other firms. Completely specific training is valuable only in the firm in which it is received and usually reflects knowledge of procedures

---

2   When the human capital model was reintroduced into economics in the early 1960s, there were heated debates about whether it was demeaning to analyze human beings as if they were capital goods. Nothing about the idea of human capital is meant to imply that people can or should be treated as if they were machinery. Many academics were particularly worried about the idea of applying investment analysis to higher education. It turned out that they had nothing to worry about. Education passed the investment test with flying colors.

3   The private costs of attending the fifth grade—those borne by the individual or his/her family—may be close to zero. Public costs, which include the cost of all resources (teachers' salaries, supplies, buildings, etc.), are certainly not equal to zero.

4   Investment in human capital may also provide external benefits, which are benefits that accrue to other persons.

and/or people that are unique to that firm.[5] Some jobs provide the opportunity to invest in a great deal of OJT; other jobs—dead-end jobs, we might call them—provide little or no opportunity to learn new skills.

Just like investments in education, investments in OJT carry costs and provide benefits. The benefits, again, are the higher earnings made possible by the additional human capital. The costs are entirely opportunity costs because workers almost never pay their employers directly for the opportunity to learn skills. Here, the costs arise because jobs that provide extensive learning (investing) opportunities will offer lower wages than otherwise identical jobs with less of an up-side. If that weren't the case, no worker would want to take the otherwise equivalent job with less OJT. Consequently, the cost is the difference between what the worker earns in a job where he or she is investing in OJT and what the same worker could earn in an otherwise similar job without investment in OJT.

Evaluating investments in human capital

Because an investment in human capital has both costs and benefits, we can investigate what the rate of return on the investment is, exactly as we might with an investment in machinery or other physical capital. Doing that correctly involves taking careful account of the fact that investment costs are incurred in the present, but the benefits are received over many years, often far in the future. For example, some of the benefits of a college education are earned at the very end of your working career, as much as 40 years in the future. Why does it matter if benefits are received in the future and costs are incurred now? Benefits received in the future are worth less than their face value in today's dollars because if an individual had that same amount of money today, he/she could invest it at the market interest rate and earn interest on it until that future date, by which time it would have grown to a much larger amount. As a result, having the money sooner, rather than later, is valuable.

For any sum of money that would be received in the future, there is some smaller sum of money today that would, if it were invested at the market rate of interest, exactly accumulate to that larger sum in that future year. That smaller current sum of money is called the **present value** of the future sum. In the appendix we review present value analysis and show exactly how it works. Here we just summarize the key points that we need for our analysis of possible gender differences in human capital investment.

To find the present value of a future sum, simply divide the future sum by $(1 + r)^T$, where T is the number of years in the future and r is the market interest rate expressed as a decimal.[6] For example, if the interest rate is 5 percent, the present value of $1,000 available in 10 years is $1,000/1.05^{10}$ or $613.91. If the $1,000 were received 20 years in the future, it would be worth even less: $1,000/1.05^{20}$, or $376.89, to be precise. Note how much smaller the present value is than its face value. It is very important to appreciate that the further in the future a sum of money is received, the lower is its present value.

An investment in human capital typically provides benefits for many years—for example, from entrance into the labor market until retirement. To calculate the present

---

5 The same general vs. specific distinction also applies to human capital more generally. There is general human capital—widely useful—and specific human capital—useful only in a narrow sphere.

6 This formula applies in the simple case where interest is received once a year at the end of the year. Today, most interest is paid continuously. In that case the formula is conceptually similar but involves that strange numerical constant, e. For our purposes, however, this formula is perfectly fine.

value of benefits received over many years, simply divide each year's benefits (the higher earnings) by $(1 + r)^T$. If the benefits are $B_1 \ldots B_T$, then the present value of the stream of future benefits as of today is

$$PV(B_1 \ldots B_T) = \frac{B_1}{(1+r)} + \frac{B_2}{(1+r)^2} + \ldots + \frac{B_T}{(1+r)^T} = \sum_{t=1}^{T} \frac{B_t}{(1+r)^t} \qquad (10.1)$$

where Σ, the Greek letter sigma, is the summation sign. Note that benefits received in the first year are divided by $(1 + r)$, benefits in the second year are divided by $(1 + r)^2$, and so on, up to year T. The term at the end involving Σ is just a compact way to express a long sum of terms; the summation starts with $t = 1$ and goes through $t = T$. This is a very important expression that you should know.

To evaluate how good an investment is, economists compute its **internal rate of return**. The internal rate of return is a measure of the net value or profitability of an investment that reflects how large the benefits are relative to the costs, after properly accounting for the different timing of the costs and benefits using present value analysis. To be precise, the internal rate of return to an investment is the interest rate at which the present value of all the benefits just equals the cost of the investment. It is the interest rate r^* that solves the following expression:[7]

$$\sum_{t=1}^{T} \frac{B_t}{(1+r^*)^t} = C \qquad (10.2)$$

The left side of this expression is the present value of the benefits, using the internal rate of return as the interest rate. The right side of the expression is the costs, which are assumed to be entirely incurred in the current time period; that's why we don't need to compute a present value for them. If the benefits are very large relative to the costs, then the internal rate of return will be large as well: It will take a high interest rate to reduce the present value of benefits to the smaller level of the costs. If the benefits are not very much larger than the costs, then the internal rate of return will be very small. An investment with a low internal rate of return is unlikely to be an attractive investment from an economic standpoint.

To determine whether any particular investment in human capital is worth making, an individual should compare the internal rate of return to the market interest rate. The market interest rate represents the rate at which an individual can borrow the funds to finance the investment or, alternatively, the rate at which he or she could invest the proceeds. The decision rule is simple: If the internal rate of return is greater than the market interest rate, then the investment makes economic sense. If the internal rate of return is smaller, however, there is no economic basis for proceeding. This means that anything that lowers

---

7 In most equations the variable being solved for (here, r^*) is all by itself on the left-hand side of the equation. Because this computation involves a long summation, that expression is impossibly complicated. Equation (10.2) shows the solution indirectly. As a practical matter, internal rates of return are almost always solved with a financial spreadsheet program that finds the solution by trial and error in an iterative procedure. To compute an internal rate of return with a spreadsheet program, set up a column of net benefits, treating the cost as a negative benefit. You provide a starting value for the internal rate of return; the program then solves for the solution by trial and error. If the present value of benefits at the starting value is greater than the costs, the program re-computes the present value using a slightly higher interest rate; if the present value of benefits at the starting value is negative, a lower interest rate is used. The process continues until an internal rate is found at which the present value of benefits equals zero.

the internal rate of return to an investment in human capital may cause an individual to forego the investment entirely. Could that apply to women and thus cause them to invest in less human capital than men?

Gender and human capital

Theory: the economic basis for gender differences in human capital

Suppose a woman expects to take some time off from working in the labor market for family responsibilities. This was, as we have seen, certainly the norm in previous generations, and even today it is certainly not uncommon. (Review Box 3.1 on the division of labor within families for more information.) In those years the monetary benefits from any investment in human capital will be zero. Alternatively, if a woman works part-time to accommodate family responsibilities, her benefits will be positive but smaller than they might otherwise be. These patterns of labor-force participation lower the internal rate of return for two related reasons: first, total benefits are lower, and, second, the benefits that are lost are those with a high present value because they typically come relatively early in a woman's adult life.

Investment in education Let's consider a specific example of how periods of not working in the labor market affect the internal rate of return. Figure 10.1 shows average earnings in 2012 by age for US women between the ages of 18 and 64 with college and high-school degrees who were YRFT workers. The data come from the US Census Bureau's annual survey of individual earnings. The earnings are averages by 5-year age brackets, which is why the two lines have flat regions and then sudden jumps. For high-school graduates, earnings start at age 18, while they start at age 22 for college graduates.

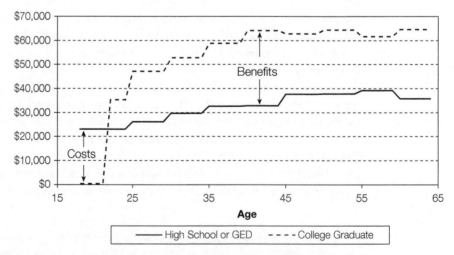

Figure 10.1 *Mean earnings by age and education, US women, year-round full-time workers, 2013.*
Source: US Census Bureau, Annual Social and Economic Census, Table PINC-04.

We can use these data to compute the internal rate of return to a college degree for women under different assumptions about work. In doing that, we follow standard practice and assume that the foregone earnings during college are measured by what is *actually* earned by the high-school graduates during those years (i.e., between the ages of 18 and 22). These are the opportunity costs. That is, admittedly, far from perfect, but it's probably in the ballpark. The benefits can be measured by the difference in average earnings between women college graduates and women high-school graduates. The earnings gap is about $20,000 at ages 25–34, $25,000 at ages 35–44, and peaks at more than $31,000 at ages 45–49.[8] To that we add an estimate of direct costs for tuition and so forth. Figure 10.1 shows these estimated costs and benefits associated with FTYR work throughout a woman's career. The area between the two lines from ages 22 to 65 represents the benefits of a college degree, while the area between them at ages 18–22 are the opportunity costs of the foregone earnings.

The internal rate of return to a college degree is the interest rate at which the present value of discounted benefits just equals the opportunity costs plus any direct costs. Suppose out-of-pocket expenses for college are $15,000 per year for four years. Then the internal rate of return to the earnings profile shown in Figure 10.1 is 11.3 percent. Using comparable data for men, the internal rate of return for college is 11.6 percent.

With rates of return like these, a college investment is a very good investment indeed. What happens, though, if a woman takes time out of her career? If both the college graduate and the high-school graduate leaves the labor market at age 25 and returned to YRFT work at age 29, the internal rate of return to the college degree falls to 8.8 percent. If she leaves the labor market for ten years (from age 25 to 34), the internal rate of return falls all the way down to 7.1 percent. And with 15 years out of the labor force, the internal rate of return is just 5.7 percent, just about half the value with full-time continuous work.

The impacts on the internal rate of return are so large because the years of absence from the labor market are early career years with high present value. It is easy to see that leaving the labor market can make a huge difference to the internal rate of return of the investment. If the rate of return is low enough, it may not make economic sense to make the investment in the first place. That, in turn, would result in women having less human capital than men.

Imagine how low the rate of return would have been for women born in the early decades of the twentieth century for whom market work often ceased with marriage. See Box 10.1 for evidence on the return to a college degree for women during the baby boom.

Box	10.1

The Return to a College Degree during the Baby Boom

Claudia Goldin estimated the internal rate of return for women to a college degree in the mid-1950s. The median female college graduate in that time period married in the year of her graduation, worked for four years, and then exited the labor force for about eight years, returning at age 35. For high-school graduates, Goldin assumed that they, too, worked four years after school, took ten years off, and then returned to work.

---

8 We are also assuming that current college and high-school graduates will, when they are older, earn what is actually earned in 2012 by older women. This assumption is not perfect but it is good enough for our purposes.

College-educated women earned about 30 percent more than high-school-educated women at the beginning of their careers and about 40 percent later on. With further allowance for out-of-pocket college costs, Goldin estimated an internal rate of return for college graduation of about 5 percent, certainly no goldmine and about half of the internal rate of return for men at that time. She notes that the income premium to female college graduates was about the same as for men. Their lower internal rate of return was entirely a function of their briefer employment.

College was, however, somewhat more financially lucrative for women if viewed more broadly. Goldin notes that college attendance and especially college graduation greatly increased the probability that a woman married a college graduate. For example, only 10 percent of high-school graduate women were married to a college graduate, compared to two-thirds of all college graduate women. And, of course, these better-educated men earned more than their less-educated counterparts. Goldin reports that, on average, the husband of a college graduate woman earned almost 40 percent more than the husband of a high-school graduate woman. Taking all this into account, Goldin estimates that the "full" internal rate of return to college for women was in the 10 percent to 11 percent range rather than the 5 percent associated with its direct labor-market impact.

Source: Claudia Goldin (1997), "Career and Family: College Women Look to the Past," in Francine Blau and Ronald Ehrenberg (eds.), *Gender and Family Issues in the Workplace*, New York: Russell Sage Foundation, 20–58.

Investment in on-the-job training Most jobs provide a worker with not only a wage rate, but also the opportunity to acquire human capital (learn skills) that will be valuable subsequently in terms of higher wages. This learning on the job is precisely what economists mean when they talk about OJT. Jobs that provide OJT will typically pay lower current wages than jobs that offer no training, but compensate for that with higher wages after the training is received. In that way, acquiring OJT is a human capital investment with costs and benefits that can be measured by its rate of return.

In the case of general training, the skills learned are widely valuable. In that case, human capital theory shows that individuals receive *all* the benefits of training and pay *all* the costs. In the case of specific training, the skills learned have a more limited market, and in the extreme case of completely specific training, the skills are valuable only in the current firm. Completely specific training often reflects knowledge of procedures and/or people that are unique to a firm. University department coordinators are a good example of workers who have a great deal of knowledge of forms, people, and procedures that are highly university-specific. In the case of specific training, it turns out that firms and workers share the costs and the benefits of investment in training.

Precisely as in the case of education, it is possible to think about the rate of return on the investment in OJT. Suppose a job has a starting salary that is $2,500 lower than another otherwise similar job but provides more OJT—enough more that your earnings would increase by $500 per year thereafter for as long as you stay on the job, starting in the next year. (Again, this is a simplified arithmetic example; in the real world the benefits might well increase over time.) If you use that OJT for ten full years, the internal rate of return on the $2,500 investment is over 15 percent. If, instead, you use the training for only six years and then drop out of the labor market, the return drops below 5.5 percent.

In the case of specific training, a firm will want to make sure that any worker that they train will stay with the firm long enough that it can recoup its costs and earn a reasonable rate of return on its investment. So here, too, women's history of intermittent labor-force participation may make firms more reluctant to offer them jobs with substantial specific training.

Differences in labor-force participation are not the only thing that could lead to differences in internal rates of return. Suppose that, because of labor-market discrimination, women don't earn as much as men for the human capital they possess. Suppose opportunities for advancement are limited, no matter how much human capital they have. In the OJT example, suppose a woman received only $400 more per year after training, rather than $500, because she wasn't promoted. Even if she expected to have the same ten-year career as a man, her rate of return would be just over 9.5 percent, not the 15 percent that a man might receive. Again, it is easy to see that if labor-market discrimination lowered rates of return sufficiently, a woman might rationally choose not to make a costly investment in human capital. "What's the point?" she might reason. I can do nearly as well without making the investment.[9]

Let's summarize the main points about the human capital approach to gender earnings differences. An investment in human capital has a financial return that can be measured by the internal rate of return. Rates of return are affected by many factors, but especially by participation in the labor market and by discrimination, both of which affect the benefits received. Individuals make decisions about investment in human capital on the basis of the rate of return it offers. If women anticipate spending some years out of the labor force for family responsibilities, this will lower the internal rate of return to human capital investment. Under these circumstances, they might well rationally choose to invest in less human capital. The ultimate source of these potential labor-market human capital differences by gender is the traditional organization of households, with its characteristic division of labor on the basis of gender that we discussed in Chapter 3. Labor-market earnings depend on the amount of human capital a worker has. If women invest in less human capital than men, they will earn less than men.

Evidence—gender differences in human capital

The actual amount of human capital that an individual has is not directly observed. For example, it is not possible to say that a certain person has 17 units of human capital or 42 units or any other number. That doesn't mean that the concept isn't useful.

---

9 This kind of argument applies with great force in the case of race discrimination in the United States, South Africa, and elsewhere. Think about the human capital investment situation facing black workers in the time period when overt discrimination was rampant and not illegal. They had very few incentives to acquire skills because they would be unlikely to reap the benefits. This means that discrimination may cast a long shadow; its labor-market effects may be felt a long time after it has been eliminated. An argument like this is sometimes used to support affirmative action programs. We discuss affirmative action programs in more detail in Chapter 12.

Human capital acquired through schooling is usually assumed to be related to the number of years of completed schooling, while human capital in the form of OJT is usually assumed to be associated with the number of years of work experience.

Years of education and years of work experience are by far the two most important factors used by economists to explain differences in wages among individuals and between men and women. If human capital differences are responsible for at least some portion of the gender gap in earnings, there must be differences between men and women in these measures. Let's look briefly at the evidence.

Gender differences in education   In Chapter 9 we reviewed gender issues in educational attainment. We concluded there that women and men have graduated from high school in equal numbers since the 1940s at least, but that two very different gender gaps in college completion have existed at different times. Through at least the early 1990s, men were more likely to be college graduates than women. From the early 1960s through the late 1970s, this difference was large—about 7 to 8 percent (14.5 percent vs. 7.0 percent in 1960, 20 percent vs. 12 percent in 1970, and 28 percent vs. 20 percent in 1979). In percentage terms, these differences are quite large, so it is clear that across the population in those years, men had more education than women. But thereafter the gender gap in college completion first narrowed, then disappeared, and finally emerged in substantial favor of women. Since 1982, women have outnumbered men among graduating college students and since 1996 they have outnumbered men as college graduates among 25- to 34-year-olds; in 2013 the difference was almost 7 percent (38.0 percent vs. 31.3 percent). By the mid-2010s, men's educational advantage has been completely eroded for the total working-age population. For younger age groups, women now thoroughly dominate in numbers in college and have at least rough parity or more with men in most professional degree programs. They still lag in the hard sciences at the postgraduate level.

These trends mean that educational differences between men and women could have played an important part in earnings differences through the 1970s and a declining but still genuine part through the early 1990s. Moving forward and especially among younger workers, it is unlikely that educational differences can be an important factor in explaining the gender gap in pay.

Gender differences in work experience   Historically, as we discussed in Chapter 7, women have been far less likely to be in the paid workforce. In the first half of the twentieth century, their participation in the paid labor market was largely confined to women before marriage and to women who did not marry. The labor-force participation rate for married women was just 5–10 percent in the early part of the century and still only 20 percent in 1950. The gender gap in participation rates didn't begin to close until the 1960s and 1970s, and even now there is a 15 percent gender difference in participation rates.

In fact, the difference in work experience among working men and women is more complex than these time trends suggest. In the early part of the century, relatively few women worked, but those who did worked more or less continuously. They were primarily either women who never married or a small fraction of married women who worked regularly. We saw in Box 7.2, for example, that in this time period most women left the labor market at about the time of marriage and relatively few ever returned to regular employment outside the home. Thus, while gender differences in average work experience for *all* men and women were very large during this time, gender differences in average work experience for *working* men and *working* women were relatively small. This was the pattern through about the middle of the twentieth century. Later in the century, more women worked but fewer worked continuously; single women were now a smaller fraction of the female labor force. As a result, a greater proportion of women working at any point in time had previously been intermittent labor-force participants. Thus differences in average years of work experience between *working* men and women were larger than in the past, even though they fell for *all* men and women.

Thus the increase in women's labor-force participation, which took the form of re-entry into the labor market, had the initial effect of increasing the gender gap in years of work experience among working women. Claudia Goldin noted that this pattern meant that relatively few married women established careers in the same way that men did.[10] Rather, "married working women who entered the labor force in their middle years had, by and large, entered a rather new world. They were not bringing to the labor market recently acquired skills. Many were, instead, reentering occupations they had left many years, or possibly decades, before, and most were inadequately prepared for their new labor market roles" (p. 23).

James Smith and Michael Ward made a similar point in their research on the historical patterns of labor-force participation by women.[11] They computed the average accumulated years of labor-market experience from 1920 to 1986 for *all* US women and for the subset of women who were *working* in those years. Although this was a time period in which the labor-force participation rate of women increased by more than 30 percent, the average labor-force work experience among working women increased very little at all. At age 35, average work experience actually fell by 0.1 years between 1920 and 1980, before rising by about two years between 1980 and 1986. Average work experience at age 45 also rose very little, not quite three years in more than 60 years. These figures are consistent with the information that Goldin presented on life cycle labor-force participation.

When Smith and Ward computed average work experience across *all* women, regardless of whether they were currently working, work experience increased much more across this time period because of the large increase in labor-force participation. At age 35, women's average work experience increased more than six years, and at age 45 it increased nearly seven years. In 1920 the difference between the average work experience of *working* women and *all* women was very large because many women almost never worked in the paid labor market. By 1986, however, this had changed: The averages for the two groups were much more similar because a much higher proportion of women now worked in the labor market at some time in their lives.

From our standpoint the most important point of all this research is that women have indeed, on average, worked fewer years in the labor market than men of the same age and that, paradoxically, the gap did not narrow when the LFPR of women first began to increase in the 1950s through the 1980s. The rising LFPR was largely the product of reentry into the labor market by women who had been absent for many years. Their presence thus prevented the gender gap in work experience from narrowing further.

---

10   Claudia D. Goldin (1990), *Understanding the Gender Gap*, New York: Oxford University Press.
11   James P. Smith and Michael Ward (1989), "Women in the Labor Market and in the Family," *Journal of Economic Perspectives*, 3 (1), 9–23.

In the next chapter we will develop a technique to determine exactly how important education and work experience differences between men and women are in explaining the gender gap in earnings.

Labor-market discrimination and women's earnings

An alternative explanation for the gender gap in earnings is that women earn less because they are discriminated against in the labor market. The standard economic analysis of discrimination is based on Gary Becker's *Economics of Discrimination,* a book written in the mid-1950s. Becker's analysis was developed in the context of racial discrimination, which was by far the most widely noted form of discrimination at that time; public awareness of possible labor-market discrimination against women was still at least a decade or two in the future.

The application of Becker's approach to gender discrimination is complicated in at least one way. Typical discrimination models are based on aversion or dislike. Whatever we may individually feel about these dislikes and their legitimacy, we understand that individuals do sometimes harbor genuine negative feelings for persons of differing races, ethnicities, religions, and so on. But what about gender? It cannot really be said that men dislike women; after all, in the non-market sphere of life, they often like them very much. So here it is primarily a matter of context. If discrimination models are to make any sense, it must be that some men feel aversion to women holding particular employment positions, rather than having an across-the-board dislike. Bear that distinction in mind as we consider the models.

The economic approach to discrimination is often puzzling to students. First, it makes absolutely no effort to explain *why* discriminatory preferences exist. In that respect, it follows the tradition in economics of treating preferences as exogenous—that is, as a given of the situation being analyzed. For example, economists make no effort to understand why certain people like broccoli, while others prefer string beans or corn, although those preferences are certainly an important part of explaining the demand for and market prices of broccoli, string beans, and corn. The economic approach simply takes likes and dislikes as givens, and then analyzes how, holding those preferences constant, demand is affected by incomes and prices.

Without a doubt, how people develop the preferences they have, particularly their discriminatory preferences, is an important issue. But it is not one that traditional economic analysis can shed much light on. Psychologists, anthropologists, and sociologists all have comparative advantages in analyzing that issue. The comparative advantage of economics is in analyzing how these preferences affect market outcomes.

Thus, in his work, Becker assumed that some individuals had what he called a **taste for discrimination.** This may seem like an odd choice of words, but it is part of Becker's effort to place likes and dislikes on the basis of gender, race, and other personal characteristics within the general economic framework of preferences. A taste for discrimination is not just a like or dislike but, rather, a like or dislike that an individual is willing to act on. In Becker's words: "If an individual has a taste for discrimination, he [sic] must act as if he were willing to pay something, either directly or in the form of a reduced income, to be associated with some persons rather than others" (p. 14).

Second, Becker's analysis of discrimination is embedded within the conventional economic analysis of utility-maximizing individuals and profit-maximizing firms, operating in markets that often constrain their behavior. Becker's approach therefore focuses on market equilibriums, and especially long-run competitive equilibrium.

Becker examined three potential sources of discrimination—employers who had tastes for discrimination regarding their employees (**employer discrimination**), employees who had tastes for discrimination regarding their coworkers (**employee discrimination**), and customers who had tastes for discrimination regarding the suppliers with whom they interacted (**customer discrimination**). We examine each in turn.

Employer discrimination

Let there be two kinds of workers, whom we call m and f for male and female. To isolate pay differences resulting from discrimination, assume that the two groups of workers are identical in all relevant respects. Technically they are **perfect substitutes** in production, exactly and identically productive, so no employer would have any reason to favor one group over the other in the absence of discrimination. In the absence of discrimination, the wages for the two groups of workers would be identical because otherwise no employer would ever choose to hire the more highly paid group.

But what happens if employers have a taste for discrimination for (are prejudiced against) f workers. (It probably makes sense to think of the employers as members of group m). To give this prejudice a quantitative measure, Becker introduced what he called a **discrimination coefficient.** It operates in the following specific way. Let d stand for the discrimination coefficient, w for the money wage that an employee receives, and W for the gross (or total) wage as perceived by the employer. For an employer with discrimination coefficient d, $W = w \times (1 + d)$. The gross wage now consists of two parts—the money wage (w) and the monetary equivalent of the taste for discrimination ($w \times d$). For example, if the money wage were $10 and $d = 0.25$, the gross wage would be $10 \times 1.25 = \$12.50$. Facing a money wage of $10, this employer would act as if the wage were $12.50, composed of $10.00 in money wages and a disutility cost equal to $2.50. A more prejudiced employer would have a higher value of d and thus a higher gross wage for any given money wage.[12] An employer with no prejudice at all would have $d = 0$.

How do discriminatory preferences affect the equilibrium wages of men and women? We begin with a simple case in which all employers have the same taste for discrimination, which we denote by $\bar{d}$. Let w_m stand for the money wage rate for men and w_f be the money wage rate for women. To get the gross wage for women, as perceived by the employer with a taste for discrimination, we multiply that wage by $(1 + \bar{d})$, getting $w_f \times (1 + \bar{d})$. If $w_m < w_f \times (1 + \bar{d})$, then women are more expensive (inclusive of all costs) than men, so that all employers would choose to hire only men. If $w_m > w_f \times (1 + \bar{d})$, just the opposite is true—the men are too expensive and even the prejudiced employers would want to hire only women because the lower wage more than compensates for the higher psychic costs of hiring the women. These employers are prejudiced but they are also capitalists.

---

12 Note that the discrimination coefficient is multiplicative, not additive. If it were additive, so that the net wage was $w + d$, the same general results would hold.

The only way both groups can find employment is when their gross wages are equal. Thus, in equilibrium, the relative wages for men and women must satisfy this relationship:

$$w_m^* = w_f^* \times (1 + \bar{d}) \tag{10.3}$$

where the asterisk (*) means this is an equilibrium wage rate. We can rewrite this as a wage ratio:

$$w_f^*/w_m^* = 1/(1 + \bar{d}) \tag{10.4}$$

Equation (10.4) shows that the women's equilibrium wages will be less than the men's, as long as $\bar{d} > 0$. If, for example, $\bar{d} = 0.50$, then $w_f^*/w_m^* = 1/1.5 = 67\%$. If $\bar{d} = 0.25$, then $w_f^*/w_m^* = 1/1.25 = 80\%$.

Now let's make the problem a bit more realistic and also a bit more complex. Instead of assuming that all employers have the same discrimination coefficient, suppose the discrimination coefficient ranges from 0 (no taste for discrimination) for some employers to some large number that we'll call d_m; the m subscript stands for the maximum. We use d_j to stand for the discrimination coefficient for each particular employer. Just as before, each employer will compare the gross wages of men and women and hire the less expensive group. When $w_m = w_f$, employers with $d = 0$ will be the only ones willing to employ women because for everyone else the gross wage for women ($w_f \times (1 + d_j)$) exceeds the gross wage for men (w_m). If w_f were just a bit lower, firms with the next lowest value of d_j would be just willing to employ women, and so on. As w_f continues to fall, more and more employers are willing to employ women, until the wage is so low that even the employer with $d = d_m$ would be willing to hire women.

Table 10.1 shows how this might work, for employers A, B, C, D, and E, arranged from lowest to highest discrimination coefficient. If $w_f = \$10.00$, the employers will view that wage as if it were $10.00 (employer A), $12.50 (employer B), and so on up to E, who acts as if the wage were $100. In each case the gross wage equals $w \times (1 + d_j)$. The final column shows the wage at which they would be just willing to hire women employees, assuming that the male wage was $10.00. This is the value of w_f, such that $w_f \times (1 + d_j)$ 5 $10.00; rearranging, this wage is equal to $\$10.00/(1 + d_j)$. It ranges from a high of $10.00 (employer A, who doesn't care whom he/she hires) to $1.00 for employer E, who clearly cares an enormous amount.

Table 10.1 *Employer discrimination coefficients and willingness to hire.*

Employer	d	Gross Wage [$w \times (1 + d_j)$] if $w_f = \$10.00$	Maximum Willing to Pay Women if $w_m = \$10.00$
A	0	$10.00	$10.00
B	0.25	$12.50	$8.00
C	1	$20.00	$5.00
D	3	$40.00	$2.50
E	9	$100.00	$1.00

Figure 10.2 illustrates this situation. Suppose, just to simplify a bit, that each of the five firms was willing to hire a maximum of ten workers and that the wage for men was $10.00.

What would the demand curve look like? If $w_f = \$10.00$, firm A is willing to hire anywhere between 0 and 10 women. (At that wage it is indifferent between hiring men and hiring women and ten workers is the maximum.)

Figure 10.2 *The demand for female employees from five firms when tastes for discrimination vary.*

That corresponds to the top short horizontal section of the demand curve. If the wage were $8.00, firm A would definitely hire ten women (it would actually do so if the wage were $9.99), and now firm B is willing to hire between one and ten women. So the demand curve is a horizontal line stretching from 10 to 20 when $w_f = \$8.00$. At a wage of $5.00, firms A and B will hire a total of 20 women, and firm C will hire anywhere from one to ten. And so on, down to firm E, whose demand for women workers kicks in when the wage for women is $1.00. The demand curve looks like a descending set of stairs.

The actual wage in the market will depend on where the supply curve intersects this strange demand curve. For the supply curve drawn in Figure 10.2, the equilibrium wage will be $5.00. At this wage, firms A and B hire only women, firms D and E hire only men, and firm C hires both. Note that if the supply were smaller, the wage would be higher, because then the women would need to deal with the less-prejudiced employers only.

If there are many firms instead of five, and if the value of d_j differs just slightly from one firm to the next, the demand curve will look like the smooth one in Figure 10.3 rather than the stair-step demand curve of Figure 10.2. In Figure 10.3 the vertical axis shows the relative wage of women, w_f/w_m rather than just women's wages, and the horizontal axis shows the number of women. When $w_m = w_f$, there is some demand for women workers, stemming from firms for whom $d_j = 0$. These employers are willing to hire women even when their wages are the same as men's wages. That demand is the horizontal portion of the demand curve at $w_f/w_m = 1$. Most employers, however, are still unwilling to hire women at that wage. But, as w_f falls further and further, more and more employers are willing to hire women. Each one is just willing to hire women when $w_f \times (1 + d_j) = w_m$. Thus the number of women workers demanded increases as the relative wage of women falls.

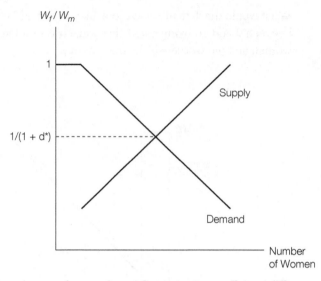

Figure 10.3 *Women's wage when employers' discrimination coefficients differ.*

The market equilibrium will be a relative wage at which the number of women willing to work just equals the number demanded. This is shown in Figure 10.3 as $1/(1 + d^*)$, where d^* is the value of d that just balances supply and demand. Women clearly continue to earn less than men. Again, it is clear that the relative wage will depend on both supply and demand; the greater the supply of women, the more prejudiced the employers they must deal with, and the lower their wages must be.

The equilibrium relative wage divides firms into two categories. For all firms with $d_j < d^*$, women are now relatively inexpensive compared to men because their own personal discrimination coefficient is low. For them, $w_f^* \times (1 + d_j) < w_m^*$, so they will employ only women and no men at all. They will pay them the market wage for women, which is lower than that for men.[13] For all firms with $d_j > d^*$, women are still too expensive relative to men because their own personal discrimination coefficient is so high. For them, $w_f^* \times (1 + d_j) > w_m^*$, so they will employ only men and no women at all. Only the marginal firm, for whom $w_f^* \times (1 + d_j) = w_m^*$, will be willing to hire both men and women.

Because of the difference in which kind of workers they hire, the profits of these two kinds of firms will differ, too. The firms hiring women have lower monetary labor costs than the firms hiring only men. Because the men and women are equally productive, the profits of the men-only firms must be lower than the profits of the women-only firms. It is easy to see why this must be true. The men-only firms could earn exactly the same revenues and have lower costs simply by replacing all their male employees with women because the women are just as productive, but cost less. That is a very powerful and important idea: *The more prejudiced firms sacrifice potential profits to indulge their prejudices. Discrimination is inconsistent with profit maximization.* It costs the firm something to indulge its discriminatory preferences.

There is one final step to the argument. Figure 10.3 might represent the state of affairs given the existing firms in the market. But the composition of the market might well

---

13 This is a subtle idea. Even firms with low discrimination coefficients pay women less than men because they take wages as given. These firms are *willing* to pay women more than that but they don't have to.

change over time in a particular way. Potential firms with relatively low d_js could enter the market to take advantage, as it were, of the lower wages of women. Precisely because they are willing to employ women, they can earn the higher profits of the women-only firms in the market. But no firms with high d_js would want to enter the market because they would face the higher costs associated with hiring men.

Figure 10.4 shows how this entry would change the market. The entry by these firms would shift the demand curve out at higher relative wages, thereby raising the equilibrium wage for women. Eventually the entry process might result in a demand curve composed only of firms with $d_j = 0$. In that case the demand curve would be horizontal at $w_m = w_f$. Discriminatory wage differences have been eliminated by competitive market processes. In a famous article, the economic theorist and Nobel Prize winner Kenneth Arrow showed that this result would be attained if there was free entry, constant returns to scale,[14] and a sufficient number of potential employers with $d_j = 0$.

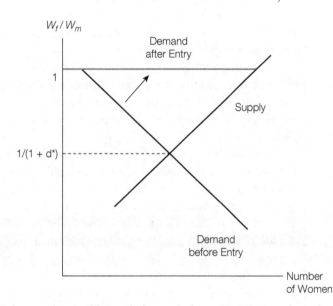

Figure 10.4 *Labor-market equilibrium before and after potential entry of new firms.*

Needless to say, this is a surprising result and an important one. As Arrow wrote: "The model predicts the absence of the phenomenon it was designed to explain."[15] It is important to appreciate the key elements necessary for the result—the ability to enter the market, the exclusive focus on monetary profits, and the existence of a sufficient pool of potential employers with low or even zero discrimination coefficients. Some economists take the results largely at face value and conclude that earnings differences between men and women or, for that matter, any two groups cannot reflect labor-market discrimination but must instead be the result of genuine differences in productivity.

---

14 The constant returns to scale means that the market is likely to be competitive rather than dominated by a single monopolist or several oligopolists.

15 Kenneth Arrow (1972), "Some Mathematical Models of Race Discrimination in the Labor Market," in Anthony H. Pascal (ed.), *Racial Discrimination in Economic Life*, Lexington, MA: Lexington Books. Arrow was one of the first US economists to receive the Nobel Prize in Economics for his work on general equilibrium theory.

(Those productivity differences could, of course, be caused by prior discrimination, perhaps public discrimination in the provision of public education.) The market will inevitably eliminate discrimination, they argue, by virtue of the profit-seeking activities of firms. For an interesting example of this process in the world of professional sports, see Box 10.2.

Box   10.2

Discrimination in Professional Sports

In a somewhat different context, discrimination in sports provides an interesting case exactly on point for both sides of the argument. For many years, discrimination in Major League Baseball was essentially absolute. No black players at all were employed. There was no relative wage at which firms were willing to hire them. Instead, an alternative league, the Negro Baseball League, was formed to provide them an opportunity to play. They played there, often with great skill and always with very low wages. This situation prevailed for many years.

Why didn't the market just eliminate the unjustified earnings differences? One critical element of the "competition eliminates discrimination" argument was missing. Entry into Major League Baseball was not open. Would-be nondiscriminators could not simply set up shop and join the league, so race discrimination in baseball persisted for many years.

Eventually, however, the Brooklyn Dodgers, under the influence of a particularly broad-minded and cagey executive, Branch Rickey, signed Jackie Robinson to a contract as the first black Major League Baseball player. He acted very much like an employer with a low value of d and recognized a great player—and a great bargain—when he saw it. The other teams acted like employers with high values of d. Within a decade, however, the color bar had been broken on every team as a result of competitive pressures.

A similar story can be told for college athletics; through the 1950s, most Southern universities fielded all-white football and basketball teams. Black athletes were not offered athletic scholarships, but this practice, too, eventually ended. When change finally came, it moved quickly across all universities.

The moral of this story is that discriminatory wage differences may persist for many years if the circumstances are right. But change, when it does come, can occur suddenly and thoroughly.

Other economists worry about the underlying conditions. Is entry sufficiently easy? Are firms sufficiently profit-oriented, or will they adhere to what may be social custom? Are there a sufficient number of unprejudiced employers? In this regard, the well-known economist and feminist Barbara Bergmann quoted the yet more famous nineteenth-century economist, John Stuart Mill. Mill wrote that "Political economists exaggerate the effect of competition. They are apt to express themselves as if they thought that competition actually does, in all cases, whatever it can be shown to be the tendency of competition to do."

Source: Barbara Bergmann (1989), "Does the Market for Women's Labor Need Fixing?" *Journal of Economic Perspectives*, 3 (1), 43–60.

Customer discrimination

The analysis of customer discrimination is quite similar to the analysis of employer discrimination. Now imagine that there are a number of firms selling an identical product in a competitive market. The firms are distinguished only by the gender, race, or other personal characteristic of the seller; the firms differ in no other important respect. If customers have no taste for discrimination, then the prices charged by the firms must be identical in long-term equilibrium. No customer would ever pay more for the product from one seller if it were available at a lower price from another seller. That would eliminate price differences.

Suppose, though, that m (male) customers have tastes for discrimination. Now, faced with a good sold by an f (female) firm, these customers would regard the gross price as $p_f \times (1 + d)$, where d is, once again, the discrimination coefficient. The gross price of the product is composed of two parts—the monetary cost (p_f) and the disutility of interacting with an f firm $(d \times p_f)$. If the f firm wants to sell its output to these customers, it must lower its price so that its gross price just equals the price of the good sold by m (male) firms. Thus it must be the case that $p_f^* \times (1 + d) = p_m^*$. The discriminatory preferences result in f firms being forced to charge a lower price. In thinking about how this might affect wage rates, imagine that the good in question is a service of some kind, where the customer interacts directly with the seller. For example, this could apply to doctors, dentists, lawyers, shopkeepers, and all kinds of retail workers. Then the price that is affected is either the worker's pay directly (as in the case of doctors, dentists, and lawyers) or the price of the good that the worker sells, which affects her pay indirectly.

If tastes for discrimination vary across customers, the analysis would follow exactly along the lines of the model of employer discrimination, where the discrimination coefficient varied. The f (female) customers would presumably have $d = 0$. Each male customer would have a critical value for p_f^*/p_m^* that was just low enough to make him indifferent between the two kinds of firms by making the gross prices equal. Market equilibrium would divide customers into those with lower discrimination coefficients who buy only from the f firms and those with higher discrimination coefficients who buy only from the m firms. As in the case of employer discrimination, the customers who are indulging their taste for discrimination pay something for exercising those preferences. They pay a higher monetary cost by buying the good from m firms rather than f firms. They are not, however, worse off in terms of their own preferences—they quite willingly pay the higher price because they prefer to do so. Unlike the case of employer discrimination where firms with high discrimination coefficients earned lower profits and could potentially be driven out of business as a result, there is no corresponding mechanism here. Nothing happens to customers who prefer to buy goods from one firm rather than another except that they are worse off than they could be if they had different (no taste for discrimination) preferences. Consequently, customer discrimination can survive in market equilibrium in the long run.

Employee discrimination

If there is employee discrimination, then employees have tastes for discrimination concerning their coworkers. Suppose that m and f employees are again perfect substitutes. Employers have no taste for discrimination, but m employees don't like to work alongside

f employees. Then, if the m money wage is w_m, their gross wage would be $w_m \times (1 - d)$ if they were working alongside women employees. Here, d enters negatively, reducing the gross wage received by m workers.

Now suppose there were two jobs that m workers could take, one with only m coworkers and one with both m and f coworkers. No m worker would take the latter job unless its money wage was sufficiently higher to offset the disutility of working with f workers. In symbols, if job 1 has only m workers and job 2 has m and f workers, then wages must be set so that $w_{1m} = w_{2m} \times (1 - d)$. The m wages in job 2 just compensate for the disutility of working alongside f workers. Women in this simple story are assumed not to care about their coworkers, so $w_{1f} = w_{2f}$. The apparent result is that men and women in job 1 will receive the same wage, but m workers in job 2 will earn more.

In fact, as Becker pointed out, an alternative result is that the workforce would be segregated by gender, thereby eliminating the need to pay higher wages to the men. Clearly, this is a lower-cost solution to the problem. So this simple model actually predicts job segregation rather than pay differences.

In more complicated production settings, it is possible to establish wage differences on the basis of employee discrimination. For example, suppose there are m and f type 1 workers who are perfect substitutes for one another, but also m type 2 workers who are supervisors of the type 1 workers. Production requires either m or f type 1 workers and type 2 workers. If there is employee discrimination among type 1 m workers, job segregation will result, but, as above, there will be no pay differences. If type 2 m workers also have a taste for discrimination, they will receive higher pay when they supervise f workers than when they supervise m workers. In this situation, pay differences could arise from employee discrimination.

Summary of discrimination models

Let's review these three models of labor-market discrimination. Employer discrimination can certainly affect wage rates in the short run—and the short run can last a very long time. Becker's insight that discrimination is costly to those who practice it is important, as is the prediction that market forces could operate to eliminate much of the earnings differences that are a result of discrimination. It is sensible to appreciate the insight but to be skeptical that it applies perfectly to labor markets in the twenty-first century.

Customer discrimination can certainly generate differences in prices for identical goods sold by different kinds of firms as long as there are tastes for discrimination. Unlike employer discrimination, this source of wage differentials will not be eroded by market forces. This model potentially applies primarily to services and retail where face-to-face contact is present. Employee discrimination probably has the least impact of all. Firms can readily avoid paying higher wages by segregating their workforce along the dimension on which discrimination operates.

Becker's models of labor-market discrimination have been very influential among economists. Many, although certainly not all, economists interpret them as indicating that labor-market discrimination is not likely to be an important factor in explaining the lower wages of women. We look at the evidence in the next chapter.

Other explanations of the gender gap in earnings

Statistical discrimination

Statistical discrimination is another form of discrimination that can arise in the labor market. It arises because employers have an interest in maximizing profits, which requires keeping costs as low as possible. Firms often bear the cost of hiring and training workers, and so it is in their interest to keep these costs low. Unfortunately, the firm does not always have exactly the information it needs to determine which employees are likely to be the easiest to train, the most productive, the most reliable, or the most committed to the firm. This is called **asymmetric information**—the employee has more information than the employer about his/her own skills and commitment.

Because of this, the employer will often rely on a signal or a credential that the employee possesses to make a determination about whether to hire that person. For example, if graduates of Ivy League colleges are, in the firm's mind and experience, more productive than other college graduates, the firm may make its hiring decision based upon this criterion. The firm is using the average characteristics of a group (Ivy League college graduates) to make decisions about individuals and their productivity. The firm is following this course because it has imperfect information; it can't be certain about each individual's productivity, but it has found that, on average, people from this group are more productive than those who do not possess an Ivy League degree.

This same kind of thing can happen to women if firms are looking to hire people into jobs where there are considerable training costs. The employer may believe that a particular woman is qualified for the job but may worry that she won't make the long-term commitment necessary to make the firm's investment in training her profitable. Perhaps in the past the firm has had many women employees who left to raise a family. Because it is costly to investigate whether a particular applicant will leave the firm after a short period of time—and difficult to verify in any case—the firm may tend to offer jobs to men because they have historically had a stronger attachment to the labor force. Thus women may find it more difficult to get hired at this firm. It isn't because employers actively dislike female applicants; it is because in the past female employees have tended to leave the firm, and the firm has had to incur the costs associated with hiring and training a new employee.

Figure 10.5 makes the point quite nicely. Suppose that some attribute—call it attachment to the workforce—is distributed normally throughout the population but is higher for men than for women. We can draw two bell curves (normal curves) in Figure 10.5 to illustrate this distribution. These curves are drawn under the assumption that there exists a distribution of labor-force attachment across men and women and that the distribution is different for each group—in particular, men have a higher degree of labor-force attachment than do women. Think of the situation that existed 30 or 40 years ago. In Figure 10.5 the average woman has a lower average attachment to the workforce (W) than the average man (M). However, the distributions do overlap a little bit: some women are more attached to the workforce than some men. Employers who are looking for someone more attached to the workforce will likely select a man, given that they cannot observe a given woman's attachment to the workforce and that they know that men, on average, have been more attached to the workforce.

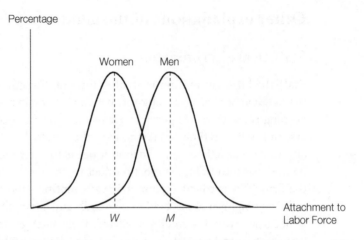

Figure 10.5 *Statistical discrimination when the distributions by gender are very different.*

One might think that, given the strong attachment that women have demonstrated to the labor force over the past 30 years, statistical discrimination would be less likely to occur; after all, as we have documented throughout this book, men and women are becoming more alike in their attachment to the labor force. However, statistical discrimination can occur even if men and women have a nearly equal attachment to the labor force. This may happen if employers are risk averse and fear making a costly mistake or if the indicator of attachment is a noisy signal—it doesn't predict attachment well. Then, even though employers understand that women are equally committed to the labor force, they may still prefer to hire men to minimize the costs associated with hiring someone who may leave the firm after a short while. Figure 10.6 illustrates this scenario with another set of bell-shaped curves. This time the distributions overlap nearly completely, indicating the near parity in labor-force attachment that we now see. This figure highlights an important observation: As men and women become more alike in their attachment to the workforce (or more alike in whatever productivity characteristic is being measured), some risk-averse employers could easily end up hiring a man who is less attached to the workforce than a woman.

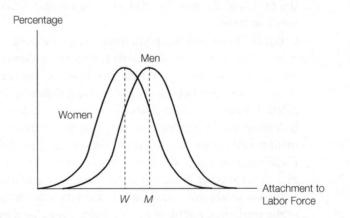

Figure 10.6 *Statistical discrimination when the distributions by gender are very similar.*

Gender differences for competition and risk

As we saw above, the standard economics explanation for the gender earnings gap focuses on human capital differences such as education and work experience or discrimination as being the drivers of earnings differences across men and women. Yet, as we saw earlier, women are becoming more like men in these attributes but a persistent gender earnings gap still exists. Relatively recently, economists have focused on other potential determinants of earnings using ideas developed from psychology. Here we focus on two of these: gender differences in preferences for a competitive work environment and gender differences regarding risk aversion. Much of this work is quite new and therefore has focused on establishing whether or not gender differences exist along these dimensions. Even where gender differentials in these traits have been established, we are only beginning to understand how well, if at all, they might contribute to explaining the gender wage gap. Nonetheless, the work here is interesting and worth discussing in some depth.[16]

Gender and competition There has long been speculation that one reason for the gender wage differential is that men are more competitive than women and that, as a result, women shy away from competitive work environments. If jobs that have a competitive environment pay more, this reluctance to compete on the part of women can then result in a loss of earnings for them. In addition, if women are more reluctant to compete, they may be less likely to seek promotions or enter male-dominated fields that tend to pay better. Hence gender differences in competition may well provide an explanation for the continuing gender earnings gap.

Establishing whether or not women are less competitive than men is difficult to do with existing survey data. As we have noted often throughout this text, economists regularly lament the difficulty of finding experimental data with random assignment and the lack of that data makes finding causal relationships between variables problematic. But sometimes economists can create their own data in the laboratory, filtering out all other complicating factors. Economists Uri Gneezy, Muriel Niederle, and Aldo Rustichini[17] conducted an experiment in which groups of three men and three women solved computerized mazes in different kinds of "competitive" environment. In one experiment, individuals were rewarded based on their own performance, a reward system called **piecework**. In this environment the men and women performed equally well. No statistically different gender differences in ability were observed.

Then the experiment was changed to what economists call a **tournament** reward structure, in which payoffs depend on an individual's relative score, just like in a golf or tennis tournament. In this experiment the individual with the highest score was paid proportional to the number of puzzles he or she solved, while the others received nothing. Labor economists have noticed that many corporate pay structures have a

---

16 For more information, see Muriel Niederle (2014), "Gender," NBER Working Paper No. w20788 and Marianne Bertrand (2011), "New Perspectives on Gender," *Handbook of Labor Economics*, 4, 1543–1590.

17 Uri Gneezy, Muriel Niederle, and Aldo Rustichini (2003), "Performance in Competitive Environments: Gender Differences," *Quarterly Journal of Economics*, 118 (3), 1049–1074.

tournament structure, with many "players" at the entry level, but only a few winners who make it to vice president and president of the company. Here, pay depends on relative, not absolute, performance—the "best player" wins and gets the best salary, the second best becomes vice president and gets the second highest salary, and so on. In other words, the tournament is a competition and one that women, if they dislike competition, may shy away from.

What happened in this experiment? The absolute performance of the women was the same as in the piecework experiment, but the absolute performance of the men improved. The competitive environment of the second experiment somehow elicited better performance from the men.

The experimenters considered one more wrinkle. In the two experiments above, men and women competed against each other in mixed-sex groups. Some research suggests that women perform better in single-sex environments, either because they are less competitive in general or because they do not like competing against men. To test this, the experiments were also conducted with same-sex groups, first with piecework and then with a tournament pay structure. Gneezy, Niederle, and Rustichini found that, indeed, the women did perform better in the tournament structure than the piecework, unlike their performance in the mixed-sex environment.

In a related paper, Niederle and Vesterlund examined whether men and women had different preferences for competitive environments.[18] The general structure of the experiment was similar to the previous one—men and women performed tasks, in this case, adding up sets of 5 two-digit numbers for five minutes—under piecework and tournament pay systems. In this experiment, however, another issue was introduced. After performing the addition task in both pay environments, each individual was told his or her absolute performance level—how many sums were added correctly—but not how he or she did relative to others in the group. Then each was asked which compensation scheme they preferred for their next task.

No absolute differences in ability level existed between the men and the women. Both groups, on average, solved the same number of problems in the piecework environment and in the tournament system. Nevertheless, more than twice as many men as women chose the tournament pay scheme (73 percent vs. 35 percent). Even low-ability men (men who solved fewer problems than average) opted for the tournament scheme, while even high-ability women opted for the piecework system. The authors conclude that men tend to be overconfident about their abilities.[19]

Economists have also used field experiments to test if women are less competitive than men. A field experiment is a blend of experimental methods with the "real world." An example of a field experiment is when a researcher sends out fictitious résumés to prospective employers to determine if there is any bias in hiring. In this example, the fictitious résumés would be identical except for gender. Field experiments have the advantage that outcomes are observed in a natural setting, rather than in a contrived laboratory

18 Muriel Niederle and Lise Vesterlund (2007), "Do Women Shy Away from Competition? Do Men Compete Too Much?" *Quarterly Journal of Economics*, 122 (3), 1067–1101.

19 Many more experiments like this have been conducted to test gender differences in competition. Interested readers should consult Muriel Niederle and Lise Vesterlund (2011), "Gender and Competition," *Annual Review of Economics*, 3, 601–630 for a review of more of these types of experiments.

environment which often uses college students as subjects. Thus their results may be more generalizable than those from an experiment.

Flory, Leibbrandt, and List used a field experiment to study gender differences in taste for competition.[20] They randomly assigned individuals who were seeking employment into two groups and exposed each group to advertisements for jobs that had differing compensation schemes. Individuals then had to decide whether or not to apply for the jobs. They report that when the compensation package was competitive in that it was greatly skewed towards rewarding the individual's performance relative to that of a coworker's, women were significantly less likely to apply.

These findings from experiments and field work as well as others that followed indicate that women may systematically underperform relative to men in competitive environments and that many women, even among the most educated, may simply prefer to avoid such environments.[21] Proponents of single-sex schooling have often argued that in a coeducational environment, boys dominate the discussion and garner more attention from teachers, thus promoting gender stereotypes. If this is the case, economists Lee, Niederle and Kang asked whether single-sex schooling could affect girls' willingness to compete.[22] If so, single-sex school could potentially be used as a policy tool to reduce the gender gap in competition. To test this hypothesis, they used data on middle-school students in Seoul, South Korea, where they conducted essentially the same experiment as Niederle and Vesterlund discussed above. The advantage of using the education system in Seoul is that in Seoul, all students are randomly assigned to either a single-sex or a coeducational school in their district and each district has both types of school. Since students are randomly assigned, concerns about nonrandom selection of certain types of student into single sex schools are not an issue. Interestingly, in this study, Lee, Niederle and Kang established that women were less willing to compete than men but their hypothesis that single-sex schooling reduces the gender gap was not supported. One notable feature of their study is that it also lends further support to other studies that have used data from various countries and established that the gender gap in willingness to compete is not unique to the United States

The finding that high-ability women choose not to compete is potentially costly to society because it indicates that those with the highest ability may not apply for the jobs for which they are best suited. What can be done to encourage women to enter competitions? The answer to this question depends on whether gender differences in competitiveness stem from "nature" or "nurture." If the former, that women are inherently less likely to compete then it may be possible to make institutional changes that will entice women to enter competitive environments. For example, Vandegrift and

---

20 J. A. Flory, A. Leibbrandt, and J. A. List (2015), "Do Competitive Workplaces Deter Female Workers? A Large-Scale Natural Field Experiment on Job-Entry Decisions," *The Review of Economic Studies*, 82 (1), 122–155.

21 It is not just the labor market where differences in competition might matter. Similar findings regarding willingness to compete have been established in terms of entry to competitive educational environments. See T. Buser, M. Niederle, and H. Oosterbeek (2012), "Gender, Competitiveness and Career Choices," NBER Working Paper No. w18576. These authors conducted an experiment regarding choosing competitive educational tracts in Norway and also report evidence that women are less likely to compete in education.

22 Soohyung Lee, Muriel Niederle, and Namwook Kang (2014), "Do Single Sex Schools Make Girls More Competitive?" *Economics Letters*, 124, 474–477.

Yavas (2009) find that gender is not as strong a predictor of tournament entry when individuals face the same task and competition repeatedly and are able to learn about their relative ability.[23] Niederle, Segal, and Vesterlund examine the effect of introducing a gender quota in an environment where high-performing women fail to enter competitions that they have the capacity to win. They show that guaranteeing women equal representation among winners increases their entry.[24] If, however, preferences for competition are a result of "nurture" or the socialization process, then it may be possible to influence such preferences so that women are more likely to engage in competition. Of course, it is likely neither nature nor nurture but rather a combination of the two that explains these differences.

Gender and risk aversion   Another source of gender differences that might affect the gender earnings gap is risk aversion. What does it mean to be risk averse? A quick example will illustrate an economic way of viewing risk aversion. Suppose that an individual has a choice between accepting $100 now or engaging in a gamble in which she will earn $200 with 50 percent probability or $0 with 50 percent probability. The $100 is a "sure thing" if she opts for that, but the gamble is not. The expected income from the gamble is $100. (We can see this by simply multiplying the dollar sums for each outcome by the probability as follows: $0.5 \times \$200 + 0.5 \times \$0 = \$100$; while she will either have $200 or $0, $100 is the average or "expected value" of the gamble.) Thus what she expected to gain on average in each case is the same, but with the gamble there is the chance she won't get anything. A risk-averse person, therefore, would prefer to have the certain $100 rather than take the risk of gaining nothing vs. having $200 (and, of course, a risk-loving person, by the same analogy, would prefer the gamble).

Jobs that involve some risk pay more to compensate individuals for taking the risk. Hence risk aversion could be a viable contributor to the gender wage gap. From numerous experiments in conducted in laboratory settings by economists, there is a great deal of evidence that women are more risk averse than men.[25] These experiments are typically conducted using college students as the subjects. The students are presented with a variety of gambles of varying degrees of risk and asked if they are willing to take them. Sometimes the gambles are merely hypothetical, but sometimes they involve actual money (though the amounts involved are typically small). In these experiments, men are more often found to be willing to engage in riskier gambles than are women.

While experimental evidence in economics on risk aversion comes almost exclusively from college students, Dohmen and coauthors complement this finding by presenting evidence of higher risk aversion among women in the general population.[26] Their research provides an important link between the experimental evidence cited

---

23   D. Vandegrift and A. Yavas (2009), "Men, Women, and Competition: An Experimental Test of Behavior," *Journal of Economic Behavior and Organization*, 72 (1), 554–570.

24   Muriel Niederle, Carmit Segal, and Lise Vesterlund (2013), "How Costly is Diversity? Affirmative Action in Light of Gender Differences in Competitiveness," *Management Science*, 59 (1), 1–16.

25   For an excellent overview of this research, see C. C. Eckel and P. J. Grossman (2008), "Men, Women and Risk Aversion: Experimental Evidence," in C. Plott and V. Smith (eds.), *Handbook of Experimental Economic Results*, Amsterdam: Elsevier.

26   Thomas J. Dohmen, Armin Falk, David Huffman, Juergen Schupp, Uwe Sunde, and Gert G. Wagner (2011), "Individual Risk Attitudes: Measurement, Determinants and Behavioral Consequences," *Journal of the European Economic Association*, 9 (3), 522–550.

above and an individual's own subjective evaluation of their level of risk aversion. They used survey data where respondents were asked to assess their willingness to take risks ("How willing are you to take risks, in general?") on a scale from 0 to 10. Then these same survey respondents were placed in a laboratory setting where they were asked to make choices in real-stakes gambles. The subjective survey question was found to be highly correlated with the laboratory results in terms of assessing risk, even after controlling for many observable characteristics, hence adding further credibility to the experimental results. They also find that those who are more risk averse as measured by the responses to the subjective evaluation of risk are more likely to work in jobs with performance evaluation and that women are less likely to work for variable pay than men. They did not, however, assess how much of the gender gap in willingness to work for variable pay could be accounted for by gender differences in risk aversion.

Croson and Gneezy offered an interesting explanation of what might explain these often-found gender differences in risk aversion.[27] They point to systematic gender differences in the emotional reaction to risk and posit that this emotional reaction may affect the utility one gets from making riskier choices. Indeed, women appear to experience more stress, fear, or dread in situations that involve the risk of a negative outcome, which may explain their greater level of risk aversion when compared to men.

As we saw earlier, experimental evidence makes clear that men are more competitively inclined than women, and women underperform when competing against men. Some researchers have asked whether these competitive differences can be explained by differences in risk aversion across men and women. In fact, studies find that these differences in competitiveness persist and are only somewhat reduced when controlling for measures of risk aversion.[28] In other words, distaste for competition by women cannot be explained by their higher degree of risk aversion.

While the laboratory and field experiments described above have established that women differ from men in terms of taste for competition and risk aversion, it's not an easy matter to know exactly what these experimental results mean for the differences between men and women in the real world of the labor market. To date there is only limited research establishing the relevance of these experimental findings in explaining labor-market outcomes. Economist Marianne Bertrand notes that most of the existing attempts to measure the impact of these factors on actual labor-market outcomes have not found a large effect.[29] She attributes this to two factors: this is a relatively new research area for economists, and databases that combine measures of these attributes with actual labor-market outcomes are difficult to find. There is, undoubtedly, more to come in this fascinating area of gender research.[30] For an overview of research on biological differences by gender and their possible impact on wage differences, see Box 10.3.

27 R. Croson and U. Gneezy (2009), "Gender Differences in Preferences," *Journal of Economic Literature*, 47 (2), 448–474.

28 For a review of more experiments, see Muriel Niederle and Lise Vesterlund (2011), "Gender and Competition," *Annual Review of Economics*, 3, 601–630 and Niederle, "Gender."

29 Marianne Bertrand (2011), "New Perspectives on Gender," *Handbook of Labor Economics*, 4, 1543–1590.

30 See also Azmat Ghazala and Barbara Petrongolo (2014), "Gender and the Labor Market: What Have We Learned from Field and Lab Experiments?" *Labour Economics* 30, 32–40.

Box   10.3

Biological Differences and the Gender Wage Gap

It's no secret that there are basic biological differences between men and women in physical strength and size, hormones, and the like. Are these differences part of the explanation for the gender gap?

Realistically, physical strength plays a far less central role in modern economies than in the past, so, except for very specialized occupations, this difference is unlikely to be important. Technical progress in medicine has helped to mitigate the effect of the career disruptions that inevitably surround childbirth. As we saw in Chapter 6, the development of the birth-control pill changed women's behavior regarding higher education, marriage, and work. Albanesi and Olivetti (2009) show how medical improvements in maternal health and the introduction of infant formula increased the labor-force participation of married women of child-bearing age. Buckles (2007) finds that easier access to infertility treatments positively affects women's labor-force participation and wages by relaxing the biological time constraint on childbearing. These developments have made biological differences less important.

What about a biological explanation for gender differences in competition and risk taking that we discuss in this chapter? Buser finds that women are less competitive both when taking contraceptives that contain progesterone and estrogen, and during the phase of the menstrual cycle when the secretion of these hormones is particularly high. However, Wozniak et al. report that in high-hormone phases women are more, rather than less, competitive. Thus although both studies suggest that hormones influence women's willingness to compete (e.g., enter tournaments) and, thus, suggest that nature matters, there is at present no consensus on the direction of such an effect.

One last biological issue concerns the possible role of menstruation. In controversial research, Ichino and Moretti suggested that women earned less than men because of increased absenteeism due to their menstrual cycle. Logically this conclusion relies on two assumptions: first, that women take more sick days than men, and second, that menstruation is a major factor in women's sick days. Using data from the personnel records of a large Italian bank, Ichino and Moretti found a cyclical 28-day pattern in absences for women, which they interpreted as being consistent with the explanation that the menstrual cycle was to blame. But follow-up work by Herrmann and Rockoff showed that their approach was quite sensitive to some minor coding errors as well as to some technical issues and, even if it were true, it is hard to know just how representative the behavior of workers in an Italian bank could be. In two further studies, one based on female teachers in the New York City public schools and the other on nationally representative data on women from the National Health Interview Survey, Herrmann and Rockoff found little or no impact of menstruation on absenteeism. Certainly, careful research is necessary here to avoid reckless inferences that could lead to statistical discrimination against women of childbearing age.

Sources:
Stefania Albanesi and Claudia Olivetti (2008), "Gender Roles and Medical Progress," National Bureau of Economic Research Working Paper # w14873.

Kasey Buckles (2007), "Stopping the Biological Clock: Infertility Treatments and the Career-Family Trade-off," Boston University, unpublished manuscript.

T. Buser (2011), "The Impact of the Menstrual Cycle and Hormonal Contraceptives On Competitiveness," Working Paper, University of Amsterdam

Mariesa A. Herrmann and Jonah E. Rockoff (2012), "Does Menstruation Explain Gender Gaps in Work Absenteeism?" *Journal of Human Resources* 47.2: 493–508.

Mariesa A. Herrmann and Jonah E. Rockoff (2012), "Worker Absence and Productivity: Evidence from Teaching," *Journal of Labor Economics* 30.4: 749–782.

Mariesa A. Herrmann and Jonah E. Rockoff (2013), "Do Menstrual Problems Explain Gender Gaps In Absenteeism And Earnings? Evidence from the National Health Interview Survey," *Labour Economics* 24: 12–22.

Andrea Ichino and Enrico Moretti (2009), "Biological Gender Differences, Absenteeism, and the Earnings Gap," *American Economic Journal: Applied Economics*: 183–218.

David Wozniak, William T. Harbaugh, and Ulrich Mayr (2014), "The Menstrual Cycle and Performance Feedback Alter Gender Differences in Competitive Choices," *Journal of Labor Economics* 32.1: 161–198

Theories of occupational differences

As we explained in Chapter 9, occupational segregation by gender is still substantial, although it is certainly declining in the United States. The intriguing question is why it exists. This is potentially a very important question: While earnings differences by gender do exist within occupations (see Table 9.2), the difference by gender in the occupational distribution is an important part of the explanation of women's lower earnings. After all, it is not just that women and men tend to congregate in different occupations; it is that women tend to congregate in occupations that pay less than those in which men dominate. A full understanding of the cause of gender differences in occupation is probably not something we can realistically expect. But we do have a number of interesting possible explanations. As with most complex phenomena, each may be partly correct.

Gender roles, gender identity, and occupational choice It is certainly possible that men and women truly prefer different kinds of occupation, as a result either of innate preferences or ubiquitous social cues about what is feminine and what is masculine. Studies of gender roles find that many individuals have definite ideas regarding what jobs or careers are suitable for what gender. These studies suggest that children as young as 4 years old show strong predilections toward occupations that are conventionally linked to a specific gender. Where these ideas of suitable occupations and roles for a specific gender came from is arguable. One idea is that jobs considered typically "masculine" demand traits considered typically masculine, such as aggression, competitive conduct, and physical strength. Jobs considered typically female entail such traits as caring, compassion, and patience. These traits are considered to be innate under this theory and each gender "self-selects" occupations because of these differences.

Economists George Akerlof and Rachael Kranton have formalized this notion of gender roles into an economic model of social identity and proposed it as a possible explanation for occupation differences.[31] They define social identify as one's sense of self, or

---

31   G. A. Akerlof and R. E. Kranton (2000), "Economics and Identity," *Quarterly Journal of Economics*, 115 (3),715–753.

one's sense of belonging to one or multiple social categories. Importantly, an individual's identity incorporates a clear view about how people that belong to that category should behave. In their model, one's identity is a source of utility and an individual's identity can influence economic outcomes because deviating from the behavior that is expected for one's identity will decrease utility. They ask readers to picture themselves as a female Marine to illustrate how gender identity can lead to occupational segregation by gender. Because Marines are essentially all viewed as men, a woman in this occupation may feel discomfort because her decision to become a Marine is in direct conflict with the behavioral prescription for her gender category in that only men, not women, are Marines. In addition, male Marines may be reluctant to accept a female Marine because this threatens their own gender identity and hence they may feel the need to tease or mistreat a female Marine. This behavior on the part of the male Marines serves to reinforce women's reluctance to enter this male profession.

Gender differences in personality traits Economists have borrowed from the psychology literature to ask whether gender differences in psychological traits might lead men and women to select different occupations. Nobel laureate James Heckman has focused on what he terms "soft skills" or "noncognitive" skills that are valued in the labor market. The most commonly used inventory of personality traits is the "Big Five" model. The Big Five personality traits are extroversion, agreeableness, conscientiousness, neuroticism, and openness to experience. Considerable research by psychologists suggests that agreeableness and neuroticism are the two traits that are most consistently associated with gender differences: women are consistently found to be both more agreeable and more neurotic than men.[32] There is evidence that workers' personality traits are often matched to the requirements of the specific occupations they have chosen. There is also evidence that these are often gendered, leading the expected benefit of entering different occupations to depend on one's personality in ways that differ for men and women.[33]

Compensating differences Whatever the underlying cause of the occupational segregation by gender, it does not, however, follow immediately that women's occupations will necessarily have lower wages. For that to be so, one of two things must be true. First, it could be that women's jobs are more attractive than men's jobs in terms of their **nonpecuniary job characteristics**, holding the level of necessary skill constant. Nonpecuniary job characteristics are everything about a job except its pay—its working conditions, hours, safety, prestige, and so on. The theory of **compensating differences** tells us that when two jobs require the same skills, but one is widely held to have more desirable nonpecuniary job characteristics, then that job will have a lower equilibrium wage. It is not difficult to find examples that seem to reflect this.

A related idea focuses on the degree of job flexibility and, in particular, the extent to which a job accommodates a work–family balance. Claudia Goldin has suggested that this dimension is particularly important and that it is the key to what she calls the "final chapter" in gender convergence in the labor market. We discuss her argument and findings in detail in the next chapter. For the moment it is sufficient to recognize that jobs that offer

---

32   See Bertrand, "New Perspectives on Gender."

33   H. Antecol and D. A. Cobb-Clark (2013), "Do Psychosocial Traits Help Explain Gender Segregation in Young People's Occupations?" *Labour Economics*, 21, 59–73.

greater flexibility about time and place and hours of work may also have associated wage penalties. Goldin proposes that in some particular employment contexts, these penalties can be quite severe. More on this later.

Second, it could be that women are "limited" to a relatively small subset of occupations and thereby increase the supply of workers there relative to a world in which no gender stereotyping occurs. If supply is larger, then wages will be lower; this is simple supply and demand. That is the essence of the **crowding hypothesis**. This hypothesis has a logical internal consistency—if women are crowded into occupations, wages probably would be lower—but economists tend to be skeptical of models in which individuals are "compelled" to do things without clear ways in which the compulsion is enforced.

Human capital and occupational choice More sophisticated models of occupational segregation focus on the characteristics of the occupations themselves in terms of human capital investment. One version is based on the theory of optimal investment in OJT that we discussed earlier in this chapter. Investment in training is costly to an individual, usually in terms of lower earnings than could be earned in a job without training. Earnings are higher after the training is received, and thus the investment has an internal rate of return. How high that rate of return is depends largely on how long an individual expects to stay in that job (for specific training) or in the labor market (for general training). It also depends on whether the individual is paid according to his or her productivity—that is, it depends on the absence of labor-market discrimination.

OJT typically is an inherent part of a job—if you have the job, you receive the training. The only way to avoid the training is to take a different job. Different occupations provide different amounts of training, so choice of the amount of training implies a choice of an occupation. Thought of this way, women might choose those occupations that offer the desired amount of OJT. In a time period when women's work was irregular, congregating in occupations that provided relatively little training might make economic sense. The changing occupational distribution of the past decades also makes sense viewed in this light: As women's lifetime labor-force participation increased, they upgraded their occupational choices and invested in more OJT.

Even though women are far more likely to participate in the labor force than in previous decades, it is still the case that many women cycle in and out of the labor force and hence we describe their labor-force participation as intermittent. For example, Goldin notes that over 40 percent of college-educated women were out of work for more than six months at some point, and 23 percent had out-of-work spells that totaled two years or more in the 15-year period following the completion of college. In contrast, only 14.1 percent of college-educated men were out of work for at least 6 months at some point, and only 3.1 percent had accumulated out-of-work spells of more than two years.[34]

It is likely that occupations have different inherent penalties to intermittent labor-force participation. In some, the impact is substantial—an individual, male or female, who leaves a job and returns to it some years later will have suffered a large wage penalty. In others, the impact is small, so that an individual could more or less pick up where he or she left off. The reasons for the difference in penalty could reflect the changing

34 Claudia Goldin (2006), "The Quiet Revolution that Transformed Women's Employment, Education, and Family," *American Economic Review*, 96 (2), 1–21.

technological nature of a job—think of a computer programmer returning to work after a long absence. It could also reflect other peculiar institutional details of a job. For example, some jobs, such as nursing, have relatively low wage premiums to seniority, so the penalty is smaller.

Figure 10.7 shows how wage penalties might work. To make it simple, we focus on just two occupations, *j* and *k*. Assume that the skill level involved in the two occupations is relatively similar (at least well in advance) so that it makes sense to think of an individual potentially choosing at some earlier point in time between working in occupation *j* and working in occupation *k*. For each occupation we've drawn two age-earnings profiles, one if the individual worked continuously and another if the individual dropped out of the labor market for a fixed interval of, say, five years. In Figures 10.7(A) and (B), the line *AB* is the likely wage path with continuous participation, and *ACDE* is the likely wage path if an individual is out of the labor force for the time period denoted by the two dashed lines. The wage penalty is shown in each figure as *DD'*.

Which job is a better choice depends on the profile selected. Occupation *k* has a higher wage, but a more substantial penalty, than occupation *j*.

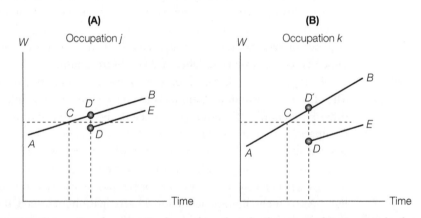

Figure 10.7 *Occupational segregation by gender—the role of wage penalties to periods of non-work.*

Clearly, for the individual who will work continuously, occupation *k* is the better choice. Technically it has a higher present value of earnings. However, if the worker plans to leave the labor market for a number of years, occupation *j* is probably better because he or she suffers a far smaller penalty. Thus the two occupations offer individuals a trade-off between wage levels and the penalty they will bear if they drop out of and then reenter the labor force. Individuals who expected to work continuously would probably congregate in occupation *k* and others like it, while individuals who expected to work intermittently would congregate in occupation *j* and others like it.

It's a small step to then argue that these factors could be part of the explanation of occupational segregation by gender. Women disproportionately end up in occupations like *j*, while men disproportionately choose occupations like *k*. The key point is that women, knowing they will likely go in and out of the labor market, pick jobs that penalize them less for doing so. For example, they choose to be a school teacher rather than a college professor, a clerk rather than a technician, a nurse rather than a doctor.

When this explanation was first proposed in the mid-1980s, it was highly contro-versial because it seemed to explain away occupational gender differences as an opti-mal choice. Like most such arguments, there probably is *something* to it. Teaching and nursing, two occupations with an obvious overrepresentation of women, are also occupations with a relatively small promotion ladder and thus a smaller penalty to lost years of experience. The empirical evidence on this explanation is mixed. The key rela-tionship is the link between an occupation's penalty rate and its share of employment of workers with intermittent labor-market attachment. If the hypothesis is correct, there ought to be a negative relationship with workers with intermittent work pat-terns choosing the low-penalty occupations. Some evidence supported this but other evidence did not.

Summary

In this chapter we have examined several major approaches for explaining why women earn less than men. Broadly put, earnings differences can exist either because the two groups of workers differ, on average, in their labor-market skills, or because they are treated differently in the labor-market, given the skills that they do have. The first of these is a human capital explanation; the second reflects labor-market discrimination. We also more briefly examined statistical discrimination and theories of occupational segregation.

A human capital explanation of male-female earnings differences does have some reso-nance. We know that married households have often utilized a gender-based division of labor, with men specializing in labor-market work and women in household production. A natural and inevitable consequence of that division is that, on average, married women spent far fewer years in the labor market than men did. This difference was quite large in earlier cohorts in which many women exited the labor market at marriage or at the birth of their first child and did not return, if at all, for many years. Differences in actual and/or expected labor-force participation rationally lead to differences in investment in human capital because the fewer years of participation lower the internal rate of return to an investment. It certainly doesn't help that the years of non-participation are those in which the present value of earnings is relatively high.

Becker's model of labor-market discrimination does a great job of showing how preju-dices could find their way into the demand for labor and could affect the relative wages that women, or other groups that are the victims of prejudice, earn. It also yields two important counterintuitive hypotheses: (1) The practice of discrimination is costly to the firms that practice it, and (2) strong competitive pressure might eliminate discriminatory firms from the market. Although this result is certainly not guaranteed, it is not an idea to ignore either.

When the human capital argument is combined with the "competition eliminates discrimination" argument, it leaves many more conservative economists believing that all earnings differences between groups in the labor market must be legitimate. In the next chapter we present statistical methods to examine the sources of the earnings gap between men and women. We then turn to studies that provide real-world evaluation and computation of the sources of the gender gap in earnings.

Appendix: present value analysis and the return to human capital

To evaluate the value of an investment in human capital, it is necessary to account for the fact that costs are incurred in the present while benefits are received in the future, often far in the future. This kind of analysis is called **present value analysis**. Here we first work through an example to show exactly why benefits in the future are worth less and then show how to use present value analysis to adjust for the time pattern of benefits and cost.

Suppose that it costs a student $75,000 to get a college education in direct and opportunity costs, and, in return, average earnings are expected to increase by $5,000 for each of 40 working years until retirement. Both of these numbers are low, and, in addition, the effect of education on income typically changes with age. The example is just meant to be illustrative and relatively easy to work with computationally. The total lifetime benefits are thus $200,000 (40 years × $5,000 per year). Has the student then made a $125,000 profit, the difference between the $200,000 return and the $75,000 costs? Absolutely not. Indeed, if we simply compare the costs to the benefits, we will have made an error of more than $100,000.

To see why benefits in the future are less valuable than current benefits, let's continue with this example. If the student had the $5,000 benefit this year instead of one year in the future, he or she could invest that $5,000 at, let's say, a 5 percent interest rate. At the end of the year the student would have the $5,000 invested (called the **principal**) plus interest earned of $250 (5% × $5,000) for a grand total of $5,250. Thus $5,000 available right now is equivalent to $5,250 in one year, at an interest rate of 5 percent. Despite the fact that the two sums look different, they are actually identical in present value—that is, once we account for the difference in the time period in which they are received.

At the end of two years, the original $5,000 would be worth $5,250 + (5% × $5,250) = $5,512.50, which is, again, the sum of principal plus earned interest. That means that $5,000 now is equivalent to $5,512.50 in two years at an interest rate of 5 percent. If the interest rate had been 10 percent, instead of 5 percent, the $5,000 today would be worth $5,500 after one year and $6,050 after two years.[35] This kind of analysis—finding the future value of current sums—is called **compounding to future value**.

Let's look more closely at the calculation of the value of $5,000 today in two years. Note that each year's value is equal to the previous year's value multiplied by $(1 + r)$, where r is the interest rate expressed as a decimal (e.g., 1.05 if the interest rate is 5 percent or 1.10 if the interest rate is 10 percent). Thus $5,250 (the value in year one) = $5,000 × 1.05 and $5,512.50 (the value in year two) = $5,250 (the value in year one) × 1.05. If we substitute for $5,250 from the first expression into the second one, we could rewrite the year two value as $5,512.50 = ($5,000 × 1.05) × 1.05 = $5,000 × 1.05^2. This is a very convenient substitution because it means that we can express the future value as a function of just the original value, the interest rate, and the number of intervening years. (This assumes that the interest rate is constant from year to year.)

Using this relationship, we can write a series of expressions for the future value of any current sum of money. Let Y_0 stand for the amount of money available now and $FV_1 (Y_0)$,

---

35 $5,000 + (0.10 × $5,000) = $5,500. $5,500 + (0.10 × $5,500) = $6,050.

FV_2 (Y_0), and FV_3 (Y_0) represent its future value in years 1, 2, and 3, respectively. Then we have the following relationships:

$$FV_1(Y_0) = Y_0 \times (1+r)$$

$$FV_2(Y_0) = FV_1(Y_0) \times (1+r) = [Y_0 \times (1+r)] \times (1+r) = Y_0 \times (1+r)^2$$

$$FV_3(Y_0) = FV_2(Y_0) \times (1+r) = [Y_0 \times (1+r)^2] \times (1+r) = Y_0 \times (1+r)^3$$

The general formula for finding the future value of any current sum in any year T is thus:

$$FV_T(Y_0) = Y_0 \times (1+r)^T \tag{10.5}$$

This equation shows that the future value of a current sum equals that sum multiplied by one plus the interest rate raised to a power equal to the number of years between now and then. This is exactly the equivalent of the arithmetic we did in the preceding paragraph. This is the basic formula for compounding.[36]

We can use these formulas to compute quickly and easily the future value of any sum in any future year at any possible interest rate. For example, at a 5 percent interest rate 0.05),

$$FV_1(\$5,000) = \$5,000 \times 1.05^1 = \$5,250.00$$

$$FV_2(\$5,000) = \$5,000 \times 1.05^2 = \$5,512.50$$

$$FV_{10}(\$5,000) = \$5,000 \times 1.05^{10} = \$8,144.47$$

$$FV_{20}(\$5,000) = \$5,000 \times 1.05^{20} = \$13,266.49, \text{ and so on.}$$

For finding the value of an investment in human capital, it is usually more convenient to reverse the problem and find the **present value** of money received in the future. That approach makes sense because the investment in human capital will yield benefits in the future; we need to compare those benefits to the costs, which are typically incurred now. Fortunately, this involves nothing more than turning the arithmetic and equations around. The present value of a future sum is the amount of money which, if it were available today, would grow (via compounding) to that sum in that year. It is the value of that future sum right now. Because we already know that $5,000 grows to $5,250 in one year, $5,512.50 in two years, and $8,144.47 in ten years (if the interest rate is 5%), it follows that the present values at a 5 percent interest rate are $5,250 in 1 year, $5,512.50 in 2 years, and $8,144.47 in 10 years are all exactly $5,000.

The general formula for finding the present value of a current sum is exactly the opposite of equation (10.5). We already know that $Y_1 = Y_0 \times (1 + r)$, where we begin with Y_0 and want to find its future value Y_1. Now suppose that we know Y_1, the amount of money available next year, and want to find its present value Y_1 at interest rate r. By manipulating the compounding equation to solve for the present value (Y_0), we have $Y_0 = Y_1/(1 + r)$.

Thus the present value in year 0 of a sum Y_1 available one year from now is that sum divided by $(1 + r)$. This makes perfect sense in terms of the definition of the present

---

36 This compounding formula applies in the simple case where interest is received once a year at the end of the year. Most interest today is paid continuously. In that case the formula is conceptually similar but involves that strange numerical constant e. For our purposes this formula is perfectly fine.

value: it is precisely the current sum that would grow via compounding to the future sum. Proceeding in exactly the same way, we can find the present value of some amount of money available two years from now. From the compounding formula, we have $Y_2 = Y_0 \times (1 + r)^2$. It follows immediately that the present value is $Y_0 = Y_2/(1 + r)^2$. More generally, for any sum of money available t years in the future, the present value is

$$PV_0(Y_t) = Y_t/(1+r)^T \tag{10.6}$$

where we have used $PV_0(Y_t)$ to stand for the present value in year 0 of Y available in some year T. This equation shows that to find the present value of some future sum, we divide that sum by one plus the interest rate raised to a power equal to the number of years between then and now. This is the famous formula for discounting to present value. If we compare equations (10.5) and (10.6), we can see that discounting to present value is just compounding in reverse. Instead of multiplying the current sum by $(1 + r)^T$ to find its future value, we divide the future sum by the same factor, $(1 + r)^T$. The term $(1 + r)^T$ is often referred to as the **discount factor**.

Using this formula and applying it to the preceding numerical example, we would have

$$PV_0(\$5{,}250_1; 0.05) = \$5{,}250/1.05^1 = \$5{,}000$$

$$PV_0(\$5{,}512.50_2; 0.05) = \$5{,}512.50/1.05^2 = \$5{,}000$$

$$PV_0(\$8{,}144.47_{10}; 0.05) = \$8{,}144.47/1.05^{10} = \$5{,}000$$

In these equations, the subscripts 1, 2, and 10 on the dollar amounts refer to the year in which that sum is received, and the 0.05 refers to the interest rate. Using equation (10.6), it is possible to find the present value of any sum in any year at any interest rate.

Table 10.2 *Finding the present value of $Y and $1,000 in various years.*

Year	Present Value of $Y Available in the Future	Present Value of $1,000 Available in the Future at an Interest Rate of 5%
1	$\$Y/(1 + r)$	$952.38
2	$\$Y/(1 + r)^2$	$907.03
3	$\$Y/(1 + r)^3$	$863.84
4	$\$Y/(1 + r)^4$	$822.70
5	$\$Y/(1 + r)^5$	$783.53
10	$\$Y/(1 + r)^{10}$	$613.91
T	$\$Y/(1 + r)^T$	$\$1{,}000/1.05^T$

Table 10.2 summarizes what we have learned about finding the present value of a future sum. The second column shows the application of the formula for discounting any sum in a given year. The third column shows the actual present values of $1,000 in years 1 to 5 and 10 at an interest rate of 5 percent. Note how the value declines quite steeply; after ten years, $1,000 is worth only about 61 percent of its face value. As you should be able to see from the present value formula for year T, the present value of a sum depends on the year in which it is received and on the interest rate. The further in the future we go and the larger the interest rate is, the smaller the present value of any particular sum is.

Now let's return to our original problem, with initial costs of $75,000 and benefits of $5,000 per year for 40 years. Table 10.3 shows the computation of the present value of the benefits using an interest rate of 5 percent. Each entry in the table is the present value of $5,000 received in the corresponding year and is calculated following exactly the form of Table 10.2 and equation (10.6). Note how quickly the present value falls. By the 14th year the $5,000 benefit is worth not much more than $2,500; by the 19th year it is worth less than $2,000; and by the 33rd year it is worth less than $1,000. The very last row shows the present value of the entire 40-year stream of benefits, and, rather than $200,000, it is just a bit under $86,000—less than half its face value. This is the $100,000 mistake referred to earlier—it is, in fact, a $114,205 mistake, the difference between the $200,000 benefits received and the $85,795 present value of those benefits (at an interest rate of 5 percent). The mistake would be even worse at a higher interest rate because the present value of each future year's $5,000 would be smaller. At a lower interest rate the mistake would be a bit less serious.

Table 10.3 *Present value of $5,000 per year for 40 years at a 5 percent interest rate.*

Year	Present Value	Year	Present Value
1	$4,761.90	21	$1,794.71
2	$4,535.15	22	$1,709.25
3	$4,319.19	23	$1,627.86
4	$4,113.51	24	$1,550.34
5	$3,917.63	25	$1,476.51
6	$3,731.08	26	$1,406.20
7	$3,553.41	27	$1,339.24
8	$3,384.20	28	$1,275.47
9	$3,223.04	29	$1,214.73
10	$3,069.57	30	$1,156.89
11	$2,923.40	31	$1,101.80
12	$2,784.19	32	$1,049.33
13	$2,651.61	33	$999.36
14	$2,525.34	34	$951.77
15	$2,405.09	35	$906.45
16	$2,290.56	36	$863.29
17	$2,181.48	37	$822.18
18	$2,077.60	38	$783.03
19	$1,978.67	39	$745.74
20	$1,884.45	40	$710.23
Total Value, Years 1–40			$85,795

More generally, the present value of any stream of benefits B_0, B_1 ... B_T at interest rate r can be written as $PV(B_1 \ldots B_T) = \frac{B_1}{(1+r)} + \frac{B_2}{(1+r)^2} + \ldots + \frac{B_T}{(1+r)^T} = \sum_{t=1}^{T} \frac{B_t}{(1+r)^t}$

where Σ, the Greek letter sigma, is the summation sign. The term involving Σ is just a compact way to express a long sum of terms; the summation starts with $t = 1$ and goes through $t = T$. This is a very important expression.

Present value analysis is an integral part of wise financial planning. See Box 10.4 for examples of present value analysis in action.

Box 10.4

What's It Worth?

We all know the story of how Peter Minuet purchased Manhattan Island from the Native Americans for the piddling sum of $24 of goods. Implicit in the story is the wonderful bargain that Minuet made.

Indeed, $24 sounds like a very small amount of money for Manhattan Island, but it was quite a few years ago—in 1626, to be exact. We can find the approximate current value of that $24 by using the future value formula. We want to find the value of something like $24 \times (1 + r)^{390}$. Letting $r = 3\%$, this is $24 million, well under the current value of Manhattan. If $r = 5\%$, the sum grows to $4.4 billion, still short of the current valuation. But if $r = 7\%$, the current value exceeds $6.9 trillion.

Here's another example. Suppose you are saving for retirement. You want to know how much you must save this year to have $10,000 when you retire. Let's call that sum S (for savings). To find that sum, you need to solve for the present value of $10,000 by using the PV formula, $PV_0(Y_t) = Y_t/(1 + r)^t$, where T is the number of years until retirement and r is the interest rate at which you can invest your savings. Necessary savings S just equals this present value.

Suppose retirement is 40 years away and a worker can lock in an interest rate of 5 percent. Then the sum the worker needs now is $S = PV_0(Y_{40}) = \$10,000/1.05^{20}$. Solving this, you will find that you only need to put away $1,420. If retirement is only 20 years away, then $S = PV_0(Y_{20}) = \$10,000/1.05^{20}$ or $3,769. If retirement is only ten years away, you better start saving: you'll need to save $6,139 this year: $S = PV_0(Y_{10}) = \$10,000/1.05^{20} = \$6,139$.

Here's another example, this time involving saving to finance a child's college education. Suppose the child will need $20,000 per year for each of four years of college, and the child's parents want to put aside an amount in each of the next four years that will be sufficient to cover that amount. How much will they need to save? Again, this is just the present value of $20,000, so the amount the parents need in each year of saving is $20,000/(1 + r)^T$, where T is number of years until the child will begin college. If college is 18 years away and the parents can lock in a 5 percent interest rate, they must put away $8,310.41: $\$20,000/1.05^{18} = \$8,310.41$. If college is only 15 years away, they need to save $\$20,000/1.05^{15} = \$9,620.34$.

In practice, the amount the parents need to save is less than these amounts because they can save each year from now until college begins, rather than save in just the next four years. The logic behind that saving problem is similar to what we have done, but it is a bit more complicated. If the parents start saving when the child is born, then to accumulate $20,000 in 18 years at a 5 percent interest rate, the parents need to save $710.92 each year. The sum of the future values will total $20,000 in 18 years: $\$710.92 \times 11.05^{18} + \$710.92 + 1.05^{17} = \$710.92 \times 1.05^{16} + \ldots + \$710.92 = \$20,000$.

Net present value and the internal rate of return

Now we are ready to find the value of this hypothetical investment in a college education. Just how good an investment is it? This involves finding the **internal rate of return** to this particular set of costs and benefits. The internal rate of return is the interest rate at which the net present value of an investment equals zero. Instead of picking an interest rate and finding the net present value of the investment, here we solve for the interest rate that makes the net present value equal to zero. Expressed as an equation, the internal rate of return, denoted as r^*, is the interest rate at which $NPV(B_1, B_T, C; r^*) = 0$.

The internal rate of return is the interest rate r^* that solves the following expression:

$$\sum_{t=1}^{T} \frac{B_t}{(1+r^*)^t} = C$$

Continuing with the example we've been working with, we have $C = \$75,000$. In Table 10.3 we showed the present value of the benefits of a college education, using a 5 percent interest rate; the present value was \$85,795. This means that the internal rate of return must be greater than 5 percent. Why? Since the net present value of this investment is positive at that interest rate, we need to discount using a higher interest rate. The interest rate is in the denominator of the discounting formula, so as the interest rate gets larger, the present value gets smaller.

If we recalculate the present value using an interest rate of 6.0 percent, the present value of the benefits falls to \$75,231. That means the **net present value (NPV)** is now \$231, so the internal rate of return must be just a hair larger than 6.0 percent. In fact, using a spreadsheet program like Excel, it is easy to solve for the exact internal rate of return, which in this case is equal to precisely 6.024 percent. At this interest rate the present value of the benefits equals \$75,000 or, equivalently, the NPV equals zero. This tells us that this hypothetical investment in human capital earns a rate of return of 6.024 percent. The rate is not bad but it's not great either. Fortunately, an investment in a college education typically pays a much higher rate of return—something closer to 10–12 percent.

Equation (10.5) shows the factors that contribute to making the internal rate of return for an investment in human capital high or low. The internal rate of return will be greater when: (1) Costs are lower, (2) benefits in each period are greater, (3) benefits are received sooner rather than later, and/or (4) the total length of the benefit period is greater.

Optimal investment in human capital

How do individuals decide whether to make a particular investment in human capital? The internal rate of return to the investment is the key piece of information, indicating how valuable or productive the investment is. (We assume that each individual has a rough enough idea of costs and benefits to compute the rate of return.) In the preceding example, if an individual could invest the \$75,000 of college education costs in some other investment at an interest rate of 6.25 percent, he or she would be better off doing that than investing in him- or herself and earning 6.024 percent. But if that alternative investment opportunity paid only 5 percent or 5.5 percent, the individual would be better off investing in him- or herself. There might be reasons to go ahead even with a poor rate of return—maybe it's something the individual has been dying to do or the opportunity has benefits other than the increase in earnings. But from a purely monetary point of view, the decision about whether to invest in more human capital depends simply on a comparison of the internal rate of return with the return that can be earned investing the money elsewhere.

How much human capital should an individual acquire? Is there some best (maximizing) amount of human capital investment? Figure 10.8 illustrates the logic. The horizontal axis measures the amount of human capital, and the vertical axis measures the internal rate of return and the cost of funds, both represented as an interest rate. Look first at the supply curve. The supply curve represents the cost of investing in human capital, measured by the interest rate available on alternative uses of the money. In Figure 10.8 the supply curve is shown as horizontal at interest rate r_m, which means that the cost of funds is constant. By drawing it as horizontal, we are assuming that an individual can always earn a rate of return equal to r_m by investing in something other than human capital. The supply curve could be upward-sloping, but that wouldn't change anything important in the analysis.

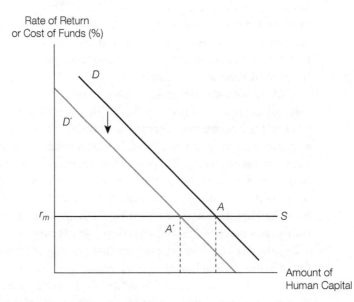

Figure 10.8 *Investing in human capital.*

With respect to the demand curve, the return to additional human capital typically falls the more human capital one has. One reason for this is the fact that working lifetimes are finite. The more time people spend acquiring human capital, the less time they have available to earn a return on it. Other things being equal, that would lower the rate of return. Imagine, for example, having multiple degrees. Of course, it's nice to acquire knowledge and to have numerous degrees, but this pursuit takes time. Most people wouldn't have the opportunity to receive the full potential value of the investment. Also, the more human capital people have, the higher their opportunity costs are, which would also reduce their internal rates of return. Human capital is probably also subject to diminishing marginal productivity. That would also lower the internal rate of return associated with additional human capital investment.

As a result, the demand curve for human capital would likely be downward-sloping, as shown in Figure 10.8. Two demand curves are shown in Figure 10.8; D' has a lower rate of return associated with every unit of human capital investment than D. This could happen for any reason that lowers the internal rate of return—higher costs, lower benefits, later benefits, and/or a shorter benefit period.

The investment rule is simple: An individual ought to invest in human capital just up to the point where the last unit acquired (i.e., the last year or last degree) yields an internal rate of return just equal to the return that could be earned elsewhere. This rule suggests that the rate of return to human capital ought to be quite close to the rate of return to physical capital. This is shown in Figure 10.8 as point A for demand curve D and point A' for demand curve D_j. Note the very important implication: Anything that lowers the internal rate of return lowers the amount of investment in human capital. An individual facing demand curve D' will invest in less human capital than an individual facing demand curve D.

11

THE GENDER GAP IN EARNINGS:
METHODS AND EVIDENCE

Introduction

In this chapter we finally examine empirical work on the gender gap in earnings, with the goal of trying to understand the core facts about the gender gap presented in Chapter 9 and the competing explanations surveyed in Chapter 10. To do that we first introduce the quantitative methods that are widely used in this kind of research. Then we discuss a series of important empirical studies of the gender earnings gap and its change over time, ranging from the 1950s through the 2010s. Then we look more briefly at employment discrimination and the interesting research methods used to analyze it. We close the chapter by looking at the effects of physical appearance on women's earnings and at the glass ceiling.

Methods for analyzing the gender gap in earnings

Regression analysis of earnings differences

Analyses of the gender gap inevitably involve using regression analysis of individual earnings. In Chapter 2 we reviewed the basics of regression analysis. Here we offer a brief summary and then show how it is used to analyze the gender gap in earnings.

Regression is a widely used statistical technique for measuring the relationship between an outcome of interest, such as earnings, and a set of potential explanatory or causal variables. The outcome is the **dependent** variable and the explanatory variables are the **independent** variables. We write a regression equation this way:

$$Y_i = \alpha + \beta_1 X_{i1} + \beta_2 X_{i2} + \beta_3 X_{i3} + \ldots + \mu_i \tag{11.1}$$

In equation (11.1), Y is the dependent variable, the Xs are the independent or explanatory variables, and μ ("mew") is the error term. μ represents the influence of factors that affect Y, but are unobserved by the researcher. μ is assumed to be normally distributed, like the familiar bell curve, with a mean of zero. The i subscript on Y, X, and μ means that each observation has his/her/its own value of Y, all the Xs, and μ. Finally, the Greek letters α and β (alpha and beta) are the **regression coefficients**. β measures the effect on Y of a one-unit change in X, holding constant or controlling for the values of all the other X variables. It corresponds to the thought experiment of changing just the one variable of interest, leaving all others the same. α is the constant term of the equation. It is the value of Y when all the Xs are equal to 0.

In regression analysis, a researcher uses information on the values of Y and the X variables to estimate the best values of α and β, written as $\hat{\alpha}$ and $\hat{\beta}$; the "hat" or "caret" indicates that these are estimated values. The best estimates make the predicted values of Y as close as possible to the actual values of Y.

In a regression analysis of individual earnings, the X variables typically include measures of human capital, like years of education and years of work experience, and usually also other personal characteristics, like race, ethnicity, and living in a big city vs. a small town or in a particular geographic area. In order to measure the effect of gender on earnings, researchers add a variable to indicate whether an individual is male or female. Obviously a variable like that does not have a natural numerical value, like years of education or experience do. It can, nevertheless, be included in a regression by constructing a **dummy variable**, which is just a clever way to assign a numerical value to a "yes/no" variable. For the male/female variable, it works this way: Create a variable called Female that equals 0 if a person is male and 1 if a person is female.

A very simple regression equation for earnings would then look like this:

$$\text{Earnings}_i = \alpha + \beta_1 \times \text{Years Educ}_i + \beta_2 \times \text{Years Work Exp}_i + \ldots + \delta \times \text{Female}_i + \mu_i \quad (11.2)$$

where the "..." means that other variables that affect earnings are also included.

In (11.2) the regression coefficient (δ) for the Female dummy variable measures the impact on earnings of being female rather than male, controlling for all the other explanatory variables included in the regression. If $\delta < 0$ and statistically significant (see Chapter 2 for details), this means that women are paid less than men with the same skills. If instead $\delta > 0$ and statistically significant, then women earn more than otherwise similar men. Finally, if δ is statistically insignificant, then there is no reliable difference in earnings between men and women with equal skills. In that case, gender has no effect on earnings. Similarly, questions about changes in the gender gap are exactly equivalent to changes in the estimated value of δ at different points in time. Is δ becoming less negative over time? Is it no longer statistically significant? Regression analysis of individual earnings is the standard way to answer these questions.

The Oaxaca decomposition of earnings differences

Regression analysis like equation (11.2) can be used to compute how much of the gender gap in earnings is due to differences in skills and how much is due to other factors, including discrimination. The most well-known technique to do this is the **Oaxaca decomposition**, named after Ronald Oaxaca, the economist who developed it.[1] It is widely used, both in economics and other social sciences, to account for differences in group averages in a wide range of outcomes, not just earnings. Using the Oaxaca decomposition, researchers can say something like "40 percent of the gender wage gap is due to gender differences in measures of skills" or "20 percent of the wage difference is due to gender differences in the market value of education." These are very useful summary statements. Here's how it works.

The gender wage gap is $\overline{Y}_M - \overline{Y}_F$, the difference in average earnings. Now suppose that earnings for men and women depend on only a single factor, denoted as X. This

---

1 Oaxaca's name is pronounced something like "wah-hocka."

simplification is only for purposes of exposition. In practice the method is always applied to the case of multiple measures, such as education and years of work experience; we will consider that case after the simple case. The corresponding regression earnings equations for men and women are then simply $Y_{iM} = \beta_M X_{iM} + \mu_{iM}$ for men and $Y_{iF} = \beta_F X_{iF} + \mu_{iF}$ for women. (Note that we have dropped the constant term, α, again just for ease of exposition.) $\hat{\beta}_M$ is the estimated effect of X on Y for men and $\hat{\beta}_F$ is the corresponding effect for women. The average values of X_M and X_F are $\overline{X}_M$ and $\overline{X}_F$.

A remarkably simple and useful arithmetic relationship links $\overline{Y}$, $\overline{X}$, and $\hat{\beta}$:

$$\overline{Y} = \hat{\beta}\overline{X} \tag{11.3}$$

This equation holds for any regression. In words, it says that average earnings for a group of workers equals their average level of skills multiplied by the per-unit value of those skills. Suppose, for example, that education was the only factor that influenced earnings and that, on average, an additional year of education increased earnings by $2,500. Then, if working women had an average of 12 years of education, their average earnings would be $30,000.

The relationship in equation (11.3) necessarily holds for both men and women. Substituting into the expression for the gender earnings gap, we have:

$$\overline{Y}_M - \overline{Y}_F = \hat{\beta}_M \overline{X}_M - \hat{\beta}_F \overline{X}_F \tag{11.4}$$

Equation (11.4) suggests that average earnings for men and women could differ either because $\overline{X}$ differs or because $\hat{\beta}$ differs—that is, either because the average level of labor-market skills differs by gender or because the market value of those skills differs. The first of these is a human capital explanation; the latter sounds a lot like discrimination. After all, if women earn less than men with the same skills, this should show up as a lower value (β) for the skills they have.

Now the key to the Oaxaca decomposition is to add and subtract $\hat{\beta}_M \overline{X}_F$ to the right side of equation (11.4); since the sum of the two terms is zero, the equality in (11.4) still holds.[2] Rearranging and combining terms yields the famous Oaxaca decomposition of differences in means:[3]

$$\overline{Y}_M - \overline{Y}_F = [\hat{\beta}_M \times (\overline{X}_M - \overline{X}_F)] + [(\hat{\beta}_M - \hat{\beta}_F) \times \overline{X}_F] \tag{11.5}$$

The first term in brackets on the right side of equation (11.5) is the gender difference in average levels of human capital, multiplied by $\hat{\beta}_M$, the value of a unit of X for men. It represents the dollar amount of the gender wage difference that can be attributed to differences in average skills. For this term to be quantitatively important there must be large gender differences in $\overline{X}$ and the skill involved must be valuable. (Men and women differ in many ways, such as average height and weight, which may be of little or no broad labor-market significance.) This portion of the gender earnings gap is usually referred to as the "explained" portion of the wage gap. This portion would exist even if there were no labor-market discrimination.

---

2 We could, instead, add and subtract $\hat{\beta}_F \overline{X}_M$ and get a slightly different version of equation (11.5). It is more common to proceed as we are doing here.

3 If we expand the terms on the right side of equation (11.5), two terms cancel out. There is a $-\hat{\beta}_M \overline{X}_F$ in the first term and a $+\hat{\beta}_M \overline{X}_F$ in the second term. That leaves us with the original difference, $\hat{\beta}_M \overline{X}_M - \hat{\beta}_F \overline{X}_F$.

The second term in brackets on the right side of equation (11.5) is the difference in the market value of skills for men and women—the difference in the $\hat{\beta}$s—multiplied by the average skill level of women. This term measures the dollar amount of the gender wage gap that is the result of differences in the monetary return or reward for skills. Think of it as how much more women would earn if they had their current skills but were rewarded for those skills as men are. It is often referred to as the "unexplained" portion of the earnings gap and is usually interpreted as evidence of discrimination. If, for example, women with the same skills as men ended up in lower-paying occupations, this would be reflected in lower values of $\hat{\beta}$ for women's education or experience. But it could also reflect different occupational choices based on preferences for the job or its other characteristics.

Researchers usually divide equation (11.5) by the total wage gap $(\overline{Y}_M - \overline{Y}_F)$ to put the two terms in percentage terms. The explained portion is then $(\hat{\beta}_M \times (\overline{X}_M - \overline{X}_F))/(\overline{Y}_M - \overline{Y}_F)$ and the unexplained portion is $((\hat{\beta}_M - \hat{\beta}_F) \times \overline{X}_F)/(\overline{Y}_M - \overline{Y}_F)$. Together, the two parts add up to 100 percent.

Table 11.1 presents a simple example of how a Oaxaca decomposition works. Suppose the mean values for the two groups are as shown in the table with $\overline{Y}_M > \overline{Y}_F$, $\overline{X}_M > \overline{X}_F$, and $\hat{\beta}_M > \hat{\beta}_F$. Note that the basic relationship between the means holds: $\overline{Y} = \hat{\beta}\overline{X}$ for both groups. The explained term is $\hat{\beta}_M \times (\overline{X}_M - \overline{X}_F) = \$3,000 \times (15 - 10) = \$15,000$. The unexplained term is $(\hat{\beta}_M - \hat{\beta}_F) \times \overline{X}_F = (\$3,000 - \$2,500) \times 10 = \$5,000$.

Table 11.1 *A numerical example of a Oaxaca decomposition of earnings differences.*

	Women	Men
$\overline{Y}$	$25,000	$45,000
$\overline{X}$	10	15
$\hat{\beta}$	$2,500	$3,000
Explained: $\hat{\beta}_M \times (\overline{X}_M - \overline{X}_F) = \$3,000 \times (15 - 10) = \$15,000$		
Unexplained: $(\hat{\beta}_M - \hat{\beta}_F) \times \overline{X}_F = (\$3,000 - \$2,500) \times 10 = \$5,000$		

In this example, of the original $20,000 difference in mean earnings, $15,000 is the result of differences in average skills, and $5,000 can be attributed to a difference in rewards. In terms of percentages, 25 percent of the gross or unadjusted difference is caused by the difference in treatment ($5,000/$20,000) and 75 percent by the difference in mean skill levels ($15,000/$20,000).

In a real-world analysis of this sort, many X variables, like education, years of work experience, and marital status, are included. It is possible to apply the same approach individually to each variable For example, if $\hat{\beta}_{ED,M}$ is the estimated value of a year of education for men, and $\overline{X}_{ED,M}$ and $\overline{X}_{ED,F}$ are the average amounts of education for men and women, then the explained contribution of education to the gender earnings gap is $\hat{\beta}_{ED,M} \times (\overline{X}_{ED,M} - \overline{X}_{ED,F})$ and the unexplained part due to education is $(\hat{\beta}_{ED,M} - \hat{\beta}_{ED,F}) \times \overline{X}_{ED,F}$. These terms are exactly like the overall measures shown in equation (11.5). Similar terms could be constructed for each variable of interest, thereby pinpointing which factors were most responsible for the difference in earnings. Dividing the two terms by the total wage gap puts them in percentage terms. So the portion of the gender earnings gap explained by differences in education is $(\hat{\beta}_{ED,M} \times (\overline{X}_{ED'M} - \overline{X}_{ED'F})) / (\overline{Y}_M - \overline{Y}_F)$, and the portion due to differences in returns to education is $((\hat{\beta}_{ED,M} - \hat{\beta}_{ED,F}) \times \overline{X}_{ED'F}) / (\overline{Y}_M - \overline{Y}_F)$.

A similar procedure can be used to examine the change in the gender wage gap over time. The formula gets much more complicated—it involves not just differences by gender but differences in differences—and we do not show it here. But the underlying idea is exactly the same. The gender gap in wages could get smaller over time either because average skill differences decrease and/or because differences in rewards decrease. By comparing mean characteristics of male and female workers and estimating the βs for men and women at two points in time, all the necessary terms can be constructed. We discuss an example of this later on when we examine the time trend in the gender gap.

Going further The Oaxaca decomposition procedure is a very valuable tool but it has its limitations. The burden of proof in this analysis is on the explanatory variables. We are not testing directly for the presence of discrimination; rather, we are looking for indirect evidence in the sense that there are wage differences unrelated to average differences in skills. This leads to two problems, both related to the X variables that are included in the model.

First, it is possible to include too many X variables, specifically to include variables that are themselves the product of discrimination. Suppose that we could somehow measure the jobs that men and women held so that we were then comparing wages for men and women doing the exact same job. We might well find that there were little or no earnings differences between men and women doing the same job and thus that all of the gender earnings difference is explained. But suppose discrimination operated to influence the jobs that men and women got, so that, for example, many women ended up in jobs that were not particularly good relative to their skills. (Think of women becoming nurses and men becoming doctors, for example.) In that case, controlling for the job controls for too much—it throws out the baby with the bath water. For example, some researchers include a measure of a worker's occupation in an analysis of the gender gap in earnings. That is usually inappropriate, however, if women and men end up in different occupations as a result of discrimination in the labor market.

In some cases, including measures of education may be inappropriate if differences in education reflect discrimination in the provision of education. The appropriate rule is this: Don't include any variables that themselves may reflect discrimination.

At the same time it is possible to have too few X variables so that the skills of men and women are not being accurately and appropriately compared. Truthfully, the information available to researchers is quite limited—race, gender, age, years of education, measures of where an individual lives, and sometimes a measure of actual years of work experience. Much is left out, and even the variables included, such as years of education, are often measured less than ideally.[4]

How do left-out variables affect the Oaxaca procedure? Suppose that a researcher leaves out some important variable in which men greatly outscore women and which is important in determining earnings for both men and women. Omitting that variable might cause the researcher to underestimate the portion of the wage gap that is explained

---

4 Certainly the quality of education varies across individuals with the same amount of education, as do majors. Don't, however, go overboard and conclude that these studies are useless. They are imperfect but helpful.

by differences in skills. This is actually just another example of omitted bias, an idea we first discussed back in Chapter 2. Here the omitted variable is correlated with gender and with earnings.

Many researchers seem to assume that omitted variables will lead to exactly that result. They may well be right. But Barbara Bergmann, a well-known feminist economist, reminds us about "the missing data that would show men's qualifications and behavior in a bad light relative to women's ... [such as] men's greater tendency to alcohol abuse, drug abuse, smoking, bad driving, back problems, [and] history of heart attacks" (p. 45).[5] Excluding information about these characteristics might cause researchers to overestimate the skills portion.

In the end, the Oaxaca technique must be used, like so many things, carefully and with an appreciation for what is included and excluded. The Oaxaca technique is valuable and far better than simply making guesses, but it is not perfect. Studies with more variables (but not the inappropriate endogenous ones discussed earlier) are likely to be more trustworthy than those with very few. Pay attention to the details.

The evidence—why do women earn less than men?

A truly enormous number of studies have examined the sources of earnings differences between men and women in different time periods and places. In this section we focus on several representative and well-known studies, especially ones that use the research methods discussed here; we organize them more or less chronologically to provide an historical overview of gender earnings differences. In this chapter our focus is on the United States, although the method has been applied to data from European countries as well. Gender earnings issues in developing countries are discussed in Chapter 14. We also briefly consider a number of narrower studies that examine earnings differences in specialized occupations or subgroups, or that focus on particular dimensions of earnings differences.

1960–1980: change beneath the surface

Between roughly 1960 and 1980 the gender median earnings ratio for YRFT workers in the United States was remarkably steady at about 59 percent. June O'Neill, a well-known economist who served as the first woman to head the US Congressional Budget Office, examined the time trend between 1955 and 1982.[6] Although the gender earnings ratio was stable over this time period, a great deal was happening beneath the surface. For example, the LFPR of women increased substantially, especially for married women, whose LFPR doubled from 25 percent in 1955 to about 50 percent in the early 1980s. It would be surprising if that kind of change didn't have some impact on the earnings ratio.

O'Neill found that in the early 1950s, women who were in the labor force had completed an average of 12 years of education, compared to just 10.4 years for men. That's an

5 Barbara Bergmann (1989), "Does the Market for Women's Labor Need Fixing?" *Journal of Economic Perspectives*, 3 (1), 43–60.
6 June O'Neill (1985), "The Trend in the Male-Female Wage Gap in the United States," *Journal of Labor Economics*, 3 (1), S91–S116.

enormous difference, which reflected primarily the more selective nature of labor-force participation for women than men in that time period. It was not true that women had more education than men overall, but rather that *working* women had more education than *non-working* women. Over the next two decades, average years of education rose steadily for working men—this was a time of rising educational attainment and growing college enrollments for men, aided by the GI Bill—all the way up to 12.7 years in 1982. But for working women there was a smaller 0.7 year increase in educational attainment because educational attainment rose more slowly and because labor-force participation became less selective. O'Neill notes that the participation rates of older married women with less education increased particularly rapidly. By the early 1980s the entire 1.6 year educational advantage of working women was eliminated.

Something fairly similar was also happening in terms of the average work experience of working women compared to working men. As "cycling" back and forth between the labor market and household production emerged as a norm in the 1950s and early 1960s, this had a negative impact on the average work experience of working women. It is not hard to see why. Women who returned to the labor market in, for example, their mid-thirties had left the labor market perhaps a decade or more ago and returned with little experience. These new entrants pulled down average years of labor-force experience of working women because, up to then, the female work force had been heavily composed of women with steadier work patterns. Combining family and work was a new development.

This decrease shows up in the data. Information on job tenure with current employer shows a pattern of rising gender differences during the mid-1950s and through the 1960s. For example, among men and women aged 35 to 44, there was a 1.4-year difference in job tenure in favor of men in 1951, which rose to 4.0 years in 1963, stayed at greater than 4 years throughout the 1960s, finally dropping to between 3.1 and 3.3 years in the mid-1970s. For men and women aged 45–54, the job tenure difference increased from 3.6 years in 1951 to 6.2 years in 1968 and was still above 5 years in 1981.

These changes in education and experience by gender have direct implications for the gender earnings ratio. Suppose that there had been no changes at all in the rewards to education and work experience by gender over this time period. Because the gap in educational attainment, which had favored women, was eliminated and the gap in work experience in favor of men expanded, women's earnings would have fallen relative to men's earnings. In fact, as we know, women's earnings did not fall relative to men's but rather stayed virtually constant. This tells us that the rewards for women's skills must have increased over this time period relative to the rewards for men's skills to offset the decline in women's average skills compared to men's.

In terms of the Oaxaca technique, virtually all the gender wage difference in the 1950s would be "unexplained." The explained portion is $\hat{\beta}_M \times (\overline{X}_M - \overline{X}_F)/(\overline{Y}_M - \overline{Y}_F)$; since $\overline{X}_M - \overline{X}_F$ was close to zero or even favored women, it follows that the explained portion would have been very low. It also makes sense that the unexplained portion, based on differences in the market value of skills, was large. Women with college degrees didn't have access to the full range of occupations but were largely in low-paying fields like nursing and teaching. Thus it follows that $\hat{\beta}_M > \hat{\beta}_F$. But by the early 1980s the gender gap reflected the greater skill differences by gender in addition to differences in treatment and opportunity, which had, in fact, declined. The "explained" portion of the gender gap thus increased and the unexplained portion declined.

Work histories and human capital

In another very well-known study, Mary Corcoran and Greg Duncan examined gender wage differences as of the mid-1970s.[7] They analyzed data from a national survey of working men and women that was specifically designed to measure many of the important but difficult-to-measure individual traits that could affect earnings and potentially explain the gender earnings gap.[8] For example, it asked very detailed questions about men's and women's work histories, including how many times an individual had stopped working and how long he/she had stayed out of the labor force since finishing school. Previous studies usually lacked this kind of detailed information and resorted to various indirect and imperfect ways to measure work history; often researchers measured total work experience as a person's age minus their years of education minus six under the assumption that schooling starts at age six. For men, who tend to have fewer workforce interruptions, this measure worked reasonably well, but since women were more likely to work intermittently, it provided a poor measure of their actual work experience.

Corcoran and Duncan estimated earnings regressions separately for men and women by race and then used those estimates to carry out an Oaxaca decomposition. Table 11.2 summarizes their basic findings concerning wage and skill differences separately for white

Table 11.2 *Explaining the US gender gap in earnings, 1976.*

A. Average Wage Rate and Human Capital			
Skill or Characteristic	White Men	White Women	Black Women
Hourly wage rate	$5.60	$3.61	$3.17
Years of education	12.9	12.7	11.8
Work history			
Years not in labor force	0.5	5.8	4.0
Years with current employer	8.8	5.7	6.5
Years other work experience	11.3	8.1	9.3
Years part-time (%)	9.0%	21.0%	17.4%
Indicators of labor-force attachment			
Hours of work missed (illness)	40.5	55.5	83.7
Placed limits on job hours or location	14.5%	34.2%	21.6%
B. Sources of the Wage Gap between White and Black Women and White Men			
Explained			
Years of education	—	2%	11%
Work history	—	39%	22%
Labor-force attachment	—	3%	0%
Total	—	44%	33%
Unexplained	—	56%	67%

Source: Mary Corcoran and Greg J. Duncan (1979), "Work History, Labor Force Attachment and Earnings Differences Between the Races and Sexes," *Journal of Human Resources,* 14 (1).

---

7 Mary Corcoran and Greg J. Duncan (1979), "Work History, Labor Force Attachment and Earnings Differences Between the Races and Sexes," *Journal of Human Resources,* 14 (1), 3–20.

8 The survey is the Panel Study of Income Dynamics, a landmark study that has interviewed a nationally representative sample of US families since 1967.

women and black women, both compared to white men. Part A of the table presents information on average differences in the measures and Part B shows the net impact of these differences on the wage gap.

Part A shows that white men earned considerably more than women (although note how low, by today's standards, average 1976 wages were). White women earned 65 percent of what white men earned and black women earned about 57 percent. Differences in years of education between white men and women were minuscule, while black women had 1.1 fewer years of education. This tells us immediately that years of education cannot be an important factor explaining earnings differences between white men and women, but it could be important for explaining the lower earnings of black women. Differences by gender do exist for measures of work history and work attachment. Both white and black women had been out of the labor force for more years than white men and had worked fewer years with their current employer and fewer years prior to their current job. They had also worked more years part-time, missed more hours of work as a result of illness (both their own and that of other family members), and were more likely to have placed limits on job hours or location. This tells us that these measures could be important factors explaining the gender earnings gap.

In Panel B the net impacts on the gender wage gap are shown. Recall that for a particular variable to be an important explanation of wage differences (1) there must be a substantial average difference between the two groups, and (2) the variable itself must be valuable to the higher-earning group. As we suggested earlier, education explained virtually none (2 percent) of the wage gap between white men and women and somewhat more (11 percent) of the wage gap between white men and black women. Work history differences were far more important, accounting for 39 percent of the wage difference between white men and white women and 22 percent of the wage difference between white men and black women. The reason for the smaller effect for black women is that the differences in work history between white men and black women were less than the corresponding differences between white men and white women. This is quite consistent with the historical pattern of labor-force participation in which black married women typically worked more than white married women. The indicators of labor-force attachment turned out to have virtually no effect, even though there were gender differences. The reason is that the measures of labor-force attachment had little or no impact on the wage rates of white men: white men with more absences or more job restrictions did not earn less than white men with fewer absences and restrictions.

The bottom line from this study is that only 44 percent of the wage gap was explained for white women and 33 percent for black women, even though the researchers used an extensive set of explanatory variables. Corcoran and Duncan concluded "that the wage advantages enjoyed by white men cannot be explained solely or even primarily by superior qualifications or more attachment to the labor force" (p. 19).

Convergence in the 1980s

As we have already seen, the 1980s were the decade when much of the increase in women's earnings relative to men's occurred. The YRFT median earnings ratio increased more than 11 percent from 60.2 percent in 1980 to 71.6 percent in 1990. In a well-known study, Blau and Kahn analyzed earnings of full time non-agricultural workers aged 18 to 65 in 1979 and 1988.[9] We can use a Oaxaca-style approach to summarize what they found. On the "explained" side of the Oaxaca decomposition, the gender gap in average work experience fell substantially between 1979 and 1988, from 7.5 years to 4.6 years, reflecting the now more continuous nature of women's labor-force participation. In 1979 the work experience difference alone caused women's earnings to be 14 percent lower than men's, even if the women had been rewarded for their work experience in the same way that men were. This is just a standard Oaxaca-style computation in which the difference in average years of work experience is multiplied by the return to experience for men. In this case, however, instead of converting the result into a percentage of the wage gap, we are expressing it as a direct wage difference in percentage terms. But by 1988 the now-smaller work experience difference would have accounted for a smaller 9 percent earnings gap, even if the wage structure had been the same as it had been in 1979. This is a cross-year Oaxaca-style term: $\hat{\beta}_{M,1979} \times (\overline{X}_{EXP,M,1988} - \overline{X}_{EXP,F,1988})$.

Other skill differences between men and women were quite small and stable over time. In 1979 women had almost the same total years of education as the men, although they were still a little less likely to be college graduates and much less likely to have an advanced degree. In 1979 these differences were responsible for making women's earnings about 2 percent less than men's. By 1988, with the continuing narrowing of the educational differences, the impact was 0.2 percent.

In addition, the wage structure changed in the 1980s, narrowing some of the rewards differences between men and women that favored men. This is related to the "unexplained" portion of the Oaxaca decomposition. The biggest change was in the constant term of the equation, which functions in a wage regression like an across-the-board addition to men's and women's earnings that is separate from returns to specific traits like education and work experience. In 1979 the difference in the constant term greatly favored men; in effect, men earned 45 percent more than women more or less independent of the particular skills involved. By 1988 this factor dropped to just 8 percent. Some other factors worked in the opposite direction, however, so the net effect was smaller than this.

The slowdown in the convergence of the gender earnings ratio in the 1990s reflected both the slowdown in the convergence of skill differences and in returns to skills. Between 1988 and 1999 the gender difference in years of full-time work experience declined by 0.7 years, just about one-third of the convergence in the 1980s. Women's gains in education partly made up for this; we already know that this is the time period in which women's college graduation rates surpassed men's, and women continued to increase their rates of professional and other postgraduate education. In addition, it appears that differences in returns to skills by gender stabilized.

The family gap

The early literature on the gender gap discussed above emphasized human capital issues, especially the lower average years of work experience of women, as a potential

9   Francine D. Blau and Lawrence M. Kahn (1997), "Swimming Upstream: Trends in the Gender Wage Differential in the 1980s," *Journal of Labor Economics*, 15 (1) (Part 1), 1–42. Information for the 1990s is derived from Francine D. Blau and Lawrence M. Kahn (2004), "The U.S. Gender Pay Gap in the 1990s: Slowing Convergence," NBER Working Paper 10853.

explanation for the lower earnings of women. In this literature, family responsibilities played an important, behind-the-scenes role. They were the primary reason that women might have less human capital than their male peers and, as a result, receive lower wages. But in those studies, this impact of family responsibilities is indirect, operating through its impact on human capital investment, exactly as we discussed in Chapter 10.

In contrast, the **family gap** literature focuses on the direct impact of family responsibilities, over and above any impact it may have on human capital investment. It does this by including measures of family and marital status in an earnings regression along with the traditional measures of human capital for both men and women. As a result, researchers can examine how family and marital status affect male and female earnings and how they contribute to the gender earnings gap. After all, we still expect that men and women will marry and, more often than not, have children. How do marriage and children affect men's and women's earnings when both are active labor-market participants?

A well-known early study of the family gap is by Jane Waldfogel, who analyzed the impact of marriage and family responsibilities on the earnings of young men and women (average age 30) in 1980 and 1991.[10] Waldfogel estimated a wage regression in which she included not only the standard measures of human capital (education and experience) but also an individual's current marital status, previous marital status, and whether he/she had one child or more than one. A summary of her findings for 1991 is presented in Table 11.3. The figures shown in the table are the standard Oaxaca decomposition percentages.[11]

In 1991 the young women earned 81 percent of what the young men earned. Human capital differences were quite small. The difference in educational attainment was slightly in favor of women and the difference in work experience was only half a year in favor of the men; remember that these are young women of a more recent cohort, many of whom had a very steady pattern of labor-force participation. Differences in the value of education and experience for men and women were also very small.

Table 11.3 *The impact of human capital and family status on earnings, US men and women, age 25–35, 1991.*

Variable	Contribution to Wage Gap	
	Explained Portion (%)	Unexplained Portion (%)
Human Capital Measures		
Years of Education	−6	13
Years of Work Experience	10	23
Family Situation		
Married	−5	22
Children	−3	40
All other variables	−4	10
Total	−8	108

Source: Figures in the table are derived from estimates presented in Jane Waldfogel (1998), "Understanding the 'Family Gap' in Pay for Women with Children," *Journal of Economic Perspectives*, 12 (1), 137–156.

---

10 Jane Waldfogel (1998), "Understanding the 'Family Gap' in Pay for Women with Children," *Journal of Economic Perspectives*, 12 (1), 137–156.

11 Waldfogel uses a different and far less common form of the Oaxaca decomposition. We have transformed her results into the standard form.

The impact of this is shown in the second row of Table 11.3. The first row shows the impact of human capital variables. Differences in educational attainment explained −6 percent of the wage gap. The negative sign is not a misprint, although it is not what is typically found in analyses like this. It does, however, make sense; the negative sign means that rather than accounting for some portion of the gender wage gap, the gender difference in education would actually cause women to have higher wages than men.[12] The small difference in work experience explained 10 percent of the wage gap. As seen in the third column, differences in the value of education for men and women accounted for 13 percent of the gap, and differences in the value of work experience accounted for 23 percent.

The next row shows the impact of marriage and motherhood on earnings. Again, the explained portion is small and is actually in favor of women. Differences in the proportions married and in the number of children accounted for −5 percent and −3 percent, respectively. The important part of the story is in the unexplained column, which summarizes differences in the impacts of marriage and children on men's and women's wages. In her regression analysis, Waldfogel found that marriage increased the earnings of men by 11 percent and of women by 4 percent (these results are not shown in the table). Having children had no effect at all on men's earnings, but it decreased women's earnings by approximately 10 percent if she had one child and 20 percent if she had two or more. Those gender differences in the impact of marriage and children yield the figures in the "unexplained portion" column. Differences in the way men's and women's earnings were affected by marriage accounted for 22 percent of the gender earnings gap, and differences in the way their earnings were affected by having children accounted for another 40 percent. Voila! We have the family gap.

In all, the differences by gender in human capital and in marriage and family variables account for −8 percent of the wage gap, meaning that they would cause women to have higher wages than men. But differences in the impacts of these variables explain 108 percent of the gap, so that together the two parts exactly explain the entire wage gap (as mathematically they must). On the basis of this evidence, Waldfogel argued that family factors, not human capital, were the primary cause of the gender earnings gap as of the 1990s.

When she repeated her analysis for 1980, she found two important differences. First, the explained portion of the earnings gap was greater—about 27 percent, which is much more in line with other studies for that time period. Second, the impact of family responsibilities was important, but much less so than in 1991. Waldfogel found that differences in the impact of family status on male and female earnings accounted for about one-third of the earnings gap in 1980, compared to more than 60 percent in 1991.

Some economists and policy analysts now argue that the family gap is the major impediment to wage equality between young men and women, like the ones analyzed by Waldfogel. Human capital differences have shrunk and will continue to shrink, an inevitable consequence of the new patterns of women's educational attainment, fertility and

---

12 Suppose that the gender wage gap was \$3.00 per hour. Then the −6% figure would mean that gender differences in years of education would cause women to have average wages that were \$0.18 per hour higher (\$0.18 = 0.06 × \$3.00). In the Oaxaca formula, the unexplained portion due to education is $\hat{\beta}_{ED,M} \times (\overline{X}_{ED,M} - \overline{X}_{ED,F})/(\overline{Y}_M - \overline{Y}_F)$. Usually the higher wage group has more of the underlying skill, so the numerator is positive. But if women have more education than men, then $\overline{X}_{ED,M} < \overline{X}_{ED,F}$, and if $\hat{\beta}_{ED,M} > 0$, the numerator will be negative.

labor-force participation. And differences in the value of education and work experience to men and women have also shrunk and will, in all likelihood, continue to shrink. That leaves primarily marriage and children as factors that disproportionately affect women and their earnings.

The last chapter?

Claudia Goldin, whose work we have seen many times in this text, presented a lecture titled "A Gender Convergence: Its Last Chapter" in her role as president of the American Economic Association in 2014.[13] Because hers is such an important and knowledgeable voice in understanding women's economic position, it is well worth taking a close look at what she says there about what does and does not explain the still lower earnings of US women. She focuses especially on occupational wage differences, because it is sometimes argued that the gender earnings gap is largely a direct result of the gender difference in occupations and, as we established in Chapter 9, many occupations remain today quite gender-segregated. Goldin shows that earnings differences by gender *within* occupations are far more important than earnings differences by gender *between* those occupations. And that finding leads her to focus on the role of flexibility on the job and its impact on earnings across occupations.

Her analysis is based on data on annual earnings, occupation, and other characteristics for more than 2.6 million US men and women in 2009–2011 from a Census Bureau survey called the American Community Survey. An individual's occupation is measured by a set of nearly 500 categories.[14] That is a very detailed list of occupations, to say the least, although there are still differences in the specific nature of jobs within even this level of detail. To evaluate the importance of occupational differences by gender, Goldin computed what the gender gap would be if women had their actual average earnings in each of these occupations but had the occupational distribution of men instead of their own. The key insight behind this comparison is that the average earnings of men or women is just a weighted average of their earnings in each occupation, where the weights are the percentage of men (or women) employed in that occupation. We can write this algebraically this way: $\overline{Y}_F = \Sigma \alpha_{jF} \overline{Y}_{jF}$, where α_{jF} is the proportion of women working in occupation j and $\overline{Y}_{jF}$ is their average earnings. For men, $\overline{Y}_M = \Sigma \alpha_{jM} \overline{Y}_{jM}$. Written this way, it is clear that average earnings by gender can differ either because the occupational distribution differs by gender ($\alpha_{jF} \neq \alpha_{jM}$) or because average earnings by occupation differ ($\overline{Y}_{jF} \neq \overline{Y}_{jM}$).

To assess the importance of occupational differences by gender, Goldin computed $\hat{Y}_F = \Sigma \alpha_{jM} \overline{Y}_{jF}$. $\hat{Y}_F$ is the average earnings women would have using the male occupational distribution (α_{jM}) to weight female earnings in each occupation, rather than their own occupational distribution. The closer $\hat{Y}_F$ is to $\overline{Y}_M$, the more important are occupational distribution differences by gender and the less important are average earnings differences

---

13 Claudia Goldin (2015), "A Grand Gender Convergence: Its Last Chapter," *American Economic Review*, 104 (4), 1091–1119. Most of this article is fully accessible to students using this textbook.

14 Each occupation is a dummy variable, coded 1 if a person works in that occupation and 0 otherwise. Including occupation as an explanatory variable is usually inappropriate in a wage equation because it may itself reflect discrimination, thereby potentially making the "explained" part of the Oaxaca decomposition too large. In this case this is not a problem because Goldin is interested in getting an upper-bound estimate of the effect of the occupational distribution on the gender gap.

within each occupation. If, instead, $\hat{Y}_F$ is close to $\overline{Y}_F$, just the opposite is true: occupational distribution differences by gender are less important and average earnings differences within each occupation more important.

When Goldin carried out this exercise, she found that $\hat{Y}_F$ was not very different from $\overline{Y}_F$. Equalizing the occupational distribution would eliminate only 15 percent of the gender gap for all YRFT workers and 35 percent for YRFT college-educated workers. This means that the gender difference in occupation, even at this level of detail, is not a particularly important factor in explaining the gender gap. She writes that "what is going on within occupations … is far more important to the gender gap in earnings than is the distribution of men and women by occupations. That is an extremely useful clue to what must be in the last chapter" (p. 1098).

Goldin emphasizes within-occupation characteristics that may affect the gender gap and, in particular, the role of workplace flexibility—an idea that resonates with the family gap literature we discussed earlier. Workplace flexibility is, she writes, "a complicated, multidimensional concept … that incorporates the number of hours to be worked and also the particular hours worked, being 'on call,' providing 'face time,' being around for clients, group meetings, and the like" (p. 1094). Her analysis emphasizes particularly work hours and the earnings premiums and penalties attached to long and short hour schedules for college-educated workers.

One way to think about this issue is to ask what difference there is between two half-time workers and one full-time worker in terms of total productivity and what this implies about likely earnings differences. If each half-time worker is working independently on tasks or if they are working on the same task but can very easily "get up to speed" on what the other has done, then there might well be little or no difference in productivity. In that case, two half-time workers are a very good substitute for one full-time worker and, consequently, a full-time worker would probably earn roughly twice as much as a half-time worker. She calls this a case of **linear pay**, meaning that pay increases more or less proportionately with hours worked. But if a task is complicated in subtle ways that are not easily communicated from worker to worker or if production requires team activities or other interpersonal face-to-face interactions, then a full-time worker may be substantially more productive than two half-timers and might earn a substantially larger salary. She calls this **nonlinear pay**, meaning that pay increases more than proportionately with hours worked and, equivalently, penalties for part-time work are large.

Goldin argues that some occupations inherently place a greater premium on hours continuity and availability because of the nature of the tasks involved and/or the specific technology. Those occupations will likely have more nonlinear pay schedules and place heavier penalties on those who value flexibility. Individuals, in turn, may choose occupations based on those premiums and penalties, so, for example, women and men might have different occupational distributions if their desire for flexibility differs. Alternatively, they may choose niches within each occupation that differ in the extent of flexibility. Think, for example, of specialties within law and medicine that fit this pattern. In that case we would expect to see gender gaps in earnings within occupations, even those as detailed as in Goldin's analysis. One interesting example is the choice between working part time and withdrawing from the labor market entirely. If the pay schedule is sufficiently nonlinear, some women may withdraw from the labor market when family pressures are greater, rather than work part time.

To test these ideas, Goldin drew on information about job flexibility from the US Department of Labor's Occupational Information Network ("O*net"), based on a survey of workers who are asked about the day-to-day nature of their work tasks. For each of the 95 highest-paid occupations, she compiled information on five measures related to job flexibility: (1) time pressure, (2) the extent of required contact with others to perform tasks, (3) the importance of maintaining interpersonal relations, (4) the extent to which a job is structured for the individual worker, and (5) the freedom to make decisions. For each of these measures, higher scores mean either less flexibility in the job or less substitutability across workers, which means that the penalty for reduced hours will likely be more severe.

If occupations differ in the degree of flexibility they offer, then the gender pay gap might well differ as well. While the details are complicated, it does, in fact, appear that occupations differ in this respect. Among these high-paid occupations, science and technology occupations offer far more flexibility and substitutability than business, law, and health occupations. For example, health ranks very high in terms of "contact with others" and "freedom to make decisions," law ranks highly in terms of "time pressure" and the importance of "maintaining interpersonal relations," and business also ranks highly in terms of interpersonal relations.

Furthermore, the hypothesized earnings relationship does hold. The higher the value of these five indices in an occupation—meaning the less is flexibility and worker substitutability—the greater is the female wage gap in that occupation. A one-standard-deviation difference in the average of these indices is associated with a wage gap that is six points larger. Goldin reports that the impact is greatest for the measures of time pressure, contact with others, and freedom to make decisions.

As case studies, Goldin focuses on business and the legal profession as occupations with nonlinear pay schedules and pharmacy as one with linear pay. In both business and law, studies have shown that there are large wage penalties for shorter hours and for time out of the labor force; these penalties cumulate with time. Not surprisingly, marriage and children are factors, as, interestingly, are spouses who, thanks to assortative mating, are often similarly employed in jobs with large penalties for time flexibility. She summarizes the situation in these two occupations this way: "Children require a modicum of parental time, high-income husbands provide little of it, and part-time work … is insufficiently remunerative for some to remain employed" (p. 1115).[15]

In contrast, pharmacy is a relatively high-paying occupation with a heavy female representation (55 percent and rising) and a high gender earnings ratio (> 90 percent). The explanation for the linear pay schedule is interesting. Because of changes in the industry, large retail chains now dominate: 75 percent of pharmacists now are employed by chains compared to 25 percent in the 1970s. As a result, pharmacists are now typically employees rather than owner-managers. Previously, women pharmacists were often the part-time assistants of male pharmacy owners, who earned the higher salary; now they are on a more equal footing with their male peers. At the same time, computerization of pharmacies enabled more flexibility, as it became easier for one pharmacist to be fully informed about a patient's record and reduced the need for interdependent hours of work.

Goldin's "last chapter" involves transforming more occupations from nonlinear to linear pay schedules. Some of this, she hopes, will be made possible by technological change that

---

15 This fits nicely with the discussion of "opting out" in Chapter 8.

makes employers better substitutes for one another (as in pharmacy). She lists healthcare, retail sales, banking and real estate as examples of occupations moving in that direction. Some occupations, however, may never make that transformation.

Gender discrimination in employment

Audit and correspondence studies

In studies of gender differences in earnings, discrimination is measured indirectly by the portion of the earnings gap that is unrelated to measured skill differences. A more direct test of discrimination, especially of discrimination in employment, is an **audit** or **correspondence study**.[16] An audit study is a kind of economic experiment in which "testers" are sent out in matched pairs, typically, one woman and one man to apply for a job. The testers are as alike as possible "on paper" (i.e., they have résumés indicating similar levels of education, work experience, etc.). They differ only by gender or, in other experiments, race.

A correspondence study is similar in concept, except that it involves sending fictitious résumés in response to genuine job openings. As in the audit studies, the résumés are constructed to be as identical as possible except for gender, race, or other personal characteristics. In both cases, researchers have the ability to make the job candidates more alike than in any regression analysis of real individuals and thus sharply reduce the problem of omitted variable bias creating a spurious gender or race effect. Differences in outcomes, such as interview or hiring rates, can then be taken as an indication of discrimination.

Probably the most famous of these studies involved race discrimination in employment,[17] but some studies have focused on gender. An often-cited audit study involved gender discrimination in employment at high-priced restaurants.[18] To see if men were more likely to be hired at these restaurants, closely matched pairs of applicants were sent to apply for positions. Each tester's résumé indicated that he or she had experience that would be valued at a high-priced restaurant. Two men and two women were used to search for jobs in order to mitigate the effect of any unique personality traits that each tester might possess that could influence the outcome. Testers were instructed to keep the same demeanor throughout all contacts with the restaurant and to dress similarly for all the restaurants they visited. The testers attempted to have the employer make a decision about interviewing based solely on résumés by handing a résumé to the first employee they encountered, which was often a host or waitperson, rather than the manager. The host or waitperson was asked to have the manager call the tester if there was any possibility of an interview. In this way, interviews were based on résumés; the manager had usually not met the job

---

16   Audit studies are also often termed "field studies" in the economics literature. We discussed field studies in chapter 10 when we described evidence about gender differences in competition and risk taking. For more information on these studies, see Jonathan Guryan and Kerwin Kofi Charles (2013), "Taste-Based or Statistical Discrimination: The Economics of Discrimination Returns to Its Roots," *Economic Journal*, 123 (572), 417–432.

17   See M. Bertrand and S. Mullainathan (2004), "Are Emily and Greg More Employable Than Lakisha and Jamal? A Field Experiment on Labor Market Discrimination," *American Economic Review*, 94 (4), 991–1013. That study did report evidence of racial discrimination in hiring.

18   David Neumark, Roy J. Bank, and Kyle D. Van Nort (1996), "Sex Discrimination in Restaurant Hiring: An Audit Study," *The Quarterly Journal of Economics*, 111 (3), 915–941.

candidate. Thus personality traits or biases of the manager that might be correlated with sex were controlled for and thus not a factor in the decision to hire.

The results showed a strong gender effect. In the high-priced restaurants, male testers received job offers in 48 percent of the cases, while female testers received offers in only 9 percent of the cases. This could reflect either employer discrimination—employers in high-priced restaurants prefer male to female servers—or customer discrimination—customers in high-priced restaurants prefer male to female servers.

Riach and Rich conducted a gender correspondence study in London.[19] They sent two standard résumés in response to job advertisements. In order to avoid detection, the résumés obviously could not be literally identical but in all essential job characteristics, such as age, qualifications and experience, candidates were carefully matched so that the only effective distinguishing characteristic was gender. Gender was identified by name, and both male and female were given traditional Anglo-Saxon/Celtic first names and surnames to avoid any possibility that the study could be confounded by racial or ethnic discrimination.

Résumés were sent to advertised job openings in four occupations: computer analyst programmer, engineer (electrical and mechanical), secretary, and trainee chartered accountant. Computer analyst programmer and chartered accountant are occupations that have a majority of male workers (21 percent and 31 percent female, respectively) so the authors referred to these as "mixed occupations," whereas secretary is a female-dominated occupation (5 percent male) and engineer a male-dominated occupation (97 percent).

Riach and Rich found that women were less likely to be called back for the engineering position and, perhaps surprisingly, they found statistically significant discrimination against men in "mixed" occupations and in "female" occupations. They attributed this to gender stereotyping on the part of those making the decisions about whom to call back.

Booth and Lehigh conducted a follow-up study to Riach and Rich in several Australian cities.[20] They were particularly interested in testing the hypothesis that women would be more likely to be called back in jobs that had a larger percentage of women. Thus they sent matched male/female résumés to four different kinds of job: wait staff (80 percent female), data entry (85 percent female), customer service (68 percent female), and sales (69 percent female).

Averaging across all jobs, they found substantial discrimination against male candidates. The typical female applicant received a callback 32 percent of the time, while the typical male candidate received a callback 25 percent of the time. Importantly, there was considerable heterogeneity across job types. For wait staff and data-entry positions, gender differences in callback rates were very large, while for customer service and sales positions they were negligible. For example, a man seeking work as a waiter would have to submit 31 percent more applications to receive the same number of callbacks, while a man seeking work as a data-entry employee would have to submit 74 percent more applications and a man in customer service would have only to submit 4 percent. Hence they concluded that there was only bias towards male candidates when the jobs were

19 P. Riach and J. Rich (2006), "An Experimental Investigation of Sexual Discrimination in Hiring in the English Labor Market," *BE Press Advances in Economic Analysis & Policy*, 6 (2), Article 1.

20 Alison Booth and Andrew Leigh (2010), "Do Employers Discriminate By Gender? A Field Experiment in Female-Dominated Occupations," *Economics Letters*, 107 (2), 236–238.

overwhelmingly female, leading them to speculate that gender stereotyping may play a role in the callbacks.

Audit and correspondence studies have certainly provided some evidence of gender bias in hiring, but not always in the direction we might expect. It is important to recognize that each may reflect the particular characteristics of the country and economy in which the study is conducted. Also, while these studies are useful, they examine only callback rates and not (for obvious reasons) whether an individual is hired or the salary that is offered. In other words, these studies can shed light on potential discrimination at entry-level jobs. They are not appropriate for measuring discrimination at higher levels of the corporate hierarchy and among jobs filled through personal networks.

A natural experiment: women's employment in symphony orchestras

Natural experiments are hard to identify in employment and earnings, but a particularly interesting and well-known one involves women's employment in top US symphony orchestras. Prior to about 1970, very few women were employed in these orchestras. The so-called top five US orchestras (Philadelphia, Boston, New York, Cleveland, and Chicago) had an average of about 4 percent female orchestra members. The proportion was a bit higher, but still quite low, in four other well-known US orchestras (San Francisco, Los Angeles, Detroit, and Pittsburgh). This low representation of women was the result of a number of factors, but one that gained attention was the hiring process itself. Candidates typically auditioned for a position in front of the music director and/or a committee of orchestra members. Because the candidate's identity was clearly known, it was possible that favoritism (primarily based on a candidate's music teacher who might have long-standing ties to the conductor) and sexism were part of the hiring process.

To remedy these problems, most orchestras eventually adopted a "blind" audition process in which a candidate performs behind a screen that completely conceals his or her identity. Elaborate procedures were implemented to prevent anything that might indicate a candidate's gender. For example, precautions were taken to mute the sound of shoes, which might indicate whether the candidate was wearing high heels. In this new setting—unlike the previous one—the evaluators knew nothing at all about the candidate—not name, race, or gender. The change in the procedures thus provided a natural experiment to evaluate the impact of gender on the selection procedure.

The effect of the change was studied by Claudia Goldin and Cecilia Rouse.[21] They collected data on auditions between 1950 and 1995 for eight major US orchestras. Some of the auditions were blind and some were not, because different orchestras adopted the blind audition format at different times. For each audition, Goldin and Rouse knew whether the audition was blind and how each candidate fared. Even better, the same individuals often auditioned in both a blind audition and one that was not blind. That enabled Goldin and Rouse to hold constant the musical ability of the candidates across the different kinds of audition to see if the *same* woman or *same* man fared differently in blind and non-blind auditions. In all, they analyzed outcomes for 588 audition rounds that involved a total of more than 7,000 musicians.

---

21 Claudia Goldin and Cecilia Rouse (2000), "Orchestrating Impartiality: The Impact of Blind Auditions on Female Musicians," *American Economic Review*, 90 (4), 715–741.

Were women more likely to be hired in blind auditions compared to non-blind auditions? The answer is "yes." Of all the men who auditioned in non-blind auditions, 2.7 percent were hired, compared to 1.7 percent of women. In the blind auditions, 2.6 percent of the men and 2.7 percent of the women were hired. So the net effect of the blind audition is a 1.1 percent increase in the proportion of women hired: 1.1= gender difference in blind auditions (0.1)—gender difference in non-blind auditions (−1.0).

These effects were confirmed in other regression analyses by Goldin and Rouse in which they controlled for other factors that could affect the outcomes. They conclude that the switch to blind auditions accounted for 30 percent of the increase in the proportion of women among the new hires and about 25 percent of the increase in the proportion of women among these orchestras from 1970 to 1996. The switch to blind auditions apparently eliminated subtle discrimination that impaired the ability of women musicians to gain employment in the top US orchestras.

Specialized studies of women's earnings

Discrimination on the basis of physical appearance

Economists have established two areas related to physical appearance where women (and men) face discrimination—both relating to physical appearance.

Beauty and earnings We often think of beauty as subjective. After all, we are all familiar with the adage "beauty is in the eye of the beholder." Nevertheless, a growing body of research has established that the beautiful are rewarded in the labor market, while less-attractive employees earn lower wages. Economist Daniel Hamermesh's book *Beauty Pays* draws on his work (and that of other economists) on the economics of beauty.[22] Hamermesh terms this branch of economics **pulchronomics** which is economics jargon for the study of the economics of physical attractiveness.

Perhaps the biggest challenge in this area of research is how to measure beauty. Most studies rely on interviewer ratings of physical appearance. Interviewers are typically shown a photo and asked to rate the person on a scale of attractiveness. In order for these ratings to be credible, they must reflect what society considers beautiful and they must be stable across interviewers. Hamermesh presents evidence that standards of beauty are well established within a culture at a given point in time and that these standards evolve slowly. He also demonstrates that interviewers' assessments of beauty are remarkably consistent. Thus what one person identifies as beauty is also beautiful to another. Attributes such as symmetric facial features are closely tied to beauty, for example. After establishing who is beautiful and who is not, Hamermesh (and other scholars) use regression analysis and include a variety of other control variables to isolate the effect of beauty on earnings. Their findings are fascinating.

How much is beauty worth? Hamermesh calculates that the least-attractive women (who score 1 or 2 on a 1-to-5-point attractiveness scale) earn 4 percent less than

---

22 Daniel Hamermesh (2011), *Beauty Pays: Why Attractive People Are More Successful*, Princeton, NJ: Princeton University Press. Hamermesh's work garnered him an appearance on *The Daily Show* on November 14, 2011.

average-looking women (who score 3). Beautiful women (who score 4 and 5) earn 8 percent more than average-looking women and 12 percent more than the least-attractive women. The best-looking men earn 4 percent more than average-looking men, while the least-attractive men earn 13 percent less than average-looking men, and 17 percent less than the best-looking men. These percentages are calculated after controlling for a host of other factors that affect earnings. Hamermesh calculates that the attractive enjoy an approximately $230,000 lifetime earnings advantage over the unattractive.

Hamermesh notes that looks are at least partly mutable in that individuals can enhance their looks by purchasing cosmetics—in fact, the cosmetics industry generated about $60 billion in revenue in the United States in 2014. Using a unique data set from China that contains data on earnings, interviewer assessments of beauty, and spending on clothing and cosmetics, Hamermesh and colleagues examined two questions.[23] First, is there a beauty premium in China? Second, can spending on clothing and cosmetics generate higher earnings for women—that is, is it a human capital investment or is it just pure consumption spending? Using the same regression methods applied to US data, controlling for education and other factors that affect earnings, they report that Chinese women who are rated as beautiful earn 10 percent more than average-looking women who, in turn, earn 30 percent more than women whose looks are below average. However, in contrast with what they found using US data, there is no effect of being above average on men's earnings. Whether this difference can be ascribed to cultural differences regarding men and women's looks in the workplace in the two countries remains to be resolved.

To answer the second question—whether women's spending on clothing and cosmetics has an investment component—they examined the relationship between the rating of a woman's beauty by the interviewer and her spending on clothing and cosmetics. They find that such spending is not significantly related to the interviewer's rating of beauty and they interpret this to mean that this spending is primarily for consumption purposes and not an investment in the woman's looks.

One potential explanation for the beauty premium is that appearance may, in fact, be positively correlated with certain skills that are important for job performance but are not easily observed and thus cannot be controlled for in an empirical study. For example, perhaps more attractive persons thereby have the ability to be more persuasive. Another is that employers may overestimate the skills of comparatively attractive people simply because they're attractive. Finally, employers may prefer hiring more attractive people, which would be consistent with Becker's model of taste-based discrimination.

Hamermesh's research does confirm a beauty premium in occupations where attractiveness may be important, such as sales. In other words, this suggests that the labor market sorts the more attractive people into occupations where their attractiveness makes them more productive.[24] In this case it would be difficult to sort out productivity from discrimination. But Hamermesh also finds beauty pays in many occupations that do not require beauty or where the requirement of attractiveness is not as obvious. This finding provides some support for the Becker model of employer discrimination. Based on this

---

23   Daniel S. Hamermesh, Xin Meng, and Junsen Zhang (2002), "Dress For Success—Does Primping Pay?" *Labour Economics*, 9 (3), 361–373.

24   As an interesting example, Hamermesh finds that better-looking college professors generate better student evaluations.

and on the fact that one's looks are not easily modified (plastic surgery notwithstanding), Hamermesh goes so far as to suggest that unattractive individuals deserve legal protection from discrimination.

Finally, we can't help but note that his work based on US data actually finds a larger wage penalty for unattractive men as compared to unattractive women. One possible explanation for this offered by Hamermesh is that women have lower LFPRs and hence perhaps the most unattractive women are not in the labor force.

Obesity and earnings With obesity rates rising in all developed countries, researchers have studied whether or not the obese pay a penalty in the labor market. Obesity is easier to quantify than beauty and many social science data sets contain good information on labor-market earnings, as well as measures of height and weight. This enables scholars to calculate an individual's **body mass index (BMI)**. The BMI is a commonly used measure of obesity; it is calculated by dividing weight in kilograms by the square of height in meters.[25] An individual who is six feet tall and weighs 180 pounds would have a BMI equal to 24.4; someone who is five feet four inches and weighs 135 pounds would have a BMI of 23.2. A BMI value greater than 30 is considered obese.

Just as in the beauty models, once we have a measure of obesity, it is straightforward to include it in a typical wage regression equation, while controlling for other factors that would also affect earnings. Numerous researchers, using data from the United States as well as from Europe, have established that the obese, particularly women, earn lower wages. Obese women are also less likely to marry, and when they do they marry men with lower earnings.[26] Unlike the studies of beauty, there is typically no effect of obesity on the earnings of men. This may be due to cultural biases about weight regarding women.

Can we interpret this finding as a causal effect of obesity on earnings? While these studies all include an extensive set of control variables to mitigate the possibility of omitted variable bias, scholars in this area have noted the potential for bias in their results and have taken careful steps to mitigate such bias. For example, there is the potential for reverse causality in this relationship. In other words, it is possible that the low wages are a cause of obesity rather than obesity causing low wages. And scholars have also noted that a third, hard to measure, factor, such as motivation or ability to delay gratification, might cause both obesity and low wages. These issues are less likely to be a problem in the beauty literature since looks are less ameliorable than weight (though there is certainly debate about how much control an individual has over their own weight). In other words, this is less of a problem in the beauty studies unless attractiveness happens to be correlated with an unobservable skill.

To be sure that the direction of causality runs from obesity to earnings requires scholars to make use of some sophisticated econometrics, because evidence from controlled or natural experiments are not likely to be available in this case. This has been accomplished in two ways. First, scholars have used longitudinal data, which include information on an individual's BMI taken before the individual enters the labor market; this earlier BMI

---

25 In terms of pounds and inches, BMI = (weight in pounds/height in inches squared) × 703. One kilogram is equivalent to 2.2 pounds and one meter is equivalent to 3.28 feet.

26 See Susan Averett (2011), "Labor Market Consequences: Employment, Wages, Disability, and Absenteeism," in John Cawley (ed.), *The Oxford Handbook of the Social Science of Obesity*, Oxford, UK: Oxford University Press, 531–552, for a review of this research.

information should be less affected by reverse causality. This longitudinal data also allow scholars to follow individuals over time (similarly to the method used to establish the effect of marriage on health that we discussed in Chapter 4). Finally, scholars have also made use of data that allow them to control for whether the individual has a genetic predisposition towards obesity—perhaps having a sibling who is obese. These studies have tended to confirm the finding that obese women have wages that could be as much as 20 percent lower than their counterparts who are not obese. Interestingly, scholars find that the obesity penalty is smaller for black rather than white women, suggesting that cultural norms about body weight may play a role in the relationship between obesity and earnings.

The glass ceiling

While women have made substantial gains in the workplace in recent decades, there is clear evidence that women remain underrepresented at the top levels of American business and politics. Is this evidence of a **glass ceiling**, that invisible barrier that keeps women from top jobs and garners considerable attention from the media? Data from Catalyst report that while the number of women CEOs at Fortune 500 companies is rising, as of January 2015, there were only 23 women CEOs out of 500 companies. The federal government is concerned about this as well and in 1991, with a reauthorization of the 1964 Civil Rights Act, the federal government created the Glass Ceiling Act. Among its stated purposes was to provide appropriate remedies for intentional discrimination and unlawful harassment in the workplace.

Why are women underrepresented at the very top corporate levels? While there is no single easy answer, two possible explanations are often advanced in the media. The first is that there are simply fewer women qualified to be CEOs than are men. For example, in 1970 only 4 percent of MBAs were awarded to women but by the mid-2010s that percentage had risen to nearly 50 percent. If the pipeline of qualified women was low, it is certainly rising now. And, of course, having an MBA is an admittedly rough measure of anyone's ability to be a CEO. Certainly, as women have increased their attachment to the work force and have surpassed men in terms of educational attainment, this pipeline argument should eventually lead to more women CEOs. Catalyst does report that the percentage of female CEOs at Fortune 500 companies has doubled in the past decade but still remains below 5 percent. Despite the narrowing of the gender gap in business education, there is a growing sense that women are not getting ahead fast enough in the corporate world.

Another explanation centers on work/life balance. The position as a corporate leader demands what often seems to be round-the-clock devotion to the job. A 2008 Pew Research Center survey asked respondents to evaluate a series of potential reasons why there are not more women in top-level business positions and high political offices. Many respondents expressed the opinion that women's family responsibilities don't leave time for running a major corporation. Women themselves were somewhat more likely than men to say this is a major reason why so few top-level business positions are held by women (37 percent vs. 32 percent).

Some interesting evidence regarding these explanations comes from a study of the careers of MBA degree recipients who graduated from the University of Chicago's Booth School of Business between 1990 and 2006. Because the data are uniquely focused on

MBAs from the same school, we know that the men and women in the sample started out with approximately the same skills. This provides an unusual opportunity to study the gender wage gap, since many studies of the gender wage gap, as we have noted, find a sizable unexplained portion. That unexplained portion may reflect discrimination, but it also may reflect unobservable characteristics of both the workers and the firms that may be correlated with earnings. For example, women may not be as committed to long-term careers as men—something that is unobservable to the economist performing the analysis. In this sample, these concerns are mitigated to some extent.

Consistent with this observation, the authors of this study, Marianne Bertrand, Claudia Goldin, and Lawrence Katz, found that at the outset of their careers, the male and female MBAs in their sample had nearly identical earnings.[27] However, a mere five years after graduation their earnings trajectories diverged greatly, with men substantially out-earning women and the differential continued to grow over time. Furthermore, despite the very substantial human capital investment in the degree, a decade after completion of their MBA, 13 percent of the women were not working compared to only 1 percent of the men.

Bertrand and her coauthors performed a more complicated version of the Oaxaca decomposition that allowed them to decompose the gender wage gap across men and women and over time. The details are too complex for this text, but the general idea is the same in that the gender gap can be decomposed into an explained and an unexplained portion. In their research they identified three factors that are together responsible for explaining 84 percent of the gender gap in earnings over time in their sample.

The first factor is gender differences in courses and grades. Men tended to take more finance courses and they had higher Grade Point Average (GPA) in business school. The return to finance courses is particularly high (as compared to courses in other disciplines such as marketing) as is the return to a higher GPA, hence these differences translate into large wage differentials. Second, women were more likely to interrupt their careers and the authors noted that any career interruption was costly in terms of earnings growth. At 10 years out, women were 22 percent more likely to have interrupted their careers than are men. Finally gender differences in weekly hours worked were an important explanation for earnings differences. Women were more likely to work part time and to choose jobs with lower hours. The authors noted that deviations from the male norm of long hours and continuous attachment to the work force was penalized particularly highly in terms of earnings in corporate and financial sectors jobs.

Not surprisingly, and consistent with the general public's belief, they find that the presence of children was the main contributor to the interrupted careers of female MBA graduates. MBA mothers have about 8 months less work experience post-MBA than men, while childless MBA women have only 1.5 months less work experience than MBA men. MBA mothers were found to actively choose jobs that were family friendly with more predicable hours and consequently less room for advancement. As our model of labor-force participation in Chapter 7 predicted, the MBA mothers with the highest-earning spouses were most likely to reduce their employment, whereas mothers with lower-earning spouses did not reduce their employment after the birth of a child.

---

27   Marianne Bertrand, Claudia Goldin, and Lawrence F. Katz (2010), "Dynamics of the Gender Gap among Young Professionals in the Corporate and Financial Sectors," *American Economic Journal: Applied*, 2 (3), 228–255. This study was used in Goldin's discussion of occupational wage differences discussed earlier.

While the above research makes clear that at least among women with similar educa-tion to men a gender gap can be explained by choices women make, those choices are constrained greatly by the inflexibility of the corporate environment. This certainly dove-tails with Claudia Goldin's discussion of a large penalty for flexible jobs that we discussed earlier in this chapter.

Although the data in the MBA study stop relatively early in the careers of the respond-ents, an oft-cited study by economists Marianne Bertrand and Kevin Hallock[28] asked how well women who do make it to the top of the corporate ladder fare compared to their male counterparts in terms of earnings and total compensation. They examined the compensa-tion of the five most highly paid executives at about 1,500 major companies that Standard and Poor's tracked from 1992 to 1997, so this reflects a somewhat earlier time period. Similarly to the MBA study, an important advantage of their data set is that the sample of women and men is much more homogenous than other samples. Because the men and women in the Standard and Poor's data set are at the highest levels of the corporate lad-der, it is safe to assume that they are probably very similar with respect to career goals, commitment to the labor force, human capital, and motivation. Thus these data provide a unique opportunity to study the gender wage gap at the top of the corporate hierarchy.

The authors found that high-ranking corporate women received only about 67 percent of the earnings that top male executives command. In 1997 the average female execu-tive earned a little less than $900,000 in compensation (1997 dollars) while the average male executive earned about $1.3 million. To help ascertain whether these women faced pay discrimination, the authors used a variation on the Oaxaca decomposition similar to that discussed in Chapter 10. Their regressions included five variables to explain wages: indicators for the top three occupations, log stock market value, and stock return in the previous year. With just these five control variables, they found that 71 percent of the total difference in compensation between male and female executives was explained. Because this group is likely a fairly homogenous group in terms of motivation, career commit-ment, and human capital investment, the unexplained portion of this differential probably comes closer to reflecting discrimination toward women—an assertion that Hallock and Bertrand make themselves. It is also likely that the men and women in this sample are more similar in their attitudes toward competition and risk—two factors that we saw dif-fered between men and women.

Their findings suggest that men and women holding similar functions in firms are treated fairly equally in terms of compensation. They also documented that women tend to be concentrated in smaller corporations than men, and it has been well established in the literature that large corporations pay better, all else being equal. However, there is no evidence that women are concentrated in lower-paying industries, though there is evi-dence that women are concentrated in the lower-paying occupational categories. Finally, women in the sample were younger than the men and had 5.6 years less seniority on aver-age, both of which tend to lower pay.

Policymakers in Europe have begun to accelerate women's growth in business lead-ership by adopting gender quotas for corporate boards of directors. Some interesting evidence from a natural experiment in Norway gives us a glimpse into how this change

---

28 Marianne Bertrand and Kevin Hallock (2001), "The Gender Gap in Corporate Jobs," *Industrial and Labor Relations Review*, 55 (1), 3–21.

in the composition of boards might affect firm's outcomes. Economists Doug Matsa and Amalia Miller take advantage of a change in Norwegian law, which occurred in 2006 and imposed a quota system for boards of directors of public companies.[29] Within two years, the law stated, at least 40 percent of directors had to be women, and at least 40 percent had to be men. (So far, underrepresentation of men has not been a problem.) After more women were added to Norway's corporate boards, the researchers compared firms in Norway who were subjected to the quota to other Norwegian firms that were not subject to the quota and to all firms in other Nordic countries and found that "larger layoffs"—those that affected more than 3 percent of the workforce—at those companies dropped by 20 percent compared to previous years. The authors report that it is mostly people at the lower salary levels who are being spared.

There is evidence that this is more than just a phenomenon specific to Norway. In particular, the authors report in a separate study that privately held firms owned by women were less likely than those owned by men to downsize their workforces during the Great Recession. The conclusion is that having more women on a company's board of directors translates into fewer layoffs.[30] While quotas have not been adopted in the United States, Spain and France have also adopted similar quotas.

Summary

In this chapter we have sampled a bit of the extensive empirical literature in economics examining women's earnings. Much of the literature attempts to sort out the relative importance of the two primary explanations for the gender gap in earnings—human capital vs. discrimination. Using regression analysis and the Oaxaca decomposition technique, it is possible to determine the proportion of the wage gap due to all human capital differences or even to specific human capital measures, such as education and experience.

The research literature shows that there is certainly something to the human capital explanation. Men and women do not, on average across the entire working population, bring equal skills to the labor market. They would not therefore have equal earnings even if labor-market discrimination could be eliminated. But despite the prediction from economic theory that market competition would eliminate discrimination due to employers, no study has found that gender differences in human capital account for all or even a substantial majority of the wage gap. In the mid-1970s, human capital differences, primarily measures of career-work attachment, accounted for roughly one-third to one-half of the earnings gap. The remainder was the result of gender differences in the value of human capital. A later study focusing on the late 1980s found that one-third of the gap was explained by human capital differences. More recent studies of gender earnings differences among younger workers have emphasized not differences in human capital but differences in the way family responsibilities affect men's and women's earnings. These analyses of the family gap have found that marriage and children have different effects on

29 David A. Matsa and Amalia R. Miller (2013), "A Female Style in Corporate Leadership? Evidence from Quotas," *American Economic Journal: Applied Economics*, 5 (3), 136–169.

30 David A. Matsa and Amalia R. Miller (2014), "Workforce Reductions at Women-Owned Businesses in the United States," *Industrial & Labor Relations Review*, 67 (2) , 422–452.

earnings for men and women, and that these differences have been an important source of the difference in pay.

Even though human capital differences may not explain the entire wage gap, changes in human capital differences are an important part of the time trend in the wage gap. One interesting study showed that the stability in the earnings ratio at about 60 percent between 1960 and 1980 was actually the result of offsetting changes in gender differences in human capital and in discrimination. During these years, women's human capital declined relative to men's as a result of the rapid influx into the labor market of women who had relatively little prior attachment to the labor market. Taken by itself, this would have led to a decline in the earnings ratio. The fact that the ratio did not decline tells us that discrimination must have eased. Many scholars are optimistic about the future narrowing of the gender gap. Women already have more education than men, and differences in LFPRs are narrowing. More and more women are establishing careers in the same way as men, by working more or less continuously without significant family interruptions. As gender differences in human capital narrow, the wage gap should narrow as well. The suggestion that the family gap may be the last remaining hurdle to gender equality is an important idea to bear in mind.

The gender gap in pay has led to the development of public policy measures that are intended to address that problem. We turn to these policies in the next chapter.

12 EMPLOYMENT AND EARNINGS POLICIES

Introduction

In this chapter we fold together several different employment and earnings-related policies that impact women and their economic lives. We begin with an examination of anti-discrimination legislation in the United States. We then turn our attention to policies intended to help women balance work and family obligations, especially maternity leave and childcare. We end the chapter with a brief look at Social Security in the United States and how its structure impacts women's economic well-being in retirement.

Anti-discrimination policies

The economic basis for anti-discrimination laws

In this section we examine laws that are currently in place to protect women against labor-market discrimination. Before we do so it is worth taking a minute to explore why society might wish to enact such laws. After all, if the labor market works well, labor should be allocated to where it is most productive, and, as we saw in Chapter 10, discrimination arising from employers should disappear in the long run (although discrimination arising from other sources might not be eradicated by market forces alone and may require government intervention).

How can we justify the existence of antidiscrimination laws? From an economics perspective, there are two ways to justify these laws. The first is on the basis of equity. If some group—such as women or racial minorities—is being treated unfairly, we may rationalize such laws on the grounds that they force employers to treat all labor-market participants equally. Why should equally qualified women or minorities be denied access to higher-paying jobs or earn less money for doing equal work?

The second justification is on the basis of efficiency. One important task of the labor market is to allocate labor across all the possible firms in the economy in an efficient way. How many workers should be employed at this firm and how many at that one? This allocation is important because it determines how much we, as a society, can produce. When labor is allocated inefficiently, we as a society end up producing—and consuming—less than we otherwise could. An allocation of workers across firms is said to be efficient when it is impossible to change the current allocation and produce a set of outputs that is more highly valued.

It turns out that discrimination leads to an inefficient allocation of labor in exactly that way. Labor-market discrimination results in economic inefficiency whenever people of one gender or race or religion are denied the opportunity to use their skills where they are best suited. Imagine, for example, a world in which talented women are employed in settings that underutilize their skills. Perhaps a woman who was a college graduate some years ago ended up as a secretary because professional jobs were not open to women. The woman in question clearly suffers financially, but society suffers, too. It loses the difference in the value of what she could have produced in a professional setting vs. the value of what she produced as a secretary. Whenever a talented person is unable to find an appropriate job for reasons of discrimination, society loses the output that is not produced. The career of Supreme Court justice Sandra Day O'Connor is a perfect example of this kind of inefficiency. See Box 12.1 for a discussion.

Box | 12.1

Sandra Day O'Connor—Economic Inefficiency in Practice

Justice Sandra Day O'Connor was the first women to serve on the US Supreme Court, serving on the court from 1981 until 2006. Her story is an interesting one because it highlights how strong labor-market discrimination against professional women was in her time period.

O'Connor graduated from Stanford Law School in 1952. She completed the degree in two years rather than the usual three, ranked third out of the 102 students in her class, and was an editor of the *Stanford Law Review*. Soon after her own graduation she married a fellow law student and attempted to find work with a private law firm in California, while her husband completed his last year of law school. Despite her lofty academic credentials, she was completely unsuccessful in her job search in the private sector because of the reluctance of many firms to hire a female attorney. Apparently, some firms offered her a position as a legal secretary rather than as an attorney.

She eventually found a position as a deputy attorney for San Mateo County and worked there while her husband finished his degree. She then followed her husband to Europe, where she worked from 1954 to 1957 as a civilian attorney for the Quartermaster Market Center in Frankfurt, Germany. When she and her husband returned to Arizona, she was again unable to find work with a local law firm; her husband had no problem. Rather than give up, she established her own law practice, later served as an Arizona assistant attorney general, a state senator, a trial judge, and a member of the Arizona Court of Appeals before being appointed to the US Supreme Court.

There seems little question that O'Connor suffered from a particularly harsh form of labor-market discrimination solely on the basis of her gender. Despite impeccable qualifications, she was completely unable to secure the kind of legal position that her male classmates readily received. A less-determined person might well have abandoned the practice of law altogether.

Note the inefficiency here. Not only was Justice O'Connor deprived of the opportunity to utilize her skills to the fullest, but society was deprived of the value of those skills. She was underutilized. The potential output that she could have produced was squandered.

There are undoubtedly thousands of similar stories of skilled women and skilled members of other minority groups who were unable to use, in the most productive way, the many skills that they had.

In the mid-2010s, three women—Ruth Bader Ginsburg, Sonia Sotomayor, and Elena Kagan—serve on the US Supreme Court.

We can also demonstrate this inefficiency more rigorously with a numerical example. Assume that men and women are equally skilled, just as we assumed in our models of discrimination in Chapter 10. Assume further that as a result of labor-market discrimination, women all work in a sector of the economy where they earn $10 per hour and men all work in a sector of the economy in which they earn $20 per hour. For both men and women, employment is set where the MRP of the last worker just equals the wage rate. Thus, given these wage rates, firms will hire men and women up to the point where the MRP of the last woman equals $10 and the MRP of the last man equals $20. This is shown in Figure 12.1. W_m and E_m represent the equilibrium wage and employment in the men's labor market, and W_f and E_f represent the equilibrium wage and employment in the market for women's labor.

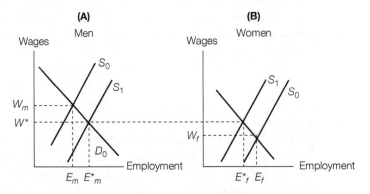

Figure 12.1 *Inefficiency in the labor market resulting from discrimination.*

This employment situation is inefficient in the sense that it is possible to reallocate the men and women and end up better off. This follows directly from the fact that the MRPs of equally productive men and women are different, which in turn follows from the fact that women earn lower wages as a result of labor-market discrimination.

To see that this situation is inefficient, consider what would happen if one woman were moved from the women's sector to the men's sector. In the women's sector, the value of output produced would fall by $10, which was the MRP of the last worker. In the men's sector, that same woman could produce output valued at just a bit less than $20, since $20 was the MRP of the last man hired. In the process of reallocating that woman from the women's sector to the men's sector, the total value of output would increase by $10. Society would therefore end up better off, with a more highly valued bundle of goods produced.

Of course, that would not be the end of the reallocation process. The next worker moved might cause the value of output to fall by, say, $10.10 in the women's sector and rise by $19.90 in the men's sector. (These numbers reflect the idea of diminishing MRP.) So the value of total output would rise by $9.80. As long as the wage differs for equally skilled men and women, then their MRPs will differ, and it will always be possible to move a worker from where her current MRP is low to where her potential MRP is higher. In the process the total value of output increases. Only when the MRPs of the last worker employed in both sectors is identical will the allocation of labor be efficient. Only then is it impossible to move a worker from one sector to the other and increase the value of total output. And that requires that the wage rates be identical. This means that wages would increase for women and decrease for men.

In Figure 12.1, this equilibrium is illustrated by a leftward shift in the supply curve for women and a rightward shift in the supply curve for men. The final equilibrium wage is reached at W^*. Of course, now there is no longer a market exclusively for men's labor because women have joined that market.

Anti-discrimination laws in the United States

Laws expressly forbidding discrimination on the grounds of race or gender are actually relatively new in the United States. Historically, women have typically experienced some sort of discrimination in the workplace. Some of the early discrimination women faced actually had its origins in an attempt at being protective toward women and was actually legal. For example, in the early 1900s, many states adopted legislation limiting how many hours per day a woman could work—it was believed to be bad for her reproductive health if she overexerted herself. Many firms also imposed marriage and/ or pregnancy "bars." A **marriage bar** often took two forms. One was a rule that stated that a woman who was single when hired and subsequently married would lose her job. Another established that a married woman could not be hired for a certain job. Similar rules often held for women who became pregnant. Marriage bars were implemented in the late 1800s and early 1900s in the United States and were not unusual in other countries as well, such as Japan. In the United States they had largely disappeared by the 1950s.[1]

The Equal Pay Act of 1963 was the first federal law to deal with sex discrimination. It is an amendment to the Fair Labor Standards Act of 1938, the same act that created the minimum wage and required overtime pay. The Equal Pay Act of 1963 makes it illegal for employers to pay different wage rates for men and women if they are doing equal work. Equal work is defined as being work that requires equal skill, effort, and responsibility and is performed under similar working conditions. This law essentially eliminated a not uncommon practice of paying women in a firm lower wages than men doing the same job.

Critics charge that the weakness of the Equal Pay Act of 1963 is its narrow focus on wages—it only covers wage discrimination. Thus a firm that segregates its employees by occupation and gender and pays the female occupations lower wages would not be violating the Equal Pay Act, even if it refused to hire women into the higher-paying male jobs or even to hire women at all.

Title VII of the Civil Rights Act of 1964 made it an unlawful employment practice for an employer "to refuse to hire or to discharge any individual, or otherwise to discriminate against any individual with respect to his [sic] compensation, terms, conditions, or privileges of employment, because of such individual's race, color, religion, sex or national origin." This act is widely regarded as the cornerstone of anti-discrimination legislation in the United States. Surprisingly, sex was only added to the Civil Rights Act at the last minute, as described in Box 12.2.

---

1 See Claudia Goldin (1990), *Understanding the Gender Gap: An Economic History of American Women,* New York: Oxford University Press, 160–178, for a discussion of marriage and pregnancy bars.

Box 12.2

On the Passage of the 1964 Civil Rights Act

In the early-1960s, sex discrimination did not receive the same attention as discrimination on the basis of race and color. In fact, sex was added as an amendment to Title VII on February 8, 1964—the day it passed—by Congressman Howard W. Smith of Virginia, chairman of the Rules Committee of the US House of Representatives. He was a conservative and known to oppose all civil rights legislation. His amendment is widely believed to have been an effort to ensure that the civil rights act would not pass. In fact, as one author notes, the addition of "sex" to Title VII was "the result of a deliberate ploy of foes of the bill to scuttle it" (Whalen and Whalen, 1985, p. 238).

However, there is another interpretation of the last-minute addition of "sex" to the legislation. Freeman argues that it was, in fact, the result of tireless work by women lawmakers and the National Women's Party whose strategy was to add "sex" to any legislation aimed at expanding or securing rights for any group in hopes of gaining rights for women. Because the National Women's Party had been lobbying Congress for the Equal Rights Amendment (ERA) for nearly 40 years, Freeman speculates that the addition of "sex" to Title VII was an attempt by some lawmakers to support the ERA.

Sources: Charles Whalen and Barbara Whalen (1985), *The Longest Debate: A Legislative History of the 1964 Civil Rights Act,* New York: New American Library and Jo Freeman (1991), "How Sex Got Into Title VII: Persistent Opportunism as a Maker of Public Policy," *Law and Inequality: A Journal of Theory and Practice,* 9 (2), 163–184.

Over the years, Title VII has been amended by Congress several times.[2] In 1972 it was amended to apply to all employers in interstate commerce with 15 or more employees, to all labor unions with 15 or more members, and to workers employed by state and local governments, federal agencies, and educational institutions. The 1972 amendment is called the Equal Opportunity Act of 1972. In 1978 the act was again amended to protect pregnant women through the Pregnancy Discrimination Act. In 1991, Title VII was amended to expand the remedies available to victims of discrimination by allowing for jury trials and the recovery of compensatory and punitive damages; previously, jury trials were possible only in a limited set of circumstances. The 1991 amendment also included the Glass Ceiling Act of 1991, which formally recognized that women remained underrepresented in management and other positions with authority in business and that there were some artificial barriers that held them back—that is, the glass ceiling. The most recent amendment came in 2009, when President Obama signed the Lilly Ledbetter Fair Pay Act, which established that pay discrimination claims on the basis of sex, race, national origin, age, religion, and disability "accrue" whenever an employee receives a discriminatory paycheck, as well as when a discriminatory pay decision or practice is adopted, when a person becomes subject to the decision or practice, or when a person is otherwise affected by the decision or practice of discrimination. See Box 12.3 for more details of this most recent amendment to Title VII.

---

2 See www.eeoc.gov/laws/statutes/index.cfm for a full discussion of these amendments.

Box | 12.3

The Lilly Ledbetter Fair Pay Act

Lilly Ledbetter was one of the few female supervisors at a Goodyear plant in Gadsden, Alabama, and worked there for close to two decades. When she began her job in 1979, she was paid the same as her male colleagues, but over the years she was awarded smaller raises and nearly two decades later she found out that she was making 40 percent less than her male supervisors. Goodyear had a policy that forbid employees to discuss their pay, and Ms. Ledbetter only realized that she was the subject of discrimination when she received an anonymous note revealing the salaries of three of the male managers she worked with. She filed a complaint with the Equal Employment Opportunity Commission (the federal agency charged with enforcing Title VII) and her case went to trial. A jury awarded her back pay and approximately $3.3 million in compensatory and punitive damages for the pay discrimination to which she had been subjected. She had been doing the same job as the male managers but been making far less than them for nearly two decades.

However, this decision was reversed by an appeals court, which ruled that her case had been filed too late. Even though she had been receiving lower pay for over a decade, the court ruled that she had to file the claim at the time she started receiving the lower pay, which is when the company's original decision on her pay had been made. This appeals court decision was upheld by the Supreme Court which, in a controversial ruling, stated that employees cannot challenge ongoing pay discrimination if the employer's original discriminatory pay decision occurred more than 180 days earlier, even when the employee continued to receive paychecks that had been discriminatorily reduced. This ruling was contentious, although it was consistent with a provision of Title VII, which stated that 180 days was the statute of limitations. It was widely believed that adhering to this 180-day standard would make it difficult to uphold pending pay discrimination cases under Title VII.

Due to concerns that this ruling would create an incentive for firms to conceal discrimination until 180 days had passed and coupled with the observation that it was unreasonable to expect individuals to know immediately if they were being discriminated against, both the House and the Senate passed the Lilly Ledbetter Fair Pay Act of 2009. Under the act, each discriminatory paycheck (rather than simply the original decision to discriminate) resets the 180-day limit to file a claim. President Obama signed the legislation on January 29, 2009.

Source: Linda. Greenhouse, "Justices Limit Discrimination Suits over Pay," *The New York Times*, May 29, 2007 and Peter Baker, "Obama Signs Measures to Help Close Gender Gap in Pay," *The New York Times*, April 8, 2014. National Women's Law Center: www.nwlc.org/resource/lilly-ledbetter-fair-pay-act-0, accessed February 7, 2015.

Title VII also addressed another type of discrimination—sexual harassment. Sexual harassment encompasses a wide range of behaviors. For example, it may take a quid pro quo form (i.e., an exchange of sexual favors for a promotion) or it may be unwanted sexual comments in the workplace that result in the creation of a "hostile environment." In 1986 the US Supreme Court ruled that sexual harassment in the form of a hostile environment at the workplace could be the basis for a sex-discrimination complaint under Title VII.[3]

One exception to Title VII has to do with what are called bona fide occupational qualifications (BFOQ). At the time of the passage of Title VII, newspapers routinely published job ads that specified whether or not a woman or a man was required for the job.[4] We have seen that there was considerable sex segregation in the 1960s (and many jobs remain highly divided along gender lines today). However, the courts have not allowed BFOQ cases to stand with one exception—that of a case in 1977 regarding male employees of a maximum security prison in Alabama where the court ruled that gender was a BFOQ. Interestingly, the court has consistently ruled that it is discriminatory to bar women of childbearing age to work in places where they might come into contact with substances that could be hazardous to a developing fetus.

Enforcement of the Civil Rights Act of 1964 takes place through the Equal Employment Opportunity Commission (EEOC). The EEOC is an independent, five-member agency appointed by the US President with the approval of the Senate. Generally, in order to take action, the EEOC must receive a sworn complaint from an individual. If the complaint appears reasonable and well founded, the EEOC then approaches the offending employer for conciliation. If conciliation is not achieved, the EEOC and the complainant may then go to the court system. The EEOC can also bring class action suits designed to redress discrimination among a group of workers, rather than just one individual at a firm.[5] Class-action suits provide more of a threat to a firm accused of discrimination. In addition, the EEOC requires employers with at least 100 employees or government contractors with 50 employees or more than $50,000 in government contracts to submit an EEO-1 Private Sector Report annually. This report is a snapshot of how many racial and ethnic minorities and women are working in a company; the EEOC uses this information to decide which firms to should be investigated. Interestingly, the first year that the EEOC was in operation it did not expect to see many sex-discrimination lawsuits. After all, the main purpose of Title VII was to eliminate racial discrimination—as we noted in Box 12.2, sex was added at the last minute. Yet that first year, one-third of all charges filed alleged sex discrimination.[6]

Affirmative action We now turn our attention to perhaps the most controversial of the anti-discrimination policies—Affirmative Action. Its official title is Executive Order 11246, which was signed in 1965 by President Johnson.[7] This order requires every firm

---

3 In 1998 the Supreme Court further clarified several aspects of the law with respect to sexual harassment. See Charles J. Muhl (July 1998), "Sexual Harassment," *Monthly Labor Review*, 121, 61–62 for details.

4 Such advertisements are now rare, if they exist at all. But they are the norm in China as a recent economic study reports: Peter Kuhn and Kailing Shen (2013), "Gender Discrimination in Job Ads: Evidence from China," *The Quarterly Journal of Economics*, 128 (1), 287–336.

5 A class action suit alleging gender discrimination was filed against Walmart on behalf of 1.5 million female employees. After nearly a decade in the legal system, in 2011 the Supreme Court ruled that the case could not proceed as a class action since there was not one specific employment policy that tied the cases together. However, notably, the Supreme Court did not rule on whether or not there had been discriminatory practices at Walmart.

6 For an engaging history of the EEOC and some landmark cases, see www.eeoc.gov/35th/milestones/1991.html.

7 It was actually not until October 13, 1967 that Executive Order 11375 expanded Affirmative Action to include women, and this was not actually enforced until the Employment Act of 1972.

with a government contract totaling $50,000 or more to develop an Affirmative Action employment plan. Because of these stipulations, only large firms or those that rely heavily on federal money, such as universities and the defense industry, are legally subject to Affirmative Action. Many large firms also use Affirmative Action plans even though they are not legally required to do so.[8]

An Affirmative Action plan outlines the program, including numerical goals and timetables, which the firm will use to increase its employment of women and minorities. Such plans in practice can be difficult to implement. The following example illustrates some of the difficulties involved. Suppose a firm believes that it employs too few women as managers. First, the firm must do a statistical analysis to decide whether it has failed to hire women in the same proportion as the labor pool; that is, the pool of qualified applicants. Thus the firm must identify the potential pool of applicants from which it will hire. Defining the labor pool of available women managers is often difficult. It probably should not be based on the firm's applicant pool because if the firm has been known to be unfriendly to women, it is likely that fewer women apply to that firm. Consequently, its applicant pool will have fewer women than it otherwise might. Another choice would be to define the labor pool of women as the fraction of all managers in the area who are women. This too is problematic. Perhaps women in the area have not trained for management careers believing that they will have difficulty finding management jobs because of the firm's discrimination.

Even if the labor pool can be properly defined and the firm can set its hiring goal, the firm also faces the difficult decision about how to get its workforce to reflect that proportion defined by the goal. If the firm finds that 40 percent of the managers should be female and only 20 percent of the managers are currently female, what should the firm do? One approach is to make sure that 40 percent of their new management hires are female. However, if there is low turnover at this firm (i.e., managers are not likely to quit or be fired), using this hiring rule will mean that it will take quite some time for the management staff to be 40 percent female. Thus the only way to quickly remedy past discrimination may be to favor women in hiring (i.e., hire disproportionately more women than men). But if the firm must turn down some better-qualified men to do so, it risks being subject to charges of reverse discrimination. Reverse discrimination is said to occur when a less-qualified woman or minority is hired in place of a more qualified applicant who is not in the protected category (e.g., a white man).

To administer Affirmative Action, the Office of Federal Contract Compliance Programs (OFCCP) was established within the Department of Labor. Like the EEOC, the OFCCP's effectiveness depends partially on the political climate. For example, it is well documented that Affirmative Action did not receive much support during the 1980s.[9] However, the OFCCP has more power than the EEOC because it can initiate investigations to determine whether discriminatory practices exist at a particular firm. It can conduct what is called a compliance review, wherein the OFCCP steps in to see if the firm has complied with

---

8 Because our focus in this chapter is on employment discrimination, we do not discuss Affirmative Action issues concerning admission to college, law school, or graduate school. Several court cases have challenged the use of Affirmative Action in education.

9 Jonathan S. Leonard (1989), "Women and Affirmative Action," *Journal of Economic Perspectives*, 3 (1), 61–75 notes that there was a lack of sanction and lack of progress with respect to Affirmative Action after 1980.

the Affirmative Action plan. Not only can it require employers to formulate Affirmative Action plans but also it can impose sanctions when discrimination is discovered.[10] In practice, however, sanctions are rarely imposed and the firms most likely to be targeted for review are generally large firms that already employ large numbers of women and minorities.[11]

The Affirmative Action program of the OFCCP has been the center of much controversy. Critics of Affirmative Action charge that it amounts to a system of employment quotas, even though Title VII explicitly forbids quotas and Affirmative Action plans themselves do not include quotas. Furthermore, many critics charge that Affirmative Action is simply reverse discrimination. This is, of course, illegal under Title VII. However, some feel that reverse discrimination may be necessary to correct for a history of past discrimination. This issue is particularly thorny because Title VII prohibits firms from firing workers of one race or gender to make room for workers of another. Another criticism of Affirmative Action is that even some women and minorities allege that it is stigmatizing. Coworkers may wonder if women and/or racial minorities hired under Affirmative Action were hired simply because they were women and not for their own qualifications. Finally, critics note that because it does not apply to all firms, Affirmative Action simply redistributes qualified women and minorities so that they are working at firms that are federal contractors and thus there may not be any net growth in their employment.

On the other hand, supporters note that Affirmative Action forces firms to look more diligently for qualified minorities and women and thus helps remove barriers to employment. Some Affirmative Action supporters also argue that even if some reverse discrimination is involved, it is justified as a compensation for past discrimination against blacks and women. Finally, even some large firms are often found to be in favor of Affirmative Action. It allows them to diversify their workforce, which can help sell products in an increasingly demographically diverse marketplace, and it helps provide protection from lawsuits—the company can claim that it was simply following its Affirmative Action plan. Furthermore, the changing demographics of the workforce, where it is predicted that white men will no longer be the majority, dictates that firms must hire a more diverse workforce to survive. Supporters argue that Affirmative Action can help firms to do this.

There is one other anti-discrimination law that merits attention. Most Americans are familiar with Title IX, the law that guarantees equal participation and opportunities for women in athletics. However, that is only one part of what Title IX is supposed to accomplish. More broadly, the Education Amendments of 1972, commonly called Title IX, are credited with the tremendous increase in opportunities for female athletes in schools and colleges, although the law as originally written never mentioned athletics. Specifically, Title IX states: "No person in the United States shall, on the basis of sex, be ... denied the benefits of ... any education program or activity receiving Federal financial assistance."

---

10 See the OFCCP's web page at www.dol.gov/esa/ofcp_org.htm for more information about this organization.

11 Jonathan S. Leonard (1984), "Affirmative Action and Employment," *Journal of Labor Economics*, 2 (4), 439–463.

Effectiveness of anti-discrimination programs

The natural question to ask is: How successful have anti-discrimination laws and policies been in terms of eliminating sex discrimination? As we have documented throughout this book, women have made tremendous progress in the labor market in terms of earnings, labor-force participation, and education. How much of this progress can we attribute to these policies?

With respect to the effectiveness of the Equal Pay Act and Title VII on the earnings and employment status of women, the answer to that question is surprisingly difficult to come by and the existing literature is rather sparse. The fundamental issue is that these were federal laws that had wide impact. This prevents identification of an appropriate comparison group that can be used to control for changes in the relative outcomes under study that are unrelated to the policy implementation. In other words, these federal-level policies do not create the kind of control and treatment groups needed to conduct a natural experiment. Thus identifying causal effects of the policies is difficult. For example, the male:female wage ratio was actually quite steady at about 59 percent in the decade following the passage of these laws which may lead one to wonder if they had any effect. However, scholars have noted that, due to the rapid rise in young women's labor-force participation (therefore a large number of inexperienced women in the workforce keeping overall wages low), this steady gender wage ratio is not necessarily a sign of the ineffectiveness of the laws. In fact, as we learned in Chapter 11, quite a bit was going on beneath the surface of that 59 percent ratio. Any analysis of whether Title VII narrowed the gender wage gap requires a comparison of changes in the male–female gap for workers covered by Title VII compared to workers not covered in the same period, otherwise it is difficult to control for changes that would have occurred even in the absence of the legislation.

To get around this issue, a study by economists David Neumark and Wendy Stock focused on state laws mandating equal pay that existed *prior* to the federal 1963 Equal Pay Act.[12] In this way the authors could compare a treatment group (states with equal pay laws) to a control group (states without equal pay laws) before and after the passage of the laws. The authors note that because an equal pay constraint raises the relative price of female labor, we would expect the relative employment of women to decline. Consistent with that prediction, they report evidence that state equal pay laws for women reduced the relative employment of both black women and white women.

Most scholars argue that it is unlikely that the Equal Pay Act of 1963 had a large impact on the earnings of women. Until recently, women did not often do the same type of work at a firm as men did and hence this law was unlikely to be effective. However, as we saw in Chapter 9, women are increasingly moving into male-dominated occupations even though, on average, their earnings still lag behind those of men. Thus the full impact of the Equal Pay Act may well be felt in the next few decades.

Because Affirmative Action is a program that specifically applies to firms that are federal contractors, it has been easier to assess its impact on employment and earnings. Scholars have compared firms that are federal contractors (and thus subject to the policy)

---

12   David Neumark and Wendy A. Stock (2006), "The Labor Market Effects of Sex and Race Discrimination Laws," *Economic Inquiry* 44 (3), 385–419.

to firms that are not. An early study examining the effectiveness of affirmative action did just that.[13] The author reported fairly large employment gains for black women and more modest gains for white women. A follow-up to that study that used data spanning 1973 to 2003 found that the overall employment of minority women increased during this time frame due to Affirmative Action.[14]

Both Title VII and Affirmative Action apply to larger firms, and, as we noted earlier, the larger firms have most often been subjected to OFCCP compliance reviews. These firms have also been found to be the most proactive in hiring women and minorities (i.e., not those most likely to discriminate).[15] In fact, many large firms undertook their own Affirmative Action plans even if they were not federal contractors. Thus, if these laws were effective at providing opportunities for women and minorities, we should see more women and minorities working at larger firms because these larger firms were under direct pressure from the OFCCP. At least one study has confirmed that that this was indeed the case and that both minorities and women moved to larger firms after the passage of Title VII and Affirmative Action.[16]

There is also evidence that Affirmative Action helped facilitate the movement of women and minorities into jobs that had been traditionally male-dominated, suggesting that at least some of the discrimination against women takes the form of occupational segregation.[17] Affirmative Action may also have incentivized women to train for these male-dominated jobs that were once off limits to women.

Some researchers have asked exactly *how* Affirmative Action works to increase the employment of minorities and women. Firms can implement Affirmative Action in many different ways. For example, firms can engage in special recruitment efforts to elicit more female and minority job applicants. This search can include running job ads in publications widely read by these groups, as well as attending job fairs aimed at women and minorities. This use of Affirmative Action in recruiting can help firms "cast a wider net" when searching for qualified women and minorities. It can increase the probability that female and minority applicants are qualified. Firms can also offer training and assistance programs to women and minorities after they are hired to ensure that their performance is up to the firm's usual standards. The latter can be important if there is concern that those hired are not as qualified.

Researchers who surveyed large firms in four major cities about their use of Affirmative Action found that firms using Affirmative Action in recruiting were found to screen applicants more intensely, rely more heavily on formal evaluation, and provide training to candidates they do hire. Thus they had more minority applicants and more minority and female hires. Their hires were not found to be less qualified than other members of

13   Jonathan Leonard (1984), "Affirmative Action and Employment," *Journal of Labor Economics*, 2 (4), 439–463 and Jonathan Leonard (1989), "Women and Affirmative Action," *Journal of Economic Perspectives*, 3 (1), 61–75.

14   Fidan Ana Kurtulus (2010), "The Impact of Affirmative Action on the Employment of Minorities and Women Over Three Decades: 1973–2003," unpublished working paper.

15   Harry Holzer and David Neumark, op. cit.

16   William J. Carrington, Kristin McCue, and Brooks Pierce (2000), "Using Establishment Size to Measure the Impact of Title VII and Affirmative Action," *Journal of Human Resources*, 35 (3), 503–523.

17   Fidan Ana Kurtulus (2012), "Affirmative Action and the Occupational Advancement of Minorities and Women During 1973–2003," *Industrial Relations*, 51 (2), 213–246.

their workforce. Furthermore, because of the intense screening, these employers were less likely to engage in statistical discrimination. [18]

On the other hand, firms that use Affirmative Action only in hiring are more likely than others to hire women or minorities with lower qualifications. This result occurs presumably because, although they use many of the same strategies as firms who also use Affirmative Action in recruiting, they do so to a lesser extent. But they tend to provide training to these hires with the result that job performance is not lower in these establishments compared to those who do not use Affirmative Action at all.[19] And, in a related study, researchers established that although there is some evidence that women and minorities hired under Affirmative Action have lower educational qualifications, there is no evidence that women perform less well on the job.[20]

The general conclusion with respect to women seems to be that Affirmative Action has had a positive and fairly large impact on the employment of black women and a positive but smaller impact on the employment of white women. It also appears to have helped women obtain jobs previously open only to men. In addition, there is some evidence that the wages of women are likely to be somewhat higher than they would have otherwise been without Affirmative Action. These higher wages may be attributed to the fact that firms subject to Affirmative Action are larger firms that tend to pay more and that the larger firms subject to Affirmative Action also have smaller sex and race differences in pay. Finally, there is some evidence that Affirmative Action has led to an increase in the number of government contracts awarded to female- and minority-owned businesses.[21]

Finally, the effectiveness of Title IX deserves mention. Back when your grandmother was in high school, women took home economics and men enrolled in wood shop. These were often required courses and students had no choice in the matter. Thanks to Title IX, those days are a thing of the past and men take cooking while women learn to weld. But probably the most dramatic impact of Title IX was on women's participation in sports in public K–12 schools and at universities. Economist Betsey Stevenson showed that Title IX dramatically increased women's participation in sports. Between 1972, when the law was passed, and 1979, the fraction of female high-school students participating in sports increased from about 4 to 25 percent.[22] Perhaps more importantly, Stevenson shows that providing women with access to sports has had important spillover effects on their education and labor-market success. As in so many other research studies discussed in this book, Stevenson used a natural experiment to evaluate the impact of Title IX on outcomes. At the time Title IX was passed, there was substantial variation across states in

---

18 Harry J. Holzer and David Neumark (2000), "What Does Affirmative Action Do?" *Industrial and Labor Relations Review,* 53 (2), 240–271.

19 Jonathan Leonard (1989), "Women and Affirmative Action," *Journal of Economic Perspectives,* 3 (1), 61–75 also found that there is no evidence that firms that used Affirmative Action were hiring less-qualified women.

20 Harry J. Holzer and David Neumark (1999), "Are Affirmative Action Hires Less Qualified: Evidence from Employer-Employee Data on New Hires," *Journal of Labor Economics,* 17 (3), 534–569.

21 Also see Jonathan Leonard, "Women and Affirmative Action," op. cit. for a review that focuses on the effects of Affirmative Action on women. His conclusion is that Affirmative Action has actually had very little effect on women's progress in the workplace.

22 Betsey Stevenson (2007), "Title IX and the evolution of high school sports," *Contemporary Economic Policy,* 25 (4), 486–505. Stevenson notes that the increase was mostly by those at the top of the income distribution.

the fraction of men who participated in high-school sports. Since Title IX required states to provide relatively equal opportunities to participate in sports for women and men, this meant that some states had to make larger changes than others. That difference by state in the response to Title IX is a natural experiment to test the impact of Title IX. Stevenson uses that to show that the post–Title IX generation of women has more education, greater labor-force participation and higher earnings than the pre–Title IX generation. She credits the increase in women's sports participation with an increase in women's educational attainment of about one-eighth of a year and an increase in women's labor-force participation at ages 25–34 of 1.5 percent.[23]

Policies to help women balance work and family

In this section we examine policies designed to help women balance work and family obligations. Given the dramatic increase in the LFPR of mothers documented earlier in this text, there has been increased policy attention on how firms and/or government can or should accommodate the needs of working mothers and families. The interactions between family life and work life have profound implications for individual's and families' economic well-being. Most workers, particularly women, have caregiving responsibilities for others, and trying to balance the competing demands of work and family is challenging. We first focus our attention on maternity leave policies and then we turn to childcare policies.

Overview of maternity-leave policies

The United States is alone among developed countries in its failure to mandate paid maternity leave at the national level. Furthermore, it was slow to adopt a national maternity-leave policy. In the United States the debate over maternity leave largely centered on the appropriate role of the government in family decisions and the costs to businesses of providing this leave. This public debate ultimately led to the adoption of the federal Family and Medical Leave Act (FMLA), which was the first piece of legislation that President Clinton signed into law. The FMLA was signed on February 5, 1993, and became effective on August 5, 1993.

Under the FMLA, employees are eligible for unpaid job-guaranteed leave of up to 12 weeks per year for family reasons or medical emergencies. During the leave time, any health-insurance premiums paid by the employer for the employee must continue to be paid. In order to be eligible, a particular employee must work at a worksite that has 50 or more employees, must have worked for at least 12 months with the employer, and must have worked for at least 1,250 hours during the previous 12 months. The law does allow firms to exclude certain highly paid employees from eligibility for leave. Currently, because of the stipulations regarding which firms have to provide leave and how long a woman must be employed before leave is offered, the FMLA is estimated to cover only about 59 percent of employed individuals in the United States. While the FMLA provides parental leave, take up by men is quite low—only about 3 percent of eligible men actual use the FMLA.

23　Betsey Stevenson (2010), "Beyond the Classroom: Using Title IX to Measure the Return to High School Sports," *The Review of Economics and Statistics*, 92 (2), 284–301.

Prior to the enactment of the FMLA, the only laws regarding maternity or family leave for employees were provided by state laws or through the **Pregnancy Discrimination Act of 1978**. This act requires employers to treat disabilities that result from pregnancy or childbirth as they would other disabilities. For example, if a firm provides disability leave or sick leave, it must allow employees to use this leave for pregnancy or childbirth-related disabilities. More generally, this act prohibits employers from discriminating against pregnant employees.

Very few women had job-protected maternity leave prior to FMLA. In fact, prior to 1993, only 12 states had maternity-leave legislation that was very similar in provisions to that mandated by the FMLA. However, three states have implemented paid leave programs since that time, the first of these being California, where paid family leave took effect in 2004. We discuss the California paid leave in Box 12.4. Some women have access to paid maternity leave from their employers. These women generally work for larger companies. As of the mid-2010s, about 11 percent of American workers have access to paid family leave. Most of this is paid maternity leave.

Box	12.4

Box 12.4 Effects of Paid Leave in California

In 2004, California became the first US state to enact paid family leave (PFL). New Jersey followed in 2009 and Rhode Island in 2014.

California's PFL offers six weeks of partially paid leave to either the mother or the father and, unlike the FMLA, almost all private-sector workers are eligible for leave. Wage replacement is 55 percent of earnings up to a ceiling based on the state's average weekly wage rate. The California PFL does not come with job protection; reinstatement and job retention rights are covered by preexisting laws, including the FMLA.

Proponents of paid leave claim that paid leave could enhance child development by increasing maternal time investment in children, promote gender equality through higher maternal employment, and encourage fertility and marriage by facilitating family and career compatibility. We reported some evidence that indicates that these claims are likely true. Opponents point to the effect of mandating leave as being costly to employers. However, if all employers face a mandate, we saw earlier that workers will pay for mandated leave with lower wages.

Economists Maya Rossin-Slater, Christopher J. Ruhm and Jane Waldfogel took advantage of the natural experiment afforded by the change in California's law to examine the effect of paid leave on leave-taking, employment, work hours, and wage income. The authors compared the leave-taking, employment, wages, and work hours of women with young infants/young children in California to mothers in California who had older children (aged 5–17). Using data from the CPS from 1999 to 2010, they found that the percent of women on maternity leave rose from 5.4 percent to 11.8 percent for women eligible for the paid leave (those with younger children) and actually fell a bit for the mothers with older children from 0.2 percent to 0.1 percent. This yields a DID estimate of the policy equal to 6.5 percent ($6.5 = 6.4 - (-.1)$), which they calculate is a doubling of the typical length of maternity leave, so that women were now taking almost seven weeks of leave.

Digging deeper, they found that increases were largest for unmarried and nonwhite women and those without a college degree. Leave-taking among high-school graduates rose 8 percent and 12 percent among black mothers. Among college-educated and white mothers, by contrast, it rose by a statistically insignificant amount. They concluded that the California law made paid leave much more accessible to lower-income women. The authors point to the importance of this result in light of what we know about the externalities associated with leave taking; that is, effects on maternal and child health.

The authors also provide evidence that California's paid leave increased the usual weekly work hours of employed mothers of 1–3-year-old children by 6–9 percent and that their wage incomes also rose by a similar amount.

A related study by economists Rui Huang and Muzhe Yang analyzed the effect of California's paid leave on breastfeeding. As we noted earlier, this is an important possible externality arising from the provision of leave. Data are from Wave I (1993–1994) and Wave II (2005–2006) of Infant Feeding Practices Study. They find that women in California increased the probability that they breastfed exclusively for the first three months of their infants life by 13 percent, while new mothers in other states increased their probability by 7.7 percent over the same time frame. This means that the law led to a 5.3 percent increase (5.3 = 13−7.7) in the probability of breastfeeding exclusively for the first three months.

Sources:

Rui Huang and Muzhe Yang (2015), "Paid Maternity Leave and Breastfeeding Practice before and after California's Implementation of the Nation's First Paid Family Leave Program," *Economics & Human Biology* 16, 45–59.

Maya Rossin-Slater, Christopher J. Ruhm, and Jane Waldfogel (2013), "The Effects of California's Paid Family Leave Program on Mothers' Leave-Taking and Subsequent Labor Market Outcomes." *Journal of Policy Analysis and Management* 32 (2), 224–245.

Considerable controversy and debate surrounded the passage of the FMLA. Opponents of the measure tended to focus on the cost of providing such leave. These costs include the continuation of health-insurance coverage for individuals on leave, the administrative costs associated with compliance, and the cost of training replacement workers. There is no wage cost for replacement workers since the FMLA mandates only unpaid leave.

Additional arguments advanced by those opposed to the FMLA included the following. First, there was concern that the law would discourage small businesses from hiring younger workers who would be most likely to take the leave. Second, mandated family leave might reduce the provision of other benefits that may be preferred by employees. Third, there was concern that women would have difficulty finding jobs and would find themselves unemployed or employed in low-skilled or menial jobs as firms shied away from hiring them due to the increased costs of providing family leave. Fourth, there was concern that women with access to leave might increase the number of children they have, thus making the leave more costly for employers than antici-pated. Finally, there was concern that job creation and entrepreneurial activity would be reduced by businesses due to increased costs imposed on them by having to offer family leave. Based on these concerns, passage of the FMLA hinged critically on the firm-size provisions. Critics argued that the costs of the FMLA would be particularly devastating to small firms.

Many counterarguments were made in defense of the FMLA. Proponents of the FMLA argued that the actual costs would be low because the leave is unpaid and because the administrative compliance costs are low. Others noted that the FMLA had the potential to reduce turnover costs (i.e., the costs incurred when employers must search for and hire new employees), which can be quite substantial. The FMLA may also bolster employee morale and increase employee loyalty and productivity. Furthermore, time off from work is arguably important for parent/child bonding and infant health, an important potential externality of such leave which we discuss later in this chapter. Proponents also argued that job-protected maternity leave would help women to retain valuable human capital investments, reduce unemployment, close the gender earnings gap, and promote gender equality.

In contrast to the United States, Europe has a long tradition of providing paid maternity leave with programs that date as far back as the end of the nineteenth century in Germany and Sweden. These early leaves were somewhat paternalistic in that they were enacted over concerns for the health of the mother and child and at times the leaves were compulsory. They were also often enacted with a pro-natalist and even nationalistic orientation. All European countries and Canada now offer paid maternity leave, although there is substantial variation across countries. Most European countries also offer paternity leave, but it is less likely to be paid. As of 2015, compared to other economically advanced countries, the United States is alone in its decision not to provide any sort of paid maternity leave at the national level, as seen in Figure 12.2.

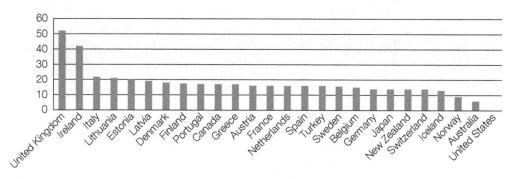

Figure 12.2 *Weeks of paid maternity leave, selected OECD countries.*

Source: OECD Family Database www.oecd.org/els/social/family/database.

Figure 12.2 shows only weeks of paid maternity leave. However, women are not necessarily paid their full salary for the weeks shown in the table. For example, in the United Kingdom, 52 total weeks of maternity leave are allowed but only 11.3 of those are at full salary. Many OECD countries also provide separate provisions for paternity leave and also for parental leave in addition to maternity-leave provisions. These leaves can be quite lengthy although it is sometimes the case that portions of the leave period are not paid. For example, Denmark provides 18 weeks of maternity leave (about half of which are paid for at full salary) plus an additional 32 weeks of paid family leave for a total of 50 weeks of paid leave during which the mother will be paid about half of her salary.[24] Table 12.1 illustrates these differences. The first column shows the total weeks of paid leave for mothers, which includes both maternity leave and parental leave. The second column shows the average payment amount which is the number of those weeks that are paid full time, and the last column shows the number of full-time paid weeks of leave for mothers. For some countries there is additional leave for fathers, which we do not show here.

Table 12.1 *Maternity leave, selected OECD countries.*

	Total Weeks of Paid Leave for Mothers	Average Payment Rate	Total Paid Leave for Mothers
Australia	18	9.8	1.8
Austria	81	39.2	31.7
Belgium	28	48.2	13.5
Canada	52	50.2	26.1
Denmark	50	51.5	25.8
Finland	158	26.8	42.4
France	42	49.1	20.6
Germany	57	61.8	35.4
Hungary	160	28.2	45.2
Italy	48	52.7	25.1
Japan	58	54.0	31.3
Luxembourg	42	64.2	27.0
Netherlands	42	49.6	20.8
New Zealand	14	46.5	6.5
Norway	36	88.9	32.0
Spain	16	100.0	16.0
Sweden	60	80.0	48.0
Switzerland	14	80.0	11.2
United Kingdom	52	22.5	11.7
United States	0	0.0	0.0

Source: OECD Family Data Base, 2013.

An economic analysis of family-leave policies

Two predictions flow from economic theory with respect to how much family leave firms should be mandated to offer. The first is that the labor market will typically provide the amount of family leave that employees desire. A simple analysis will help you understand this prediction. Begin by assuming that employees get utility or satisfaction from both wages and benefits, and assume for the moment that family leave is the only benefit

---

24 See the OECD family database for details of the policies of OECD countries: http://www.oecd.org/els/family/database.htm#public_policy.

offered and that it is of value to all employees at the firm (although not necessarily of the same value to all employees).[25] Employees are willing to trade off between wages and benefits in part because some benefits are usually taxed (they may confer other advantages as well). Further assume that employers can compensate their employees in two ways: either they pay employees cash or they provide family leave.

From the employer's perspective, as long as the costs are the same, it doesn't matter how the employee is compensated because the firm's profits will be the same.[26] Thus the firm is willing to provide many different combinations of family leave and wages as long as its profits remain the same. Employees who value family leave will negotiate a benefits package that includes family leave, presumably by accepting lower wages. Employees will then sort themselves into those jobs that offer the wage/leave combination that maximizes their utility.

An example illustrates how this would work. Suppose that family leave costs an employer $200 to provide and that this leave is worth $300 to an employee. In this case the employer could provide the leave and reduce the wages paid to the employee by between $200 and $300, leaving both the employee and the employer better off. In the end, family leave will be provided up to the point where an extra dollar spent by employers on family leave is valued by the employee at $1.

The second implication of economic theory is that as long as labor markets are perfectly competitive, profit-maximizing firms will provide the amount of family leave that employees want and thus no government intervention is needed. This second implication requires the assumptions of perfectly competitive labor and product markets. This means, in part, that workers must be well informed and must be highly mobile—that is, it must be easy (not very costly) for them to move from job to job. There also must be many firms and many workers, and employers and workers must have perfect information, including information on wages and benefits.

This model and its corresponding implications that the market will provide family leave without government intervention provided ideological support for those who opposed the passage of the FMLA. They simply argued that the market would provide such benefits if they are valued by employees, and there would be no need to mandate them.

Those in favor of the FMLA acknowledged the predictions of this economic model but stressed that the assumptions of perfect competition and perfect mobility must be examined carefully. As evidence for this, FMLA supporters note that the rapid rise in the labor-force participation of mothers did not coincide with a rapid rise in the provision of family-friendly benefits—this might have indicated that the market may be slow to respond to the needs of working families, thus opening the door for government intervention. Of course, the failure of the market to provide such leaves could be interpreted in an opposite manner—that is, given the rise in dual-earner families and particularly the labor supply of mothers, if the market is competitive and we have not seen an increase in

---

25 Obviously this is not the case. Most firms offer a wide array of employment benefits. However, the outcome of our analysis is not changed by assuming that maternity leave is the only benefit.

26 In reality, some benefits may be less expensive to provide than cash. For example, large firms can often negotiate health insurance that is less costly than an extra dollar of salary because of economies of scale—that is, they are buying so many policies, they may be able to purchase an insurance policy worth $300 for only $250. Some benefits may also make employees more productive, also saving the firm money. We ignore this complication for now since incorporating this does not change the results of our analysis.

job-protected family leaves provided by firms, perhaps the benefits from such leaves are overstated and they are not a benefit that employees desire.

However, as you are probably aware, often markets are not perfectly competitive. A firm operating in an imperfectly competitive environment may be able to offer family leave to its employees without lowering wages if it does not face as much pressure from competition to keep costs low. Even if markets were perfectly competitive, there may nevertheless be a reason for government to intervene and mandate that firms provide family leave. As you may recall from your introductory economics course, government intervention in perfectly competitive markets introduces inefficiency (think of rent control), and distorts the price signals sent to buyers and sellers. In the example of rent control, keeping rents artificially below the market level means that there are more people who want to rent apartments than there are apartments available.

An important exception is the case of **externalities**. An externality occurs when an activity undertaken either in production or consumption has a spillover onto a third party who is not directly involved in the transaction. You may remember examples of externalities from your principles of economics course. One oft-used example of a **positive externality** involves a bakery that emits a pleasant aroma. People who walk by the bakery are able to enjoy the smell. The key is that the aroma was not a product of the bakery, and the bakery cannot stop others from enjoying the aroma, even if people walking by were not buying baked goods. When a positive externality exists, it can be shown that a competitive market will produce too little of the good with the positive externality. A **negative externality** occurs if, rather than a bakery, an oil refinery emitted toxic pollution into the air. Certainly nobody enjoys the smell of this production process, and it may be bad for our health and the environment. However, it is simply a by-product of the particular production process. Yet this odor has an adverse impact on others in the area, hence creating a negative externality. In the case of a negative externality, a competitive market will produce too much of the good in question.

How does this apply to family leave? Family leave, since it enables a parent to be home with a very young child, might lead to that child's receiving better healthcare and other improved outcomes. As we noted in Chapter 5, children, particularly when they are young, are time-intensive. As a result of this better care, children might be healthier and incur fewer medical costs. To the extent that these medical care expenditures are not paid for entirely by the family (as is the case with most health-insurance coverage in the United States), the parent may undervalue family leave and thus not take enough of it in the absence of mandated family leave. This is an example of a positive externality of mandated family leave. We review other externalities below when we discuss the effects of family leave on various outcomes.

Another argument in favor of providing family leave is the presence of **adverse selection** under **asymmetric information**. To understand this argument, start by noting the obvious: Employees and employers have different information about the likelihood that the employee may take a leave. The employee knows whether she will likely become pregnant, but the employer does not necessarily know her plans. This difference in information is called asymmetric information by economists and it refers to the fact that one party (the employee) has more information about whether she will need family leave than the other party (the employer).

This asymmetric information creates what we call **adverse selection**. This refers to the fact that those individuals with a high probability of using family leave will look for and try to obtain jobs at firms that provide leave. Adverse selection occurs if only some of the firms, but not all of them, offer maternity leave. Suppose that only a few firms offered leave and the others did not. Those individuals who do not plan to avail themselves of leave will search out higher-paying jobs at firms that do not offer leave. It is possible that some of those individuals will then have amounts of leave that are "too small"—that is, they have amounts of leave that may be less than socially optimal, particularly if leave generates a positive externality as discussed above. Furthermore, the few firms offering leave will find themselves attracting workers with a higher probability of using leave than the average worker in the workforce. Thus these firms would find their leave costs higher than anticipated, which would put additional downward pressure on wages. In the end, these few firms, because they will attract all the workers who want maternity leave, may find it too costly to offer family leave and cease to offer it. In this case, market forces tend to discourage the provision of family leave.

This problem can be avoided by mandating family leave so that all firms must offer leave. Otherwise, this adverse selection under asymmetric information would likely result in the firms that offered leave having very few men as employees—assuming men do not plan to use the leave. As we noted earlier, most of the individuals who take family leave are women. Men may not plan to use leave; thus they will look for jobs that do not offer leave so that they can earn higher wages. The Pregnancy Discrimination Act of 1978 made it illegal to offer a different benefits package to men and women, so firms could not avoid the potential loss of men by offering them a different benefits package.

In the case of family leave, the government chose to intervene by mandating that employers provide unpaid leave. However, the government could have intervened in other ways. For example, it could have taxed all employers and then used the revenue from the taxation to fund a public family leave program. We will point out other ways the government can intervene later in this chapter when we talk about the childcare market.

To recap, mandating family leave is justifiable on economic grounds in at least two cases: if such leave generates a positive externality or if there is adverse selection under asymmetric information. In the next section we examine some of the research done by economists and others to understand how the passage of the FMLA has affected the economic well-being of families.

The effects of family leave on women and children

In this section we examine the considerable amount of research that exists that has tried to ascertain if providing family leave has improved women's economic outcomes. We often refer to family leave as maternity leave since many of the studies focus on women's economic outcomes. And, as we have stressed earlier in this chapter, take-up of family leave by men is low in the United States as it is in most of the developed world. Many of the studies described below use data from Europe which, as noted, has a longer history of providing leave to women.

Wages Considerable research has been done on the effect of maternity leave on women's wages. In the United States, some of this research was conducted before the passage of the FMLA in order to assess the probable effects of the FMLA on women's economic status by examining how women who had job-protected maternity leave prior to the passage of the FMLA fared compared to those who did not have such leave. The passage of the FMLA guaranteed the leave taker the right to return to her pre-birth employer in the same job (or one at the same level). To the extent that a given woman is more likely to return to her pre-birth employer now that she has job-protected leave, the FMLA has the potential to raise earnings, assuming that earnings rise with general and firm-specific human capital. Thus the FMLA may facilitate advancing a woman's career.

However, the positive effect of leave-taking on women's pay may be offset if the leave is for an extended period of time and a woman's human capital depreciates. This is not likely to be an important consideration under the FMLA since the job-protected leave is only for a maximum of 12 weeks. Furthermore, as we discussed earlier, women may have to accept lower wages in exchange for the leave.

There is empirical evidence that, pre-FMLA, women in the United States who returned to their pre-birth employers after giving birth, regardless of whether they had leave, did, in fact, have higher wages than those women who did not return to the same employer.[27] Some evidence also showed that women who had employer-provided job-protected leave prior to the FMLA and returned to their jobs post-childbirth had higher wages than those who did not.[28] This supports the human capital argument that job retention allows women to continue building their firm-specific human capital. A study that examined the wage effects of the FMLA documented that there was no effect of the FMLA on women's earnings, a finding that is most likely attributable to the fact that any negative wage effect is likely counteracted by the positive effect of having job-protected maternity leave.[29]

In contrast, a study that used data from nine European countries from the years 1969 to 1993 documented that women receive lower wages in exchange for maternity leave and that this is particularly likely when the leave is of long duration.[30] Because the FMLA provides for unpaid leave of a relatively short duration, we may be less likely to see negative wage effects in the United States.

Studies that have focused on particular countries have reported mixed results. For example, a study using data from Denmark which expanded maternity leave from 14 to 20 weeks in 1984 reported some evidence that this change raised mother's earnings.[31] However, another study, using data from Norway, found no evidence that lengthening paid leave affected women's earnings.[32]

While is it difficult to draw a firm conclusion from this evidence, it appears that wage effects, if they exist, are small. In other words, women's earnings are not changing dramatically with maternity leave.

Employment In addition to its potential effects on earnings, access to maternity leave is also likely to affect the employment decision of mothers. A change in maternity leave

27 Jane Waldfogel (1998), "Understanding the Family Gap in Pay for Women with Children," *Journal of Economic Perspectives*, 12 (1), 137–156.
28 Jane Waldfogel (1998), "The Family Gap for Young Women in the United States and Britain: Can Maternity Leave Make a Difference?" *Journal of Labor Economics*, 16 (3), 505–535.
29 Jane Waldfogel (1999), "The Impact of the Family and Medical Leave Act," *Journal of Policy Analysis and Management*, 18 (2), 281–302.
30 Christopher J. Ruhm (1998), "The Economic Consequences of Parental Leave Mandates: Lessons from Europe," *Quarterly Journal of Economics*, 113 (1), 285–318.
31 Astrid Würtz Rasmussen (2010), "Increasing the Length of Parents' Birth-Related Leave: The Effect on Children's Long-Term Educational Outcomes," *Labour Economics*, 17 (1) , 91–100.
32 Gordon B. Dahl, , Katrine Vellesen Loken, Magne Mogstad, and Kari Vea Salvanes (2013), "What Is the Case for Paid Maternity Leave?" IZA Discussion Paper, No. 7707.

can affect employment through two possible mechanisms. A woman who might have dropped out of the paid labor force upon giving birth might find that the leave is just long enough for her to decide to stay on the job and thereby maintain employment continuity. Thus maternity leave might increase women's commitment to the work force and hence increase their employment. Conversely, the leave period might be longer than a woman was planning on taking and hence she might stay out of the work force for a longer period of time.

The effect of the FMLA on employment in the United States has been mixed, with one study reporting that that the employment of mothers increases when leave is offered[33] while another found little evidence that the FMLA increased postnatal employment rates.[34] A study based on data from nine European countries from 1969 to 1993 established that paid leave rights were associated with a rise in female employment, but there was a reduction in women's relative wages for longer durations of leave.[35] And research based on data from Canada indicates that changes in maternity-leave policies in that country increased job continuity with the pre-birth employer.[36]

Germany is an interesting case study as it has changed its leave entitlements many times over the years. In 1979, paid leave length was tripled from 2 to 6 months. In 1986, paid leave increased from 6 to 10 months, and in 1992 it was extended to 36 months. Each expansion in maternity leave was found to encourage women to delay their return to work.[37] The delay was strongest for the increase in job-protected leave from 2 to 6 months in 1979, and weakest for the increase from 18 to 36 months in 1992. Hence the reforms succeeded in increasing the time mothers spend with their children after childbirth. Despite this strong short-term impact on labor supply, the expansions had little impact on mothers' LFPRs in the long run. The authors of the study interpret this as an indication that the expansions in leave coverage failed at promoting employment continuity of mothers.

In 2007, Germany made yet another change in its leave policy by making the wage replacement more generous, but reducing the length of paid leave. The dual objective of this change was to increase fertility and to enhance incentives for women to return to the labor force after childbirth. A study that analyzed the effect of this new regulation found, similar to the effects of previous legislation, that women timed their return to work postpartum to coincide with the end of their leave, but again there was no long run effect on mother's labor-force participation.[38]

33 Jane Waldfogel, (1999), "Family Leave Policies and Women's Retention after Childbirth: Evidence from the United States, Britain, and Japan," *Journal of Population Economics*, 12, 523–545, and Christopher J. Ruhm (1998), "The Economic Consequences of Parental Leave Mandates: Lessons from Europe," *Quarterly Journal of Economics*, 113 (1), 285–318 find support for this.
34 Katherine E. Ross (1999), "Labor Pains: The Effect of the Family and Medical Leave Act on the Return to Paid Work after Childbirth," *Focus*, 20 (1), 34–36.
35 Christopher J. Ruhm (1998), "The Economic Consequences of Parental Leave Mandates: Lessons from Europe," *Quarterly Journal of Economics*, 113 (1), 285–318.
36 Michael Baker and Kevin Milligan (2008), "How Does Job-Protected Maternity Leave Affect Mothers' Employment?" *Journal of Labor Economics*, 26 (4), 655–691.
37 U. Schönberg and J. Ludsteck (2007), "Maternity Leave Legislation, Female Labor Supply, and the Family Wage Gap," (No. 2699), Institute for the Study of Labor (IZA).
38 Jochen Kluve and Marcus Tamm (2013), "Parental Leave Regulations, Mothers' Labor Force Attachment and Fathers' Childcare Involvement: Evidence From a Natural Experiment," *Journal of Population Economics* 26 (3), 983–1005.

Fertility Maternity leave, whether it is paid or unpaid, lowers the cost of a birth, and this creates a fertility incentive. Many European countries have enacted or enhanced their maternity-leave policies to explicitly encourage families to have more children, such as the change made by Germany in 2007 as noted earlier in this chapter. This has not been a stated goal in the United States, which, as we saw earlier, enjoys higher fertility than its European counterparts.

Frequent changes in family policies in many European countries provide ample opportunities for studying their effects on fertility trends. It is worth keeping in mind that even the very generous European paid-leave policies only cover a small part of the costs of raising a child, which are incurred for roughly 21 years for families. Also, while the leave lengths are long in Europe, women are not typically paid their full pre-birth salary while on leave; in other words, the opportunity costs are not zero. Still, there is empirical evidence that more generous parental leave policies do influence fertility, particularly second and third births.

As an example, Lalive and Zweimüller focus on changes in Austria's parental leave policies. In 1990, Austria doubled the leave period from 1 to 2 years.[39] Lalive and Zweimüller viewed changing leave regulation as a natural experiment and investigated subsequent childbearing among women who had a child in June 1990 vs. having a child in July 1990, that is during the month preceding and following the change in parental leave rules. Their research design took advantage of the fact that women having a child, say, on June 30, were still only entitled to a shorter period of parental leave, while those having a child on July 1 would benefit from an extended leave period. They identified a strong increase in fertility after this change in the policy. Some have termed this a **speed premium** as it encourages women to have a second child by making it easier for them to take extended leave after the birth of a first child. Similar results have been found for Sweden.[40]

The 2007 policy change in Germany provided additional evidence that births are responsive to economic incentives. On January 1, 2007, women giving birth were entitled to a much more generous payment than those who gave birth in 2006. There is evidence that the change in benefits caused women currently pregnant and due to deliver just before the policy change to attempt to postpone births until January 1, 2007, when the policy became effective, to take advantage of the more generous birth allowance.

Maternal and child health As we discussed earlier, one of the main arguments for mandating maternity leave is that it might have positive effects on both maternal and child health, thus generating positive externalities for society. The general guideline among US doctors is that it generally takes a woman 6 weeks to recover from childbirth and perhaps longer for mothers who give birth via Cesarean section. Women in the United States take shorter leaves on average than their European or Canadian counterparts. There is concern that such short leaves could be detrimental to a child's health. For example, it takes some time to establish breastfeeding, and mothers who must return to work in just 6 weeks may decide not to breastfeed, feeling it will conflict with their work or make it difficult to

---

39 Rafael Lalive and Josef Zweimüller (2009), "How Does Parental Leave Affect Fertility and Return to Work? Evidence From Two Natural Experiments," *The Quarterly Journal of Economics*, 124 (3), 1363–1402. They also focus on a 1992 reform using a similar method.

40 Anders Björklund (2006), "Does Family Policy Affect Fertility?" *Journal of Population Economics*, 19 (1), 3–24.

transition back to work. Research confirms that the length of time a woman breastfeeds depends partly on how long a leave from work she takes.[41] A study based on Canadian data found that the generous leave provisions in that country are associated with a substantial increase in breastfeeding duration and rise in the proportion of mothers who breastfeed exclusively for 6 months, which is an important public health benchmark.[42] Another study using United States data found that leave coverage is associated with more breastfeeding and that children whose mothers did not have family leave coverage scored lower on tests of their cognitive ability administered when they were ages 3 and 4. This same study further documented that women who return to work between 0 and 6 weeks following the birth of a child are less likely to breastfeed, less likely to have taken their child to a well-baby visit, and less likely to have had their child immunized.[43]

Maternal health may also be positively affected by maternity leave. Empirical evidence from the United States shows that state leave mandates that were adopted before enacting the FMLA increased the length of maternity leave by about one week, and this longer leave was associated with a drop in postpartum depressive symptoms of the mother and fewer outpatient doctor visits for the mother.[44] A study based on 16 countries observed from 1969 to 2000 found that paid maternity leave entitlements reduced mortality during the post-neonatal period (between 28 days and 1 year) and in early childhood (between 1 and 5 years). For example, a 10-week extension of paid leave could reduce post-neonatal deaths by 3.7–4.5 percent and could decrease child mortality by 3.3–3.5 percent.[45] A follow-up to that study, which expanded both the number of countries and the time frame to 2000, corroborated these initial findings and also found reductions in the incidence of low-birth weight babies.[46] Thus there is some evidence that maternity leave, by providing time for parents to invest in the health of their young children, has the potential to increase child health.

Childcare costs and childcare policy

Data from the US Census Bureau indicate that every week in the United States nearly 11 million children younger than age five whose mothers are working are in some type of childcare arrangement.[47] On average these children spend 36 hours a week in childcare. A quarter of children, nearly 3 million, are in multiple childcare arrangements because of the need to accommodate the working hours of their parents. The most

---

41 Brian Roe, Leslie A. Whittington, Sara Beck Fein, and Mario F. Teisl (1999), "Is There Competition Between Breast-Feeding and Maternal Employment?" *Demography*, 36 (2), 157–171.

42 Michael Baker and Kevin Milligan (2008), "Maternal Employment, Breastfeeding, and Health: Evidence from Maternity Leave Mandates," *Journal of Health Economics*, 27 (4), 871–887.

43 Lawrence M. Berger, Jennifer Hill, and Jane Waldfogel (2005), "Maternity Leave, Early Maternal Employment, and Child Health and Development in the U.S.," *Economic Journal*, 115, F29–F47.

44 Pinka Chatterji and Sara Markowitz (2005), "Does the Length of Maternity Leave Affect Maternal Health?" *Southern Economic Journal*, 72 (1), 16–41.

45 Christopher J. Ruhm (2000), "Parental Leave and Child Health," *Journal of Health Economics*, 19, 931–960.

46 S. Tanaka (2005), "Parental Leave and Child Health Across OECD Countries," *Economic Journal*, 115, F7–F28.

47 These data typically focus on children under the age of 5, because children typically start kindergarten at age 5 and hence the school system functions as a childcare provider for at least part of the day. Many parents also rely on after-school care at least until their children are 12 or so.

often reported arrangement is a relative, typically a grandparent, caring for the child. The next most common arrangement is a formal childcare center, followed by a family daycare home.[48]

Childcare costs vary widely across the type of arrangement and across states.[49] In 2013, one survey of childcare providers across the United States reported that the average annual cost of full-time care for an infant in center-based care ranged from $5,496 in Mississippi to $16,549 in Massachusetts and from $4,560 (Mississippi) to $12,272 (Virginia) for an infant in a family childcare setting. Like many service industries, over three-quarters of the cost of a childcare program is for labor. The average income for a full-time childcare professional in 2013 was only $21,490, making childcare one of the lowest-paying professional fields.[50]

Most childcare arrangements are made privately and the costs are borne mostly by families. In 1996 the United States dramatically changed its support system for low-income families, replacing a program called AFDC with a new one called TANF. A major goal of this reform was to incentivize low-income mothers to work. In order to provide these women with affordable childcare, the United States introduced the Child Care Development Fund (CCDF). Similarly to the case of maternity leave, subsidies for childcare are often more generous in other developed countries than in the United States Hence, as shown in Figure 12.3, as a percentage of the average wage, the United States is at the higher end of childcare costs.

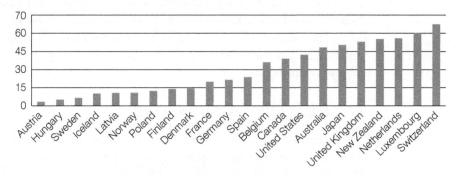

Figure 12.3 *Childcare fees for two-year-old attending an accredited facility as a percentage of average wages, selected OECD countries, 2012.*

Source: OECD family database.

CCDF subsidies exist to assist low-income families with the cost of childcare so that they may work or prepare for employment. The benefit is provided in the form of either a contracted childcare slot or a voucher that may be used to access care by any childcare provider that meets state requirements. Families typically pay a monthly copayment, based on factors such as income, family size, and the number of children in care. The

---

48 Who's Minding the Kids? Child Care Arrangements: Spring 2013. www.census.gov/prod/2013pubs/p70-135.pdf

49 Data on costs of childcare by state can be obtained at husa.childcareaware.org/sites/default/files/19000000_state_fact_sheets_2014_v04.pdf.

50 US Department of Labor, Bureau of Labor Statistics (2013, March 29). Occupational employment and wages—May 2012 [News Release]. Retrieved May 24, 2013, from http://www.bls.gov/news.release/pdf/ocwage.pdf. Does not include preschool teachers and assistant teachers.

CCDF subsidy—typically paid directly to the provider—covers the difference between the copayment and the full cost of care, up to a maximum state payment rate. CCDF subsidies are not a federal entitlement, meaning that eligible applicants do not necessarily receive subsidies. While the federal government establishes broad requirements for state CCDF programs, including a maximum income eligibility limit of 85 percent of state median income, states maintain considerable discretion in terms of designing their programs and determining income limits, work requirements, and family copayments. States spent $9.5 billion of CCDF funds in 2010.[51]

The provisions in the 1996 Welfare Reform Bill provide an extra incentive for low-income mothers to work—generally, they can only collect benefits for a maximum of 5 years during their lifetime. Thus the hope is that by providing them with childcare subsidies, they can participate in the labor market and build the human capital and work experience they need to become self-sufficient. It is important to remember that many of the jobs available to former welfare recipients require little skill and hence pay very little. These are jobs that typically do not lead to promotions or offer much opportunity for advancement. Thus it is unclear whether just working will make these women economically self-sufficient. However, it has long been posited that childcare costs are a significant barrier to employment among the low-income population.

A number of empirical studies have established that childcare subsidies do encourage low-income women to work.[52] In addition to encouraging work, the 1996 welfare reform also wanted to provide incentives for women to increase their human capital to improve their labor-market skills and hence help them increase their wages and hence promote economic self-sufficiency. There is also evidence that these subsidies have increased women's human capital.[53]

In addition to the CCDF, tax policies assist some families in paying for childcare. Employed parents can use the Child and Dependent Care Tax Credit to receive a tax credit of up to 35 percent of their expenses to care for two or more children. Because this tax credit is nonrefundable, it is used primarily by middle-class families, as lower-income families often do not have a large enough tax liability to qualify. Flexible spending accounts which allow families to set aside money for childcare before taxes are another source of childcare funding. These too are aimed more at higher-income families.

While most childcare in the United States is privately provided, two programs are not. Head Start, a federal program which has operated since 1965, provides educational and other services to children from low-income families. Some states are now offering pre-K programs. These programs are aimed at 3- and 4-year-olds and primarily serve children from low-income families. Like Head Start, pre-K programs are typically provided five days a week but there is substantial local variation and children attend from 2 to 8 hours per day depending on the local offerings.

51 Erdal Tekin (2014), "Child Care Subsidy Policy: What It Can and Cannot Accomplish," IZA World of Labor.

52 David Blau and Erdal Tekin (2007), "The Determinants and Consequences of Child Care Subsidies for Single Mothers in the USA," *Journal of Population Economics*, 20 (4), 719–741.

53 Chris M. Herbst and Erdal Tekin (2011), "Do Child Care Subsidies Influence Single Mothers' Decision to Invest in Human Capital?" *Economics of Education Review*, 30 (5), 901–912.

Many scholars report that the quality of childcare in the United States is not high.[54] Studies have established that process quality is low—this refers to the interactions between caregiver and child. There are also concerns that the structural quality of care is low. Structural quality refers to the size of the group, the ratio of staff to child, and caregiver training and pay. States often mandate these structural aspects of care.

The age of the child is a critical determinant of the appropriate type of care. Experts stress that infants and toddlers (children aged 1–3) need more intensive care that emphasizes their health and safety. Preschoolers—aged 3 to 5—generally benefit from a more educationally focused environment. In the United States, many parents send their children to preschool even if the mother is not working, often at their own expense. The US system is most similar to those of Canada, the United Kingdom, and Switzerland, which all rely on a market-driven decentralized approach to childcare for most of the preschool period. Other countries take a more integrated approach. For example, the Nordic countries have a universal system of early childhood education, which starts with maternity leave and progressively gets more educational until the child enters school at the relatively late age of 7. In Belgium, France and Italy there are fewer childcare services in the first three years of life, but once children turn three they begin formal schooling and receive care in that setting.[55] The United States spends a relatively low percentage of gross domestic product (GDP) on childcare compared to other OECD countries.[56]

A related and important policy question is the effect of childcare subsidies on the quality of childcare purchased. Investments in children are generally seen as investments in the future economy. A large literature in economics (as well as psychology) makes clear the importance of early childhood education.[57] Similarly to the provision of maternity leave, childcare may provide important externalities to society. Hence, one goal of the CCDF is to increase the quality of the care provided.

Women and Social Security

As most Americans are aware, the Social Security system pays benefits to a wide array of individuals, including the elderly and the disabled. In this section we focus on retirement benefits, with an emphasis on how the structure of the current system poses problems of equity between one-earner married couples as compared to two-earner married couples, unmarried couples and single individuals. We present just enough information about the system for you to understand our discussion, but we leave the more complicated details to the Social Security Administration staff.

The Social Security Act was signed into law in 1935. The purpose of the act was to ensure that the elderly and the disabled had financial security. Social Security is financed

---

54 See Christopher J. Ruhm (2011), "Policies to Assist Parents with Young Children," in *The Future of Children*, Center for the Future of Children, The David and Lucile Packard Foundation 21 (2), 37.

55 Information on other countries is adapted from Christopher J Ruhm (2011), "Policies to Assist Parents with Young Children, in *The Future of Children*, Center for the Future of Children, The David and Lucile Packard Foundation 21 (2), 37.

56 Olivier Thévenon (2011), "Family Policies in OECD Countries: A Comparative Analysis," *Population and Development Review*, 37 (1), 57–87.

57 Janet Currie and Douglas Almond (2011), "Human Capital Development Before Age Five," *Handbook of Labor Economics* 4, 1315–1486.

through a payroll tax. This means that, for all workers, 12.4 percent of their earnings are paid into the Social Security system each year up to some maximum level of earnings which is adjusted annually (in 2015 this maximum was $118,500). The payroll tax is split equally between the employee and the employer.[58]

To receive Social Security benefits based upon their own earnings record, individuals must have worked for 40 quarters and must have reached a certain threshold level of pay. An individual is eligible to collect Social Security at age 62, although full benefits can only be collected by those aged 66 and above.[59] Monthly Social Security benefits are based upon how long an individual worked and what his or her earnings were.

The Social Security system is structured such that individual workers pay the Social Security tax, but families receive the benefits. This creates some inequities where women are concerned. Some examples will illustrate this point. In our examples, we assume that wives are the secondary earners (i.e. earn less than their husbands). We assume this to make our point, but it is worth noting that in 2012 the Bureau of Labor Statistics reported that 30 percent of wives out-earned their husbands.

When a single woman works and pays Social Security payroll taxes for ten years, she is eligible to collect benefits based on her own earnings. When a married woman works and pays into Social Security (by paying the payroll tax described earlier) for at least ten years, she is also eligible to collect benefits based on her own earnings. However, she can also apply to receive 50 percent of her husband's benefit (i.e., a spouse's benefit), but she cannot collect both. Because men tend to work longer and earn more, many married women are eligible for a larger benefit based on their husband's earnings record than on their own earnings record.[60]

A woman who specialized in household production rather than market work will also be eligible for 50 percent of her husband's Social Security benefit upon retirement. A widow can receive 100 percent of her husband's Social Security benefit as long as she is aged 65 or above. Finally, a divorced woman is entitled to collect benefits based on her ex-husband's Social Security, if he is receiving Social Security or is deceased, as long as the marriage lasted at least ten years and the recipient is unmarried. However, a divorced woman can only collect 50 percent of her ex-spouse's benefits.[61]

To provide some idea of the magnitude of these benefits, Table 12.2 presents the average monthly Social Security benefit received by different groups of individuals in 2014. Note that a man collecting on his own earnings record receives the highest benefit per month. It is not surprising that a widow collecting on her husband's earnings record collects the second greatest amount. The lowest-paid group is men who collect based on their wives' earnings record.

The family structure that benefits the most from the current structure of the Social Security system is the one where the husband worked in the formal labor market and the

---

58 The employee and employer each pay an additional 1.45 percent on all the employee's earnings for Medicare, the health insurance system for elderly individuals in the United States.

59 Since 2003, the age at which full benefits are payable has been gradually increasing and will reach age 67 in 2027.

60 The Social Security benefits formula provides a higher replacement rate for workers with low earnings. For the median female retiree, Social Security replaces 54 percent of average lifetime earnings compared to 41 percent for the median man.

61 There are some other stipulations for collecting benefits from an ex-spouse, which we won't detail here.

wife specialized in household production. In this case only the husband is paying into Social Security through the payroll tax and upon his retirement the family receives 150 percent of his benefits—he gets his full benefits and his wife is eligible for 50 percent of his benefits.

Table 12.2 *Average monthly Social Security benefits by gender, December 2014.*

Type of Beneficiary	Men	Women
Retired worker collecting on own earnings record	$1,451	$1,134
Spouse of retired worker	$474	$655
Widows/widowers	$1,084	$1,248

Source: "Fast Facts and Figures about Social Security, 2014."

In the case of a two-earner family where the wife earns substantially less than the husband and/or only worked for a few years, they both pay the payroll tax and they receive 150 percent of his benefits, assuming her earnings were low enough that she is better off collecting as his spouse. Thus they get the same benefits they would have gotten had the wife not worked at all, even though they both paid into the system. In the case where the wife has worked continuously for relatively high earnings and the husband has as well, they will likely receive higher benefits than the family where the wife did not work at all. But they will have both paid the payroll tax and being married does not increase their benefits at all (i.e., they each collect what they would collect if they were single).

Social Security clearly provides an incentive for couples to follow a "traditional family structure." In fact, this was the most common family structure that existed when Social Security first began, which, in part, explains this payment system. Edward McCaffery, author of a book on gender bias in the US tax system, notes that when it comes to Social Security, wives who work in the formal labor market essentially subsidize those who do not.[62] From the standpoint of Social Security, it doesn't pay to be a secondary earner.[63]

Despite its bias toward a traditional family structure, Social Security is an important component of income for older women. Currently, women represent about 56 percent of all Social Security beneficiaries aged 62 and over, and 68 percent of all beneficiaries 85 years and older. In general, women face greater economic challenges than men when they reach retirement age. First of all, they have a longer life expectancy—women reaching age 65 in 2012 are expected to live, on average, an additional 21.4 years compared with 19.1 years for men. Second, as we have seen in several other places in this book, women earn less than men. Elderly women are less likely than elderly men to have significant family income from pensions other than Social Security. In 2012, only 22 percent of unmarried women aged 65 or older were receiving their own private pensions (either as a retired worker or survivor), compared to 27.7 percent of unmarried men.[64]

---

62 Edward J. McCaffery (1997), *Taxing Women*, Chicago, IL: University of Chicago Press.

63 For a more detailed analysis of the issues surrounding women in the Social Security System, see Andrew G. Biggs, Gayle Reznik, and Nada Eissa (2010), "The Treatment of Married Women by the Social Security Retirement Program," available at SSRN 1711932.

64 Figures in this paragraph are taken from "Social Security Is Important for Women," Social Security Administration, March 2014. www.ssa.gov/news/press/factsheets/women.htm.

Given that labor-force participation rates for women have risen drastically over the past three decades, more and more women are expected to receive Social Security benefits based solely on their own earnings history rather than on their husband's. Nevertheless, proposals have been brought forth to help eliminate the bias in Social Security toward single-earner couples. One proposal is called "earnings sharing" because it assigns an equal share of household earnings to each spouse and eliminates dependent benefits. This approach explicitly recognizes that the division of labor in the home represents a joint decision and, unlike the present system, would not penalize dual-earner couples.[65]

Conclusion

In this chapter we have sought to provide an overview of the various polices in place that affect women's economic lives. From anti-discrimination legislation to family leave, childcare and Social Security, we have provided some history related to each policy and identified the current state of the policies both in the United States and in other countries.

While it has been difficult to ascertain the efficacy of anti-discrimination policies, the evidence we have suggests that such policies have been effective in improving the labor-market situation of women, particularly women of color. They do not appear to have had any negative effects on worker productivity.

The United States provides relatively limited support for the efforts of household with preschool aged children to balance the competing demands of work and family. In the United States the FMLA has likely raised (albeit modestly) time at home with infants and increased the job continuity of mothers, with little effect on earnings but clear benefits to both maternal and child health. In Europe there is evidence that longer leaves have little discernible effect on the long-term labor supply of women but that there is some positive effect on higher-order fertility. In the United States, childcare remains largely a private responsibility, whereas most other OECD countries have moved toward universal provision of such care by the time a child is age 3 or 4, if not earlier.

Paid family-leave policies fall into the category of what Blau and Kahn recently called "family- friendly" policies—that is, policies that increase mothers' attachment to the labor force during her childbearing years. They report that up to 28 percent of the United States' relative decline in female labor-force participation in comparison to other developed countries since 1990 may be attributable to such policies.[66] Similar results are found by Cipollone, Patacchini, and Vallanti[67] in assessing differences in female employment outcomes across 15 European Union countries. Their work indicates family-oriented policy changes may explain up to 25 percent of young women's increased labor-force participation in these countries in the last 20 years. Thus the United States may suffer in terms of productivity if it does not adopt more family-friendly employment policies.

---

65 For more details about this proposal, see Marianne Ferber, Patricia Simpson, and Vanessa Rouillon (2006), "Aging and Social Security: Women as the Problem and the Solution," *Challenge*, 49 (3), 105–119.

66 Francine D. Blau and Lawrence M. Kahn (2013), "Female Labor Supply: Why is the US Falling Behind?" *American Economic Review*, 103 (3), 251–256.

67 Angela Cipollone, Eleonora Patacchini, and Giovanna Vallanti (2014), "Female Labour Market Participation in Europe: Novel Evidence on Trends and Shaping Factors," *IZA Journal of European Labor Studies*, 3 (1), 18.

13 MARRIAGE AND FERTILITY IN DEVELOPING COUNTRIES

Introduction

This is the first of two chapters that focus on women in developing countries. In this chapter we focus on the economics of marriage and fertility in developing countries; in the next we focus on labor-market issues. The field of economic development did not explicitly acknowledge the relationship between gender and economic development until 1970 when Ester Boserup, a Danish economist, examined what happens to women in the process of economic and social growth throughout the developing world in her landmark book *Women's Role in Economic Development*. In this chapter and the following, we carry her work forward and document the role of women in developing countries, the specific issues they face, and their contribution to the economy.

Measuring economic development

There is no "official" definition of a developing country. The UN refers to all of Europe and North America, Japan, Australia, and New Zealand as more developed regions, while other regions and countries are referred to as less developed regions. Countries with the lowest indicators of socio-economic development are classified as **Least Developed Countries** (LDCs).[1] As of 2013, 48 countries were officially classified as LDCs, including Angola, Chad, Ethiopia, and Liberia in Africa and Nepal, Cambodia and Bangladesh in Asia. In the Western hemisphere, only Haiti is classified as an LDC. Some developing countries, such as Brazil, China, and India, are classified as emerging economies or newly industrialized countries (NICs). NICs are nations with more advanced and developed economies than those in the developing world, but not yet with the full signs of a developed country.

For many years the most commonly used measure of economic development was per capita income. However, economic growth as measured by per capita income does not always reflect human development in terms of education and health—that is, the ability of people to lead the lives they wish to lead. In 1990 the UN introduced the Human Development Index (HDI), which is a broader measure of development. The HDI takes into account three factors: life expectancy at birth; the educational attainment of adults and the expected educational attainment of children; and income per capita, adjusted

---

1 A current list of Least Developed Countries and the criterion for defining a country as such can be found at unohrlls.org/about-ldcs/criteria-for-ldcs/.

for differences in prices. Each term is expressed as a percentage between 0 and 1, where 0 means the country has the lowest observed value and 1 is the highest observed value. The overall score is a weighted average of the three components, with each component counting equally. As of 2013, the last year for which data are available, Norway had the highest score of 0.944, which means that, on average, its component scores were 94.4 percent of the maximum. Among the countries included, Congo and Niger were at the bottom with HDI scores of 0.338 and 0.337, respectively. North Korea, South Sudan, and Somalia are not included because their data are unavailable; their HDI scores would likely be the lowest.

Figure 13.1 summarizes the HDI scores for several developed countries and regions and for LDCs. The United States has an HDI score of 0.914, which put it in fifth place, behind not only Norway but also Australia, Switzerland, and the Netherlands. The UK ranked 14th with a score of 0.892. Brazil and China are typical intermediate development level countries; Brazil has a score of 0.744 (tied for 79th) and China has an HDI score of 0.719 (91st). India is further below at 0.586 (135th). The LDCs as a group have an average HDI score of 0.493. The low scores for South Asia and Sub-Saharan Africa reflect the fact that many of the countries in those areas are LDCs. The low HDI score for the LDCs reflects all three components of the index. They have an average life expectancy of 59.5, compared to 80 for the top 25 percent of countries. The average education of the adult population is less than four years, compared to 11.5 for the top 25 percent, and their per capita income is about one-sixth of the average income of the top 25 percent.

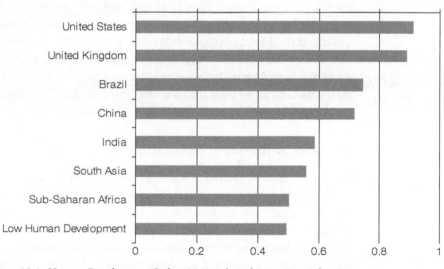

Figure 13.1 *Human Development Index, 2013, selected countries and regions.*

Source: UN Development Reports, Human Development Report 2014, Table 1. hdr.undp.org/en/data.

In the next section we turn to a discussion of the economics of marriage in the context of a developing country. While much of our analysis is similar to that of Chapter 3, applying our models to a developing country context yields some interesting insights into the lives of women around the world.

Marriage in developing countries

Overview

As we have just discovered, the term "developing country" is quite broad and masks considerable heterogeneity across countries in terms of economic growth and standards of living. Thus, as we would expect, marriage rates and age at first marriage vary widely in developing countries. In general, however, women in developing countries marry earlier than do women in more developed countries. Similar to women in developed countries, there is an upward trend in the age at first marriage.

Data from the Population Reference Bureau for 2013 show that of women residing in the least developed countries, 47 percent of women aged 20–25 were married by age 18 and 16 percent were married by age 15. Data from the UN reveal that one-third of girls in the developing world are married before the age of 18 and 1 in 9 are married before the age of 15. While these rates are lower than even ten years ago, they are still quite high compared to those of developed countries.[2]

Just as in developing countries, the choice to marry is usually based on a comparison of utilities while single vs. married. However, in some countries, marriage is not a choice and although the accepted international age at marriage is 18, there are many cases across the world where girls younger than 18 are married, some of them even as young as 12. In many cases these are also driven by economic decisions—desperately poor parents may marry their daughters off at a young age so they do not have to feed them. Even when it is a choice, early marriage is relatively more common in developing countries for reasons related to economic development. Because women are less educated and have fewer opportunities in the formal labor market, the opportunity cost of marriage (and childbearing) is lower, and in many developing countries, individuals marry early in part because childbearing prior to marriage is not socially acceptable. However, as we established above, just like in the developed world, marriages are occurring later in developing countries. What economic factors have led to this trend?

Marriage and women's education

One explanation for the rising age at first marriage in the developing world is that women are obtaining more education and education delays marriage by increasing the opportunity cost of marriage. Development economists have asked to what extent has the increased education of women been responsible for the increased age at first marriage in developing countries? Answering this question is not straightforward because it is also possible that delaying marriage facilitates women's educational attainment. Furthermore, there could be other factors that influence both age at marriage and women's educational attainment simultaneously. For example, if women who have a strong preference for schooling also

---

2 See B. S Mensch,. S. Singh, and J. B. Casterline (2005), "Trends in the Timing of First Marriage Among Men and Women in the Developing World," in C. L. Lloyd et al. (eds.), *The Changing Transitions to Adulthood in Developing Countries: Selected Studies*, Washington, DC: National Academies Press, 118–171.

have a strong preference to marry later, we might see a correlation between education and marriage that is spurious—not indicative of a causal relationship.

Ascertaining the direction of causation here is certainly of interest to policymakers, who may be willing to fund initiatives aimed at increasing women's education levels if these initiatives also have spillover effects on marriage. Phrasing this in economic terms, increasing women's education in developing countries may have the positive externality of delaying the onset of marriage (and hence of fertility). For these and other reasons we discuss in Chapter 14, many policymakers in developing countries have made educating women a priority.

As we saw earlier in this book, women invest in education based on the costs and benefits of that investment, and the returns to education include increased productivity in both the labor market and in home production. Increased labor-market productivity increases the opportunity cost of marriage, while increased household production increases the returns to marriage. Both of these may affect the timing of marriage. In addition, rapid economic development increases economic opportunities for women and hence implies a greater opportunity cost to marriage.

Economists have made some inroads into untangling the potential causal impact of education on marriage and there is some empirical evidence that indicates that education may actually cause a delay in marriage. Most of the studies in this area focus on a particular country and use a natural experiment to identify exogenous variation in schooling.

For example, in 1997, Turkey extended its compulsory schooling duration from five to eight years, and the percentage of ever-married women at age 15 dropped by 50 percent after the implementation of the policy.[3] The authors of the study note that this fall can be explained by two channels: the fact that marriage and schooling are incompatible events, and that schooling raises human capital and hence wages and perhaps also influences preferences for marriage. Other studies have documented that education delays the age at marriage in Indonesia,[4] and a study of marriage timing in Malaysia found that later age at marriage among Malaysian women can also be explained largely by increases in education.[5]

Other factors influencing delayed marriage

Of course, it isn't just opportunities for women that may delay marriage. For example, in some developing countries men are now postponing marriage because of greater expectations about job status and employment stability, and the material possessions needed to form a household. To put this in economic terms, they delay marriage because, until they can form an independent household, the gains from marrying are not as great as the gains from remaining single.

Studies of marriage in Egypt reveal that increased material expectations and increased consumerism among youth are a factor in the rising age at marriage, which can be traced

3 Murat G. Kırdar, Meltem Dayıoğlu Tayfur, and İsmet Koç (2011), "The Effect of Compulsory Schooling Laws on Teenage Marriage and Births in Turkey," IZA Discussion Paper 5887.

4 L. Breierova and E. Duflo (2004), "The Impact of Education on Fertility and Child Mortality: Do Fathers Really Matter Less than Mothers?" NBER Working Paper 10513.

5 M.J. Brien and L.A. Lillard (1994), "Education, Marriage, and First Conception in Malaysia," *Journal of Human Resources*, 34 (4), 1167–1204.

to the migration of Egyptian men to Gulf countries such as Saudi Arabia in search of employment. Their remittances—the money they send home to their families—have increased the material standard of living in that country.[6] Furthermore, some scholars have noted that there has been a decline in labor-force participation among women aged 20–24 and that marriage may give them more material assets than they could earn on their own—hence further evidence for an economic rationale for marriage.[7]

Gender preference and the marriage market

South Korea provides an interesting illustration of the workings of the marriage market that we studied in Chapter 3 and a fascinating example of how economic development can change women's economic prospects.[8] The widespread availability of sex-screening technology for pregnant women since the 1980s has resulted in the birth of a disproportionate number of boys in South Korea and an associated shortage of girls to marry. In addition, South Korea's growing wealth through economic development has increased women's educational and employment opportunities and led to plummeting birthrates—birthrates in South Korea are among the lowest in the world. These changes have disrupted the South Korean marriage market and have led South Korean men to pursue foreign brides. Currently, China and Vietnam are the countries of choice for South Korean men to find a bride. The so-called "marriage tourism" business began in the late 1990s by matching South Korean farmers to ethnic South Koreans in China. However, by the early 2000s the majority of customers were urban bachelors, and the foreign brides came from a host of countries. Now in South Korea, billboards advertising marriages to foreigners are ubiquitous, and fliers advertising such are scattered on the Seoul subway. Many rural South Korean governments, faced with declining populations, subsidize the marriage tours, which typically cost around $10,000.

Figure 13.2 shows how sex-screening and marriage tours might affect the marriage market. The general analysis is very similar to the case of gender imbalance that we presented in Figure 3.12. The basic idea is to represent the number of potential brides with the supply curve and the number of potential husbands with the demand curve. The "price" is the wife's share of marital output. The market equilibrium is the price at which supply-and-demand balance.

In Figure 13.2, S_1 and D_1 are the supply-and-demand curves that would exist in the absence of any sex screening. We have drawn the curves with equal numbers of men and women—the vertical portions of the curves are lined up just above one another. The market equilibrium is at S_{F1}^* and N_1^*. With sex screening that favors men, more boys and fewer girls are born than would occur naturally. Thus the demand curve shifts outward to D_2 (an increase in demand), and the supply curve of brides shifts inward to S_2 (a decrease

6 D. Singerman and B. Ibrahim (2003), "The Costs of Marriage in Egypt: A Hidden Variable in the New Arab Demography," in N. Hopkins (ed.), *The New Arab Family, Cairo Papers in the Social Sciences*, 24 (1/2): 80–116.

7 Amin Sajeda and N. Al-Bassusi (2003), "Wage Work and Marriage: Perspectives of Egyptian Working Women," Policy Research Division Working Paper 171, New York: The Population Council.

8 Much of this section is based on Norimitsu Onishi, "Korean Men Use Brokers to Find Brides in Vietnam," *New York Times*, February 22, 2007 and Norimitsu Onishi, "Wed to Strangers, Vietnamese Wives Build Korean Lives," *New York Times*, March 30, 2008.

in supply). In addition, the rising education for women shifts the curve inward yet again. With higher education and better opportunities for self-support, the women will marry only if they receive a better deal.

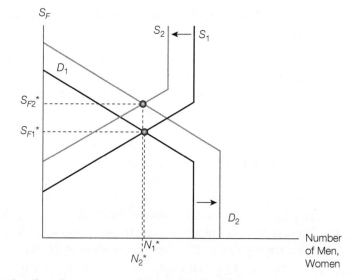

Figure 13.2 *The effect of sex screening on the marriage market.*

The new marriage market equilibrium would be something like $S_{F2}{}^*$ and $N_2{}^*$. A much smaller proportion of men are able to find brides, and even those who do must offer a better deal (higher S_F) to their wives. So, paradoxically, the widespread South Korean preference for boys ends up improving the marriage market position of daughters and harming the marriage market position of sons. The marriage tours are a way of increasing the supply of potential brides by shifting the supply curve back out toward S_1, thus increasing the proportion of men who marry and decreasing the wife's share of marriage output.

In addition to the shortage of women in South Korea, South Korean men complain that South Korean women are not family-oriented enough and their standards are too high—they want a highly educated, tall man with a good profession. This is exactly what our marriage model would predict: When there is a shortage of women, women get a bigger piece of the marital pie. Bachelors in China, India, and other Asian nations, where the traditional preference for sons has created a disproportionate number of men now fighting over a smaller pool of women, are facing the same problem.

Brideprice, dowry, and polygyny

Although much of the decision-making process with respect to marriage in developing countries is quite similar to developed countries, the cultural norms surrounding marriage are often very different. For example, developed countries are almost exclusively **monogamous**, meaning that marriage is between two partners only.[9] In developing countries, **polygamy**—a man with more than one wife or a woman with more than one

---

9   In fact, Utah was not admitted to the United States as a state until it agreed to disavow polygamy.

husband[10]—is still common in parts of Africa and the Middle East. Similarly, marriage in developed countries rarely involves an explicit transfer of wealth from one family to another at the time of marriage. But in some developing countries, **dowry** (a payment from the bride's family to the groom's) or **brideprice** (just the opposite) are still practiced. Finally, arranged marriages are far more common in developing countries than in developed ones.

Marriage payments: brideprice and dowry The use of brideprice tends to occur in relatively homogenous societies and correlates strongly with polygyny, because the women are usually involved in agricultural work. Income transfers from the family of the bride to the groom (or his family) are another form of payment at the time of a marriage and are referred to as dowry. Most societies at some time had payments at the time of marriage. Historically, dowry was far more common in Western countries than brideprice, but neither is widespread in the west at this time.[11]

Becker's theory of marriage can be used to help us understand more about why marriage payments arise in the first place. Recall that Becker regarded marriage as a joint venture whereby each person seeks to maximize his or her utility. If the marriage market is in equilibrium, no person can be made better off by marrying someone else rather than staying single. If, however, the division of output within the marriage is inflexible, perhaps by social custom, and if one partner does not get an adequate share as under the market solution, then an upfront payment will be made between the spouses' families to compensate for this. In economic terms, dowry reflects a negative price for a bride, whereas brideprice reflects a positive price. In this framework, brideprice and dowry are two sides of the same coin and differ only in the direction of transfer. Both dowry- and brideprice-paying societies tend to be **patrilineal** (children belong to the lineage of their father) and **patrilocal** (a bride joins the household of the groom and his family upon marriage). These marriage payments can be large enough to affect savings patterns and to have implications for the wealth of a family. From an economic viewpoint, these payments represent a form of intergenerational transfer of wealth from the old to the young.

Another explanation for the existence of dowry has been offered by two economists, Botticini and Siow.[12] They note that sons receive a bequest (a bequest is an inheritance) after their parents die, but daughters receive a dowry at the time they are married. They term a dowry a "pre-mortem"—that is, a "bequest" received before the death of a parent. They note that this type of arrangement is common in agricultural families, where women leave their birth families and move to live with their husband's families upon marriage, while sons continue to work on their parents' farms.

Their explanation for this practice is that if parents leave both the son and the daughter a bequest, the son, who stays with his parents' family, has less incentive to work hard on the family farm. Even if he works hard, he will not receive all the benefits because he and

---

10 The more general term, polygamy, encompasses both polygyny, where a man has several wives, and polyandry, where a woman has several husbands. Polygyny is far more common than polyandry.

11 Siwan Anderson (2007), "The Economics of Dowry and Brideprice," *Journal of Economic Perspectives*, 21 (4), 151–174.

12 Maristella Botticini and Aloysius Siow (2003), "Why Dowries?" *American Economic Review*, 93 (4), 1385–1398.

his sister will share the bequest. Thus, to incentivize their sons to work hard, parents give their daughters a dowry. The sons then know that, if they work hard, they will inherit the full efforts of their work. Essentially, by offering a dowry to daughters, the parents avoid a "free rider" problem—that is, the problem that the daughter will leave the family home upon marriage but still receive a bequest.

As economic development occurs, other employment opportunities arise and sons no longer work on their parent's farms. Economic development means that education becomes more important and hence parents move toward spending their money on educating their children.

In her work on dowry and brideprice, economist Siwan Anderson notes that brideprices tend to be more uniform in value, but dowries, which occur more often in socially stratified societies, are much more variable. In both India and Pakistan, the payment of dowry is nearly universal, despite the fact that in India the payment of a dowry was prohibited in 1961. In fact, not only has the dowry persisted in India despite rapid economic growth and modernization, but the amount of dowry required to entice a man to marry has increased rapidly. What can account for this dowry inflation?

Dowry-paying societies, unlike brideprice societies, tend to be economically stratified. India has experienced rising inequality as a byproduct of its rapid economic growth over the past few decades. In a caste-based society such as India's, women desire to marry up and hence are competing for a limited pool of men in castes above their own, which results in dowry inflation. Increasingly unequal incomes make it possible for the price of a scarce resource, in this case a high-caste husband, to be bid up much higher than it would if incomes were more uniform.[13] Similarly, rising levels of dowry are correlated with increasing levels of the grooms' education, lending support to the idea that a higher dowry might be a reflection of the amount brides and their families are willing to pay for a high-quality groom[14] For an engaging look at how the Indian marriage market functions, see Box 13.1.

Box 13.1

Discrimination in the Marriage Market: The Role of Caste and Income in India

In Chapter 11 we introduced the idea of **correspondence studies**. These studies were used to ferret out discrimination by sending fictitious résumés in response to posted job openings. Because the résumés could be manipulated to differ only by sex (or race), they isolated the impact of that factor on outcomes. An interesting study of the marriage market in India made use of the correspondence study framework to investigate whether economic incentives can overcome discriminatory behavior.

In India, the caste of an individual is a prominent indicator of his or her socioeconomic status. Marriage across castes is quite rare, in part because a high-status woman will

---

13 S. Anderson (2007), op. cit.
14 S. Munshi (2012), "Education and Dowry: An Economic Exploration," *IIM Kozhikode Society & Management Review*, 1 (2), 111–120.

experience a decline in her social status if she marries a low-status man, as a husband's caste determines that of the wife and children.

The authors of the study were interested in determining whether economic incentives could diminish the incidence of this status-based discrimination on the part of high-caste women. In India (as in some other countries), newspapers are a popular venue for advertising for a spouse. The authors posted matrimonial advertisements for fictitious grooms in a leading Bengali-language newspaper that has been publishing matrimonial advertisements (both "brides wanted" and "grooms wanted") for decades in the state of West Bengal, India. Because this is such a common way of finding a spouse, the authors did not have to worry about "adverse selection"—that is, that only the less desirable women will be searching the ads for grooms.

They constructed nine groom advertisements that differed either in terms of the monthly income or in the caste status of the grooms. In some cases, income was the same but caste varied, and so on, so they could identify the impact of each separately. To assess whether status-based discrimination occurs, they examined whether individuals from a specific high-caste group responded less frequently to lower-caste grooms than their own-caste grooms, even when both types of groom shared the same advertised monthly income and nearly identical other marital attributes.

The nine advertisements, published in two different editions of the newspaper, elicited over 1,000 responses. The findings confirmed significant caste discrimination in that high-caste women were less likely to respond to an advertisement from lower-caste grooms. However, grooms from a given lower-caste group, who were otherwise observationally identical to each other, received a significantly larger number of responses from higher-caste women as their advertised monthly incomes went up. The authors caution that their data does not permit them to observe whether or not the response results in a marriage—the grooms are, after all, fictitious—but their findings do present evidence that income may overcome caste-based discrimination. They note that the finding that potential brides are willing to consider lower-caste grooms with more income is potentially hopeful. India remains quite segregated by caste even as it is undergoing rapid economic development. Such economic development may be able to reduce caste discrimination over time.

Source:
Subhasish Dugar, Haimanti Bhattacharya, and David Reiley (2012), "Can't Buy Me Love? A Field Experiment Exploring The Trade-Off Between Income And Caste-Status In An Indian Matrimonial Market," *Economic Inquiry* 50 (2), 534–550.

A dowry may also affect a woman's bargaining power within the household. One study of marriages in China investigated how the size of a women's dowry affected the intra-household allocation of time between household chores and leisure, as well as the share of household spending that goes to women's goods. The author reported that women with larger dowries had better bargaining power within the household, as evidenced by the finding that their husbands were more likely to participate in household chores, and they spent more of their own time in leisure activities.[15] This finding indicates that dowries may make women better off by increasing their bargaining power in their households.

Monogamous or polygynous? Wealthy men have historically had multiple wives, but in developed countries where considerable inequality exists, we don't see polygyny. Economists Gould, Moav and Simhon offer some insights into why this might be the case.[16] They note that just as inequality among men results in polygyny, just the opposite exists among women—that is, where there is inequality across women, we see monogamous societies. Why would this be the case? Gould and colleagues show that as an economy develops, labor income from human capital (education) becomes more important than land (nonlabor) income. If better-educated men would prefer to have better-educated children, they will likely want a wife who is also better educated. This will lead to better-educated men demanding better-educated women as wives, thereby increasing the brideprice of educated wives and leading to better-educated men preferring only one wife. In fact, better-educated men would prefer to have one educated wife to many uneducated wives.

However, the same is not true for less-educated men who have considerable nonlabor (land) income. These men will not share this preference for educated wives because they still need multiple wives to help farm, and these will generally be women without human capital. The process of economic development gradually increases income from human capital relative to income from land and hence there are fewer and fewer men whose wealth comes from nonlabor sources. In this manner a society changes from polygynous to monogamous.

Polygyny and economic development Interestingly, some research suggests that polygyny might hinder economic development. As we've seen, having multiple wives can be thought of as a type of economic investment and hence it is not a stretch to think that this might also be related to economic development. Research by economist Michèle Tertilt has linked polygyny and economic development in a most intriguing way.[17] In polygynous countries, men "buy" wives as an investment, not only to work the land, but also because they expect that they will have children. Because men in polygynous societies pay a brideprice, having multiple wives is expected to yield a return in terms of daughters who can then be sold in 20 years or so as brides. This selling of daughters for marriage is lucrative for these men because they receive a brideprice.

By the time their daughters are ready to marry, the male heads of household are getting older and not working as much. Thus we can also think of the brideprice as a form of old-age support. After all, in the countries where polygyny is practiced, well-developed state-supported Social Security does not typically exist. The proceeds, which are often cash but can also be cows and even camels, are usually used to meet current consumption needs.

---

15 P. H. Brown (2009), "Dowry and Intra-Household Bargaining: Evidence from China," *Journal of Human Resources*, 44 (1), 25–46.

16 Eric D. Gould, Omer Moav, and Avi Simhon (2008), "The Mystery of Monogamy," *The American Economic Review*, 98 (1), 333–357.

17 Michèle Tertilt (2006), "Polygyny, Women's Rights, and Development," *Journal of the European Economic Association*, 4 (2/3), 523–530 and (2005), "Polygyny, Fertility, and Savings," *Journal of Political Economy*, 113 (6), 1341–1371.

Tertilt argues that this practice impedes economic growth because the money from brideprice is not used to invest in physical capital, which would lead to economic growth. Tertilt notes that in a polygynous marriage system, competition for women drives up the price of women. This investment in women as assets then crowds out investment in physical capital. Her work suggests a strong negative correlation between the practice of brideprice and economic development.

Should polygyny be legal? Polygyny is illegal in all developed countries. Although the UN has adopted a resolution aiming to discourage the practice because it is widely believed to exploit women, many countries in Sub-Saharan Africa are still highly polygynous. The percentage of polygynous unions ranges from 10.2 percent in Malawi to 55.6 percent in Cameroon. Polygynous countries are poorer than similar nonpolygynous countries and are characterized by higher fertility, higher spousal age gaps, and lower savings rates.[18]

Economist Gary Becker notes that the most frequently encountered argument against polygyny is that it exploits women and is a continuation of the traditional suppression of women by men. Indeed, these arguments are certainly the main reason why developed countries have long moved away from polygyny. Yet Becker provocatively argues that the practice of polygyny should not be outlawed as long as women are free to choose their own husbands.[19] Women, he argues, can refuse to marry men whom they do not want to marry, regardless of their parents' feelings or how much the man wants to marry them. In other words, a woman has a choice as to whether she wants to enter into a polygamist household. While his arguments may have some merit if women are truly able to choose, evidence strongly suggests that women in polygynous households often do not have a say in the matter. Becker's arguments have not gained traction in any developed countries.

Divorce in developing countries

Unlike developed countries, access to divorce varies widely across the developing world. For example, Brazil introduced the right to divorce in 1977, while Chile only introduced a law granting couples the right to divorce in 2004, and divorce remains illegal in the Philippines. No-fault divorce is typically allowed in Muslim societies, although normally only with the consent of the husband. A wife seeking divorce is normally required to give one of several specific justifications.

There is evidence, though, that divorce may be an inevitable outgrowth of changing social norms as developing countries advance economically, and also of women's empowerment. An interesting study in Brazil found that exposure to TV shows where women are depicted as divorced or unfaithful to their husbands may have helped fuel a substantial increase in divorce in that country between 1970 and 1991.[20]

Because divorce is particularly rare in some parts of the developing world, such as South Asia, couples who want to divorce but cannot for legal or cultural reasons often

18 Michèle Tertilt, (2005), "Polygyny, Fertility, and Savings," *Journal of Political Economy*, 113 (6), 1341–1371.

19 G. S. Becker. 2006, October 22, "Is There a Case for Legalizing Polygamy?" www.becker-posner-blog.com/archives/2006/10.

20 A. Chong and E. L. Ferrara (2009), "Television and Divorce: Evidence from Brazilian Novelas," *Journal of the European Economic Association*, 7 (2–3), 458–468.

have to figure out a way to live together. We saw in Chapter 3 where we discussed household bargaining models that focused on a divorce threat, a woman's well-being within marriage depends in part upon her options outside the marriage. In this case a breakdown of bargaining within the marriage results in a divorce. Hence options outside the marriage are the relevant threat utilities.

A related model is termed the "separate spheres" bargaining model and focuses on the situation that might arise when a couple cannot reach an agreement when bargaining and would prefer to divorce but cannot do so given culture norms, concern for the well-being of children or religious prohibitions.[21] In this case the threat point refers to non-cooperative behavior within the marriage. In other words, the utility that each person derives by behaving noncooperatively within marriage may be the relevant threat point as opposed to their opportunities outside the marriage. What this means is that if negotiations (bargaining) between a husband and a wife break down (i.e., they cannot agree) and divorce is not possible, each may now ignore the fact that their actions impinge on the well-being of the other person and may act in their own individual best interest, essentially assuming that the other person's actions are beyond their control. When this happens, economists say they have retreated into their separate spheres as defined by their traditional gender norms.

What would this mean? We can use an example from the production and specialization model of marriage introduced in Chapter 3. Suppose that the wife has a comparative advantage in household production and the husband has a comparative advantage in market work. When behaving cooperatively, they each specialize according to their comparative advantage and then share their output. This is the situation we illustrated in Chapter 3 when we looked at the model of the gains of marriage when there are productivity differences. For example, the wife will do the housework for both of them and the husband will do the market work for both.

In a noncooperative situation, the wife might curtail some of her household production (perhaps she only cooks for herself and only does her own laundry, not his). She might even take a job outside the home. Because the wife has cut back on her household production, the husband may have to curtail some of his market work to attend to his own household needs. In other words, when they retreat into their separate spheres, each ignores the effects of his or her actions on the actions of their spouse.

A subtle but interesting distinction between the divorce threat and the separate spheres model is that in the divorce threat model both a woman's earned and non-earned income affect her threat point—in both cases the more she has of either type of income, the greater her opportunities outside the marriage and hence she will have greater bargaining power.

In the separate spheres model, when noncooperative behavior within marriage is the threat point, then the receipt of income by the wife may have well have a different effect on the utility of the husband depending on the source of that income. If the income is unearned income (perhaps the wife has been left a bequest by her parents), it is logical that she will spend at least part of it on household public goods—perhaps on clothes or books for their child. In this case, because children are a public good, the receipt of the unearned income also benefits her husband: Since children are a public good, he gets

---

21 Shelly Lundberg and Robert A. Pollak (1993), "Separate Spheres Bargaining and the Marriage Market," *Journal of Political Economy*, 101 (6), 988–1010.

utility from his child being well clothed or well educated. But if the income comes from labor-market earnings of the wife, we might find that the utility of the husband has gone down because, when the wife starts working outside the home, she will naturally reallocate some of her time from household production to market work and thus her husband, who benefits from her household production, will be worse off.

Fertility in developing countries

Overview

Fertility rates are higher in developing countries than developed countries, yet in all countries fertility rates have been declining. Figure 13.3 presents the TFR over time across countries grouped broadly by UN income levels.[22] We introduced the TFR in Chapter 5; it is the number of births a woman today would have over her lifetime if she had the age-specific fertility rates that prevail currently.

The figure makes clear two important facts. First, in lower-income countries, fertility is higher than in higher-income countries. Second, across all regions of the world, fertility rates have been declining.

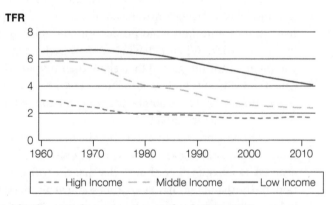

Figure 13.3 *Total fertility rates by country income level, 1960–2012.*

Source: Data from: http://data.worldbank.org/indicator/SP.DYN.TFRT.IN.

Within these broad income categorizations of economic development, we see wide variations in fertility, as seen in Figure 13.4. In this figure we present the TFR for selected countries and regions in 2012. China has the lowest TFR followed closely by high-income countries—a grouping that includes the United States, Western Europe, and other highly developed countries. At the high end are African countries, with Somalian women having nearly 7 children. Sub-Saharan Africa has a TFR of 4.78. India and Bangladesh have TFRs of 2.51 and 2.21. Brazil also has a low TFR; we discuss an interesting fertility development in this country later in this chapter.

Finally, one commonly observed feature of fertility in several developing countries is a preference for sons. See Box 13.2 for a discussion of this phenomenon.

---

22   See http://data.worldbank.org/country for a discussion of the country income groupings.

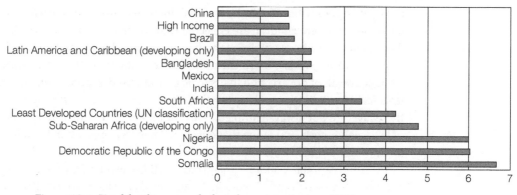

Figure 13.4 *Total fertility rates of selected countries/regions, 2012.*

Source: http://data.worldbank.org/indicator/SP.DYN.TFRT.IN.

Economic explanations for higher fertility in developing countries

In order to understand why women in developing nations have more children on average, while at the same time fertility rates are falling, we have to broaden our understanding of why parents have children. In the developed world, as we discussed in Chapter 5, children are primarily a source of utility or satisfaction for their parents. However, in the developing world where financial markets are often not as established and where many families subsist on less than $1 per day, children may provide other important benefits to their parents. We consider several of these below.

Child-replacement effect Fertility behavior cannot be examined in isolation from child mortality in a developing country, as child mortality can affect a family's decision about the number of children to have in order to replace the children who have died. This fertility response is called the **replacement effect**. Developing countries have higher infant mortality rates compared to developed countries and, hence, if families are aiming for a desired family size, fertility rates will have to be higher to compensate for this higher infant mortality.

Old-age security In most poor developing countries, capital markets are often nonexistent. That often means that there is no formal Social Security pension system. In these countries, children are the Social Security system, and the elderly are the responsibility of their children. This so-called **old-age security hypothesis** maintains that when parents face uncertainty about their ability to support themselves in old age, they have children in order to provide that security. The agreement, although unspoken, is that parents care for their children when they are young, and then children care for their aging parents. It would not be surprising to find therefore that fertility is higher in these countries, compared to developed countries with well-established capital markets and publicly financed Social Security systems. A number of empirical studies of fertility in both Asia and Africa support this theory.

Children as a productive asset Children are often viewed as a beneficial economic resource in addition to the utility that they provide their parents. Economically struggling parents may choose to bear children because they believe that children will be able to substantially contribute to the household's income. This is particularly true in rural agrarian societies, where children are expected to work on the family farm or in the household. As a result, the value of children is higher than in developed countries, and higher fertility is a likely result. Today, more than one in five children in the world work.[23] Most child labor is a result of poverty and tends to be concentrated in poor countries. Although strict laws forbid child labor and curtail the amount and type of work that children can do, these laws are not always enforced. Some developing countries allow child labor because of lower labor costs and argue that developed nations' opposition to child labor is only an attempt to eliminate economic competition.

The International Labour Organization (ILO) estimates that 218 million children between the ages of 5 and 17 work in developing countries. Of these, 122.3 million children work in the Asia-Pacific region, 49.3 million work in Sub-Saharan Africa, and 5.7 million work in Latin America and the Caribbean. Most working children in rural areas are found in agriculture; many children in both rural and urban areas work as domestics; urban children tend work in trade and services, with fewer in manufacturing and construction. Thus women in developing countries may face strong pressure to have more children because their children can directly contribute to a family's income.

Thus in many countries there is an economic link between high fertility and the need for children's productive capabilities, even if those capacities are less than those of an adult. It is important to remember, as economist Eric Edmonds has noted, that most children who work are helping their parents meet basic needs, and most children work in the family business or on the family farm. Unfortunately it is also not unusual to see parents in developing countries bonding their children in order to meet family expenses, including medical care and schooling for other children. Child-bonded labor refers to situations where a child's labor services are offered in exchange for a loan.[24]

| Box | 13.2 |

What Happened to the Girls?

In 1990 the Nobel Prize–winning Indian economist Amartya Sen wrote an essay in *The New York Review of Books* lamenting the "missing women." This widely cited essay shed light on the fact that in some developing countries, notably China and India, the proportion of women is far lower than what would be expected if girls and women were born and died at the same rate as boys and men. Estimates from a 2012 World Development report estimated that excess female mortality after birth and "missing" girls at birth account every year for 3.9 million "missing" women below the age of 60. About two-fifths of these missing women are never born, one-fifth go missing in infancy and childhood, and the remaining two-fifths do so between the ages of 15 and 59. Development economist Esther Duflo noted that for each missing woman there are many more women who fail to get an education, a job, or a political responsibility

---

23 This statistic is from E. V. Edmonds and N. Schady (2011), "Poverty Alleviation and Child Labor," *American Economic Journal: Economic Policy* 4 (4), 100–124.

24 Eric V. Edmonds (2008), "Child Labor," in T. Schultz and J. Strauss (eds.), *Handbook of Development Economics 4*, Amsterdam: North Holland Elsevier.

that they would have obtained if they had been men. There are ethical consequences in terms of gender inequality to consider, as well as economic consequences because of the effect of this gender imbalance on the marriage market and on crime rates.

Technological advances have been partially responsible for the missing women who are never born. The availability of inexpensive ultrasound scans in Asian countries within the last 25 years has made it possible for the vast majority of women to discern the sex of their unborn child. Sex selection in countries such as China, South Korea, and India is now achieved mainly through ultrasound, followed by an abortion if the fetus is female, even though in these countries sex-selective abortion is now illegal. In India it is estimated that about 2 percent of annual pregnancies end with a sex-selective abortion. While the natural sex ratio is about 105 boys per 100 girls at birth, data from the Population Reference Bureau indicate that in India it has climbed to 110 boys per 100 girls. After prenatal sex determination technology became widely available in South Korea in the mid-1980s, the country experienced a steep rise in the sex ratio at birth.

China's One Child Policy, which became formal in 1979 and restricts urban dwellers to having one child, exacerbated an already culturally strong preference for sons. In more rural areas, couples are allowed to have a second child if the first is a girl. The current sex ratio in China is about 118 boys per 100 girls, and in the more prosperous provinces it is even higher. Recent research indicates that the sex ratio at birth in China has been rising since the introduction of the One Child Policy. This rigorously enforced policy made it more costly to have multiple births to ensure the birth of a son, effectively raised the opportunity cost of having another child of the "unwanted" sex, and led to both lower fertility and higher sex ratios. Economists Chen, Li and Meng show that much of the increased sex ratio in China can be explained by the differential introduction of ultrasound throughout China during the 1980s. The introduction of this technology significantly reduced the cost of prenatal sex selection. This changing sex ratio is not without consequences, as Ebenstein and Sharygin note. They worry particularly about large numbers of unmarried men and how that will affect the prevalence of prostitution and sexually transmitted infections, the economic and physical well-being of men who fail to marry, and China's ability to care for its elderly, especially elderly men who do not marry. Also, as we saw earlier, it has effects on the marriage market, as shown in Figure 13.2.

South Korea has had some success in reducing its sex ratio disparity at birth in part due to rapid economic development, which brought increased female labor-force participation, and greater retirement savings. This lessened the traditional reliance on the presence of a son to provide old-age care and hence led to a decline in son preference.

Although son preferences have been thought to be a cultural factor linked to the need for a son to carry on the family name, there is likely an economic rationale as well. Daughters often marry out of the family and old-age support is often expected of sons but not daughters. A clever study by economist Dan Rosenblum sheds some light on this issue. Using data from India, he examined the economic differentials between families whose first-born child is a son vs. those whose first-born child is a daughter.

He argues that in India families are less likely to abort their first child and hence the sex of a first child is more likely to be random than a higher-order birth (where presumably the parents may avail themselves of an abortion if the fetus is female). He finds that families with a first-born daughter are more likely to be in poverty and have lower per capita yearly incomes, providing indirect evidence that a son is an economic benefit for a family.

Sources:

S. Anderson and D. Ray (2010), "Missing Women: Age and Disease," *Review of Economic Studies*, 77 (4), 1262–1300.

P. Belluck (2011), "If You Really, Really Wanted a Girl …," *The New York Times*, August 20, 2011.

Y. Chen, H. Li, and L. Meng (2013), "Prenatal Sex Selection and Missing Girls in China: Evidence from the Diffusion of Diagnostic Ultrasound," *Journal of Human Resources*, 48 (1), 36–70.

E. Duflo (2012), "Women's Empowerment and Economic Development," *Journal of Economic Literature*. *50*(4), 1051–79.

A. Y. Ebenstein, and E.J. Sharygin (2009), "The Consequences of the "Missing Girls" of China," *The World Bank Economic Review*, 23 (3), 399–425.

A. Ebenstein (2010), "The 'Missing Girls' of China and the Unintended Consequences of the One Child Policy," *Journal of Human Resources*, 45 (1), 87–115.

K. Gilles and C. Feldman-Jacobs (2012), "When Technology and Tradition Collide: From Gender Bias to Sex Selection," Population Reference Bureau.

P. Jha, Kesler, M., Kumar, R., Ram, U., Aleksandowicz, L., Bassani, D., Chandra, S., and J. Banthia (2011), "Trends in Selective Abortions in India: Analysis of Nationally-Representative Birth Histories from 1990 to 2005 and Census Data from 1991 to 2011," *Lancet*, 377 (9781), 1921–1928.

D. Rosenblum. (2014), "Economic Incentives for Sex-Selective Abortion in India," Centre for Health Economics Working Paper No. 2014-13.

A. Sen (1990), "More Than 100 Million Women Are Missing," *The New York Review of Books*, 37(20).

World Development Report (2012), accessed 10/30/2014: http://go.worldbank.org/GPLFFB9PQ0.

Economic explanations for falling fertility in developing countries

Economic development and rising educational opportunities An explanation for falling fertility rates in developing countries lies partly in the process of economic development and modernization. Economies generally begin as rural agricultural economies and then develop from this base through the adoption of labor-saving technology that frees up labor for use in other activities, such as manufacturing. Factories are likely to be located in urban areas and thus the population starts to migrate from rural to urban areas. With migration from rural to urban areas, children's economic productive value falls. In addition, the enactment and enforcement of child labor laws and minimum schooling requirements further reduce the value of children as productive inputs. There are increased opportunities for education for women and families rely less on child labor to meet their needs. Thus many view falling fertility rates as a direct measure of economic development. Declines in infant mortality and rising literacy and education rates are also important indicators of economic development. The increasing educational levels of women raise the value of their time and hence they are less likely to have children.

We learned in Chapter 5 that more education for women, which translates into higher wages, tends to dampen fertility in developed countries by increasing the cost of time used in producing child services. Figure 13.5 demonstrates that the same is true in developing countries. The data in the figure are from 2007, but the relationship is undoubtedly similar today. The figure shows that women with a secondary or higher level of education have one-third to one-half as many children as women with no education.

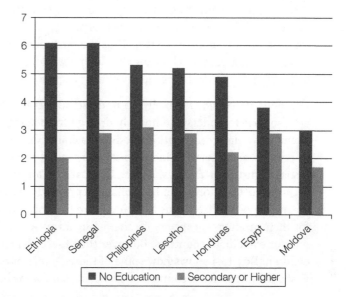

Figure 13.5 *Lifetime births per woman by highest level of education, 2007.*

Source: Population Reference Bureau, 2007 World Population Data Sheet.

Economic theory suggests several reasons why fertility might fall when education is increased. First, as noted above, the value of a woman's time increases, making children more expensive. Second, education may lower fertility through improvements in child health and reduced rates of child mortality, so that women can have fewer births to yield the same desired family size. Finally, female education may lower fertility rates through knowledge and more effective use of contraception or by increasing female bargaining power in fertility decisions. In Chapter 3 we introduced the idea of bargaining power in families and the idea that higher earnings, which result from more education, might increase a woman's ability to bargain with her husband over how many children to have. (However, see Box 13.3, which explains that in developing countries, many families have unmet contraceptive needs.) Thus it seems natural that increasing women's education will have a spillover effect of reducing their fertility.

Several carefully done studies that rely upon the natural experiment framework have confirmed the existence of a likely causal effect of women's education on fertility. One study used data from Nigeria and variation in the introduction of a universal primary education (UPE) program implemented for the non-western regions of Nigeria during the petroleum boom of 1976–1981.[25] This study found that the UPE program increased female schooling and thereby decreased fertility by age 25 by 0.11 and 0.24 births for each additional year of completed schooling. Another study based on Turkish data found that when Turkey increased its compulsory schooling laws from 5 to 8 years, the probability of

---

25 U. O. Osili and B. T. Long (2008), "Does Female Schooling Reduce Fertility? Evidence from Nigeria," *Journal of Development Economics*, 87 (1), 57–75.

marriage by age 16 was reduced by 44 percent and the probability of giving birth by age 17 fell by 36 percent.[26]

Rising age at first marriage In many developing countries, individuals marry early in part because childbearing prior to marriage is not socially acceptable. This is particularly true, for example, of Islamic societies. Thus the postponement of marriage, which appears to be occurring across much of the developing world, contributes to reduced fertility rates by shortening the total reproductive life of women.

Economic development Finally, to understand fertility decline in developing countries, we also have to understand how children go from being considered productive inputs in a family to being consumption goods. As a country develops its infrastructure and ability to provide social services increase. At some point the state takes over as the provider of Social Security for families, and children are no longer as necessary to provide old-age security. Furthermore, as industrialization proceeds in a country, work in the formal manufacturing or service sector becomes more the norm and children are no longer needed for their productive capacity on the family farm. All of these changes do not happen at once or even in all countries. But over time these changes act to reduce the demand for children. Box 13.4 shows how some of these factors have lowered fertility in the Middle East and North Africa, countries which had some of the highest fertility rates in the world.

Box   13.3

Family Planning Policies

Interestingly, declines in fertility in most developed countries started before the introduction of the birth-control pill. Abortion and barrier methods of birth control have been available for centuries, although abortion is not legal in many developing countries. Concerns over rapid population increases in developing countries led many countries, including the United States, to offer family planning assistance to developing countries. The existence and efficacy of such programs has been a matter of debate.

From the perspective of the developing countries, rapid population growth and high fertility are thought to be detrimental to economic development, and most have adopted policies that are aimed at lowering fertility. In addition, the overwhelming majority of all countries today, both developed and developing, favor access to contraception, many through direct government support to family planning programs.

The role of family planning in fertility decisions can be viewed in economic terms. Couples have a demand for children. Biologically, the capability to bear children far surpasses the fertility of even the countries with the highest TFRs. Thus couples need a way to control the timing and spacing of births. This generates a demand for contraception. Family-planning programs lower the cost of contraception by providing it at a reduced cost or even free. They also provide information about health and pregnancy that allows couples to control their fertility better. The advent of modern,

---

26 Op cit. Kirdar, Tayfur, and Koc (2011).

highly effective contraceptives such as the pill and the IUD as well as more recent LARCs (long-acting reversible methods) have all been credited with reducing fertility. There is evidence that in some countries, where overall economic development is low, family planning has had a measureable impact on reducing fertility. Despite the existence of family-planning programs in most countries, there is still concern that many women have unmet contraceptive needs—that is, they are married or never married and sexually active; they are able to become pregnant but they do not wish to have a child in the next two years; or they have completed their childbearing but are not using contraceptives. Often they lack access to contraception due to financial constraints, or a lack of education means that they have a fear of some methods or do not know how to use them properly. Sometimes their husbands or partners do not wish them to use contraception. Estimates indicate that of the 80 million unintended pregnancies in developing countries in 2012, 79 percent occurred to women with an unmet need for modern contraceptives.

Sources:

H. Boonstra, S. Barot, and M. Lusti-Narasimhan (2014). "Making the Case for Multipurpose Prevention Technologies: The Socio-epidemiological Rationale," *BJOG: An International Journal of Obstetrics & Gynaecology*, 121.s5, 23–26.

T. P. Schultz (2007), "Population Policies, Fertility, Women's Human Capital, and Child Quality," *Handbook of Development Economics*, 4, 3249–3303.

J. R. Seltzer (2002), "The Origins and Evolution of Family Planning Programs in Developing Countries," Rand: Santa Monica, CA: www.rand.org/publications/MR/MR1276.

A. Sonfield (2006). "Working to Eliminate the World's Unmet Need for Contraception," *Guttmacher Policy Review*, 9 (1), 10–13.

Box	13.4

Fertility and Marriage in the Middle East and North Africa

The Middle East and North Africa (MENA) constitutes an area of mainly Arab countries where most of the population is Islamic. This region has experienced tremendous population growth in the past 50 years. Many people believe that the high fertility rates in this region were mainly a function of Islamic beliefs, which place a high value on family and often limit the role of women in society. Yet this area's population growth has been slowed by changes in marriage and fertility patterns in recent decades. Figure 13.6 shows fertility rates for four of the countries in this region. Overall the TFR of this region was seven children per woman in 1960 and it now stands at about three children per woman. How did this decline come about? Several factors have been implicated in the fertility decline in this region.

Some countries—notably, Egypt, Iran, and Tunisia—adopted policies aimed at limiting fertility as a way to slow population growth, including public advertisements in Egypt exhorting couples not to have children if they cannot pay for them, access to contraceptives in Iran, and family planning help in Tunisia. Aside from policies aimed at reducing fertility, rising economic aspirations and delayed marriage have also contributed to the fertility decline in these countries.

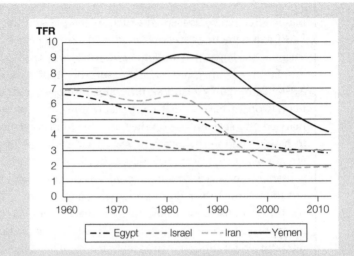

Figure 13.6 *Patterns of fertility decline, selected Middle Eastern and North African countries.*

Source: UN Population Division, *World Population Prospects: The 2006 Revision* (2007) http://esa.un.org.

In these countries, the family was the epicenter of life because it provided economic security for the elderly and for relatives in need of assistance. Thus nearly all couples married, and large families were the norm and were highly valued. Strict negative views of premarital and extramarital sexual relationships encouraged girls to marry young and to bear children soon thereafter. Only rarely did women remain single and childless. However, more and more women are not married by the time they reach their late thirties, and an increasing number of these women never will marry. For example, in Lebanon one-fifth of women aged 35–39 are still unmarried. In contrast, less than 5 percent of women stayed single into their late thirties in most of the Arabian Peninsula countries. The average age at marriage in the region is rapidly changing. While the average age at first marriage for women was between 18 and 21 years in most MENA countries in the 1970s, it has risen to 22.7 in Egypt and 23.7 in Iran in the 2010s.

Demographers also note that acceptance and access to family-planning services and to female education helped delay marriage and reduce fertility. In addition, in some of these countries, laws that limited women's rights and ability to participate in wider society have been relaxed. Rising economic aspirations have also played a role. Rather than living with their parents, couples increasingly wish to live alone and to have fewer children. Thus demographers believe that the high fertility rates that persisted in the region for so long were not just due to religious beliefs but reflected social and economic factors.

The fertility decline of the past few decades is likely to continue, even accelerate, as education, economic opportunities, and access to family-planning services expand, according to experts.

Sources:

Barbara S. Mensch, Susheela Singh, and John B. Casterline (2005). *Trends in the Timing of First Marriage Among Men and Women in the Developing World.* New York: Population Council, Policy Research Division.

Farzaneh Roudi-Fahimi and Mary Mederios Kent (2007). "Challenges and Opportunities—The Population of the Middle East and North Africa," *Population Bulletin* 62 (2).

Changing social norms regarding fertility A final explanation for declining fertility has to do with changing social norms about what constitutes the ideal or desired family size. While this may seem outside of the purview of economics, there is evidence that economic factors may well influence social norms. One way social norms regarding desired family size may change is through migration. Migrants tend to go from lower-income countries to higher-income countries in search of greater economic opportunities, and this kind of migration has been increasing over time. For example, data from the US Census Bureau indicates that the foreign-born population in the United States has increased from 4.8 percent in 1970 to 12.9 percent in 2010.[27] In the United States and much of Europe, immigrant women also tend to have more children than native-born women, mirroring their countries of origin, although the immigrant–native difference has declined among the most recent immigrants as fertility levels have fallen around the world. The children of immigrants may assimilate toward native levels of labor supply and fertility as they become acculturated to work and family size norms in the destination country. Several studies have documented support for this latter hypothesis.[28]

Another interesting way that social norms can affect fertility is through the media. A documented example of this has occurred in Brazil. There, the TFR rate fell dramatically from 6.3 in 1960 to 5.8 in 1970, 4.4 in 1980, 2.9 in 1991, and 2.3 in 2000. The only other developing country comparable in size to have experienced such a sharp and generalized decline is China, where the decline was the result of deliberate government policy; that is, the One Child Policy.

What might have caused such a dramatic drop in a relatively short time frame? A fascinating explanation is offered by the economists La Ferrara, Chong, and Duryea, who hypothesized that the popularity of the Brazilian soap operas, called novellas, exposed the vast majority of Brazilians to female characters with no children or only one child and thereby spurred a drop in the demand for children.[29] The vast majority of the Brazilian population, across all social classes, regularly watches the 8 p.m. novella broadcast by Rede Globo, the network that has a virtual monopoly on the production of Brazilian novellas. A content analysis of 115 Globo novellas aired between 1965 and 1999 in the two time slots with the largest audience between 1965 and 1999 reveals that 72 percent of the five main female characters (aged 50 or below) had no children at all, and 21 percent had only one child. This is in marked contrast with the prevalent fertility rates in Brazilian society over the same period.

To measure the causal impact of these novellas on fertility, the authors took advantage of yet another natural experiment, this time involving geographic and time variation in when TV was introduced throughout Brazil. Women living in areas covered by Globo have significantly lower fertility than other women. As additional evidence to bolster their claim that this is a causal effect, the authors present evidence regarding the naming of children, many of whom born during this time frame are named after characters in this

---

27 US Bureau of the Census, www.census.gov/prod/2012pubs/acs-19.pdf, accessed October 31, 2014.
28 See, for example, M. Beine, F. Docquier, and M. Schiff (2013), "International Migration, Transfer of Norms and Home Country Fertility," *Canadian Journal of Economics*, 46 (4), 1406–1430, and F. D. Blau, L. M. Kahn, A. Y. H. Liu, and K. L. Papps (2013), "The Transmission of Women's Fertility, Human Capital, and Work Orientation Across Immigrant Generations," *Journal of Population Economics*, 26 (2), 405–435.
29 Eliana La Ferrara, Alberto Chong, and Suzanne Duryea (2012), "Soap Operas and Fertility: Evidence from Brazil," *American Economic Journal: Applied Economics*, 4 (4), 1–31.

TV program. Along similar lines, the introduction of cable and satellite TV into rural parts of India have been shown to have reduced the fertility of women in these areas.[30] The effect of the media on fertility may be an international phenomenon: Recall the discussion in Chapter 6 about the effect of MTV's *16 and Pregnant* on teen fertility in the United States

Summary

In this chapter we have offered an overview of the family lives of women in developing countries. At times their lives are quite different from the lives of women who live in highly industrialized countries. They have more children on average than women in the developed world. Many times children serve as a source of production/income for their families.

Marriage customs differ as well. Marriage payments such as dowry and brideprice remain common in many countries. Early marriage is still the norm in many developing countries. In addition, some developing countries face a shortage of women in the marriage market, and, perhaps surprisingly, in some countries, polygyny is still practiced.

Yet despite these differences it is perhaps the similarities that are the most surprising. Fertility rates are falling in nearly all developing countries and the age at first marriage is rising. Divorce is becoming more common in many developing countries. Despite differences in cultural norms and infrastructure, our basic economic analysis of women's lives is applicable to developing nations as well, and, indeed, as we saw, the economic approach does a credible job of explaining the trends we see in these countries.

In the next chapter we turn to an investigation of the labor-force participation and earnings of women in developing countries.

---

30 Robert, Jensen and Emily Oster (2009), "The Power of TV: Cable Television and Women's Status in India," *The Quarterly Journal of Economics* 124 (3), 1057–1094.

14 WOMEN'S WORK AND EARNINGS IN DEVELOPING COUNTRIES

Introduction

There is no better way to start a chapter examining women's work and earnings in developing countries than by reminding readers of the importance of the work that women do around the world. That importance was underscored by the UN in 2000 when it established the Millennium Development Goals (MDGs), which included attaining gender equity in education and the paid labor market. These goals were reaffirmed in 2010. In this chapter we examine women's work and earnings in developing countries and provide some context for why the UN has selected these as MDGs. In much of the developing world, women are still disadvantaged when compared to men in virtually all aspects of life. Women are often deprived of equal access to education, healthcare, capital, and decision-making powers in the political, social, and business sectors.

As in the last chapter, much of the evidence we present in this book comes from the subfield of development economics. Broadly speaking, development economists seek to understand why some countries are poor while others are relatively rich. Development economists want to learn from the successes of some countries and the failures of others. Poverty is a fact of life in developing countries. Women make up half of the world's population and 70 percent of the world's one billion poorest people.

In this chapter we focus specifically on women and their work in developing countries. While we cannot hope to do this vast literature justice, we attempt to provide an overview of the issues and key research findings to provide a starting point for further exploration. As you will see, this is a fascinating and rich area of study.

Women and work in developing countries

Facts and trends

Labor-force participation Figure 14.1 presents LFPRs of women and men in several regions of the world. We include the United States and an average of all developed countries for comparison purposes. As evidenced in the figure, in all regions shown and, indeed, in virtually all countries of the world, women are less likely to participate in the work force than are men. Yet there are striking differences across regions.

The LFPRs of women are lowest by far in the Middle East where cultural norms often dictate that women do not work outside the home. Sub-Saharan Africa and East Asia have the highest rates. Sub-Saharan Africa is a region containing many of the least-developed countries in the world. Yet the LFPRs of women are high, with women contributing to the work force, particularly in agriculture.

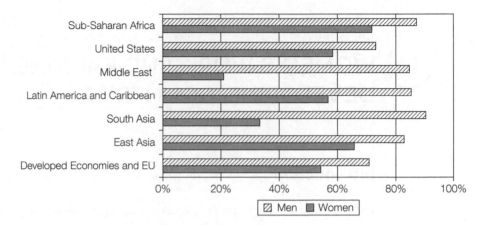

Figure 14.1 *Women's and men's LFPRs, 2012, by region.*

Source: Data from International Labor Organization. 2014. "Global Employment Trends".

In Figure 14.2 we present trends in the ratio of female-to-male labor-force participation in various regions of the developing world and also from high-income countries for comparison. Between 1990 and 2010 the ratio of female to male labor-force participation showed mixed trends across developing country regions. Women's participation rates in the Latin American/Caribbean region showed the most gains, increasing by 18 percent in the last two decades, although the size of the participation gap remains large—only two-thirds of men's participation rates. Some improvements also occurred in Sub-Saharan Africa (+8 percent) and the region (+3 percent). On the other hand, the South Asia region experienced a slight widening of the gender gap in participation (−3 percent), and in the East Asia and Pacific and the Europe and Central Asia regions (both fell by 1 percent).

Interestingly, high-income countries do not have the smallest gap between male and female labor-force participation rates. Both East Asia and Sub-Saharan Africa have higher ratios of female-to- male labor-force participation. And the MENA countries have strikingly lower ratios of female to male labor-force participation.

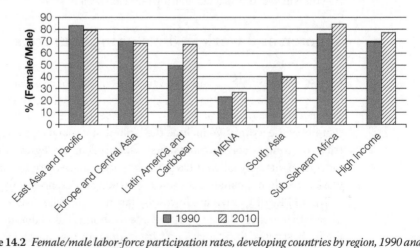

Figure 14.2 *Female/male labor-force participation rates, developing countries by region, 1990 and 2010.*

Source: Data from World Development Indicators: http://data.worldbank.org/news/women-less-likely-than-men-to-participate-in-labor-market, Updated 1/30/2015

The trends in women's labor-force participation over time are perhaps somewhat surprising when we consider other dimensions in which women's lives have changed over time in developing counties, as shown in Table 14.1.

Table 14.1 *Indicators of women's well-being: low- and middle-income countries, 1990–2010.*

Human capital measures	1990	1995	2000	2005	2010
Life expectancy at birth	65	66	67	68	70
TFR (births per woman)	4	3	3	3	3
Maternal mortality ratio (per 100,000 live births)	440	400	350	290	230
Ratio of female-to-male primary school enrollment (%)	n/a	n/a	92	95	97
Ratio of female-to-male secondary school enrollment (%)	n/a	n/a	90	94	96
Literacy rate, women ages 15–24	76	n/a	82	n/a	86
Gender gap in labor-force participation					
Ratio of female-to-male labor-force participation rate (%)	67	68	68	69	68

Source: Data from World Bank Data. http://data.worldbank.org/news/women-less-likely-than-men-to-participate in-labor-market

Education Increasing the schooling attainment of girls remains a challenge in much of the developing world. The multiplier effect of education on several aspects of development as well as its impact on economic growth is now commonly accepted: education reduces high fertility rates, lowers infant and child mortality rates, lowers maternal mortality rates, and increases labor-force participation and women's earnings. Although Table 14.1 shows that women and men's school enrollment rates have become more equal, that aggregate data masks some important variation. For example, World Bank statistics indicate that in the 2010s, 42 countries reported gender gaps in secondary school enrollment rates exceeding 10 percent.

Economist T. Paul Shultz argues forcefully that increasing investments in women's human capital, especially education, should be a priority for countries seeking to increase both economic growth and human welfare.[1] In fact, he goes so far as to suggest that countries should even reallocate public educational resources to favor women. While he notes gender equity is a possible rationale, he makes his arguments based on three observations gleaned from empirical research.

First, women tend to be concentrated at lower levels of education than men, and returns are generally higher at these lower levels of schooling. Thus closing the gender gap in years of schooling will garner higher returns as compared to increasing equally men's and women's levels of education.

Second, he notes that numerous empirical studies of child development find that increased schooling for mothers is associated with larger improvements in childquality outcomes than is the increased schooling of fathers. Men who want better-educated (healthier) children are thus motivated to marry a better-educated woman with increased capacity to produce child human capital.

---

1 T. Paul Schultz (2002), "Why governments should invest more to educate girls," *World Development* 30 (2), 207–225.

His last argument is that better-educated women tend to have higher LFPRs. They work in the formal labor market and pay taxes, thus broadening the tax base in their country. He cites evidence that countries that have equalized their educational achievements for men and women in the last several decades have on the average grown faster.

Doepke and Tertilt[2] have proposed another mechanism through which higher returns to education can have spillovers to gender equality in other areas. They argue that men want expanded legal rights for their daughters but restricted rights for their wives. A key benefit to a man if his daughter acquires more rights through his son-in-law is that his grandchildren will be given more education, since women tend to invest more in children's education. Thus when the returns to education increase, men are tipped toward endorsing legal rights for women.

The economics of labor-force participation in developing countries

A woman's labor-supply decision is composed of two important economic determinants. The first is the opportunity cost of her time, which equals the prevailing wage for a woman with her skills, experience, and level of education. The second is her non-earned income, which for a married woman is often her husband's earnings. Typically, as we saw in the model in Chapter 7, her participation is higher when her own potential labor-market earnings are higher and when her husband's earnings are lower. In this section we consider two related topics, the U-shaped relationship between economic development and women's labor-force participation and the influence of the plough on gender inequality in the labor market.

Economic development and women's labor-force participation Research on women's labor-force participation has established that female labor-force participation is high in low-income countries and high-income countries, and relatively lower in middle-income countries, creating a U-shaped relationship between national income and female participation.[3] This is shown clearly in Figure 14.3, which presents LFPRs for men and women by level of development in the early 2010s. This U-shaped relationship also holds for a single country across time—that is, as an economy develops, this is a typical pattern of labor-force participation for women.

What accounts for this U-shape? Economists Kristin Mammen and Christina Paxson provide an explanation.[4] While they necessarily make some generalizations across countries to make their point, their work provides a framework for considering how women's work has evolved over time as countries develop.

Consider a low-income country with little to no industrial development. Much of the work is agricultural, and women are often heavily involved in this work. Thus LFPRs of women are quite high. As the economy develops, an industrialized nonagricultural sector

2   M. Doepke and M. Tertilt (2009), "Women's Liberation: What's in It for Men?" *Quarterly Journal of Economics*, 124, 1541–1591.

3   C. Goldin (1995), "The U-Shaped Female Labor Force Function in Economic Development and Economic History," in T. P. Schultz (ed.), *Investment in Women's Human Capital and Economic Development*, Chicago, IL: University of Chicago Press, 61–90.

4   K. Mammen and C. Paxson (2000), "Women's Work and Economic Development," *Journal of Economic Perspectives*, 14, 141–164.

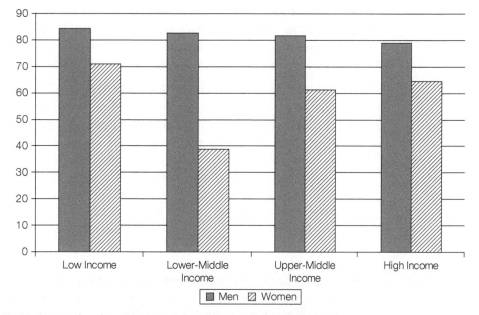

Figure 14.3 *Labor-force participation rates by level of development.*

Source: Data from World Bank Gender Statistics: http://data.worldbank.org/news/women-less-likely-than-men-to-participate-in-labor-market

opens up. The jobs in this new sector are often dominated by men, and they pull men out of agriculture and into manufacturing. These jobs pay more, leading to a rise in the earnings of men. This rise in male earnings tends to reduce women's labor-force participation because this becomes an increase in a woman's non-earned income. As economic development continues further, the white-collar sector tends to grow, providing new employment opportunities for women. These jobs pay more than agriculture, and this higher wage draws many women back into the labor force because the price of their time in the labor market has increased.

In this scenario the sequencing of opportunities available to men and women in the formal labor market plays a key role in determining how women's labor-force participation changes with development. Improvements in men's opportunities without corresponding increases in women's wages may reduce the labor-force participation of women. Subsequent increases in women's earnings may draw women back into the labor force. However, if wage opportunities for women arise at the same time as those for men, we may see no change in female labor-force participation as a country develops.

Of course, we have assumed that women are free to choose whether to work in the formal sector. But there may be constraints limiting the ability of women to work outside of the sphere of the family farm or nonfarm family enterprise. For example, laws may restrict women from working outside the home, as was the case in Afghanistan under the Taliban. Cultural norms may also dictate the extent to which women can work outside their homes.

Female labor-force participation rates in MENA countries are low and cultural norms are often invoked as a reason for this. For example, economist Seema Jayachandran notes that concern for women's and girls' safety and "purity" constrains their physical mobility in many developing countries, particularly, but not exclusively, in MENA countries. Jayachandran stresses that it is hard to know how much of this limited mobility is out of genuine concern for women's welfare, aimed at protecting them from harassment and sexual violence, and how much is simply a way to stifle female autonomy.[5]

The influence of the plough on modern-day labor force participation   Pioneering development economist Ester Boserup, whose research we mentioned in Chapter 13 as being among the first to focus on women's role in economic development, had some interesting insights about the origins of cultural norms regarding the economic roles of men and women. In particular, she argued that cultural norms about the economic roles of the sexes can be traced back to traditional farming practices thousands of years ago. Research by economists Alberto Alesina, Paola Giuliano, and Nathan Nunn finds striking evidence that ancient agricultural techniques have influenced these cultural norms today.[6] We talked at length about this work at the end of Chapter 8 but we briefly revisit it here.

Digging into a vast amount of historical information on ancient farming practices across most regions of the world, they established a remarkable link between historical farming practices and modern-day attitudes toward women. Historically, women were much more likely to be involved in the agricultural sector among those groups that did not use the plough. Why was this? Farming requires work digging in the ground and much of this was done using a hoe, which is a farming implement that is relatively easy for both men and women to use. On the other hand, the plough is a heavy tool, requiring quite a bit of strength to use, and hence in those countries that adopted the plough, agriculture quickly became the domain of men.

Despite industrialization and increased participation of women in the workforce, the authors of the study find that even today, variation between countries in the fraction of adult women who work outside the home can be explained rather well by the farming practices of their ancestors. If their ancestors used the plough, then women are less likely to be in the workforce today. In countries such as Rwanda, Botswana, Madagascar or Kenya, whose people are predominantly descended from hoe-users, women are far more likely to be in the labor force than women in historically plough-using places such as India, Syria, and Egypt.

The authors of the study show that the choice of whether or not to adopt the plough was a function of the type of farmland and the climate, and not due to their preexisting notions of whether or not women should work. In general, the authors found that ploughs are particularly useful for crops that require a large amount of land to be worked in a small time—examples they give include wheat, barley and rye, which all have relatively short growing seasons. Conversely, roots and tubers benefit less from the use of the plough. Using this information, the authors of the study could predict which parts of the world were likely to adopt the plough and they found that those groups whose ancestors would have been predicted to adopt the plough have very proscribed and differentiated gender roles for the sexes even today.

---

5   Seema Jayachandran (2014), "The roots of gender inequality in developing countries," National Bureau of Economic Research, Working Paper # 20380.

6   Alberto Alesina, Paola Giuliano, and Nathan Nunn (2013), "On the Origins of Gender Roles: Women and the Plough," *Quarterly Journal of Economics*, 128 (2), 469–530.

Informal employment

Labor markets in developing countries often have a large informal sector. Jobs in the informal sector are generally low quality. Workers in these jobs do not have a formal employment contract and are not offered benefits or job stability. They are typically self-employed. Unable to afford spells of unemployment, many people in developing countries use informal employment as a survival strategy. Others may use informal employment as a means of avoiding taxes.

In most cases, informal employment means lower, more volatile pay and worse working conditions than employment in formal arrangements. Women face a higher risk of informal employment than men as they often have less legal and social protection. Informal employment is particularly widespread in Africa, the Asian regions, and Latin America and the Caribbean.

One reason to be concerned about moving women from the informal to the formal sector is that the latter offers better pay and job security and hence also increases a woman's bargaining power within her household. In fact, decision-making power within the household receives a great deal of attention from economists and policymakers. A woman's say in household decisions (and hence her empowerment) is one aspect of her well-being and thus an end in itself, but the intense interest in female empowerment is in large part because it is believed to be a means of improving children's outcomes.[7]

Women's work and women's empowerment

Research shows that the poorer a country is, the less influence women have over household spending decisions or even over such things as whether to visit family and friends. As GDP per capita rises, women have more say in decision making. The pattern seen across countries also holds within countries, with women above the median wealth level for their country having more decision-making power and less tolerance for gender-based violence than those with below-median wealth.[8]

You may recall from Chapter 3 that household decisions are the result of a bargaining process between husbands and wives, who often have different preferences. One of the most important factors determining the relative bargaining power of husbands and wives is their earnings options outside the marriage. Given that women's empowerment is a potential driver of economic growth, it is important to examine how bargaining power shifts in response to changing labor-market opportunities for women. This is particularly important in the context of a developing country.

When trying to measure changes in spouses' bargaining power within households or to examine the effect of changes in women's bargaining power on household decisions, researchers face two challenges. The first challenge is that we do not observe spouses' bargaining power directly. Because of that, researchers usually examine the changes in household outcomes over which spouses might likely have different preferences. For example, we saw in Chapter 3 that a famous study examined spending on clothing in response to a policy change in the UK in which non-earned income went directly to

7 E. Duflo (2012), "Women's Empowerment and Economic Growth," *Journal of Economic Literature*, 50 (4), 1051–1079.
8 Jayachandran, op. cit.

mothers.[9] Examples of outcomes that are often examined in the literature include spending on men's, women's, and children's clothing, and children's health and education.

The other challenge is to find what economists call an exogenous determinant of bargaining power. An interesting study using longitudinal data from Mexico by economist Kaveh Majlesi surmounts these two issues and provides some interesting insights into how the opportunity for employment in the formal labor market can benefit women.[10] Husbands and wives were asked about various decisions they made in the household. These can be divided into decisions made by each individual on private consumption goods and on household public goods. As we have stressed throughout this text, the most important household public good for most couples is children. In Mexico, like many other developing countries, the manufacturing sector is a major source of employment for women. The theory of household bargaining predicts that an increase in the number of jobs available for women compared to those for men improves women's outside options, regardless of whether or not a woman actually decides to participate in the labor market. Thus Majlesi used changes in demand for manufacturing employment to measure women's bargaining power. Majlesi found that women did experience increased bargaining power in their households when they had an increase in their labor-market opportunities. Women's relative power particularly went up concerning decisions on whether the woman should participate in the labor market, the amount of money that is given to the wife's parents, the use of contraception, and children's health and medicine.

A study by Nancy Qian shows how economic reforms can influence women's labor-market participation and hence their bargaining power.[11] In the late 1970s, China undertook economic reforms that made growing cash crops more profitable. She noted that women have a comparative advantage in picking tea leaves, which grows on short bushes. The leaves are delicate and hence women's height and smaller hands give them a comparative advantage as compared to men who have a comparative advantage in picking fruit from trees. Thus the economic reforms that favored tea-growing regions should have favored women. In fact, she finds fewer "missing girls" in these areas, a finding consistent with families having fewer sex-selective abortions and/or less infanticide of girls.[12] Her hypothesis is that as women's share of household income increased, they gained bargaining power in their families and their preferences prevailed in household decision making.

Another study using data from India reached a similar conclusion. In some parts of India the soil is quite coarse and requires what is known as deep tillage. This is physically demanding work and is typically performed by men. Hence women have less bargaining power. Carranza[13] showed that in those parts of India, the female labor-force participation rate is lower and the sex ratio favors men.

Overall, a great number of studies indicate that empowering women seems to facilitate increased labor-market activity and hence better outcomes for their families. And,

---

9   As a reminder, this study was Shelly Lundberg, Robert Pollak, and Terrence Wales (1997), "Do Husbands and Wives Pool Their Resources? Evidence from the United Kingdom Child Benefit," *Journal of Human Resources,* 32 (3), 463–480.

10 Kaveh Majlesi (2014), "Labor Market Opportunities and Women's Decision Making Power within Households," *Unpublished Manuscript.*

11 Nancy Qian (2008), "Missing Women and the Price of Tea in China: The Effect of Sex-Specific Earnings on Sex Imbalance," *The Quarterly Journal of* Economics, 123 (3), 1251–1285.

12 See Box 13.2 on the missing girls in developing countries.

13 Eliana Carranza (2012), "Soil Endowments, Production Technologies and Missing Women in India."

of course, the process of economic growth itself may facilitate women's empowerment. Is there a synergy between the two? Box 14.1 provides some interesting insights into this issue.

Box 14.1

The "Virtuous Cycle": Economic Development and the Empowerment of Women

As we have discussed in several places in this chapter, there appears to be a strong correlation between economic development and the economic empowerment and hence well-being of women. Economist Esther Duflo notes that the process of economic development in a country reduces poverty and hence increases the well-being of everyone in that country, including women. Importantly, because women are more likely to be in poverty, reducing poverty disproportionately benefits women. Thus economic development by reducing poverty also has a spillover effect in that it lessens gender gaps in health and earnings. There is also empirical evidence that empowering women by providing them with more education, better access to healthcare, increased political participation/representation and increased labor-market opportunities has the added benefit of increasing economic development. The existence of this bi-directional relationship between economic development and women's empowerment leads Duflo to question whether a "virtuous cycle" could be set in motion, whereby economic development empowers women, and empowering women further spurs economic development.

While this idea is intriguing, Duflo presents compelling evidence that economic development by itself is not enough to reduce gender gaps. One example she cites is the persistent difference in sex ratios at birth in some developing countries. This illustrates the fact that economic development, and the concomitant availability of new technologies, can have perverse effects on gender equality if it decreases the cost of discriminating against girls. She further advances two rationales for supporting active policies to promote women. The first is simple equity: Women are currently worse off than men, and she terms this "repulsive in its own right." The second is that women play a fundamental role in development. To illustrate this point, she notes that decades of research by economists has established that, when women have more money or power, they invest the money in goods and services that improve the well-being of families; that is, in goods that are conducive to development. This finding has been the basis for numerous policy initiatives: Many conditional cash transfer benefit programs in developing countries, such as PROGRESA/Opportunidades in Mexico, direct the transfer to women, not men, and measures to enforce women's access to political positions through quotas have been instituted in 87 countries, including India, where a 1993 constitutional amendment required that one-third of rural village council seats and village presidencies be reserved for women. Duflo concludes that neither economic development nor women's empowerment alone will erase gender gaps, and she argues that equity between men and women is only likely to be achieved by continuing policy actions that favor women at the expense of men, possibly for a very long time.

Source: E. Duflo (2012), "Women's Empowerment and Economic Growth," *Journal of Economic Literature*, 50 (4), 1051–1079.

Improving infrastructure and women's work

One reason that women's formal labor-force activity is lower in developing countries may have to do with the amount of time that women in these countries spend on tasks that a woman in the developing world do not have to undertake. Two of the most common are gathering water and firewood for cooking. Many families in developing countries do not have plumbing and thus must walk to a water source at least once a day, if not more. Also, in developing countries, cooking indoors with wood is still quite common but requires that someone gathers the wood. These tasks fall disproportionately on women.[14]

Furthermore, given that water (unlike fuel) has few alternatives and that access to water in rural areas is often limited to wells, public standpipes, or natural sources, substantial time can be spent collecting water. The burden of collecting water may fall on women in large part because of its link to domestic tasks, such as cooking and childcare. Indeed, a lack of infrastructure has been identified as one factor constraining women's economic opportunities in developing countries.

Thus it is natural to ask whether the improvement of infrastructure will lead to higher LFPRs for women? And, if so, will this increased labor-force participation lead to an increase in women's bargaining power and have spillover effects in terms of their children's well-being? These questions were posed by economists Koolwal and Van de Walle.[15] They note that the presence of a well in town where many women work outside their homes might lead us to conclude that the well has facilitated the work of the women. However, this might be misleading because the decision about where to place a new well is not made in isolation. In particular, women's decision to participate in labor markets may well be jointly determined with infrastructure placement, making it difficult to determine if the infrastructure is merely correlated with women's labor-force participation or if there is a causal link from the placement of infrastructure and women's work outside the home. In other words, did working women locate near the water supply because it was convenient or did the acquisition of a new water supply in the area make it easier for women to then work outside the home? It is the latter question that interests economists and policymakers.

Using data from across several countries, Koolwal and Van de Walle do not find that access to water comes with greater participation in the labor market for women, although in countries where substantial gender gaps in schooling exist, both boys' and girls' enrollments improve with better access to water. In addition they find some signs of impacts on child health for some of the countries in their sample. Because they find no effects on women's labor-force participation, they conclude that the positive effects on children's outcomes cannot be driven by increased bargaining power of women. They surmise that the increases in children's health and education must be a direct function of women having more time for childcare now that they do not have to travel so far for water and that the quality of the water likely improved.

---

14 See the UN for statistics on water collection at http://www.un.org/waterforlifedecade/gender.shtml.
15 Gayatri Koolwal and Dominique Van de Walle (2013), "Access to Water, Women's Work, and Child Outcomes," *Economic Development and Cultural Change*, 61 (2), 369–405.

Remittances and women's work

Many women in developing countries work abroad and send money, called **remittances**, back home to their families. In 2013, women accounted for 48 percent of international migrants. Remittances are often an important source of income for the home country. In 2013, officially recorded remittances to developing countries were an estimated $404 billion, an increase of about 3.3 percent over the previous year.[16] After foreign direct investment, remittances are the most important source of external financing in developing countries.

A growing body of research by economists investigates the effect of this migration and the resulting remittances on the well-being of women. Women who migrate to find work are typically working in low-skills areas, such as domestic work or low-skill work in the tourism industry. Women tend to send home as much money as male migrants, but they earn less while abroad, hence they send a larger portion of their income back to their families at home. Depending on the age at migration, a woman may be helping to support her parents and siblings or she may be sending money home to someone who is caring for her children.

Another important channel to consider is the possibility that one parent's international migration may also result in a change in bargaining power among household decision-makers if one parent travels abroad while the other remains in the sending country. If parents have different preferences over goods, this might also affect the allocation of resources and thus outcomes for children.

There is some evidence for this in work by Francisca Antman, who demonstrates that families with migrant household heads spend a smaller fraction of resources on boys relative to girls in both clothing and education.[17] And, in related research, she uses longitudinal data to investigate whether this relationship is causal and finds support for the idea that when a household head migrates, families spend more on girls relative to boys, and once the household head returns, the reverse is true.[18] These findings are consistent with a shift in bargaining power toward women when men migrate and a shift back toward men once they have returned to the household. These results are consistent with growing evidence from other studies that increasing women's bargaining power results in improvements in girls' health outcomes and not boys.

In addition, some studies focus more directly on the labor-supply responses of women left behind. When a husband migrates and sends money home, that creates an income effect that, all else being equal, reduces a woman's labor-force participation, as our model in Chapter 7 predicts. There is evidence that remittances are accompanied by a drop in women's labor supply in informal and non-paid work in rural areas of Mexico.[19] Additional evidence for this prediction is found in Nepal and also in Egypt.[20]

16   Figures from World Bank 2014 Migration and Development Brief. See http://siteresources.worldbank. org/INTPROSPECTS/Resources/334934-1288990760745/MigrationandDevelopmentBrief22.pdf.

17   Francisca M. Antman (2011), "International Migration and Gender Discrimination Among Children Left Behind," *American Economic Review*, 101 (3), 645–649.

18   Francisca M. Antman (2010), "International Migration, Spousal Control, and Gender Discrimination in the Allocation of Household Resources," University of Colorado at Boulder, Department of Economics Working Paper 10–15.

19   Catalina Amuedo-Dorantes and Susan Pozo (2006), "Migration, Remittances, and Male and Female Employment Patterns," *American Economic Review*, 96 (2), 222–226.

20   MichaeLokshin, l and Elena Glinskaya (2009), "The Effect of Male Migration on Employment Patterns of Women in Nepal," *The World Bank Economic Review*, 23 (3), 481–507 and Christine Binzel, and Ragui Assaad (2011), "Egyptian Men Working Abroad: Labour Supply Responses by the Women Left Behind," *Labour Economics*, 18, S98–S114.

Women's earnings in developing countries

Overview

As we might expect, in all countries for which data are gathered, women earn less than men. Figure 14.4 shows the ratio of female to male earned income for selected countries in 2010. These figures are not directly comparable to the figures we showed for the United States in Chapter 9 since those were median earnings of YRFT workers. While these are not perfect measures, they are the closest we have for measuring the gender earnings ratio across a broad range of countries. Unlike the United States and other developed countries, developing nations do not always have good household survey data, and when they do it is often not collected annually.

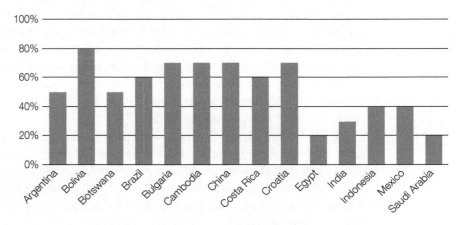

Figure 14.4 *Ratio of female-to-male earned income, selected developing countries.*

Source: Data from World Economic Forum, "Table D3: Estimated earned income," The Global Gender Gap Report 2011 (2011). Available at: http://www3.weforum.org/docs/WEF_GenderGap_Report_2011.pdf.

The figure shows some stark differences across countries. For example, in many developing countries, the ratio of female to male earnings is 70 percent or greater. Yet some countries, such as India, Egypt and Saudi Arabia, have much lower ratios.

Just as in developed countries, whether these gender differences arise because of differences in human capital endowments, in occupational choices, or because of discrimination is an empirical question. Given the heterogeneity that exists across labor markets in developing countries, it is impossible to generalize on this issue. The authors of an ambitious survey of numerous gender wage gap studies around the world that applied the Oaxaca decomposition reported two important findings: Worldwide, over time, unadjusted wage differentials have fallen substantially, and most of this decrease is due to better labor-market endowments of women.[21] Another set of scholars established that across 64 countries the gender wage gap ranged from 8 to 48 percent, with wider gaps in South Asia and Sub-Saharan Africa.[22] The results of this same study indicated

---

21 Doris Weichselbaumer and Rudolf Winter-Ebmer (2005), "A Meta-Analysis of the International Gender Wage Gap," *Journal of Economic Surveys*, 19 (3), 479–511.

22 Hugo Ñopo, Nancy Daza, and Johanna Ramos (2011), "Gender Earnings Gaps in the World," IZA Discussion Paper 5736.

that the unexplained portion of the gender gap is more pronounced among part-time workers and less-educated workers.

Country studies of the gender gap

In this section we apply the Oaxaca decomposition technique[23] to learn more about the gender gap in specific countries. We consider four interesting cases—China, the Russian Federation, the transition from socialism to a market-based economy in Eastern Europe, and the transformation of jobs requiring physical strength to those requiring more human capital.

China Our first application comes from a study that uses Chinese data.[24] Gender pay differentials in China are increasingly important, as China continues to move towards a more market-oriented economy and wages are increasingly used to allocate labor. China has an interesting history in terms of its treatment of women in the economy. From 1950 to 1979, when the economy was largely centrally planned, the LFPR for women living in urban areas was 90 percent—far above that of Western economies. Since that time, China has gradually moved away from a socialist economy to a more market-based system and incentives were put in place to link earnings of individuals to their productivity.

Lin and Gunderson report a female/male earnings ratio of 0.75 in China. Their estimates suggest that about one-third of the pay gap reflects the fact that men have endowments or characteristics that tend to be associated with higher pay, especially supervisory responsibilities, general labor-market experience, occupational skills, education, and membership of the Communist Party. Interestingly, marriage has a large positive effect on the earnings of women in China but no effect on men's earnings—just the opposite of what we often see in developed countries. Childcare responsibilities for children under the age of six have a large negative effect on the earnings of women. However, the negative impact of childcare responsibilities are offset almost completely if an elderly family member is present in the household, highlighting that childcare responsibilities disproportionately fall on women unless an elder family member is present. Pay premiums for higher-level skills and higher supervisory ranks are remarkably small for both men and especially women. The remaining two-thirds of the pay gap is unexplained (often labeled as discrimination). This potential role of market forces in determining wages is likely to be the most interesting issue with respect to the future of the gender pay gap in China.

The Russian Federation A fascinating study based on Russian data is among of the first to consider whether or not personality differences can explain the gender wage gap.[25] You may recall that we discussed this emerging explanation in our discussion of occupational differences in Chapter 10. Using data from the 2000s from 2,600 Russian employees, the authors focused on whether two specific personality traits—locus of control (LOC) and the need for challenge and affiliation—can explain the gender wage gap.[26]

---

23 See Chapter 11 for a discussion of the Oaxaca decomposition technique.

24 Lin, Xiu and Morley Gunderson (2013), "Gender Earnings Differences in China: Base Pay, Performance Pay, and Total Pay," *Contemporary Economic Policy* 31 (1), 235–254.

25 Anastasia Semykina and Susan J. Linz (2007), "Gender Differences in Personality and Earnings: Evidence from Russia," *Journal of Economic Psychology* 28 (3), 387–410.

26 It is worth noting that it is not often that a dataset has both measures of earnings and human capital characteristics along with personality traits.

LOC can be either internal or external. Individuals with an internal LOC believe that the outcomes that they experience (e.g., wages, employment, or marriage) are consequences of their own behavior, ability or effort. Those with an external LOC believe that the outcomes that they experience are a function of luck or fate and that they cannot control them. Challenge and affiliation (CA) refers to two opposing traits. Broadly speaking, the authors characterize challenge as "getting ahead" and affiliation as "getting along." Individuals with a preference for challenge are motivated and more likely to undertake demanding tasks, and hence are expected to perform better in the labor market.

In their work they test several hypotheses:

1. Men are more likely than women to have an Internal LOC.
2. Men are more likely than women to exhibit a need for challenge.
3. Individuals with an internal LOC are more likely to have higher earnings than those with an external LOC.
4. Individuals who exhibit a need for challenge are more likely to have higher earnings than those who exhibit a need for affiliation.
5. Gender differences in personality contribute to gender differences in earnings.
6. The "explained" component of the gender wage gap increases when personality traits are included.

In their sample (we leave the details of how LOC and CA are actually calculated to interested readers), they find support for the first four hypotheses. They use a form of the Oaxaca decomposition to address the last two hypotheses. In their sample there are differences in human capital characteristics that favor men. In particular, women have fewer years of schooling, a lower probability of having supervisory responsibilities, a lower probability of holding jobs in manufacturing, and a greater probability of holding jobs in state-owned enterprises. Women, however, do have more years of experience with their current employer. Overall, they report a gender wage gap of 0.31. In a model that only controls for the aforementioned characteristics, 0.072 or 23 percent of this gap is explained by these controls (0.23 = 0.072/0.31). When they add controls for personality differences, the percentage explained rises to 0.093 or 30 percent. Furthermore, they report that in their data, personality traits are more important in explaining the gender wage gap than are education and work experience, the traditional human capital explanations.

Eastern Europe and the economic transition Some interesting work has also been done analyzing the gender wage gap in economies as they transition from socialism to more market-based economies. Eastern Europe and the former Soviet Union are the focus of this research. Under socialism in these countries, women fared well. LFPRs were 90 percent or above, and wages were not set by market factors but rather determined by the state. Maternity leave was generous, as were childcare benefits. Thus the female-to-male earnings ratio was quite high, often better than that in developed countries.

Most East European countries initiated economic reforms in 1990 and 1991, and these were notable for how rapidly they took effect. While it is difficult to generalize overall about the reforms, they all involved a movement towards a more market-based economy with greater emphasis on supply and demand to determine wages and prices, an opening of international trade, and the privatization of many previously state-owned enterprises.

How did women fare in the aftermath of these reforms? Elizabeth Brainard gathered data from various countries pre- and post-reform and found some surprising results.[27] The ratio of median women's to men's earnings fell from 77.1 to 50 percent in Ukraine and from 83.3 to 65.8 percent in Russia. However, that same ratio increased from 73.4 to 83.2 percent in Poland and from 66.7 to 71.5 percent in the Czech Republic. She attributes the positive increase to a reduction in discrimination against women. Indeed, in six of the eight post-communist countries explored by Brainard, the female relative wage position improved after reform.

Structural change in developing countries As countries develop, the type of jobs available change from those requiring "brawn," which may be more suited to men and their physical strength, to those that require more "brain" and are hence suitable for both men and women. This process is part of the U-shaped curve between development and women's labor-force participation that we discussed earlier in this chapter. How, though, does this change translate into earnings and, in particular, can this shift help close the gender wage gap?

In a study that used data from four developing countries—Thailand, Brazil, Mexico, and India—economist Michelle Rendall explored how female labor-force participation and earnings evolved over time in these four countries as the labor force changed to jobs requiring less physical strength.[28] Because it is difficult to decide exactly how to classify jobs as to whether they require brains or brawn, Rendall took advantage of earlier research based on US data that provided a detailed classification of jobs according to the amount of physical strength vs. human capital they required. She argues that transferring these classifications to the context of these four developing countries is legitimate because the physical requirements of the job are the same regardless of the country in which the job is being performed. She cites three example occupations to make her point—farmer, waiter, and accountant—and notes that those will have the same physical strength requirements in other countries. This earlier research documented that in the United States, as jobs became more brain-oriented, that helped explain some of the narrowing of the US gender wage gap. Might it also explain closing wage gaps in developing countries?

Using data from 1990 to 2008 (the exact years vary slightly for each country due to data availability), Rendall reports that in Thailand, Brazil, and India, female labor-force participation and the ratio of female to male earnings rose during this time period commensurate with a shift away from brawn-based occupations and an increase in service-sector jobs. Mexico is slightly different in that the wage ratio was essentially unchanged over this time period, while female labor-force participation rose. The magnitudes of the changes vary across the four countries, in part because they are all at differing stages of economic development. For example, in Brazil, female labor-force participation rose from 46 percent in 1990 to 61 percent in 1998, and the female-to-male wage ratio rose from 0.67 to 0.78 during that same time period.

Using a variation of the Oaxaca decomposition, Rendall decomposes this narrowing of the gender wage gap into changes in brain and brawn requirements of occupations as well

27 Elizabeth Brainerd (2000), "Women in Transition: Changes in Gender Wage Differentials in Eastern Europe and the Former Soviet Union," *Industrial & Labor Relations Review*, 54 (1), 138–162.

28 Michelle Rendall (May 2013), "Structural Change in Developing Countries: Has it Decreased Gender Inequality?" *World Development*, 45, 1–16.

as changes in human capital to show how the change from brawn to brain over time has partially explained the narrowing of the female/male gender gap in each of the countries studied. For Brazil, about half of the narrowing of the gender wage gap can be attributed to the changing skill requirements of jobs from brawn to brain. The results for Thailand are similar to those of Brazil, as it saw an increase in brain demand and a decline in brawn demand. Mexico is unique in this study in that in the 1990s there was an increase in brawn demand due to the rise of manufacturing companies, sometimes called "maquiladoras".

India, on the other hand, has a much lower female LFPR than the other countries, although it did rise from 33 to 41 percent between 1990 and 2005, while the gender wage ratio increased from 0.36 to 0.55 during the same time frame. Rendall attributed this large labor-market inequity to a larger share of the workforce working on brawn jobs primarily due to subsistence needs. She concludes her paper by noting that expanding the service sector in developing countries and hence the return to brains will help women.

Globalization and women's earnings

Finally, in our increasingly global work environment, you might wonder how international trade affects the earnings of women in developing countries. Economic activity is increasingly global in nature, with goods and services produced at home and abroad. For example, technology has lead to the outsourcing of many services; for example, X-rays taken in the United States are often read by radiologists in other countries. Most of us are also probably aware that, when we call for technical support for our electronic devices, our calls are often routed to call centers abroad, often in developing countries. Globalization can affect women through an increased demand for their labor and hence higher earnings. How does this translate into their economic well-being? Economist Robert Jensen has provided some answers.[29]

Jensen studied the impact of the rapid growth of the business process outsourcing industry (BPO) in India. BPO is a term used to describe the outsourcing of some of a company's tasks to a third party for completion (e.g., the reading of an X-ray taken in the United States by a radiologist in India). To ascertain whether or not these new job opportunities had the predicted effects on women's decision making, he took advantage of the rapid growth of this industry to conduct an experiment. He provided three years of recruiting services to help young women in randomly selected rural Indian villages get jobs in the BPO industry. Because the industry was so new at the time of the study, there was almost no awareness of these jobs, thus this recruiting was, in effect, an exogenous increase in women's labor-force opportunities for the rural households in his study.

He reports that young women in the randomly selected villages were significantly less likely to get married or have children during this period, choosing instead to enter the labor market, or obtain more schooling or post-school training. Women also report wanting to have fewer children and to work more steadily throughout their lifetime, consistent with increased aspirations for a career.

There are also numerous researchers who have sought to determine whether or not globalization and trade liberalization have improved women's earnings and their household

---

29 Robert Jensen (2012), "Do Labor Market Opportunities Affect Young Women's Work and Family Decisions? Experimental Evidence from India," *The Quarterly Journal of Economics*, 127 (2), 753–792.

bargaining power. Most of the studies in this area find that increased trade for developing countries tends to create improvements in women's economic well-being.[30]

While it appears that globalization is a good thing for women's economic well-being in developing countries, we would be remiss not to caution that differing labor standards across countries means that some women are undoubtedly exposed to unsafe and unhealthy working conditions. The most egregious of these violations often find their way into the media in more-developed countries.[31] The economist Drusilla Brown presents an engaging history of labor regulation and discussion of the debate about international labor standards.[32] The arguments hinge on those who want a global standard of working conditions pitted against those who argue that individual countries should retain the right to decide upon acceptable working conditions, and that the standards might well vary with respect to the level of economic development and cultural norms. And some high-profile companies, Apple among them, have gone so far as to declare that their products when produced abroad adhere to US labor practices.[33]

Microcredit and women's well-being

You are probably familiar with the term **microcredit**. Dr. Mohammed Yunus, an economist who holds a PhD from Vanderbilt University, founded the Grameen Bank in Bangladesh in 1976 with the purpose of offering microcredit—the lending of small amounts of money to people who would not ordinarily qualify for a bank loan—to the poor. In 2006 he was awarded the Nobel Peace Prize for his work.

The Grameen Bank was founded on three principles: (1) Loans were to be repaid and on time; (2) only the poorest villagers (those without land) were to be given loans; (3) lending would primarily be to women, because women were the most impoverished and because the most immediate beneficiaries of the loans to women were generally their children.

The loan process at the Grameen Bank is far from traditional. Rather than demonstrate that she has a certain level of assets, a borrower must show that her family assets fall below a certain threshold. No collateral is required. Lack of collateral in developing countries, particularly for women, makes it quite difficult for them to escape poverty as they cannot obtain small loans to start businesses. Banks do not want to lend to individuals who they do not believe will repay the loan, and many individuals in developing countries are **unbanked**, a term used to define those who do not have their own bank accounts.

Grameen bank borrowers must join a five-member group (community) of other bank borrowers, attend weekly group meetings, encourage "loan discipline" within the group (this consists of adhering to 16 decisions, which include keeping families small and not paying a large dowry for a daughter's wedding), and assume responsibility for the bank

---

30 Interested readers should consult Chinhui Juhn, Gergely Ujhelyi and Carolina Villegas-Sanchez (2014), "Men, Women, and Machines: How Trade Impacts Gender Inequality," *Journal of Development Economics*, 106 (C), 179–193 or Niklas Potrafke, and Heinrich W. Ursprung (2012), "Globalization and Gender Equality in the Course of Development," *European Journal of Political Economy*, 28 (4), 399–413 for more information on this topic.

31 See M. Anderson. "Clothed in Misery," *The New York Times*, April 29, 2013.

32 Drusilla K. Brown (2001), "Labor Standards: Where Do They Belong on the International Trade Agenda?" *Journal of Economic Perspectives*, 15 (3), 89–112.

33 See the article by Charles Duhigg and David Barboza, "In China, Human Costs are Built into an iPad," *The New York Times*, January 25, 2012.

loans of all the group members. A borrower's continued access to bank credit is conditional on the prompt loan repayment by all of her group members. Most loans have been for a two-year period with an annual interest rate of 20 percent calculated on a declining principal.

Loan repayment rates at the Grameen Bank are high, typically over 90 percent. This high repayment rate is attributed to the group lending. Groups are typically formed within communities where individuals have close ties that span many years. Borrowers face tremendous pressure to repay lest they jeopardize the ability of other members of their group to borrow at a later date. Failure to repay a loan often means that no one else in the lending group will be offered a microloan.

Since the founding of the Grameen Bank, Microfinance institutions (MFIs) have expanded rapidly. By one account the number of very poor families with a microloan has grown from 7.6 million in 1997 to 137.5 million in 2010. Microcredit has generated considerable enthusiasm because it appears to promise a fast route to poverty alleviation.[34] Most but not all focus their lending towards women following the model of the Grameen Bank.

Microloans aim to facilitate upward mobility by loaning money to start small businesses. Thus they should directly increase the well-being of the borrowers. In addition, they may well have a positive spillover on the borrower's family. As we've noted many times in this text, an important dimension of women's empowerment concerns their control over household spending. The main assumption is that by providing credit to poor women, their direct control over expenditure within the household increases, with subsequent implications for the status of women, and the well-being of women and other household members.

It is difficult to ascertain the efficacy of microcredit in terms of the well-being of the borrowers and their families. The classic problem, which we have raised numerous times in this text, is that it is difficult to sort out the true causal effects of receiving a loan on various outcomes from a selection effect. Borrowers are not selected at random and lending groups are not formed at random. Thus a simple comparison of the outcomes of those with a loan to those without is not informative. And results from existing empirical work on this question are inconclusive, with some reporting positive effects of microcredit on women's outcomes and others reporting no effects.[35] Yet the importance of ascertaining if there is a causal effect of these loans on women's economic outcomes is paramount since they are often viewed favorably by many agencies promoting economic development.

A randomized trial, conducted in India, presents some of the most reliable evidence to date about the effects of microfinance on women's economic outcomes and their families' well-being.[36]

The experiment itself, set in Hyderabad, the fifth largest city in India, can be described in general terms as follows. In 2005, 52 of 104 poor neighborhoods were randomly selected for the opening of an MFI branch by one of the fastest-growing MFIs in the area, Spandana, while the other 52 neighborhoods did not have a branch of this MFI. Randomization ensures that, on average, the only difference between residents is the

---

34 http://www.microcreditsummit.org/uploads/resource/document/web_socr-2012_english_62819.pdf.

35 Abhijit V. Banerjee (2013), "Microcredit under the Microscope: What Have We Learnt in the Last Two Decades, What Do We Need to Know?" *Annual Review of Economics*, 5, 487–519.

36 Abhijit V. Banerjee et al. (2013), "The Miracle of Microfinance? Evidence from a Randomized Evaluation," Department of Economics, Massachusetts Institute of Technology.

greater ease of access to microcredit of those who are in the treatment area. Some 15–18 months later, a comprehensive household survey was conducted in an average of 65 households in each neighborhood, for a total of over 6,800 households.

Only women were eligible for loans and they had to form lending groups based on specific criteria, including age, homeownership, and length of residence in the area. Groups were formed by women themselves, not by Spandana. Thus although Spandana did not determine loan eligibility by the expected productivity of the investment, selection into groups could screen out women who could not convince fellow group-members that they were likely to repay.

The authors of the study reported no changes in any of the development outcomes that are often believed to be affected by microfinance, including expenditures on health, education, and indicators of whether or not women make spending decisions in the household (the latter is a measure of women's empowerment). The results of this study, while certainly not the last word on this important question, will surely stimulate further study of this key issue.

Conclusion

In this chapter we have established two basic facts about women's work and earnings that are consistent with what we know about the United States and the rest of the developed world. In the developing world, women are less likely to participate in the labor force and when they do they have lower earnings. However, women in developing countries face different constraints when making decisions about labor-force participation. These include cultural norms that may limit their ability to work outside the home, and a lack of infrastructure that may mean that basic household tasks disproportionately occupy their time.

Women's earnings, education, and labor-force participation have increased over time in developing countries. Some of this is due to the process of development itself, which tends to open more jobs to women and rewards human capital investment in women. Yet, as we've seen, persistent gender gaps still exist and are sizable in some countries. Research suggests that some of these persistent gender differences can be traced back to ancient agricultural practices.

One theme that emerges from this chapter is that economic development and women's empowerment are closely related. The idea of bargaining power, first introduced in Chapter 3, plays a prominent role in the development economics literature. Scholars are engaged in determining to what extent empowering women through better control over their fertility, better job opportunities in the formal labor market, and access to education can improve women's lives. There is much to suggest that women's lives improve, as do those of their children, when they have access to education and jobs.

We closed with a discussion of microcredit for women. While, in theory, microcredit appears to offer a potential way for women to advance economically, in practice, evidence of its success is decidedly mixed.

Women represent half the world's population, and gender inequality exists in every nation. While we have not done justice to the enormous field of economic development and its research on women's contributions to, and benefits from, economic development, we hope that after reading this chapter you are motivated to read more and perhaps even conduct your own research.

REFERENCE INDEX

INDEX